Definition in Greek Philosophy

Definition in Greek Philosophy

EDITED BY

David Charles

OXFORD

UNIVERSITY PRESS

OXFORD
UNIVERSITY PRESS

Great Clarendon Street, Oxford OX2 6DP

Oxford University Press is a department of the University of Oxford.
It furthers the University's objective of excellence in research, scholarship,
and education by publishing worldwide in

Oxford New York

Auckland Cape Town Dar es Salaam Hong Kong Karachi
Kuala Lumpur Madrid Melbourne Mexico City Nairobi
New Delhi Shanghai Taipei Toronto

With offices in
Argentina Austria Brazil Chile Czech Republic France Greece
Guatemala Hungary Italy Japan Poland Portugal Singapore
South Korea Switzerland Thailand Turkey Ukraine Vietnam

Oxford is a registered trade mark of Oxford University Press
in the UK and in certain other countries

Published in the United States
by Oxford University Press Inc., New York

British Library Cataloguing in Publication Data
Data available

Library of Congress Cataloging in Publication Data
Data available

Typeset by SPI Publisher Services, Pondicherry, India
Printed in Great Britain
on acid-free paper by
MPG Books Group, Bodmin and King's Lynn

ISBN 978-0-19-956445-3

Preface

This collection of essays originated in a seminar Paolo Crivelli, Annamaria Schiaparelli, and I organized on *Ancient Theories of Definition* in Oxford in summer 2003. In the course of the term, Lesley Brown, Jane Hood, Vasilis Politis, and the three of us gave talks on definition in Plato, Aristotle, the Stoics, Galen, and Plotinus.

It soon became apparent that there were interlocking issues concerning essence, causation, and signification which recurred in different ways in the various authors we discussed and that these deserved further study. It was also clear that the diachronic study of definition, in which we were engaged, was best done as a collaborative project, involving people with specialist research interests in each of the areas we studied. At this point, when we were considering how best to proceed, we were delighted to elicit essays from Kei Chiba, Gail Fine, Mary Louise Gill, Lindsay Judson, James Lennox, Deborah Modrak, and Richard Sorabji, whose contributions considerably extended the range of topics discussed.

The resulting collection of essays focuses on a number of questions concerning the nature and role of definition in Greek philosophy. It makes no claim to cover all the issues in this area. Nor does it consider the role of definition in mathematical or Hippocratic writings. Still less does it attempt to present one shared overview of the field. Indeed, the contributors disagree amongst themselves on a number of important topics. Its goal is the modest one of rekindling interest in this important area of philosophical enquiry.

All the essays in this volume are unpublished elsewhere with one exception. Richard Sorabji's essay will also appear in *Ancient Interpretations of Aristotle's Posterior Analytics*, edited by F. de Haas, M. Leunissen, and M. Martijn, Leiden, forthcoming. I am grateful to Frans de Haas for his permission to include it.

I wish to thank Peter Momtchiloff for his unfailing support in the preparation of this volume and the excellent but anonymous Oxford University Press readers for their helpful and detailed comments.

David Charles

1 September 2009

Contents

Part III. Post-Aristotelian Writers on Definition

Contributors

LESLEY BROWN is Centenary Fellow in Philosophy at Somerville College, Oxford. She has published several articles on Plato's *Sophist*, including a recent contribution to *The Oxford Handbook of Plato* ('The Sophist on Statements, Predication and Falsehood'). She wrote a new introduction and explanatory notes for the 2009 Oxford World Classics reissue of *Aristotle's Nicomachean Ethics*.

DAVID CHARLES is Research Professor of Philosophy at Oriel College, Oxford. He is the author of *Aristotle on Meaning and Essence* (Oxford, 2000) and *Aristotle's Philosophy of Action* (London, 1984).

KEI CHIBA is Professor of Philosophy in the Graduate School of Letters, Hokkaido University, Japan. He is the author of *Aristotle on the Possibility of Metaphysics: Complementary Development between Dialectic and Natural Philosophy* (Tokyo, 2002).

PAOLO CRIVELLI is Fellow and Tutor in Classical Philosophy at New College, Oxford. He has written articles on Plato's philosophy of language and epistemology, Aristotle's philosophical logic, and Stoic logic. His book on *Aristotle on Truth* was published by Cambridge in 2004.

GAIL FINE is Professor of Philosophy at Cornell University and Senior Research Fellow at Merton College, Oxford. She is the author of *On Ideas* (Oxford) and of *Plato on Knowledge and Forms* (Oxford), and the editor of *The Oxford Handbook of Plato*.

MARY LOUISE GILL is Professor of Philosophy and Classics at Brown University. She is the author of *Aristotle on Substance: The Paradox of Unity* (1989), co-translator and author of the *Introduction, Plato: Parmenides* (1996). She is currently working on a book on Plato's later metaphysics and epistemology.

JANE HOOD is a Fellow in Philosophy in Oriel College, Oxford, specializing in ancient philosophy. She has written on ancient medicine and is completing a book on the epistemology of medical and philosophical skill.

LINDSAY JUDSON is Official Student and Tutor in Philosophy at Christ Church, Oxford. He is General Editor of the Clarendon Aristotle Series, and (with Julia Annas) of Oxford Aristotle Studies. His recent publications include 'Aristotelian Teleology', in *Oxford Studies in Ancient Philosophy* (2005), and *Remembering Socrates: Philosophical Essays* (with Vassilis Karasmanis, Oxford, 2006).

JAMES G. LENNOX is Professor of History and Philosophy of Science at the University of Pittsburgh, and holds secondary appointments in both the Department of Philosophy and Department of Classics. He is the author of a translation, with introduction and commentary, of *Aristotle, On the Parts of Animals* (Oxford, 2001); and of *Aristotle's Philosophy of Biology: Studies in the Origins of Life Science* (Cambridge, 2001).

DEBORAH MODRAK is Professor of Philosophy at the University of Rochester. She has written numerous articles on ancient Greek theories of mind and perception and philosophy of language and epistemology. She is the author of *Aristotle: The Power of Perception* (Chicago, 1987) and *Aristotle's Theory of Language and Meaning* (Cambridge, 2001).

VASILIS POLITIS is Senior Lecturer in Trinity College Dublin. He has published mainly on Plato and Aristotle, and is currently working on an extended project on *aporia*, and its place in philosophical enquiry, in Plato, Aristotle as well as ancient scepticism. For the year 2009–10 he is Fellow at the Wissenschaftskolleg zu Berlin.

ANNAMARIA SCHIAPARELLI is Lecturer at The Queen's College, Oxford. Her areas of research are in ancient philosophy. She has published several articles on Aristotle and on Plotinus. She is co-author with C. D'Ancona of *Plotino: La discesa dell'anima nei corpi: Enn. 4.8[6]* (Padua, 2003). She is the author of *Galen and the Linguistic Fallacies* (Venice, 2002).

RICHARD SORABJI is a fellow of Wolfson College, Oxford and Global Distinguished Professor at New York University. He is the general editor of 81 volumes of translations from philosophy of 200–600 AD, has written a 3-volume sourcebook on the philosophy of that period and co-edited a 2-volume book of essays on philosophy between 100 BC and 200 AD. He is the author of three books on the physical world (*Necessity, Cause and Blame*; *Time, Creation and the Continuum*; *Matter, Space and Motion*) and three books on mind and morals (*Animal Minds and Human Morals*; *Emotion and Peace of Mind*; *Life and Death*).

Introduction

DAVID CHARLES

1 Why Study Definition in Greek Philosophy?

Definition was a central topic in Greek philosophy. Socrates' most significant philosophical innovation, in Aristotle's view, was to focus on the search
for definitions, raising and attempting to answer his famous 'What is it?'
question (*Metaphysics* 1078b22ff.). In many of Plato's dialogues, Socrates asks
such questions as 'What is virtue?', 'What is knowledge?', 'What is justice?'
and hunts, often unsuccessfully, for an adequate answer. Aristotle, in the
Topics, *Analytics*, and *Metaphysics*, devoted considerable time and effort to
determining what counts as a good definition. Later philosophers pursued
these issues further, developing their own accounts of the nature and role of
definition. The topic remained, from Socrates onwards, an important
concern in Greek philosophy.

Although definition was a major preoccupation for ancient philosophers,
it has received relatively little attention in recent scholarly discussions of
ancient philosophy. Indeed, since Richard Robinson and J. M. LeBlond,[1]
few have examined it as a topic in its own right.[2] For roughly the same

---

[1] R. Robinson, *Plato's Earlier Dialectic*, 2nd edn., Oxford, 1953, pp. 55–60; J. M. LeBlond, 'Aristotle on
Definition', reprinted in *Articles on Aristotle*, ed. J. Barnes, M. Schofield, and R. Sorabji, London, 1979, vol.
3, pp. 63–79. (The first edition of Robinson's book appeared in 1941, LeBlond's article in 1939.)

[2] These have included notable contributions such as J. L. Ackrill's 'Aristotle's Theory of Definition:
Some Questions on *Posterior Analytics* II.8–10', R. Sorabji's 'Definitions: Why Necessary and in What
Way?'(both in *Aristotle on Science*, ed. E. Berti, Padua, 1981), G. Vlastos's 'What did Socrates Understand
by his "What is F?" Question?', in *Platonic Studies*, 2nd edn., Princeton, 1981, pp. 410–17, C. Kahn's 'The
Priority of Definition: From *Laches* to *Meno*', in his *Plato and the Socratic Dialogue*, Cambridge, 1996,
pp. 148–82, and C. Brittain's 'Common Sense: Concepts, Definitions and Meaning in and out of the
Stoa', in *Language and Learning*, ed. D. Frede and B. Inwood, Cambridge, 2005, pp. 164–209. However,
M. Deslauriers's *Aristotle on Definition* (Leiden, 2007), published while the present volume was in
preparation, is the first book-length discussion of this topic for many years.

period, it has ceased to be of much interest to contemporary philosophers. Few have shared A. J. Ayer's view that 'the propositions of philosophy . . . express definitions or the consequences of definitions'.[3] Indeed, it is only in the last few years that some, explicitly influenced by Aristotle, have begun again to reassess its role and significance.[4]

In this context, a reconsideration of ancient views of definition seems timely. Since these have not been extensively explored, we need to think afresh about which issues to address. One central question must be 'What is definition?' or 'What type of answer should one seek when, following Socrates, one asks the "What is it?" question?' To make progress one needs to answer three sets of more specific ones:

(a) What is to be defined: linguistic expressions, concepts or entities in the world? Can all these be defined? Or only some? If so, which?

(b) What counts as a good definition? What should be included, what excluded? And why?

(c) Is there only one type of good definition? If there are several, how are they connected?

In this collection several ancient philosophers' responses to these basic questions will be discussed. If scholars do not grasp these, they cannot satisfactorily address further questions such as:

(d) Did [Plato's] Socrates think that one cannot know anything at all about (e.g.) virtue until one knows a definition of virtue (or what virtue is)?[5] or

(e) Did Aristotle think that the entities required to make definitions true were individual or general forms?[6]

---

[3] A. J. Ayer, *Language, Truth and Logic*, London, 1936, pp. 61–2.

[4] See, for example, D. Wiggins's *Sameness and Substance Renewed*, Cambridge, 2001, pp. 11–12, 21, and 'Three Moments in the Theory of Definition or Analysis', *Proceedings of the Aristotelian Society* 107 (2007), pp. 73–109. K. Fine discusses definitions in his 'Essence and Modality', *Philosophical Perspectives* 8 (1994), pp. 1–15. They are in the minority. J. Fodor summed up the orthodox view, writing, 'Many philosophers are now very sceptical about definitions,' in his *Concepts*, Oxford, 1998, p. 47.

[5] See, for example, H. Benson, 'The Priority of Definition and the Socratic Elenchus', *Oxford Studies in Ancient Philosophy* 8 (1990), pp. 19–65 for a comprehensive review of a protracted discussion.

[6] For a fine review of recent discussion of this topic, see J. Whiting, 'Metasubstance', *Philosophical Review* 100 (1991), pp. 359–77.

In answering (d), one needs to consider what type of definition Socrates required if one is to have any knowledge at all about virtue. Must one know the essence of virtue? Or is it enough that one knows some distinguishing feature? Similarly, to answer (e), one must grasp what role (or roles) Aristotle required of the entities referred to in definition. In these ways, the study of definition is central for the proper understanding of many epistemological and metaphysical issues.

Since many ancient philosophers were interested in definition, their differing accounts can be usefully compared. Aristotle took a critical interest in the views of his immediate predecessors. Some of his successors rejected or modified his suggestions, others attempted to apply them in various fields. The diachronic study of their views reveals the differing roles and value they attached to definition. It also helps to indicate what was seen as problematic in the work of earlier philosophers, encouraging us to consider for ourselves where they withstand criticism and where they do not.

In the remainder of the Introduction, I shall indicate some issues addressed by all contributors to this volume, taking as a starting point (in Section 2) three specific problems raised in (and by) Plato's dialogues. My aim in this and in subsequent sections is to point to common problems and note which essays address them. It is not to give a full survey of all the issues discussed, still less to resolve them.

2 Socrates and Plato: Three Problems about Definition

Two important problems arise in the *Meno*, a third emerges in Plato's discussion elsewhere. The first concerns what counts as a good definition, the second what is to be defined, the third the variety of permissible definitions.

2.1 Problem 1: Requirements for Good Definition

In his remarks on definition in the *Meno*, Socrates states that what he seeks is

[A]   that one thing in virtue of which all cases of F are F (72c7ff.).

Here, and elsewhere, he is looking for some one feature which makes all (e.g.) cases of virtue cases of virtue, a feature which (in some way) accounts for their being cases of virtue. His idea is a powerful one, which imposes a basic constraint on what is to count as a good definition. In his view, an adequate definition cannot merely point to features which are present only in some cases of virtue or simply indicate features (one or more) which all and only virtuous things possess. Rather, what is sought must be in some way fundamental, the one feature which makes them all cases of virtue, the primary source of their virtue. It is not enough to find a property which all and only instances of virtue necessarily possess (such as, for example, being worthy of moral admiration) if this is not what makes them cases of virtue.

Although Socrates' idea, expressed in [A], is a powerful one, it needs careful analysis. Properly to understand it, one needs to grasp: [A 1] What is it for a case of virtue to be made a case of virtue? [A 2] In what way does the feature sought make virtuous things virtuous? and [A 3] What type of unity should it have? Socrates, according to Aristotle, thought of the feature sought in raising his 'What is F?' question as the starting-point of explanation (demonstration). But what is to be explained? What type of explanation did he have in mind? What are its appropriate starting-points? Let us consider these questions in turn.

Take question [A 1]: In the *Meno* Socrates mentions the case of bees (72b3ff.). What does it mean to look for something which makes a bee the object it is? Is what is to be explained what makes each bee an animal with certain distinctive features *or* what makes each of them a bee *or* what makes each of them the very object it is? How, if at all, are the answers to these three questions connected? Is there, for example, one feature which explains the presence of the other features bees possess and accounts for each bee being a bee? Does this feature also explain why each bee is the individual bee it is?

Or consider question [A 2]: How does the basic feature invoked explain the other features of bees? Is it, to use Aristotelian terminology, their efficient cause (what brings them about) or their teleological cause (what they are for)? Can it be discovered by empirical investigation? Or is it an instance of a distinctive type of cause, a purely formal cause (what it is to be a bee), grasped by philosophical reflection on the identity of the object in question? If the formal cause accounts for what makes this a bee, and bees must have other properties, will it also explain the latter? What type of entity does the basic feature in question have to be? How does knowledge of its essence make the bee intelligible to us? What kind of intelligibility is sought? Answering the latter questions would throw light on some of Plato's requirements for knowledge.

Finally, consider [A 3]: What does it mean to say that the definitional account must invoke one thing? What kind of unity should this feature possess? Should the explanation begin with simple atomic entities, not capable of further analysis or decomposition of any kind? Or should they be unities only in being one efficient or teleological cause? Should the type of unity be self-evident, graspable by rational reflection alone? Further, why does Plato assume (as he seems to) that anything which is truly called (e.g.) virtuous (whether people, constitutions, laws, punishments, or cities) all share the same one basic feature, which makes them all virtuous in precisely the same way? How does he defend this assumption?

While these issues emerge in the *Meno*, similar questions can be asked about other Platonic dialogues. Thus, for example, a version of question [A 1], concerning the connection between definition and (e.g.) teleological causation, arises about the role of the Form of the Good in the *Republic*. Is it the starting-point in a distinctive definitional order? Or is it the fundamental teleological cause? Or does it play both roles? If so, how are they connected? Did Plato achieve a clear view on this problem? Similarly, versions of question [A 3] are central for an understanding of the significance of Socrates' dream in the *Theaetetus* and the method followed in his examination of justice in the *Republic*.

Socrates and Plato attached great importance to the search for definitions, presenting it as a route to knowledge of fundamental features of reality, starting from rational reflection on information of a type available (in principle) to Socrates and his interlocutors. Their conception of a distinctively philosophical, definition–directed, investigation proved, despite its problems, exceptionally influential. Even though (as we shall see) it was challenged and modified by their immediate successors, it remained for centuries a central philosophical project.

2.2 *Problem 2: What is to be Defined? The Problem in the* Meno

In the *Meno*, when Socrates seeks an account which will answer his 'What is F?' question, his target is described in the following terms:

[A]   it is that one thing in virtue of which all cases of F are F (72c7ff.);
[B]   it is graspable without specialized knowledge by intelligent interlocutors (75d2–7);

[C] it is such that if one does not know it, one cannot know any other feature of F (71b3–7);

[D] it is such that if one does know it, one will be able to distinguish on its basis any case of F from any case which is not F (72c8–d1).

There is, however, an immediate difficulty. Why did Socrates believe that there is just one thing which meets these four conditions? Was he correct to do so? Here is one way to raise this difficulty.

The idea motivating [A], which (as we have already seen) involves explanation, is expressed in terms of the basic nature of F (using Plato's term, its form or *eidos*). But why believe that this can be grasped without specialized knowledge by all intelligent interlocutors? Or why think that if one does not know it, one will not know any other feature of F? F's basic nature might only be graspable by those with specialized scientific knowledge. F might be a natural kind, like water, whose basic nature (one might assume) is to be H_2O. This truth was only grasped after the scientific revolutions of the seventeenth century. Nor is it at all clear why failure to know water's scientific nature entails a failure to know that it has other properties (such as being colourless or odourless). Surely people knew these facts about water long before they knew its scientific nature.

There is another way to raise the same difficulty. If one knows what something is and can thereby distinguish it from everything else, one will be able to identify Fs as a distinct group. Perhaps if one cannot identify Fs as a distinct group, one will not be able to know which features belong to Fs. But why think that one must know F's basic nature in order to do so? In the example just considered, skilled people could identify water as a distinct kind and pick out all and only instances of water without knowing its basic nature. More specialist knowledge, not available to all intelligent interlocutors, was required to discover the latter.

Richard Robinson saw this problem clearly and suggested that there was a crucial vagueness in Socrates' original 'What is F?' question. In his view, Socrates sometimes raised this question when searching for a description true of all and only Fs, sometimes when looking for a basic description, which gives the basic nature (or *eidos*) of Fs, sometimes when asking what the term 'F' means. In Robinson's cautious words, there is a 'certain duality in Socrates' conception of the "What is F?" question' which misled him into attempting to provide an answer 'without first discovering precisely *what* question it is [he] desired to answer'. His mistake is revealed in his thinking that there is one answer which simultaneously satisfies all of [A] to [D].[7] No such answer is to be found. In Robinson's account, Socrates' basic error was to have failed to frame a sufficiently precise question.[8]

Robinson's criticism becomes even more pressing if Socrates (as has been recently argued) subscribed not only to [C] and [D] but to an even more demanding condition on a good definition:

[E]   if one does not know it, one cannot distinguish any case of F from any case which is not F.

Why believe that there is one answer to the 'What is F?' question which meets all five conditions? In particular, why think you need to know the underlying essence of Fs (as required to satisfy [B]) if you are to be able to distinguish Fs from anything else?

Socrates' mistake, according to Robinson, arose from his failure to consider carefully the precise form of his question. However, in the *Meno* and elsewhere (as in the *Hippias Major*) he repeatedly attempted to clarify this question, setting out conditions for the answer he required. His mistake, if such it was, was not simply the consequence of failing to analyse his question. He made it because, after considerable reflection, he imposed conditions on a satisfactory answer to his 'What is it?' question which cannot be jointly satisfied.

Why, then, did Socrates impose these conditions on definitions? Why did he fail to distinguish different types of definition, appropriate for differing purposes? Why did he not separate, for example, definitions which say what words mean from definitions of kinds in the world?[9] What were the consequences of his mistake? Did he ever rectify it, developing the resources to separate various kinds of definition? If so, where? Later in the *Meno*? Are

---

[7] Robinson, *Plato's Earlier Dialectic*, pp. 55–60.

[8] P. T. Geach agreed with Robinson that Socrates erred in thinking that an adequate answer to the 'What is it?' question must simultaneously satisfy all of conditions [A] to [D]. However, in Geach's view, Socrates' error was the result of mistaken philosophical doctrine: the belief that one could not understand a term without being able to distinguish its bearer from everything else by grasping its basic essence. (See his 'Plato's *Euthyphro*', *Monist* 50 (1966), pp. 367–82.)

[9] Some doubt whether Plato and Aristotle were concerned with *meaning* at all. See, for example, T. H. Irwin's 'Aristotle's Concept of Signification', in *Language and Logos*, ed. M. Nussbaum and M. Schofield, Cambridge, 1982, pp. 241–66. Much, of course, depends on what is to count as 'meaning' (see, for example, D. Charles's *Aristotle on Meaning and Essence*, Oxford, 2000, pp. 106–7). Full discussion of this issue lies outside the scope of the present volume.

his varying definitions of justice in the *Republic*, for example, a symptom of this error or an attempt to overcome it?[10]

2.3 Problem 3: The Variety of Definitions

Socrates sometimes phrases his definitional question in different terms, seeking not that one thing 'in virtue of which' all cases of F are F but rather that 'by being which all Fs are F'.[11] The answers to these questions may differ. The second, but not the first, could be answered simply by pointing to some feature which all and only F things possess, one which separates them from everything else. Its presence might be sufficient for a thing to fall into the class of Fs even if it did not explain what made each (and every) F an F. To take an example from the *Euthyphro*, pious objects might differ from all others in being the unique object the gods love, even though this was not what made them pious.

Socrates certainly gives different types of answer to definitional questions in Plato's dialogues. In the method of division in the *Sophist* and the *Politicus*, he aims to find a feature which Fs alone possess, the possession of which is sufficient for their being F. However, this need not be the explanatorily basic metaphysical ground, that feature which makes F objects the ones they are. It will be good enough if it divides Fs from all other objects.

The method of division gives rise to its own difficulties. Can there be several equally good definitions of the same object, arrived at by different definitional trees? Or does something make one division-based definition better than the others? Why select some features as *differentiae*? These issues are important in their own right and for what they reveal to us about Plato's goals in the dialogues where this method is applied.

There is, however, a more general problem. Plato, as we have seen, discussed definition in varying ways in different dialogues, sometimes using the method of division, sometimes connecting definition with an explanatory answer to the 'What is it?' question, sometimes (as in *Theaetetus*

---

[10] In the *Republic*, several characterizations of justice are considered, such as doing one's own and not interfering with others (433a8–9), possessing internal psychic harmony (443c9ff.), abstaining from acting unjustly so as to avoid being unjustly treated (359a5f.), doing what is good for another (343c2ff.). Are these rival definitions of the same thing? Or do some give an account of what 'justice' means, others specify which things are just, still others say what the basic nature of justice is? Did Plato succeed in achieving a clear view on this question?

[11] See, for example, *Euthyphro* 6d11 (with *eidos*), *Hippias Major* 294b1f. (without *eidos*).

201e1ff.) aiming to account for complexes in terms of simples. How are these different approaches connected? Did he think of division-based definitions as alternatives to ones connected with explanation or as supplements? Did he consider one method as preferable in some contexts (and not in others)? And why? Or was he open-mindedly investigating different styles of answer to Socrates' 'What is F?' question, perhaps never fully satisfied with any of them? Did Plato achieve a satisfying overview in which these differing types of definition fit together? Or was his investigation an extended case of work in progress?

2.4 In this Collection

Although the essays on Plato in this collection do not focus exclusively on the three problems just noted, they contain much that is relevant to them.

Lindsay Judson and Vasilis Politis investigate important aspects of *Problem 1* in considering parts of the *Euthyphro* and the *Phaedo* respectively. Judson discusses the explanatory asymmetries Socrates uncovered in the *Euthyphro*, examines their basis and their relevance to definition. His essay raises, in acute form, the question of what type of priority Socrates attributes to piety over the property of being loved by the gods. Since Socrates took definitions to be of essences (*ousiai*) in some way prior to other properties, Judson's question is central for the study of definition. Politis focuses on the explanatory role of Plato's Forms in the *Phaedo*, which, he suggests, are best conceived as a distinctive type of essences. Politis notes the stringent requirements imposed on Form-involving explanation and argues that it is distinct from (and irreducible to) other types of explanation (such as involve teleological or material causation), even though some of Plato's Forms may be (in Aristotle's terminology) both teleological and formal causes. Both essays raise questions with relevance to other dialogues. Did he, for example, reach in the *Republic*, or elsewhere, a stable view as to how teleological and definitional concerns are to be connected? Or was it left to Aristotle to do so?

Deborah Modrak and David Charles examine aspects of *Problem 2*. While Modrak focuses mainly on Aristotle, she connects his discussion with Plato's account of names in the *Cratylus*, in which (as she notes) names encapsulate definitions. But here, as she and others have remarked, it is not always clear how the definitional accounts themselves are to be understood.

Sometimes they serve merely to distinguish the object named from other things, sometimes to convey its essence.[12] Charles suggests that Socrates imposed (in the *Meno*) the apparently incompatible demands on answers to his 'What is . . . ?' question (noted by Robinson) because he failed systematically to distinguish two distinct definitional questions: 'What is virtue?' (a question about the nature of virtue) and 'What is "virtue"?' (a question about what the term 'virtue' signifies). Both essays raise the more general issue of whether Socrates succeeded in clearly distinguishing questions about the meaning (or signification) of terms from ones about the nature of the objects or kinds signified (and, if so, where). Or did his conflation of these topics, if such it was, have further consequences for his philosophy?

Lesley Brown and Mary Louise Gill consider Plato's division-based approach to definition. Brown argues that this method cannot, in Plato's view, be satisfactorily applied to defining the sophist because there is no definable art of deception which the sophist masters. She suggests that the inconclusive outcome of the *Sophist* results from the nature of its subject-matter rather than problems or limitations in the method itself. Her essay raises the issue of what range of items Plato sought to define in this way and of why he restricted this method (as she suggests) to certain cases. Gill focuses on the method itself, as developed in the *Sophist* and in the *Politicus*, suggesting that Plato in these dialogues addressed the questions set out above. Her essay points to a number of important, and frequently overlooked, suggestions and modifications to this method which Plato makes in these dialogues. Although Gill and Brown disagree as to whether the *Sophist* rules out the possibility of a division-based definition of the sophist, both essays raise important questions about the range and defensibility of this style of definition and its connection with the explanation-involving style of definition employed elsewhere. (These issues, relevant to *Problem 3*, are further considered by Aristotle in the *Analytics* and elsewhere.)

None of the essays in this volume attempts to give an overview of Plato's varied attempts at definition in different dialogues, still less to explain what led him to modify his approach in the way (and to the extent) he did. There remains a need for a study of this issue and for a more sustained examination of whether his differing accounts of definition withstand Aristotle's subsequent criticism.

---

[12]   For further discussion of this issue see D. Sedley, *Plato's Cratylus*, Cambridge, 2003, p. 83.

3 Aristotle: Attempts to Resolve Plato's Problems

Many of Aristotle's views on definition arise from difficulties he saw in Plato's and Socrates' approach. In the *Topics* and the *Posterior Analytics*, he is often preoccupied with diagnosing and resolving problems concerning definition that had arisen in the Academy. I shall consider aspects of his varying accounts relevant to the three problems outlined in the previous section, beginning with his remarks in the *Analytics*.

3.1 Problem 1: Requirements for Good Definition

Aristotle, in *Posterior Analytics B*, closely connects questions of explanation and definition. In answering the definitional 'What is it?' question, one should, in his view, also answer the further question 'Why is it as it is?' There is one feature which is the centre of the answer to both explanatory and definitional questions (90a32).

In Aristotle's favoured examples (of thunder and eclipse) the efficient cause explains the occurrence of a given type of noise in the clouds (or deprivation of light: 93a30–b10). Further, in both cases, the type of noise (or light deprivation) in question is made the type it is by being caused in this way. In the case of thunder, its distinctive causal ancestry determines the specific type of noise that occurs and marks it off from other types of noise (see, for example, 94a5). In both, efficient causal ancestry makes what happens the type of thing it is: it fixes its identity.

In Aristotle's account, one finds the best causal explanation of thunder when one finds that cause which fixes the feature which determines the identity of the phenomenon. Similarly, a successful search for the definition of thunder requires one to find the efficient cause of its occurrence. So understood, both definitional and explanatory projects are guided by, and directed towards, the idea of essence (or nature), understood as that which makes the kind the one it is and explains why it has the qualities it does. Indeed, these projects are two sides of the same coin, variants of one basic method differing only in 'presentation' (see, for example, 94a1–3).

To see, in general terms, the significance of Aristotle's suggestion, consider Socrates' conditions on good definition in the *Meno*. In his favoured case of bees, there will be, in Aristotle's account (if applied to substances), just one feature which explains the presence of the other features bees possess and accounts for each bee being a bee. The essence of bees is central to answering two distinct questions: 'What makes bees bees?' and 'What accounts for the distinctive features bees possess?' It is both explanatorily basic and what fixes the identity of each and every bee (as the animals they are). The essence teleologically explains the presence of the other features bees possess (assuming that the teleological cause is what fixes the identity of bees) and, as such, will be grasped (in large part) on the basis of empirical, biological investigation. While the essence must possess the kind of unity required (in this case) for it to be one teleological cause, there is no requirement that it be absolutely simple, incapable of further analysis or description in general terms. There is no suggestion that the type of unity in question be self-evident, graspable *a priori* by reflection alone.

While this rough outline of Aristotle's approach might be generally agreed, crucial specific questions remain. Here are four:

[AR 1]   How precisely did he understand the connection between causal explanation and definition? Did it, in his view, have a metaphysical basis? Or was it simply that causal explanation offered a good way of coming to know the essence (captured in the definition)? How precisely are the two roles that essences play (those of making the kind the one it is and explaining why it has the qualities it does) connected?

[AR 2]   What motivated his account? Did he take it as a requirement for a fully perspicuous (scientific) account of how things are that there are causally basic essences which determine the identity of the kind in question? Was this the goal of an ideal science? Or did he think that his account was (or would be) vindicated by the actual success of science in finding such essences? Or was it rather a generally shared, pre-philosophical, assumption that objects or kinds have natures which it is the task of definers and explainers to uncover?

[AR 3]   Did Aristotle succeed in applying this account to substances in the *Metaphysics* and to biological kinds in his biological researches? If he did not, what accounts for his failure to do so? Is there, perhaps, some fundamental problem in his approach to definition? Or do these difficulties suggest that we should understand his account in the *Analytics* in different terms?

[AR 4]   How do essences, so understood, relate to the objects or kinds whose essences they are? Are they identical with the kinds in question? Or do they rather make the kinds the ones they are? Are there individual essences as well as essences of kinds?

Although each of these questions is important, only the first and part of the third are addressed in this volume.

3.2 Problem 2: What is to be Defined? 'The Problem in the Meno'

In the *Analytics*, Aristotle distinguishes accounts of what terms signify from accounts of the nature of the objects or kinds signified (93a29–32, 92b26). While the former need to be grasped at the outset of the quest for knowledge, the latter are arrived at in the final stage of investigation. Enquiry, involving the acquisition of new information, is possible because one can proceed from the former to the latter stage in one's quest for knowledge. Aristotle distinguished (at least) two types of definition, one of which meets one of the conditions mentioned in the *Meno*:

[A]   it is that one thing in virtue of which all cases of F are F (72c7ff.)

and, if successful, indicates the (basic) essence of the object (or kind) to be defined. Another type seems designed to meet two other conditions noted in the *Meno*:

[B]   it is graspable without specialized knowledge by intelligent interlocutors (75d2–7);
[C]   it is such that if one does not know it, one cannot know any other feature of F (71b3–7).

The second type will give an account of what the term in question signifies.
   Although Aristotle's distinction is an important (and generally accepted) one, many interpretative issues remain about his account. I shall mention four, adding to the list of specific questions raised in the previous section:

[AR 5]   What information or knowledge is required if one is to possess an adequate account of what a term signifies? How is it acquired?

[AR 6]   Do accounts of what terms signify give us information about the world? Or about concepts? Or both?

[AR 7]   What is the role of accounts of what terms signify? Do they determine the extension of the term? Or do they provide just enough information for a scientific investigation to begin into the nature of the kinds they signify?

[AR 8] Are all accounts of what terms signify definitions? Can there be definitional accounts of this type even when the terms fail to signify any existing object or kind? Can one acquire an account of what a term signifies without knowing of the existence of the object signified?

These specific issues intersect with questions about Aristotle's views about the signification of terms and remain controversial.

3.3 Problem 3: The Variety of Definitions

Aristotle, like Plato, employs several models of definition. While in some sections of the *Analytics*, as already noted, he uses a causally explanatory model, elsewhere (e.g. in the *Topics*, *Metaphysics*, and biological works) he employs definitions based on *genus* and *differentia* and on occasion (as in the *Metaphysics*) matter and form (or potentiality and actuality). How do these three different types of definition fit together? LeBlond argued that Aristotle 'muddled' these three quite distinct types of definition, concluding that 'This confusion is so pervasive that Aristotle's arguments are often difficult to follow.'[13]

LeBlond held that the three styles of definition just mentioned are on the same level and aspects of each were intended to refer to the same phenomenon in different ways. Thus, in analysing Aristotle's definition in terms of

cause	:	effect
form	:	matter
differentia	:	*genus*

he assumed that his aim was to identify (in the case of substances) the form with the cause and the *differentia*. LeBlond argued that this goal could not be achieved for two reasons.

(i) The causal model of definition developed in the *Analytics* cannot be applied to substances. For while (according to LeBlond) the causal model

---

[13]   LeBlond, 'Aristotle on Definition', p. 72.

requires there to be two separate things, cause and effect, no such independent [or separate] causal elements are present in the case of substances. Form and matter are not, in his view, two separate entities. If (as it appears) Aristotle sought to apply his causal model to substances, the result must be a failure. LeBlond concluded that since substances are the basic objects of Aristotle's definition, causal definition (of the type developed in the *Analytics*) is not genuine definition.[14]

(ii) While Aristotle legitimately applied the *genus/differentia* model in defining substances, he conflated this with a wholly different style of definition in terms of matter and form. LeBlond suggested that since the former style of definition is concerned with classification, with comparison with neighbouring cases, and not with the nature of substance, it cannot be assimilated to definitions using matter and form (or, for that matter, cause and effect) since the latter focus on the substance by itself.

Both LeBlond's arguments deserve careful scrutiny. The first will be successfully challenged if the matter/form style of definition is a legitimate extension to the case of substance of *Analytics*-style, causal definitions. So understood, the introduction of matter and form (and potentiality and actuality) will constitute Aristotle's attempt to apply his *Analytics*-style, causal model, to substances. Much depends on whether LeBlond is correct to see form and matter as lacking the type of independence required for causal definition. Form may, after all, be teleologically prior to its effect even if both co-occur. In Aristotle's terms, they may be separable *in being* but not in existence.

LeBlond's second argument assumes that Aristotle, in treating substances, treated form/matter and *differentia/genus* definitions as equally basic. But this assumption is controversial. Aristotle may have preferred causally based, or matter/form, definitions to those phrased in terms of *differentia/genus*. Perhaps only the former capture the type of unity and priority he required of good definitions. If so, definitions by *genus* and *differentia* may be useful only at a preliminary stage of investigation. Or, alternatively, they may be finally

---

[14] 'Aristotle on Definition', p. 71. He further claimed: 'Definition by matter and form is inspired by a different analogy. . . . which also only works (in the case of artefacts) when you have matter with pre-existing properties' (p. 75).

reconstituted with matter as the relevant *genus*. Or perhaps, more radically, they were finally discarded in favour of definitions by matter and form. However, in none of these ways do they constitute an equally basic rival to the other styles of definition Aristotle considers.

LeBlond's arguments flow from a more general concern: how do the definitions developed in the *Topics* fit with those proposed in the *Analytics*, *Metaphysics*, and biological works? His question remains even if his particular arguments fail to establish a radical discontinuity between them.

One way to address LeBlond's basic concern begins by suggesting that the *Topics* is part of a 'logical' investigation which does not explicitly invoke causal notions. The appropriate constraints on definition in this style of investigation will differ from those appropriate in other causal ('analytical') or metaphysical contexts. In the *Topics* Aristotle refers in considering definitions to the order to be found in a science with its distinctive starting-points (*archai*) and demonstrative consequences (141b7–8, a29–30: compare *Post. An.* 72b5). The *Analytics* may be seen as making clear (in causal terms) what the relevant type of science will be, while parts of the *Metaphysics* further enrich this picture by introducing ideas derived from physics (such as matter and form).[15] So understood, Aristotle's discussions of definition in the *Topics*, *Analytics*, and *Metaphysics* are distinct but complementary, with different levels of analysis appropriate in different areas. In some 'logical' contexts, it is enough to point to the genus and *differentiae* in a completed science (whatever it may be). In 'analytical' contexts, he adds the causal terms in which the relevant sciences are to be conducted. In metaphysical contexts, he introduces general physical terms (such as matter and form) required if these causal terms are to be applied. In biological contexts, he specifies the type of matter, form, and causality required for the study of animals.[16]

[15] For somewhat differing versions of this view, see M. Ferejohn 'The Definition of Generated Composites in Aristotle's Metaphysics', in *Unity, Identity and Explanation in Aristotle's Metaphysics*, ed. T. Scaltsas, D. Charles, and M. L. Gill, Oxford, 1994, pp. 291–318; A. Code, 'Aristotle's Metaphysics as a Science of Principles', *Revue Internationale de Philosophie* 51 (1997), pp. 357–78; and M. Burnyeat, *A Map of Metaphysics Zeta*, Pittsburgh, 2001.

[16] For differing accounts of the interconnections between these levels, see D. Charles, *Aristotle on Meaning and Essence*, Oxford, 2000, chs. 8–11; D. Modrak, *Aristotle's Theory of Language and Meaning*, Cambridge, 2001, ch. 6; and M. Deslauriers, *Aristotle on Definition*, Leiden, 2007, ch. 5.

This approach, although promising, raises several more specific questions about Aristotle's project (to add to the eight already mentioned):

[AR 9]   While it predicts that Aristotle, in his biological works, will attempt to implement in a more determinate fashion the project outlined in the *Analytics* and parts of the *Metaphysics*, is this what he, in fact, does? Are his biological definitions causally based? Do they connect with definitions using matter and form? Or does he revert to definitions based on *genus* and *differentiae*?

[AR 10]   The *Topics'* account of definition requires further study, both in its own right and for its connection with Aristotle's discussion elsewhere. Does it yield clear and determinate conditions on definition which Aristotle satisfies by drawing on causal material drawn from the *Analytics* and elsewhere? Or does it contain incomplete (or indeterminate) conditions for definition which are made precise by considering the type of unity and priority required for good definition in the *Analytics*? Are *Topics*-style definitions subject to revision by ones drawn from scientific investigation? Or do they represent a style of definition which is adequate in its own terms for the distinctive purposes at hand? Or, more radically, should scientific-style definitions be made to cohere with those presented in the *Topics* (if they were to appear inconsistent)?

3.4 In this Collection

Each of the major issues, captured in *Problems 1, 2,* and *3,* is discussed in this collection. Kei Chiba considers aspects of *Problem 1*, focusing on issues raised in the *Topics*. He argues that Aristotle is concerned there with analysing and modifying Plato's 'dialectical' method, distinguishing varying types of 'What is F?' question and noting differing styles of answer. He claims that Aristotle draws an important distinction in the first book of the *Topics* between the *definiens* (defining term: *horos*) and the whole definition (which includes both *definiens* and *definiendum*) as part of a 'logical' theory of dialectic, which is to be distinguished from the practice of dialectical argument. He further suggests that the key Aristotelian phrase 'what it was to be that thing' was introduced in these chapters with the aim of referring back to Socrates' search for definitions through discussion. His essay, which points forward to Aristotle's discussion of definition in the *Analytics* and the

Metaphysics, also suggests that Aristotle's discussion of varying categories of predication and entity in *Topics* A.9 is motivated, in part, by his wish to distinguish between the types of definition appropriate for (e.g.) substances and properties.

Deborah Modrak also addresses *Problem 1* in her account of Aristotelian 'scientific definitions' of essences which she discusses with reference to his views on definition in the *Metaphysics* and *Physics*. She further argues that while only scientific definitions of essence are definitions in the strictest sense, accounts of what terms signify can, in certain cases, be definitions. Indeed, the more closely they approximate to scientific definitions, the better their claim to be definitions proper. However, in her view, not all accounts of what names signify are definitions as there can be no definitions in the case of vacuous names, such as 'goatstag'. Modrak connects Aristotle's account of definition with his views on signification in *De Interpretatione*, where she sees him as making signification dependent on a general correspondence between linguistic concepts and extra-linguistic reality.[17] Using these resources, she gives an interesting and distinctive account of Aristotle's response to *Problem 2*, underlining the ways in which it differs from that later offered by Stoic writers. Throughout her paper, she connects issues of definition closely with those of division, noting the points of similarity and dissimilarity between Plato's and Aristotle's discussion and that found in some of the Stoics. In these sections, she addresses *Problem 3* concerning the unity of Aristotle's account of definition. Her essay offers, as well as detailed analysis of a range of texts (some also discussed by Chiba, Charles, and Crivelli), an admirable overview of Aristotle's varying treatments of definition.

David Charles considers aspects of *Problem 1*, suggesting, on the basis of an account of the *Analytics*, that for Aristotle the search for definition (in this context), so far from offering a separate, distinctively philosophical, route to knowledge, is inseparable from the 'scientific' search for features which are causally basic (in, for example, efficient or teleological modes). He argues that, for Aristotle, this interconnection between definitions and explanation is metaphysically grounded in the essences of the relevant phenomena. In the second part of his essay, Charles addresses one of LeBlond's criticisms of Aristotle's account of definition, arguing that he based his discussions of

---

[17] She discusses the issue of signification further in *Aristotle's Theory of Language and Meaning*, ch. 1.

substance, matter (potentiality), and form (actuality) in central chapters of the *Metaphysics* on his *Analytics* view of definition.

James Lennox's essay is concerned with *Problem 3* (and another of Le-Blond's concerns), focusing on the role of definition in biology. Lennox argues that Aristotle, in his biological writings, was attempting to apply his *Analytics* style of definition to biological kinds. Where some have maintained that the study of such kinds poses a problem for this style of definition,[18] Lennox suggests that Aristotle deploys the notion of 'a way of life' (*bios*) to express the basic unity of the kind, around which the definition is to be constructed. While such lives are made up of a variety of activities, they are not reducible to a set of them. Rather the activities are, in some measure, the ones they are because they are aspects of a given animal's life. If he is correct, Aristotle in his biological works takes major steps to carrying through the definitional project outlined in the *Analytics*. If Lennox's account can be sustained, it shows a substantial measure of continuity between the views on definition in the *Analytics*, *Metaphysics*, and biological works. Lennox also considers the precise interconnection between formal and teleological cause in the biological works. Is this exactly the same as that sketched elsewhere? Or should Lennox's account of their connection in the biological works call into question the account some have offered of the other texts? These important issues are left open here.

4 Post-Aristotelian Developments

Post-Aristotelian discussion of definition is a fascinating and under-explored area. I shall merely point to some issues raised by contributions to this volume, focusing on the first two problems raised above.

4.1 Problem 1: Requirements for Good Definition

Stoic definition appears importantly different from Aristotle's. Its basic goal is not to capture essences but, as Paolo Crivelli argues in this collection, to clarify and elucidate our *preconceptions*, forming in the process *conceptions* which can be used in physical and ethical discourse. There can be several

---

[18] See, for example, Charles, *Aristotle on Meaning and Essence*, pp. 310–47.

acceptable definitions of the same concept, each stating in some appropriate form conditions necessary and sufficient for its application. Definitions are useful when they improve our ability correctly to apply individual concepts or assist in organizing a number of concepts, revealing their differences and showing how they fit together in a harmonious way. The best definitions will be phrased in terms which are clear and well understood. While definitions can be used for various purposes in different contexts, there is not a variety of types of definition. In Aristotelian terms, their definitions most resemble accounts of what terms signify. They are not put forward as accounts of the unitary, causally basic essences of the objects or kind signified. Indeed, essential definitions of the latter type seem to play no role in their account.[19]

There are important questions about the detail of the Stoic account of definition, even abstracting from their particular views about *preconceptions* and *conceptions*. Here are three:

[S 1] While good definitions are, in the Stoic view, to be expressed 'fittingly and analytically', their conditions stand in need of further specification. What is required over and above co-extensiveness?

[S 2] What counts as a properly clarified concept? Is it simply one clear enough to be used in successful scientific or ethical investigation? Or should it be thoroughly perspicuous to us, meeting some further, more demanding, condition on clarity or intelligibility?[20]

[S 3] Why was it important that, in giving definitions, one seeks to ensure that several concepts fit together in a 'harmonious way'? Is this merely a way of ensuring that they can all be used in a successful scientific enterprise? Or does it require that the concepts should fit together in a fully intelligible way?

These specific questions raise a more general issue. Did the Stoics see good definitions simply as providing a clear grasp on the conceptual tools to be

---

[19] While, in some contexts, Stoics speak of 'men as mortal in that and in so far as they are men' (Philodemus, *On Signs* 4.10ff.), they do not connect this talk with definition of essences. These phrases may mean no more than that man is necessarily mortal. For an apparently opposed view (which, however, does not distinguish between essential and necessary features), see A. A. Long and D. Sedley, *The Hellenistic Philosophers*, Cambridge, 1987, vol. 1, p. 265.

[20] For discussion of this question, see M. Frede's 'Stoics and Sceptics on Clear and Distinct Impressions', in *Essays in Ancient Philosophy*, Minnesota, 1987, pp. 151–76.

used in scientific or ethical enquiry? If so, was the sole purpose of their definitions to give the resources properly to investigate these differing areas? On this account, once the enquirer has an adequate set of concepts, his scientific or ethical enquiry will, if successful, lead him to discover how things are in the world. While the enquiry must begin with a clear and defensible tool-kit of concepts, what is discovered depends on how things are with the world. Different definitions of the same concept will be useful for different investigators with different background information or in different contexts. Perhaps, as enquiry progresses, they may be led to further alter their earlier definitions in the light of new information. We need a firmer grasp on the role definition played for the Stoics before we can finally answer these important questions.

It is a striking feature of Stoic definitions that they are primarily confined to concepts and do not involve the essences of objects or kinds. What led to this radical departure from the views of their immediate predecessors?

One suggestion, consistent with the one just made, is that they took the task of scientific investigation to be that of uncovering necessities or laws in nature. If the best explanation of what occurs is given solely in these terms, they will have no role in their account for essences distinct from the necessary properties of kinds (or individuals). The goal of uncovering essential features which ground the necessary or law-like properties of objects, which was central to their predecessors, would have been rejected. Indeed, if laws and necessary properties were, for them, explanatorily bedrock, there would have been no need for definitions involving essences (as opposed to necessary properties). If the world is fundamentally constituted by objects with necessary properties standing in law-like necessary connections, there will be no space for further essence-involving definitions. The most one can do is outline an object's necessary properties.

There may be other explanations of the Stoic reluctance to propose essence-involving definitions. Further, the suggestion just made is incomplete since it leads to the further question of why they treated necessity as their bedrock notion. Did they regard it as a better understood (or clearer) concept than that of essence (and, if so, why?). Or did they think that scientific explanation was complete without talk of essence? Or did they have some further metaphysical qualms which led them to avoid essences and get by with necessities alone? These questions remain unresolved.

Despite these gaps, it may be instructive to compare the Stoic view with Plotinus' approach to definition (discussed by Annamaria Schiaparelli in this volume). Plotinus, who was aware of Stoic discussions on this issue, was happy to talk of definitions as capturing the formal causes of objects in the material world. Further, essences (so understood) are interconnected in an intelligible order, fitting together in a harmonious system of universals, graspable by rational reflection alone.[21] However, while essences (in his account) play an explanatory role, it is (it appears) to be understood in terms of logical entailment, not of (Aristotelian) efficient, teleological, or material causation. If the Stoics gave up on talk of essences and preferred to ground their view on the necessities uncovered by scientific explanation of the world, Plotinus maintained talk of essences but separated it from scientific explanation of the material world. In this respect, Plotinus' approach resembles that followed by Socrates in the *Phaedo*, where the search for definition is distinguished from scientific enquiry in terms of material or teleological explanation and confined (in the 'second journey') to the Forms.

There are several specific questions to be raised concerning Plotinus' account of definition. I shall mention three:

[PL 1]   How did he attempt metaphysically to ground claims about what is essential for an object or kind (as opposed to what is merely necessary), once he had abstracted away from efficient, teleological, or material explanation? (This problem resembles the one Aristotle raised for advocates of the 'logical syllogism' in *Posterior Analytics* B.4–6. In these passages, Aristotle argued that it could not be resolved without invoking real-world explanations in his theory of demonstration.)

[PL 2]   What was the metaphysical basis, if any, for Plotinus' use of the method of division in arriving at definitions? What generates the relevant divisions and excludes others? What makes certain features *differentiae* and others not? (This problem engaged both Plato and Aristotle, as noted above.)

[PL 3]   How did Plotinus account for our coming to know which features are essential and relevant to definitions and which are not?

---

[21]   For further discussion of this issue, see E. E. Emilsson, *Plotinus on the Intellect*, Oxford, 2007, chs. 3–4, and M. Wagner, 'Plotinus on the Nature of Physical Reality', in *The Cambridge Companion to Plotinus*, ed. L. Gerson, Cambridge, 1996, pp. 130–70.

What epistemological resources did he deploy in addressing this issue? (He cannot have depended, as Aristotle seems to, on grasping the explanatory role of essences in efficient, teleological, or material explanation.)

What seems absent from Plotinian and Stoic accounts of definition is the distinctively Aristotelian mid-position in which definition and scientific explanation are strongly interconnected, both based on essences which simultaneously fix the identity of the object (or kind) and explain its necessary properties. Plotinus retained the definitional project but separated it from scientific explanation (in terms of efficient, teleological, or material causation). In this, he may have followed Plato's earlier approach. The Stoics, by contrast, seem to have focused on scientific explanation, couched in terms of necessary connections in nature, but to have divorced this concern from the search for definitions involving essences. Each party, in effect, retained one aspect of Aristotle's account but rejected the other.

What led to this unravelling of Aristotle's view? Did Stoics and neo-Platonists have specific objections to connecting definition and explanation in the way Aristotle suggested? Or were they led to their different views by differing concerns and projects? If so, how are these differences to be understood? There are major historical questions to address at this point.

The differing Stoic and neo-Platonist approaches, so understood, point in radically opposed directions. The Stoic account (on one interpretation) encourages the view that we should (after some preliminary definitional work) engage in scientific investigation, unconstrained by the ideal of essence-directed definition, to uncover laws and necessities in nature. If definition has any role in this latter project, it is simply (as for more recent scientific essentialists) to record the results of empirically based scientific enquiry, governed by independent explanatory principles. Plotinus' approach, by contrast, suggests that we should, in seeking for definitions, focus on questions answerable by reason alone. We do not need empirical scientific investigation to find what grounds the identity of an object or kind. These questions can be resolved by 'armchair' reflection alone. From either perspective, Aristotle's attempt to interconnect definitions and scientific explanation appears mistaken, an unsustainable hybrid, made up of different elements that cannot fit properly together. Is Aristotle's view, as many since have believed, doomed? Or is it rather that his later critics, in their contrasting ways, rejected the best available approach to definition? A great deal rests on the answer to this question.

Despite their differences, there is one point on which Stoics and Plotinus agree while disagreeing with Aristotle. Both maintain that the search for definitions has its own distinctive subject-matter. For the Stoics, it is the investigation of concepts, distinguished from the scientific exploration of objects and kinds in the world. For Plotinus, it is a search for universals whose identity and existence is independent of ordinary causal explanation. For both, the philosopher (like Plato's Socrates) will hunt for definitions without reliance on the methods or results of ordinary 'scientific' explanation. Stoic and neo-Platonist alike reject Aristotle's suggestion (in the *Analytics*) that the methods appropriate for the study of definition and scientific explanation are, when fully spelled out, fundamentally the same. The point at issue is a basic one: is the philosophical search for definitions a distinct, *sui generis*, activity with its own unique domain (of concepts, meanings, or transcendent universals)? Or is it best understood as part of an investigation, shared with a theoretically sophisticated science, into aspects of the world around us? How is 'philosophy' itself to be defined?

4.2 Problem 2: What is to be Defined? 'The Problem in the *Meno*'

The Stoics, as already noted, saw definitions as clarifying and elucidating our *preconceptions*, forming in the process *conceptions* to be used in physical and ethical investigation. In their account we can, it appears, gain knowledge by first achieving a grasp on suitably clarified conceptions (meeting, for example, the conditions sketched above) and then by employing these to discover necessities in nature. A broadly similar view was, it seems, taken by the Epicureans.[22] Galen, although he differed from the Stoics on some issues, accepted the outlines of this approach, as did the majority of Aristotelian commentators. Sextus, too, understood the Stoics in this way and proceeded to raise questions about their account.

There are several issues to be raised about the *preconceptions* which definitions refine and organize. I shall mention three relevant to our present study, to add to the three already noted:

[S 4]   Are *preconceptions*, like conceptions, concerned with universals which are grasped as universals? Is their content itself universal in charac-

---

[22] See, for example, Long and Sedley, *Hellenistic Philosophers*, vol. 1, pp. 88–9. For further discussion of this issue, see M. Tuominen, 'Analysis in Epicurus' Arguments for the Existence of Void?', forthcoming.

ter? Or do they solely concern particulars, grasped in non-universal terms? If one thinks (using a *preconception* of man) that Kallias is a man, does one grasp in some unclear way the universal man (as a given kind of animal)? Or does one's *preconception* consist simply in one's being able to spot that Kallias is like other men, without having any thought of there being one universal they all instantiate?

[S 5]   How much do we need to grasp to have a *preconception*, albeit unclear or incomplete? To have a preconception concerning man, we must be able, it would seem, to apply it correctly on some occasions and to withhold it correctly on others. But how demanding is this condition? Do we, for example, have a preconception of man if although we sometimes apply it and sometimes withhold it correctly, we sometimes (even in favourable conditions) apply it incorrectly to mountains or the sea? Or is it required that one is always able to apply and withhold it correctly in good conditions, even if one sometimes errs in more difficult circumstances? Or could some errors, even in unfavourable conditions, call into question the claim that one's *preconception* was of man (rather than, for example, of something that merely looks like a man)?

[S 6]   When one grasps a *preconception* of man, does one have knowledge (whether of the universal or of the cases that fall under it)? Or does one only have beliefs about these matters? Further, if one uses one's *preconception* in understanding the term 'man', does one know what that term means? Or does one only have beliefs about its meaning?

With regard to [S 4], many take *preconceptions* to be concerned with universals and expressed in universal terms.[23] If this is correct, the Stoic account will differ from Aristotle's, if (as some have suggested) he took the stage characterized as 'experience' to involve only judgements about particulars expressed in non-universal terms.[24] If so, the Stoics, and others influenced by them, will have discarded Aristotle's account of the origin of conceptual thought in distinctive particular-orientated judgements. As a result they will not be able to employ his explanation of how we come to acquire, on the

---

[23]   This issue is discussed in Modrak's essay in this volume.

[24]   This interpretation is favoured by D. Modrak in *Aristotle: The Power of Perception*, Chicago, 1987, p. 167; R. D. McKirahan, *Principles and Proofs: Aristotle's Theory of Demonstrative Science*, Princeton, 1992, p. 243; S. Everson, *Aristotle on Perception*, Oxford, 1997, pp. 223f.; and Charles in 'The Paradox in the *Meno* and Aristotle's Attempts to Resolve it' in this volume.

basis of experience, our grasp of universal concepts. Without the support his account provides, it may seem unexplained how we are equipped at the outset (albeit in an incomplete form) with the very universal concepts we need for scientific enquiry.

If [S 4] is correctly addressed in the terms just used, one needs to know why the Stoics (and others) turned away from Aristotle's experience-based account and to assess their grounds for doing so. Did they regard his account as unnecessary? Or did they entertain suspicions about its usefulness or coherence? Were they simply unaware of it? Or did they understand it differently? Once again, quite apart from these historical questions, there is a more general philosophical one: Did the Stoics have a good explanation of why we are (generally) in possession of such good preconceptions at the beginning of our route to knowledge? Can they satisfactorily account for the acquisition (or possession) of preconceptions without using Aristotle's particular-orientated account of experience. These questions, raised in an acute form by the Stoics' approach to definition, require further investigation.

[S 6] is raised in a challenging form by sceptical criticism of the Stoic view, discussed in Gail Fine's essay. They called into question the claim that we have knowledge of our preconceptions and challenged the suggestion that we are entitled even to beliefs about them. (Their question is pressing if, on the Stoic account, we simply find ourselves at birth with a set of preconceptions. Why, after all, should we believe claims we are 'saddled with' by nature?) However, there is an interesting problem in the sceptic's own account of these matters. If they are correct, they need to show what my understanding of the terms I grasp (on the basis of preconceptions) amounts to. Can I, indeed, understand a term (such as 'man') if I lack both knowledge and belief concerning which objects fall under it? If I do not have beliefs about which are the objects to which this term is correctly applied, I will be unable to distinguish them from those to which it appears to apply (but does not, in fact, do so). But if I cannot draw this distinction (even in principle), what understanding do I have of the term in question?

4.3 In this Collection

Paolo Crivelli and Annamaria Schiaparelli discuss aspects of *Problem 1*, considering the differing views on what is to count as a good definition suggested by the Stoics and Plotinus respectively. Both essays raise, in addition to the issues noted above, important questions about the detail and direction of their differing approaches.[25]

Richard Sorabji, Jane Hood, and Gail Fine focus mainly on *Problem 2*, discussing the variety of views of the Aristotelian Commentators, Galen, and some of the sceptics on the issues concerning preconceptions and conceptions outlined above. Sorabji notes that many of the Commentators understood Aristotle's remarks in *Posterior Analytics* B.19 as favouring a view of the acquisition of concepts which takes as its starting-point an incomplete grasp of a universal. Their adherence to this view may call into question the alternative, particular-content, interpretation of Aristotle's 'pre-conceptual' experience sketched above. Or perhaps they were influenced by the Stoic account and interpreted Aristotle so as to make his views resemble theirs. To answer these questions there is need for further specification of the project in which the Commentators themselves were engaged.

Jane Hood's essay on Galen notes the continuity between certain aspects of his account of definition and Aristotle's, while also commenting on important points of difference. Galen, like Aristotle, drew a clear distinction between accounts of what terms signify and accounts of the things signified but understood the former in ways which correspond closely to the views of the Stoics and some of the Aristotelian commentators. Hood's essay points to the importance of definition in Galen's writings, opening up a further relatively unexplored area for future discussion. It would be a major task to uncover and analyse the various philosophical motivations at work in his treatment of this topic.

Gail Fine's essay, in assessing sceptical criticism of the Stoic view, raises new and important questions both about its effectiveness and about the defensibility of the sceptics' own account of our understanding of the meaning of terms. Although she argues that their account is a tenable one, she points to several serious difficulties. Her essay considers the views of both Stoics and their critics about accounts of what terms signify and points to a number of intriguing issues about the sceptic's grasp of meaning which have been left aside in recent discussions of the beliefs a sceptic may have.[26] Fine

---

[25] Crivelli's account may profitably be compared with a recent discussion by C. Brittain, 'Common Sense: Concepts, Definitions and Meaning in and out of the Stoa', in *Language and Learning*, ed. D. Frede and B. Inwood, Cambridge, 2005, pp. 164–209. Brittain also considers Cicero's views on definition.

[26] See, for example, the essays collected in *The Original Sceptics: A Controversy*, ed. M. Burnyeat and M. Frede, Indianapolis, 1997.

throughout connects the issues which divide Stoics and sceptics with the paradox in the *Meno*, examining some of the ways in which Hellenistic philosophers re-considered questions which had pre-occupied Plato and Aristotle.

In conclusion: philosophers from Socrates to the logical positivists regarded the search for definition as a, perhaps the, central task of philosophy. This collection is part of an attempt to understand this project and assess its philosophical value.[27]

[27] I am indebted to Kei Chiba, Paolo Crivelli, Michail Peramatzis, Annamaria Schiaparelli, and Marco Zingano for their comments.

PART I
Plato on Definition

1

Carried Away in the *Euthyphro*

LINDSAY JUDSON

At 9e1–3 Euthyphro offers his second definition of piety: 'Well, then, I would say that the pious is this, whatever all the gods love; and that its opposite, what all the gods hate, is impious.'[1] Socrates asks if they are to examine this definition, or merely accept it because someone has stated it—not the first implicit attack in the dialogue on the idea of relying on appeals to authority.[2] The examination begins with the famous question: 'Is the pious loved by the gods because it is pious, or is it pious because it is loved?' The argument which begins with this question (10a1–11b5) is much stronger than is often claimed: this argument, and the role of definition in it, are the subjects of this paper.

The *Euthyphro* on Definition

Although in his characteristic fashion Socrates offers no set-piece discussion of what kind of definition he has in view, we can nonetheless glean a certain

---

[1] Ἀλλ' ἔγωγε φαίην ἂν τοῦτο εἶναι τὸ ὅσιον ὃ ἂν πάντες οἱ θεοὶ φιλῶσιν, καὶ τὸ ἐναντίον, ὃ ἂν πάντες θεοὶ μισῶσιν, ἀνόσιον.

[2] 4b4–c2 and 6a7–d4 are also designed to provoke the reader to think about what is problematic about appeals to authority. Euthyphro's definition itself—at least in the way it is understood in the dialogue—can also be thought of as authoritarian: cf. S. M. Cohen, 'Socrates on the Definition of Piety: *Euthyphro* 10A–11B', *Journal of the History of Philosophy* 9 (1971), 1–13, at p. 2 (this article is reprinted in G. Vlastos (ed.), *Socrates* (Garden City, 1971), pp. 158–76). In the present passage Burnet takes ἀποδεχώμεθα only to indicate 'accept as a starting point for discussion' (J. Burnet, *Plato's Euthyphro, Apology of Socrates, and Crito* (Oxford, 1924), p. 47); but the contrast here is with ἐπισκοπῶμεν ... εἰ καλῶς λέγεται. ἀποδέχομαι at 6a8 also means 'accept', not 'accept as a starting-point'.

amount about this, partly from what he does say and partly from the role
which definition plays in the argument with which we are concerned. Two
well known remarks are particularly relevant. The first is at 6d9–e6:

Do you remember that it was not this that I was bidding you to do—to teach me
some one or two of the many pious things—but to teach me that very form by
which all pious things are pious? For you said, surely, that it is by one form that the
impious things are impious and the pious things pious. . . . So teach me what this
form itself is, so that looking to it and using it as a model, I may say that whatever
actions (whether yours or anybody else's) are of this sort are pious, and those that
are not of this sort are not pious.[3]

The expression 'by which all pious things are pious' is hardly transparent.
Some light is cast on it by the second remark, at 11a6–b1:

though you were asked, Euthyphro, what the pious is, you are in danger of not
wanting to make clear to me its essence, but only to tell me of some feature that it
has. . . . But what it *is*, you have not yet said.[4]

The sort of definition that Socrates is after is a specification of whatever it is
about a pious thing (or person[5]) which makes it pious. Though this idea is to
a large extent indeterminate, it at least excludes the idea of what merely
produces or brings about the piety of pious things: Socrates' reference to the
οὐσία of piety rules this out.[6] It might then be natural to construe 'by which
all pious things are pious' in terms of identity or of constitution; but there
might be other possibilities too. Participation in a Platonic Form, for
instance, might resist analysis in these ways without resting on a relation
of efficient causation either; if so, a more abstractly specified analogue of

---

[3] Σ. Μέμνησαι οὖν ὅτι οὐ τοῦτό σοι διεκελευόμην, ἐν τι ἢ δύο με διδάξαι τῶν πολλῶν ὁσίων, ἀλλ'
ἐκεῖνο αὐτὸ τὸ εἶδος ᾧ πάντα τὰ ὅσια ὅσιά ἐστιν; ἔφησθα γάρ που μιᾷ ἰδέᾳ τά τε ἀνόσια ἀνόσια εἶναι καὶ
τὰ ὅσια ὅσια· ἢ οὐ μνημονεύεις; Ε. Ἔγωγε. Σ. Ταύτην τοίνυν με αὐτὴν δίδαξον τὴν ἰδέαν τίς ποτέ ἐστιν,
ἵνα εἰς ἐκείνην ἀποβλέπων καὶ χρώμενος αὐτῇ παραδείγματι, ὃ μὲν ἂν τοιοῦτον ᾖ ὧν ἂν ἢ σὺ ἢ ἄλλος τις
πράττῃ φῶ ὅσιον εἶναι, ὃ δ' ἂν μὴ τοιοῦτον, μὴ φῶ.

[4] καὶ κινδυνεύεις, ὦ Εὐθύφρων, ἐρωτώμενος τὸ ὅσιον ὅτι ποτ' ἐστίν, τὴν μὲν οὐσίαν μοι αὐτοῦ οὐ
βούλεσθαι δηλῶσαι, πάθος δέ τι περὶ αὐτοῦ λέγειν, ὅτι πέπονθε τοῦτο τὸ ὅσιον, φιλεῖσθαι ὑπὸ πάντων
θεῶν· ὅτι δὲ ὄν, οὔπω εἶπες.

[5] The shifts in focus in the dialogue between pious actions and pious people are a topic I shall explore
on another occasion.

[6] Not everyone accepts this. For discussion see Terence Penner, 'The Unity of Virtue', *Philosophical
Review* 82 (1973), 35–68 (reprinted in H. H. Benson (ed.), *Essays on the Philosophy of Socrates* (New York
and Oxford, 1992); and Gregory Vlastos, 'What Did Socrates Understand by his "What is F?" Question?', in Vlastos, *Platonic Studies* (2nd edn., Princeton, 1981).

such an account might be available even without the idea of Platonic Forms.[7] I do not mean to suggest, however, that we are to suppose that Socrates has one of these possibilities determinately in mind—nor even that Plato does in presenting Socrates in the way that he does.[8] All that we can do is to delimit the constraints which Socrates is made to place on definition and hence the conceptual space within which a more determinate account would have to be located. This is not the only case of significant indeterminacy in the argument, as we shall see.

Two further constraints emerge in the *Euthyphro*. One is epistemological, and is hinted at in the first of the quoted passages: knowledge of the definition provides the ability to recognize its instantiations. And it is clear from elsewhere in the *Euthyphro* that this constraint is actually much stronger: knowledge of the definition is *required* for knowledge of the instances.[9] The nature and scope of this claim is of course controversial, but for present purposes we need only note that it introduces some form of epistemological *dependence*, of knowledge that X is pious on knowledge that X satisfies the definition of piety: the definition must be such as to make this dependence possible. As we shall see, the refutation of Euthyphro's definition reveals an ontological or metaphysical dependence too: being pious depends on satisfying the definition. This idea will come into more focus when we discuss the argument. Dependence of this sort seems to rule against identity as the relation between *definiens* and being pious;[10] although we might find it natural to think in terms of constitution at this point, other relations may not be excluded, as I said above, and there is no discussion of the nature of this relation in the *Euthyphro* itself.

---

[7] Richard Sharvey makes the suggestion that the relationship might be something like an Aristotelian formal cause ('*Euthyphro* 9d–11b: Analysis and Definition in Plato and Others', *Noûs* 6 (1972), 119–37, at pp. 128ff.).

[8] I shall leave for another occasion the question of what gaps there might be between Plato's thoughts and aims in writing this part of the dialogue and those which he presents Socrates as having; for this reason I shall usually (mis)speak as if Socrates rather than Plato were the one actually at work.

[9] Thus, e.g. at the end of the *Euthyphro*, Socrates says that Euthyphro must know what piety is, since if he did not he could not think that he knew that his prosecution of his father was pious (16d–e).

[10] This despite the way Socrates refers to Euthyphro's definition at 10e10–11: 'if they really were the same, Euthyphro my friend—the god-loved and the pious...': see pp. 49–50 below.

Socrates' Argument in Outline

Socrates' line of argument does not proceed in exactly the way with which we are familiar from the so-called 'Euthyphro dilemma' argument, though there are some close connections, as we shall see. His argument falls into three main sections. In the first (10a5–c13) he sets up some distinctions which will enable him to secure Euthyphro's agreement that a pious thing's being god-loved is due to its being the object of the gods' activity of loving it; as we shall see, Socrates assumes that this in turn is due to the gods' activity of loving it. In the second section (10d1–8) Socrates secures Euthyphro's assent to what I shall call the 'reasons agreement'—the agreement that when the gods love something pious, they do so *because* it is pious. In the third (10d9–11b1) Socrates uses the points established in the first two parts to show that Euthyphro's definition of the pious will not do. In the light of the result of the first section, he argues, Euthyphro cannot hold both to the reasons agreement and to his definition. This is because a thing's being loved by the gods—and hence its being 'god-loved' ($\theta\epsilon o\phi\iota\lambda\acute{\epsilon}s$), as Socrates puts it—cannot both be that on which the thing's being pious depends and at the same time be due to the thing's being pious.

The First Section of the Argument: Distinctions

S: Well, then, I shall try to make it clearer. We speak of a thing being carried and carrying, being led away and leading away, being seen and seeing; and with all things of this sort you understand that they are different from each other and in what way they are different? **E:** I *think* I understand. **S:** Is there not also something which is loved, and, different from this, that which loves? **E:** Of course.

S: So tell me, is that which is carried a thing carried because it is carried, or for some other reason? **E:** No, for this reason. . . .

S: Then it is not because it is a thing seen that it is seen, but the opposite—because it is seen, it is a thing seen. . . .

S: Is it clear, then, Euthyphro, what I wish to say? It is that, if something comes to be or is affected in some way, then it does not come to be because it is a thing coming to be, but because it comes to be it is a thing coming to be; nor is it affected because it is a thing affected, but it is a thing affected because it is affected. Or do you not agree that this is so? **E:** I do.

S: Then is that which is loved too either something which is coming to be or which is affected in some way by something? **E:** Certainly. **S:** Then this too is like the previous cases: it is not loved by those who love it because it is a thing loved, but it is a thing loved because it is loved? **E:** Necessarily so. (10a5–c13, with omissions)[11]

It is notoriously hard to translate phrases such as φερόμενόν ἐστι and φέρεται in such a way as to make the machinery which Plato deploys in the text at least as evident in English as it is in the original without over-translating them. Plato intends to mark some distinction by means of these two phrases (as he does between θεοφιλές ἐστι and ὑπὸ τῶν θεῶν φιλεῖται: see below). But what might seem to be the natural translation—'it is carried' and 'it is carried', or 'it is god-loved' and 'it is loved by the gods'—would not show up any distinction between them. I shall discuss the sense of φερόμενόν ἐστι later; but although rendering it, as I wish to, as 'is a thing carried'[12] helps a little, we still have to remind ourselves that there is supposed to be an important difference between 'it is a thing carried' and 'it is carried'.

It is important to see how Plato in this passage combines an analytical goal with a relatively informal procedure. It might be natural to say that he is trying to make a number of quite sophisticated distinctions, but lacks any well-established technical vocabulary with which to mark them—and it is certainly right that the obscurity of the passage is at least partly due to the fact that he lacks any such vocabulary. But this way of putting the point contains an ambiguity of scope. I do not think that we should endorse it if read as 'There are a number of quite sophisticated distinctions such that Plato is trying to make *them*': that implies that there are precisely specifiable distinctions delineated, however obscurely, in the text. Rather we should

<hr />

[11] Σ. Ἀλλ' ἐγὼ πειράσομαι σαφέστερον φράσαι. λέγομέν τι φερόμενον καὶ φέρον καὶ ἀγόμενον καὶ ἄγον καὶ ὁρώμενον καὶ ὁρῶν καὶ πάντα τὰ τοιαῦτα μανθάνεις ὅτι ἕτερα ἀλλήλων ἐστὶ καὶ ᾗ ἕτερα; Ε. Ἔγωγέ μοι δοκῶ μανθάνειν. Σ. Οὐκοῦν καὶ φιλούμενόν τί ἐστιν καὶ τούτου ἕτερον τὸ φιλοῦν; Ε. Πῶς γὰρ οὔ;
Σ. Λέγε δή μοι, πότερον τὸ φερόμενον διότι φέρεται φερόμενόν ἐστιν, ἢ δι' ἄλλο τι; Ε. Οὔκ, ἀλλὰ διὰ τοῦτο ...
Σ. Οὐκ ἄρα διότι ὁρώμενόν γέ ἐστιν, διὰ τοῦτο ὁρᾶται, ἀλλὰ τὸ ἐναντίον διότι ὁρᾶται, διὰ τοῦτο ὁρώμενον· ... ἆρα κατάδηλον, ὦ Εὐθύφρων, ὃ βούλομαι λέγειν; βούλομαι δὲ τόδε, ὅτι εἴ τι γίγνεται ἤ τι πασχει, οὐχ ὅτι γιγνόμενόν ἐστι γίγνεται, ἀλλ' ὅτι γίγνεται γιγνόμενόν ἐστιν· οὐδ' ὅτι πάσχον ἐστὶ πάσχει, ἀλλ' ὅτι πάσχει πάσχον ἐστίν· ἢ οὐ συγχωρεῖς οὕτω; Ε. Ἔγωγε.
Σ. Οὐκοῦν καὶ τὸ φιλούμενον ἢ γιγνόμενόν τί ἐστιν ἢ πάσχον τι ὑπό του; Ε. Πάνυ γε. Σ. Καὶ τοῦτο ἄρα οὕτως ἔχει ὥσπερ τὰ πρότερα· οὐχ ὅτι φιλούμενόν ἐστιν φιλεῖται ὑπὸ ὧν φιλεῖται, ἀλλ' ὅτι φιλεῖται φιλούμενον; Ε. Ἀνάγκη.

[12] This is also how Burnet recommends translating the phrase (*Plato's Euthyphro,* ..., p. 48), though he does not explain what he takes this to signify.

take it that Plato's formulations are aimed at capturing some precisely specifiable distinctions—which carries no such implication. Of course, we must try to work out, as well as the text will allow, what distinctions Plato is after. But there can be no guarantee in advance that Plato—and still less his text—has a fully determinate grasp of any such distinctions; and in the case of our passage I think that the insistence that there is such a grasp, waiting to be discovered, would be misplaced.

(a) *The φερόμενον/φέρον distinction*   This is drawn at 10a5–9. A number of recent commentators think that Socrates is making a *grammatical* distinction between the passive and active voices of verbs;[13] and Emlyn-Jones, for instance, recommends translating 10a10 as: 'Is "being loved" one thing and "loving" something else?' (p. 79). But it is very hard to read the text this way; moreover, Socrates' point ought to tie up in some way with the claim that follows, that *X* is a thing carried because it is being carried and not vice versa—and that is plainly neither about grammar nor about linguistic expressions.[14] The grammatical interpretation appears to confuse the question of what Socrates is distinguishing between with the question of what devices he uses to present the distinction. The simplest interpretation of the distinction is that it is between being the *subject* of an action or activity and being the *object*. Note that this distinction is meant to be very general in scope, since 'action or activity' needs to be understood so as to include, e.g. seeing and loving: the crucial point is that seeing and loving are things that one *does*. It is also important to note that *X*'s being the object of an activity is not the same as *X*'s having something done to it. That is one way of being the object of an action; but being the object of certain psychological activities (e.g. seeing and loving) is another way. Likewise, being the object

[13] For example, Burnet, *Plato's Euthyphro*, . . . , pp. 47–8; Chris Emlyn-Jones, *Plato: Euthyphro* (London, 1991), pp. 78–9; Cohen, 'Socrates on the Definition of Piety', p. 3; A. Kim, 'A Chiastic Contradiction at *Euthyphro* 9e1–11b5', *Phronesis* 49 (2004), 219–24, at p. 219.

[14] Cohen might seem to hold that both distinctions are grammatical: 'whereas Socrates' first distinction was between active and passive voices, this second distinction is between two different passive forms' ('Socrates on the Definition of Piety', p. 4). Likewise he claims that 'Socrates wants to say that substituting the participle for "p" and the inflected passive for "q" [in sentences of the form "p because q"] will yield a truth, whereas substituting the inflected passive for "p" and the participle for "q" will yield a falsehood' (pp. 4–5). But Socrates says no such thing; at best this—or some highly qualified version of it—might be entailed by what he says. Gunther Patzig rejects the idea that the first distinction is grammatical in 'Logic in the "Euthyphro"', in S. M. Stern, A. Hourani, and V. Brown (eds.), *Islamic Philosophy and the Classical Tradition* (Oxford, 1972), p. 297.

of an action may involve being moved or altered—a point that some commentators have fastened on, as we shall see—but it need not, and in two of the four cases which Socrates mentions it does not involve this.[15]

(b) The φέρεται/φερόμενόν ἐστι *distinction*   Socrates' second distinction (10a9–c13) is marked on the one hand by passive verbs such as φέρεται and on the other by phrases of the form φερόμενόν ἐστι. The latter type of expression is perhaps a little odd, but in ordinary Greek one might well take these two different types of expression to have just the same meaning; and as I indicated earlier it is certainly hard to translate them in such a way that they clearly have different meanings. Plato used participles when setting out the first distinction; so we might at first glance expect φερόμενον here to indicate what it did in the first distinction—i.e. being the object of some action or activity. Three considerations undercut the force of this, however. First, it now occurs not on its own but as part of a different expression, with ἔστι: the new expression might if anything be expected to indicate something new. Second, when θεοφιλὲς εἶναι is introduced into the argument at 10d9–10, it seems to be doing the same work as ὑπὸ θεῶν φιλούμενον εἶναι;[16] and of course θεοφιλὲς is not a participial expression. Third, it is very hard to see what φέρεται is supposed to indicate if *it* does not in some way invoke the idea of being the object of an activity.[17] So it seems more likely that φερόμενόν ἐστι should indicate something different.

A common view[18] is that φερόμενόν ἐστι and its counterparts signify *being in a certain state*—and so a common translation for φερόμενόν ἐστι is 'is in a state of being carried'—while φέρεται and its counterparts signify an *activity*. Holders of this interpretation typically construe the distinction as one which involves a causal connection between the state and the activity: they take the state in question to be an *altered condition* of the object, and the activity to be a process which causes or produces that altered state. Thus what Plato is supposed to be claiming is that these states are caused by the correlative

---

[15] See below.

[16] So e.g. Cohen, 'Socrates on the Definition of Piety', p. 8.

[17] See p. 39 below.

[18] To be found, e.g. in B. Jowett, *Dialogues of Plato*, vol. 1 (4th edn., Oxford, 1953), pp. 307 and 318–19; R. G. Hoerber, 'Plato's *Euthyphro*', *Phronesis* 3 (1958), 95–107, at pp. 102–3; Peter Geach—though he does not use the term 'state'—in 'Plato's *Euthyphro*: An Analysis and Commentary', *Monist* 50 (1966), 369–82, at pp. 378–9; Emlyn-Jones, *Plato: Euthyphro*, pp. 78–9. See also Lane Cooper's translation of 10c1–3 in E. Hamilton and H. Cairns (eds.), *The Collected Dialogues of Plato* (Princeton, 1961).

activities.[19] The commentators then complain that while 'X is in a state of being carried *because* it is being carried' is a true claim about causal relations, 'X is in a state of being loved because it is being loved' is not about a causal relationship at all, and then they conclude that Plato is confused. Now the fact that the idea of a causal relationship does not fit the case of being loved casts some doubt on the interpretation. This doubt is not, perhaps, decisive: we might suppose that the error is Plato's, and that he mistakenly extends to the 'target' case—being loved—a view that holds of his illustrative cases. But the interpretation in question does not fit one of these illustrative cases either—that of being seen—and this makes the interpretation impossible to sustain.[20]

Whatever the ontological character of X's being carried by Y is, it is obviously relational in some way. One might think of it as having two co-subjects, or, to use a slightly picturesque metaphor, as jointly owned by X and Y. In distinguishing φερόμενόν ἐστι from φέρεται, Plato, I suggest, has in view a notion of something which is related to this jointly owned item, but which has a *single* owner, X. This is arrived at by building the role of the second owner into the thing which is singly owned: X's being Y-carried or god-loved.[21] One can think of this as the idea of how things are with X, considered in itself, provided that this construal is not understood in too loaded a way: being Y-carried or god-loved is still a relational matter, and is not something which X could have were Y not to be appropriately related to it (I shall return to this point below). It has to be said that Plato's notion is vague or indeterminate: if we ask whether it involves properties, states of affairs, facts, or something else again, the text presents no answer at all. Note that although Plato applies the notion more widely, so as to include being

[19] This line of thought is sketched, but not endorsed, by Cohen ('Socrates on the Definition of Piety', pp. 4–5).

[20] The most thorough exposition of the view that the problem is Plato's is David Wolfsdorf's 'Euthyphro 10a2–11b1: A Study in Platonic Metaphysics and its Reception since 1969', Apeiron 38 (2005), 1–72, at pp. 32–49). I am unpersuaded, however, by his arguments that Plato does take being loved and being seen in the Euthyphro to be states involving change, and that the confusion surfaces again in Socrates' claim at 11a6–b1 that Euthyphro's definition reveals (only) a πάθος of the pious. In a similar, if less sympathetic, vein, Geach criticizes Plato for confusing the logical structures of verbs like 'carry', which imply that the object is 'shifted or altered', and of verbs like 'love', which do not ('Plato's Euthyphro', pp. 378–9). But Plato is only open to the charge of confusion if his argument relies on ignoring or trading on this difference; Geach provides no evidence that it does, and, as we shall see, it does not.

[21] Plato sometimes says 'is a carried (loved) thing' without mentioning the second owner; but this is, I think, just a convenient abbreviation.

Y-carried, and so on, he presumably formulates the idea because his principal interest is in the role played by his target case, being Y-loved, in a *definition*: the assumption is that the condition of having or sharing in the essence of piety must be something of a kind which can belong to pious things in themselves—it must be a matter of how things are with those pious things.

I suggest therefore that Plato uses the first distinction to introduce the notions of being the subject and being the object of an activity (broadly construed), and that he uses the second distinction to arrive at two types of thing which we can discern in the case of the occurrence of an activity:

(1)   how things are with X: its being Y-ϕ-ed.

(2) X being ϕ-ed by Y—understood as equivalent to the union, as it were, of (2_{Obj}), X's being the object of Y's activity of ϕ-ing and (2_{Subj}), Y's being the subject of that activity.

On this view Plato uses expressions such as $\phi\acute{\epsilon}\rho\epsilon\tau\alpha\iota$ to pick out, not X's being the object of the activity alone, but the 'jointly owned' conjunction of this and Y's being the subject of the activity.

(1) and (2) are symmetrically related: necessarily, (1) holds iff (2) holds. Nonetheless we find Socrates claiming that there is an asymmetrical relationship between them. Thus he says that X is a Y-carried thing (call this $(1)^{carried}$) because X is being carried by Y ($(2)^{carried}$), and not vice versa. If we do not mind things being a little loaded, metaphysically, this seems quite plausible. We arrived at $(1)^{carried}$ only by taking the jointly owned relation between X and Y and deriving a single-owner item from it: it thus seems reasonable to think that things are this way with X because X and Y stand in this relation, and hence because of $(2)^{carried}$. Socrates does not discuss the type of connection he signals by 'because' here, and we shall return to this below. Some commentators take the point of the distinction to be to show the 'agent-dependence' of being a carried thing—in my terms, the dependence of $(1)^{carried}$ on $(2_{Subj})^{carried}$ rather than on $(2)^{carried}$.[22] While I agree

[22] So Terence Irwin, 'Socrates and Euthyphro: The Argument and its Revival', in Lindsay Judson and Vassilis Karasmanis (eds.), *Remembering Socrates: Philosophical Essays* (Oxford, 2006), p. 59; cf. Mark L. McPherran, *The Religion of Socrates* (University Park, PA, 1996), pp. 43–4. Cohen adopts a variant of the agent-dependence interpretation ('Socrates on the Definition of Piety', pp. 7–8).

that Socrates will—quite reasonably, as it turns out—rely on this sort of
agent-dependence in the third section of the argument, when it comes
to the particular case of being a god-loved thing,[23] I think the idea that
agent-dependence applies quite generally in all these cases is mistaken, and
that Socrates does not appeal to it here. It is true that the dependence
of $(1)^{\text{carried}}$ on $(2)^{\text{carried}}$ means that we can say that X's being Y-ϕ-ed depends
on the subject of the activity, Y; but we can equally say that it depends
on the object of the activity, X: nothing has been yet said to establish any
asymmetry between the status of the subject and that of the object (nor,
for that matter between them and the holding of the relation). Suppose
one thinks, in a particular case, that the relation must hold because of
something further, on which the holding of the relation thus depends.
There is no reason why this further item must have a closer connection
to the subject of the activity than to its object. A good way to see this
is to consider what changes one might need to bring about in order to
terminate the holding of the relation.[24] In the case of carrying, these
might be changes in the subject which are, or which bring about, its
dropping the object (I speak sharply to the cat so that it drops the mouse);
but they also could be changes in the object, which are, or which bring
about, its jumping out of the subject's grasp (before I can speak, the mouse
leaps from the cat's paws)—and there might be changes of the relevant
sort which it was hard to characterize other than as changes to the
subject and the object jointly.[25] I see no reason to ascribe to Socrates
here the false, strong claim of agent-dependence, rather than the more
plausible weaker claim that (1), X's being a Y-ϕ-ed thing, depends on
(2), X being ϕ-ed by Y. As I have said, Socrates' argument *will* rely on
agent-dependence when it comes to the case of being loved: my present
point is that he does not base this on a claim that agent-dependence holds
for all activities.

---

[23] See pp. 54–5 below.

[24] Just as the distinctions which I am ascribing to Plato presuppose some sort of a special status for
subjects or owners of properties, the present line of argument presupposes a distinction between genuine
and something like merely Cambridge changes.

[25] Perhaps this is the case when the melting ice-cube becomes too slippery for me to hold, and slides
from my grasp.

The Second Section: The Reasons Agreement

S: Well, then, what is it that we are saying about the pious, Euthyphro? Surely that it is loved by all the gods, as your account stated? **E:** Yes.

S: Is it loved because of this—because it is pious—or because of something else? **E:** No, because of this. **S:** Then it is loved because it is pious, but it is not pious because it is loved? **E:** So it seems. (10d1–8)[26]

Neither Socrates nor Euthyphro expands the point on which they agree at the end of this brief passage, but it is clear that the idea is that being pious essentially involves being in some way *attractive*: this might be because piety itself is intrinsically attractive, or it might be because it essentially involves some attractive property—e.g. being good—and it is the attractiveness of this which explains why the gods love it. As we shall see, Socrates and Euthyphro also assume *transparency*: it is taken for granted that if the gods do love pious things because those things are pious, the gods are correct in thinking that pious things are essentially attractive in one or other of these ways, and in thinking that that is why they love these things.[27]

It is helpful to approach this section by considering how Socrates' strategy differs from the core of the latter-day 'Euthyphro dilemma' argument. First, Socrates' conclusion is about piety rather than about morality in general. Second, and more important, his argument—if one can call it that—is a 'short-circuited' version of the dilemma argument. Indeed, as we shall see, it is short-circuited twice over. The modern dilemma argument as standardly presented offers two alternatives—that God does have reasons for wanting the things he wants, and that he does *not* have reasons—and it offers some arguments to rule out the second alternative, or at least to try to make it unappealing. Socrates, by contrast, does not offer any such arguments: he does not even give Euthyphro the option of saying that the gods love the pious for no reason, and Euthyphro makes no attempt to introduce it. This is the first and more important 'short-circuiting': I call it this because Socrates apparently bypasses the need to argue against the alternative that the gods do not have reasons for loving what they love. Next, Euthyphro

---

[26] Σ. Τί δὴ οὖν λέγομεν περὶ τοῦ ὁσίου, ὦ Εὐθύφρων; ἄλλο τι φιλεῖται ὑπὸ θεῶν πάντων, ὡς ὁ σὸς λόγος; Ε. Ναί. Σ. ˚Αρα διὰ τοῦτο, ὅτι ὅσιόν ἐστιν, ἢ δι᾽ ἄλλο τι; Ε. Οὔκ, ἀλλὰ διὰ τοῦτο. Σ. Διότι ἄρα ὅσιόν ἐστιν φιλεῖται, ἀλλ᾽ οὐχ ὅτι φιλεῖται, διὰ τοῦτο ὅσιόν ἐστιν; Ε. Ἔοικεν.

[27] I return to this assumption on p. 55 below.

simply offers the view that the reason the gods have for loving pious things is that those things are pious: this is the second short-circuiting, since no argument is produced to rule out the alternative. Let us call this two-part agreement the 'reasons agreement'.

Not surprisingly, some commentators are unhappy about the reasons agreement. In particular, they are unhappy about its most crucial feature: why doesn't Euthyphro say—why doesn't Plato allow Euthyphro to say—that the gods have *no* reason for loving the pious—that it is a basic fact, not further to be explained, that they love these things and hate their opposites? The text does not even acknowledge this as an option in the text, since Plato has Socrates ask Euthyphro, '[do the gods love the pious] because of this—because it is pious—or because of something else?'. Emlyn-Jones offers a good example of this reaction:

E.'s admission, although essential for S.'s argument, does not follow inevitably from what precedes [that is, the material about carried and being carried, etc., at 10a5–c13]. He could have argued, without violating S.'s distinctions at 10b1ff., that the love of all the gods still *defines* the holy as a 'loved thing'. E., somewhat predictably, accepts S.'s suggestion, and agrees that the gods love the holy because it is holy and not for any other reason.[28]

The claim that Euthyphro's agreement that the gods love the pious because it is pious 'does not follow inevitably from what precedes' is an understatement: the preceding argument offers no basis whatever for the reasons agreement.[29] Emlyn-Jones's own (implicit) explanation of why Euthyphro makes the reasons agreement is unsatisfactory: 'E., somewhat predictably, accepts S.'s suggestion. . . .' This smacks of what we might call the *transcript fallacy*. The explanation which it implies might be acceptable if the dialogue were a plain transcript of an actual conversation: if that were the case, a reasonable explanation of why Euthyphro makes the reasons agreement might be that he was simply acting in character. But the *Euthyphro* is not a transcript, but a very carefully constructed drama. The proper question is not, 'Why does Euthyphro assent to the reasons agreement?', but 'Why does *Plato make* Euthyphro assent to the reasons agreement?' Viewed in this light (and assuming that Plato is concerned at least to some degree with the

---

[28] *Plato: Euthyphro*, p. 80; cf. p. 102.
[29] Cf. John C. Hall, 'Plato: *Euthyphro* 10a1–11a10', *Philosophical Quarterly* 18 (1968), 1–11, at p. 5; see also pp. 43–4 and p. 46, n. 39 below.

philosophical argument) the explanation comes to this: Plato saw the need for this step if the argument was to go through, but could not think of a better way of securing it than to portray Euthyphro as ready to go along with anything. But if there is no good reason available for someone defending a position like Euthyphro's to accept the reasons agreement, Socrates' argument loses all philosophical interest.[30] John H. Brown also sees that the reasons agreement does not follow from what precedes, and says, 'So far as I can see, Socrates suggests this premise because he believes it to be true (assuming for the argument that the gods love the holy).'[31] But if this is all we can say, and the reasons agreement is needed to refute Euthyphro's definition, then Socrates is simply begging the question against Euthyphro.

A third explanation would start from the fact that we get this same type of interchange between Socrates and Euthyphro earlier on in the argument, at 10b1–3, in connection with being a carried thing. So it could be that Plato has been carried away by his earlier examples:

S: So tell me, is that which is carried a thing carried because it is being carried, or for some other reason? **E:** No, for this reason. . . .

If so, this would be a bad mistake on Plato's part, because the cases are different:[32] its being a loved thing certainly does require an explanation, just as its being a carried thing does—an explanation given by its being loved and its being carried, respectively. But it does not follow that its being loved requires an explanation, any more than its being carried does. Mark McPherran's rather compressed remark may suggest a similar interpretation to the one rejected here:

[30] I do not of course mean to suggest that philosophical dramas are just like philosophical text-books—quite the contrary—or that the only reason that Plato can interestingly have for making Socrates say that *p* is that *p* is philosophically defensible. There are many cases in which Plato makes Socrates (or one of his interlocutors) say something philosophically inadequate or even inept in order to reveal or confirm the speaker's personality, and/or to reveal the sort of muddle one can get into if one holds a certain view, and/or to provoke the reader into thinking about just what it is that makes *p* inadequate or inept. But I do not think that any explanation of this sort is plausible for the reasons agreement. Kim thinks that Socrates aims to show *only* that Euthyphro has inconsistent beliefs ('A Chiastic Contradiction', p. 223); but unless the demonstration has some interesting pay-off, this seems a nugatory aim.

[31] 'The Logic of the *Euthyphro* 10A–11B', *Philosophical Quarterly* 14 (1964), 1–14, at p. 3.

[32] Cf. Brown, 'The Logic of the *Euthyphro*', p. 3.

Socrates provides a series of examples ('being seen' versus 'seeing', 'being loved' versus 'loving') that display the agent-dependent nature of passive properties, with the analogy to the 'god-loved' clearly implying that this too is an agent-dependent passive property; that is, something only comes to possess the property 'god-loved' by being loved by some god(s). Once Euthyphro recognizes this, he is able to see that proper explanations of the possession of such properties must make reference to the agent-cause of the property in question, and thus, ultimately, what initial property it is in the object of the agent's attentions that elicits the agent-response.[33]

If the second sentence is meant to characterize a move supposed to hold good for all 'agent-dependent' properties, it commits Plato to this same error. Even if the possession of such a property requires an explanation by citing the agent's activity, it does not follow that there is *any* explanation of why the agent engaged in that activity; and if there is such an explanation, it is plainly false for properties such as carrying that the explanation must cite some feature of the object of the activity which elicits the agent's response: I might carry something unwittingly, for instance.[34]

But a much better explanation is available, namely that Plato thinks that the claim that the gods love the pious for a reason is *unavoidable*—not because Plato thinks that it follows from the material about carrying and being carried, since it quite clearly does not follow, but on some other basis. What might this basis be? There could be more than one answer to this, but an obvious one is that Plato thinks that the 'no reason' option is ruled out by the sort of considerations which are advanced in the modern Euthyphro dilemma. If the gods love the pious for *no* reason, then they are being arbitrary, whimsical; and this, Plato may think, is unacceptable—indeed, it is just the sort of picture of the gods which was put in doubt earlier in the dialogue,[35] and which we will find Euthyphro himself committed to rejecting later in the dialogue when he endorses the idea of the gods as perfect and

---

[33] *The Religion of Socrates*, p. 44.

[34] As I said earlier, of course, I do not in any case think that being carried is (in the relevant sense) agent-dependent: see pp. 39–40.

[35] 5d8–6d4, 9a1–d5—both passages in which the reader's doubts about this picture of the gods are provoked as much by Socrates' repeated setting aside the issue of the nature of the gods as by the little that he says directly about it.

lacking nothing.[36] Moreover, if there is no reason for the gods to love the pious, why should *we* love it?[37]

If the gods' having *no* reason for loving pious things is ruled out, this leaves the two options which Socrates actually offers to Euthyphro: the gods love what is pious because it is pious, or they love it for some other reason. Here we come to Plato's second piece of short-circuiting: neither Socrates nor Euthyphro is made to argue for the former view or against the latter. This too may give the impression of philosophical sleight of hand; but once again this impression will be dispelled if we can suppose that Plato had reason to find the bypassed view hard to swallow. In the modern Euthyphro dilemma, this option is dealt with by the thought that we are considering whether God is the *source* of morality, and for that idea the claims that God loves moral requirements because of some intrinsic or essential feature and that he does so because of some accidental feature are equally problematic. But this is not the context of the argument in the *Euthyphro,* for here we are considering only the weaker claim that the gods' love of pious things is what constitutes the essence of their being pious; and it seems quite compatible with that claim that the gods should have a reason for loving these pious things. I suggest that the answer lies in an unquestioned assumption which underpins the whole dialogue, that an action's piety or impiety constitutes a powerful reason for doing it or refraining from it, and for commanding our respect or abhorrence.[38] Suppose that the gods love the

[36] 13c6–d3 and 15a5–6. Notice that Euthyphro does not have a unified view of the gods in the dialogue: he embraces the Homeric picture of the gods—anthropomorphic, far from perfect, and at war with each other (for references see the previous note)—then he supposes that they do agree about what is just and unjust, and finally expresses the more 'Xenophanean' view just cited. This (understandable) plethora of views seems to me to undercut the long-standing debate over Euthyphro's (un)orthodoxy; it is also relevant to Myles Burnyeat's claim that in the *Euthyphro* we see radical, rationalist theology (Socrates) confronting 'traditional polytheism' (Euthyphro) ('The Impiety of Socrates', *Ancient Philosophy* 17 (1997), 1–12). I shall take up these issues elsewhere.

[37] Another possible line of thought is that Plato might suppose quite independently that loving X necessarily involved responding to some intrinsically attractive feature of X. (This conception of love has often been detected in the *Lysis;* for the view that the point of the *Lysis* is actually to reject such a conception, see Catherine Osborne, *Eros Unveiled: Plato and the God of Love* (Oxford, 1994), pp. 58–61.) It may be that McPherran has something like this in mind in the passage quoted above; but if so it is a line of thought which would disassociate the demand for an explanation in terms of something eliciting the agent's love from the material on being carried and being seen. A disadvantage of ascribing this move to Plato here is that it seems to come perilously close to begging the question against someone who holds that what makes things pious is that the gods love them; for this reason, among others, I prefer the line of thought sketched in the main text above.

[38] This is brought out, for example, in the emphasis throughout the dialogue on a connection between piety and δικαιοσύνη—an emphasis which is of course fully explicit in the development of

pious for some extrinsic reason, and that it is the gods' love which makes things pious. Then we can ask, why should we respect *the pious*, as opposed to whatever incidental feature of it that the gods love? It could be, for example, that the gods love pious acts because such acts make people happy—and that this is not what make the acts pious, but is simply a feature which pious actions happen to have. It could be also that what the gods love in this case is genuinely worthy of love. Then it would appear that what we ought to be concerned with in our attitudes and actions are things which make people happy, and the piety of some or all of these ought to be of no interest. This problem does not arise, on the other hand, if the gods love the pious *because it is pious*, or *for itself*: then the idea would be that there is something good about piety *itself*, and the gods love that. In this case we would have a reason to be concerned with piety—namely whatever is good about piety itself.[39]

The Third Section: Consequences

[i]   **S:** But it is precisely because it is loved by the gods that it is a thing loved and god-loved? **E:** Of course.

[ii]   **S:** Then the god-loved is not pious, Euthyphro, nor is the pious god-loved, as you say they are, but the one is different from the other. **E:** How so, Socrates?

Euthyphro's third definition, but is also in play earlier. Thus the piety of Euthyphro's prosecution depends on the justice or injustice of the killing of the hired hand by his father (4b7–e3; 8b7–9b3); and the discussion of what the gods dispute over, and what they love and hate, at 7e1ff., relies on a connection between being pious and being δίκαιος.

[39]   So what is the connection between the reasons agreement and what precedes it? Cohen thinks that the material on carrying, being carried, and being a carried thing is Socrates' explanation of what he meant by his original question at 10a2–3, 'Is the pious loved by the gods because it is pious, or is it pious because it is loved?' ('Socrates on the Definition of Piety', p. 3). But although this material is introduced by Euthyphro saying that he does not understand the question and Socrates responding that he will speak 'more clearly' (σαφέστερον φράσαι), this material does *not* clarify that question. I suggest that the reader is meant to understand that Euthyphro fails to grasp not merely the question but where the argument is going; and the material on carrying etc., does clarify *that*. The δή which introduces the reprise of the original question at 10d1—the reprise which brings us to the reasons agreement—does not mark the start of an inference from what goes before, but rather signals that what goes before now puts Socrates and Euthyphro in a position to proceed to the next step in the argument.

[iii] **S:** Because we agreed that the pious is loved because of this—because it is pious—but that it is not pious because it is loved. Is that right? **E:** Yes.

[iv] **S:** But on the other hand, in the case of the god-loved, we agreed that it is because it is being loved by the gods that it, *precisely in virtue of this being loved*, is god-loved; but that it is not being loved because it is god-loved. **E:** You are right.

[v] **S:** But if they really were the same, Euthyphro my friend—the god-loved and the pious—then if the pious were loved because of its being pious, the god-loved too would be loved because of its being god-loved; and if the god-loved were god-loved on account of its being loved by the gods, then the pious would be pious too on account of its being loved. [vi] But as things are, you can see that the two things are oppositely placed, as being altogether different from each other; for the one is such as to be loved because it *is* loved, while the other is loved because it is such as to be loved. [vii] Though you were asked, Euthyphro, what the pious is, you are in danger of not wanting to make clear to me its essence, but only to tell me of some feature that it has, when you say that the pious has received this feature, namely being loved by all the gods; but what it *is*, you have not yet said. (10d9–11b1)[40]

Does Socrates appeal to substitutivity? In this final section Socrates brings together the conclusions of the first two sections in an argument to show that Euthyphro's definition must be rejected. The passage at 10e10–11a6 (steps [v] and [vi]) is often taken to deploy a substitutivity argument: if 'pious' and 'god-loved' are not interchangeable *salve veritate*, then they do

---

[40] [i] Σ. Ἀλλὰ μὲν δὴ διότι γε φιλεῖται ὑπὸ θεῶν φιλούμενόν ἐστι καὶ θεοφιλές. Ε. Πῶς γὰρ οὔ;

[ii] Σ. Οὐκ ἄρα τὸ θεοφιλὲς ὅσιόν ἐστιν, ὦ Εὐθύφρων, οὐδὲ τὸ ὅσιον θεοφιλές, ὡς σὺ λέγεις, ἀλλ' ἕτερον τοῦτο τούτου. Ε. Πῶς δή, ὦ Σώκρατες;

[iii] Σ. Ὅτι ὁμολογοῦμεν τὸ μὲν ὅσιον διὰ τοῦτο φιλεῖσθαι, ὅτι ὅσιόν ἐστιν, ἀλλ' οὐ διότι φιλεῖται ὅσιον εἶναι· ἦ γάρ; Ε. Ναί.

[iv] Σ. Τὸ δέ γε θεοφιλὲς ὅτι φιλεῖται ὑπὸ θεῶν, αὐτῷ τούτῳ τῷ φιλεῖσθαι θεοφιλὲς εἶναι, ἀλλ' οὐχ ὅτι θεοφιλές, διὰ τοῦτο φιλεῖσθαι. Ε. Ἀληθῆ λέγεις.

[v] Σ. Ἀλλ' εἴ γε ταὐτὸν ἦν, ὦ φίλε Εὐθύφρων, τὸ θεοφιλὲς καὶ τὸ ὅσιον, εἰ μὲν διὰ τὸ ὅσιον εἶναι ἐφιλεῖτο τὸ ὅσιον, καὶ διὰ τὸ θεοφιλὲς εἶναι ἐφιλεῖτο ἂν τὸ θεοφιλές, εἰ δὲ διὰ τὸ φιλεῖσθαι ὑπὸ θεῶν τὸ θεοφιλὲς θεοφιλὲς ἦν, καὶ τὸ ὅσιον ἂν διὰ τὸ φιλεῖσθαι ὅσιον ἦν·

[vi] νῦν δὲ ὁρᾷς ὅτι ἐναντίως ἔχετον, ὡς παντάπασιν ἑτέρω ὄντε ἀλλήλων. τὸ μὲν γάρ, ὅτι φιλεῖται, ἐστὶν οἷον φιλεῖσθαι· τὸ δ' ὅτι ἐστὶν οἷον φιλεῖσθαι, διὰ τοῦτο φιλεῖται. [vii] καὶ κινδυνεύεις, ὦ Εὐθύφρων, ἐρωτώμενος τὸ ὅσιον ὅτι ποτ' ἐστίν, τὴν μὲν οὐσίαν μοι αὐτοῦ οὐ βούλεσθαι δηλῶσαι, πάθος δέ τι περὶ αὐτοῦ λέγειν, ὅτι πέπονθε τοῦτο τὸ ὅσιον, φιλεῖσθαι ὑπὸ πάντων θεῶν· ὅτι δὲ ὄν, οὔπω εἶπες.

(I have added numbers for ease of reference.)

not denote the same thing.[41] Step [v] (10e10–11a3), might seem to apply this move to the sentences

> (S1) (a) The pious is loved because it is pious, and (b) it is not the case that it is pious because it is loved. (10e2–4)

and

> (S2) (a) The god-loved is god-loved on account of its being loved by the gods and (b) it is not the case that it is loved because it is god-loved. (10e6–8)[42]

(S1)(a) is agreed to be true; the truth of (S1)(b) shows that the substitution of 'god-loved' for 'pious' in (S1)(a) yields a falsehood—and the same procedure could be applied to (S2)(b) substituting 'pious' for 'god-loved'. Socrates is supposed to infer that 'pious' and 'god-loved' cannot refer to the same thing. The problem is, of course, that substitution cannot be relied on to preserve truth-value in intensional contexts, and 'because' (whatever sort of connection it invokes) introduces just such a context.[43] Some of these commentators detect a weaker conclusion to try to avoid this problem; in particular, Cohen takes it to be about failure of 'definitional equivalence'. But definitional equivalents too will not always preserve truth-value if substituted in intensional contexts—otherwise there would be no unknown definitions. Cohen admits this, but claims that 'the principle of substitutivity

---

[41] So Cohen ('Socrates on the Definition of Piety', pp. 8–10), Emlyn-Jones (*Plato: Euthyphro*, pp. 78 and 101), Geach ('Plato's *Euthyphro*', pp. 376–7), Patzig ('Logic in the "Euthyphro"', pp. 298–9), Lynn E. Rose ('A Note on the *Euthyphro*, 10–11', *Phronesis* 10 (1965), 149–50); see also Wolfsdorf cited in n. 45. These commentators differ as to whether the conclusion is non-identity, non-equivalence, or something else. Thomas D. Paxson ('Plato's *Euthyphro* 10a to 11b', *Phronesis* 17 (1972), 171–90, at pp. 185–6), Kim ('A Chiastic Contradiction', p. 222), and Panos Dimas ('Euthyphro's Thesis Revisited', *Phronesis* 51 (2006), 1–28, at pp. 10–11) claim that the argument involves a substitution of 'god loved' or 'loved by the gods' for 'pious' which they think is indeed—given Euthyphro's definition—truth-preserving, although they differ from the other commentators cited in seeing Socrates as using the substitution to derive an unacceptable conclusion of one sort or another, rather than merely arguing that truth has not been preserved (cf. McPherran, *The Religion of Socrates*, p. 43, n. 43).

[42] Note that there is some indeterminacy in how, as a rendering of 10e6–8, (S2) is to be understood: see below, p. 51.

[43] So, e.g. 'She wanted to marry him because he was the handsomest man in Britain' could be true while 'She wanted to marry him because he was the richest man in Britain' was not, even though the handsomest man in Britain was also the richest man in Britain. Cf. Geach, 'Plato's *Euthyphro*', p. 376. (Of course, we could simply rule that 'because' was in general extensional, but only by giving up the substitutivity test or by making our ontology unacceptably fine-grained; for the idea that 'because' in the context of Socrates' argument is extensional, see n. 45.)

of definitional equivalents does not seem to be one which will break down in the intensional contexts in question'.[44] I think that something like this claim is correct; but if it is, there must be an explanation of what is special about these contexts which licenses the principle, and this suggests that the burden of the argument really lies elsewhere. On the substitutivity interpretation, there are two main ingredients in the account of Socrates' argument. One is the claim that Socrates applies the substitutivity test (in whatever form) to (S1)(a), and appeals to the truth of (S1)(b) to show that truth-value is not preserved; the other is an explanation of why he can insist that (S1)(b) *is* true, on the basis of (S1)(a). This second ingredient is, of course, the heart of the matter, since it would appear that Euthyphro's definition *requires* him to deny (S1)(b) if he can. I shall suggest that once we have given the explanation for this, there will be no need to see the text as containing any appeal to substitutivity.[45]

'Because' We must consider first, however, the nature of the connection(s) which Plato means Socrates to signify when he says that something is a god-loved thing *because* it is being loved by the gods, and not vice versa, and when he says that the gods love the pious *because* it is pious. Once again, Socrates offers no explanation of the connection(s), and we must be careful about how determinate an account we ascribe to him. On the surface, as we shall see, Socrates' argument involves a matrix of connections of a single (if unspecified) type, which is, apparently, transitive and, in at least some cases, asymmetrical. These features make it natural, though not inevitable, to construe the connection as one of *dependence*; and this construal receives some confirmation from that the fact that it certainly reveals much about the

---

[44] Cohen, 'Socrates on the Definition of Piety', p. 10.

[45] Wolfsdorf subscribes to a variant of the substitutivity interpretation, but floats the idea that Plato takes the relation signalled by Socrates' 'because's to be extensional (*'Euthyphro* 10a2–11b1', pp. 64–7) (so that the 'because's in what I call the reasons agreement do not directly signal the gods' reasons for loving the pious, but a more generic causal relationship). Wolfsdorf deploys a highly fine-grained ontology for the relata—'that which is holy qua holy (that is, holiness)', 'that which is god-beloved qua god-beloved (that is, god-belovedness)' (p. 2; cf. p. 64), and this seems to be needed if the extensionality in question is to be plausible. Given this machinery, however, Plato could have gone straight from the reasons agreement in the second section to his conclusion without any need for either the first or third sections: from 'it is loved because [understood extensionally] it is pious, but it is not pious because it is loved' (10d6–7) it will follow immediately that being loved by the gods (understood in the 'qua being loved' way) is not the same thing as being pious (qua pious). We have good reason, then, to see the argument as working in a different way.

argument's points of difficulty and success. There are many items in this matrix, all but one invoked by the term 'because': Socrates and Euthyphro use ὅτι, διότι, and διά interchangeably for this purpose, over 40 times in our passage (10a1–11b4). Only one item is not so invoked—Euthyphro's definition itself, which enters the matrix at 10e10–11. I think we should infer that Socrates, as Plato presents him here, construes definition as itself involving dependence: a thing's being pious depends in some way on the essence of piety.[46] How this definitional dependence figures in the argument will be explored below.

Trouble begins when we consider the connections invoked in the matrix in more detail. In the argument's first section, the only plausible asymmetrical connection which we could identify between items such as X's being Y-carried and X's being carried by Y was some sort of metaphysical or ontological dependence of the former on the latter. When in the same breath Socrates denies that the latter holds because of the former we would expect that he is speaking of the same relation. Moreover, the context is such that were he to intend a different one, he would have to signal this in some way: his question is plainly of the form 'Is it the case that p because q or vice versa?', and questions of that form obviously presuppose that no equivocation on 'because' is intended.[47] In the case of the reasons agreement in the second section, however, it is hard to avoid taking the connection— signalled once again by 'because'—to be a matter of the gods' reasons for loving the pious:[48] and though it is easy enough to see this as a form of

---

[46] As I noted earlier, the definition too should be understood as involving a dependence relation, despite Socrates' use of 'the same' at 10e10. David Charles has suggested to me that Plato might be advancing, or fluctuating between, two different conceptions of definition, and I do not think that these possibilities can be entirely ruled out. It is unclear, however, what Plato might expect to gain in this context from introducing an alternative conception, and the argument's steadfast reliance on dependence makes it much more plausible that Plato here simply takes definition to introduce a dependence relation than that his use of 'the same' is philosophically scrupulous or careful.

[47] *Pace* Cohen, who thinks (i) that Socrates *equivocates* in his use of 'because' here ('Socrates on the Definition of Piety', pp. 5–8), and (ii) that he does so non-fallaciously. According to Cohen, the 'because' in 'Is X a ϕ-ed thing because it is being ϕ-ed?' is a sort of logical 'because', but in the converse question—'Is it being ϕ-ed because it is a ϕ-ed thing?'—the 'because' has a quite different sense: it now indicates the idea of the reason Y has for ϕ-ing X. But it is bizarre to suppose that, without any signal or contextual indication, a double question of this form is meant to involve two quite different senses of 'because'—senses which mean that the alternatives are actually not opposed to each other. (This is a matter of some delicacy: that Socrates is presented as taking the connection to be of the same type in both halves of the question is compatible with his not being presented as taking a view about the precise type of explanatory connection in question.) The case of 10e6–8 is more difficult, for the reasons given below.

[48] For discussion of a different view, see n. 45 above.

dependence, it seems to be dependence of a very different form from the one we identified in the first section. Socrates acknowledges no difference, and simply plugs the new connections into the matrix. 10e6–8 presents one difficulty which this causes but which I shall not pursue:

in the case of the god-loved, we agreed that it is because it is being loved by the gods that it, *precisely in virtue of this being loved*, is god-loved; but that it is not being loved because it is god-loved.

This has the same form as the claim familiar from the first section, and so may invoke the relation which we identify as one of metaphysical dependence. On the other hand, the reasons agreement has intervened, and has just been repeated (10e2–5): so perhaps 10e6–8 concerns the gods' reasons for loving what they love instead.[49] A much more important difficulty, however, is that since more than one form of dependence is involved, the transitivities and asymmetries on which Socrates relies must come under suspicion: indeed, without more justification than he gives, the argument simply will not go through. We can respond to this problem in a number of ways. One would be to suppose that for Plato (or at least for Socrates as he presents him here), the reasons of the gods just do involve specifically the same form of metaphysical dependence as being Y-carried etc.; or we could suppose that in some other way Socrates construes one or both of these forms of dependence differently from us. Plato's silence on the matter should make us disinclined to pursue either of these options: Socrates behaves as if he does not have a determinate or specific view of the nature of the dependence connections he invokes. This in turn might suggest a counsel of despair—the view that Plato does not realize that there are differences in these connections, or does not see that these differences undermine the argument. But there is no need for such despair either: it will emerge that considerations specific to particular premises entitle Plato to use the argument despite his indeterminate grasp of the dependencies involved.

---

[49] Once again, I think we cannot suppose that Socrates is to be read as deliberately deploying one of these forms of dependence in the first half of the claim and the other in the second half: see previous note. We shall encounter a similar difficulty at 11a1: see pp. 55–8 below on propositions (3) and (3′).

Socrates' argument   If it is not a substitutivity argument, what are we to make
of steps [v]–[vii]? The argument is compressed, and needs to be unpacked: I
suggest that it is a reductio argument whose basic strategy is to arrive at two
consequences of Euthyphro's definition—(3) and (5) below—which Socrates will insist are false. Socrates draws out these consequences by advancing two conditionals to whose antecedents he and Euthyphro are already
committed: the focus is really on the consequents. We shall see that Socrates
thinks that both of these consequents are false: in both cases this is because
the dependence they assert runs in the wrong direction. The argument runs
as follows.

Step [v]   Consider some pious thing, *P*:

[A]   Suppose (1) *P*'s being pious depends on *P*'s being a god-loved
thing (from Euthyphro's definition).

(2) *P*'s being loved by the gods depends on *P*'s being pious (from the
reasons agreement together with a further premise to be supplied:
see below).

So (3) *P*'s being loved by the gods depends on *P*'s being a god-loved
thing.

[B]   Suppose (1) *P*'s being pious depends on *P*'s being a god-loved
thing (from Euthyphro's definition).

(4) *P*'s being a god-loved thing depends on *P*'s being loved by the
gods (agreed in the section on carrying, seeing, and loving).

So (5) *P*'s being pious depends on *P*'s being loved by the gods.

Step [vi]   But (3) and (4) cannot both be true, and (2) and (5) cannot
both be true. Since (4) is true, (3) must be false; and since (2) is true,
(5) must be false.

Step [vii]   The derivation of (3) and (5) was from (4), (2), and (1).
Therefore (1), and Euthyphro's definition, are false.

I have set out [A] and [B] as arguments with two premises, whereas Socrates
presents them as conditionals: 'If (1), then if (2), (3)' and 'If (4), (5)'.[50] But no

---

[50] 'S: But if they really were the same, Euthyphro my friend—the god-loved and the pious—then if
the pious were loved because of its being pious, the god-loved too would be loved because of its being
god-loved; and if the god-loved were god-loved on account of its being loved by the gods, then the

violence is done to his argument by recasting it in this way: (1) is being supposed as the target of the reductio,[51] and Socrates plainly thinks that (2) and (4) have been established by what has gone before in the first and second sections.

If we combine (3) and (4), and (2) and (5) we obtain:

(4)+(3) P's being a god-loved thing depends on P's being loved by the gods *and* P's being loved by the gods depends on P's being a god-loved thing.

(5)+(2) P's being pious depends on P's being loved by the gods *and* P's being loved by the gods depends on P's being pious.

Arguments [A] and [B] thus appear to show that P's being pious and P's being a god-loved thing stand in the same, bi-directional dependence relations to P's being loved by the gods. I suggest that it is this, and not the opposition of a true sentence to a false one, that Socrates objects to in step [vi], the climax of the argument:

But as things are, you can see that the two things are oppositely placed, as being altogether different from each other; for the one is such as to be loved because it *is* loved, while the other is loved because it is such as to be loved. (11a3–5)

The two things in question are the pious and the god-loved. Step [vi] insists that, rather than being related in the same way to being loved by the gods— by each having dependence relations to it running in both directions—the pious and the god-loved are 'oppositely placed' because they stand in opposite dependence relations to it. When Socrates says 'the one [i.e. the god-loved] is such as to be loved because it *is* loved', he has (4) in mind, and is implying that because it is true, (3) must be false; when he says 'the other [i.e. the pious] is loved because it is such as to be loved', he is thinking of (2), and again is implying that because it is true, (5) must be false. The relations he affirms are of course those he takes himself to have established in the first and second sections. Since the derivation of (3) and (5) relied, in essence, on

pious would be pious too on account of its being loved' (10e10–11a3). Although he does not repeat (1) when he derives (5) from (4), it is plainly needed; so argument [B] also relies on Euthyphro's definition.

[51] The opening clause 'If they really were the same–the god-loved and the pious' clearly refers to Euthyphro's definition, and hence is meant to be equivalent to 'if the god-loved is the οὐσία of the pious'. If we consider some pious thing, P, the definition yields (1).

(2), (4), and Euthyphro's definition, (1), Socrates can reject this definition as false (step [vii]).

We can put this another way, in terms of dependence trees. Arguments [A] and [B] aim to establish the following trees (in which lower items depend on higher ones):

[A] P's being loved by the gods
      The gods loving P
      P's being pious
      P's being a god-loved thing

[B] P's being pious
      P's being a god-loved thing
      P's being loved by the gods

Putting these together reveals each item as symmetrically related to all the others. Socrates believes that at least some of the items are asymmetrically related—i.e. that for them, at any rate, dependence runs only in one direction. He also believes in these two dependencies:

D1 P's being loved by the gods
     P's being pious

D2 P's being a god-loved thing
     P's being loved by the gods

His argument is that adding Euthyphro's definition would yield

D3 P's being pious
     P's being a god-loved thing

and it is this which links D1 and D2 together so as to generate the unacceptable symmetries. For this reason he concludes that Euthyphro's definition is false.

How well does Socrates' argument work?   In addition to Euthyphro's definition, Socrates uses two further premises, (2) and (4). Premise (4) is simply an instance of the conclusion of the first section on carrying, seeing, etc. Premise (2) follows from the reasons agreement established in the second section provided that we also accept:

(6) P's being loved by the gods depends on the gods loving P.

For the reasons agreement asserts that the gods loving P depends on P's being pious. Now one could ask how (6) can be justified if, as I argued earlier, there is no general 'agent-dependence' of X's being Y-ϕ-ed on Y's being the subject of that activity.[52] As before, it is helpful to think of how we might set about terminating the relationship—how we might stop X being Y-loved. It seems to be true in the case of *loving* (though, as I have said, it is not true for every case), that it is Y that must be changed, not X, if X is to cease being Y-ϕ-ed. Of course, one might end Y's love for X by bringing about a change in X;[53] but that can only be effective if the change in X brings about a change in Y. It is thus plausible that P's being loved by the gods depends on the gods loving it.

Socrates first argues from (1) and (2) to (3). As the excursus through (6) reminds us, the dependence in (2) differs from that in (1) in being a matter of the gods' reasons for loving P. This sort of dependence is an intensional matter; so that we cannot rely on a general transitivity across it to establish the conclusion. What I suggest licenses the inference to (3) is Socrates' conception of definition together with what in the discussion of the second section I called his assumption of *transparency*: if the gods love the pious because of its piety, and if the essence of that piety (specified by its definition) is E, then the gods will grasp both of these facts, and will correctly regard E, or some aspect of it, as what attracts them about the pious. This seems sufficient to enable Socrates to infer (3); and with this defence of (3), his next inference, from (1) and (4) to (5), is in order too. Is the transparency assumption problematic? It would of course be problematic on the Homeric conception of the gods advanced by Euthyphro early in the dialogue, since on that conception the gods can be deceived; but it seems entirely in order on the sort of 'Xenophanean' conception which Socrates has all along accepted and which, as I have said, Euthyphro himself also turns out to endorse.[54]

---

[52] See above, pp. 39–40.

[53] Thus Dr Watson hopes that the disfigurement of Baron's Gruner's face by vitriol will end Violet de Merville's love for the Baron (Arthur Conan Doyle, *The Illustrious Client*).

[54] See pp. 44–5 and n. 36 above. Note that the transparency assumption would not save the argument from substitutivity *salve veritate*: even if she knows that they are one and the same person, it might still be the case that 'She wanted to marry him because he was the handsomest man in Britain' was true while 'She wanted to marry him because he was the richest man in Britain' was not. The same holds in the case

Socrates' argument involves not only these two inferences, of course, but also the twin claims that because (4) is true, (3) must be false and that because (2) is true, (5) must be false—i.e. that the dependencies in question are asymmetrical. Why does Socrates think this? He plainly needs an argument, since the dependence of A on B does not necessarily exclude the dependence of B on A; this latter dependence might in principle be of the same sort—as in cases of mutual dependence such as we encounter in arches and card-castles—or of a different one.[55] One might be tempted to suppose that (3) was already shown to be false by the considerations advanced in the first section, where the metaphysical dependence of X being Y-ϕ-ed on X being ϕ-ed by Y did indeed seem asymmetrical. If Socrates thinks this he is mistaken, however, since the purport of (3) is to some extent indeterminate: the deduction of (3) rests in part on (2), and hence invokes a distinct form of dependence, as we have seen. In other words, we could concede that the metaphysical dependence involved in (4) is asymmetrical, but understand (3) as nonetheless true because the dependence it involves can be construed as a different sort—as a matter of the gods' reasons for loving P. Thus the asymmetry implied by (4) does not require (3) to be false. If Socrates thinks that (3)'s truth is ruled out on *general* grounds—that is, grounds which can be specified in terms of dependence in general—it is very hard to see what these could be. He does, however, have a good response available, which focuses on the specific content of (3). The objection to Socrates which I have sketched says, in effect, that (3) is true, and compatible with (4), if understood along the lines of:

(3′) The gods love P because of P's being a god-loved thing.

But (3′) faces a problem of its own which is familiar to all students of the *Euthyphro*, since it also arises in relation to our next question, why Socrates thinks that (2) and (5) cannot both be true: if Socrates can defend this incompatibility, he can reject (3′). Let us put (3′) to one side for the moment, and turn to (2) and (5).

---

of necessary truths, too: the Pythagoreans admired the number 10 because it is the sum of the first four natural numbers, and not because it is the immediate predecessor of 11.

[55] Once again, we could recast the point in terms of dependence trees. As David Charles has suggested, the argument that D1 and D2 are incompatible with D3 might simply embody the assumptions that there is one linear order of dependency and that no item can appear in two different positions in that order; but the problem is that on the general level these assumptions seem quite unfounded.

(5) relies entirely on what seem (to us) to be metaphysical dependencies—of the sort we identified in the argument of the first section, and of the sort we inferred to be at work in Socratic definition. Both of these relations are plausibly asymmetrical, and the asymmetry of the dependence asserted in (5), construed as a metaphysical dependence, is secure. Once again, however, this will not suffice to establish the incompatibility of (2) and (5), since the form of dependence in question in (2) is different in the now familiar way. As in the case of (3) and (4), the prospects for a highly general basis for the desired incompatibility seem bleak. Perhaps the least unpromising route would be to try to argue that, although even the asymmetrical dependence (of a given sort) of A on B is in principle compatible with dependence of some other sort running in the opposite direction, the *complete* (asymmetrical) dependence of A on B is not. If this were true, then since Euthyphro's definition and (4) together establish that P's being pious depends completely on P's being loved by the gods, any form of dependence in the opposite direction would be ruled out, and so (2) would be incompatible with (5) after all. This is a tempting line of thought, but it faces two very severe difficulties (which are possibly related): first, it is not obvious how to give a non-circular account of complete dependence, and second, it is hard to see how to justify, in general terms, the principle that complete dependence in one direction rules out *any* form of dependence in the other.[56]

Since no general argument seems to be available, we should look at considerations specific to the particular case of (2) and (5)—and here we find ourselves on familiar ground. The reasons agreement commits Euthyphro to the view that piety is intrinsically attractive, or that it essentially has some attractive property, and that it is this attractiveness which inspires the gods' love for pious things. But then if *being god-loved* were the essence of piety, the gods would be inspired to love pious things by the fact that they love them: read as 'each god is inspired to love pious things by the fact that he/she loves them', this either is incoherent, or amounts to the claim that after all the gods love the pious for no reason. Exactly the same problem makes (3′) untenable: so a move to (3′) cannot secure the compatibility of (4) and (3). Note that the assumption of transparency is crucial here: were the gods in loving the pious to be labouring under a misapprehension as to the

---

[56] We will encounter the need to appeal to a different—and much easier—type of completeness below, namely the completeness of a definition: see n. 59.

nature of piety, we might well feel able to affirm both (5) and (2), if the latter were understood in terms of modes of presentation or descriptions under which the gods love the pious.

Someone might try to counter this account by supposing that each god loves the pious because all the gods do. This situation does not seem to me to escape the difficulty, since (given that all the gods have only the reason now alleged for loving the pious) this reason for loving the pious is as vacuous as the original reason—i.e. it cannot operate as a reason.[57] If it is somehow not vacuous in this sense, then we would have to agree that the gods in this situation would have a reason for loving what they love; but it is one which fails to satisfy the objections which I sketched on Plato's behalf as grounds for the reasons agreement—the objections to saying that the gods have no reason, or only an extrinsic reason, for loving the pious. Though armed with a reason, the gods in this situation seem to be whimsical in their choices (albeit in a different way) and imperfect (since they should have better reasons); and the fact that they love the pious offers us no reason to do so.[58]

We have, one might say, arrived back at Socrates' famous question at 10a2–3, 'Is the pious loved by the gods because it is pious, or is it pious because it is loved?' Once the question is understood in the light of the reasons agreement and Euthyphro's definition, we can see that Euthyphro is committed to answering '*both*'—and that this answer is unacceptable. We should conclude that the essence of piety must be constituted (at least in part[59]) by something other than being god-loved—something which either

---

[57] Compare the following. 'Obey this command' is vacuous in the sense that nothing counts as obeying or disobeying it. 'Obey all these commands', when a member of a set of commands, need not be vacuous ('Keep quiet; shut the door; obey all these commands'); but the vacuity re-emerges if the set consists of a number of commands all of the form 'obey all these commands'.

[58] Couldn't I love something today only because I loved it yesterday? Possibly—but eventually we shall get back to a day when I had some other reason for loving it, or loved it for no reason at all. But couldn't the gods love something each day only because they had loved it the day before, so that we never get back to a day when things are different? Again, possibly—but although in this situation the gods always have reasons for loving what they love, as with the case discussed in the main text, the gods do not seem to emerge as perfect or unwhimsical, and the fact that they love the pious again offers us no reason to do so.

[59] If being loved by the gods were only *part* of the definition of piety, it would be quite compatible with the claim that the gods love pious things because of their piety, as I have understood that claim. If being pious were, essentially, being loved by the gods *and* being F, the gods could love the pious because of its essential F-ness. This is the sense in which the argument relies on the idea that Euthyhpro's definition is (meant to be) *complete*.

PLATO ON DEFINITION 59

is or includes the attractive property which inspires the gods' love—and thus that Euthyphro's definition is incorrect.

Conclusions: The Body of the Argument

Plato's commitment to the introduction and deployment of very general structures in the refutation of Euthyphro's definition makes it tempting to suppose that the argument is meant to proceed at an entirely general level— that is, solely on the basis of general features of dependence relations. As we have seen, however, these general structures cannot provide the resources to make the argument go through. We could, of course, suppose that Plato simply failed to see this; but since considerations specific to the subject-matter of the argument (the gods' love of the pious) do make the argument at least plausible, we have no reason to ascribe this mistake to Plato— especially since these considerations are ones we have reason to see Plato as in any case having in mind in relation to the reasons agreement.

It is a cliché for commentators to say that such-and-such a philosopher of the past has provided the skeleton of an argument, and that what is needed is to put some flesh on the bones. Something more like the reverse is true of parts of Socrates' argument here. As we have seen, both the technical resources he deploys (especially the notion of definition and the distinctions drawn in the first section) and the lines of arguments he constructs display crucial and pervasive indeterminacies, so that the argument as presented is (to change the metaphor) rather lacking in philosophical musculature. Despite this, we have been able to supply (or in some cases perhaps detect) enough support for key moves to reveal an argument with an impressively strong overall structure whatever its minor deficiencies. Its most vulnerable point is the reasons agreement—not so much, I think, because the case for voluntarism is stronger than the argument supposes, but because it shares with voluntarism a conception of the gods' love of the pious as based on something like decisions or choices—a conception which, for all Socrates' efforts to avoid making the gods in man's image, may not entirely escape the charge of anthropomorphism. The idea that the gods' love is more like an expression of their essential nature than it is like a choice might offer a more promising way for a defender of Euthyphro's definition to avoid the reasons agreement. To press this point, however, would be to trade on a good deal of philosophical hindsight.

In any case, I hope that what has emerged is a picture, not of a limping argument struggling to approach its goal, but of one whose philosophical ambitions, as to techniques, methods, and conclusion, are bold and exciting—so that we should praise it for what it attempts rather than complain about its weaknesses. It is not to Plato's discredit if ambitions of this calibre run ahead of themselves from time to time.[60]

Bibliography

John H. Brown, 'The Logic of the *Euthyphro* 10A–11B', *Philosophical Quarterly* 14 (1964), 1–14.

J. Burnet, *Plato's Euthyphro, Apology of Socrates, and Crito* (Oxford, 1924).

Myles Burnyeat, 'The Impiety of Socrates', *Ancient Philosophy* 17 (1997), 1–12; reprinted in Rachana Kamtekar (ed.), *Plato's* Euthyphro, Apology, *and* Crito (Lanham, MD, 2005).

S. M. Cohen, 'Socrates on the Definition of Piety: *Euthyphro* 10A–11B', *Journal of the History of Philosophy* 9 (1971), 1–13; reprinted in G. Vlastos (ed.), *Socrates* (Garden City, 1971), and in Rachana Kamtekar (ed.), *Plato's* Euthyphro, Apology, *and* Crito (Lanham, MD, 2005).

Panos Dimas, 'Euthyphro's Thesis Revisited', *Phronesis* 51 (2006), 1–28.

Chris Emlyn-Jones, *Plato: Euthyphro* (London, 1991).

Peter Geach, 'Plato's *Euthyphro*: An Analysis and Commentary', *Monist* 50 (1966), 369–82; reprinted in Rachana Kamtekar (ed.), *Plato's* Euthyphro, Apology, *and* Crito (Lanham, MD, 2005).

John C. Hall, 'Plato: *Euthyphro* 10a1–11a10', *Philosophical Quarterly* 18 (1968), 1–11.

E. Hamilton and H. Cairns (eds.), *The Collected Dialogues of Plato* (Princeton, 1961).

R. G. Hoerber, 'Plato's *Euthyphro*', *Phronesis* 3 (1958), 95–107.

Terence Irwin, 'Socrates and Euthyphro: The Argument and its Revival', in Lindsay Judson and Vassilis Karasmanis (eds.), *Remembering Socrates: Philosophical Essays* (Oxford, 2006).

B. Jowett, *Dialogues of Plato*, vol. 1 (4th edn., Oxford, 1953).

[60] An earlier version of this paper was given at London University: I am grateful to Mary Margaret McCabe, Richard Sorabji, and Harold Tarrant for their comments on that occasion, to David Charles for his comments on later versions, and to an anonymous reader.

A. Kim, 'A Chiastic Contradiction at *Euthyphro* 9e1–11b5', *Phronesis* 49 (2004), 219–24.

Mark L. McPherran, *The Religion of Socrates* (University Park, PA, 1996).

Catherine Osborne, *Eros Unveiled: Plato and the God of Love* (Oxford, 1994).

Gunther Patzig, 'Logic in the "Euthyphro"', in S. M. Stern, A. Hourani, and V. Brown (eds.), *Islamic Philosophy and the Classical Tradition* (Oxford, 1972).

Thomas D. Paxson, 'Plato's *Euthyphro* 10a to 11b', *Phronesis* 17 (1972), 171–90.

Terence Penner, 'The Unity of Virtue', *Philosophical Review* 82 (1973), 35–68; reprinted in H. H. Benson (ed.), *Essays on the Philosophy of Socrates* (New York and Oxford, 1992).

Lynn E. Rose, 'A Note on the *Euthyphro*, 10–11', *Phronesis* 10 (1965), 149–50.

Richard Sharvey, '*Euthyphro* 9d–11b: Analysis and Definition in Plato and Others', *Noûs* 6 (1972), 119–37.

Gregory Vlastos, 'What Did Socrates Understand by his "What is *F*?" Question?', in Vlastos, *Platonic Studies* (2nd edn., Princeton, 1981).

David Wolfsdorf, '*Euthyphro* 10a2–11b1: A Study in Platonic Metaphysics and its Reception since 1969', *Apeiron* 38 (2005), 1–72.

2

Explanation and Essence in Plato's *Phaedo*

VASILIS POLITIS

Introduction

This paper examines how, through the narration of Socrates' intellectual journey (*Phaedo* 95e8ff.), Plato searches for an adequate account of explanation, and how this search culminates in an account which says that explanations are, primarily, essences. I conclude that the account which says that explanations are, primarily, essences, and indeed the claim that there are essences, can be defended by setting out to provide an adequate account of explanation, and that this is how Plato defends it here. The wider upshot of the paper is that Plato thinks explanation and essence belong inseparably together.

Let me begin by briefly clarifying what I mean, and what I think Plato means, by 'explanation' ($αἰτία$) and 'essence' ($οὐσία$).[1] An explanation is what is signified by the answer, if the answer is true, to the question '*Why* is this thing as it is?' or '*Why* is this thing, x, f (supposing it is f)?' An essence is what is signified by the answer, if the answer is true, to the—Socratic-type—question '*What* is this thing, x?' or '*What* is this quality, f?' This shows that the concepts of explanation and essence are not technical or narrowly philosophical ones, much less narrowly Platonic; on the contrary, they are readily familiar. For the questions '*Why* is it as it is?' and '*What* is it?' are readily familiar. It also shows that the two concepts are distinct, and that

---

[1] For the translation of $οὐσία$ as 'essence', see section 3, where I also consider the relation between the notion of essence ($οὐσία$) and the notion of form ($εἶδος$). For the translation of $αἰτία$ as 'explanation', see section 4.

we do not have immediate reason to suppose that they are related in any particular way. For the two questions are distinct and we do not have immediate reason to suppose that they are related in any particular way. I would like to begin by emphasizing both the fact that these two concepts, and the corresponding questions, are familiar and that they are distinct. For this shows that the immediate import of Plato's argument, which defends the conclusion that explanation and essence belong inseparably together, is unquestionable.

I shall, however, be using a technical-sounding term, but one which I think is both useful and harmless: 'explanans' (and the plural 'explanantia'); and from now on I shall formulate Plato's claim as being that *explanantia* are, primarily, essences. In English, the word 'explanation' is ambiguous between, on the one hand, the whole sentence 'x is f because E', or what is signified by this sentence, and, on the other hand, the term 'E', or what is signified by this term if the sentence in which it figures is true. But in general it is useful to reserve the word 'explanation' for the former use and introduce the term 'explanans' for the latter. This term, 'explanans', I intend to correspond to Plato's phrase 'that because of which' ($\delta\iota$' $\ddot{o}\tau\iota$, as used in e.g. 97b3–5), and this phrase in turn appears to be used interchangeably with, and apparently as a clarification of, precisely, $a\dot{\iota}\tau\dot{\iota}a$ (see section 4).[2]

The claim that there are essences ($o\dot{v}\sigma\dot{\iota}a\iota$) is introduced early in the *Phaedo* and remains prominent throughout the dialogue.[3] Later in the dialogue, however, when Socrates narrates his intellectual journey, the attention becomes focused on explanations ($a\dot{\iota}\tau\dot{\iota}a\iota$) and the aim is to search for an adequate account of explanation. A particular account of essence is introduced, but it is situated within and motivated by the search for an account of explanation. This search issues in the claim that explanantia are, primarily, essences. When spelled out fully, the claim is that the explanation of why a thing, x, has a quality, f, is *either* that x is appropriately related directly to the essence of this quality (the simple schema, 100b1–102b3), *or*

[2] Plato tends to use $\tau\dot{o}$ $a\ddot{\iota}\tau\iota o\nu$ for what I have called the explanans and $\dot{\eta}$ $a\dot{\iota}\tau\dot{\iota}a$ for the explanation. For this point, both in general and about the *Phaedo*, see M. Frede, 'The Original Notion of Cause', in M. Schofield, M. Burnyeat, and J. Barnes (eds.), *Doubt and Dogmatism* (Oxford, 1980), 222–3.

[3] This statement ought not to be particularly controversial, especially since I intend it to be compatible with the statement that the claim that there are forms ($\epsilon\ddot{\iota}\delta\eta$) is introduced early in the *Phaedo* and remains prominent throughout the dialogue. However, I shall defend it, with particular attention to Plato's text, in section 3.

that x is appropriately related to something, e.g. a physical thing, which, though not itself an essence, is in turn appropriately related to the essence of this quality, f (the complex schema, 102b3–105c7).[4] Plato is committed to, and he defends, both schemata.[5] His account of explanation, therefore, is not that explanantia are simply essences, but that explanantia, whatever else they may involve, are primarily essences.

Socrates' narration of his intellectual journey describes a path from confidence in and enthusiasm about traditional explanations of natural phenomena and in general things that are subject to generation and destruction, to complete loss of trust in such explanations and indeed in explanations altogether. It emerges that this extreme state of *aporia* about explanations is generated not simply by the question, 'What is the explanation of generation and destruction?' (this question is raised at the outset of the narration, at 95e10–96a1), but by the more radical question, 'What is an explanation, whether of generation and destruction or anything else?' (hence the liberal choice of examples, which include just as much why 10 is greater than 8, at 96e1–3, as why human beings grow, at 96c7–d6). It is this radical—Socratic-type—question about explanation that the account which says that explanantia are, primarily, essences is supposed to answer.

I shall (in the first two sections of the paper) concentrate on two central issues. First, what is the source of Socrates' radical *aporia* about explanations? Second, how is this *aporia* resolved by the introduction of the account which says that explanantia are, primarily, essences? It is very important to recognize this overall structure of Plato's argument: he first (95e8–99d3) articulates a particular and fundamental *aporia*, in the sense of a particular problem, about explanation (we shall consider in a moment what the problem is); and this gives rise to the need to raise the radical question 'What is an explanation?' He then (99d4–105c7) defends a particular answer to this question, which says that explanantia are primarily essences; and a central aim of this answer is the resolution of the original *aporia*. It is also important to recognize that we can understand the *aporia*, and that it articulates a real

---

[4] It is traditional to refer to this as Plato's theory of forms (εἴδη), but it is just as much a theory of essences (οὐσίαι)—see section 3. I prefer to speak of Plato's theory of essences, because we will see that Plato's argument defends the conclusion that explanantia are, primarily, *essences*, and the argument depends on his core notion of essence.

[5] My use of 'either...or...' here is, therefore, meant to be inclusive, not exclusive.

problem, independently of accepting or even considering its resolution, the claim that explanantia are primarily essences.[6]

The first section of the paper is addressed to the first issue: What is the source of Socrates' radical *aporia* about explanations? Socrates loses trust in traditional explanations, and especially explanations that appeal purely to physical things (we may call these, 'physicalist' explanations), because he comes to think that such explanations do not satisfy certain fundamental requirements of explanation.[7] Two requirements of explanation are at the source of his *aporia*. The one says that same explananda must have same explanantia; the other says that, conversely, same explanantia must have same explananda (a fuller formulation will follow). We will see that it is appropriate to characterize these requirements as embodying the constraints of the uniqueness, generality, and uniformity of explanation. It appears that they are supposed to be requirements precisely of explanation, i.e. it is in so far as something is an explanation that it must satisfy them. Because Socrates comes to think that traditional, and especially physicalist explanations do not satisfy them, he comes to doubt that they are explanations at all. But this loss of trust extends to all explanations, even such familiar and apparently unobjectionable ones as that human beings grow because they eat and drink or that 10 is greater than 8 because it is the sum of 8 and 2.

The second section is addressed to the second issue: How is the radical *aporia* about explanations resolved by the introduction of the account which says that explanantia are, primarily, essences? This account restores trust in explanations because Plato thinks that explanations in conformity with it, and such explanations alone, satisfy the two fundamental requirements of explanation. It is relatively easy to see why he thinks this account is sufficient to satisfy the requirements; it is more difficult, but not, I think, impossible, to establish why he thinks it is also necessary.

I conclude that the account which says that explanantia are, primarily, essences, and indeed the claim that there are essences, can be defended by

---

[6] A number of critics have recognized a similar structure in Plato's argument (see below). My account differs in two major respects. First, I argue that the *aporia* is well-motivated and a genuine one (see section 1). Second, I argue that Plato succeeds in resolving it, and does so without appeal to such question-begging principles as: causes must be like their effects (see section 2).

[7] For the notion of a 'physical' thing, see below. It is tempting to use the term 'material' here, and 'materialist' for explanations that appeal purely to such things; but the terms 'physical' and 'physicalist' are preferable and closer to Plato's concepts.

setting out to satisfy certain fundamental requirements of explanation, and in general to provide an adequate account of explanation; and it appears that this is how Plato defends it here. This does not mean that the search for an adequate account of explanation is the sole origin of the account of essence, in Plato generally or the *Phaedo* in particular. It is notable that earlier in the dialogue a conception of essence was introduced without reference to explanation. What it means is that Plato thinks the account of explanation is sufficient to generate a particular account of essence, and indeed to defend the claim that there are essences. Plato, therefore, defends, in the *Phaedo*, the claim that there are essences.[8] He does this by arguing that only if there are essences can there be an explanation ($a\mathit{i}\tau\mathit{i}a$) of why a thing is as it is. This is a powerful defence, for few would be willing to give up on the possibility of explanation and of there being true answers to the question '*Why* is it as it is?'

A note about the structure of the paper. The first two sections follow what I consider to be Plato's method of argument: the articulation of a particular *aporia* about explanation (95e8–99d3, which I examine in section 1), followed by the defence of a particular solution to this *aporia* (99d4ff., which I examine in section 2). However, Plato's argument, and the question of how we ought to interpret it, gives rise to a number of further issues, which I prefer to address individually and separately, in five further sections. These sections are as central to the paper as are sections 1–2. Sections 3 and 4 are addressed to the clarification of the concepts of essence ($o\mathring{v}\sigma\mathit{i}a$) and explanation ($a\mathit{i}\tau\mathit{i}a$), and the reader is invited to consult them in conjunction with the reading of sections 1 and 2. Section 5 asks why, at 97b8–99d3, Plato considers teleological or good-based explanations. Section 6 considers how Plato defends not only the simple schema of explanation (defended at 100b1–102b3; it says that, e.g. things are hot because of their relation to the essence of heat), but also the complex schema of explanation (defended at 102b3–105c7; it says that, e.g. things are hot because of, first, their relation to fire, and, second, its relation to the essence of heat). It is crucially important that Plato defends both these schemata of explanation, for this shows that his conclusion is not that explanantia are

---

[8] We may note that the claim that there are essences (and forms) is referred to as a hypothesis ($\mathring{v}\pi\acute{o}\theta\epsilon\sigma\iota s$) at 92d7 and again at 101d2. Plato, therefore, not only makes use of this claim as a hypothesis (in particular for the purpose of defending the conclusion that the soul is immortal), he also defends it.

simply essences, but rather that explanantia, whatever else they may involve, are primarily essences. This, we will see in section 7, allows Plato to accommodate physical things, such as snow and fire, within the account of explanation. He does so by conceiving of physical things not merely as necessary and sufficient conditions for the things to be explained, but as elements in explanantia, and, therefore, as genuinely parts of explanations.

1 Plato's *aporia* about Explanation (*Phaedo* 95e8–99d3)

Socrates opens the narration of his intellectual journey with the remark:

A thorough examination is, therefore, needed of the explanation of generation and destruction in general. ὅλως γὰρ δεῖ περὶ γενέσεως καὶ φθορᾶς τὴν αἰτίαν διαπραγματεύσασθαι.[9] (95e10–96a1)

This examination is needed because, in spite of the extended discussion and argument (going back virtually to the beginning of the dialogue, at 63b), no agreement has been reached on the question under discussion, whether the soul is or is not subject to generation and destruction. Socrates, therefore, proposes to make another attempt at answering this question, by shifting the attention from the question whether in particular the soul is or is not subject to generation and destruction, to the more general and radical question: *Why* is any thing that is (or is not) subject to generation and destruction subject to (or not subject to) generation and destruction?[10] Eventually he will apply the results of this examination to the soul (105c8f.).

However, to understand why the dialogue takes this more general and radical turn, we must ask why Socrates turns to the question *why* any thing that is (or is not) subject to generation and destruction is (or is not) subject to

---

[9] I read the scope of the ὅλως to be περὶ γενέσεως καὶ φθορᾶς. The point of the ὅλως is to shift the discussion from the question whether a particular thing, the soul, is or is not subject to generation and destruction, to the more general and radical question: *Why* is any thing that is (or is not) subject to generation and destruction subject to (or not subject to) generation and destruction? I read the γὰρ to mean 'therefore', rather than 'for'. The point of the γὰρ is that, since the extended discussion and argument (going back to 63b) has failed to establish agreement (on the question whether or not the soul is subject to generation and destruction), *therefore* a more general and radical examination *is needed* (δεῖ).

[10] That the question is, in the first instance at least, about the explanation of things that are subject to generation and destruction is also indicated by the repeated use of the phrase: 'why something is, or comes to be, or ceases to be' (96a8–9, 97b4–5, c7). The issue is, in the first instance at least, about the explanation of natural phenomena (cf. περὶ φύσεως ἱστορίαν, 96a7).

generation and destruction. It is here that the general appeal to αἰτίαι and the question 'Why?' is introduced for the first time in the dialogue. It appears that this turn of the dialogue is motivated by the outcome of the extended preceding discussion and argument about the soul and the question of its immortality. This goes back virtually to the beginning of the dialogue (63b), when Socrates begins defending the claim that the soul is immortal, and in particular it goes back to Kebes' initial challenge (at 69e–70b) of Socrates' initial defence. Socrates' narration of his intellectual journey is a response to Simmias' and Kebes' views about the relation between soul and body, and these views have emerged in the course of and as a result of this extended discussion and argument. On their views, the soul depends on the body: either on the individual body (which is Simmias' view, see 85e–86d), or on the body in general (which is Kebes' view, 86e–88b). From this they infer that, since the body is subject to generation and destruction, the same must be true of the soul (this was indeed the point of Kebes' initial challenge, at 69e–70b). It appears, therefore, that they think the relation between the soul and the body not only implies *that*, it also explains *why* the soul is subject to generation and destruction: *because* it depends on something which is subject to generation and destruction. It is, therefore, natural and appropriate that Socrates, when he broadens the discussion, should precisely take up the question concerning the *explanation* of generation and destruction. It is also notable that, as soon as he begins the narration, he focuses especially on those explanations that appeal purely to physical things (96b2–c1), which is the kind of explanation favoured by Simmias and Kebes.

What, we ought to ask, is distinctive of the explanations favoured by Simmias and Kebes—what I have been calling 'physicalist' explanations, i.e. explanations that appeal purely to 'physical' things? Socrates refers to such explanations generically as: the explanations traditionally favoured by those who engage in 'the science of *nature*' (*phusis*, 96a5–7). He goes on (96b2–c1) to clarify what is distinctive of such explanations, by citing some examples of the things appealed to in them as being *aitiai*: the hot and the cold; blood, air, and fire; the brain. Does Plato provide a general account of such things—'physical' things? Here (96a7–9) he describes these things as things that are subject to generation and destruction; and in general he describes such things as the things that are, first, capable of being perceived and, second, subject to change (or, the kind of change that is capable of being perceived; see e.g. 78e–79a). We may, therefore, also introduce the notion of a 'physical constituent' to mean a constituent, of a physical thing, which is capable of being perceived and subject to change (or, the kind of change that is capable of being perceived). For it is notable that blood, air, fire, and the brain, as well as (later) bones and sinews and (later again) fire and snow would appear to be physical constituents of things.

We may note, incidentally, that the introduction, at this point of the dialogue, of a general appeal to αἰτίαι and the question 'Why?' accords with, and hence would also appear to prepare for, the methodological recommendation later in the narration, when Socrates says that we ought to investigate the truth about any thing not directly, but through statements (λόγοι), and in particular statements that put forward explanatory hypotheses (see 99d4–100a8). For it appears that what this methodological recommendation says is that an adequate investigation of *whether* p is the case (e.g. whether the soul is immortal) must involve an investigation of *why* p is the case, if it is the case, and *why* p is not the case, if it is not the case (e.g. why the soul is immortal, if it is, and why the soul is not immortal, if it is not). I shall not in this paper, however, look any further at this—highly suggestive and intriguing—methodological passage.

Socrates begins the narration of his intellectual journey with the question, 'What is the explanation of generation and destruction?', but when we look closer at the narration, it emerges that the question he wants to address includes the more radical one, 'What is an explanation, whether of generation and destruction or anything else?' He appears to move directly from the former to the latter question. For he begins by recounting how he lost trust especially in those explanations of generation and destruction which appeal purely to physical things (96b2–c1), but immediately goes on to describe how this directly led him to lose trust in explanations altogether, even such familiar and apparently unobjectionable ones as that human beings grow because they eat and drink (96c7–d6) or that 10 is greater than 8 because it is the sum of 8 and 2 (96e1–3). He must, apparently, think that the question about the explanation of generation and destruction is directly associated with a more radical *aporia* about explanation, the kind of *aporia* it would be natural to express through the Socratic-type question, 'What is an explanation?'[11]

---

[11] Socrates does not formulate this *aporia* in so many words, but he describes his intellectual journey as a path from youthful confidence in explanations of natural phenomena to a state, as he grew in maturity, of loss of trust in such explanations and indeed in explanations altogether. It is, I think, natural and appropriate to describe this as a path from his being concerned entirely with the question 'What is the

This reading will be corroborated when we consider why Socrates lost trust in physicalist explanations. He did so, we will see, because he came to think that such explanations do not satisfy certain fundamental requirements of explanation. But these requirements, we will see, are not specifically about physicalist explanations, and they are not specifically about the explanation of generation and destruction, rather, they are about any explanations and about explanation itself. This also shows why he lost trust in explanations altogether, even familiar and apparently unobjectionable ones. He did so because he came to doubt that any familiar explanation satisfies these requirements of explanation.

It is the following two requirements of explanation that traditional explanations fail to satisfy:[12]

REQ1   If same explanandum, then same explanans.
        i.e. it is impossible for numerically different particular things, in so far as they have the same quality, to have different and incompatible explanantia.
        i.e. it is necessary that, if E1 is the explanans of why x is f, and E2 is the explanans of why y is f (where x and y are numerically different particulars), then E1 = E2.[13]

REQ2   If same explanans, then same explanandum.

explanation of this or that?' to his being motivated, because of a particular *aporia*, to concentrate rather on the question 'What is an explanation?' We may note that, in a later dialogue, the *Sophist* (243b7–10), Plato uses the very same topos, the contrast between youthful confidence and mature *aporia*, to describe a similar path: from being concerned entirely with the question 'What things are there?' to being motivated, because of a particular *aporia* (expressly so called), to concentrate rather on the question 'What is being?'

[12]   See G. Fine, 'Forms as Causes: Plato and Aristotle', in A. Graeser (ed.), *Mathematics and Metaphysics in Aristotle* (Bern and Stuttgart, 1987), 69–112, pp. 89–90; also J. Annas, 'Aristotle on Inefficient Causes', *Philosophical Quarterly* 32 (1982), 311–26, pp. 314–18 (see also Annas, note 14 for further critics of a similar view). However, my account differs in a number of ways. First, I consider how these requirements ought to be formulated. Second, I consider why it is supposed that physicalist explanations do not satisfy them. Third, I argue that the same charge is levelled at teleological explanations as traditionally conceived. Fourth, I consider what is the motivation behind these requirements and why they are supposed to be plausible. I argue that they are well-motivated, but not because of the principle 'causes must be like their effects' (which I think it would be question-begging to invoke). Finally, I consider how it is that explanations in conformity with the account which says that explanantia are primarily essences/forms is supposed to satisfy them (I argue that Fine's and Annas's response is not satisfactory, unless, as Annas thinks we are forced to do, we add the principle 'causes must be like their effects').

[13]   See 96e6–97b3, read together with 101b10–c9. See below for paraphrase and comments.

i.e. it is impossible for numerically different particular things, in so far as they have different and incompatible qualities, to have the same explanantia.

i.e. it is necessary that, if E is the explanans of why x is f, and E is the explanans of why y is g (where x and y are numerically different particulars), then $f = g$.[14]

It is appropriate to characterize these requirements as embodying the constraints of the uniqueness, generality, and uniformity of explanation. They are requirements of the uniqueness of explanation because they imply that each explanandum has a single explanans, the one proper to it, and conversely each explanans explains a single explanandum, the one proper to it. They are requirements of the generality of explanation because they imply that, if a particular thing, x, has an explanation, it does so in virtue of having a general quality, f. This is a general quality in the sense that numerically different particular things, x and y, can have the same quality, f. What the requirements assert is that explanations must be uniform, indeed to articulate the constraint that explanations must be uniform is precisely to state these requirements.

It appears that these requirements are supposed to be requirements precisely of explanation, i.e. it is in so far as something is an explanation that it must satisfy them. Otherwise their apparent breach would not be grounds for Socrates' loss of trust in explanations altogether, even in such familiar and apparently unobjectionable ones as that human beings grow because they eat and drink or that 10 is greater than 8 because it is the sum of 8 and 2. If, on the other hand, they are indeed supposed to be requirements of explanation in general and as such, that is, requirements that contribute to the very essence of explanation and to the question, 'What is an explanation?', then Socrates' being in a state of radical *aporia* is readily intelligible. For by coming to think that traditional explanations, whether the sophisticated ones offered by physicalist philosophers (e.g. 96b2–c1) or perfectly everyday ones (e.g. 96c3f.), fail to satisfy these requirements, he came to think that traditional explanations are not explanations at all.

[14] See 98e5–99a4 (also 96d8–e4), read together with 100e8–101b8. See below for paraphrase and comments.

Remarkably, no general and abstract defence, indeed no general and abstract formulation is offered of these requirements. They are, rather, articulated and made plausible entirely through the appeal to apparent examples of their breach; and, no less, through the appeal to Socrates' reaction of radical *aporia* in the face of these examples—a reaction we are invited to recognize as perfectly natural and reasonable. What we gather from Socrates' narration of his intellectual journey is that the apparent breach of these requirements by traditional and in particular physicalist explanations is what led him to lose trust in such explanations and to suspect that they are not explanations at all. He even lost trust in explanations altogether, presumably because, and for as long as, he thought that he did not know how to satisfy these requirements.

Let us for a moment look at how, in particular, these requirements are supposed to emerge through the appeal to apparent examples of their breach. In the argument at 96e6–97b3 Socrates considers whether we may suppose that the explanation of why some particular thing, x, 'comes to be two' is that some other thing is added to it and joined together with it. And he objects (97a6–b3) to this attempted explanation on the grounds that, if it were an adequate explanation, we could expect to find ourselves in the position, with regard to some other thing, y, of having to say that the explanation of why this thing 'comes to be two' is that it is divided and some thing is taken away from it. The objection is that this latter explanans, the one in terms of division (σχίσις, 97a7), is 'contrary' (ἐναντίον, 97a8, see below for the meaning of ἐναντία) to the original one, the one in terms of addition (πρόσθεσις, 97a1), but that one and the same explanandum, *coming to be two*, is involved. The objection, therefore, relies crucially on the appeal to the requirement, if same explanandum (*coming to be two*), then same explanans, which is articulated and made plausible through the appeal to an apparent example of its breach.

In the argument at 98e5–99a4 Socrates considers whether we may suppose that the explanation of why he, Socrates, stays imprisoned in Athens and does not run away to, e.g. Megara or Boeotia, is his bones and sinews. And he objects to this attempted explanation on the grounds that, if it were an adequate explanation, it could equally have explained why the same thing, he Socrates, had run away to Megara or Boeotia, in the hypothetical situation in which he had judged that it is better to run away than to stay imprisoned. The objection, therefore, appears to rely crucially on the appeal to the requirement, if same explanans (*the particular constituents of a particular body*), then same explanandum, which is articulated and made plausible through the appeal to an apparent example of its breach.

This famous argument demands particular care. As I read it, its main purpose is to exhibit the requirement, if same explanans, then same explanandum, by appealing to an apparent example of its breach. On a common reading, however, its purpose is simply to reject physicalist explanations, that is, explanations that appeal only to physical things, in favour of teleological or good-based ones.[15] Let us briefly compare the two readings. In general, I agree that the purpose of the argument is to reject physicalist explanations in favour of teleological or good-based ones— though we must not forget that traditional good-based explanations will disappoint Socrates no less—but I think this purpose is supposed to be achieved precisely by arguing that physicalist explanations fail to satisfy those requirements of explanation.

First, if the purpose of the argument were simply to reject physicalist explanations, explanations that appeal only to physical things, it would plainly fail. For, suppose a physicalist philosopher asserts that the explanation of why a particular thing, x, behaves in a particular way, W, is that it has a particular physical constituent, M. And suppose another philosopher, for no other purpose than to reject physicalist explanations, objects that, if this were an adequate explanation, it could equally have explained why this thing, x, behaved in a different way, W*. Evidently all the physicalist philosopher needs to do, to defend his favoured type of explanation against this objection, is respond that, had this thing, x, behaved in a different way, W*, the explanation would have been not that it has this physical constituent, M, but rather that it has a different physical constituent, M*.

Second, it is of course true that, in this argument and its context (i.e. 98b7–99c6), Socrates objects to physicalist explanations. But his grounds for objecting are precisely that physicalist explanations do not satisfy those requirements of explanation, and in particular the requirement, if same explanans, then same explanandum. We should note that the force of the objection is not that a physicalist philosopher could not simply require of us

---

[15] See e.g. C. C. W. Taylor, 'Forms as Causes in the *Phaedo*', *Mind* 78 (1969), 45–59. Likewise Fine and Annas, who suppose the appeal to teleological explanations is independent of the objection against physicalist explanations based on their not satisfying the above requirements ('Forms and Causes: Plato and Aristotle', 90; 'Aristotle on Inefficient Causes', 314).

that we formulate our statements, or hypotheses, of physicalist explanations in conformity with these requirements. Evidently he could require this—and we could try our best to comply (see previous paragraph).[16] The force of Socrates' objection is that nothing in what it is to be a physicalist explanation, i.e. an explanation that appeals only to physical things, implies that physicalist explanations satisfy these requirements. And that, therefore, we (or the physicalist philosopher) have nothing to appeal to for the purpose of justifying the claim (regarding whether physicalist explanations satisfy the requirement, if same explanans, then same explanandum):

> (Q) Necessarily: if a particular thing, x, is f because it has a particular physical constituent, M (i.e. its having this physical constituent, M, is the entire explanation of why it is f), then it is impossible for a numerically different thing, y, if it has a quality, g, that is different from and incompatible with the quality f, to be g because it has that same physical constituent, M.

(An analogous formulation may be offered of the corresponding claim regarding whether physicalist explanations satisfy the converse requirement, if same explanandum, then same explanans.) But evidently this claim, Q, needs justification. For it is not at all obvious, nor does it in any way go without saying, that physicalist explanations, or indeed any of the explanations with which we are readily familiar (such as that human beings grow because they eat and drink or that 10 is greater than 8 because it is the sum of 8 and 2), satisfy these requirements of explanation. This, I submit, is the force of Socrates' objection that physicalist explanations, and indeed any of the apparently unobjectionable explanations with which we are readily familiar, fail to satisfy the requirements of explanation.

This means, we should note, that Plato at this point leaves open the possibility that, on a reformed conception of them, explanations that appeal to physical things may, provided that this is not all that they appeal to, satisfy these requirements—in which case they will be of good standing. We will see (in sections 6 and 7) that Plato defends such a reformed conception, for he argues that if physical things are appropriately related to essences, and if essences are conceived as the primary elements in explanantia, then physical

---

[16] Of such a physicalist philosopher we might say, echoing a Kantian slogan, that he would conceive of the requirements as being only regulative principles of scientific enquiry, not constitutive principles of things.

things can be elements in explanantia, and can, therefore, be genuinely parts of explanations.

Third, it is of course true that, in this argument and its context (i.e. 97b8–99c6), Socrates sets teleological or good-based explanations against physical ones, and objects against the latter but holds out hope for the former. But it is equally true that his hopes, to the extent that they were founded in good-based explanations traditionally available, were dashed (98b7), and that, as a result of this, he turned to essence-based or form-based explanations. We must ask, therefore, why his hopes in good-based explanations were dashed and why he does not fear that his turn to essence-based or form-based explanations may suffer a similar fate. I shall address these questions in section 5, and I shall argue that the reason why Socrates despairs of traditional good-based explanations, like the reason why he despairs of traditional physicalist explanations, is that he thinks that, as traditionally conceived, they do not satisfy those requirements of explanation.

How does Plato intend that these requirements should be formulated? What Socrates claims, when he describes how traditional explanations breach these requirements, is that same explananda cannot be explained by contrary (ἐναντία) explanantia, and that, conversely, same explanantia cannot explain contrary explananda.[17] What does he mean by 'contrary' here? It appears that he means 'different and incompatible'. Explananda are contrary if they ascribe different and incompatible qualities to one and the same particular thing. For example, the explananda *Socrates' staying in Athens* and *Socrates' running away to Megara* (see 98e5–99a4) are evidently contrary in this sense. In general, two qualities are incompatible if, and only if, one and the same particular thing cannot (at the same time, in the same respect, etc.) have both qualities. Similarly, explanantia are contrary if, and only if, they explain things in terms of different and incompatible kinds of things. In general, two kinds of things are incompatible if, and only if, one and the same particular thing cannot instantiate both kinds. For example, the explanations in terms of the appeal to addition (πρόσθεσις, 97a1) and division (σχίσις, 97a7), which are expressly referred to as contrary (ἐναντία, 97a8), are contrary in this sense. For the same particular thing, in this case it is a particular process, cannot at once be the process of addition and a

---

[17] See e.g. 97a8–b1 and 101a5–b2.

process of division. Socrates' claim, therefore, is that same explananda cannot be explained by different and incompatible explanantia, and that, conversely, same explanantia cannot explain different and incompatible explananda.[18]

Is the lack of a general and abstract defence, indeed formulation, of these two requirements of explanation (i.e. REQ 1 and 2) a defect of Plato's argument? That depends on what the aim and ambition of the argument is supposed to be. If it were to demonstrate the requirements, or in general to address the question of their ultimate plausibility and their truth, then certainly this would be a defect. It appears, however, that the aim is a different one, namely, first, to introduce the requirements in a way that exhibits their immediate plausibility, and second, to appeal to them in order to defend a particular account of explanation, namely, the account which says that explanantia are, primarily, essences. In that case, a general and abstract defence of the requirements is not part of Plato's aim. Indeed it appears that we ought to understand his overall conclusion as having the form of a conditional: on the supposition of the truth of these requirements of explanation, it follows that explanantia are, primarily, essences. If this is the force of his overall conclusion, then what is required in order to avoid the impression that the whole thing is merely hypothetical is, precisely, some appropriate indication of why it is plausible to believe in these requirements, and this is just what the narration of Socrates' intellectual journey aims at providing. In that case, it may also be appropriate that no general and abstract formulation is given of them. For it is plausible to think that it is precisely through particular examples, examples that are supposed to strike us by their exemplifying, or failing to exemplify, this or that general principle, that general principles first become familiar and plausible to us. It may also be appropriate that the requirements should be articulated and made plausible primarily through the appeal to apparent examples of their breach. For it is plausible to think that it is precisely when it appears to us that some particular case fails to satisfy them that these requirements first strike us. As long as things run smoothly, we need not wonder how they work.

[18] For convenience, we will often say simply that same explananda cannot have *different* explanantia (and *different* explanantia cannot explain same explananda) to mean that same explananda cannot have *different and incompatible* explanantia (and *different and incompatible* explanantia cannot explain same explananda).

We must ask, finally, why Plato thinks that these requirements are plausible, and why he thinks they belong to the essence of explanation. Apparently, he thinks that they are plausible because he thinks that

(INTELL)   If things do not satisfy these requirements of explanation (i.e. REQ1 and REQ2), then their behaviour is not intelligible (or, what is equivalent, if the behaviour of things is intelligible, then they satisfy these requirements).[19]

The reasoning behind this central claim would appear to be along the following lines:

(1) If numerically different things, though they have the same qualities, have different explanantia, then we want to ask why this is, that is, what is the relevant difference in the things which explains why they have different explanantia; and likewise,

if numerically different things, though they have different qualities, have the same explanans, then we want to ask why this is, that is, what is the relevant similarity in the things which explains why they have the same explanans.

(2) Unless we suppose that there is an answer to this question, the behaviour of the things will appear not to be intelligible. But

(3) we can be satisfied that there is an answer to this question if, and only if, we suppose that these requirements (i.e. REQ 1 and 2), are true, and that they are true of the things in question.

It follows that,

(INTELL) If things do not satisfy these requirements, then their behaviour is not intelligible (or, what is equivalent, if the behaviour of things is intelligible, then they satisfy these requirements).

Moreover, if we suppose that there is an essential relation between a thing's being subject to explanation and the thing's being intelligible (I will consider this supposition in a moment), it follows that these requirements belong to

---

[19] By 'intelligible' I mean 'subject to explanation' (see below for a defence of this). It is worth pointing out that Plato is not committed to the converse claim: If things satisfy these requirements of explanation, then their behaviour is intelligible. For this claim would depend on the view that these (i.e. REQ 1 and 2) are the *only* requirements of explanation, and we do not have reason to think that Plato holds this view.

the essence of explanation. This line of reasoning, I suggest, is what is supposed to motivate and indicate the immediate plausibility of these requirements, and of the view that they belong to the essence of explanation.

Let me clarify this line of reasoning, and indicate how it is suggested by the text. The central claim, INTELL, says that if things do not satisfy these requirements of explanation, their behaviour is not intelligible (or, what is equivalent, if the behaviour of things is intelligible, then they satisfy these requirements). First, we must avert a possible misunderstanding. This claim does not say, and it does not imply, that things are intelligible, or that they satisfy these requirements of explanation. What it says is, rather, that *if* things are intelligible, *then* they satisfy these requirements of explanation. It would, therefore, be misplaced to think that Plato's argument rests on the supposition that nature (*phusis*)—the totality of things subject to generation and destruction—is governed by reason (*nous*)—reason as the source of intelligibility. If Plato's argument rests on a supposition about the relation between nature and reason, it is that *if* nature is governed by reason, *then* it is subject to these requirements of explanation. The central claim, we may say, is about the essence of explanation and intelligibility, not about what things, if any, are subject to explanation and intelligible.

Second, what, in the central claim, is supposed to be the relation between a thing's being subject to explanation and the thing's being intelligible? Suppose that being subject to explanation and being intelligible are, precisely, one and the same thing. In that case, the claim says that if things do not satisfy these requirements of explanation, their behaviour is not subject to explanation. Is this uninformative or tautologous? I think not. What is perhaps uninformative and tautologous is the claim that if things do not satisfy *any* requirements of explanation (i.e. do not satisfy *whatever it may be* that explanation requires), their behaviour is not subject to explanation. But the claim is genuinely informative, and far from tautologous, which says that if things do not satisfy *these* requirements of explanation, *viz. REQ1 and REQ2*, then their behaviour is not subject to explanation. I do not, therefore, see any immediate objection against supposing that a thing's being subject to explanation and the thing's being intelligible are, precisely, one and the same thing. It also seems plausible to suppose this, if we bear in mind the relevant meaning of 'a thing is subject to explanation', namely, 'there is something, whatever it is, which is *that because of which* (the δι' ὅτι, see e.g. *Phaedo* 97b3–5) the thing, or some quality of it, is as it is' (for this being the relevant meaning, see section 4). For it seems plausible to think that there being something which is *that because of which* a thing, or some quality of it, is as it is, and the thing's, or some quality of it, being intelligible, are, precisely, one and the same thing.

Third, we must suppose that the relation between a thing's being subject to explanation and the thing's being intelligible, even if it is not that of identity, is a particularly close one. Otherwise the main claim, INTELL, would not directly imply—as evidently it is supposed to imply—that there is anything wrong with supposing that a thing satisfies the requirements of explanation (i.e. satisfies the requirements of explanation, *whatever they may be*) but that, nevertheless, it is not the case that its behaviour is intelligible. It seems plausible to think, moreover, that what is wrong with supposing this is, precisely, that it is a necessary truth, and one apparently rooted in the essence of explanation and intelligibility, that if a thing satisfies the requirements of explanation (i.e. satisfies the requirements of explanation, *whatever they may be*), then its behaviour is intelligible. In general, this necessary truth indicates what, minimally, we must suppose to be the relation between a thing's being subject to explanation and the thing's being intelligible.

Let me comment briefly on the premises, 1–3, of the argument—its validity being evident. With regard to premise (1), I suppose it is evident that we do want to ask this. My six-year-old daughter does. Recently she asked me why I was wearing rubber shoes in the pool. I said, because of the need to avoid foot infections. She objected, in her insistent fashion, that in the sea I would swim barefoot. I said something to the effect that there is a difference, but that I would some other time tell her what it is. It appears that what my daughter said was an expression of some grasp of the requirement, if same explanantia (*the need to avoid foot infections*), then same explananda (*the wearing of rubber shoes*). Of course, her grasp did not involve, or imply, her being able to formulate this requirement in abstract and general terms, it involved rather, if anything, her being sensitive to a case of its apparent breach (and no doubt its real breach, as my behaviour is not always intelligible). What is striking is that Socrates, when he describes the radical *aporia* that befell him in his youth about explanations, describes his reaction, in the face of the would-be explanations offered him by his elders, philosophers and non-philosophers alike, as being similarly childlike—and no less insistent. This is of course a deliberate literary device on Plato's part, and one that appears to be modelled on something like a topos, the topos of the innocence and apparent simple-mindedness needed for philosophy (cf. εὐήθως ἔχω παρ' ἐμαυτῷ, 100d4).

With regard to premise (2), the point is not, of course, that, unless we suppose that we know the answer to the question 'What is the relevant difference (or similarity)?', or that we are capable of finding this out, the behaviour of the things will appear not to be intelligible. We may have no clue what the answer to this question is, or how to discover it. The point is that, unless we suppose that there is an answer to this question, the behaviour of the things will appear not to be intelligible. That is, it will appear that there is no *that because of which* (the δι' ὅτι) the things, or some qualities of them, are as they are. Of course, we may indeed suppose that the behaviour of the things is not intelligible. There need not be anything puzzling about supposing that. What is puzzling—whence Socrates' radical *aporia*—is to suppose that the behaviour of the things is not intelligible while at the same time supposing that the things are subject to explanation. We have seen that the reason why this is altogether puzzling is that, apparently, it involves a contradiction.

Premise (3) ought to be evident. The supposition that precisely these requirements (i.e. REQ 1 and 2) are true, and, moreover, that they are true of the things in question, is precisely what allows us to justify the supposition that there is an answer to the question 'What is the relevant difference (or similarity)?'

2   Plato's Response to the *aporia* about Explanation (*Phaedo* 99d4–102b3): Explanantia Are, Primarily, Essences

Socrates' intellectual journey culminates in the introduction of the account which says that explanantia are, primarily, essences (100b1f.). This is a journey from complete loss of trust to perfectly restored trust in explanations, and it is the account which says that explanantia are, primarily, essences that restores this trust. Trust is restored, we will see, because Plato thinks that explanations in conformity with this account, and such explanations alone, satisfy the two fundamental requirements of explanation.

It is notable that the two requirements of explanation are invoked both during Socrates' description of how he lost trust in traditional explanations (up to 99d3) and when his trust in explanations has been restored by the introduction of the account which says that explanantia are, primarily, essences (beginning at 99d4).[20] This provides further indication that, just as the apparent breach of these requirements by traditional explanations is the source of his loss of trust in explanations, so the restoration of trust in explanations is due to the satisfaction of these requirements by the account which says that explanantia are, primarily, essences.

As it is formulated when it is first introduced (100b–101c), this account says that:

1. The explanation of why x is f is that x is appropriately related to—it 'partakes in', or 'communes with', or 'has present in it'—the essence of the quality f, Ess(f).[21]

Here x is a changing thing, and f is a quality of that thing. It is pointed out more than once that x is a changing thing, and apparently it is changing in respect of the quality f.[22] It is, therefore, natural to think that f is, as we would say, an accidental and contingent quality of x. The essence of the quality f, Ess(f), is the entity properly referred to as *the f itself by itself*.[23] Shortly later this entity is referred to as, precisely, the οὐσία of the quality f, or of things in so far as they are f (101c3).[24] We may single out this passage as central, for it says that explanations (αἰτίαι) are essences (οὐσίαι):

And you would cry out loud that you know of no other way in which any thing comes to be [including, that is, comes to be f] than by partaking in the proper essence of any thing, whichever it may be that it partakes in; and also in this case you know of no other *aitia* of coming to be two, save the participation in twoness. . . .

---

[20] For REQ1, compare 97a8–b3 with 101b10–c9; for REQ2, compare esp. 96d8–e4 with 100e8–101b8.

[21] Remarkably, David Sedley thinks the schema ' "It is because of the F that F things are F" ' is 'treated as [an example of] self-evident truths' ('Platonic Causes', *Phronesis* 43 (1998), 114–32, pp. 116–17). I confess I cannot see how it could be so treated by Plato. Plato intends 'the F' here to signify an essence/form, and he could hardly think it is self-evident that causes are essences/forms.

[22] See 96a8–9, 97b4–5, c7.

[23] See e.g. 100b5–7: [τὸ καλόν, ἀγαθόν, μέγαν, etc.] αὐτὸ καθ' αὑτό. Earlier in the dialogue simply f *itself* (αὐτό).

[24] See section 3 for why it is plausible to think that οὐσία here means 'essence', and for why, at any rate, the term οὐσία as used here refers not only to forms, but likewise to essences.

καὶ μέγα ἂν βοῴης ὅτι οὐκ οἶσθα ἄλλως πως ἕκαστον γιγνόμενον ἢ μετασχὸν τῆς
ἰδίας οὐσίας ἑκάστου οὗ ἂν μετάσχῃ, καὶ ἐν τούτοις οὐκ ἔχεις ἄλλην τινὰ αἰτίαν τοῦ
δύο γενέσθαι ἀλλ' ἢ τὴν τῆς δυάδος μετάσχεσιν. (101c2–5)

The term εἶδος ('form') is used a little later, with the same reference as
οὐσία.[25] The relation between the changing thing which is f and the essence
of the quality f is variously called 'participation' (μετάσχεσις, μέθεξις),
'communion' (κοινωνία), and (for the converse relation) 'presence'
(παρουσία, ἐνουσία), but its exact nature appears deliberately to be left
open (see 100d4–8).

This is evidently an account about explanantia, which says that explanantia are (primarily) essences.[26] But it is just as much an account about
explanation, that is, about explananda, explanantia, and their relation, *A
because B*. Indeed, the account is introduced as an attempt to satisfy the
requirements, REQ 1 and 2, which embody the constraints of the uniqueness, generality, and uniformity of explanation. But evidently these requirements are specifically about how explananda and explanantia must be
related to each other, that is, in such a way that explanations are unique,
general, and uniform. So the account, though certainly about explanantia, is
above all about explanation, that is, about the whole triad: explananda,
explanantia, and their relation.

The account appeals to explananda, but how is an explanandum understood here? Is it understood simply as an unanalysed whole, *something's being
such and such*, or is it already analysed into a particular, x, and a quality, f?
Initially at least, it appears that it is understood as an unanalysed whole.
For this is the way in which natural phenomena present themselves to us in
experience and when we begin to ask simple and immediate 'Why?' questions, such as the question why human beings grow. And in his narration
Socrates appears deliberately to present such 'Why?' questions as arising
naturally and directly from our experience of natural phenomena. Unless,
therefore, we have particular reason to think that Plato understands explananda as already analysed into particulars and qualities, we ought to leave it

---

[25] See 102b1; also 103e3 and 104c7. For the claim that these two terms are used here with the same
reference, and in general for their use in the *Phaedo*, see section 3.

[26] I put 'primarily' in brackets because, in this passage (100b–101c), the account says simply that
explanantia are essences. It is only later that it will emerge that the account is not that explanantia are
simply essences, but that explanantia, whatever else they may involve, are primarily essences. See section 6.

at that. We do, however, have such reason, and this is that, precisely because of the requirements of explanation, Plato needs to analyse explananda into particulars and qualities. For, in order to state that explanations must be uniform, it is necessary to introduce the idea of the sameness or difference of a quality, and to suppose that the sameness or difference of a quality is independent of the sameness or difference of the things which have it.

Why, then, does Plato think that any explanation in conformity with this account satisfies the two fundamental requirements of explanation?[27] Why, that is, does he think that the account which says that explanantia are (primarily) essences *is sufficient* to satisfy these requirements, REQ 1 and 2?[28] The account says that:

1.   x is f because x is appropriately related to the essence of the quality f, Ess(f).

But if we reflect for a moment on the notion of essence, it is evident that:

2.   The essence of a quality f is that which determines and constitutes the very identity of this quality: *what* quality this is.

If, however, we put together these claims, we obtain the following, central claim:

[27] That this is indeed what Plato thinks is pointed out by, e.g. Fine ('Forms as Causes: Plato and Aristotle', 96) and Annas ('Aristotle on Inefficient Causes', 314–18). However, I do not think their account is satisfactory of why Plato thinks this. Fine says: 'Plato's SA [i.e. the simple schema] disallows this [i.e. explanations by opposites]; something is, or comes to be, F just in case it is, or comes to be, suitably related to the Form of F, and no Form (Plato assumes) consists of opposites.' Annas says: 'The Form F explains an F instance by its guaranteed freedom from being the opposite of F.' But this, surely, is not sufficient to ensure uniformity. We can see this if we name the form of F 'N' and ask why it should not be possible that N sometimes causes F in things, sometimes G (opposite to F) in things; or, conversely, why it should not be possible that things that are F should sometimes be caused to be F by form N, sometimes by a different form, M. As far as I can see, what Fine and Annas say does not address this crucial question. Nor, in my view, would it be advisable to address it by invoking the principle 'causes must be like their effects', for this would be to beg it. (Annas appears to suppose that the question can only be addressed by invoking the principle 'causes must be like their effects', and this is why she concludes that 'Plato's demand on explanation is one which we no longer find compelling; it applies convincingly only to a few simple cases where the explanandum is a quality that can be transmitted from one thing to another' (317). I agree with her inference to her conclusion, but not with the supposition behind it, hence not with her conclusion.) What Fine and Annas fail to point out is that the form F is the essence of the quality F. This, and this alone, is why, if the form is the cause, it can only cause F (see my analysis below).

[28] Sedley ('Platonic Causes') invokes the principle 'causes must be like their effects' to explain why Plato thinks it is because of the f that things are f (123–4); and he argues that Plato thinks this principle is self-evidently true (116f.).

CC.   That which explains why a particular thing has a certain quality, f, and that which determines which quality this is and constitutes the identity of this quality, *are one and the same thing.*

This is a striking claim, which indicates the precise way in which Plato thinks that these fundamental concepts, *explanation* (αἰτία) and *essence* (οὐσία), are related.

But this claim, CC, has an immediate consequence, and this is the truth of the requirements REQ1 and REQ2. On the supposition of this claim, the demonstration of REQ1 and REQ2 is straightforward. It is impossible for different particulars, in so far as they have the same quality, to have different explanantia; for, according to claim CC, if they have different explanantia, then they have different qualities. So REQ1 is true. Likewise, it is impossible for different particulars, in so far as they have different qualities, to have the same explanans; for, according to claim CC, if they have the same explanans, then they have the same quality. So REQ2 is likewise true. On the supposition, therefore, of the account which says that explanantia are (primarily) essences, the requirements of explanation, REQ1 and REQ2, are true. This account is, therefore, sufficient to satisfy the requirements of explanation.

A brief comment on premise 2—having already commented on premise 1. This premise is supposed to articulate no more than Plato's core concept of essence, which says that the essence of any thing, x, is *what it is to be this very thing, x.* (We should also note the expression εἶναι ὅπερ ἦν, 'to be the very thing it is', which is used twice later in the dialogue, at 103d7 and 12.) Or, to say the same thing in a different way, the essence of any thing, x, is what is signified by the answer, if it is true, to the Socratic-type question, 'What is this very thing, x?' We are of course familiar with this Socratic-type question from dialogues we consider to be earlier than the *Phaedo*. Earlier in the *Phaedo* itself, however, Plato reminds us of this type of question, and he associates it directly with the theory of forms (see section 3).

It is worth observing that this defence of the requirements of explanation appears to conform to the method of hypothesis, as this method is introduced here (100a3–8 and 101d1–8). That is to say, on the hypothesis of the account which says that explanantia are (primarily) essences, it follows that these requirements are true. So the requirements of explanation, which perhaps had the status of hypotheses when initially introduced, are now logically derived 'from something higher' (see ἄνωθεν, 101d8), that is, from the account which says that explanantia are (primarily) essences. Indeed it appears that this account is itself referred to as a hypothesis.[29]

Plato, therefore, thinks that the account which says that explanantia are (primarily) essences *is sufficient* to satisfy the requirements, REQ 1 and 2, that embody the constraints of the uniqueness, generality, and uniformity of explanation. Indeed he is right. Does he also think that this account *is necessary* to satisfy these requirements? This does appear to be his view. When he comments on the method of hypothesis here (in 101d6–8), he says that if one is requested to defend (διδόναι λόγον) a particular hypothesis, one must put forward a further hypothesis, namely *'the one that would appear best of those above* (ἥτις τῶν ἄνωθεν βελτίστη φαίνοιτο), until one arrives at something adequate (ἱκανόν)'. But if the requirements of explanation were initially hypotheses, and if the task now is to defend them by relying on a 'higher' hypothesis, that is, the account which says that explanantia are (primarily) essences, then this comment on the method of hypothesis shows that Plato thinks that there may be other and competing 'higher' hypotheses for defending the requirements, and that his own account must be shown to be not only a good means of defence, but the best. But to show this is to show that this account is not only sufficient, but also necessary to satisfy the requirements of explanation.

To consider why Plato thinks that the account which says that explanantia are (primarily) essences is necessary to satisfy the requirements of explanation, we need to distinguish the various elements in this account and to ask why he thinks each of them is necessary to satisfy the requirements of explanation. We need to distinguish the following elements in the account:

(i) the general schema of explanation, x is f because E;
(ii) the analysis of the explanandum into a particular and a quality had by it;
(iii) the claim that the quality f has an essence, $Ess(f)$;
(iv) the claim, CC, which says that the entity, E, that explains why a particular thing, x, has a particular quality, f, and the essence of this quality, $Ess(f)$, are *one and the same thing* (i.e. $E = Ess(f)$); and

---

[29] See 101d2–4, supposing that the ὑπόθεσις mentioned here includes the general statement of the account that explanantia are, primarily, essences, in 101c2–4, and not only its particular application to the present case, in 101c4–5, i.e. the case of one thing coming to be two.

(v) the relation between the explanandum and the explanans, which
Plato variously refers to as 'participation', 'communion', and (for
the converse relation) 'presence', but whose exact nature he appears
deliberately to leave open (see 100d4–8).

The question, therefore, is why Plato thinks each of these elements in
the account of explanation is necessary to satisfy the requirements of
explanation.

With regard to the first element, it ought to be evident that the general
schema of explanation, *x is f because E*, is necessary to satisfy the requirements of explanation, and one could hardly think otherwise. This is evident
if we consider that all this schema does is set out the form of any answer to
the question 'Why is this thus and so?': 'This is thus and so because such and
such.' The variables in the original formulation, x, f, and E, are simply
placeholders and do not add anything to the blueprint.

With regard to the second element, we need to ask why it is justified to think
that explananda should be analysed into particulars and qualities had by
them. But we saw that this is justified precisely by the constraint which says
that explanations must be uniform, that is, by the requirements REQ1 and
REQ2. For, in order to state that explanations must be uniform, it is
necessary to introduce the idea of the sameness or difference of a quality,
and to suppose that the sameness or difference of a quality is independent of
the sameness or difference of the things which have it. This, in turn,
provides us with the appropriate, and minimal notion of a particular here:
a particular is a *this* and something that can be counted; it is a bearer of
qualities; and it is such that one and the same quality can be had by
numerically different particulars. This shows that the analysis of explananda
into particulars and qualities had by them is necessary to formulate, and
therefore to satisfy, the requirements of explanation.

One might object that it would be no less justified to think that explanantia should be analysed into objects (e.g. Socrates) and states of affairs (e.g.
Socrates' being in a state of growing). We ought to reply that, if this analysis
is to allow for the formulation of the requirements of explanation, it will
need a means of indicating that the following two states of affairs have an
element (what we have called, the quality) in common: *Socrates' being in a
state of growing* and *Plato's being in state of growing*. But once such a means is
provided, it will be evident that this analysis is equivalent to ours: what is

indicated by this means corresponds to what we have called the quality, and the object appealed to in the analysis corresponds to what we have called the particular. We can, therefore, avail ourselves of both analyses without needing to choose between them.

With regard to the third element, it is striking that the view that qualities have essences is a presupposition of the requirements of explanation. This is because, in order to state that explanations must be uniform, it is necessary to introduce the idea of the sameness or difference of a quality, and to suppose that the sameness or difference of a quality is independent of the sameness or difference of the particulars which have it. We can see this also if we ask how it is possible to dispute the requirements of explanation. For it appears that one way in which this is possible is precisely by arguing that they cannot be true *of* anything; and that this is so because *either* qualities do not have determinate identity conditions or essences at all, *or*, if they have identity conditions of a sort, these depend in each case on the particulars that have them. The truth of the view that qualities have essences, and that the essence of a quality is independent of the particular that has it, is, therefore, a necessary condition for the truth of the requirements of explanation, or rather for the possibility of there being any thing that satisfies them.

With regard to the fourth element, we can, I think, readily recognize why Plato may think that claim CC is necessary to satisfy the requirements of explanation—though we will see that this is not quite his view. Suppose that CC is not true, i.e. the essence of the quality f, Ess(f), is not identical with the explanans, E, that explains why a particular thing, x, is f. In that case, it appears, the explanandum, *x's being f*, will be independent, for its essence, i.e. for its being the very one it is, of the explanans, E. (As we might say, echoing Hume, there will be no necessary connection between the effect and the cause.) But then, it appears, there will be nothing to appeal to for the purpose of showing that the putative explanation, 'x is f because E', satisfies the requirements of explanation.

To recognize the force of this reasoning, we ought to recall why, if CC is true, then the explanandum, *x's being f*, will indeed be dependent, for its being the very one it is, on the explanans, E. Evidently the essence of the quality f, i.e. *what* quality this is, is part of the essence of this explanandum, *x's being f*, i.e. part of what it is for this explanandum to be the very one it is. But, according to CC, the essence of the quality f is identical with the explanans, E. Therefore, if CC is true, the explanandum, *x's being f*, will be dependent, for its being the very one it is, on the explanans, E. It was precisely this dependence and necessary connection that we made use of earlier for the purpose of showing that, if CC is true, then the requirements of explanation, REQ1 and REQ2, are true.

We may, however, object to this reasoning, that even if claim CC is false, i.e. even if Ess(f) and E are not identical, there may still be a necessary connection between them. But in that case the explanandum, *x's being f*, may still be dependent, for its being the very one it is, on the explanans, E— though the dependence may be less immediate, and less immediately evident, than if it is based on the identity of Ess(f) and E. It may, therefore, be possible, even if CC is false, to show that a putative explanation, 'x is f because E', satisfies the requirements of explanation. Therefore, it is not the case that CC is necessary to satisfy the requirements of explanation.

However, Plato can acknowledge and accommodate this objection. For we will see (in section 6) that he will argue (at 103c–105c) that the explanans, E, of *x's being f* may not be the simple one, Ess(f), but may be rather a complex, conjunctive one, [S + Ess(f)]—where S is, for example, a physical constituent of x. For example, the explanans, E, of *this body's being hot* may be not simply the essence of heat, but may be rather the conjunction of fire (supposing the body has fire in it) and the essence of heat. Plato, that is, defends not only the simple schema of explanation, but also a complex one, and he thinks the complex schema is dependent on the simple one. It is evident, however, that if the explanandum, *x's being f*, is dependent, for its being the very one it is, on the simple explanans, Ess(f), then it is also dependent, for its being the very one it is, on the complex explanans, [S + Ess(f)]. For the complex explanans is a conjunction of the simple one and a further explanatory element. On the complex schema of explanation, there-fore, it will still be true that the explanandum, *x's being f*, is dependent, for its being the very one it is, on the explanans. In this way Plato can acknowledge and accommodate the objection. Of course, if he acknowledges and accom-modates the objection in this way, this means that he does not after all think CC is necessary to satisfy the requirements of explanation. What he thinks is necessary to satisfy the requirements of explanation is rather:

$CC^{qualified}$ Either (E = Ess(f)) or (E = [S + Ess(f)]),

where this disjunction ought to be understood as being inclusive rather than exclusive.

With regard to the fifth element, it is notable that Plato here appears deliberately to leave open how exactly the relation between explananda and explanantia is to be understood (see 100d4–8). This is indeed appropriate, if he thinks that each element of the present account of explanation is necessary to satisfy the requirements of explanation. For then the relation between a particular explanandum and a particular explanans must be specified simply as: that relation, whatever it is, which, if it obtains, implies that the particular explanandum, *a particular thing's being f*, is explained by the particular explanans, E. Suppose, on the other hand, that Plato had a particular conception of the relation between explananda and explanantia in mind here, such as, for instance, the view that it must be a relation between separate and distinct things, where separation implies more than the view that the essence of a quality is independent of the particular that has it. In that case it would not be at all plausible for him to think that this relation is necessary to satisfy the requirements of explanation. But I doubt that we have grounds for thinking that Plato has a particular conception of this relation in mind here, and he appears to indicate the contrary (see 100d4–8).

We may conclude that Plato thinks, for good reason, that the account of explanation which says that explanantia are (primarily) essences is both sufficient and necessary to satisfy the fundamental requirements of explanations, REQ 1 and 2, which embody the constraints of the uniqueness, generality, and uniformity of explanation. This account, therefore, is both necessary and sufficient for the purpose of resolving the original, radical *aporia* about explanation.

Conclusion to Sections 1 and 2

We have seen that Plato's method of argument is to articulate a radical *aporia* about explanation, and then work towards a solution to it by introducing an account of explanation, that is, an answer to the question, 'What is an explanation?' The argument proceeds as follows. First, Plato indicates the source of the *aporia*. The source of the *aporia* is that, on the one hand, it appears that any explanation must satisfy certain fundamental requirements, in particular the requirements REQ 1 and 2, which embody the constraints of the uniqueness, generality, and uniformity of explanation, but, on the other hand, it appears that no familiar explanations, whether scientific or everyday ones, satisfy these requirements. Next, he asks what an account of explanation must look like in order to satisfy these requirements. Finally, he argues that an account which says that explanantia are (primarily) essences, and such an account alone, satisfies these requirements. The purpose of this argument is to establish this account of explanation, and to do so by showing that it, and it alone, resolves the original, radical *aporia* about explanation.

It appears, moreover, that a central aim of this part of the *Phaedo* is precisely to bring together the account of essence and the account of explanation. When Plato introduces (at 100b1f.) the account which says that explanantia are (primarily) essences, he says that it is meant to be thoroughly familiar to his interlocutors. This is, in part at least, a reference to the account of essence earlier in the dialogue, though there, too, the account of essence was described as familiar. There is, however, this important difference. For the account of essence earlier in the dialogue was not, apparently, associated with explanations or an account of explanation. This suggests that Plato's aim in this part of the *Phaedo* is to bring together the account of essence and the account of explanation.

There are, however, two ways in which we may understand this aim. We may think that an already fully developed account of essence is now being associated with an account of explanation, or we may think that the account of explanation serves to develop an account of essence. It seems to me that the latter interpretation is the more plausible one. For we have seen that the account which says that explanantia are (primarily) essences, and indeed the claim that there are essences, can be defended by setting out to satisfy certain fundamental requirements of explanation, and in general to provide an adequate account of explanation; and this is how Plato defends this here. This does not mean that the search for an adequate account of explanation is the sole origin of the account of essence, in Plato generally or the *Phaedo* in particular. It is notable that earlier in the dialogue a conception of essence was introduced without reference to explanation. What it means is that Plato thinks the account of explanation is sufficient to generate an account of essence, and indeed to defend the claim that there are essences. Plato, therefore, defends, in the *Phaedo*, the claim that there are essences. He does this by arguing that only if there are essences can there be an explanation (αἰτία) of why a thing is as it is. This is a powerful defence, for few would be willing to give up on the possibility of explanation and of there being true answers to the question '*Why* is it as it is?'

This conclusion about Plato's view of the relation between explanation and essence may require further clarification. In particular, it may be thought that it is ambiguous between a weaker reading, on which it says that:

(1)   We see in explanation an important use for essences, and, what is more, a use which allows us, first, to argue that if there are explanations, then there are essences, and, second, to introduce the very idea of essence by reflecting on what is required to satisfy certain fundamental requirements of explanation;

and a stronger reading, on which it says that:

(2)   Part of what it is to be an essence is that essences play this role in explanations, i.e. the role of being the primary explanantia.

I am inclined to think that Plato is committed to the latter, stronger claim, but it may be that the *Phaedo* argument, on our interpretation of it, only provides grounds for thinking that he holds the former, weaker claim. Still, the *Phaedo* argument, on the present interpretation, allows us to conclude that Plato thinks that essences are explanations, indeed, that essences are, *necessarily*, explanations. What it may or may not allow us to conclude is that Plato thinks essences are, *essentially*, explanations—that it is part of what it is to be an essence that essences are explanations. On the other hand, I doubt whether anything in the *Phaedo* argument suggests, much less implies that he thinks essences are only necessarily, and not also essentially explanations. To answer this question, however, goes beyond the purpose of this paper.

However, Plato's argument, and the question of how we ought to interpret it, raises a number of issues, which I prefer to address individually and separately, in the following sections.

3   The *Phaedo* on Forms ($\epsilon\check{\iota}\delta\eta$), Essences ($o\dot{\upsilon}\sigma\acute{\iota}\alpha\iota$), and their Relation

In the *Phaedo* Plato repeatedly refers to forms ($\epsilon\check{\iota}\delta\eta$).[30] But does he also refer to essences ($o\dot{\upsilon}\sigma\acute{\iota}\alpha\iota$; i.e. what is signified by a true answer to the Socratic-type

---

[30] The term $\epsilon\check{\iota}\delta\sigma$ is not used until 102b1 (and later at 103e3 and 104c7). Earlier, forms are referred to in other ways (see below).

question, 'What is f?')?[31] And if he refers to both, what is the relation between the two? I want to defend the following answer, which I intend to be relatively unexciting and readily acceptable on evident textual grounds:

A.   In the *Phaedo* Plato repeatedly refers to both forms and essences. And when he is referring to forms, he is also referring to essences; and, at least generally, when he is referring to essences, he is also referring to forms.

I would like to emphasize that this view is not supposed to imply, nor is it part of my aim to defend any of the following claims regarding the *Phaedo*: (a) the terms εἶδος and οὐσία (for 'essence') are used synonymously, or interchangeably; or (b) there is no difference between forms and essences; or (c) forms are simply essences. It is, however, supposed to imply the claim that:

B.   Forms in the *Phaedo*, whatever else they also are, are essences as well. And the theory of forms, whatever else it also is, is also a theory of essence.[32]

This view, we may note, is compatible both with affirming and with denying the following view, which makes up a central part of a traditional (though no longer generally accepted, if it ever was) developmentalist interpretation: (i) there is a philosophically significant distinction between early and middle dialogues, and (ii) it is part of this distinction that the early dialogues are committed only to essences whereas the middle ones, to which (according to this view) the *Phaedo* belongs,[33] are also committed to forms. In general, the present paper is neutral on the question of developmentalism.

Of course, if we are committed to these claims (A and B), but not to the claim that there is no difference between forms and essences, we must consider what the difference may be between Plato's being committed

---

[31]   The term οὐσία is used at 65d13, 92d9, and 101c3, but it is not clear whether in any of these instances it is used to mean 'essence' (rather than 'being'). I will argue that at 92d9 it is rather used to mean 'being', but at 65d13 and 101c3 it is plausible to think that it is used to mean 'essence'. But at any rate essences are also referred to in other ways in the *Phaedo* (see below).

[32]   This is also how Aristotle reads Plato (see *Metaphysics* I. 9, 991a12–14 and b1–3 [= XIII. 5, 1079b15–18 and 1079b35–1080a2], if we suppose that when he talks of the οὐσία of certain things here, he means to signify, in the first instance at least, the essence of those things).

[33]   It is notable that, on purely stylometric criteria for distinguishing between early and middle dialogues, which are supposed to be neutral on the question of the philosophical significance, if any, of this distinction, the *Phaedo* is classified as early. See Charles Kahn, 'On Platonic Chronology', in J. Annas and C. Rowe (eds.), *New Perspectives on Plato, Modern and Ancient* (Harvard, 2002), 93–127.

only to essences and his being committed also to forms. It is not, however, part of my aim to consider this difficult question. One difference that suggests itself, and would appear to be a good candidate for a central difference, is due to Plato's claim that the things with which forms are contrasted, that is, the things it is possible to perceive directly by the senses (for short, the sensibles), are somehow 'deficient' (ἐνδεές) when compared with forms (see 74d4f. for this claim). In general, we may suppose that the meaning of this claim is that the sensibles are dependent, for being what they are and indeed for being real, on the forms, whereas the forms are not dependent, for being what they are and for being real, on the sensibles. The suggestion would be that Plato can be committed to essences without being committed to this further claim, but that this further claim is part of his commitment to forms. I think this is a plausible suggestion, but I shall not pursue it further. What is important for present purposes is that the suggestion is compatible with, and is a way of giving substance to, claim B. On this suggestion, forms are essences conceived as being the ontologically independent things, and the theory of forms is a theory of essences, thus conceived, and of the relation (commonly referred to as 'participation', μέθεξις, and 'communion', κοινωνία, as at 100d6) between sensibles, conceived as being the ontologically dependent things, and essences.

These claims (A and B), which I shall defend presently, are centrally important to the overall aim of this paper. For this is to show that in the *Phaedo* Plato argues that explanantia are, primarily, *essences*, and to examine his argument for this thesis. We have seen (in sections 1 and especially 2) that Plato's argument depends basically on the core notion of essence, which says that the essence of a quality, f, is what it is to be this very quality, f. In general the essence of a thing is what it is to be this very thing. Plato's argument depends, therefore, on his theory of essence. It also depends on his theory of forms, but it does so because this theory, whatever else it also is, is also a theory of essence. I would like to emphasize that the truth of this view, i.e. the view which says that Plato's argument for the claim that explanantia are, primarily, essences depends basically on his core notion of essence, is not something I am assuming, it is something that has been shown by the examination of Plato's argument (see section 2).

The first reference in the dialogue to either forms or essences is a reference to a particular essence, that of death (64c2–9), when, early in the dialogue and at the beginning of the extended argument that will see us through the whole of the *Phaedo*, Socrates puts forward the view that death and dying consists in precisely this (see μὴ ἄλλο τι ᾖ ὁ θάνατος ἢ τοῦτο, 64c8; same as in c4–5), namely, the separation of the soul and the body. Socrates introduces this account of the essence of death by the question: ἡγούμεθά τι τὸν θάνατον εἶναι; 'Do we suppose that death is something?' (64c2). Practically the entire dialogue depends on this account of the essence of death, a central of whose implications—viz. that the soul can survive the body—is challenged by Kebes at 69e–70b, then further defended by Socrates, only to be further challenged by Simmias and Kebes, and defended by Socrates to the satisfaction of all only by the end of the dialogue.

The first reference to forms is, we may suppose, the reference to 'just itself' (δίκαιον αὐτό) at 65d4–5, if we suppose that the function of αὐτό here is to mark a form-referring use of the adjective. The question Socrates asks here is: φαμέν τι εἶναι δίκαιον αὐτὸ ἢ οὐδέν. This question is notably similar to the one that served to introduce his view of the essence of death (ἡγούμεθά τι τὸν θάνατον εἶναι; 64c2), and this already suggests that the reference to the form of just is likewise a reference to the essence of just. The suggestion is established if we translate the question at 65d4–5 as: 'Do we assert that just itself is something, or nothing?' (i.e. taking δίκαιον αὐτό as subject). If instead we translate: 'Do we assert that there is something just itself, or nothing?' (i.e. taking δίκαιον αὐτό as complement of εἶναι), the suggestion, though still standing, will need further confirmation. Confirmation, however, is immediately forthcoming, when Socrates says that by the terms 'just itself' (also 'beautiful [itself]', 'good [itself]', 'size [itself]', 'health [itself]', and 'strength [itself]'), he is, in sum (ἑνὶ λόγῳ), referring to (λέγω περὶ): τῶν ἄλλων . . . ἁπάντων τῆς οὐσίας ὃ τυγχάνει ἕκαστον ὄν ('the being [or: essence] of all the others, what each [of them] is', 65d12–e1). It is the phrase ὃ τυγχάνει ἕκαστον ὄν ('what each [of them] is', literally, 'what each [of them] happens to be') that marks a reference to the essence of each of the things—as it does typically in Plato. This, therefore, confirms that the first reference to forms in the *Phaedo*—and this is an important reference to forms in the dialogue—is likewise a reference to essences.

Does the term οὐσία here (65d13) mean 'essence'? Though we cannot be certain (it may mean rather 'being' and serve to refer to the being peculiar of the forms), it is plausible to think that it does. First, οὐσία is here used with the genitive ('the οὐσία of something'), and this is a mark (though not of course a conclusive one) of the use in the sense of 'essence'. We may contrast the occurrence of οὐσία at 92d9, which is not used with the genitive and appears to mean rather 'being' and indicate the being peculiar of the forms. Second, the phrase ὃ τυγχάνει ἕκαστον ὄν in general serves to mark a reference to the essence of things, and this phrase is used in apposition to and as a clarification of the term οὐσία and the phrase τῶν ἄλλων ἁπάντων τῆς οὐσίας.

Suppose, however, that οὐσία here means rather 'being' and serves to indicate the being peculiar of the forms. This is how it is often read.[34] Still, since the phrase ὃ τυγχάνει ἕκαστον ὄν stands in apposition to and is epexegetic of τῶν ἄλλων ἁπάντων τῆς οὐσίας, we may conclude that 'being' (οὐσία) here is used not only in a complete way (signifying what we might call 'existence' but ought perhaps rather call 'being real'), but also in an incomplete, predicative way, in which, moreover, what is predicated is predicated essentially.[35] The supposition that οὐσία here means 'being' and serves to indicate the being peculiar of the forms is, therefore, consistent and coherent with the supposition that the reference to forms here is likewise a reference to essences.

A later, and central series of references to forms begins with the reference to 'the equal itself' (αὐτὸ τὸ ἴσον) at 74a12. This is then generalized to being a reference to 'all things of that kind' (σύμπαντα τὰ τοιαῦτα, 75c10), such as the beautiful, good, just, and holy itself (75c10–d1). The object of this reference is then generically described by the remarkable characterization: περὶ ἁπάντων οἷς ἐπισφραγιζόμεθα τοῦτο, τὸ "ὃ ἔστι", καὶ ἐν ταῖς ἐρωτήσεσιν ἐρωτῶντες καὶ ἐν ταῖς ἀποκρίσεσιν ἀποκρινόμενοι ('[the present argument, ὁ νῦν λόγος, is] about all the things to which we add this stamp, "that which it is", both in our questions when we are asking questions and in our answers when we are proposing answers', 75d2–4).[36] There can be little doubt that a central, if not *the* function of this characterization is to indicate that the things referred to by this kind of reference, i.e. forms, are essences (I do not mean to imply that

---

[34] e.g. David Gallop, *Plato: Phaedo* (Oxford, 1975 and 1983), pp. 10 and 227.

[35] I say '*not only* in a complete way, *but also* in an incomplete way' because, as Lesley Brown has shown, we ought not think that we must choose between the two ways of using the verb εἶναι ('to be'), but may suppose that it is used at once in both ways ('Being in the *Sophist*: A Syntactical Inquiry', *Oxford Studies in Ancient Philosophy* 4 (1986), 49–70).

[36] Later in the dialogue this characterization is repeated, when the realm of forms is referred to as ἡ οὐσία ('being') and described as 'having the title of the "ὃ ἔστιν"' (ἔχουσα τὴν ἐπωνυμίαν τὴν τοῦ "ὃ ἔστιν", 92d9–e1).

they are simply essences).³⁷ The mention of what 'we', i.e. Socrates and his friends, are doing in asking questions and proposing answers shows that the ἔστι in the ὅ ἔστι is not used only in a complete way; for evidently the questions and answers are not only about what exists or is real. It must, therefore, be used in an incomplete, predicative way, or also in such a way. But it is plausible to suppose the questions and answers mentioned are meant to include, even primarily, questions and answers about the essence of things—the kind of questions and answers typical of the dialogue between Socrates and his friends. This is also suggested by the requirement, stated shortly later (76b4–6), that if one knows something (and in particular if one knows a form, which is what is at issue here), then one must be able to give an account (λόγος) of it—if, that is, we make the plausible supposition that this account is meant to be, or be based on, an account of the essence. I would like to emphasize, however, that the ὅ ἔστι may, in addition to serving as a mark of the reference to essences, serve to indicate the being peculiar of the forms—if the ἔστι is used not only in an incomplete, but also in a complete way. I conclude that this, central series of references to forms in the *Phaedo* is also, and practically expressly, a reference to essences.

Without pretending that this is an exhaustive survey of the references to forms and essences up to this point in the *Phaedo*, we may turn briefly to the same issue in the latter part of the dialogue (95eff.)—which is our present concern—when the claim is introduced that αἰτίαι ('explanations', 'causes', see next section) are εἴδη and οὐσίαι. When this claim is first expressly stated in these terms (at 101c2–5), it is formulated as saying that αἰτίαι are οὐσίαι (the term οὐσία is used at 101c3). The term εἶδος, with reference to the claim that αἰτίαι are εἴδη, is first used later (at 102b1; see also 103e3 and 104c7), and it is used with the same reference as οὐσία. That the reference is the same is clear from the fact that when the term εἶδος is first introduced (viz. at 102b1), this occurs in the summary of the claim that αἰτίαι are οὐσίαι. Does, then, the term οὐσία here (at 101c3) mean 'essence'? Though we cannot be certain (it may mean rather 'being' and serve to indicate the being peculiar of the forms), it is plausible to think that it does. The term οὐσία is here used with the genitive (ἡ ἰδία οὐσία ἑκάστου, 'the proper

---

³⁷ R. D. Archer-Hind, *The Phaedo of Plato* (London, 1883), comments on 75d2–4: '"on which we stamp the character of essence". ὅ ἔστι is Plato's technical term to denote the essentiality of the ideas' (p. 83). We may understand other occurrences of ὅ ἔστι, and variants thereof, in a similar way (see e.g. 74d6, 75b6 (ὅτι ἔστιν, 'what it is'), and 92d9–e1).

οὐσία of each thing'), and this is a mark of the use in the sense of 'essence'. That the genitive has this function here is perhaps also suggested by the ἰδία ('proper', in the sense of 'its own' and 'not shared by others'); for the essence of each thing is evidently in this sense 'proper' to it, whereas the being peculiar of a form may be common to each and every form. Furthermore, the term οὐσία here is used in exactly the same way as at 65d13, and there we found further reason for thinking that it means 'essence'. However, I would like to emphasize (as previously) that, due to the possibility that 'being' is used both in a complete and in an incomplete, predicative way, the term οὐσία here may serve both functions at once: to indicate the being peculiar of a form, and to indicate an essence.

4 Plato's Concept of αἰτία, and the Unitariness of his Account of αἰτίαι

First, there is a primarily terminological issue. It is a delicate question how to translate αἰτία: as 'explanation' (or 'reason') or as 'cause'. Difficulties are attached to both options. For some readers the term 'explanation' may be associated with certain typically modern views about explanation, in particular the view that explanantia are propositions or propositionally structured entities such as facts or states of affairs; or the view that explanations are dependent on our explanatory theories. Certainly we ought not to assume that the term αἰτία carries such associations. Further, the term 'explanation' is ambiguous between, on the one hand, the relation between a particular explanandum and a particular explanans, *A because B*, and, on the other hand, the explanans itself, *B*.

However, the translation 'cause' has its own problems. As Plato uses the term αἰτία, an αἰτία is that thing, whatever it is, that is designated by a true answer to a 'Why?' question. For example, if the question is 'Why do human beings grow?', and if the answer is that human beings grow because they eat and drink (see 96c–d), then, if this answer is true, eating and drinking is the αἰτία, that is, *that because of which* (the δι' ὅτι, see e.g. 97b3–5) human beings grow. But the use of the term 'cause' in English appears to be narrower. For example, Plato is happy to suggest that the αἰτία why 10 is greater than 8 is that 10 is the sum of 8 and 2 (96e1–2), but it is strange to say that the cause of 10 being greater than 8 is that 10 is the sum of 8 and 2—apparently the strangeness is due to our tending to think of causation as involving activity between cause and effect.[38] Further, the term 'cause', unlike the term 'explanation', cannot be used for the relation of explanation between a particular explanandum or effect and a particular explanans or cause, *A because B*; it can only be used for the explanans or cause, *B*. But Socrates' *aporia* about αἰτίαι is not only about the nature of causes or explanantia, it is just as much about the relation of explanation between particular explananda or effects and particular explanantia or causes. The same is true of the account which he offers in response to this *aporia* and which says that αἰτίαι are, primarily, essences.

This primarily terminological issue is related to one of substance. Does the fact that Plato uses a single term, αἰτία, for that which is designated by a true answer to any 'Why?' question, indicate that he thinks all explanations, irrespective of what they explain, are of the same type? Certainly Plato does not—as do some of his modern critics—begin the investigation of αἰτία by supposing that there are fundamentally different types of αἰτίαι, e.g. those concerning factual issues and those concerning conceptual issues.[39] But this may be a mark of the deliberate method of his investigation rather than its conclusion; for he may think that an investigation must not presuppose anything that may be thought of as one of its possible conclusions.

There can be no doubt, however, that Plato defends a unitary account of explanation, i.e. an account that is supposed to be true of each and every explanation without distinction. For he argues that all explanations depend on essences, and, therefore, that all explanation is fundamentally of the form: *x is f because it is appropriately related to the essence of the quality f, Ess (f)*. But we ought to observe that thinking that Plato defends this unitary account of explanation is compatible with thinking that he may distinguish different kinds of explananda and explanantia, and may assign to them different places within this unitary account of explanation (see section 6 below). It is also compatible with thinking that he may distinguish between teleological (i.e. good-based) and non-teleological explanations. Of course,

---

[38] For this point, see Frede, 'The Original Notion of Cause', esp. 217–21 and 246. Frede offers a general account, both historically and more generally, of the distinction between causation and explanation, and of the relation between the two.

[39] I am thinking of G. Vlastos ('Reasons and Causes in the *Phaedo*', *Philosophical Review* 78 (1969), 291–325), and Taylor ('Forms as Causes in the *Phaedo*').

what Plato cannot do is distinguish between teleological and formal (i.e. essence-based) explanations. For he thinks that all explanations are formal and essence-based. But he can distinguish between those essence-based explanations that, ultimately, appeal to the essence of the good, or to the essence of the good of the thing whose explanation is in question, and those that do not; and this is sufficient to distinguish between teleological and non-teleological explanations (I return to this point in the next section).

5 The Interlude about Good-Based (Teleological) Explanations (*Phaedo* 97b8–99d3)

Why, in the course of recounting his disillusionment with traditional explanations, does Socrates turn to good-based (teleological) explanations, only to become disappointed with them too (97b8–99d3)? And why, in response to this disappointment, does he turn to essence-based explanations? The question is: First, why does Plato introduce good-based explanations at this point of the dialogue? Second, why does he nevertheless go on to defend not them, but essence-based ones? And third, what does he think is the relation between good-based (teleological) and essence-based (formal) explanations?

One answer to the first question is clearly mistaken: Plato introduces good-based explanations because his complaint against traditional explanations is just that they are not good-based.[40] This interpretation is mistaken because Socrates' complaint against traditional explanations is independent of and prior to his becoming hopeful about good-based ones. The complaint is lodged before the mention of good-based explanations, and they are introduced because of the expectation that they at any rate are not subject to it. Indeed, if the complaint were simply that traditional explanations are not good-based, we would have been given no reason for thinking that explanations ought to be good-based.

In a central passage of the interlude about good-based explanations (98e5–99a4), it is clearly indicated what the complaint is that good-based explanations are expected to escape. As we saw, the complaint is that

---

[40] This answer was defended by Taylor ('Forms as Causes in the *Phaedo*').

traditional explanations, and in particular physicalist explanations (i.e. explanations that appeal only to physical things) do not satisfy the following requirement: it is impossible that the same explanantia (e.g. Socrates' bones and sinews) should explain opposite explananda (e.g. his running away to Megara or Boetia as opposed to his staying imprisoned in Athens). It is clearly indicated that it is just this complaint that good-based explanations are expected to escape, because what is immediately inferred from the objection that physicalist explanations do not satisfy this requirement is that the real explanation of Socrates' behaviour is his judgement of what is best (ἡ δόξα τοῦ βελτίστου, 99a2). A corresponding complaint, however, was made before good-based explanations were mentioned (see esp. 97a8–b3, the complaint was that traditional explanations do not satisfy the requirement which says that it is impossible that opposite explanantia should explain the same explananda). This shows that Socrates' complaint against traditional explanations is independent of and prior to his hopeful appeal to good-based ones.

We may suppose, therefore, that good-based explanations are introduced because of the expectation that they at any rate will satisfy the requirements of explanation, REQ 1 and 2 (same explanans if, and only if, same explanandum); but that, as it turns out, this expectation is satisfied not by them, at least not as they are traditionally conceived, but by essence-based explanations. This also accords with a natural reading of the characterization of the upcoming defence of essence-based explanations as a δεύτερος πλοῦς ('second sailing', 99d1). Apparently, the phrase δεύτερος πλοῦς originally referred to 'those who use oars when the wind fails' (LSJ, πλόος 3). It is, therefore, natural to understand the present occurrence of this phrase as meaning a slower and more laborious means to one's original destination.[41] The first sailing was the attempt, which has turned out unsuccessful, to defend good-based explanations, that is, to show that they at any rate satisfy the requirements of explanation. The second sailing is the upcoming attempt to defend essence-based explanations in the same way, and this will in fact succeed. The two sailings have one and the same destination: to satisfy the requirements of explanation and thus answer the original *aporia* about

---

[41] See also Fine ('Forms as Causes: Plato and Aristotle', 92). But she does not associate the original destination with the requirements of explanation.

explanation. The first sailing set up high hopes of being quick and painless, but failed; the second will require more time and effort, but will succeed.

But why is the attempt to satisfy the requirements of explanation by appeal to good-based explanations represented as unsuccessful, while the same attempt by appeal to essence-based explanations is represented as successful? The following answer suggests itself. Plato thinks good-based explanations must, somehow, be capable of satisfying the requirements of explanation, otherwise he would not have been so hopeful about them—and indeed associated them so intimately with reason (νοῦς). But he thinks good-based explanations can satisfy the requirements of explanation if, and only if, it is supposed that each thing has its own proper (ἴδιον) good, and that the good that is proper to each thing depends on what the thing is, its essence.[42] Without this supposition, there is nothing to ensure that there being a good that is proper to a particular thing (e.g. the earth) stands in a necessary connection with the thing's having one particular quality (e.g. being round) as opposed to its having a different and incompatible quality (e.g. being flat). Hence, without this supposition, it is impossible to satisfy the requirement, if same explanans (e.g. the earth's good), then same explanandum (e.g. the earth's being round). Whereas, with this supposition, the satisfaction of this requirement is ensured if it is supposed that this quality (e.g. being round) does indeed stand in a necessary connection with (i.e. is either part of or a consequence of) the thing's being the very thing it is, its essence. This, however, shows that good-based explanations depend on essence-based ones. It also shows that, even if this dependence should be mutual (see previous note), essence-based explanations must, for the purpose of satisfying the requirements of explanation, REQ 1 and 2, be defended first. If essence-based explanations are not defended first, the attempt to satisfy the requirements of explanation by appeal to good-based explanations is premature and bound to fail—as it did, Plato thinks, for Anaxagoras.

We have, then, found the answer to the question: What, in this part of the *Phaedo*, is supposed to be the relation between good-based (teleological) and essence-based (formal) explanations? Good-based explanations must, if

---

[42] I intend the claim that the proper good of each thing depends on the essence of that thing to be compatible with the claim that, conversely, the essence of each thing depends on the proper good of that thing. Plato may hold both claims. That is, he may think the dependence between the essence of each thing and the good of that thing is mutual.

they are to satisfy the constraints of the uniqueness, generality, and uniformity of explanation, i.e. the constraints embodied in the requirements of explanation, REQ 1 and 2, depend on essence-based explanations.

Plato, we ought to note, does not think essence-based and good-based explanations are two different kinds of explanation. For he thinks all explanations are essence-based (formal). Rather, he thinks good-based explanations are a kind of essence-based explanations. We are perhaps accustomed to thinking of the distinction between teleological and formal explanations as a distinction between two kinds of explanation. Perhaps we are accustomed to think this because it is from Aristotle, or from a certain interpretation of Aristotle, rather than from Plato that we have become familiar with this distinction. But this is not the only way of conceiving of the distinction, and Plato's is an alternative. If we think that Plato, in order to be able to draw such a distinction at all, must conceive of the distinction between teleological and formal explanations as a distinction between two kinds of explanation, then we cannot make sense of the argument of the *Phaedo* for the claim that explanantia are, primarily, essences. For the argument defends a single account of *all* explanation, not only of formal or essence-based explanations. This is because the argument, as we have seen, is motivated by, and conceived as an answer to, the question 'What is an explanation?', and the answer it defends, we have seen, is a unitary one. The unifying feature is indicated by the claim that *any* explanans, whatever other elements it may contain (such as, we will see, physical things), must first and foremost contain an essence, the essence of the quality figuring in the explanandum.

It is worth emphasizing that although the account of explanation is addressed, in the first instance, to explanations in which the explananda are changeable things—for it is, in the first instance, an account of the explanation of generation and destruction—the account is one of explanation in general and as such, hence of all explanations. This implies that Plato must suppose that explanantia are, primarily, essences, not only in the case in which the explananda are changeable things, but also in the case in which they are, for example, changeless forms or ideas. Thus, for example, he says in the *Republic* (VI. 508d10f.) that the idea of the good is the αἰτία of, on the one hand, the things that are and that are capable of being known, and, on the other hand, the capacity of the rational soul to know them. But it is natural to suppose that by the things that are and that are capable of being known he has in mind (at least primarily) the other ideas or forms. This means that the other ideas are said to have an αἰτία, namely, the idea of the good. Can this view be accommodated within the *Phaedo* account of explanation? One might object that the *Phaedo* account is about the αἰτία of changeable things. But we have seen that this objection is mistaken. Or one might object that it is about formal αἰτίαι, not teleological ones. But we have seen that this also is mistaken. In fact there appears to be no problem with thinking that the claim that the idea of the good is the αἰτία of the other ideas can be directly accommodated within the account of explanation of the *Phaedo*. The idea of the good is after all an idea, hence, whatever else it also is, an essence.

6 The Simple and the Complex Schema of Explanation (*Phaedo* 102b3–105c7)

Let us refer to the original schema of explanation (set out at 100b1–102b3 and recalled at 105b5–c6) as the simple schema. This schema is of the form, *x is f because of its relation to the essence of the quality f, Ess(f)*. For example (taken from 105c2–4), this body is ill because of its relation to the essence of illness. And let us refer to the later schema of explanation (set out at 102b3ff., esp. 103c10–105c7, and contrasted with the original schema at 105b5–c6) as the complex schema. This schema is of the form, *x is f because of its relation to S and S's relation to the essence of the quality f, Ess(f)*. For example (from the same passage), this body is ill because of its relation to fever and fever's relation to the essence of illness. It is crucially important that Plato defends both these schemata of explanation. For this shows that his conclusion is not that explanantia are simply essences, bur rather that explanantia, whatever else they may involve, are primarily essences.

How are the two schemata of explanation related? The simple schema was originally described as 'safe' (ἀσφαλές, 100e1, and 101d2, indeed 'perfectly safe', ἀσφαλέστατον, 100d8), and this characterization is recalled when it is contrasted with the complex schema (105b5–c2). What does this safeness consist in? Not, certainly, in the simple schema's being empty of content or information—not in its being trivial, much less tautological.[43]

---

[43] Taylor writes: 'But the safety of the answer seems to lie in its total lack of information' ('Forms as Causes in the *Phaedo*', 47).

If 'being safe' meant 'being contentless' or 'being uninformative', the complex schema of explanation could not be characterized as it, too, being safe; for it, at any rate, is evidently contentful and informative. But this is how the complex schema is characterized (ἐκ τῶν νῦν λεγομένων [i.e. the description of the complex schema] ἄλλην ὁρῶν ἀσφάλειαν, 105b7–8). In respect of safeness, the simple and the complex schema are on an equal footing.

I would like to suggest that the safeness of the simple schema of explanation consists in the fact that at any rate explanations in conformity with this schema meet the basic constraint for being explanations, namely, the constraint of the uniqueness, generality, and uniformity of explanations.[44] That explanations in conformity with this schema satisfy this constraint is not, however, something evident, for it is the upshot of the *aporia* about what constitutes a genuine explanation and the solution to this *aporia* provided by the simple schema. Hence the simple schema is anything but contentless or uninformative. The simple schema states that explanantia, whatever else they may involve, are primarily essences. It is only natural that Socrates should refer to such explanations as safe, trustworthy, and reliable, since his concern is to find a method of explanation which he can rely on as being genuinely explanatory. This interpretation of the safeness of the simple schema also makes good sense of the fact that the complex schema, too, is described as safe (105b7–8). For Plato thinks the complex schema is dependent on the simple one (see end of this section for this dependence), and, therefore, if explanations in conformity with the simple schema are genuinely explanations, so too are explanations in conformity with the complex one.[45]

---

[44] See also Fine ('Forms and Causes: Plato and Aristotle', 96).

[45] Fine, who raises the question of the safety of the complex schema, answers as follows: 'Whereas the SA [i.e. the simple schema] specifies necessary and sufficient conditions, the CA [i.e. the complex schema] need specify no more than sufficient conditions. Further, the CA allows some explanations involving opposites. Fever, e.g. is adduced to explain illness; but, as Gallop notes, the opposite of fever—hypothermia—can also explain illness' ('Forms as Causes: Plato and Aristotle', 97). However, it seems to me that, far from showing that the complex schema is safe too, what Fine says here suggests that, compared with the simple schema, the complex schema is not safe at all. With regard to the apparent objection that the appeal to fever does not satisfy the one requirement of uniformity, we may respond that it is not fever by itself that is adduced to explain illness, but fever appropriately related to the essence of illness (the same would be true of hypothermia). But it seems clearly fallacious to argue: fever and hypothermia (if they are explanantia at all) are opposite explanantia; therefore, fever, if appropriately related to illness (e.g. if understood as an effect of one kind of illness) and hypothermia, if appropriately related to illness (e.g. if understood as an effect of a different kind of illness) are opposite explanantia.

We may note that, on this interpretation, we must understand as playful and ironical Socrates' description of his attachment to the simple schema as 'simple-minded' (cf. εὐήθως ἔχω παρ' ἐμαυτῷ, 100d4) and 'ignorant' (ἀμαθῆ, 105c1), and of the complex schema as 'more sophisticated' (κομψότεραν, 105c2). What is the point of this irony? Apparently, it is yet again directed at those who look for complex and sophisticated explanations without first pausing to ask what an explanation really is. It is to them that the simple schema, especially when compared to more complex explanations, will appear 'simple-minded', 'ignorant', and 'plain', when in reality it is the basis of any more complex explanations. This continues the irony which goes back to Socrates' initial description of himself as 'unfit' for the traditional method of scientific investigation (ἀφυής, 96c2) and of his own alternative method as 'random confusion' (ἀλλά τιν' ἄλλον τρόπον [τῆς μεθόδου] αὐτὸς εἰκῇ φύρω, 97b6).

Let us look closer at the two schemata and their relation. The schemata can be understood as follows.

(Simple Schema) x is, accidentally, f[46]
        because
        x is appropriately related (by relation R) to the essence of f, Ess(f).

For example (based on 105bc), this body is hot because it is appropriately related to the essence of heat. Or, this thing has an odd number of parts because it is appropriately related to the essence of odd.

(Complex Schema) x is, accidentally, f
        because
        (1) x is appropriately related (by relation R1) to S, and
        (2) (i) S is distinct from the essence of f, Ess(f), and
            (ii) S is essentially f, and
            (iii) S is essentially f because it is appropriately related (by relation R2) to the essence of f, Ess(f).

---

[46] 'Accidentally' because, as we saw, x is subject to change, and subject to change in particular with regard to its being f.

For example (based on the same passage), this body is hot because (1) it is appropriately related to fire, and (2) fire, which is distinct from the essence of heat, is essentially hot, and is essentially hot because it is appropriately related to the essence of heat. Or, this thing has an odd number of parts because (1) it is appropriately related to the unit, and (2) the unit, which is distinct from the essence of odd, is essentially odd, and is essentially odd because it is appropriately related to the essence of odd.

We should note that the complex schema must be understood as representing a single, unitary explanation, not a conjunction of two independent explanations. It is of the form, *a because (b and c)*, and not of the form, *(a because b) and (b because c)*. If the complex schema represented a conjunction of two independent explanations, then *x is, accidentally, f because x is appropriately related to S* (i.e. the first conjunct of the schema) would by itself be an explanation. But in that case there would after all be genuine explanations whose explanantia do not involve essences, e.g. *this body is hot because it is appropriately related to fire*—but this precisely Plato denies. It follows, we ought to note, that Plato rejects the following principle, we may call it the principle of the distributivity of explanation: if *a because (b and c)*, then *(a because b) and (b because c)*.

Let me make a few comments in clarification and defence of this reading of the two schemata and their relation.

First, Plato distinguishes between a thing's being accidentally f and a thing's being essentially f (see esp. 102b8–103a3). I am thinking of a passage such as the following: 'Because it isn't, surely, by nature that Simmias overtops him [Socrates], by virtue, that is, of his being Simmias, but by virtue of the largeness that he happens to have. Nor again does he overtop Socrates because Socrates is Socrates, but because of smallness that Socrates has in relation to his largeness?' (102c1–5; this passage does not, of course, say or imply that Simmias or Socrates have an individual essence, rather it illustrates the distinction between a thing's being accidentally f and a thing's being essentially f, by offering a positive instance of the former and a negative instance of the latter).

Second, he distinguishes between, on the one hand, things that are essentially f while being distinct from the essence of f (e.g. fire, which is essentially hot but distinct from the essence of heat), and, on the other hand, the essence of f itself (e.g. the essence of heat, see esp. 103c10–104c10). That the former side of this distinction concerns *being essentially f*, rather than merely *being necessarily f*, is indicated by the fact that the expression $\epsilon \hat{\iota} \nu a\iota$ $\ddot{o}\pi\epsilon\rho$ $\mathring{\eta}\nu$ ('to be the very thing it is') is used of snow and fire in relation to cold and heat (see 103d7 and 12). If so, the phrase *being <u>always</u> f* and *being <u>always</u> f for as long as it exists* (see e.g. 103e2–5 and 104a1–3), which appears to be a gloss on this notion, indicates *being essentially f* rather than merely *being necessarily f*.

Third, are fire, snow, the triad, etc., themselves essences? There is good reason to think that they are not, and I have supposed this in the interpretation of the complex schema of explanation. First, Plato expressly sets fire, snow, the triad, etc., against $a\mathring{v}\tau\grave{o}$ $\tau\grave{o}$ $\epsilon\hat{\iota}\delta o\varsigma$ ('the form itself', 103e2–5) and $\tau\grave{a}$ $\epsilon\check{\iota}\delta\eta$ ('the forms', 104c7–9). Second, he allows for the possibility that fire, snow, the triad, etc., are subject to destruction and movement (103d5–12, 104b10–c3). But essences and forms could not be subject to any such thing. If we ask how something that is essentially f and always f, such as fire, snow, the triad, etc., can nevertheless be subject to destruction, the answer is that such things are always f, *for as long as they exist* (see $\ddot{o}\tau a\nu\pi\epsilon\rho$ $\mathring{\eta}$, 103e5). Essences, on the other hand, are eternal, everlasting, or timeless. Third, that fire is hot, that snow is cold, that the triad is odd, etc., is supposed to stand in need of explanation by appeal to something which is emphasized as being distinct from them, that is, by appeal to the essence of hot, cold, odd, etc. And yet it is indicated that hot, cold, odd, etc., are essential qualities of fire, snow, the triad, etc. But Plato is not likely to think that an essence's having a particular quality needs to be explained by appeal to something distinct from this essence; on the contrary, it is because of themselves that essences are what they are. It follows that fire, snow, the triad, etc., though they have essential qualities, are not themselves essences.

Fourth, the complex schema of explanation indicates (see esp. 104c11–105c7) that Plato distinguishes between explananda that consist in a thing's being accidentally f (e.g. this body's being hot) and explananda that consist in a thing's being essentially f while being distinct from the essence of f (e.g. fire's being hot). And he assigns to these two kinds of explananda different places in the unitary account of explanation. For while accidental explananda (e.g. this body's being hot) can figure only as explananda and not as explanantia, essential explananda that are distinct from essences (e.g. fire's being hot), though themselves subject to explanation in terms of essences (e.g. the essence of heat), can be elements in the explanation of accidental explananda (e.g. this

body's being hot). Essences, on the other hand, have just one place in explanation, that is, as primary explanantia.

Plato thinks that, first, the simple schema of explanation is primary, and,
second, the complex schema is dependent on it. The simple schema is
primary because it gives expression to the fundamental claim that explanantia, whatever else they may involve, are primarily essences—and this
claim is fundamental because it is what allows for the satisfaction of
the requirements of explanation (REQ 1 and 2)—the requirements that
embody the constraints of the uniqueness, generality, and uniformity of
explanation. But why does Plato think the complex schema of explanation
is dependent on the simple one? What this view means is that the complex
schema is true *because* the simple schema is true (but not conversely). But
why does Plato think that? To see this, let us recall that the complex schema
is of the form:

A.   x is f because [(x-R_1-S) and (S-R_2-Ess(f))];

meaning that x is f because: x is appropriately related to S, and S is
appropriately related to the essence of f. And the simple schema is of the
form:

B.   x is f because x-R-Ess(f);

meaning that x is f because: x is appropriately related to the essence of f.
Now, it is true that Plato does not provide an account of these relations, R_1,
R_2, and R. But it is just as important to observe that he thinks there is a
crucial difference between relation R (in the simple schema), on the one
hand, and relations R_1 and R_2 (in the complex schema), on the other. For
he thinks the obtaining of R between x and Ess(f) is sufficient for an
explanation, E, of why x is f, whereas it is not the case that the obtaining
of R_1 between x and S, or the obtaining of R_2 between S and Ess(f), are
individually sufficient for an explanation of why x is f. (We recall that the
complex schema is of the form *a because (b and c)* but not of the form *(a
because b) and (b because c)*.) Rather, he thinks that (a) the obtaining of R_1
between x and S is one conjunct in a conjunctive explanation, E*, of why x
is f, and the obtaining of R_2 between S and Ess(f) is a further conjunct in this
same conjunctive explanation, E*, and (b) the conjunction of these two
conjuncts, which is E*, is sufficient (but not necessary) for the explanation,

E (the same as in the simple schema), of why x is f. This shows that A implies B (but not conversely), and why A is true *because* of B (but not conversely).

6.1 ἡ τῶν τριῶν ἰδέα, 104d5–6

One may object that the above interpretation of Plato's complex schema of explanation, which depends on thinking that Plato does not conceive of fire, snow, the triad, etc., as essences or forms,[47] is impossible, since he makes use of the expression ἡ τῶν τριῶν ἰδέα ('the ἰδέα of the three', 104d5–6), and therefore, it seems, expressly refers to the three as an idea or form. However, I suspect this objection may rest on a grammatical misunderstanding. The expression ἡ τῶν τριῶν ἰδέα picks up and illustrates the expression τὴν αὑτοῦ ἰδέαν ('the ἰδέα of itself', 104d2) in the previous sentence. This expression is part of the clause: ἃ ὅτι ἂν κατάσχῃ μὴ μόνον ἀναγκάζει τὴν αὑτοῦ ἰδέαν αὐτὸ ἴσχειν, ἀλλὰ καὶ ἐναντίου αὖ τῳ ἀεί τινος ('the things which, whatever thing occupies them compels this [i.e. that which it occupies] to have not only the ἰδέα of itself, but also always in turn the ἰδέα of some opposite', 104d1–3). But the function of the genitive of the reflexive pronoun in the expression τὴν αὑτοῦ ἰδέαν is to attribute something, τὴν ἰδέαν, to the subject, ὅτι (e.g. 'the three', which is the example the next sentence gives of this subject); it is evidently not its function to identify this subject and specify which subject it is—since evidently the expression 'the ἰδέα of itself', if it meant 'the ἰδέα which is itself', could not serve to identify any particular ἰδέα. We may, therefore, suppose that the genitive in ἡ τῶν τριῶν ἰδέα must likewise be understood as attributive and possessive: it means 'the ἰδέα possessed by the three' and indeed 'the triadic idea'—as in ἡ περιττὴ μορφή/ἰδέα at 104d12, which itself confirms the attributive reading of the genitive in ἡ τῶν τριῶν ἰδέα. The genitive in ἡ τῶν τριῶν ἰδέα must not, therefore, be understood as predicative and identifying ('the ἰδέα which is the three', i.e. the ἰδέα of which *being the three* is predicated as uniquely identifying). But when a genitive refers to an idea or form (as in ἡ τοῦ ἀγαθοῦ ἰδέα in *Republic* 505a2), it must, of course, be understood as predicative and identifying (it means 'the ἰδέα which is the good', i.e. the ἰδέα of which *being the good* is predicated as uniquely

---

[47] For the view that they are not forms, see also Fine ('Forms as Causes: Plato and Aristotle', 95).

identifying). This shows that ἰδέα in ἡ τῶν τριῶν ἰδέα does not refer to the idea or form of the three.

For the same use of the attributive genitive, see also ἔχει δὲ τὴν ἐκείνου μορφὴν ἀεί, ὅταυπερ ᾖ ('but it always has the μορφή of that thing, for as long as it exists', 103e4–5), meaning 'the μορφή possessed by that thing', and not 'the μορφή which is that thing'. We should note that μορφή and ἰδέα are used interchangeably at 104d–e. The use of ἰδέα at 104b9, which refers to one or the other of a pair of opposites present in, e.g., fire or snow, may likewise be understood as referring not to the εἶδος which denotes the opposites themselves (e.g. the form of the hot or the cold), but rather to the essential quality of fire or snow, its hotness or coldness.

What, then, is that which is possessed by the three (or by fire, snow, etc.), and likewise by odd (or hot, cold, etc.), and such that when things have this they are, precisely, three (or fire/fiery, snow/frosty, odd, hot, cold, etc.)? It is, evidently, *the quality* of being three (or fire/fiery, snow/frosty, odd, hot, cold, etc.). In general, it will be true that irrespective of how Plato conceives of the triad, fire, snow, etc., or odd, hot, cold, etc., he will need a term to refer in general to *the quality* taken on by a thing, and especially a concrete particular or body, when it is characterized by such things. So it is not surprising that this is how he uses the terms ἰδέα and μορφή in the present passage (104c11–105c7). For his concern in this passage is not the nature of these things themselves; this issue was addressed in the previous passage (103c10–104c10), and there the triad, fire, snow, etc., were expressly set against the εἴδη (see esp. 103e2–5). His concern here is how these things are related to concrete particulars or bodies.

We should also note that this reading makes good sense of the otherwise incongruous expression ἡ περιττὴ μορφή/ἰδέα ('the odd μορφή/ἰδέα') at 104d12. To refer to the idea or form of the odd as 'the odd idea' would surely be bizarre. But it is perfectly correct to refer to a particular quality of odd things as 'the odd quality' (or 'the odd characteristic'; compare 'the red colour').

7   The Place of Physical Things in Explanation

Had Plato defended only the simple schema of explanation, his view would have been that the physical constituents of a body (e.g. the fire in a particular body), since they are not themselves essences, cannot be an element in the explanation of why the body has a particular quality (e.g. hot). Physical constituents, since they are not essences, would simply have been excluded from being part of explanations. But the fact that he also defends the complex schema means that he allows that the physical constituent of a body can be an element in the explanation of why the body has a particular quality. The physical constituents of a body can be an element in the explanation of why the body has a particular quality, if they are conceived as satisfying the following conditions (see previous section for these conditions in general): (i) the physical constituent must have essentially the quality that the body, whose constituent it is, has accidentally (e.g. fire is essentially hot); (ii) it must be distinct from the essence of this quality (e.g. fire is not identical with, but distinct from, the essence of heat); and (iii) it must have this quality essentially in virtue of being appropriately related to, and being dependent on the essence of this quality. By being conceived as depending on essences, physical constituents, though not themselves essences, and though all explanation ultimately depends on essences, can thus be accommodated within explanations.

It is true that, at a particular juncture (98e–99b) of the argument that leads up to the introduction of the thesis that explanantia are, primarily, essences, Socrates says that physical constituents are not explanantia, but at best necessary conditions (conditions *sine qua non*) for the explanantia being explanantia (see ἄλλο μέν τί ἐστι τὸ αἴτιον τῷ ὄντι, ἄλλο δὲ ἐκεῖνο ἄνευ οὗ τὸ αἴτιον οὐκ ἄν ποτ᾽ εἴη αἴτιον, 'it is, in truth, one thing to be the explanans, another thing to be that without which the explanans could not be an explanans', 99b2–4). But we ought to observe that in this earlier passage Socrates is still criticizing the appeal to physical constituents as conceived by the traditional physicalist explanations, and has not yet introduced the new conception of physical constituents, now conceived as depending on essences. Plato would appear to think that physical constituents, if they are not appropriately related to essences, are not even sufficient conditions, let alone explanations of the things they are supposed to explain; they are at best necessary conditions, since, e.g., Socrates evidently cannot either stay or go unless he has bones and sinews appropriately put together. At the same time, Plato defends the view that physical constituents, if they are appropriately related to essences, can be part of explanations.

This clarifies the nature of Plato's initial criticism, presented through the description of Socrates' intellectual journey, of physicalist explanations (see e.g. 96b; we may note that the traditional explanations which he chooses as an example of the target of the criticism appeal to precisely such things as 'the hot and the cold' and 'fire' (96b2–4), the very physical constituents which later he chooses to illustrate the complex schema of explanation). Plato's criticism is not that physical constituents cannot be part of explanations; it is, rather, that they cannot themselves be explanations. We must, therefore, understand Socrates' disillusionment with physicalist explanations as resulting not in his throwing them out, but in his setting them to one side, for the sake of first examining what an explanation really is; but only in order to return to them and readmit them once this examination has got under way and has established the crucial point—that explanations ultimately depend on essences. What is readmitted, however, is not the appeal to physical constituents as originally conceived by the physicalist explanations, but a new conception of physical constituents, now conceived as depending on essences.

A consequence of this account of the place of physical constituents in explanation is that a body's having certain physical constituents (e.g. this body's having fire in it) may be both a necessary and a sufficient condition for this body's having a particular quality (e.g. hot). So the bi-implication may be true which says that this body is hot if, and only if, it has fire in it. Indeed, since the physical constituent (e.g. fire) will depend, for being the one it is, on its relation to the essence of this quality (e.g. the essence of the quality, hot), this bi-implication, if it is true, will be true *necessarily*. However, it will still be the case that the physical constituent is not the explanation of why this body has this quality; it is only an element in the explanation, and the explanation ultimately depends on the essence of the quality. This shows that Plato distinguishes between *necessarily, p if and only if q* and *p explains q*, and he does not think the former implies the latter.

This is what we ought to expect. A necessary bi-implication indicates a symmetrical relation; but the relation of explanation is asymmetrical (or at least non-symmetrical); the two cannot, therefore, be equivalent. Elsewhere Plato appears to make precisely this point. In the *Euthyphro* 9–11 he argues that we ought to distinguish between bi-implications, even necessary ones, and explanations. For a particular bi-implication, even a necessary one (e.g. that something is holy if, and only if, it is loved by perfect beings such as gods) does not determine in which direction the explanation goes: are holy things loved by gods *because* they are holy or are holy things holy *because* they are loved by the gods? Likewise, the necessary bi-implication which says that this body is hot if, and only if, it has fire in it, does not determine whether this body is hot *because* it has fire in it or this body has fire in it *because* it is hot. An explanation which ultimately depends on an essence will, however, determine the direction of explanation. For such an explanation will ultimately depend *either* on the essence of a quality, such as hot (as it does on Plato's account), *or* on the essence of a physical constituent, such as fire—but not both at once.

We have seen (in this and the previous section) that Plato accommodates physical constituents, such as snow and fire, within an account of explanation. It is important to recognize that he does so by conceiving of physical constituents not merely as necessary and sufficient conditions of explananda, but as elements in explanantia and parts of explanations. Why, we may ask, are physical constituents, according to the complex schema of explanation, not merely necessary and sufficient conditions of explananda, but elements in explanantia? Because, on the reformed conception of physical constituents, they are supposed to be essentially related to essences, which are the primary elements in explanantia. For example, it is supposed that fire is part of the explanation of why a particular thing is hot because it is supposed that fire (i) is essentially hot, (ii) is distinct from the essence of heat, and (iii) is essentially hot, while being distinct from the essence of heat, by virtue of being appropriately related to and being dependent on the essence of heat. The fact that physical constituents, on the reformed conception of them, are supposed to be essentially related to essences shows that they are supposed to be not merely necessary and sufficient conditions of explananda, but elements in explanantia and parts of explanations. For it is striking that the things to which physical constituents are supposed to be essentially related are, precisely, the primary elements in explanantia, essences; and if

physical constituents were conceived as being merely necessary and sufficient conditions of explananda, there would be no reason to relate them
to the elements of explanation. It appears, therefore, that Plato wants to
relate physical constituents to the elements of explanation—and to the
single primary element, essence—and to do so in such a way as to enable
physical constituents to be elements in explanantia and genuinely parts of
explanations.[48]

Bibliography

J. Annas, 'Aristotle on Inefficient Causes', *Philosophical Quarterly* 32, 1982, 311–26.

R. D. Archer-Hind, *The Phaedo of Plato*, London, 1883.

L. Brown, 'Being in the *Sophist*: A Syntactical Inquiry', *Oxford Studies in Ancient
Philosophy IV* (1986), 49–70.

G. Fine, 'Forms as Causes: Plato and Aristotle', in A. Graeser (ed.), *Mathematics and
Metaphysics in Aristotle*, Bern and Stuttgart, 1987, 69–112.

M. Frede, 'The Original Notion of Cause', in M. Schofield, M. Burnyeat, and
J. Barnes (eds.), *Doubt and Dogmatism*, Oxford, 1980, 222–3.

D. Gallop, *Plato. Phaedo*, Oxford, 1975 and 1983.

C. Kahn, 'On Platonic Chronology', in J. Annas and C. Rowe (eds.), *New
Perspectives on Plato, Modern and Ancient*, Harvard, 2002, 93–127.

D. Sedley, 'Platonic Causes', *Pronesis* XLIII (1998), 114–32.

C. C. W. Taylor, 'Forms as Causes in the *Phaedo*', *Mind* 78 (1969), 45–59.

G. Vlastos, 'Reasons and Causes in the *Phaedo*', *Philosophical Review* 78 (1969),
291–325.

---

[48] This paper has been a long time in the making, and is likely to be indebted to more people than
I can be certain to remember. My thanks are due above all to Daniel Watts and David Charles for their
close reading of recent drafts and extended and invaluable comments. Originally, and in Cambridge,
I am grateful to Dominic Scott. In Dublin, to: John Connolly, John Dillon, Peter Dudley, Brendan
O'Byrne, and Scott O'Connor. In Oxford: Paulo Crivelli and David Charles. In Edinburgh: Panos
Dimas, Anthony Hatzistavrou, Fritz-Gregor Herrmann, Vassilis Karasmanis, Dory Scaltsas, and David
Sedley. In Leiden, to Berg van den Berg. I am also grateful to the anonymous referee of Oxford
University Press.

3

The Paradox in the *Meno* and Aristotle's Attempts to Resolve It

DAVID CHARLES

1 Introduction

Aristotle mentions 'the paradox in the *Meno*' on several occasions in the *Analytics*, once in the first chapter of *Post. An.* A.1 (71a29). While these short discussions do not engage in detail with the famous paradox as it is developed by Socrates, Aristotle does pay considerable attention to the issues it raises in the *Analytics*. He seeks to undermine (or so I shall argue) the assumptions on which it is based and to address the problems to which it gives rise. I shall suggest a diagnosis of the paradox and then consider Aristotle's attempts to resolve it.

2 An Initial Diagnosis of 'the Paradox in the *Meno*'

In the *Meno*, after some unsuccessful attempts to define virtue, Meno, somewhat exasperatedly, asks the following question:

[M] How can you search for something if you do not know at all what it is? Which of the things that you do not know will you take as your aim in your search? And even if you do come across it, how will you know that this is the thing you did not know? (80d5–8)

His question (I shall suggest) arises in the following way: if (as Socrates professes) one does not know at all what virtue is, one does not even know what (in reality) is signified by the term 'virtue'.[1] However, if one lacks even

---

[1] Compare: if one does not know who Meno is (71b4ff.) one does not know what the name 'Meno' signifies.

this amount of information, one cannot search for the nature of virtue. For without an account of what the term signifies, one will not know what thing or feature it is whose nature one is seeking. Indeed, as Meno notes, one would not even know that one had found it if one came across it (80d6–8). One must know what the term signifies before one can search for the nature of the thing (or feature) in question. Since Socrates (on his own admission) does not know what the term signifies, he cannot engage in any such search.

Socrates reformulates Meno's question, taking it to exemplify a contentious (*eristic*) argument:

[S] A person cannot search either for what he knows or for what he does not know. He cannot search for what he knows because he already knows it (and there is no need for him to search). Nor can he search for what he does not know, since he does not know what he is searching for. (80e2–5)

In Socrates' version, Meno's problem has become more acute: either one has a full account of what virtue is or one altogether lacks such an account. In the former condition, not mentioned by Meno, enquiry is impossible since one already knows what virtue is. But in the latter condition enquiry is also impossible because one does not know what one is searching for. If enquiry is understood as the successful search for information one does not already possess, one cannot enquire into what virtue is if one altogether lacks an account of what virtue is. Nor can one enquire if one already has the information sought. Either way enquiry is impossible.

Why did Socrates reformulate Meno's question in this *all or nothing* way?[2] Meno had not, in his initial question, ruled out the possibility of enquiry. He had merely pointed out (in the terms used above) that an enquiry cannot begin (or be successfully completed) if one lacks an account of what the term 'virtue' signifies. He had not committed himself to the view, implicit in Socrates' reformulation of his question, that if one has the amount of

---

[2] Socrates' *all or nothing* reformulation of Meno's question, and his subsequent interest in it, needs an explanation. It is difficult to see why Socrates (or anyone) should take seriously the suggestion that one either knows (or grasps) everything about (e.g.) Pericles or one knows (or grasps) nothing at all about him. If he was simply repeating a contentious (*eristic*) argument, he could have gone on to dismiss it with ease. Similarly, if his reformulation had depended simply on a scope for ambiguity in Meno's phrase 'does not know completely', Socrates could have resolved the paradox without difficulty. Dominic Scott saw the need for a proper account of how the paradox arises in *Recollection and Experience*, Cambridge, 1995. pp. 26ff. However, his reconstruction begins with the assumption that one cannot know anything at all about virtue (even that something is a case of virtue) without knowing its definition (27–8). In this essay, my aim is to understand why Socrates made such a counter-intuitive assumption.

knowledge required for an account of what 'virtue' signifies, there is nothing left to find out. Indeed, he could have thought that, *pace* Socrates, if one were initially to know an account of what the name signifies (for example, an account that is of something found in all and only cases of virtue), one would be in a very good position to search for further information about the relevant essence.

Socrates' *all or nothing* reformulation of Meno's question is, I shall suggest, best explained on the assumption that he is (at this point) failing to distinguish two distinct questions raised by their previous discussion:

(1)   What is it of which 'virtue' is the name?
(2)   What is virtue?

Question (1) is to be answered by identifying the thing called 'virtue', Question (2) by specifying the essence of virtue. Question (1) is about a linguistic expression: it asks what object in the world it names. Question (2), by contrast, is about an object in the world: it asks what is its nature.[3] If he fails to distinguish these questions, an enquirer will be in the *all or nothing* state Socrates describes. In order to begin his (or her) enquiry, he needs (let us assume) an account of what the term signifies (an answer to Question (1)). However, if Questions (1) and (2) are conflated, he cannot answer Question (1) without a grasp on the essence of virtue (an answer to Question (2)). Hence, either the enquirer grasps everything there is to grasp about the virtue at the beginning of the enquiry or else he does not even have the resources to get an enquiry under way. There is no possibility of his having enough resources to begin an enquiry (an answer to Question (1)) and then going on to find out something he does not already grasp about the essence of virtue (an answer to Question (2)).

Socrates, according to this suggestion, reformulates Meno's question in an *all or nothing* way because he makes three assumptions:

[A]   One cannot start a successful enquiry into what virtue is without having an account of what 'virtue' signifies.
[B] One cannot possess an account of what 'virtue' signifies without grasping the essence of virtue.

---

[3] I assume that Socrates is being straightforward at this point. Charles Kahn has suggested that Plato (in effect) distinguished throughout between accounts of what terms signify and accounts of essence but conflated them in the *Meno* 'as part of [his] art' (*Plato and the Socratic Dialogue*, Cambridge, 1996, p. 160).

[C]   Enquiry is the successful acquisition of information one does not possess.

Given [A] and [B], one can only start an enquiry into what virtue is if one already grasps the answer to the question one seeks. But, given [C], if one already possesses all this information one cannot acquire it. If so, enquiry is impossible. In the next section I shall argue that commitment to Assumption [B] is an integral part of Socrates' discussion throughout the *Meno*. However, before doing that, several points should be noted about the interpretation under consideration.

(1) Assumption [A] does not mean that one cannot talk meaningfully about virtue without grasping an account of what 'virtue' signifies. One can certainly do that—as Meno's earlier career as an orator amply demonstrates. What he lacked was enough information to begin an enquiry into what virtue is. For that, in Socrates' view, he needed an account which picks out some general feature present in all and only cases of virtue. Only thus can one have sufficient grasp on the phenomenon to be studied.

(2) Assumption [B] is crucial. Assumption [A], by itself, is consistent with the possibility of enquiry. For one might, as already noted, come to find an account of what the term signifies and then go on to discover the essence of the object signified. Meno himself (in formulating his own question) did not require Assumption [B]. He could, indeed, be taken as asking how one can come to acquire the required account of what the term signifies. His question and Socrates' paradoxical reformulation of it differ in that only the latter essentially involves both Assumptions [A] and [B].

(3) Assumptions [A], [B], and [C] (as stated) do not essentially involve the term 'knowledge'. The paradox, as formulated by Socrates, could arise even if the relevant cognitive state were true belief or some form of cognitive grasp less than knowledge. More specifically, it can be generated in the following way:

[A]★   One cannot start an enquiry into what virtue is without believing a complete true account of what 'virtue' signifies.
[B]★   One cannot believe a complete true account of what 'virtue' signifies without having the complete set of true beliefs about the essence of virtue.
[C]   Enquiry is the successful acquisition of information one does not possess.

If one lacks the relevant true beliefs about the essence of virtue, one will lack an account of what 'virtue' signifies and so will be unable to start an enquiry into what virtue is. Conversely, if one begins one's enquiry with the complete set of true beliefs about the essence of virtue, one will not come to acquire new true beliefs about what virtue is in the course of one's enquiry. Hence, given [C], enquiry will be impossible. Since the paradox arises whether true belief or knowledge is involved, it cannot be overcome solely by separating these states.[4] For if the enquirer begins with the complete set of true beliefs about the essences in question he cannot acquire any more information about what virtue is in the course of the enquiry.

If there is to be the successful acquisition of new information, the account with which one begins one's enquiry will have to contain less information than the one with which one ends. The resolution of the paradox, so understood, requires a difference in informational content, not just one in the epistemic attitude of the enquirer. In the terms used above, accounts of what the term signifies need to involve less information than accounts of the essence of the object (or kind) signified.

3 Assumption [B] at Work in the *Meno*

Socrates, on occasion, asks his famous question,

'What is F?'

Thus, for example, he asks

'What is virtue?' (77b9)

and is keen to find out what virtue is (72c9ff.). In considering answers to this question he outlines a number of well-known (if somewhat ill-defined) conditions. The answer to the question 'What is F?' should have (at least) the following three characteristics:

---

[4] For a contrasting account, see G. Fine, 'Inquiry in the Meno', in *The Cambridge Companion to Plato*, ed. R. Kraut, Cambridge, 1992, pp. 200–26, and 'Knowledge and True Belief in the Meno', *Oxford Studies in Ancient Philosophy* 27 (2004), pp. 41–80. It is worth noting that, in Fine's account, the enquirer, at the outset of the enquiry, will only have true beliefs about what 'F' signifies. She will lack knowledge of what her terms signify.

(1) it should specify one *eidos* (form) which all virtues possess;

(2) it should specify the one *eidos* (form) by being which all virtues are virtues;

(3) it should specify that in virtue of which (*di'ho*) all virtues are virtues.

Let us call this Question 1 and answers to this question Type 1 accounts.[5] However, Socrates sometimes poses a different question. In the case of shape, he asks:

'Do you call something (*kaleis*) boundary?' (75e1)[6]

The latter question is naturally interpreted (in a language which possesses quotation marks) as

'Do you call something "a boundary"?'

Socrates indicates the kind of answer he expects:

'I speak of the type of thing which is exemplified by a limit or end . . .' (75e1–2)

This answer suggests that the original question is to be understood as

'Do you speak of some specific type of thing as "a boundary"?'

To answer this question it is not enough to say:

'Yes: I do speak of something as "a boundary".'

One needs to say what type of thing is spoken of as 'a boundary':

'I speak of a limit as "a boundary".'[7]

---

[5] *Question 1 vocabulary:* What is virtue? (77a9, see *Laches* 190d7: courage). What do you say (*phanai*) virtue is? (71d5, 79e5: see *legein:* 76b1).

[6] This question, '*ti kaleis* . . .' is to be distinguished from '*kaleis ti* . . .' in 76a1, which appears to be the existential question: 'Is there something you call . . . ?' For similarly existential formulations, see also *Protagoras* 330d3 and *Cratylos* 385b2. It is not clear, however, that the first question ('What do you call . . . ?') could be answered if nothing existed which was called by that name. (I leave this issue unresolved in this essay.)

[7] See *Gorgias* 454c6ff.: 'Do you call something *having learned*?' 'Yes.' What?' 'Having been persuaded.' 'Is this the same as having learned . . . ?' They then proceed to discuss whether these are the same. For a similar pattern of thought see *Protagoras* 332a4ff. 'Do you call something folly?' 'Yes.' 'Is wisdom completely opposite to this thing?' In both cases, attempts are made to work out what is called ' . . . '. See also *Meno* 88a6–b2.

In answering this latter question, one is addressing the question:

'What do you speak of as "a boundary"?'

Elsewhere Socrates asks more generally

'What is that of which this is the name, shape?' (74e11)

This question, or so I shall suggest, is one which we would express as follows:

'What is it to which the name "shape" applies?'[8]

To answer this question (which I shall call Question 2), Socrates aims to specify one thing to which the name 'shape' applies. Thus, he asks:

'What is it that is the same in all cases of shape?' (75a4–5)

The answer to this question will be:

'What I call by the name "shape" is . . . '

where the ellipsis is filled by a description of the thing to which the term 'shape' applies. I shall call such answers Type 2 answers.

Socrates' preferred answer to this question is introduced as follows:

'So now you may learn from this what I call shape (*o lego schema*). I say that, in every case of shape, shape is that in which a solid comes to a limit.' (76a5ff.)

The introductory phrase (*o lego schema*) seems equivalent to the longer phrase,

'what I say is shape'

or

'what I specify by using the name "shape"(what I mean by "shape")'.

If so, Socrates' answer,

'I say that shape is that in which a solid comes to a limit,'

should be taken as equivalent to

---

[8] The Greek could also be interpreted to mean: 'What is the nature of the thing which is called "shape"?' I shall return to this possible ambiguity below.

'I use the name "shape" to specify the limit of solid.'[9]

In answering Question 2, what is sought is an answer adequate to pick out shape. This is clear in the first example which Socrates offers: shape is the one thing which always accompanies colour (75b7ff.). While this is adequate as an answer to Question 2, it fails to answer Question 1 because it does not specify what makes shapes shapes. The weakening of this condition on an acceptable answer, encapsulated in Socrates' statement that he is seeking what is the same in all cases of shape (75a4f.), suggests that the original question in 74e11 is best understood as 'What is "shape" the name of?' not as a version of Question 1 (such as 'What is the nature of the thing called "shape"?'). For there is no suggestion that the first answer specifies the form (*eidos*) of shape, let alone the feature in virtue of which shapes are shapes.

Answers to Questions 1 and 2 differ in a further respect: in answering Question 2, there is no requirement that there is one and only one correct answer. Indeed there can be several provided that all pick out the object in question. Thus, as Socrates notes, shape can be specified correctly both as

---

[9] In the immediate context, he uses the terms '*lego*' and '*kalo*' interchangeably (75e1: *lego*, *kalo*; 75e2: *lego*; 75e3: *kalo*; 75e4: *lego*; 75e6: *kalo*; 76a1: *kaleis*; 76a3: *kalo*; 76a4: *legeis . . . eipo*: 76a7–b2). So, the phrase *o lego schema* seems to be treated as equivalent to *o kalo schema*. Elsewhere, when the latter phrase is used,

'they call (*kalousi*) this the diagonal',

it is treated as equivalent to

'"Diagonal" is the name for this . . . ' (85b6–8)

If so, the phrases

'they call this, the limit of solid, shape'
'they call shape this . . . the limit of solid'

should be taken as equivalent to

'"Shape" is the name of the limit of solid.'

In a similar way,

'I say this (the limit of solid) is shape.'

should be equivalent to

'I call this (the limit of solid) "shape".'

and to

'"Shape" is the name of the limit of solid.'

'the limit of solid' (76a4)

and as

'that which always accompanies colour'(75b10f.).

Since he seems to find both answers acceptable, he is best understood as engaged with Question 2. Had he been answering Question 1:

'What is the nature of the object which is named "shape"?'

only one answer would have been correct, assuming (with Socrates) that the object has only one essence. More is needed to answer Question 1 than is provided simply by giving an identificatory account of the object named 'A'. Since the latter is good enough to answer Question 2, it seems that Socrates is engaging with Question 2 not Question 1 in this passage.

Socrates professes himself satisfied with an answer to a 'What is it?' question which meets constraints appropriate to specifying what the term signifies. A definitional account, it appears, is good enough by his lights if it states necessary and sufficient conditions for identifying the object in question (75c1).[10] However, had he concentrated solely on Question 1, he would not have been satisfied with a definition of this type. Indeed, elsewhere, in the *Euthyphro*, he rejects 'being god-loved' as a good definition of piety because it merely points to a property of the thing to be defined and not its essence. If he is focusing in both dialogues on answering Question 1, it is difficult to see how it could be regarded as a satisfactory definition in the *Meno* but not in the *Euthyphro*. It is not sufficient to respond that in the *Meno* an account of the type suggested in 75c1 is a useful staging-post on the long and arduous journey to finding a Type 1 definition of virtue. To do so is to confuse a point on the journey with the destination itself. When Socrates states that he would be satisfied with this as an answer to a 'What is it?' question (75c1), he is allowing that the (merely coextensive) account proposed is an acceptable answer to some definitional question, not a point to be achieved en route to finding a satisfactory one. It seems better to understand Socrates as satisfied with an acceptable answer to Question 2 rather than with a plainly inadequate answer to Question 1.

---

[10] I take 'thus' in 75c1 as referring to an acceptable answer to the 'What is . . . ?' question mentioned in 74b8, as exemplified by the proposed 'What alone always accompanies colour?' in 74b9–11. What is required, in the case of virtue, is an equally adequate answer to a definitional ('What is it?') question.

There are two further advantages in taking Socrates as concerned with Question 2 in these sections of the *Meno*. First, it does justice to his use of 'I call' (*kalo*) interchangeably with 'I say/mean' (*lego*) in this part of the dialogue (noted above). These expressions indicate an interest in what terms are applied to rather than in the nature of the things to which they are applied (as required in Type 1 accounts). Indeed, this is what is signalled in his introductory question by his apparent concern with what it is that is named by 'shape' (74e11f.). Second, if Socrates is focusing on Question 2 (and so providing an account of what the term signifies), his demand (introduced in 75a4f.) that the answer be an account coextensive with the object signified is readily explained. Indeed, this condition would be required if satisfactory accounts of what terms signify apply to all and only items that fall within the extension of the term. Many have thought that such accounts must play this role as they fix the reference of the term. To do so, such accounts must distinguish the object signified from all others.[11] If we lack such an account, we will not know what the term signifies and for this reason be unable to begin to investigate the nature of its bearer.

By contrast, had Socrates simply wished to 'identify' the item in question (unconstrained by what is needed in an account of what is 'named' by the term), he would have needed only an account which picked it out in situations where he encountered it. For, on this basis he could have begun an enquiry, advancing in time to grasp features which it alone possesses in all contexts. If he is not attempting to answer Question 2, his introduction of such demanding conditions on 'identification' at the start of an enquiry would seem unmotivated.[12] Indeed, it is far from obvious why, in order to begin enquiry, one has to possess resources uniquely to identify the kind in

---

[11] Perhaps this is why 'the many' take knowledge of an object to consist in being able to specify some sign (*sēmeion*) which differentiates it from everything else (*Theaetetus* 208c5ff.). The many could reach this view by making two assumptions: (i) to know what a term signifies is to know which object it signifies; and (ii) to know which object is signified is to have an account which distinguishes it from everything else. The many, so understood, would focus on the type of knowledge of (e.g.) 'who Meno is' (71b5) required in the account of what the name 'Meno' signifies. Further examination of this suggestion lies outside the scope of the present essay.

[12] For an alternative view, see T. H. Irwin, 'Socrates and Euthyphro', in *Remembering Socrates*, ed. L. Judson and V. Karasmanis, Oxford, 2006, p. 64. One could, of course, insist that Socrates (for some further, unspecified, reason unconnected with signification or naming) required that the accounts in question uniquely identify the object in question. If one further accepts (on the basis of 75c1) that such accounts (however motivated) are acceptable as definitions, one will attribute to him (in addition to Type 1 accounts) 'identificatory definitions'. This proposal would parallel the one offered here (with 'identificatory definitions' replacing accounts of what the terms signify).

all contexts in which it could be found. One can surely begin an investigation into the nature of gold (or dogs) even when one cannot distinguish these from all other objects in all conditions.

However, while Questions 1 and 2 seem (as I have argued) to be distinguished in these passages, Socrates fails to separate them in a consistent manner throughout the *Meno*. I shall give three examples:

(1) The language which Socrates uses blurs the very distinction he has drawn. Thus, while in 74e11 he appears to ask the question

'What is it of which this is the name "shape"?',

his first answer in 75b8 seems to be an answer to the question

'What is shape?'

where the absence of the article (*to*) may suggest that he is talking about the phenomenon in the world not the linguistic expression. Of course, he may be answering the question

'What is shape?'

in the way required to answer the question

'What does "shape" name (or signify)?'

but his language does not suggest that he is keeping the two issues clearly separate by using the linguistic resources he possesses to distinguish them.[13] Similar problems arise in the second definition proposed. For while, as suggested above, Socrates appears to be answering the question

'What do I say shape is?'

understood as

'What does "shape" signify?',

the answer he gives is of the form

'I'd say that shape is the limit of solid',

---

[13] The possible ambiguity of the question raised in 74e11 (see note 6 above) may help to explain Socrates' shift from Question 2 towards Question 1 at this point.

which appears to be an account of shape as a phenomenon in the world and not 'shape' as a linguistic expression. Once again, he is not using the type of vocabulary which keeps the answers to the two questions clearly distinct.[14]

(2) The definition of colour offered in 76d4–5 is generally taken as an attempt at a real or essential definition of colour, not as merely picking out what 'colour' signifies. However, the proposed definition

Colour is the effluence of shapes . . .

is compared by both Socrates and Meno with the earlier answers given (such as 'Shape is the limit of solid'), as if they were all answers to the same question (75d6–8, 9ff.). But on the account offered in the previous section this would be a mistake. For while this definition is an attempt to provide an essential definition, the first and second say what a name signifies.

Plato's language at the point of transition from the second to the third definition is revealing. Meno begins by asking

'*to de chroma ti legeis;*' (76a8)

which appears to be a version of Question 2:

'What do you say "colour" is?'

and in this way continues the discussion of Type 2 accounts begun at 75a3. But Socrates immediately takes up the issue by asking, in Question 1 mode:

'What does Gorgias say virtue is . . . ?' (76b1),

and continues in a similar vein up to 76d5, without apparently noting the shift of perspective he has introduced. Socrates, it appears, has slipped from discussing Question 2 to considering Question 1 without acknowledging the important differences between them. Nor is this slip difficult to understand. The two forms of question are so similar in Greek that the crucial transition from what is 'A' (e.g. *to de chroma ti legeis*) to what is A (e.g. *ten de areten ti legeis einai*) could easily escape attention. After all, it is made simply by the addition of the apparently innocuous verb 'to be'. Plato's failure to

---

[14] Socrates is using Question 1 vocabulary to answer Question 2 in 76b8 (*ti esti schema*) in a context where Question 2 is being answered (see the phrase *eipein areten . . .* in 75c1), without any indication that he is aware of the shift.

detect this transition (if such it be) is the more readily understandable since ancient Greek lacked the resources (such as quotation marks) which allow one unambiguously to distinguish between the use and mention of a linguistic expression. Nor had his predecessors formulated the technical terminology required to draw the relevant distinction. Indeed, some of their bolder claims seem to have been vitiated by their failure to do so.[15]

(3) At the beginning of the dialogue, Socrates first claims that one cannot know what features something has unless one knows what it is (71b2–6) and then gives an essence-involving account of the answer to the question 'What is . . . ?' (72c5–7). Putting these claims together, it follows that one cannot know what features a thing possesses unless one knows its essence. However, if Socrates had focused (at this point) on the distinction between Questions 1 and 2, he would not have proceeded in this way. Rather he would have insisted that, while one may need to know an account of what the term signifies in order to know what qualities the object signified possesses, one need not know its essence. But nowhere, in the present context, does he invoke the required distinction. This omission is surprising since to answer the question 'Is Meno tall?' one needs only some way of identifying the man in question; one does not need to know his essence. Socrates would have seen, had he securely grasped the distinction between Questions 1 and 2, that one does not need to know what F is (the essence of F) before one can know what qualities F has.[16] To know that Meno is tall, it is enough that one has the identifying knowledge of F (plausibly) required to answer the question: 'Who is Meno?' (or 'What does "Meno" signify?'). If at the beginning of the dialogue, Socrates assumes that one cannot know what 'F' signifies without knowing the essence of F, he will also think (mistakenly) that one cannot know (eidenai) that Meno is tall without knowing his essence. Indeed, if essences are causes, he will also think that

---

[15] For example, is Heraclitus' use of the term account (logos) free from all confusion between use/mention? Does he use it to refer to the statements we make or to the subject-matter of such statements (e.g. an order in the world) or does he conflate the two? A proper study of the pre-history of the use/mention distinction could profitably examine this and several other key pre-Socratic terms (such as being, not-being and truth).

[16] The claim in 71b3ff. that one cannot know that a is F unless one knows what a is does not require that one knows what a is prior to knowing that a is F. It is consistent with this claim that one cannot know what a is without knowing (for some F) that a is F. For all that is said here, knowledge of what a is and of what properties a has might emerge together. In this passage, Socrates uses know (eidenai) and grasp (ginoskein) interchangeably.

one will not be able to know how tall Meno is without knowing what causes him to be (e.g.) 6 foot tall. Socrates' subsequent attachment to the claim that knowledge (*episteme*) always involves knowledge of causes (98a2–5) may stem from his conflation of accounts of what terms signify and accounts of the essences of what is signified.[17]

4 Socrates' Response to the Paradox in the *Meno*

Does Socrates draw the relevant distinction between Questions 1 and 2 after his initial reformulation of Meno's question? Does he employ (in a more systematic way) the distinction he has suggested to undermine the contentious argument he introduced? As the dialogue develops, it is far from clear that this is the case.

Socrates' first move is to suggest that since the soul is immortal it has seen *everything* beforehand: there is nothing it has not already learned (81c7). Since the soul has already learned everything and all nature is akin, it can (in principle) recover everything if it recovers just one thing. So understood, enquiry and learning are the recovery of information one already possesses (recollection: 81d4–5). In terms of the diagnosis offered in the previous section, Socrates is, in effect, denying

[C]   Enquiry is the successful acquisition of information one does not possess.

In successful enquiry, we do not acquire new information but rather improve our epistemic status with regard to information we already have. More precisely, we always have true beliefs which need to be 'aroused' in us (85c10) and then converted by some means into knowledge (85d1ff.). We may not be aware (at the outset) that we have these beliefs or be able to distinguish them from other false beliefs we also possess. Nonetheless, they are present and can be 'aroused' in the thinker (under certain favourable

---

[17] Socrates' claim about knowledge (*episteme*) involving knowledge of causes (98a2–5) is exceptionally (indeed implausibly) demanding, ruling out knowledge (*episteme*) of one's own name or height, when one does not know what causes this to be your name or height. One can, however, see how he could have been led to accept this view of knowledge had he conflated answers to Questions 1 and 2 (where the latter, but not the former, is required for knowledge of one's name or height).

conditions). Enquiry consists in 'stirring up' such beliefs and converting them into knowledge.[18] Both stages are involved in recollecting information one already has.[19]

If one is prepared to reject Assumption [C], there is no need to call into question either Assumption [A] or [B]. One can conduct an enquiry (so understood) into virtue even if one already grasps (or has true beliefs about) its essence. For enquiry will consist in accessing and securing one's true beliefs about what 'virtue' signifies and about the essence of virtue. Indeed, a commitment to [A] and [B] would serve to explain why Socrates took the apparently paradoxical step of denying [C] by suggesting that the slave all along has true beliefs about certain geometrical shapes which need to be 'aroused' and converted into knowledge.

Contrast how the dialogue would have developed had Socrates systematically distinguished between Questions 1 and 2. He would have turned (after reformulating Meno's question in 80e1ff.) to further reflection on Question 2, showing how it can be answered without grasping an answer to Question 1.[20] However, in his dialogue with the slave, Socrates is concerned to establish that learning is recovering information one already possesses (82b1–2). The slave is encouraged to follow a line of argument and arrive at a conclusion of which he was not previously aware. Socrates claims that, since the slave has not been taught the answer, he (in fact) is recovering information he already had. This claim enables him to support his rejection of [C] without challenging either Assumption [A] or [B].

As the dialogue continues, Socrates shows no interest in questioning Assumption [B] by separating Questions 1 and 2. When he ascertains that the slave grasps (*gignoskei*) what a square is (82b10), first by presenting an example and then by noting some of the general features of the example ('figure with these four equal sides'), he does not consider whether the slave has a (partial) answer to Question 2 or to Question 1. Neither here nor in the later discussion of the diagonal does he consider a case where one has an

---

[18] Socrates sometimes speaks of the enquirer as already having such knowledge (85d12), sometimes merely as having beliefs which can be turned into knowledge (85d1). His lack of care in specifying the original state of the enquirer suggests that he is concerned more with the transition to 'exact knowledge' (the final state) than whether this is from specific beliefs or dispositional knowledge of specific claims.

[19] In 98a5ff. the latter process alone is described as recollection. However, as the context indicates, Socrates is there concerned with only the second of the two stages described as 'recollection' in 85c9ff.

[20] This is what one would have expected had Socrates' reformulation of Meno's question been merely to connect it with an unfounded (and easily resolved) 'eristic' argument.

answer to Question 2 but no answer to Question 1. Nor should this surprise us: given his commitment to the recollection doctrine there can be no such case.

What of Assumption [A]? The slave is not offered a fully general account of what a square is (at 82b10f.) as Socrates' suggestion involves the demonstrative expression ('these lines'). Similarly, in the discussion of the diagonal, Socrates makes sure that the slave understands what 'diagonal' signifies (85b5ff.) (in the case he is considering) on the basis of his grasping that it is the line which cuts a given (demonstrated) figure into two (85a5). Here too the slave does not have a general account of what 'diagonal' signifies or of what the diagonal is. Do these comments show that the slave, in fact, begins his enquiry without already possessing a general account of what the terms signify? It might look as if, in being able to speak Greek and say that a given figure is a square, he has grasped enough to get the enquiry under way. If so, does his predicament constitute a challenge to Assumption [A]?

There is, however, little reason to believe that Socrates is advocating a weakening of Assumption [A] in these contexts. Given his commitment to the recollection doctrine, he is entitled to assume that we all already possess answers to Question 2 and can recover them (if placed in suitable conditions). If so, while he did not make his answer to Question 2 fully explicit in his discussion, the slave too must have a general account of what 'square' signifies which he could recover (if pressed). Had Socrates been considering a weakening of Assumption [A], he should have made what he intended clearer by sketching (in outline) the new minimum conditions for enquiry. Earlier in the dialogue, Meno was taken to task for seeking to answer the 'What is it?' question without having a satisfactory general answer to Question 2. He (and the reader) would have been entitled to an explicit account of (and justification for) the new weaker conditions now being imposed on answers to this Question.

Nor do matters change when Socrates turns to the method of hypothesis. He assumes that virtue is a good (87d2–3), *en route* to his (interim) conclusion that it is a form of knowledge. However, he does not say what kind of account (if any) of what 'virtue' signifies is involved in making this assumption. Need the hypothesizer have a true general account of what 'virtue' signifies? Will this involve a true account of the essence of virtue, even though he has not as yet recovered his knowledge of it? Once again, Socrates fails to specify the minimum grasp of what 'virtue' signifies that is required for this form of enquiry. We are certainly not given any indication of the weakening of the conditions required (in this context) for an adequate answer to Question 2. It seems that Socrates is once again assuming that we do possess an account of what 'virtue' signifies 'within us' when we come to apply the method of hypothesis, even though we have not as yet properly recovered it.

Socrates does not, it appears, seek to address his own reformulation of Meno's paradox by calling into question either Assumption [A] or [B].[21] As the dialogue proceeds, both Assumptions remain unchallenged. Socrates is, it appears, looking for ways to allow for the possibility of enquiry consistent with their truth. By contrast, Aristotle (or so I shall argue) engaged with the paradox Socrates raised in the *Meno* by rejecting Assumption [B] and separating accounts of what terms signify from accounts of the essence of the object signified. He also subjected Assumption [A] to critical scrutiny by considering in more detail what is required at the outset of an enquiry into essence.

5 Aristotle's Explicit Comments on 'the Paradox in the *Meno*' in the *Analytics*

Aristotle, on occasion, refers explicitly to Meno's paradox in the *Analytics*. Thus, at *Post. An.* A.1, 71a29–31, he considers examples in which one comes to have knowledge of some particular (or specific) fact on the basis of knowledge of some universal claim. Such cases would be among those to which the Socratic account of learning as recollection, exemplified in the *Meno* by the case of the slave, should apply. One runs as follows:

(1) S knows that everything G is F,
(2) a is G,
(3) S does not know that a exists, and
(4) S does not know that a is F.

Aristotle comments that S knows that a is F *in some way* since he knows the universal but does not know it *without qualification*. He then notes that 'if this

---

[21] For further aspects of the *Meno* which reflect this pattern of thought, see my 'Types of Definition in the *Meno*', in *Remembering Socrates*, ed. L. Judson and V. Karasmanis, Oxford, 2006, pp. 121–6.

were not so, the paradox (*aporia*) in the *Meno* would arise' (71a29–30). For if S knew without qualification that a is F, he could not come to know it by inference from the syllogism.[22]

In what sense does S know that a is F (in this example)? It appears that he has the ability to infer it from what he already knows (viz. (1)) if he also grasps that a exists and is G. In this way, as Aristotle notes elsewhere, S knows this conclusion potentially not actually (*Post. An.* A.24, 86a25–7). Had he known it actually in virtue of knowing the universal he could not have gained this knowledge by means of the syllogism. He would have already possessed it (albeit non-occurrently) and there would have been no actual acquiring of knowledge.

What is involved in S's knowledge that everything G is F? Aristotle comments on this in *Pr. An.* B.21, 67a15ff. Here, too, he envisages an example in which

(1)   S knows that everything G is F,
(2)   a is G,
(3)   S does not know that a exists,
(4)   S does not know that a is F.

Aristotle proceeds to disambiguate the phrase

(1)   S knows that everything G is F.

It can mean, he suggests, that

[1]   one knows that the following universal is true:

'Everything G is F' or

[2]   one knows of every individual case of G that it is F.

Aristotle notes that S, in this case, knows the universal claim in sense [1] but not in sense [2]. If he had known it in sense [2], he would already have known that a is F. In which case, as Aristotle remarks, he would not actually

---

[22] Alternatively, if one lacks the universal knowledge expressed by (1) one will learn nothing as a result of this inference. As Aristotle remarks, without the distinction he draws, 'either one learns nothing (lacking universal knowledge) or one learns what one already knows (possessing universal knowledge)'. In this formulation, Aristotle captures both horns of Socrates' version of Meno's paradox. For an alternative view of this passage, see Scott Labarge, 'Aristotle on "Simultaneous Learning" in *Posterior Analytics* I.1 and *Prior Analytics* II.21', *Oxford Studies in Ancient Philosophy* 27 (2004), pp. 177–216.

have acquired the information that a is F but only recollected it (as is claimed in the *Meno*).[23]

What does knowledge of type [1] amount to? One may know [1] without knowing *each* case to which it applies. This claim is consistent with the thought that if one knows that

'Everything G is F'

one knows that there is some G and perhaps even that one knows of some individual that it is G. All that is ruled out is that one knows of the existence and identity of *each* thing that is G. One may understand and use the relevant universal claim without such extensive knowledge.[24]

The two sets of comments in *Post. An.* 71a29–31 and *Pr. An.* 67a15ff. do not engage with the assumptions underlying the paradox set up in the *Meno* (as set out above). Rather Aristotle argues that Socrates' defence of the claim that we have pre-existing specific knowledge is unsuccessful in the cases under discussion. Inference (from a universal) gives no support to Socrates' rejection of Assumption [C]. If so, the slave's epistemic progress in the *Meno* (in so far as it is based on inference) will also not be evidence for his doctrine of pre-existing knowledge. Aristotle, in these passages, calls into question Socrates' grounds for his claim that learning is recollection.[25] Further, he shows, through these examples, that we are not in the 'all or nothing' epistemic condition described in the *Meno*: we do not have either complete knowledge or complete ignorance with regard to the items in question. While he has undermined a consequence of Socrates' reformulation of Meno's question, he has not engaged with the assumptions which (I have suggested) give rise to the paradox.

Aristotle does, however, address the basis of 'the paradox in the Meno' later in the *Post. An.* B when he shows how we can grasp what the relevant terms signify without already grasping the essence of the kind itself. There,

---

[23] Aristotle adds a further note. It will not help to defend claim [2] to say that if one knows that everything G is F one knows that everything one knows to be G is F. For this type of claim is too limited to account for what one knows when one knows that

'Everything G is F.'

For this claim is one about everything that is G not just about everything one knows to be G.

[24] So understood, the unqualified claim 'Everything G is F' may always be referential and only understood by someone who has knowledge of some actual case that is G. For a contrasting view, see Michael Ferejohn, *The Origins of Aristotelian Science*, Yale, 1991, pp. 43–4.

[25] For a similar pattern of thought see *De Memoria* 452a2ff.

he makes explicit the disastrous consequences of failing to separate these accounts (in *Post. An.* B.7) and proposes (in *Post. An.* B.8–10 and elsewhere) a positive account in which they are clearly separated. This is his way to undermine Assumption [B].[26] Or so I shall now argue.

6 'The Paradox in the *Meno*' and *Post. An.* B.7

Post. An. B.7 concludes with the following provocative remark:

It is not possible to grasp what something is by definition or by proof. (92b38)

Aristotle derives his startling conclusion from a complex series of arguments. Most are directed against the claim that definitions can establish what something is. Aristotle produces several considerations to support his contention. First he argues that there can be no one proof both of what something is and that it exists (92b4–11). If so, since definitions will be different from the conclusions of demonstrative syllogisms, it will be possible to know a definition without establishing by demonstration that the object to be defined exists. But this, Aristotle claims, is impossible (92b12–18). Further, if definitions are different from the conclusions of syllogisms, demonstrations cannot be useful in establishing definitions. For the conclusion of the syllogism will not be directly connected to the object to be defined (92b20–22).

Aristotle notes that one could avoid these specific problems if one took definitions to be accounts of what the name in question signifies. One could then grasp an account of what the term signifies without knowing that the object signified exists (and so avoid the first problem). Further, if the relevant accounts were of the form

'"Thunder" signifies the same as "noise in the clouds".'

---

[26] Some see *Post. An.* A.1, 71a24–30, as Aristotle's main attempt to resolve Meno's paradox (e.g.) by accepting that the enquirer in some way already knows what he is looking for (e.g. the essence of the kind in question). So understood, his strategy follows that developed by Plato in the *Meno*. See, for example, Jonathan Barnes, *Aristotle, Posterior Analytics*, 2nd edn., Oxford, 1993, p. 88. My suggestion is that Aristotle engages with the paradox in the Meno in the centre of *Post. An.* B and arrives at his own, non-Platonist, solution.

one could immediately grasp that the *definiens* (noise in the clouds) was related to the *definiendum*. However, if one takes such accounts to be definitions one encounters a range of serious problems:

(1) Some of the accounts derived will not be proper unities but will be like the *Iliad* (92b28–32).
(2) Some of the accounts will be of essences since they are not of existents at all (92b26–28).
(3) These accounts will be unconnected with demonstration since no demonstration can prove that

' "Thunder" signifies a type of noise in the clouds.'

Aristotle faces a dilemma: if definition is of what the object in question is but is distinct from the conclusion of the relevant demonstration, we confront the set of problems mentioned above. However, if we avoid these by taking definitions to be accounts of what the name signifies, we violate some basic conditions on what it is to be a definition (as pointed out in (1) to (3) above). There seems to be no one type of definition which can simultaneously (a) connect the *definiens* and the *definiendum*, (b) be grasped without knowing of the existence of the kind, and (c) meet other basic conditions on being a definition (picking out an essence, etc.). The first type of definition meets the latter conditions but not the former (since it is not directly connected with the *definiendum* and cannot be grasped without knowing of the existence of the kind); the second type meets the former conditions but not the latter.[27]

The paradox (*aporia*) which Aristotle formulates at the end of B.7 rests on the assumption that there is just one type of definition which is an account both of what the term signifies and of what the object in question is. The chapter as a whole shows that if one holds this assumption one faces epistemic disaster. However, the assumption in question just is Assumption

---

[27] Since the discussion in B.7 is *aporetic*, one cannot take one section of the chapter by itself (such as 92b27–32) to show that Aristotle held that accounts of what names signify cannot all be definitions (of some type). For a contrasting view, see R. Bolton, 'Essentialism and Semantic Theory in Aristotle', *Philosophical Review* 85 (1976), pp. 515–44; R. Sorabji, *Necessity, Cause and Blame*, London, 1980, p. 198; and D. DeMoss and D. Devereux, 'Essence, Existence and Nominal Definition in Aristotle's Posterior Analytics II.8–10', *Phronesis* 33 (1988) pp. 133–54. Aristotle's most conservative approach to the *aporia* raised by the chapter as a whole would be to show that all the accounts mentioned there are definitions (albeit of different types). I argue below that this is the approach he followed in B.10.

[B] (noted in the Introduction): that there is one definition which is an account both of what the name signifies and of the essence of the thing signified. In B.7 Aristotle, we can conclude, succeeds in identifying the Assumption which leads to the paradox in the *Meno* and in showing that it must be rejected if knowledge by definition is to be possible. In B.8–10 he proceeds to show enquiry can proceed once Assumption [B] is discarded.[28] There can be no one type of definition which plays both the roles specified.

7 Aristotle's Rejection of Assumption [B] in *Post. An.* B.8–10 and Elsewhere

In *Post. An.* A.1, Aristotle introduced a crucial distinction about what has to be known at the beginning of an investigation. He noted that one needs to grasp in advance 'what the term used is . . . such as what does "triangle" signify' (71a13–15), separating this from knowledge that something is the case. In his example, one may need to know both what the 'monad' signifies and that the monad exists (71a15–16). These two pieces of knowledge are further distinguished from the knowledge generated by subsequent demonstration of the relevant causes (A.2) leading to discovery of the essence of the object or kind at issue. In the terminology of B.7, the latter type of knowledge concerns what the thing in question is. Knowledge of what the term 'monad' signifies, by contrast, will be given by a different type of account, which signifies the same as the name (92b26–28). Aristotle, in effect, distinguishes two answers to the 'What is it?' question: one is an account of what (e.g.) the term 'triangle' signifies, the other of what the triangle is: the very distinction which Socrates (in the *Meno*) had gestured towards but failed to maintain.

Aristotle aims to resolve the paradoxes in B.7 by distinguishing different types of definitional account (answers to the 'What is it?' question). B.10 opens as follows:

[28] R. D. McKirahan notes Aristotle's distinction in B.7 between accounts of 'what it is' and 'what it signifies' in *Principles and Proofs*, Princeton, 1992, pp. 124–5. He does not, however, connect it with Meno's paradox in the way outlined here.

Since a definition is said to be an account given in reply to the 'What is it . . . ?' question, it is clear that one type of definition will be an account given in reply to the question 'What is it that a name or other name like expression signifies?' An example of such a question is: 'What does "triangle" signify?' When we discover that what is signified exists, we seek to answer the 'Why?' question. (93b29–32)

Aristotle separates three stages in scientific enquiry.

> *Stage 1*: this stage is achieved when one knows an account of what the name 'triangle' signifies.
> *Stage 2*: this stage is achieved when one knows that what is signified by the name exists.
> *Stage 3*: this stage is achieved when one knows the answer to the 'Why?' question, an answer which (it emerges later in B.10) is given when one grasps what the kind in question is, the essence of the thing in question.

In his account, one can complete *Stage 1* without knowing that the object signified exists or what its essence is. The latter knowledge is achieved at *Stages 2* or *3* of scientific investigation. If so, it cannot be a requirement that in grasping what a name signifies one has knowledge of either the existence or the essence of the thing signified. In a scientific enquiry, one begins with knowledge of what the term signifies and proceeds to discover whether there is a genuine kind marked out by this term and (finally if all goes well) what its essence is.

Enquiry is possible if one rejects Assumption [B] by separating accounts of what terms signify and accounts of the essence of the things signified. Both accounts are definitions (of some type) as both answer some 'What is it?' question. Once Aristotle has distinguished these, he can show that the differing definitional tasks mentioned in B.7 can be discharged separately by them. Accounts of what terms signify link *definiens* directly with *definiendum* and can be grasped without knowledge of the existence of the object in question (at *Stage 1*). Accounts of what the kind is (at *Stage 3*) pick out the essences of existing kinds and cannot be grasped without knowledge of the existence of the kind to be defined (grasped at *Stage 2*). Although neither account is adequate by itself to fulfil all the relevant definitional purposes, taken together they do so (each playing a different definitional role).

To secure this promising result, Aristotle needs to show that one can grasp what a name signifies without knowing that the kind in question exists or what its essence is. In B.7, accounts of what names signify appear to be of the form:

The name signifies *this*.

where '*this*' is replaced by an account signifying the same as the name. As the immediate context makes clear, there can be accounts of this type whether or not there is an object or kind in the world signified by the term in question. For there can be an account of what 'goatstag' signifies. Such an account might be as follows:

'"Goatstag" signifies the same as "offspring of goat and stag".'

In the case of the term 'triangle' the relevant account might be:

' "Triangle" signifies the same as "plane figure with three angles".'

One can grasp both without thereby knowing (in grasping the account) whether or not there are goatstags or triangles. One will come to know this at *Stage 2*.

Aristotle comments that there can be two distinct types of relevant account. In one, it is required that 'one thing is predicated of one thing non-accidentally', in the other, the account is tied together in some way (like the *Iliad*: 93b37). The example given of the account of what 'triangle' signifies will meet the first condition if 'being three-angled' is predicated non-accidentally of plane figure. This case exemplifies the type of unity which is underwritten by the natural unity of the kind in question. In the case of 'goatstag', by contrast, the expressions 'offspring' and 'goat and stag' are tied together by us without any underlying natural unity being present to support the connection. If so, there will be distinct types of account depending on whether or not there is a natural unity present which is signified. If such a unity is present, the expression must signify some non-accidental feature of the kind (in an appropriate way), if it is to signify the same as the linguistic expression. Both accounts are to be classified as definitions because both answer the version of the 'What is it?' question appropriate for names (e.g. 'What is "triangle"?' or 'What is "goatstag"?').

Although there are different types of account required in these two cases, there is no requirement that the enquirer at the outset knows into which category the account in question fits. That is, even if he grasps that

'"Triangle" signifies the same as "plane figure with three angles",'

he need not know that (in this account) one thing is predicated of one thing non-accidentally. For all he need know, this case could be like the following:

'"Void" signifies the same as "place deprived of body".'

For here, if there is no such place as the void, there will be no natural unity to sustain the predication as one in which one thing is said non-accidentally of another. The most one knows at the outset would be

'"Void" signifies place deprived of body, if there is such a place.'

Similarly, in the case of the term 'triangle' the most one need know in grasping the account of what the term signifies is

'"Triangle" signifies three-angled plane figure, if there is such a figure.'

In neither case need one know of the existence (non-existence) of the kind in question.

At *Stage 1*, one might know what it is to be a triangle: to be a triangle is to be a three-angled plane figure. But one does not yet know that triangles exist. It would be a further step to hypothesize (let alone believe) that they do so. It is a step beyond accepting that

'To be a triangle is to be a three-angled plane figure'

to believe that

'Triangles exist as three-sided plane figures,'

or

'All triangles are three-sided plane figures,'

if accepting the latter claim commits one (as it does for Aristotle) to the existence of triangles. Knowledge of what the term signifies should be sharply distinguished from beliefs about the existence of the kind signified. One can have the former without beliefs or hypotheses about the latter. This is why Aristotle can separate accounts of what terms signify (a species of *theses*) from hypotheses (or beliefs) that the kind in question exists (71a11–17, 72a18–24). It may be that at *Stage 1*, one will know that

' "Triangle" signifies the same as "three-sided plane figure",'

or that

' "Triangle" signifies plane figures with three internal angles (if there are any such),'

or that

'To be a triangle is to be a three-angled plane figure,'

or that

'All triangles, if there are any such, are plane figures with three internal angles.'[29]

But none of these claims is equivalent to the following hypothesis:

'Triangles exist as three sided figures,'

or

'All triangles are three-sided figures,'

where the latter involve commitment to the existence of triangles with specific qualities.

Aristotle spells out his approach in B.8 as follows:

In those cases in which we grasp something of the what it is, we proceed thus: let A be eclipse, moon be C and screening by the earth B. To ask whether or not the moon is eclipsed is to seek whether B is or is not.... When we discover [that B exists] we know at the same time that the moon is eclipsed and why it is eclipsed. (92a29ff.)

Here, our original grasp of eclipses cannot involve grasp on their existence or on their essence. For these are established later in the enquiry. At the first stage, the most one can know is that eclipses, if they exist, have certain features. This is precisely what is provided by the account of what the term 'eclipse' signifies. For we can grasp that:

[29] See note 21 above. In this formulation the conditional phrase 'if there are any such [figures]' is used to cancel the implication of existence of some triangles conveyed by the universal claim (in its unqualified form). There is no need to interpret Aristotle's statements about meaning as referring to a separate type of Platonist universal. For a contrasting view, see Ferejohn, *Origins of Aristotelian Science*, p. 44.

'Eclipse' signifies the same as 'a specific type of light deprivation from the moon'

without yet knowing whether there is such a specific type. One does not yet know whether or not there is natural unity at issue here. There might turn out to be no such specific type. One's knowledge at *Stage 1* is not to be represented by claims which require the existence of the type of phenomenon in question.[30]

At *Stage 1*, the enquirer is in a condition similar to that in which

One asks of which of a contradictory pair of statements there is an account: of a triangle's having or not having internal angles equal to two right angles. (93a33–5)

At this point, one does not know whether triangles have an internal angle sum of two right angles or not. When one finds a proof one will know which of these claims is correct. The proof will establish that triangles do have such an angle sum and why this is so. Prior to this stage one does not know whether this is the case. As at *Stage 1*, one does not yet know whether or not the phenomenon (having an angle sum equal to 180) exists.

What one grasps at *Stage 1* is a distinctive type of definition (93b38f.), one to be distinguished from genuine definitions which capture the essence of the kind itself. Aristotle mentions three types of the latter:

[A] definitions which express all of the demonstrative syllogism;
[B] definitions which express the conclusion of such a syllogism;
[C] indemonstrable postings of what something is (of a kind which might appear as the starting-point of a demonstration).[31]

These differ from accounts of what names signify since all state (or presuppose) the existence of the kind in question. Take [B]: the conclusion of demonstrative syllogism might state,

---

[30] It is important to distinguish two questions about *Stage 1* accounts. (i) Do they assert (or presuppose) that the phenomenon exists? (ii) Are they all definitional (in some way)? The three-stage view secures a negative answer to (i). Although Aristotle (if I am correct) returned an affirmative answer to (ii), this is not required by the three-stage view.

[31] In the first, thunder might be defined as the type of noise which is caused by quenching of fire (where causal ancestry is used to define the type of noise in question), in the second as the noise in the clouds, which is caused by quenching of fire (where the noise is not defined in terms of its causal ancestry). They would, nonetheless, both be definitions of the same thing as (i) they have the same extension and (ii) they are derived from the same demonstration. J. L. Ackrill noted this issue in his 'Aristotle's Theory of Definition: Some Questions on *Posterior Analytics* II.8–10', in *Aristotle on Science*, ed. E. Berti, Padua, 1981, pp. 359–84.

'Having internal sum of 180 belongs to plane figures,'

a statement which asserts the existence of plane figures with this property. It could only be asserted knowledgeably by one who knew this to be the case. This statement is to be contrasted with

'"Triangle" signifies the same as "plane figure with internal angle sum of 180".'

For the latter does not assert the existence of such figures and could be asserted knowledgeably by one who was unconvinced that were any such figures. Similarly, in the case of [C]: it is one thing to assert

'Monads are indivisible units,'

which commits one to the existence of monads, and another to assert

'"Monad" signifies the same as "indivisible unit".'

as the latter (but not the former) can be asserted knowingly by one who is sceptical as to the existence of monads.[32]

8 What is Involved, for Aristotle, in Grasping an Account of what the Term Signifies? His Attitude to Assumption [A]?

In rejecting Assumption [B], Aristotle has, I have suggested, undermined the basis of the paradox formulated by Socrates in the *Meno*. However, there remains Meno's original question: If one does not have an account of what 'virtue' signifies, how can one proceed to find what virtue is? This question survives even if one rejects Assumption [B]. For Meno's question can be phrased as follows: If we can engage in an enquiry only if we possess an account which notes a general feature present whenever virtue is found, how can we begin an enquiry when we lack such an account? His question arose in a context in which neither he nor Socrates had succeeded in

---

[32] Aristotle focuses on these three types of definition in 93b39–94a14, but does not mention the first, fundamentally different type of answer to the 'What is it?' question in summing up the chapter. I defend this interpretation in *Aristotle on Meaning and Essence*, Oxford, 2000, pp. 43–8.

producing such an account.[33] It is best seen as asking: How are we to obtain the minimum initial conditions for enquiry (whatever they are)?

What is Aristotle's attitude to Meno's question? Did he think that we need accounts of what terms signify of the type required in the *Meno*? Are they necessary if we are to recognize (*ginoskein*) the kind in question in the way required for us to investigate it (at *Stage 1* of enquiry)? Or did he think that we could begin an enquiry into the nature of (e.g.) virtue without such an account? If so, how?

Some of Aristotle's examples of what is required at *Stage 1* of enquiry appear relatively undemanding. Thus, in the *Analytics*, he talks of man as a certain kind of animal or of thunder as a certain kind of noise in the clouds (B.8, 93a22ff.). As there are animals other than men and noises in clouds other than thunder, these descriptions are not sufficient to pick out the relevant kinds. Further, the use of the phrase 'a certain' is most naturally taken as specifying one determinate kind of animal without spelling out what features mark out that kind.[34] There is no requirement that one be able (at this point) to specify in general terms what features mark out the relevant kind. There is a gap to be filled by further investigation. One specifies virtue as a certain kind of good in the soul or the square as a certain kind of figure (perhaps one with four equal sides) without spelling out what distinguishes virtue or the square from other objects in the same genus. If so, Aristotle is, in effect, weakening Assumption [A]: one does not need to grasp a uniquely identifying feature of man or virtue to be able to begin an enquiry into the relevant essence. At this point, his account diverges from the one suggested by Socrates' remarks in the *Meno*.

Aristotle's suggestion gives rise to a further question: If this is all the information possessed at the beginning of the enquiry, can the (would-be) enquirer recognize the kind in question in the way required to get an enquiry under way? How can he do this if he lacks a uniquely identifying description of the kind in question?

[33] Of course, one could answer Meno's question on the basis of the recollection doctrine, claiming that we already have information in general terms about the kinds in question, waiting to be made explicit. Indeed, this answer might seem attractive if one thought (i) that we can engage in enquiry in a given area, (ii) that we can engage in that enquiry only if we possess an account of this type, and (iii) that we are not able explicitly to formulate such an account.

[34] For further discussion of this issue, see Charles, *Aristotle on Meaning and Essence*, p. 38. For a contrasting view, see Bolton, 'Essentialism and Semantic Theory in Aristotle'.

In *Posterior Analytics* B.19, Aristotle, in offering an account of how we come to grasp the universals required for enquiry, provides the resources to answer this question. Here, as in *Metaphysics* A.1, he points to a route that proceeds from perception via memory and experience to thought of universals. In his account, we begin with a grasp of particulars (gained by perception: 99b35) and proceed (by means of memory and experience: 100a5) to a grasp on the relevant universals. This account, when properly spelled out, shows how an enquirer can recognize the kind in question without having a uniquely identifying general description of it.

For Aristotle, the problematic notion of *experience* is key. Empirical workers have knowledge of particulars, failing to grasp the relevant universals (*Metaphysics* A.1, 981a8–10, 16, 22f.). However, while in this respect they resemble animals (981a1, b27ff.), their grasp also opens the way to a grasp of universals. Indeed, on occasion, Aristotle refers to experience as providing universals or starting-points in astrology (*Pr. An.* 46a17–22). How can this be if it is confined to particulars? Doesn't it, in any event, need to involve some general notions (*ennoemata*) if we are to proceed, on its basis, to grasp universals? Surely those with experience must have some grasp of the groups in nature with which they are engaged, not simply be confined to knowing the particulars that fall within those groups? How can they proceed to knowledge of universals without this?

Empirical workers can see when new cases are like ones they have previously encountered even though they need not be able to state in general terms what the relevant similarity is. Their judgements are of the form, 'This illness or this taste or this face is like that one,' but do not rest on an ability to say in general terms what the relevant likeness is. They can track objective similarities in nature without being able to specify in general terms in what those similarities consist. They will be able to separate distinct groups of illnesses, tastes, or faces without being able to articulate in general terms the differences between them.[35]

---

[35] For further details of this type of account, see my *Aristotle on Meaning and Essence*, pp. 149–61. I understand *Post. An.* 100a5ff. as saying: 'from experience or rather from the whole universal resting in the soul' (taking the 'ē' in 100a6 as corrective: for examples of this latter use, see *NE* 1136a21). For a similar view of the use of 'ē', see McKirahan, *Principles and Proofs*, p. 243. For an alternative account see Travis Butler's '*Empeiria* in Aristotle', *Southern Journal of Philosophy* 41 (2003), pp. 329–50, and Scott Labarge, 'Aristotle on *Empeiria*', *Ancient Philosophy* 26 (2006), pp. 23–44. I am indebted to them and to Pieter Sjoerd Haspers for discussion of this issue. Deborah Modrak analyses the relevant texts in the present volume.

Let us take a specific example: an empirical doctor may have the ability to spot a similar medical condition when he (or she) encounters it. They may say, 'This case is like that one,' and reason that if one treatment worked well in the first case it should work well in this one also. They may have expectations about what will happen in a new case on the basis of their experience of previous ones. They can also group together cases which are similar in this way, labelling one group of cases as group A, another as group B and thinking of the illness as what these cases suffer. However, when they use general terms (such as group A or illness C), these are labels for the groups of instances which are like one another. What it is for a case to belong to group A or illness C (for an empirical worker) is for it to be like other particular cases which he has seen as similar. He can place a case in a group even though he is not able to specify in universal terms a feature they all share.[36] In this way the general concepts (*ennoemata*) of the empirical doctor fall short of being universals: they cannot be specified except in terms which refer essentially to particulars (using such terms as 'being like this one'). The empirical doctor in question has not grasped a universal separately from ('over and above', *Post. An.* 100a7) the particulars on which his judgements are based.[37]

The step required of the empirical doctors in grasping the universal is a small one. They can take it when, in investigating the group of particular cases they have isolated (group A, illness C), they find that they all have certain general features (e.g. some distinctive inability on the part of the patient). They can also take it by speculating that the groups they have encountered are natural ones with distinctive general characteristics (a type of illness) even before they know what such general features are. In neither

---

[36] If this is correct, the facts (*to hoti*) which empirical doctors know (981a29) will not be described in the same universal terms as are used at *Stage 2* of scientific enquiry. When empirical doctors talk of (e.g.) illness A (or food B) they will understand it in terms of groups of cases like this one (or these ones).

[37] For Hippocratic examples which suggest this stage of enquiry, see the discussion of '*sphakelos*' (a type of gangrene) in *Coan Prenotions* 183–4, in Hippocrates, *Opera Omnia*, ed. E. Littré, vol. 5, Paris, 1860, pp. 624–5 (analysed by Littré on pp. 581–2). There was, it appears, some uncertainty as to whether this term named one condition that affected bone and brain or two. So, at the outset of an enquiry, a doctor might speculate whether or not there was one condition which affected the patients under investigation. (Compare Aristotle's discussion of the varieties of pride in *Post. An.* B.13, 97b15ff.) I am indebted to Jane Hood for bringing this medical case to my attention. Aristotle's description of the universal in the soul as 'over and above (*para*) the many particulars' (100a7) is striking, as his universals are not separable in existence from particulars. The phrase may simply be a quasi-quote from a Platonic text. Or alternatively, it may be used to indicate that the universal with which skill is concerned (unlike the ideas (*ennoemata*) of the experienced) is defined independently of any particulars.

case need they have any idea of what the essence of the kind is. They may even be agnostic as to whether there is an essence. Nonetheless, in making the transition from experience to thought, the doctor conjectures that he has encountered a type of illness or patient with their own characteristic natures and so has placed himself in a position scientifically to investigate their distinctive causal structure. He stands at the first stage of the three-stage enquiry outlined in the *Analytics*, even if he lacks a uniquely identifying general description of the kind in question, thinking of them only as 'a specific type of illness' or 'a specific type of patient'.

How does the thinker at the first stage of his enquiry pick out (or recognize) the kind in question? He can use the examples which he previously grasped in experience to do this, thinking of the kind as the one which (if it exists) has these cases (or some of them) as instances.[38] On this basis he can begin to investigate the kind (if it exists) even though he as yet lacks a general description which is uniquely true of it. One might, as before, represent him as thinking of the kind as the one which (if it exists) has these cases (or at least some of them) as its instances. This is enough to allow him to begin an enquiry into the existence and nature of the kind in question. Further, if the kind exists and is genuinely exemplified by the examples encountered, the name that the doctor introduces (such as 'gangrene' or 'melancholic') will stand for the kind. For he has been in appropriate causal contact with the kind in question, even though he does not yet know that this is the case. The signification of these terms is determined by the kind with which he interacts, not by his ability to formulate a general description which uniquely identifies it.[39]

Three points are distinctive of Aristotle's response to Meno's question.

(1) Aristotle thinks that one can be at the first stage of an enquiry without having the type of answer to Question 2 officially required by Socrates. One can begin without possessing a general description which fixes the reference

---

[38] It would be inappropriate at *Stage 1* of the enquiry for the doctor to think of the kind as the one of which these cases are actual examples. For that would be to prejudge the outcome of *Stage 2* of the enquiry. At this point, Aristotle's account differs from the one developed by Hilary Putnam in 'The Meaning of "Meaning"', in *Philosophical Papers*, vol. 2: *Mind, Language and Reality*, Cambridge, 1975, pp. 229–34.

[39] I offer an interpretation of Aristotle's account of these issues in *Aristotle on Meaning and Essence*, ch. 4, arguing that (by *Stage 1* of the enquiry) something of the form of the illness has been transferred to the doctor even though he need not know that this has happened.

of the term by distinguishing the kind signified from all others. Paradoxically, as was noted above, in his discussion with the slave Socrates seemed (for a moment) to allow that one can begin an enquiry with an incomplete description of the square and the diagonal, similar to those which Aristotle accepts. However, Socrates did not take these as adequate answers to Question 2. Further, he deployed them against the background of his commitment to the recollection doctrine, with its implication that we do (in fact) possess the required universal descriptions of the kind (even if we cannot yet access them).

(2) At the beginning of the enquiry, one need not, in Aristotle's account, be able to pick out the kind in all circumstances. There may be cases in which one's initial grasp of the kind is not sufficient for this purpose. Indeed, it may be only in the course of the investigation that one comes to grasp some feature of the kind which permits one to do this. One's grasp of the kind can be improved as one comes to understand more of its causal structure and so can determine in all contexts what is a member of the kind. Indeed, one's experience-based recognitional capacities are fallible, sometimes appearing to pick out a kind which turns out (in enquiry) not to exist (as one kind). For Socrates, by contrast, one needs at *Stage 1* of the enquiry a universal description of the kind which successfully marks it out in all circumstances. Without this demanding recognitional capacity, Socratic enquiry cannot get under way.

(3) Aristotle emphasizes the importance of a less demanding recognitional capacity (manifested by the empirical doctors) which precedes and generates our grasp in thought of an account of what the term signifies.[40] Experience provides the springboard for the grasp on the kind required at *Stage 1* of enquiry. We are not 'parachuted' into the world already in contact with the relevant universals (as in the recollection account). Rather, for Aristotle (but not for Plato) there is a way of justifying one's claim to grasp these universals (in universal terms) on the basis of more primitive, particular-orientated, experience of the world.

---

[40] Experience, in this account, does not consist in the incomplete grasp of a universal (as a universal). For if it did, Plato's question would be apposite: Where did this type of grasp of this universal come from? For an alternative account of experience, see R. Bolton, 'Aristotle's Method in Natural Science', in *Aristotle's Physics*, ed. L. Judson, Oxford, 1991, pp. 1–29. The nature of experience, as the essays by Richard Sorabji and Jane Hood in this volume show, remained a major preoccupation of post-Aristotelian philosophers.

9 Conclusions

Socrates' reformulation of Meno's question in the *Meno* rests (I have argued) on the three assumptions:

[A]   One cannot start a successful enquiry into what virtue is without having an account of what 'virtue' signifies.

[B]   One cannot possess an account of what 'virtue' signifies without grasping the essence of virtue.

[C]   Enquiry is the successful acquisition of information one does not possess.

Socrates' response consists in accepting Assumptions [A] and [B] and seeking for a way to reject [C], using the Recollection doctrine. Aristotle, by contrast, aimed in the *Analytics* to defuse this paradox by rejecting Assumption [B] and by weakening the conditions required of accounts of what terms signify (on the basis of his account of how we can come to acquire the relevant accounts through of particular-orientated experience).

These differences have many important consequences. I shall mention just three.

(1) If one accepts the Recollection doctrine, the essences one knows about must exist independently of this world, since they are grasped by us prior to our existence in it. If so, it cannot be essential to their existence that they are instantiated here. While Forms (or essences) may explain why contingent things work as they do in this world, it cannot be essential to their existence that they do so. As with numbers, the relevant essences could have existed even if they had not been instantiated around us (*The separability of the Forms*).

(2) If it is a requirement of successful investigation that we possess *a priori* an essence-involving account of what our terms signify, one route to knowledge of essence will consist in making such accounts explicit. In doing this we will gain (or regain) knowledge of the essences in question. Clarification and articulation of what we already know, aided by dialectical discussion, can lead us to grasp what has to be the case (*The ambitions of dialectic*).

(3) The essences we grasp in answering Question 1 cannot simply be basic explanatory factors in some chain of causation, grasped by *a posteriori* or empirical investigation. They must also be capable of being known *a priori*, since we have knowledge of them prior to any empirical investigation when

we grasp accounts of what the terms signify (as answers to Question 2). Specific essences must be both basic starting-points in explanation and capable of being known *a priori* by us (*A distinctive notion of essence*).[41]

My conjecture is that Plato was attracted to the consequences just noted and constructed some of his distinctive metaphysical and epistemological theory on their basis. No doubt, he modified some of them and had further reasons for others. But, there is, nonetheless, a line of argument which runs directly from accepting Assumption [B] to these radical conclusions. Plato, I suspect, had such confidence in Socrates' philosophical insight that he was prepared (as Socrates perhaps was not) to 'bite the bullet' and accept the consequences that flowed from the thought that we grasp *a priori* accounts of what terms signify encapsulating knowledge of the essences of the things signified. For Plato, Assumption [B] was a suitable basis for ambitious and distinctive philosophical doctrine, not the product of confusion (as between use and mention).

Aristotle, by contrast, saw that Socrates in the *Meno* had been right to call into question Assumption [B] and distinguish (albeit briefly) Questions 1 and 2. As a result, he investigated what is involved in grasping an account of what terms signify and challenged Assumptions [A] and [B], both central to the paradox in the *Meno* (as understood in this essay). Indeed, several important sections of the *Analytics* constitute his attempt to undermine Assumption [B] and (with it) some of the motivations which led Plato to his transcendental metaphysics and super-rationalist epistemology. In these ways, by developing different strands in Socrates' *aporetic* remarks in the *Meno*, Plato and Aristotle came to radically differing accounts of knowledge and definition, enquiry and reality.[42]

Bibliography

J. L. Ackrill, 'Aristotle's Theory of Definition: Some Questions on *Posterior Analytics* II.8–10', in *Aristotle on Science*, ed. E. Berti, Padua, 1981, pp. 359–88.
J. Barnes, *Aristotle, Posterior Analytics*, 2nd edn., Oxford, 1993.

[41] This issue is highlighted by G. Vlastos in his 'What Did Socrates Understand by His "What is F?" Question?', in *Platonic Studies*, 2nd edn., Princeton, 1981, pp. 410–17.
[42] I am indebted to David Bronstein, Gail Fine, Deborah Modrak, Michail Peramatzis, Miira Tuominen, and the anonymous Oxford University Press commentator for their help and advice on the topics discussed in this paper.

H. Benson, 'The Priority of Definition and the Socratic Elenchus', *Oxford Studies in Ancient Philosophy* 8, 1990, pp. 19–65.

E. Berti (ed.), *Aristotle on Science*, Padua, 1981.

R. Bolton, 'Essentialism and Semantic Theory in Aristotle', *Philosophical Review* 85 (1976), pp. 515–44.

R. Bolton, 'Aristotle's Method in Natural Science', in *Aristotle's Physics*, ed. L. Judson, Oxford, 1991, pp. 1–29.

T. Butler, '*Empeiria* in Aristotle', *Southern Journal of Philosophy* 41 (2003), pp. 329–50.

D. Charles, *Aristotle on Meaning and Essence*, Oxford, 2000.

D. Charles, 'Types of Definition in the *Meno*', in *Remembering Socrates*, ed. L. Judson and V. Karasmanis, Oxford, 2006, pp. 110–28.

D. DeMoss and D. Devereux, 'Essence, Existence and Nominal Definition in Aristotle's *Posterior Analytics* II.8–10', *Phronesis* 33 (1988), pp. 133–54.

M. Ferejohn, *The Origins of Aristotelian Science*, Yale, 1991.

G. Fine, 'Inquiry in the *Meno*', in *The Cambridge Companion to Plato*, ed. R. Kraut, Cambridge, 1992, pp. 200–26.

G. Fine, 'Knowledge and True Belief in the Meno', *Oxford Studies in Ancient Philosophy* 27 (2004), pp. 41–80.

T. H. Irwin's 'Socrates and Euthyphro', *Remembering Socrates* (eds.) L. Judson and V. Karasmanis), Oxford 2006, pp. 58–71.

C. Kahn, *Plato and the Socratic Dialogue*, Cambridge, 1996.

S. Labarge, 'Aristotle on "Simultaneous Learning" in *Posterior Analytics* I.1 and *Prior Analytics* II.21', *Oxford Studies in Ancient Philosophy* 27 (2004), pp. 177–216.

S. Labarge, 'Aristotle on *Empeiria*', *Ancient Philosophy* 26 (2006), pp. 23–44.

R. D. McKirahan, *Principles and Proofs: Aristotle's Theory of Demonstrative Science*, Princeton, 1992.

H. Putnam, 'The Meaning of "Meaning"', in *Philosophical Papers*, vol. 2: *Mind, Language and Reality*, Cambridge, 1975, pp. 229–34.

D. Scott, *Recollection and Experience*, Cambridge, 1995.

R. Sorabji, *Necessity, Cause and Blame*, London, 1980.

G. Vlastos, 'What Did Socrates Understand by His "What is F?" Question?', in *Platonic Studies*, 2nd edn., Princeton, 1981, pp. 410–17.

4

Definition and Division in Plato's *Sophist*

LESLEY BROWN

I Introduction

In Plato's late dialogues *Sophist* and *Politicus* (*Statesman*), we find the chief speaker, the Eleatic Stranger, pursuing the task of definition with the help of the so-called method of division. This procedure, together with that of collection, had been described in the well-known passage which comes late in the dialogue *Phaedrus*. After delineating the pair of procedures, Socrates there goes on to claim that he himself was a lover of 'divisions and collections' and that he called those who followed the procedures dialecticians.

A major preoccupation of many of the earlier dialogues, where Socrates is chief speaker, is that of finding the answer to the question: What is it? Plenty of indications are given of what makes for a satisfactory answer to such a question. A good definition of F must give that one thing which is common to all and only Fs, and which is that *through* which all the Fs are F. A definition must give the 'what it is', the essence of F, i.e. that which explains why all the Fs are F. These connections between definition, essence, and explanation are well known. In *Republic* the nature of dialectic is expounded at some length. In addition to many contested features, including the requirement that dialectic be pursued entirely by the intellect with no input from the senses, that it must use hypotheses in a certain way and reach an unhypothetical beginning—the knowledge of the Form of the Good, readers find a familiar feature reiterated, and said now to belong to the method of dialectic: *it's the enquiry which attempts, for each thing just by itself, to grasp what that thing is* (533b2–3). A page later: 'do you call dialectical

the person who grasps a *logos* of the being of each thing? ... Of course'
(534b3–7). In *Republic*, then, for all its grander and more elaborate metaphysical ambitions, dialectic still involves, at least in part, that search for the
essence described and pursued in the earlier dialogues. What *Republic* adds
(*Rep.* 537c) is the point that the dialectician must be *sunoptikos*, capable of an
overview of reality, of discerning the structure of the whole.

So it is natural to ask whether the earlier ideas of what makes a good
definition are retained in stretches of argument found in *Sophist* and *Politicus*,
the dialogues which approach their targets using the method of division.
Does a correct definition-by-division, expounded in a long formula (in-
corporating the genus and all the sub-branches down to the thing defined),
satisfy the requirements on a definition with which a reader of the earlier
dialogues of Plato has become familiar? In particular, is there still a conviction that a good definition must give the essence of the thing defined, in a
manner connecting essence with explanation?

However, there are major and well-known problems in evaluating the
method as practised in the two dialogues, but especially so in the *Sophist*.
The project of defining the sophist/sophistry (these are taken to be equivalent in effect) occupies the outer parts of the work. Replete with humour,
mockery, and absurdity, seven definitions in all are provided, each presented
as giving *what the sophist is*. They are (D1) a paid hunter of young men who
purports to teach excellence; (D2) a travelling salesman of knowledge; (D3)
a stay-at-home retailer of products for the soul, whether produced by
others, or (D4) by himself; (D5) a combative controversialist who deals in
disputation for money; (D6) an educator who separates better from worse,
revealing contradiction through cross-questioning; and finally (D7) a producer of images in men's souls, an imitator of the wise person, who is aware
of his own ignorance when teaching via private cross-questionings. The first
five locate sophistry in one or other branch of acquisitive art (*techne*); the
sixth makes the sophist a kind of cleanser of false opinions, while the seventh
(after the long and philosophically far more satisfying interlude on not-being
and falsehood) declares the sophist to be a certain kind of producer of
images.[1] I investigate below some of the many scholarly responses to this

---

[1] For D1–D6 see the résumé at *Soph.* 231c9–e6. Most commentators regard D6 as portraying the
method of Socrates, and not, therefore, as to be read as any kind of account of a sophist. However,
Crivelli (2004) denies D6 is supposed to portray Socratic method, while Taylor (2006) holds that it does,
and thereby portrays Socrates as a sophist.

bewildering display of the much-vaunted method of division. I divide scholars into a 'no-faction', those who hold that we should not try to discern, in any or all of the dialogue's definitions, a positive outcome to the investigation into what sophistry is (Ryle, Cherniss), and a 'yes-faction': those who think an outcome is to be found (Moravcsik, Cornford, and others).[2] I shall conclude that in spite of the appearance of many answers (Moravcsik) or one answer (Cornford, Notomi), the reader is not to think that any of the definitions give the (or a) correct account of what sophistry is. But while I side with the no-faction, my reasons differ from those of Ryle and Cherniss, who, in their different ways, located the failure in the nature of the method of division. In my view the failure lies not, or not primarily, in the method of division itself, but in the object chosen for discussion and definition. Sophistry, the sophist: these are not appropriate terms to be given a serious definition, for the simple reason that a sophist is not a genuine kind that possesses an essence to be discerned.[3] If we try to carve nature at the joints, we cannot hope to find that part of reality which is sophistry, for there is no such genuine kind as sophistry—especially not under the genus of *techne*, art, skill, or expertise.

II Preliminaries on the Method of Division

Here is how the method of division is described in *Phaedrus*. After a brief description of 'collection' Socrates goes on to describe another procedure, division, as:

Soc. The reverse of the other, whereby we are enabled to divide into forms, following the objective articulation {literally: according to the joints}; we are not to attempt to hack off parts like a clumsy butcher ... (*Phaedr.* 265e, tr. Hackforth)

Soc. Believe me, Phaedrus, I am a lover of these divisions and collections, that I may gain the power to speak and to think; and whenever I deem another man able

---

[2] The views of Moravcsik, Cornford, and Notomi are discussed in the text of section III; those of the 'no-faction' in note 17.

[3] I use 'genuine kind' to indicate something with a wider extension than that of 'natural kind' familiar from Locke, Putnam, etc. I use it to mean the kind of entity which Plato would allow to have an *ousia* (essence) or *phusis* (nature) of its own (cf. *Tht.* 172b). Virtues, senses like hearing and sight, and crafts like angling would be recognized as genuine kinds in the intended sense.

to discern an objective unity and plurality, I follow in his footsteps where he leadeth as a god . . . those who have this ability I call dialecticians. (ibid. 266b)

Taxonomy or Definition?

As announced in the above passage of *Phaedrus*, the method seems designed to produce a synoptic view of a whole as it is divided into its natural parts. The method is apparently fitted to the goal of displaying a taxonomic, classificatory scheme, showing how an abstract whole has internal divisions; what those subdivisions are and how they are related to each other and to the whole.[4] So is the method one of taxonomy, that is, finding all the species of a genus, and showing their interrelations? So it seems in the *Phaedrus*, where Socrates' two speeches had made a start on displaying the different kinds of madness, *mania*, and locating love as one of these. Or is its goal definition: the careful delineation of a single species, found by successive subdivisions of a very general kind? Even if we do not go so far as Pellegrin[5] in finding a complete dichotomy between the *Phaedrus*' use of the method for taxonomy, and that in *Sophist* and *Politicus* for definition, it must be agreed that the use in *Sophist* and *Politicus* is predominantly for definition, not taxonomic classification.[6] That is, it is interested not in delineating the whole tree-structure, but in locating its target—the kind under investigation—at the end node of just one branch. But this is especially puzzling, for several reasons. First, when the method is introduced at *Phaedrus* 266, in connection with discerning all the kinds (branches) of madness, the terminology suggests that classification—that is, setting out the whole structure, with all the branches—is its prime use. Second, this fits well with the burgeoning interest in a synoptic understanding, and with the explicit interest in the interrelations of kinds both described and manifested in the central part of the *Sophist*.[7] And finally, recall the opening of the *Sophist*.

---

[4] *Gorgias* 463a–c, often thought to be an early appearance of the method of division, presents the interrelations of two pairs of four arts or pseudo-arts.

[5] Pellegrin (1986) p. 38.

[6] It is true that at some points, e.g. 266a–d, a rather elaborate taxonomy is offered, but overwhelmingly the focus is on dividing down until a definition of the sophist is reached. See especially 264d11–265a2 for a description of the procedure's aim.

[7] I do not discuss the complex passage at 254c–e, where the ES presents a cryptic and much contested account of dialectic. See Gomez-Lobo (1977) and (1981), with Waletzki (1979). I accept the overall conclusion of Ackrill (1997, p. 96) (against Ryle) that this passage shows that Plato saw 'at least a close connection between division and the philosophical task of mapping the interrelations of concepts'. Cf. n. 17.

The query posed by Socrates to the Eleatic Stranger, which sets the agenda for *Sophist* and *Politicus*, concerns these three: sophist, statesman, philosopher. Socrates asks what view the people of Elea take on the question: Do we have here three names for just one kind, or is each different from the other? (*Soph.* 217a). The question is made to arise from curiosity about the Stranger himself, and from Socrates' odd claim that real philosophers wander from city to city like the *Odyssey*'s gods[8] in disguise, appearing sometimes as sophists, sometimes as statesmen, and taking on other guises too because of the ignorance of the onlookers (216c–d). In linking the *Sophist* dramatically with the *Theaetetus* (a dialogue full of intertextual references to the *Apology* and whose closing lines recall the impending trial of Socrates), Plato has reminded the reader of the fatal consequences of confusing philosopher with sophist.[9] What we expect, then, is a systematic exploration of the relations between the three types. And the method of division, which can lay out a map of interrelated kinds, displaying interconnections in a particularly helpful way, might seem well suited to the project of displaying the relations between the three. Instead, however, the method is used—at least ostensibly—primarily to 'define' the sophist and the statesman in their respective dialogues; it is not used to explore and display the relations of one to the other, for which at best a few hints are given.[10] Why not? Once again, I shall argue that the answer lies in the nature of the objects of enquiry, sophist, and statesman, and their relation to the philosopher. In particular, I shall argue that sophistry at least is not a genuine *techne*.

Some Questions of Terminology, Logic, and Ontology

Plato designates the procedure that of dividing *kat'eide* or *kata gene*; dividing into (or according to) forms or kinds. Below I defend the translation of *kata* 'into'; first some points about the terms *eidos* (form), *genos* (kind), and *meros* (part). An exchange between Moravcsik and Marc Cohen[11] explored the question whether these terms should be taken extensionally or intensionally: are what gets divided classes or properties or what? But, as both authors agree, neither a fully extensional nor a fully intensional reading of the key

---

[8] *Odyssey* 17, 485–7.

[9] Cf. Frede (1996), Long (1998), Sedley (2004).

[10] Hints in final division at 268c–d, cf. section IV; also 253e–254a, a passage which does distinguish sophist from philosopher but not via a division, referred to in VI below.

[11] Both in Moravcsik (ed.) (1973).

terms is possible.[12] In addition, it is clear that Plato often uses the terms *eidos* (form) and *genos* (kind) interchangeably, and in particular that he uses both labels for his method—dividing *kat'eide*, and dividing *kata gene*—without intending any distinction between them. That the terms *genos* and *eidos* may be used interchangeably rules out what might otherwise be an attractive line of interpretation of the ontology of division—one whereby *gene* are classes and *eide* the properties according to which classes are divided.

The term part (*meros*) is also used, like *eidos* and *genos*, for the product of a division, and like them, for something that can itself be further subdivided. *Pol.* 262–3 contains a famous distinction drawn by the Stranger (hereafter ES) between *eidos* and *meros* (form and part), such that any *eidos* is also a *meros*, but the converse does not hold. 'Barbarian' (says the ES) names a part (*meros*) of the human kind which is *not* also a form, presumably because it does not pick out a genuine kind, but is a label for all non-Greek races, 'unlimited in number, . . . and sharing no common language'. Later I shall exploit this distinction into terms which name forms, i.e. genuine kinds, and those which do not, by arguing (as I have already indicated) that Plato may well have expected the reader to reflect that 'sophist', too, does not name a genuine kind. But in *Sophist* itself the results of a division may be labelled forms and parts (*eide* and *mere*) interchangeably.[13]

To turn to the meaning of *kata* in the locution: dividing *kat' eide* or *kata gene*, or *kata mere*, found in *Phaedrus, Sophist, Politicus,* and *Philebus.* This is commonly translated '*according to* forms' (or kinds, or parts, depending on the term following *kata*). Though this is a perfectly common meaning for *kata* with accusative, indeed more common than the well-attested distributive sense of 'into', I am convinced that the translation 'into' is to be preferred.[14] But not a lot hangs on this, since division of a whole into

---

[12] An extensional reading is ruled out by the fact that the 'kinds' *being, same,* and *different* would be only one kind if kind = class, since *ex hypothesi* anything which is is also the same (as itself) and different (from everything else). A fully intensional reading is difficult, given the terminology of parts; footed creature is part of creature, but if we stick with intensions, the converse is true: *creature* is a part of the intension *footed creature.*

[13] 223c6–7 is a particularly clear example.

[14] Confirmed by *Phdr.* 265e quoted above: division is *kat'eide* (into forms) according to the articulations (*kat' arthra*). See LSJ, s.v. *kata* B II, and Kühner-Gerth II.1, p. 323 n. 5. It might be objected that we divide according to some distinguishing mark or property, and the result of the division is something marked off by that distinguishing mark; and further that forms, *eide,* fit the former role better than the latter. Hence, the argument continues, dividing *kat'eide* should be translated *according to* forms. But we have already seen that Plato does *not* reserve the term *eidos* for the principle of division. See also next note.

forms (or kinds) is never a *de novo* division, rather, it is a division of a whole into *its* forms (or its kinds), just as the butcher divides a carcass into its parts, according to the joints, i.e. the place at which the limbs join.[15] Correct dividing into forms is presented as a matter of *discerning* pre-existing distinctions in the subject, and, to that extent, dividing according to those distinctions. But it is this very presumption that raises the most acute difficulties for understanding the method of division, especially as demonstrated in *Sophist*. For the metaphor of cutting up a carcass into parts according to its joints strongly suggests both that the divisions are objective, and (though less definitely) that there is only one correct way to divide a given subject-matter. But when the Stranger claims to discern divisions in *Sophist* and *Politicus*, these often seem arbitrary, whimsical, or designed to make a particular point. And, as we shall see, not only do the different definitions of sophistry locate it in different branches of *techne* (first in the acquisitive and later in the productive branch), but, more seriously, two quite different first cuts in the concept of *techne* are made in the two dialogues. In *Sophist* we are told that all *technai* are either acquisitive or productive; in *Politicus* that all are either practical or theoretical.[16] To sum up, Plato characterizes division as into kinds or into forms, using these terms interchangeably. Correctly done, and on an appropriate subject-matter, the division follows the objective articulation of the subject-matter; that is, we divide a kind into its pre-existing sub-kinds or forms.

III Obstacles to Finding a Successful Outcome in the Search for the Sophist via the Method of Division

In this section I explore and criticize a range of views that claim to discern a successful outcome to the search for the sophist.[17] On one view, that of

---

[15] It might be objected that it *does* matter how we translate *kata*, since that *according to* which we divide (a distinguishing property, say) cannot be the same as that *into which*, the result of the division, the part (whether understood extensionally or intensionally) marked off by the property. But it is clear that Plato is happy to use the same term for the principle of division as for the result of division. For a clear example see *Pol.* 262, where dividing number by the odd and the even yields two forms, the odd and the even. See Cavini (1995) on the logic and terminology of *diairesis*.

[16] See section V below.

[17] Ryle (1966) and Cherniss (1944) are among those who deny a positive outcome. Ryle found the outer core of the *Sophist* with its definitions by division so tedious that he concluded that for Plato

Moravcsik, the presence of six or seven *logoi* of the sophist (Moravcsik eschews the word 'definition' here) is explained by their being, each of them, a *correct unique characterization of sophistry*. Just as there are several correct ways of uniquely identifying the number two, so also with sophistry. 'The existence of a plurality of divisions is in no way an argument against their being grounded in reality' (Moravcsik 1973, p. 166). If such a development in Plato's views on definition had indeed occurred, such that he no longer searches for the single essence, but for one or more unique characterizations, this would be of considerable interest. But the evidence of the *Sophist*—the six or seven 'definitions' of the sophist—does not vindicate this claim by Moravcsik, as I now show.

The problem for Moravcsik's view is that several of the definitions contain inconsistent elements. The major inconsistencies are (a) in the content of the teaching/peddling ascribed to the sophist and (b) more seriously, in the branch of *techne* in which sophistry is located. On the first point, the first four *logoi* explicitly confine the subject of the sophist's dealings to matters concerning virtue, and this is echoed in the fifth *logos* where the focus is on *antilogike*, the art of controverting, and the subject-matter is confined to matters of justice and injustice. But the run-up to the seventh *logos*, despite it being a development from the notion of the sophist as controversialist, explicitly extends his range to speaking and controverting on *all things*. The argumentation has many oddities—I mention one of them below—but for now we notice simply the flat inconsistency in the alleged field of the sophist. If it be replied that the subject-matter of sophistry is not essential to it, it remains strange that this inconsistency is so prominent, and it remains true that inconsistent characterizations cannot all be correct ones.

A more important inconsistency derives from the initial division of *techne* into acquisitive and productive—a division I explore later—together with

---

'constructing kind-ladders' was a mere propaideutic to genuine philosophy, i.e. dialectic as seen at work in the central section of the dialogue. But in so doing Ryle rode roughshod over the difficult passage at 253c–e. Against Ryle, Ackrill (1997) convincingly demonstrates that 253c–e, in the heart of the central section of the dialogue, presents the method of division as a seamless whole with the investigation of the greatest kinds which forms of the central part of the *Sophist*. Cherniss held that in the *Sophist* and *Politicus* the method is 'a useful means of narrowing the field of search but the formal method alone may lead one to any number of definitions of the same thing unless one has the additional power of recognising the essential nature that is being sought'. (Here Cherniss quotes *Soph.* 231c–232a.) He concludes that 'diairesis appears to be only an aid to reminiscence of the idea'.

the fact that Definitions 1–5 locate sophistry within acquisitive *techne*, while the seventh proclaims it to be a branch of productive art.[18] If, as the evidence suggests, all divisions are intended to be exclusive, even where not exhaustive, it follows that sophistry cannot be truly characterized both as a branch of acquisitive art and as a branch of productive art.

But are divisions intended to be exclusive? While this has been denied,[19] the evidence in the *Sophist* and *Politicus* strongly suggests that Plato envisages that one and the same kind cannot appear on both sides of a given division. Consider, for instance, the initial division of *technai* into acquisitive and productive. The very definition of acquisitive art at 219c1–8 includes the clause 'does not produce (*demiourgei*) anything, but. . . .' In other words, to be acquisitive is to be not productive. Excluding 'producing' from the acquisitive art is striking, especially since the ES tells us that one kind of acquirer, the stay-at-home retailer of D4, may make the products he sells. The very practice of asking, 'Are we to place X in A or B?' strongly suggests that these are seen to be exclusive; the interlocutor is never offered the option of finding the desired kind in both branches of a given division. If I am right that division is always exclusive, Plato cannot have held that sophistry belongs in both the acquisitive and productive branches of *techne*.

But the ES makes it quite plain that the seventh and final attempt starts in a different branch, the productive, even though the discussion of the sophist as a producer of images (D7) emerges from the idea of him as an expert in refutation (D5), allegedly a branch of acquisitive art. He does so at 265a8, remarking that earlier the sophist had put in an appearance for us in various parts of the acquisitive art. (This is the oddity I mentioned above.) Those who believe we are to see some truth about the nature of the sophist in all seven (or even in all bar the sixth) cannot surmount this difficulty: however tricksy a character the sophist is, sophistry cannot have incompatible properties. I conclude that by having the ES emphasize that the last definition starts from a different branch of *techne* from the earlier ones, Plato is signalling that something is amiss, and at the very least that we are not to see all seven (or all except D6) as true characterizations, let alone definitions, of 'the sophist'. Of course, each might have been correct as a characterization of a *type* of

[18] See section I for a résumé of the seven definitions. I ignore for now the problematic sixth definition of the sophist as a practitioner of the elenchus, which places sophistry in a third branch of *techne*, the separative.
[19] Cohen in Moravcsik (1973), p. 189.

sophist. Indeed, the different definitions remind us of the very different kinds of intellectual who get labelled 'sophist' in earlier dialogues. Definitions 1–4, which present the sophist as a paid teacher of virtue, and as a seller of knowledge of a variety of kinds, recall Protagoras, Hippias, and others from *Protagoras*. D5, the sophist as *antilogikos*, one who engages in disputation, invokes those very different types, the brothers in the *Euthydemus*. Henry Sidgwick noted how little in common the first group ('windy declaimers' or 'professors of conduct') have with the 'shifty disputers' of the second type, apart from the mere label 'sophist'.[20] Bearing this in mind, we might well expect the ES to offer us different, and even incompatible accounts of different *types* of sophist.

But this is not how he presents his findings. As noted above, sophistry is consistently treated as the *endpoint* of a division, as something to be divided down to, not as a generic kind whose branches are to be discerned. The definitions present themselves as definitions of 'the sophist', and not of various types of sophist. So the problem for Moravcsik's view remains: the seven accounts cannot all be true characterizations of 'the sophist'— which is how they are presented.

What of the other line which finds a successful outcome, discerning it in the last definition only? This is the view favoured by Cornford,[21] and by Notomi (though the latter's discussion is highly nuanced and finds a different role for the six earlier divisions).[22] The diagram below shows this last 'definition', together with the 'cuts' leading to it.

I briefly rehearse many puzzling features of this last definition, to display how unlikely it is that it is supposed to represent the essence of sophistry. First, all the earlier aspects of sophistry as acquisitive and specifically agonistic are dropped. The second puzzle arises from the distinction at 235d–e between

[20] Sidgwick (1872). See also Irwin (1995), who accepts much of Sidgwick's position but seeks to find more common ground than Sidgwick allows between the two groups of sophist.

[21] Cornford (1935, p. 187): 'the first six divisions actually, though not formally, serve the purpose of a collection preliminary to the seventh. They bring before us the types to be surveyed before we can fix on the really fundamental character of Sophistry.' He also speaks of discovering 'the really fundamental trait, the generic form that will finally yield the correct definition of the essence of Sophistry' and of 'the final serious analysis of the essential sophist'.

[22] '[T]he first five definitions represent at least some aspects of the sophist's art, and hence they can be regarded as true appearances seen from certain viewpoints . . . The final definition . . . will be the true appearance, namely the likeness of the sophist, which the philosophical inquiry finally attains' (Notomi 1999, pp. 277–8). In places (e.g. pp. 85–7, 300) Notomi shares my reservations about whether sophistry is a *techne*; elsewhere (pp. 43, 46) he is content to speak of the essence of sophistry.

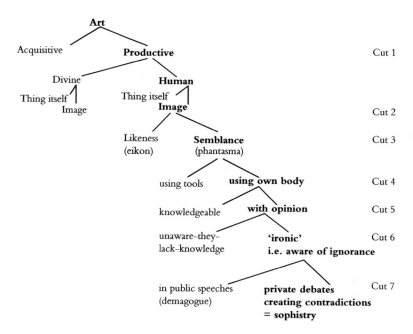

Diagram showing the seventh 'definition' of the sophist/sophistry (*Sophist* 265a–268d) after Bluck (1975).

two types of image, likenesses and semblances, a distinction whose import is disputed; it would take us too far afield to discuss it fully. Some suppose that it is meant to correspond to the distinction between production of true images (including true *logoi*) and false ones. But though the placing of the sophist in the latter branch—the production of falsehoods—would fit this interpretation, it is not, I think, what is intended.[23] It is highly problematic, for that reading, that *within the semblance-producing branch*, we find a kind of imitation which proceeds from knowledge. For how could a species of imitation which proceeds from knowledge lie in a division whose hallmark is that it is the production of falsehoods? This has been inserted to hint that the wise person (*sophos*) and the *politikos* are to be found in this nearby branch, the 'knowledgeable' one, so it remains a puzzle that knowledgeable persons are found in the semblance-producing branch. Surprisingly little mileage is gained from

---

[23] 260c–d tells against it. There the ES argues from the existence of deceit and falsehood to the possibility of images in general (and not of just one subset of images). This strongly suggests (though it does not entail) that it is *false* statements/beliefs, not statements/beliefs in general, which are regarded as images.

the distinction between two types of image-making, and by cut 5 the ES seems to have forgotten that the branch which gets divided into those who know and those who don't is itself a branch (and the 'worse' one at that) of image-making. (See 267e5–7: 'the sophist was not among those who know but among those who imitate'.) The next-but-last cut, cut 6, divides the remaining branch of imitators into those who are aware of their lack of knowledge and those who are not, and the triumphant discovery of the sophist is that he is one of the aware-he-lacks-knowledge ones, the one who speaks in private, while his public-speaking counterpart is labelled demagogue.

These last moves bring starkly into focus a point I believe to have been not far below the surface throughout the attempts to define the sophist. It reminds us of the point stressed earlier, that it is hard to separate sophistry from philosophy, at least in the guise of Socrates. For the final definition of the sophist seems to fit Socrates almost equally well, as we shall see. It's strange to find sophists placed firmly in the branch of 'aware-they-lack-knowledge imitators' since some sophists (Protagoras, perhaps, and Hippias) were portrayed by Plato as unaware that they lack knowledge. Furthermore, many genuine strivers after truth, who are no sophists, fit the description 'aware of their own ignorance' and the label *eirōnikos* inevitably calls to mind the figure of Socrates, especially when this practitioner is described as 'carrying on in private and with short speeches, compelling the person he is talking to to contradict himself' (268b3–5). In fact it becomes clear that at none of the cuts in this division is the practice of philosophy firmly distinguished from that of sophistry on our intuitive understanding of Plato's distinction between them. That is, there is no explicit reference to what from earlier works we have been led to hold is a key difference between true philosophy and sophistry, that the former undertakes its investigations seriously and aiming to discover the truth, while the latter is careless of truth but aims instead at prestige, victory, or money. Instead, the so-called distinguishing features at each of the cuts fit some philosophers as well as sophists.

For however we construe the distinction between the two types of image, it seems the philosopher as much as the sophist can produce the 'semblance' type of image (cut 3); both sophists and philosophers use their bodies, not an implement (i.e. they speak) (cut 4); philosophers can get things wrong, as well as have knowledge (i.e. they can be on both sides of cut 5), and those who lack knowledge, like Socrates, are aware of their own ignorance (cut 6).[24] Being ignorant but creating the impression of being an expert: is that not just what befell Socrates (*Apology* 23a), whose ability to refute the experts gave the impression that he himself possessed knowledge? Yet here it is given as the defining mark of a sophist!

IV Is Sophistry a *techne*, Distinct from that of Philosophy?

The fact that frequent allusions to or reminders of Socrates are found within the divisions defining the sophist has met with a variety of responses from scholars. A particularly challenging one is given by C. C. W. Taylor.[25] He holds that Plato firmly dissociates philosophy, now seen as the comprehensive knowledge of true reality, from Socratic practice, which Plato now sees as more akin to sophistry since it shares with it sophistry's distinctive mark, the production of contradiction by questioning. Among many reminiscences of Socrates he discerns in the earlier divisions, Taylor points particularly to the label *goēs*, magician or illusionist, which is prominent in the lead-in to the final division of the sophist as a producer of images of a certain kind.[26] Taylor surmises that Plato now regards Socrates' unaccountable power to identify false beliefs, in his practice of examination of people's beliefs, as mysterious. In this Socrates is akin to the sophist as a kind of *goēs*, though the sophist's magic is to instil false beliefs, while that of Socrates is to rid men of them.[27]

The novelty of Taylor's reading is his suggestion that Socrates is now being classed as a sophist and by implication not as a philosopher (since Socrates lacks the knowledge which now, according to Taylor, Plato sees as the philosopher's hallmark). Taylor has certainly mounted a powerful case, but a major problem with his account is that he accepts the apparent

---

[24] Notomi (1999, p. 297) disagrees. He writes, 'while the ironical sophist conceals his ignorance, the philosopher openly admits it'. This requires understanding the difficult clause at 268a4 to mean that the sophist *pretends* to know things he suspects he does not. Cornford translates neutrally: 'has the air in the eyes of the world <of being knowledgeable>'. No doubt Plato held that sophists (unlike Socrates) deliberately fostered the belief that they were wise, but the point is not explicitly made at cut 6.

[25] Taylor (2006).

[26] For *goēs* in *Sophist* see 234c5, 235a1, a9, 241b6. Note that at *Pol.* 303c actual *politikoi* (i.e. non-ideal ones, not real *politikoi* at all, in fact) are also labelled *goētai* and *sophists*.

[27] Taylor (2006), p. 167.

premise of the work, that philosophy and sophistry is each a distinct *techne* with an essence of its own. I believe that the data he marshals can be accounted for differently, and that we are not obliged to conclude that Plato's message is that Socrates is now seen as that distinct kind of expert, a sophist, and not after all a philosopher.

My alternative account points up the major false start, which we need to notice: the assumption that sophistry is a *techne*, with an essence distinct from that of philosophy. As indicated above, I believe the frequent allusions, in the course of the divisions, to Socrates and his practices are there to show us that if you approach the attempt to define sophistry in so unprincipled a manner, starting from unquestioned assumptions about its being a *techne*, then it can indeed seem similar to philosophy, at least as practised by Socrates.

Surprisingly little attention has been paid to two salient features of the attempt to define the sophist. First, the assumption that sophistry is a *techne* is unquestioned, despite the well-known denial of this in the famous *Gorgias* passage (462–3), where it is classed, along with rhetoric, as an *empeiria*, a knack, not a *techne*, and despite the very weak ground offered for its being a *techne*.[28] Second, no explicit or even implicit attention is paid to the question of how one *techne* is to be distinguished from another. And yet these are issues in which Plato has throughout his oeuvre shown considerable interest.[29] So it is doubly surprising that no rationale is offered for sophistry being a *techne*, that no rationale for the different cuts of the genus *techne* is given, and that little or no use is made of the important points about the nature of a *techne* that appear in earlier dialogues.

V Plato on the Criteria for Being a *techne*

What is a *techne*? It is a reasoned capacity to achieve a (worthwhile) goal. Qua possessing a *techne*, the expert must understand the causes of success or

---

[28] The ES gains Theaetetus' agreement that sophistry is a *techne* in a particularly weak exchange. Asked whether the sophist is an *idiôtes* (amateur) or a *technites* (craftsman), Theaetetus replies that, with the name sophist, he could hardly be an amateur; the reply plays on the *-istes* ending of the word. Contrast 268b10.

[29] Irwin (1977), p. 71 and p. 288, n. 19 with references; Sedley (2003), p. 43 among many treatments.

failure, and as such must be able to teach the expertise to another.[30] So a key feature of a *techne* is that it has a goal. If there is such a thing as the essence of a *techne*, the account of the essence must make reference to the goal.

Does sophistry have a goal essential to it? We know from earlier dialogues that a major complaint against the sophists was that they pursued their intellectual discussions not for the sake of the truth but for the prestige they gained from the defeat of opponents, and the fees paid by a host of paying pupils attracted by this prestige. We know also that Plato regarded their intellectual pretensions as, by and large, unfounded. All these points emerge implicitly, with wealth featuring in D1–4 (sophistry as a kind of hunting, then of merchandising), victory as well as money in D5, while the unfounded nature of the intellectual prestige is prominent in D7.[31] Does any of these give a unique goal for sophistry? No. Characterizing the sophist as someone hunting rich pupils (D1) or as someone aiming to sell his intellectual property to rich young men (D2–4) does not distinguish him from genuine experts, such as doctors or geometricians, who take paid pupils whom they instruct in their *techne*. D5, the combative controversialist who deals in disputation for money, combines the goals of defeating the opponent in controversy with money-making; it is only this last point that distinguishes him from Socrates, whom we are surely intended to recognize in the adjacent *adolesches* (chatterer), since this is how Socrates has described himself at *Theaetetus* 195b–c. Neither goal—money nor victory—is distinctive of a sophist, though both are goals associated with them by Plato. Most serious of all, and not previously remarked, the seventh definition—the one many hold to be definitive—singularly fails to reveal a goal of the sophist, as I now argue.

The last definition proceeds from a well-known but problematic analogy between painters and sophists, on the ground that each produces a kind of image. The images the sophists produce are identified as false beliefs about matters of justice and virtue, and in particular the false belief that the sophist himself is an expert on these matters.[32] An immediate disanalogy here is that

---

[30] *Gorg.* 465a, 501a.

[31] The goal of the sophist in his sixth appearance is education, or rather its essential preliminary, removing a false conceit of wisdom. Since the sixth appearance is explicitly bracketed off, we can pass over it.

[32] 267c: the sophists cultivate the appearance of virtue; 268c1: the sophist is an imitator of the wise man, echoing 233b–c. P. Kalligas (in Karasmanis 2004, p. 224), in his comment on Taylor's article, makes

painters intend their images to be recognized as such: their expertise precisely is that of producing skilful and realistic visual representations which are recognized as such. This is true even if, as the ES fancifully suggests, some painters deceive young persons into thinking their products are the real thing; that cannot be their main goal, and it is bizarre to find it suggested as any part of the painter's art.[33] The suggestion that painters' images may deceive is no doubt made to smooth the way to the claim that the sophist is a producer of images. As just noted, the images in question are the false beliefs acquired by the sophist's audience, and, chief among them, the belief that the sophist himself is a wise man. Hence the designation (offered by Theaetetus, 267c1): imitator of the wise person. So it is crucial to the sophist's success that the images (i.e. false beliefs, especially in his own wisdom) are *not* recognized as such. *But producing deceptive images is not his goal.* His goal is not, *de dicto*, to create false beliefs; rather it is to create a belief in his own wisdom. That the belief is a false one follows from the fact that the sophist is a *sham* wise person. Deception is the means to his goal, but it is not his goal. Once this is spelled out, it becomes clear why sophistry is not a genuine *techne*. There may be a trick or two involved in getting people to think you are wise when you are not, but that does not make it a *techne*. The nub of Plato's complaint against those he labels sophists may be their uncanny ability to appear wise when they are not, but again, that does not mean there is a *techne* whose aim is precisely this.

The seven definitions, then, fail to suggest a consistent goal for sophistry. While the first four gesture at goals familiarly associated with sophists (wealth, victory), these aims are not exclusive to sophistry but may be shared by other experts such as architects, doctors, and dramatists. The final definition, with its emphasis on being a kind of imitator, signally fails to mark a goal (and the analogy with painting is thereby a flawed one). Imitating a wise person, i.e. contriving to be thought wise when one is not, is a means to what, as the discussion at this point reveals, is the sophist's goal, viz. getting a reputation for wisdom, but is not the goal itself.

a different assumption. He takes the reference to the sophists producing images to be referring to their use of certain literary techniques, such as the epideictic model-speeches used by Gorgias and Antiphon. This is an ingenious suggestion, and it would allow the parallel with painters much more force. But it does not do justice to the theme of the deceptiveness of sophists, their attempts to appear wise when they are not.

[33] It is curious that both in the *Sophist* and in the *Republic* this implausible suggestion is made.

Does sophistry pass the test whereby a *techne* must have reasoned procedures, which involve understanding the causes of success and failure? Here we come up against the plethora of characterizations of sophistry in the divisions. Is there a reasoned procedure in connection with being a hunter after rich young men? Hunters after rich young men are not necessarily frauds. For instance, Theodorus, with his variety of mathematical expertises, no doubt attracted a number of pupils impressed by his wisdom, and perhaps they paid him for the instruction he gave. Is he thereby a sophist? Presumably not, since he *is* credited with wisdom. In any case, his *techne* consists in the understanding he has of the subject-matter; his ability to acquire a reputation for wisdom and, with it, rich pupils (supposing he did so) is not what constitutes his *techne*. Turning to the characterization of sophists as *antilogikoi* (experts in controversy or disputation), we have already noted that, in this aspect, their only difference from Socrates comes at the last cut: Socrates *loses* money by his examinations; they *make* money. To judge by their performance in *Euthydemus*, the *antilogikoi* Euthydemus and Dionysodorus do have an understanding of how to refute an opponent, just as Socrates did. So expertise in *antilogike* is not peculiar to sophistry.[34] Once again, sophistry seems to be used as a label for what, done properly, with the right motives and by a truly skilled person, is a respectable intellectual activity. It does not have a set of techniques and procedures peculiar to itself; rather, according to the treatment in *Sophist*, it is a fraudulent practice of what in other hands is a respectable and genuine *techne*. It fails that test for being a *techne*.[35]

Let us turn to the vexed issue of the subject-matter of a *techne*. Must a single *techne* have a single and well-defined subject-matter? Or must the goal play a part too? At this point we may note an important point about the first cut of the genus *techne*, which is different in *Sophist* and in *Politicus*. Whereas the major distinction in *Sophist* is said to be the division of *technai* into *productive* and *acquisitive*, in *Politicus* we get the far more familiar distinction

[34] Cf. *Phdr.* 261b–e.

[35] See, for a contrary view, Kato (1995), pp. 162–72, at p. 165 (*techne*) '. . . functions as the factor which uncovers one after another the various disguises of the sophists's pseudo-art, and finally discloses its essence as pseudo-art, i.e. imitative art'. Kato is assuming that being a pseudo-art is the essence of sophistry; a strange kind of essence, especially for a *techne*. And I have argued that (in contrast to painting) being imitative is not of the essence of sophistry.

into *practical* and *theoretical*. Now some subjects, such as geometry, may be pursued either theoretically or for practical purposes, as an aid to land-measurement (the literal meaning of geometry). From the fact that theoretical/practical forms the first cut of *techne* in *Politicus*, one might infer that difference in aim (practical versus theoretical) means that pure and applied geometry are different *technai*. But recall *Republic* 7, which rehearses the five *technai*/branches of knowledge that the would-be philosopher-ruler must study en route to dialectic—arithmetic, plane geometry, solid geometry, astronomy, harmony. There Socrates insists—though with considerable irony—that the disciplines have practical uses as well as their value to the trainee philosopher: their ability to lead the soul towards truth. This suggests that geometry is one and the same *techne* whether pursued for its practical uses or for enlightenment's sake.[36] From Plato's treatments of genuine *technai*, then, it is unclear what role subject-matter has in the delineation of a *techne*.

To sum up: it is clear from the above that producing definitions, and a taxonomy, even of genuine *technai* is a hard enough task, for such a taxonomy needs to find a place for, and to order in terms of importance, the criteria of purpose, of whether the *techne* is practical or theoretical, and of subject-matter, and it also needs to establish, for a genuine *techne*, that it has standards by which success and failure can be measured. It is even clearer that no serious attempt is made in *Sophist* to justify the poorly founded claim that sophistry is a *techne*, nor, a fortiori, to show, by the acknowledged criteria for *technai*, what its essential nature is.[37]

VI Conclusion

Let us distinguish four questions. First, can the method of division yield a unique definition of the *techne* of sophistry? To this I have already indicated my answer 'No, Plato cannot have intended the reader to think so, because sophistry is no genuine *techne*, indeed it lacks any essential nature.' Second,

---

[36] The analogy between the parts of difference and the parts of knowledge (*Soph.* 257c–d) also suggests that a branch of knowledge gets its specific nature from its subject-matter (regardless of whether it is employed for practical purposes or not).

[37] Cf. n 28, on the evidently weak 'argument' offered for the sophist being an expert.

can the method yield a unique definition for any *techne* or branch of knowledge? Here my hunch is that, while Plato was convinced there are objective criteria for what is a *techne*, and for what distinguishes one from another, he would have been less sanguine about finding, via the method of division, a unique correct definition, let alone a unique classificatory scheme encompassing all *technai*, for reasons sketched in the previous section. Third, are there *any* kinds for which Plato can have hoped the method of division would yield a definitive essence-revealing definition? All we can say here is that the evidence of the *Sophist* does not enable us to give an affirmative answer to the question, but that does not mean that it did not remain an aspiration; the evidence is that it did. Fourth, what if any enlightenment has the entire discussion in the *Sophist* yielded about the nature of the sophist and the philosopher, and the relationship between them?

An adequate answer to this fourth question would require an extensive study. It would need to set out in detail how, in all parts of the work, Plato is *showing* the reader, rather than formally stating, how close true philosophy is to sophistry in its various guises, how and why they are easily confused, but how at bottom there are crucial differences between philosophy and the various approaches he labels sophistry.[38] The one official statement of the difference is couched in metaphorical terms at 254. There we read that the philosopher—by now identified as the dialectician, the person with the knowledge to discern how kinds combine—clings, through reasoning, to 'what is', and is hard to discern given the brightness of reality, while the sophist too is hard to discern but for the opposite reason: he escapes into the darkness of what is not. Suggestive though this description is, it can only be fully understood in the light of a reading of the whole work. In addition to familiar points of difference—sophists aim for wealth and take paid pupils; they desire victory and renown rather than enlightenment, and a seeming refutation which defeats an opponent, not the genuine one which benefits him—a new point emerges in the argumentation from 239 to 264. The newly displayed difference beteen sophist and true philosopher lies in their respective uses of *aporia*—and here I draw on Frede's important paper, 'The Literary Form of the *Sophist*'.[39] Both

---

[38] Such a study would also need to take account of the *Theaetetus* and *Politicus*, cf. Frede's paper referred to in the next note.

[39] Frede (1996).

sophists and philosophers make use of *aporia*, but the philosopher 'does not leave us with this *aporia* [about what is not], but goes on to break the impasse by showing us that we can say, after all, that what is not is, because the claim that we cannot say this turns out to rest on confusion'. As Frede emphasizes, the *aporiai* of the *Sophist* are used constructively, to help us get clear on a subject; this is the hallmark of the philosopher, as against that group of sophists (personified by the brothers in *Euthydemus*) in whose hands such puzzles are used to refute opponents, not to get clearer about the truth of important matters. The dialogue has revealed to the reader a great deal about the contrast between the approach and interests of the philosopher and those of sophists, but it has done so *not* by producing a definition-by-division of the sophist that is intended to be correct. As such, it leaves open the question how high Plato's hopes were for the method if used on a more promising subject-matter than sophistry.[40]

Bibliography

Ackrill, J. L. (1997), 'In Defence of Platonic Division', in J. L. Ackrill, *Essays on Plato and Aristotle*, Oxford.

Bluck, R. (1975), *Plato's Sophist*, Manchester.

Cavini, W. (1995), 'Naming and Argument: Diairetic Logic in Plato's Statesman', in C. Rowe (ed.), *Reading the Statesman*, Sankt Augustin.

Cherniss, H. F. (1944), *Aristotle's Criticism of Plato and the Academy*, Baltimore.

Cohen, S. M. (1973), 'Plato's Method of Division', in J. M. E. Moravcsik (ed.), *Patterns in Plato's Thought*, Dordrecht.

Cornford, F. M. (1935), *Plato's Theory of Knowledge*, London.

Crivelli, P. (2004), 'Socratic Refutation and Platonic Refutation', in *Socrates: 2400 Years since his Death*, ed. V. Karasmanis, Athens.

Frede, M. (1996), 'The Literary Form of the *Sophist*', in C. Gill and M. M. McCabe (eds.), *Form and Argument in Late Plato*, Oxford.

Gomez-Lobo, A. (1977), 'Plato's Description of Dialectic in the *Sophist* 253d1–e2', *Phronesis* 22.1: 29–47.

Gomez-Lobo, A. (1981), 'Dialectic in the *Sophist*: A Reply to Waletzki', *Phronesis* 26.1: 80–3.

---

[40] I am very grateful to David Charles for helpful discussions and comments on this paper. Thanks also to an anonymous reader and to T. Irwin.

Irwin, T. H. (1977), *Plato's Moral Theory*, Oxford.

Irwin, T. H. (1995), 'Plato's Objections to the Sophists', in A. Powell (ed.), *The Greek World*, London.

Karasmanis, V. (ed.) (2004), *Socrates: 2400 Years since his Death*, Athens.

Kato, S. (1995), 'The Role of *paradeigma* in the Statesman', in C. Rowe (ed.), *Reading the Statesman*, Sankt Augustin.

Kühner, R. and Gerth, B. (1898), *Ausführliche Grammatik der Griechischen Sprache*, Hanover and Leipzig.

Long, A. A. (1998), 'Plato's Apologies and Socrates in the *Theaetetus*', in J. Gentzler (ed.) *Method in Ancient Philosophy*, Oxford.

Moravcsik, J. M. E. (1973), 'Plato's Method of Division' in J. M. E. Moravcsik (ed.), *Patterns in Plato's Thought*, Dordrecht.

Moravcsik, J. M. E. (ed.) (1973), *Patterns in Plato's Thought*, Dordrecht.

Notomi, N. (1999), *The Unity of Plato's Sophist*, Cambridge.

Pellegrin, P. (1986), *Aristotle's Classification of Animals*, tr. A. Preus Berkeley.

Rowe, C. (ed.) (1995), *Reading the Statesman*, Sankt Augustin.

Ryle, G. (1966), *Plato's Progress*, Cambridge.

Sedley, D. (2003), *Plato's Cratylus*, Cambridge.

Sedley, D. (2004), *The Midwife of Platonism*, Oxford.

Sidgwick, H. (1872), 'The Sophists', *Journal of Philology* 4: 288–307.

Taylor, C. C. W. (2006), 'Socrates the Sophist', in R. L. Judson and V. Karasmanis (eds.), *Remembering Socrates*, Oxford; also in *Socrates: 2400 Years since his Death*, ed. V. Karasmanis, Athens, 2004.

Waletzki, W. (1979), 'Platons Ideenlehre und Dialektik im *Sophistes* 253d', *Phronesis* 24.3: 241–52.

5

Division and Definition in Plato's *Sophist* and *Statesman*

MARY LOUISE GILL

The *Sophist* and *Statesman* search for definitions, and both dialogues focus on the search. The *Sophist* speaks often of the hunt in which we are engaged and of the sophist as our quarry. In this hunt the sophist time and again eludes us, taking cover in the darkness of not-being, reappearing occasionally to dispute the very existence of the kind to which we wish to assign him. How can we define the sophist at all, if we cannot get hold of him or accurately characterize the kind to which he belongs? The *Statesman* repeatedly notices the road we are travelling—longer roads and shorter roads that will take us to our destination or lead us astray. The dialogue often reflects on better and worse methods of seeking the goal. The word 'method' itself—μέθοδος—calls attention to the route (ὁδός) we take in our enquiry. The *Sophist* and the first part of the *Statesman* represent the search by means of an elaborate system of branching roads. We travel down these roads; at each fork we must choose which branch to take in the hopes of finding our quarry, and that quarry alone, at the terminus. This method of discovery is called division, and in its most usual form it is the repeated dichotomy of a general kind into subordinate kinds.[1] Enquirers use division to locate a target kind; the definition of that kind recounts the steps of a completed division.[2]

---

[1] I will often use the word 'division' when I mean more strictly dichotomous division. As we shall see below, Plato introduces a different sort of division in the later part of the *Statesman*, which the Stranger calls 'division by limbs'. I regard this as a distinct procedure and will use the longer phrases when distinguishing the two or when there might be some ambiguity.

[2] Because the divisions in the *Sophist* and *Statesman* seem so clumsy and yield such unsatisfactory results, some scholars have thought that Plato could not have taken division seriously as a method of discovery. Ryle (1966, 135–41), exasperated by the technique, suggested that division is at best a

In this paper I will argue that dichotomous division yields a good defin-ition of a target kind only in the simplest and most uncontroversial cases. Plato also uses division in defining more complex kinds, but then it serves as a preliminary strategy, which undertakes to expose some puzzle about the kind under investigation, which the enquirers must resolve in some other way, or at least in conjunction with some other method.

We have trouble catching the sophist, because we find him, not at the end of a single branch, but at many different termini, allowing multiple definitions. We find the statesman at a single terminus, but he has many rivals there, who claim to share his expertise; the definition of the statesman reached by dichotomous division, though very detailed, turns out to be much too general. These disappointing results serve a purpose. Plato wants us to see that something about the sophist explains why he turns up all over the map, and that something about the statesman explains why he has company at the terminus. In each dialogue, reflection on the peculiar outcome of division enables the enquirers to recognize something about the kind in question which helps to explain the peculiarity. The enquirers aim to discover a real definition that applies to all and only instances that fall under a kind, and which specifies its essence—the feature or complex of features that explains why in the case of the sophist he turns up in too many places, and why in the case of the statesman he is not alone at the terminus.

The Angler and the Sophist

Theodorus brings with him to the day's meeting a visitor from Elea, an associate of Parmenides and Zeno and himself a philosopher. Mention of the guest as a philosopher initiates the main discussion of the *Sophist*. What is a genuine philosopher? Philosophers appear in various guises—sometimes they look like statesmen, sometimes like sophists, and sometimes they appear completely mad (216c2–d2). Socrates wants the visitor to tell them what people where he comes from mean by the terms 'sophist', 'statesman', and 'philosopher'. Do the three names label one kind, two, or three (216d3–217a9)? The answer is easy,

preliminary to dialectic for philosophical novices. Crombie (1963, 2: 380–3), too, found division useless in discovering correct definitions and suggested that Plato merely used it in the exposition of them. Cf. Moravcsik (1973), 344. The divisions are indeed odd, but they are odd for a reason, as I hope to show.

says the Stranger. The three names pick out three distinct kinds, but the kinds are not at all easy to define (217b1–4). He defines the first two kinds in the *Sophist* and *Statesman*, and both dialogues anticipate a third dialogue on the philosopher, but we do not have the final dialogue.[3]

The visitor tackles the sophist first, but cautions Theaetetus, whom he selects as his respondent, that they may disagree about what a sophist is:

You must seek in common with me and start first, as it now appears to me, with the sophist, seeking and revealing by means of an account (λόγῳ) what he is (τί ποτ' ἔστι). For at the moment you and I possess only the name (τοὔνομα) in common. The work (τὸ ἔργον) to which each of us gives that name we may perhaps each have privately ourselves, but we should always in every case be in agreement about the thing itself (τὸ πρᾶγμα αὐτό) through accounts (διὰ λόγων), rather than agree on the name alone without an account. It is not the easiest thing in the world to grasp the tribe we now intend to seek—the sophist—what it is. (218b6–c7)

The enquirers must recognize at the outset that people use the word 'sophist' in conversation and think they mean the same thing by the name, when in fact they may mean quite different things. To ensure mutual understanding, speakers need to have more than the name in common: they must agree on the object the name picks out. Furthermore, as the upcoming conversation will demonstrate, they need to understand that object in more than a merely accidental way. The Stranger wants to get hold of the thing itself (τὸ πρᾶγμα αὐτό),[4] and more particularly, what it is (τί ποτ' ἔστι): its essence.

Continuing his previous statement, the Stranger suggests that they need a model, which will help them in their investigation.

[3] For the promises, see *Sph.* 216c2–217b4, with 218b6–c1; 253b9–254b6; *Stm.* 257a1–c2, with 258b2–3. Some scholars (e.g. Frede (1996), 147–50; Notomi (1999), 23–5, 287–8, 297–301) think that we find the philosopher in the *Sophist*. We do encounter him unexpectedly in the discussion of dialectic, the philosopher's method, and on that occasion the Stranger coyly remarks that we will investigate the philosopher more clearly soon, if we still want to (254b3–4). But we never get a portrait of the philosopher and his expertise on a par with those of the sophist and statesman. In my view Plato promised the *Philosopher* and left it unwritten on purpose to stimulate us to use the cues from the *Sophist* and *Statesman* to work out the final portrait ourselves.

[4] The Stranger first speaks of the work (τὸ ἔργον) and then of the thing itself (τὸ πρᾶγμα αὐτό), and this makes sense, because the work—the characteristic activity—makes the expert the sort of expert he is. Cf. *Sph.* 221b2, where αὐτὸ τοὔργον refers to the angler's activity. In the angler's case the characteristic activity expresses the angler's nature, but that is not always the case, as the efforts to define the sophist will show.

When great things need to be elaborated well, it has seemed to everyone even long ago that one should practice them first in small and relatively easy things, before [practicing them] in the greatest things themselves. So now, Theaetetus, that is my advice to us: Since we think the kind, sophist (τὸ τοῦ σοφιστοῦ γένος), is difficult and hard to catch, we ought to practice the pursuit (μεθόδον) of him on something else relatively easy, unless you have some other route (ὁδόν) to suggest, easier to pursue.—No, I have none.—Then shall we pursue one of the lesser things and try to make it a model (παράδειγμα) of the greater thing? (218c7–d9)

Elsewhere Plato speaks of immaterial forms as models (παραδείγματα), and sensible particulars as likenesses of them, which somehow fall short of the original. This notion of a model recurs in the *Sophist*, in the discussion of imitation (235d7), but the *Sophist* and *Statesman* use a different conception of a model as well, which the Stranger introduces in the passage quoted here.[5] This conception of a model involves a mundane example which has a feature—sometimes an essential feature—relevant to the more difficult topic under investigation. The most important models in the *Sophist* and *Statesman* are the angler, which serves as a model for the sophist, and the weaver, which serves as a model for the statesman. Because the example is trivial and can be observed and readily pictured, the instructor can use visual aids if the student has trouble following the verbal account. The enquirers practice giving and receiving an account of the example, and then apply the method to a more difficult case, which cannot be pictured and so can only be understood by verbal means (*Stm.* 285d9–286b1).

A model is not merely an example (or paradigmatic example) of some general concept, such as hunting (angler) or intertwining (weaver), or more generally expertise (both). The search for the definition of the example reveals a procedure, which the enquirers can transfer to the harder case, independent of content. Different models introduce different procedures. In the simple case of the angler, the definition of the example recounts the steps of its discovery, and this structural feature recurs in the definition of the more difficult type. Plato's models in the *Sophist* and *Statesman* reveal a productive next move or series of moves in an investigation. A model

---

[5] For a previous use of this notion, see *Meno* 77a9–b1, where Socrates calls his three sample definitions of shape and color παραδείγματα and intends them to guide Meno's definition of virtue. I thank Glenn Rawson for this reference.

indicates how to go on, how to begin an enquiry or how to get beyond an impasse.[6]

The *Sophist* presents its most important model at the start of the enquiry and demonstrates the way to begin. The model of the angler displays in a straightforward way the method of dichotomous division which the enquirers will use in the upcoming search for the sophist. The divisions are divisions of arts (angling, sophistry), and only secondarily of the experts who possess those arts. The art and its associated activity make the expert the sort of expert he is.[7] An angler has a humble profession, familiar to everyone (218e3–5): he hunts water creatures using a special sort of hook. The visitor arrives at his definition by first locating the angler's profession in a wide kind, art or expertise (τέχνη). Next he divides art into two subordinate kinds, productive and acquisitive, and then continues to divide the acquisitive branch until he reaches angling, fully marked off as what it is apart from everything else (see Diagram 1).[8]

Concluding his discussion of the angler, the Stranger shows Theaetetus the relevance of the example. Just as the angler has a certain expertise, so we expect the same of the sophist. The visitor establishes this connection by reflecting on the sophist's name.

Should we say that the angler is a layman (ἰδιώτην) or has some expertise (τέχνην)?—Yes [some expertise].—And now shall we set this [other] one down as a layman or as altogether truly a sophist (σοφιστήν)?—In no way a layman, for I understand what you mean, that in having that name ['sophist'] he is very far from being such [i.e. a layman].—So, it seems, we have to take him as having some expertise (τέχνην). (221c9–d6)

By reflecting on the sophist's name, which shares the same root as σοφός ('wise man'), the Stranger and Theaetetus agree that he belongs in the same wide kind as the angler, since they both have some expertise (τέχνη).[9] The

---

[6] I discuss models in more detail in Gill (2006).

[7] See n. 4 above. As for expertise and the expert, see *Stm.* 259d4–5, where the Stranger combines statesmanship and statesman and kingship and king into one group.

[8] The definition of angling: 'Of art as a whole, one half portion was acquisitive, and of acquisitive half was taking-possession, and of taking-possession half was hunting, and of hunting half was animal-hunting, and of animal-hunting half was aquatic-hunting, and of aquatic-hunting the whole segment from below was fishing, and of fishing half was striking, and of striking half was hooking. And of hooking the half concerned with a blow drawn up from below—its name assimilated from the work itself—has proved by name to be the thing sought: angling (ἀσπαλιευτική)' (*Sph.* 221b2–c3).

[9] Cf. Notomi (1999), 75. See also *Sph.* 268b10–c4.

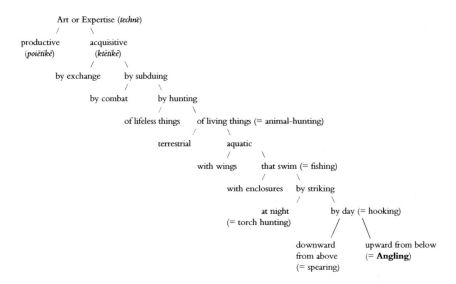

Diagram 1 Angling

Stranger then announces that the two experts have a more intimate connection: both are hunters (221d8–13). In this way the angler guides the first division of the sophist down to hunting, after which the branches diverge, since the sophist hunts creatures that live on dry land, while the angler hunts creatures that inhabit the water. By this division the sophist emerges as a hired hunter of rich young men (see Diagram 2: division leading to Definition 1).[10]

So far the model of the angler seems admirably well-suited to reveal a correct procedure and to guide the enquirers some distance toward their goal. Set on the right track, they readily complete the rest of the division. But at the end of this first division, the Stranger says:

Still, let's look at it also in the following way, since the thing now being sought partakes of no ordinary art, but one that is really quite complicated (ποικίλης). For even in what we said earlier it presented an appearance (φάντασμα) that it is not what we are now saying it is but some different kind. (223c1–4)

---

[10] Definition 1: 'So, Theaetetus, according to the present account, it seems, the hunt for rich and reputable young men, which belongs to appropriative art, hunting, animal-hunting, on dry land, human hunting, <hunting by persuasion>, hunting privately, money-earning, seemingly educative, must be called, as our present account turns out: sophistry' (223b1–6). Cf. 231d2–3.

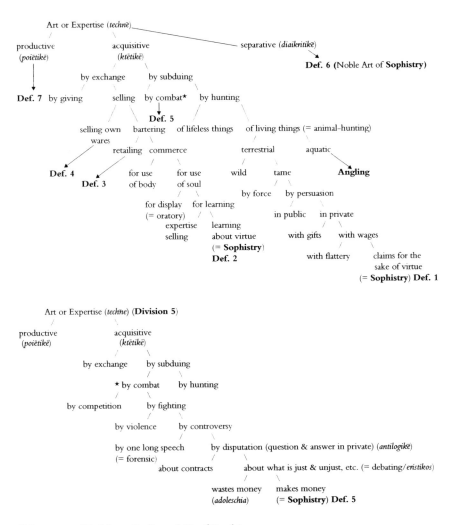

Diagram 2 Divisions (1, 2, and 5) of Sophistry

Now the visitor attends to a feature of the sophist mentioned toward the end of the first division—the sophist earns wages from those he hunts and has a product to sell. Returning to acquisitive art, the Stranger this time ignores the branch that leads to hunting, and instead follows the other branch, beginning from the art of acquisition by exchange, and defines the sophist as someone engaged in commerce, who sells products for the soul, lessons about virtue (see Diagram 2: division leading to Definition 2).[11] In the pages that follow, the Stranger focuses on various activities of the sophist and defines him in five different ways. Each time the sophist turns up at the tips of branches that stem from acquisitive art. Then on a sixth round the Stranger makes a fresh initial division of expertise, marking off the art of separation, and finds the sophist at the terminus of a branch originating from there. We shall return to the sixth division.

What should we make of the fact that the sophist turns up all over the map, and not at a single terminus like the angler? The angler differs from the sophist in two main respects. First, the essence of the angler is evident from his activity and is easy to spell out using dichotomous division. We can observe the angler's essential activity, fishing with a hook. The essence of the sophist, too, might seem easy to observe from his activities, but he is complicated (ποικίλης), and because he engages in a variety of activities, we might define him in several different ways. The essence of the sophist, as we soon discover, is none of those things: the sophist's essential activity cannot be observed and pictured, as angling can.

Second, the nature of angling is uncontroversial—from the start the Stranger and Theaetetus designate the same activity by the name 'angling' (218e4–5; 221a7–b2). By contrast, people conceive of sophistry in different ways, witnessed by the numerous divisions. Because the nature of sophistry is not obvious, people may disagree about what it is, and some conceptions may be simply mistaken.

Appearances

The sophist is not unique in his tendency to turn up in many different places. Any object, including very simple ones, can do the same, because people experience the same thing in different ways and so have different conceptions of it.[12] Whereas most people share the same conception of an

---

[11] Definition 2: 'Sophistry has been revealed a second time as the selling that belongs to the acquisitive art, exchange, trading, commerce, soul-commerce concerned with accounts and sorts of learning about virtue' (224c9–d2). Cf. 231d5–6.

[12] Consider a very simple object, the letter Θ. Socrates in the *Theaetetus* argues that we may not know the letter, even though we get it right every time we spell the name 'Theaetetus' in Greek. Getting the letter right in that name does not assure correct use in other words. We know the letter only if we can

angler, because he engages in a single observable activity, they may well have different views of complex things which engage in several activities. Some conceptions may capture the entity by a feature or activity essential to it, but many others will capture it in some accidental way. Division does not itself guarantee that one attends to essential features. Furthermore, disputes might arise about virtually any object, but we can often settle them by perception or by some recognized test (we can settle disputes about number by counting; disputes about size or weight by measuring or weighing).[13] Plato's late dialogues investigate complex and controversial kinds, and disputes about them cannot be readily settled.

The anomalous sixth division of the sophist (226b1–231b8) reveals that sophistry itself is a disputed type. Whereas the first five divisions locate the sophist somewhere under acquisitive art, the sixth division locates the sophist in a quite different place, under the art of separation, which the Stranger did not mark off in the original dichotomous division (see Diagram 3). This sophist purifies souls of beliefs that interfere with learning, and he looks a lot like Socrates. The visitor queries using the label 'sophist' in this case and calls the art he has just uncovered the 'noble' art of sophistry, saying that the noble sophist resembles the others as a dog resembles a wolf. The sixth division exploits the fact that many people mistook Socrates for a sophist.[14] This definition fails to capture the sophist by even an accidental feature, but instead captures a distinct type, which merely shares the same name owing to a superficial resemblance.[15]

---

reliably use it in the whole range of contexts in which it occurs, and to have that flexibility we must grasp the letter by its essence, those features it must have regardless of context. Recognizing Θ as the first letter in Theaetetus' name is an instance of grasping something correctly but by an accidental feature. I discuss the significance of this example in Gill (2003).

[13] See *Euth.* 7b7–c9. *Phdr.* 263a2–c12 differentiates words like 'iron' and 'silver' from words like 'just' and 'good'. We have straightforward procedures to decide whether something is iron, but not for disputed concepts, like justice.

[14] Aristophanes' *Clouds* parodied Socrates as a sophist. Socrates acknowledges at his trial (as represented by Plato in the *Apology*) that many people associated him with the sophists, and he defends himself from that association, especially on the matter of charging fees.

[15] The *Phaedrus* presents an analogous case. The first part of the dialogue discusses two quite different things called 'love'—one characterized as a human sickness, the other as divine inspiration. In the second part of the dialogue, Socrates locates both under a higher kind, madness (265e1–266b1). Though both types are called 'love' and fall under the same wide kind, they are two distinct sub-kinds of madness, one human, the other divine.

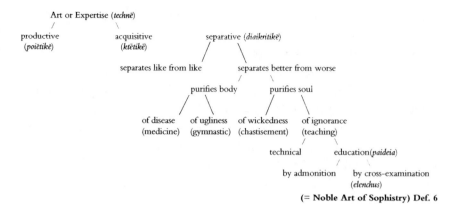

Diagram 3 Sixth Division of the Sophist

By the end of the sixth division Theaetetus is perplexed. The sophist has appeared in so many ways that the boy wonders what a sophist really is (231b9–c2). His perplexity prepares him to make a discovery.

The sophist is special not because he turns up in so many places, or because some conceptions pick out different types altogether which merely share the same name. The sophist is unique because the multiplicity in his case reflects not only something about us and our experience, but also something about him and his art. The Stranger restates the six definitions of the sophist (231c9–e7), and then observes:

Do you know that, when someone appears to know many things, and is called by the name of one art, this appearance (φάντασμα) is not sound, but it is clear that the person experiencing (ὁ πάσχων) it in relation to some art is unable to see that [feature] of it toward which all these sorts of learning look, and so he addresses the person having them by many names rather than one? (232a1–6)

The Stranger has defined the sophist as a hired hunter of rich young men, as engaged in selling his own and other people's wares for the soul, as an expert in disputation about justice and injustice, and so on. Six times he called the type defined by the name 'sophist'. But we can also call that kind by many names rather than one: a 'hunter', a 'merchant', an 'eristic', a 'teacher', and so forth.[16] Our judgement is unsound because we, who experience the sophist's appearance of manifold expertise, fail to recognize that feature of

---

[16] I thank John Ferrari for helping me see this. Cf. Notomi (1999), 80.

his art 'toward which all these sorts of learning look'—something about the
sophist that explains why he seems to know so much, something about him
that would justify our calling him by one name: 'sophist'.

What is that one thing we are missing? The Stranger suggests that they
take up an earlier point about the sophist, which reveals him especially
clearly. The fifth definition characterized the sophist as someone skilled in
dispute (ἀντιλογικόν) (see Diagram 2: division leading to Definition 5),[17]
who claims he can teach others to do the same thing. The Stranger now
asks, *about what* (περὶ τίνος) does the sophist claim to make others skilled in
dispute (232b2–c1)? What is the special *object* of his expertise? Sophists
dispute about divine matters and profess to make others competent to do
so; they dispute about things on earth and in the heavens; they dispute about
generation and being; they dispute about laws and all sorts of political issues.
In short, their capacity seems sufficient to engage in controversies *about
everything* (περὶ πάντων) (232c1–e4). But how can anyone know and dispute
about everything? The sophists' secret is their ability to make people *think*
they are wise about everything—otherwise no one would pay them fees.
We are missing the feature of sophists that explains how they can successfully *appear* wise (σοφοὶ ... φαίνονται) in all things to their students, when
they *are not* in fact wise (οὐκ ὄντες γε) (233c6–8). The guest and Theaetetus
carefully defined the sophist in terms of many of his activities but none of
those make him what he is. They have so far missed the essence of the
sophist, and for that reason they mistakenly call him by many names rather
than one.

The Stranger introduces a new model (παράδειγμα, 233d3) to help reveal
the special nature of the sophist's art. Consider someone who claims to *make*
all things by means of a single art. The art of imitation might enable him to
do that, since one can make products with the same names as the originals
(234b1–10). The imitator might fool children, who gaze at his products from
a distance, into thinking he can make anything he wants (234b5–10).
Someone might also achieve that result with statements (λόγοι), and make
large things appear small, and easy things hard (234c2–e2). This person, too,
could fool young people who do not know. In short, the sophist is a sort of
wizard, who imitates things with words (234e7–235a4). What links all the

---

[17] Notomi (1999), 246–61 helpfully links the sophist's imitative ability to his art of disputation
(*antilogikē*) in the fifth division.

appearances together is the sophist's skill at imitating people who truly know the things he appears to know.

With that insight, the Stranger announces that we have nearly caught the sophist, and he sets out in pursuit (he finally completes this seventh division at the end of the dialogue). This time the visitor ignores the entire branch of acquisitive art from which the first five divisions set out and instead takes the branch of productive art down to image-making, which he divides into two parts: copy-making ($\epsilon i\kappa a\sigma\tau\iota\kappa\eta$), and appearance-making ($\phi a\nu\tau a\sigma\tau\iota\kappa\eta$). Whereas a copy-maker preserves the proportions of the model ($\pi a\rho\acute{a}\delta\epsilon\iota\gamma\mu a$ in its more usual sense) and keeps the appropriate colors and other details, an appearance-maker distorts the true proportions of the original, so that the image appears beautiful from a distance (235e5–236c7).[18] In which group should we locate the sophist? The Stranger's declared uncertainty on this point takes him into the dialogue's main project, the investigation of not-being.[19] He has to make sense of appearances:

This appearing ($\tau\grave{o}\dots\phi a\acute{\iota}\nu\epsilon\sigma\theta a\iota\ \tau o\hat{v}\tau o$) and seeming ($\tau\grave{o}\ \delta o\kappa\epsilon\hat{\iota}\nu$), but not being ($\epsilon\hat{\iota}\nu a\iota\ \delta\grave{\epsilon}\ \mu\acute{\eta}$), and stating things ($\tau\grave{o}\ \lambda\acute{\epsilon}\gamma\epsilon\iota\nu\ \mu\grave{\epsilon}\nu\ \mathring{a}\tau\tau a$), but not true [things] ($\mathring{a}\lambda\eta\theta\hat{\eta}\ \delta\grave{\epsilon}\ \mu\acute{\eta}$), all these were always full of difficulty in the past and they still are. It is very hard, Theaetetus, to find terms in which to say that there really is false stating or judging, and to utter this without being caught in a contradiction. (236e1–237a1)

In essence the sophist *produces appearances*, and more precisely *false* appearances. So to understand the sophist, the enquirers have to make sense of appearances and their production, and to do that the Stranger investigates not-being and false statement. This is not the occasion to explore those complex issues, but let me conclude our discussion of the sophist with some observations.[20]

Later in the dialogue the Stranger analyzes appearing as a combination of perception and judgement ($\delta\acute{o}\xi a$), and judgement as a silent statement (264a4–b4).[21] Since an appearance contains a judgement, and judgement is a silent statement, the Stranger's analysis of statements reveals something also about appearances: appearances are *structured*. The simplest statement

---

[18] Think of the statues on medieval churches, which look ill-proportioned when seen from close up in a museum: their large heads and small legs are designed to look right when viewed from the ground high up on a building.

[19] For claims identifying this as the key uncertainty, see 235d2–3, 236c9–d3; cf. 264c4–8.

[20] I develop these ideas further in Gill (2005/2009), §§ 5–6.

[21] Cf. *Tht.* 189e6–190a7.

contains two parts, a noun and a verb, each with a distinct function. The noun refers to an object, and the verb states something about the object. A statement must be about something, since the visitor shows in a series of puzzles about not-being that we cannot speak coherently of nothing (237b7–239c8)—a point he recalls later in the dialogue (263c9–11). Every statement, and so every appearance, is a statement or appearance of something. A statement is true or false depending on whether the verb states something that is or is not the case about the subject. The verb 'is sitting' in 'Theaetetus is sitting' states something that is the case about Theaetetus, if Theaetetus is sitting, while the verb 'is flying' in 'Theaetetus is flying' states something that is not the case about him (262e13–263b13).

To make a statement is to *produce* an appearance, one that can be true or false. The many appearances of the sophist from which we set out reflect *our* judgements about things to which we apply the name 'sophist'. Most of those appearances were true but characterized the sophist by some accidental feature. His final appearance as someone who produces false appearances is true, and a definition of that appearance specifies his essence.

The final division, though it yields a definition of the sophist's essence, is still incomplete. Remember that the seventh division stalled with the Stranger's question whether he should class the sophist as a copy-maker or appearance-maker. The analysis of appearance, via the enquiry into not-being and false statement, enables the enquirers to locate the sophist's art in the kind *phantastikē* (appearance-making). The Stranger then completes the rest of the division fairly quickly by separating off in steps the kind that includes the sophist from other appearance-makers—appearance-makers who use other things as tools, then informed imitators, simple imitators, and demagogues (see Diagram 4). Division 7 terminates with a definition of what the sophist essentially is (268c8–d4), and the structure of the definition echoes that of the angler at the start.[22] In essence, the sophist creates the false appearance that he is wise, and thus imitates a man who really is wise (268b10–c4).

Grasping the essence of the target does not ensure our understanding of it, and Division 7 has done no more than map the right terrain. How can we

---

[22] Definition 7: 'The imitator who belongs to the insincere part of the art of conjectural contradiction-making, the part that conjures in words, which belongs to the appearance-making kind of image-making, marked off in the human, not divine, portion of productive art—whoever says that the true sophist is 'of this blood and lineage' will, as it seems, speak things most true' (268c8–d4).

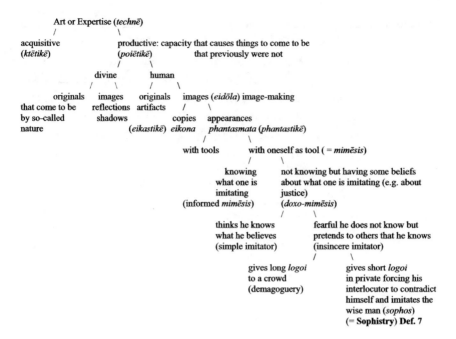

Diagram 4 Seventh Division of the Sophist

know the sophist without knowing the wise man he imitates? Who is the *sophos*? One might think that the wise man is the philosopher, but the *Statesman* reveals that there are wise men and dangerous pretenders in any field that deals with humans and their welfare. The statesman has many imitators who rule various sorts of degenerate states, whom the Stranger calls 'the greatest sophists among the sophists' (*Stm.* 303c4–5). There are others as well—the quack who charges large fees and has no business treating the sick imitates the true doctor; and the incompetent steersman, who risks sinking the ship, losing the cargo, and drowning the sailors, imitates the true helmsman (*Stm.* 298a1–e3).

The Statesman and the Herdsman

The *Statesman* embarks on its opening division without a model. The angler from the previous dialogue appears to be an acceptable guide for the method of dichotomous division itself.[23] To get started, the Eleatic visitor relies on a different procedure, identified in the *Phaedrus* as collection (*Phdr.* 265d3–5). A collection gathers into one kind (εἰς μίαν ἰδέαν) disparate items that have some common feature relevant to the investigation.[24] The technique gives the enquirers a single kind which either focuses the whole investigation or can itself be divided into subordinate kinds.[25] The *Statesman* opens its investigation with a collection of entities that appear to belong to the target kind:

Shall we posit the statesman, the king, the slave-master, and further the household manager, as one thing, although we call them all these names, or should we say there are as many arts as the names used? (258e8–11)

The visitor points out that, despite the difference in names, all these people have in common a power to maintain their rule (ἀρχή) by the strength of their understanding with little use of their hands and bodies (259c6–8).[26] This group of features allows a rough and ready description of the kind to be defined, which the enquirers hope to find at the terminus of their division.[27]

[23] In retrospect the herdsman is called a model (παράδειγμα) (275b3–7), but he is not introduced as such. The association of the statesman with a herdsman was probably conventional, relying on the Homeric epithet of Agamemnon as shepherd of the people (e.g. *Il.* 2.243, 254 [ποιμὴν λαῶν]). For discussion, see Miller (1980), 40–3.

[24] In practice, the items collected can be so diverse that virtually the only feature they have in common is the one the Stranger wishes to single out. The *Sophist* includes many instances of collection. At 219a10–c1, the visitor collects farming and generally care of all mortal bodies, and the kind concerned with things put together and fabricated, and imitation into one group, which he calls productive art; at 219c2–9, he collects the whole kind to do with learning, and that of recognition, and money-making, combat, and hunting into one group, which he calls acquisitive art. Cf. the collection at 226b2–c8 to yield the art of separation. Collections can occur at any stage of a division—for an intermediate kind, see 222c5–7, where a collection of activities yields hunting by force. Thus I differ from Lane (1998), 14, who denies a role to collection in the *Sophist* and *Statesman*.

[25] Collection without division often occurs in the Socratic dialogues, at the start of an investigation. When Socrates asks 'What is X?' the interlocutor often initially gives some sort of list—e.g. *Euth.* 5d8–e2; *Meno* 71e1–72a5; *Tht.* 146c7–d3. Socrates always objects to the list and insists that he wants to know what all the items have in common, what it is that makes them all examples of one kind. Although Socrates objects, the list is very important in getting the investigation started, because reflection on the items enumerated can help one recognize the common character they share.

[26] Aristotle opens his *Politics* by recalling Plato's collection, which he then criticizes. Whereas Plato thought the statesman, king, household manager, and slave-master belong to the same kind and differ from each other only in the number of their subjects (*Stm.* 259b9–10), Aristotle thinks these rulers and managers differ in kind (*Pol.* I.1, 1252a7–23). Given how seriously he takes Plato's proposal, one suspects that Aristotle may have missed the preliminary nature of the collection, whose purpose is simply to reveal some common features which the enquirers take to characterize the target kind, the statesman. This is the very beginning of Plato's investigation, not his conclusion.

[27] The idea of ruling/controlling (ἄρχειν) recurs throughout the dialogue, and especially at the end. See e.g. 260e8–9; 275a3–6; 304b11–c1, c5; 305a1, d1–5, e2; 311b7–c7.

Since the members of the target kind can direct and control other people by means of their understanding without physical manipulation, the Stranger starts his division from the wide kind knowledge (ἐπιστήμη) and immediately divides it into practical and theoretical. He then seeks to locate the target at a terminus stemming from theoretical knowledge.[28]

The opening division takes place in two stages—a first stage that focuses on the statesman's knowledge, followed by a lecture on method, and a second stage that focuses on the object of that knowledge (see Diagram 5). Both phases of the division are peculiar but in quite different ways.

Consider stage one. Having set off down the theoretical branch in search of the statesman, the Stranger divides theoretical knowledge into two subkinds. One kind recognizes difference, judges things recognized and then leaves off (the Stranger locates the art of calculation here); the other kind recognizes difference and judges things recognized, and then directs on the basis of that selection (he locates statecraft here) (259d7–260c5). Directing suggests practical, if not hands-on, knowledge. Keep in mind that the Stranger marked off practical knowledge and abandoned it at the start. Next he divides directive knowledge into two sorts: one sort passes on the directions of others (heralds belong here), while the other passes on its own directions for the sake of generation (γένεσις) (the statesman belongs here) (260c6–261b3). Knowledge for the sake of generation/production again suggests practical knowledge.[29] The statesman's knowledge looks ever more practical as the division continues. At the next division one kind passes on its own directions to generate inanimate things (the master-builder belongs here), whereas the other generates animate things (the statesman belongs here) (261b4–d3). The Stranger then divides this latter

---

[28] At 258e4–5, the visitor says that one sort of knowledge is practical, the other *only* theoretical (τὴν δὲ μόνον γνωστικήν). This move supports Cavini's (1995) provocative treatment of diaeretic arguments in the *Statesman*, according to which the two branches are exclusive. The statesman has either practical knowledge or theoretical knowledge; since he has theoretical knowledge, he does not have practical knowledge (127). But Cavini ignores the division after the first two steps, and the actual division poses a problem for his analysis. At the very next step, as we shall see, the Stranger starts mixing practical knowledge into the theoretical branch. He has prepared us for this development, because he asks Young Socrates at the outset whether the king is *more akin* (οἰκειότερον) to theoretical knowledge than to manual and in general practical knowledge (259c10–d2). The king's expertise may be more akin to the one than the other, and still involve both.

[29] Compare the original characterization of practical knowledge: 'The sorts of expertise concerned with carpentry and all manufacture have their knowledge contained as it were in their actions, and use it to complete the bodies generated by them that previously were not (τὰ γιγνόμενα ... σώματα πρότερον οὐκ ὄντα)' (258d8–e2, with 258e4–5).

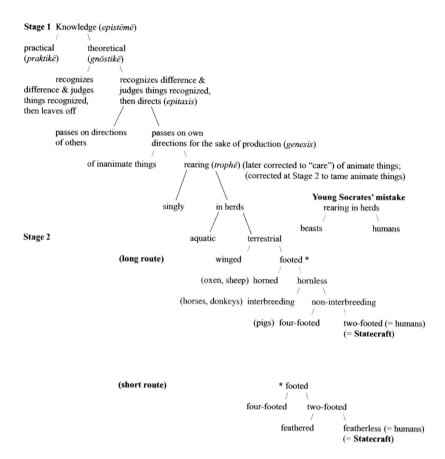

Stage 1 Knowledge (*epistēmē*)

practical   theoretical
(*praktikē*)   (*gnōstikē*)

recognizes   recognizes difference &
difference & judges   judges things recognized,
things recognized,   then directs (*epitaxis*)
then leaves off

passes on directions   passes on own
of others   directions for the sake of production (*genesis*)

of inanimate things   rearing (*trophē*) (later corrected to "care") of animate things;
               (corrected at Stage 2 to tame animate things)

Young Socrates' mistake
rearing in herds

singly   in herds   beasts   humans

Stage 2

(long route)   aquatic   terrestrial

winged   footed *

(oxen, sheep) horned   hornless

(horses, donkeys) interbreeding   non-interbreeding

(pigs) four-footed   two-footed (= humans)
                (= **Statecraft**)

(short route)   * footed

four-footed   two-footed

feathered   featherless (= humans)
               (= **Statecraft**)

Diagram 5 Division of Statecraft (dichotomous division)

kind into those who generate and rear single animate things (ox-drivers and grooms belong here), and those who generate and rear them in herds (the statesman and herdsman belong here) (261d4–11). Once the statesman merges with the herdsman, the theoretical branch has become thoroughly mixed up with the practical branch originally discarded. The knowledge of horse-breeders, cowherds, shepherds, and swineherds is practical and scarcely theoretical.

At the end of the first stage of the division, when the enquirers have reached herd-rearing, the Stranger invites Young Socrates to make the next division himself. By now Socrates sees where the division is heading and proposes to mark off the rearing of humans (= statecraft) from the rearing of beasts (θηρίων) (ordinary herding) (262a3–4). The Stranger objects that that is like dividing the human race into Greek and barbarian—we have a name 'barbarian', but it merely refers to humans who do not speak Greek. The mistake is like marking off the number 10,000 from all the other numbers (262a9–263a1); numbers other than 10,000 share merely a negative property—being numbers other than 10,000. The Stranger insists that Young Socrates divide through the middle of things, not break off one small part, leaving many large ones behind, which fail to constitute a kind. This statement seems to recall Socrates' rule about division in the *Phaedrus*: Divide at the natural joints—don't hack off bits like a bad butcher! (*Phdr.* 265e1–3).

Although the visitor admits that they are wandering from their topic and should put off this discussion until another occasion, he tarries a little longer to give a lecture on the difference between mere parts of a thing and parts that are themselves genuine kinds (263b2–11). Apparently real kinds include only members that have some positive feature in common, while some parts have members that share merely a negative feature. Scholars have taken the Stranger's lecture very seriously as indicating Plato's views about proper procedure and the metaphysics on which division relies.[30] But before we assess Young Socrates' mistake and the Stranger's lecture, we should consider the second stage of the division, which purportedly demonstrates correct procedure.

First the visitor retraces his steps and points out that in speaking of rearing animate things, they had already in effect divided living creatures into wild and tame (264a1–3). All rearing deals with tame creatures, and some of that rearing devotes itself to tame animals in herds. He then divides herd-rearing into aquatic and terrestrial (the branch he pursues). Next he marks off the winged from the footed (the branch he pursues); then the horned (oxen, sheep) from the hornless (the branch he pursues); then the interbreeding (horses, donkeys) from the non-interbreeding (the branch he pursues); and finally the four-footed (just pigs are left) from the two-footed (humans). He now defines statecraft as rearing the two-footed, non-interbreeding, hornless, footed, terrestrial, tame herd: humans (267a8–c3).

---

[30] See the subtle and resourceful discussions of Moravcsik (1973), Cohen (1973), and Wedin (1987).

This division has given Platonic division a bad name. Why does Young Socrates go along with it, when there is so much to query?[31] When the Stranger presents longer and shorter divisions that yield the same result, why does Young Socrates not object that the longer route marks off the terrestrial kind into the footed, hornless, non-interbreeding, two-footed kind, whereas the shorter route marks off the same kind into the footed, two-footed, featherless kind (266e4–11)? Why do we need featherless in the short division but not in the longer one? Why, indeed, does the short route require a final division into feathered and featherless, given an earlier division (common to both routes) into winged and footed (264e6)? Perhaps a division of two-footed herds into feathered and featherless yields two relatively equal groups and so counts as dividing through the middle of things, but divisions in the long route into horned and hornless, interbreeding and non-interbreeding appear to make the same error the Stranger chastised Young Socrates for making—of cutting off a small part and leaving many large ones behind.[32]

In retrospect Young Socrates' division of herding into the herding of humans and the herding of other animals seems to have considerable merit and to apply two lessons from earlier in the day. First, according to the *Sophist*, a property and its negation, such as large and not-large or beautiful and not-beautiful, are both forms with their own natures (*Sph.* 257e9–258c5).[33] If the not-beautiful is a form, Socrates made no error in treating animals other than human as a form—the form even has a positive name: 'beast' (θηρίον). Second, the Stranger said in the *Sophist* that parts of knowledge derive their names from the objects they are set over (*Sph.* 257c7–d2).[34] Relying on those earlier guidelines, Young Socrates reason-

---

[31] For a detailed critique, see Dorter (1994), 181–95.

[32] At 265a1–5 the Stranger claims that the short route, in contrast to the long route, fails to follow the advice he gave Young Socrates at 262a9–b2. In fact, both routes appear to make Socrates' mistake.

[33] Wedin (1987, 223–4 and n. 20) also compares the passage on negative forms in the *Sophist* with the Stranger's lecture on parts and kinds in the *Statesman*, though we draw different conclusions.

[34] This idea was also emphasized early in the *Theaetetus*, a dialogue dramatically linked to the *Sophist* and *Statesman*. When Socrates first asks Theaetetus to define knowledge, the boy lists various sorts of knowledge: disciplines Theodorus teaches, like arithmetic and geometry, and crafts like cobbling. As I remarked in n. 25 above, Socrates criticizes the list because he did not ask for kinds of knowledge distinguished by their objects; he wants to know what all those different kinds have in common (*Tht.* 146c7–e11). But when it comes to distinguishing branches of knowledge from one another, appeal to their different objects is highly relevant. The idea will recur later in the *Statesman* in the dichotomous division that leads to weaving. See *Stm.* 279c7–280a6 and Diagram 6.

ably thinks that he can distinguish the statesman's knowledge from other forms of herding by their objects: humans and beasts.

Socrates made the right cut, but he is thinking of the objects in the wrong way, given the target of the investigation. The Stranger exploits the mistake in the second stage of the division, relying on Socrates' assumption that herding is a single undifferentiated activity, whose branches can be differentiated by the physical traits of the animals herded. But how are the physical features of humans relevant to statecraft? One notices that something has gone awry when the swineherd turns up more closely akin to the statesman than he is to the cowherd and shepherd.

At the end of the division, the Stranger points to a major difference between the herding of humans and the herding of all other animals. Only the statesman faces rivals who claim that they rear humankind. The cowherd takes care of all the needs of his herd, and no one disputes his role: he is their match-maker, their doctor, and their trainer. The same is true of all other herdsmen, with the sole exception of the herdsman of humans, the statesman. In his case everyone competes for the title of care-taker: farmers provide humans with food, doctors cure their diseases, physical trainers guide their exercise, and so on (267c8–268c11; 275d8–e2). Some important difference between humans and other animals accounts for the rivalry in one case and not in the others, but it is not biological difference.

Human beings are the objects of many sorts of expertise—human biology, anthropology, human medicine, psychology, sociology, statecraft, and others. Different branches of knowledge deal with the same object, but they do so from their own perspective. The perspective on humans determines the wider kind to which humankind belongs—for instance, human biology studies humans as biological beings and sociology studies them as social beings. Young Socrates went wrong in assuming that humans are the objects of statecraft in the same way that other animals are the objects of the various kinds of herding. There was no need for the complicated second stage of the dichotomous division—it merely shows Young Socrates that if he does not think before he sets out on his divisions he will waste a great deal of time on something unnecessary.

The Stranger's lecture on parts (e.g. barbarian) and kinds (forms characterized by some positive feature) is misleading, because it suggests that division starts at the top of a tree with some wide kind, which breaks at natural joints into sub-kinds. But that is not the way dichotomous division works.[35] The target at the *bottom* of the tree—however vague or even misguided the initial conception of it—determines the selection of the wide kind at the start, the proper first division, and relevant next steps.[36] Different target kinds (the angler, the sophist, the statesman) prompt the investigators to carve up the world in different ways.[37] At the beginning of the *Statesman*, the Stranger pretends that the wide kind divided in the *Sophist* was knowledge (ἐπιστήμη) (in fact it was τέχνη) and claims that in the search for the statesman we must divide the sorts of knowledge (τὰς ἐπιστήμας) as we did with the sophist, but not in the same place (258b2–e5). In the search for the sophist he made a first division into acquisitive and productive, whereas in the search for the statesman he made a first division into practical and theoretical.[38] Thus what counts as a 'natural joint' (*Phdr.* 265e1–3; cf. *Stm.* 262a9–b2), a proper break between kinds, depends on the goal of the investigation. The present target is statecraft, and its definition, when ultimately discovered, will mention humans, since the city is the object of the statesman's knowledge, and humans make up a city, but the essence of statecraft depends on its *perspective* on humans, as members of a city.

The upcoming myth, which I will not discuss, reveals that the difference between humans and other animals relevant to statecraft is not their biological difference but their way of life, and for humans that means their culture and expertise (274b1–d8). But refocusing attention away from the physical features of the animals herded to their ways of life still misses the chief difference between statecraft and other forms of herding, since the statesman, unlike other herdsmen, faces competition. Why does the statesman *alone* deserve the name 'statesman', when the farmers and doctors and physical trainers also tend the needs of humans who live in a city (275b1–7)?

This is the puzzle of the statesman. To solve it we must grasp the *manner* (τρόπος) of the statesman's rule (275a4)—the *structure* of his expertise—since this is what differentiates the statesman from others engaged in the care of

---

[35] We should note that in continuing his digression on parts and forms the Stranger warns Young Socrates not to think that he has ever heard a clear account of the matter from him (263b2–4), and thus alerts us that the present distinction does not match other things he has said (e.g. in the *Sophist*).

[36] Thus, if the target were Greek-speaker, a division of humankind into Greek and barbarian would be quite appropriate.

[37] Cf. Ackrill (1970), 384; Cavini (1995), 131.

[38] Recall, too, that the Stranger added a third branch in the *Sophist* when he went looking for the noble sophist in the sixth division.

humans.[39] The Stranger articulates that structure by means of a different divisional method.

The Weaver and the Statesman

The first stage of the earlier division, as we noticed, tangled the threads of theoretical and practical knowledge. That difficulty arose because, as we finally learn, the art of the statesman, though theoretical, is also a practical expertise.[40] Because of the nature of his art, the statesman is closely connected with everyone engaged in the care of humans: he looks out for the good of the city as a whole and coordinates the activities of the citizens who compose it. So their business is also his business. The tangling of threads suggests a model. Perhaps the statesman somehow *combines* theoretical and practical knowledge in managing his flock. Indeed, perhaps his essence is or includes the art of combining, like a weaver. The last part of the dialogue recognizes this connection and takes weaving as its model. Weaving shares with statecraft the same business ($\pi\rho\alpha\gamma\mu\alpha\tau\epsilon\acute{\iota}\alpha$), but on a very small scale (279a7–b6).

The Stranger quickly presents a dichotomous division that yields the art of weaving. As in the second stage of the earlier division, the Stranger targets the object of weaving—clothes—and defines weaving as the art in charge of clothes, which takes its name from the object: clothes-working ($\acute{\iota}\mu\alpha\tau\iota\upsilon\rho\gamma\iota\kappa\acute{\eta}$) (279c7–280a6) (see Diagram 6). Like the definition of the statesman reached in the first part of the dialogue, this definition suffers from being too general, since many arts compete for the same title: carding, spinning, spindle-making, mending, clothes-cleaning, and others. The dichotomous division fails to isolate the *perspective* on clothes proper to weaving and the special *manner* in which it deals with clothes.

The model of weaving serves two main functions. First, it introduces a new procedure, which shows how to mark off the art to be defined from others akin to it, which are all housed in the lowest kind reached by the earlier

---

[39] Cf. Lane (1998), 44.

[40] 284c1–4 and 289d1–2 describe the statesman as concerned with practical activity ($\pi\rho\hat{\alpha}\xi\iota s$). Later the statesman's practical knowledge is denied (305d1–5), but at the very end of the dialogue the Stranger once again speaks of the statesman's practical expertise (311b8).

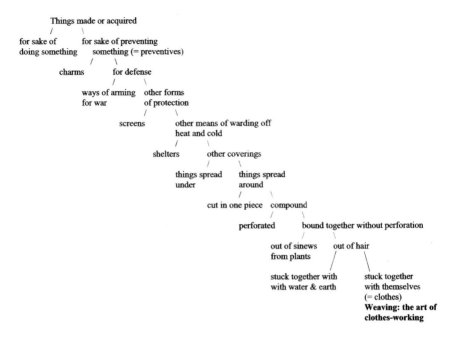

Things made or acquired
/   \
for sake of   for sake of preventing
doing something   something (= preventives)
/   \
charms   for defense
/   \
ways of arming   other forms
for war   of protection
/   \
screens   other means of warding off
heat and cold
/   \
shelters   other coverings
/   \
things spread   things spread
under   around
/   \
cut in one piece   compound
/   \
perforated   bound together without perforation
/   \
out of sinews   out of hair
from plants   /   \
/
stuck together with   stuck together
with water & earth   with themselves
(= clothes)
**Weaving: the art of
clothes-working**

Diagram 6 Weaving (dichotomous division)

dichotomous division (see Diagram 7). The visitor characterizes the new procedure as division 'by limbs (κατὰ μέλη), like a sacrificial animal' (287c3–5).[41]
Whereas dichotomous division separates by halves, and then ignores at each step
the branch that does not lead to the goal, division by limbs breaks off parts of an
original whole, whose members are interrelated and share a common object. All
the arts of clothes-working have clothes as their object, but they deal with
different aspects of clothes, and so differ in the manner of their care.

   The Stranger first divides these arts (dichotomously) into helping causes
(συναίτιοι) and causes (αἰτίαι). All the competing arts of clothes-working,
whether helping causes or causes, somehow serve the art of weaving. Some
subordinate arts relate to it more closely than others. The Stranger divides
the art of wool-working (dichotomously) into arts that separate and
those that combine; he identifies carding as an art that separates the wool

---

[41] I am grateful to Dimitri El Murr, Mitchell Miller, and David Charles for stimulating me to think
more about division by limbs and how it relates to dichotomous division. El Murr (2005) sees more
similarity between them than I do, and he argues that the *Statesman* is unified by the development of a
single division.

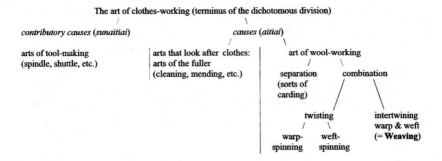

Diagram 7 Weaving (division *kata melē*: by limbs)

(282b10–c3), and both spinning and weaving as arts that combine it. Once spinning twists the wool into the threads that will constitute the warp and weft, weaving uses those products and intertwines the two (282c11–283a8). Weaving is a master craft, and the Stranger defines it in relation to the arts whose activities it oversees and whose products it uses. The same procedure will define the statesman's art in relation to its subordinate arts (see Diagram 8).

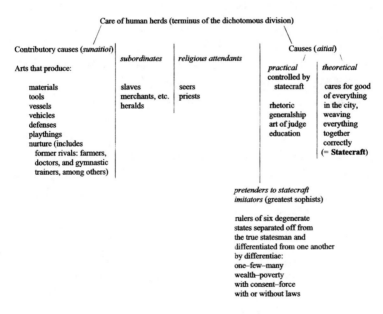

Diagram 8 Statecraft (division *kata melē*)

Second, like the model of angling, weaving not only indicates a useful procedure that yields a definition of the art, but also serves as an example. The essence of weaving—intertwining different kinds of threads—indicates an essential feature of statecraft. The statesman weaves in a number of ways. In particular, he weaves together into one fabric the virtues of courage and moderation, which often clash in the city. People prone to courage serve as the sturdy warp of his fabric, while those prone to orderliness provide the soft and abundant weft (309a8–b7).

In addition to intertwining, the statesman and the weaver use a special art of measurement (283b1–287b2). Whereas ordinary people measure the more and the less in relation to each other, weavers and statesmen and other experts measure the more and the less in relation to some good and fine thing they aim to achieve (284a1–b2).[42] Like the weaver, too, the statesman directs the subsidiary experts, whose products and activities he uses (308d1–e2). The statesman directs the experts who are, as it were, the practical arms of his expertise: the orator, the general, the judge, and the teacher. The statesman must be an expert in timing to determine when the general should go to war, though he leaves it to the general to work out the details of military strategy and to carry them out.[43] He must determine the good that rhetoric will serve, though he leaves the techniques of persuasion and its practice to the rhetorician; he must decide whether to achieve a particular goal through force or persuasion and then delegate the tasks to the appropriate experts; he must also decide what is just and lawful, though he leaves it to the judges to implement his judgement. The statesman must further determine what mix of courage and moderation will most advance the good in the city, though he leaves it to the teachers to instil in the youth the right belief about what is good (308e4–310a5).

The statesman cares for every aspect of things in the city, *weaving* things together in the most correct way (305e2–6). He resembles other herdsmen after all in that he too cares for all the needs of his herd—he oversees their marriages, their education, their health and safety (310a1–5), but he does so in a quite distinctive way, since he delegates tasks to his subordinates. His

---

[42] The Stranger says that they measure excess and defect 'in relation to the generation of the measured' (πρὸς τὴν τοῦ μετρίου γένεσιν, 284c1), or simply in relation to the measured, the fitting (τὸ πρέπον), the timely (τὸν καιρόν), what ought to be (τὸ δέον) and 'everything that has moved house from the extremes to the middle' (284e6–8). Sayre (2006) discusses the second art of measurement in detail.

[43] Lane (1998) emphasizes the role of timing in the statesman's art.

single and whole task is to weave all the good but diverse elements together into a smooth and well-fashioned fabric, the city.

Earlier the Stranger said that the statesman does not act but rules those who act, at one remove from the day-to-day practical affairs of the city (305d1–5). At that stage he seemed different from the weaver who not only directs her subordinates but engages in her own practical work at the loom (308d6–e2). Yet once we look inside the statesman's expertise—at his particular mode of intertwining—and consider the nature of his fabric, his work proves to be practical, as well as theoretical. The statesman stands at one remove from the practical knowledge of his subordinates and works things out theoretically, but he has his own higher-order practical knowledge as well, since he applies his theoretical knowledge in managing the city. In the final summary, the visitor speaks of the end of the web of *political action* (πολιτικῆς πράξεως) (311b7). The statesman, an expert in timing, knows when to set parts of his agenda in motion, so as best to preserve and enhance the lives of the citizens and the well-being of the city as a whole.

The Role of Division

Dichotomous division plays a major role in Plato's search for definitions in the late dialogues, but not the comprehensive role often attributed to it. Only in defining the simplest kinds, like angling, does it suffice to uncover the essence. We cannot adequately define even a simple observable kind like weaving by dichotomous division, because the procedure fails to mark off weaving from other kinds that share its domain and whose activities it directs and uses. Dichotomous division enables the enquirers to uncover some puzzle about the target kind whose solution will allow them to define its essence, and thus points a way forward. The dichotomous division that targets the sophist finds him in many different places; the division that targets the statesman finds him in a single place but surrounded by others who dispute his claim to look after humans. Dichotomous division brings these puzzles out into the open. Reflection on why the first six divisions fail in the *Sophist* points the enquirers to a problem—appearance—whose solution, via the analysis of not-being and false statement, enables them to locate the essence of the sophist. In turn, reflection on the inadequacy of the original division in the *Statesman* points the enquirers toward a model—weaving—which enables them to distinguish the statesman from his rivals and to define him in relation to them as overseeing and coordinating their activities for the good of the city and the people. Both dialogues are philosophical exercises. Their mistakes as well as their correct moves demonstrate how to investigate kinds, and not only the ones discovered by the Stranger here.[44]

Bibliography

Ackrill, J. L., 1970, 'In Defence of Platonic Division', in O. P. Wood and G. Pitcher, (eds.), *Ryle*, London: Macmillan, 373–92. Reprinted in J. L. Ackrill, *Essays on Plato and Aristotle*, Oxford: Oxford University Press, 2001, 93–109.

Cavini, W., 1995, 'Naming and Argument: Diaeretic Logic in Plato's *Statesman*', in C. J. Rowe (ed.), *Reading the Statesman*, Proceedings of the Third Symposium Platonicum, Sankt Augustin: Academia Verlag, 123–38.

Cohen, S. M., 1973, 'Plato's Method of Division', in J. M. E. Moravcsik (ed.), *Patterns in Plato's Thought*, Dordrecht: Reidel, 181–91.

Crombie, I., 1963, *An Examination of Plato's Doctrines*, 2 vols., London: Routledge & Kegan Paul.

Dorter, K., 1994, *Form and Good in Plato's Eleatic Dialogues: The Parmenides, Theaetetus, Sophist, and Statesman*, Berkeley: University of California Press.

El Murr, D., 2005, 'La division et l'unité du *Politique* de Platon', *Les études philosophiques* 3: 295–324.

El Murr, D., 2006, 'Paradigm and *diairesis*', *Journal of the International Plato Society* 6, 9 pp.

Frede, M., 1996, 'The Literary Form of the *Sophist*', in C. Gill and M. M. McCabe (eds.), *Form and Argument in Late Plato*, Oxford: Clarendon Press.

Gill, M. L., 2003, 'Why Does Theaetetus' Final Definition of Knowledge Fail?' in W. Detel, A. Becker, and P. Scholz (eds.), *Ideal and Culture of Knowledge in Plato*, Stuttgart: Franz Steiner, 159–73.

---

[44] The sections of this paper on the *Sophist* profited from being aired and discussed in the first of three seminars at the University of California, Berkeley, in 2005. I am grateful to the audience for their helpful questions. My treatment of models and division benefited from Dimitri El Murr's commentary (2006) and from discussion with him and others at the Universities of Notre Dame and Pittsburgh. I thank an anonymous referee at Oxford University Press for helpful suggestions, and I especially thank David Charles and Dimitri El Murr for comments, which stimulated me to rethink several central issues.

Gill, M. L., 2005/2009, 'Method and Metaphysics in Plato's *Sophist* and *Statesman*', in *The Stanford Encyclopedia of Philosophy*, ed. Edward N. Zalta. http://plato.stanford.edu/entries/plato-sophstate/.

Gill, M. L., 2006, 'Models in Plato's *Sophist* and *Statesman*', *Journal of the International Plato Society* 6, 16 pp.

Lane, M. S., 1998, *Method and Politics in Plato's 'Statesman'*, Cambridge: Cambridge University Press.

Miller, M., 1980, *The Philosopher in Plato's Statesman*, The Hague: Nijhoff. Reprinted with supplementary material, Las Vegas: Parmenides, 2004.

Moravcsik, J. M. E., 1973, 'The Anatomy of Plato's Divisions', in E. N. Lee, A. P. D. Mourelatos, and R. M. Rorty (eds.), *Exegesis and Argument* (= *Phronesis* Suppl. 1), New York: Humanities Press, 324–48.

Notomi, N., 1999, *The Unity of Plato's 'Sophist': Between the Sophist and the Philosopher*, Cambridge: Cambridge University Press.

Ryle, G., 1966, *Plato's Progress*, Cambridge: Cambridge University Press.

Sayre, K. M., 2006, *Method and Metaphysics in Plato's Statesman*, Cambridge: Cambridge University Press.

Wedin, M. V., 1987, 'Collection and Division in the *Phaedrus* and *Statesman*', *Revue de Philosophie Ancienne* 5: 207–33.

PART II
Aristotle on Definition

6

Aristotle on Essence and Defining-Phrase in his Dialectic

KEI CHIBA

1 Introduction

At the centre of Aristotle's metaphysical thought, there is a theory of substance concerning 'primary and simple being' (1028a30f.). It is often said that his theory of substance has its own centre in his theory of essence. But what does 'essence' mean? The word itself is a translation of the Greek phrase, '*to ti ên einai*', literally 'the what it was to be', which was probably introduced, or at least given precise philosophical sense, by Aristotle himself. Although it is frequently translated as 'essence', there is little agreement among scholars as to why he adopts it or what it means.[1]

My aim, in this essay, is to clarify the meaning and role of '*to ti ên einai*' ('the what it was to be') and its account, called '*horos*', which I shall translate as 'defining-phrase', in Aristotle's dialectic. The essay falls into five parts.

---

[1] T. Wagner and C. Rapp recently report that 'Die genaue Rekonstruktion dieses Begriffs ist immer noch Gegenstand von Kontrversen'. T. Wagner and C. Rapp, *Aristoteles Topik* (Stuttgart, 2004), p. 276. M. Loux writes that 'There is much discussion in the literature on the origins of the expression "*to ti ên einai*" and its precise sense. . . . But any account of the expression is conjectural.' M. Loux, *Primary Ousia: An Essay on Aristotle's Metaphysics Z and H*, (Ithaca, NY, 1991), pp. 73f. n. 5. J. D. G. Evans offers the ill-supported conjecture that '*to ti ên einai* is a novel formula, introduced instead of the normal expression of "*ti esti*" to avoid the paradox of the third man argument'. J. D. G. Evans, *Aristotle's Concept of Dialectic*, (Cambridge, 1977), p. 112. I shall offer a contextually based interpretation of this expression. Previous writers have suggested that this phrase be interpreted by means of the notion of Form, but this ignores the context in which '*to ti ên einai*' is introduced. D. Ross said that '*Logos* and *to ti ên einai* are always used as synonym with the form'. D. Ross, *Aristotle* (Oxford, 1923), p. 74. S. Mansion, J. Owens, etc. follow Ross. S. Mansion, 'La notion de matière en Métaphysique Z10 et 11', in *Étude Sur La Métaphysique D'Aristote* (Paris, 1979), p. 188; J. Owens, *The Doctrine of Being in the Aristotelian Metaphysics* (Toronto, 1963), p. 183; cf. R. Sorabji, *Necessity, Cause, and Blame: Perspectives on Aristotle's Theory* (London, 1980), p. 213.

In the first part, I shall locate these terms in their historical context, arguing that Aristotle develops his theory of dialectic in an attempt to systematize and improve on the Socratic method of dialogue. It is important to distinguish, as Aristotle himself does, between the *theory* of dialectic and its *practice*. He introduces the main constituents of the theory, including 'the what it was to be' (*to ti ên einai*), on the basis of 'the method of formal argument' (*logikôs*),[2] which is employed both in dialectic and in metaphysics.

[2] While '*logikôs*' considerations were developed by Eleatics, Socrates, and Plato, '*physikôs*' considerations were discussed by Ionian *physiologoi* as scientific claims supported by appeals to empirical data. In the past, '*logikôs*' was translated as 'dialectically', but more recently as 'logically', which is preferable, although as Burnyeat notes, 'logically' is 'a transliteration rather than a translation' (M. Burnyeat, *A Map of Metaphysics Zeta* (Pittsburgh, 2001), pp. 19, 89; cf. D. Charles, *Aristotle on Meaning and Essence* (Oxford, 2000, p. 286, n. 25)). There is no doubt that when Aristotle founded Logic, he created it in a *logikos* fashion. But the method itself has a wider application as is shown by the fact that it can sustain claims to existence. Thus, for instance, Aristotle argues in a *logikos* fashion about essence and concludes that it must be a single item for each thing (*Top.* VI.4) and primarily belong to the category of substance (*Met.* Z.4–6). I take it that the precise meaning of '*logikôs*' is conveyed by an expression such as 'the method of formal argument based on the principle of non-contradiction and general terms such as sameness and difference'.

Elsewhere I have examined all the occurrences of the adjective *logikos* (19 times) and of the adverb *logikôs* (13 times) in the corpus. See chapter 1 of my *Aristotle on the Possibility of Metaphysics: Complementary Development between Dialectic and Natural Philosophy* (Keiso Shobo, 2002). My conclusion is that the *logikos* method is a worthwhile philosophical one, never understood 'pejoratively' by Aristotle. The pejorative reading is seen in works such as D. Ross, *Aristotle's Metaphysics II* (Oxford, 1924), p. 168; Le Blond, *Logique et Méthode chèz Aristote* (Paris, 1939), p. 205. It is not an accident that 'theology' and 'astrology' have *logikê* as their suffix (46a19f., 291b21, 1026a19). Further, *logikôs* enquiry is not confined to conceptual analysis or to logical reasoning but can make a claim about 'how a thing in the world is (*pôs echei*)' based on argument grounded in 'how one ought to speak (*pôs dei legein*)' (I agree with M. Burnyeat and M. Wedin that Z4–6 is as a whole argued by the *logikôs* method (Burnyeat, *Map of Metaphysics Zeta*, pp. 22ff.; M. Wedin, *Aristotle's Theory of Substance* (Oxford, 2000), p. 201)). Further, the principle of non-contradiction itself is a *logikos* notion which we cannot understand without referring to 'sameness' and 'difference'. This shows that any item of discussion can be analysed at a general level in the *logikôs* manner.

Although the role of the method '*logikôs*' has sometimes been confined to 'conceptual analysis' (see e.g. G. E. L. Owen, 'Tithenai ta phainomena', in *Logic, Science and Dialectic* (London, 1986), p. 240; E. Berti, 'Does Aristotle's Dialectic Develop?', in *Aristotle's Philosophical Development*, ed. W. Wians (Lanham, MD, 1996), p. 114), I agree with Burnyeat that it is not 'merely verbal' (Burnyeat, *Map of Metaphysics Zeta*, p. 20). Frede and Patzig characterize '*logikôs*' as 'Untersuchungen als sprachlich, begrifflich, im Gegensatz zu inhaltlich, wissenschaftlich' and say 'sie durch inhaltliche Überlegungen ergänzt werden müssen' (M. Frede and G. Patzig, *Aristoteles Metaphysik Z Kommentar* (Munich, 1988), S.59. However, the concept/content distinction between the *logikôs* method and others is misleading. In some places, Aristotle argues that one can reach the same conclusion by both a *logikos* and *physikos* argument (e.g. G.C. I.2, 316a5–14; *Phys.* III.5, 204b4–11; G.A. II.8, 747a24–749a6). Similarly, *logikôs* and '*analytikôs*' (analytically) one can argue for the same conclusion (84b1f.). This implies that *logikos* argument is not merely confined to conceptual analysis and that it need not always be supplemented by a different 'contentful' style of argument.

Consider the following example: Aristotle offers physical and formal arguments for the conclusion that the whole of the mule kind is sterile (G.A. II.8, 747a24–748a7). Aristotle gives 'a *logikê* demonstration' (747b28) by appealing to the two contrary universal concepts: sameness and difference. His presuppos-

The *theory* of dialectic, so conceived, is to be contrasted with its *practice*, which is described using a different adverb, 'dialectically' (*dialektikôs*). Dialecticians (*dialektikoi*) *dialectically* examine any proposition that has been proposed, offering *pro* and *contra* arguments in the realm of opinion. The *theory* of dialectic, by contrast, is based on the theories of (what are traditionally called) predicables (i.e. types of term) and of categories of predications and entities as part of a philosophical analysis of being and identity (see note 2). This theory constitutes Aristotle's attempt to set out the distinctions which the *practice* of dialectic should respect and the rules, such as the theory of *topoi* (points), it should follow.

In the second part of the essay, I shall investigate Aristotle's theory of the predicables in *Topics* I.4 and 5. My suggestion is that these, which are all called 'definitory (boundary markers)' (*horika*), point to possible answers to the Socratic 'What is F?' (*ti esti;*) question. A dialectician, on the basis of the theory of the predicables, can examine any proposition whatsoever without having an answer to the 'What is F?' question. This aspect of Aristotle's account was designed to solve some difficulties which had beset Socratic enquiry into definition. Against this background, we can see why Aristotle introduced the concept of 'the what it was to be' (*to ti ên einai*) and the name of its account, i.e. 'defining-phrase' (*horos*). They are variants respectively of 'the what a thing is' (*to ti esti*) and of 'the practice of defining' (*horizein horismos*). Aristotle needed the term 'defining-phrase' to examine, in a theoretical way, the sub-sentential (or sub-propositional) components employed in the practice of defining.

In the third part of this essay, I shall focus on the role that 'defining-phrase' and 'the what it was to be' play in specifying the type of account used in successfully defining a thing. The defining-phrase can replace either a name or another phrase which signifies the object to be defined. I shall

---

itions in this proof are (1) that from male and female of the same species (say xx) are born male and female of the same species (x) and (2) that from parents of different species (say xy) is born something different in species (say z). Because of (1) x is begotten from xx, because of (2) z is begotten from xy. Now, mules cannot produce another kind because of (1). Mules cannot produce a mule because a mule is in fact the product of horse and ass which are different in form and also (2) was presupposed. Thus mules cannot produce a mule or another kind of animal.

This general demonstration of why a mule cannot beget a mule is said by Aristotle to be 'too general and empty' (748a7f.). While this is not a criticism of the *logikos* argument itself, it shows that it cannot be applied to a biological subject. However, for our present concerns, it is enough to note that *logikos* arguments are established by appealing to general notions such as sameness and difference and can lead to the same conclusion as physical explanations.

suggest, in contrast with the standard interpretation, which sees no difference between 'defining-phrase' (*horos*) and 'definition' (*horismos*),[3] that
defining-phrase is the sub-sentential component of the proposition used
to express a definition. In my account, what is signified by the phrase 'the
what it was to be' is a definable entity, specified in a successful 'defining-
phrase' and grasped by a process which differentiates it from the other three
predicables. The phrase 'the what it was to be' (*to ti ên einai*) is designed to
capture the ideal answer which Socrates was seeking for in his 'What is F?'
(*ti esti;*) question. I shall offer a grammatical analysis of this phrase, suggesting
how it arises within the context of Socratic enquiry. In my view, it emerges
from Aristotle's reformulation of the Socratic 'What is F?' question in a
context in which the interlocutor had overlooked what Socrates sought.
The question 'What was then it for F itself to be F?', in using the past tense,
reminds the interlocutor that he has overlooked *the thing F itself* in his initial
answer, offering, for instance, only an example of F.

In the fourth part of my essay, I shall elucidate the dialectical origin of the
theory of categories by considering *Topics* I.8 and 9. Aristotle confirms in I.8
that one will find in all propositions one or other of the four possible replies
to the 'What is F?' question. In I.9, he presents two corresponding lists of
categories, one of predications (CP), the other of entities (CE). He distinguishes ten genera of predications (CP) by considering various ordinary
interrogative forms and shows that all the Academicians' attempts at defini-

---

[3] For instance, Philoponus comments *Analytica Posteriora* B.10, 93b38, by using both the words '*horos*'
and '*horismos*' interchangeably. *Commentaria in Aristotelem Graeca*, ed. M. Wallies (Berlin, 1909), ad. loc.
J. Barnes also translates 93b38, 'One definition of definition (*horos horou*) is the one we have just stated.'
Aristotle's Posterior Analytics (Oxford, 1993), p. 58 H. Bonitz says that '*horos* and *horismos* are employed to
signify definition almost indistinguishably (fere promiscue)'. H. Bonitz, *Index Aristotelicus* (Berlin, 1870),
S.530. R. Smith claims that 'There seems to be no difference in meaning between the two, but it is at
least worth noting that *horismos* predominates outside the *Topics* and that in the *Analytics* the word *horos*
almost always has the different technical sense "term".' *Aristotle, Topics Books I and VIII* (Oxford, 1997),
p. 58 D. Bostock says that 'From as early as the *Topics* (101a19–23, and *passim*) this phrase ["the what [it]
was (for a thing) to be"] has been used interchangeably with "definition".' D. Bostock, *Aristotle,
Metaphysics Books Z and H* (Oxford, 1994), p. 86. Wagner and Rapp translate *horos* as 'definition' as
well (Wagner and Rapp, *Aristoteles Topik*, ad. loc.). Recently, even an emendation of the text has been
proposed. I. Ludlam says that 'I propose, with arguments based on philosophical and philological
considerations, that *horos* must most cases be emended to hor◁ism▷os'. 'Defining Terms in Aristotle's
Topics: *horos* or hor◁ism▷os?', *Mnemosyne* 53.3 (2000), p. 267.

As a translation of *horos*, '*definiens*' should be avoided. Aristotle introduces *horos* in the context of
setting out four predicables (types of terms) which are located in advance of definitional practice. *Horos* is
the name of an account which signifies an essence that can be defined. A name (*onoma*) and its replaced
horos signify a definable thing. By contrast, '*definiens*' presupposes an already existing definition in that it
together with *definiendum* (*horisthen*) is the analysed part of a definition. See also section 5.

tion can be understood within his new theory of predications. By establishing a correspondence between kinds of interrogatives and kinds of entities, Aristotle succeeds in determining a background *theory* which will avoid confusion in debates and so facilitate the practice of dialectic.

In the final section of the essay, I shall examine some *topoi* (places or points) about defining-phrases and suggest that the formal analysis of the what a thing is (*to ti esti*) in the *Topics* provides a background theory for the account of causal knowledge in the *Posterior Analytics* and the analysis of being in the *Metaphysics*.

2 Distinction between the Practice of Dialectic and its Theory

While the theory of dialectic, as developed in the *Topics*, applies to argumentative arts such as rhetoric (dealing with persuasion), eristic (dealing with victory in discussion) and logic (dealing with valid reasoning), it has its own distinctive aims. Its goal is to set out a general way of establishing whether a discussion is properly conducted by presenting *topoi* (points) through (or by) which one can confirm or overturn propositions put forward by the interlocutor (172a35f.). Unlike particular sciences, but like philosophy, dialectical argument is 'not concerned with any definite genus' (172a12). It considers universal statements at a level distinct from that characterized by the proper principles of a science. These statements can be examined using arguments or considerations based on the theories of categories, predicables, and universal terms such as 'sameness' and 'difference'.

Aristotle claims that one and the same proposition or problem can be discussed 'dialectically' in the sphere of opinion and 'philosophically' with respect to its truth. 'Of propositions and problems', he says, 'there are three divisions, ethical, physical and formal (*hai de logikai*) . . . Philosophically we must treat these things according to the truth, but dialectically in terms of opinion (*dialektikôs de pros doxan*). All propositions should be obtained in the most universal form possible' (105b19–32 with a gap). When one considers ethical or physical propositions 'in their most universal form', they are analysed at a level higher than that of their particular genus, by dialectically or philosophically using formal and general (*logikai*) concepts and propos-itions. For instance, the physical terms 'hot and cold' (105b37) or the ethical terms 'good and evil' (105b36) can be treated dialectically in terms of the concepts of 'the same' and 'the opposite'. The formal (*logikê*) proposition, 'Knowledge of opposites is the same' (105b34f.), can be applied to both ethical and physical issues.[4] Dialectical practice examines propositions at this distinctively universal level (172a28, cf. 171b3–8).

Dialectic, in contrast with philosophy, is 'the art of examination', 'which a man may possess, even though he lacks knowledge' (*Soph. El.* 11, 172a21, 171a21–23). The dialectician, who is confined to the realm of opinion (*doxa*), should carry out his distinctive examination following Aristotle's instructions about method. While the philosopher, engaged in a superior academic discipline, can make use of the dialectical examination of some proposition for his own purposes, he can also engage in a dialectical practice by suspending (as a dialectician would) his own ontological commitments. In philosophy and dialectic, our intellectual ability is employed for different goals. In *Metaphysics* Γ.2, Aristotle says that 'Philosophy differs from dialec-tic in the orientation of the ability (*tôi tropôi tês dynameôs*) . . . Dialectic is merely critical while philosophy claims to know' (1004b23–25). The practice of dialectic is contrasted with demonstrative science and with philosophy,

---

[4] In discussing 'three broad types of question that emerge in dialectical debate' in *Topics* I.14, Burnyeat claims that '*logikos* in this passage, uniquely in Aristotle, singles out a particular field of inquiry, contrasted with ethics and physics. A tripartite division of philosophy into "logic", physics and ethics is credited to Xenocrates, third head of the Academy, and *Topics* I.14 is probably relying on readers' acquaintance with it. It is thus particularly significant that Aristotle does not adopt *logikê* as an overall term for the subject-matter of his logical writings' (Burnyeat, *Map of Metaphysics Zeta*, pp. 88f.). In his account of three 'divisions of philosophy', Burnyeat fails to see that the concrete opposites in ethics and physics can be reduced to more universal and *logikos* terms such as 'the opposites' and discussed in general terms in a dialectical fashion and *logikos*, i.e. philosophical, fashion. I take it that general notions such as 'being', 'sameness', and 'what it is' can be the subject-matter of *logikos* enquiry not only in *Organon* but also in *Metaphysics*.

Burnyeat's basic understanding of *logikos* as 'familiar from the *Organon*' generates more questions than it solves (p. 15). Is there, in fact, a unified account of *logikos* discussion which applies to all methods, including 'dialectical' and 'analytical' ones found in *Organon*? If not, how are these methods related? Can some issues be discussed both analytically and logically? Formal concepts, I shall argue, can be discussed both in the *logikos* and in the dialectical fashion depending on the purposes in question. Burnyeat fails to grasp Aristotle's distinction between the practice of dialectic, carried out by the '*dialektikos*' method, and the theory of dialectic, constructed by the '*logikos*' method (cf. pp. 89, 102).

Wedin's interpretation of this method is subject to similar criticisms. He claims, referring to Burnyeat's work, that 'These remarks [two kinds of *per se* relations in 1029b13–22] are "logical" because they aim to situate the concept of essence within the range of relations that are set out in the logical works' (Wedin, *Aristotle's Theory of Substance*, p. 201).

which claim to have necessary knowledge about the causal structure of nature. Since the practice of dialectic remains at the level of opinion, it cannot yield knowledge. But it is still possible for the dialectician to present counter-examples and refute claims, and so avoid false opinions. Further, insofar as he follows the rules established by the theory of dialectic, he can gain legitimate agreement from others and so confirm his belief. Dialectical practice may, indeed, be useful in the acquisition of knowledge, when the relevant ability is redirected towards philosophical practice (163b2–11). In these passages, Aristotle marks out the different goals of these two activities (105b30f., cf. 72a7–11, 100a27–b21, 162a15f., 162b31–33, 141a29).

While the practice of the dialectician is critically to examine any proposed proposition, the theory on which he depends is grounded in a philosophical analysis of issues such as being and identity. A general or formal (logikê) account of these topics, involving the predicables and the categories, is put forward in the Topics as the proper basis for dialectical and philosophical practice.

Aristotle uses two adverbial expressions to show the different ways in which universal concepts and propositions can be examined: 'dialectically' (dialektikôs) and 'by the method of formal argument' (logikôs). The first term describes the practice of dialectic, which examines pro and contra propositions endorsed by opposing viewpoints (e.g. 105b31, 161a33, 183b3, cf. 403a2). By contrast, the second term describes his general analysis of being or identity based on (e.g.) the predicables and categories, which is a prolegomenon to dialectical practice (e.g. 82b35–83a1, 1030a25f.). Thus, for example, the term 'the what it was to be' (to ti ên einai) is introduced by the phrase 'to speak formally (logikôs)' in the Metaphysics (e.g.1041a28). While the dialectician seeks to examine propositions dialectically, the theory which underlies his practice is philosophically grounded. Put differently, when Aristotle writes of the theory of dialectic, he does so not as a dialectician but as a philosopher.[5]

---

[5] Philoponus discusses whether 'The formal argument and dialectic' (Hê logikê te kai dialektikê pragmateia) is 'a part' of philosophy or 'a tool' for philosophy. He claims while Stoics regard it as a part, Peripatetics see it as a tool for philosophy. Here Philoponus uses the conjunction 'and' (kai) epexegetically. If he means dialektikê to be the theory of dialectic, this discipline must be a part of philosophy. Otherwise, he and others fail to understand what 'logikê' means. I. Philoponus, In Aristotelis Analytica Priora Commentaria, ed. M. Wallies (Berlin, 1905), p. 6, cf. Alexander Aphrodisiensis, In Aristotelis Analyticorum Priorum Librum I Commentarium, ed. M. Wallies (Berlin, 1883), p. 3.

It is important to distinguish between the practice and theory of dialectic as some Aristotelian scholars have been led astray by overlooking this distinction. T. H. Irwin, for example, was led to separate 'strong' from 'pure dialectic' and forced to admit that 'I have to say that Aristotle has no answer to the puzzles about dialectic and objective first principles.' His difficulties arose because he asked the apparently non-Aristotelian question: 'Does strong dialectic support Aristotle's claim to find objective, and not merely *endoxic*, principles?'[6] Irwin failed to see that *endoxic* premises are useful only in the realm of dialectical *practice* which is confined to examining a proposition by offering *pro* and *contra* arguments based on premises of this type. In a similar way, he misunderstood the point of the *theory* of dialectic: Aristotle, in developing this as a theory, was intending to advance a general account of (e.g.) being and identity in a 'formal manner' (*logikôs*), not to derive first principles from merely *endoxic* premises or practices.

It may be helpful, at this point, to consider the relationship between Aristotle's and Plato's dialectic. They are both similar and dissimilar. Dialectic, based on synthesis and division, as Plato understood it, was the noblest intellectual activity, a universal philosophical method for enquiry into real being (e.g. *Resp.* 532a–d, 534b, 537d; *Soph.* 253d; *Phileb.* 55d–59e). Aristotle, by contrast, downgraded dialectic, confining the practice of dialectic to the sphere of opinion.[7] Further, since sciences are classified according to their objects or regions and methods, dialectic cannot be, for Aristotle, the (or even a) universal science. Nonetheless he inherited from Plato a belief in the philosophical significance of dialectic and developed it as a theory of being and identity, outlining it in a formal manner (*logikôs*) not

---

[6] T. H. Irwin, *Aristotle's First Principles* (Oxford, 1988). While Irwin ascribes to 'strong dialectic' the role of reaching objective first principles within the science of being, he ascribes to 'pure (ordinary) dialectic' the role of examining commonly held belief as an intellectual exercise (pp.8, 476). As he admits, this distinction is not as clear as it should be. However, Irwin further claims that 'Strong dialectic requires us to stick to premises that we have some good reason for accepting, beyond the fact that they are matters of common belief', although he admits that strong dialectical premises are 'a subset' of dialectical premises and thus are 'matters of common belief' (p. 476). Finally he suggests that there is some obscurity in Aristotle's account of dialectic when he says that 'Aristotle is quite non-committal at some of the crucial points'. However, these are the very points at which Irwin sees him as engaged in the non-Aristotelian project of investigating 'how dialectic can lead to objective principles . . . beyond common belief' (p. 479).

E. Berti similarly distinguishes between 'scientific use' and 'public use' within the practice of dialectic. Berti, 'Does Aristotle's Dialectic Develop?', p. 106.

[7] G. Ryle says that 'We get the impression that in the Academy at the same moment the word "dialectic" is being used in two entirely different ways.' G. Ryle, *Plato's Progress* (Cambridge, 1966), p. 127.

to be found in any of Plato's writing (cf. *Theae.* 164c). My suggestion is that he introduced the term 'by the method of formal argument' (*logikôs*) to indicate his own understanding of certain aspects of Plato's dialectic.

Some have suggested that the *Topics* is merely a systematization of the practice of dialogue in the Academy, taking over most of its technical terms and methods.[8] However, in my view, while Aristotle developed his own account of dialectic by building on the basis established by Socrates and Plato (cf. 120b11–29), he went beyond what they had achieved. Within this perspective, I shall consider his initial introduction of the phrase 'the what it was to be' (*to ti ên einai*) and its account called 'defining-phrase'.

3 Aristotle's Heritage: Shortcomings of Socrates' Dialectic

When Aristotle discusses the characteristics and limits of Socrates' dialectic, he represents his own theory, despite some differences, as an extension of Socrates' approach. He writes:

Socrates occupied himself with the excellences of character, and in connection with them became the first to raise the problem of how to define universally (*horizesthai katholou*). . . . But it was reasonable that Socrates should seek the what a thing is (*to ti esti*) . . . For at that time, dialectic was not strong enough to enable people even without the what a thing is (*chôris tou ti esti*) to speculate about contraries and enquire whether the same knowledge deals with contraries. For two things may be fairly ascribed to Socrates, that is, inductive arguments and universal definitions, both of which are concerned with the principles of know-ledge. (1078b17–30 with two gaps)[9]

---

[8] e.g. P. M. Huby, 'The Date of Aristotle's Topics and its Treatment of the Theory of Ideas', *Classical Quarterly* 12 (1962), p. 76, cf. J. Barnes's review of *Aristotle, On Dialectic; The Topics*, ed. G. E. L. Owen, *Philosophical Review* 79.4 (1970), pp. 558–65.

[9] Alexander takes this criticism of Socrates to depend on Aristotle's distinction between dialectic and demonstrative science. Socrates is criticized, in Alexander's view, because, although he sought for the type of exact demonstration carried out by geometers, he could not achieve it on the basis of dialectical syllogisms. Alexander says that 'Since definition is the principle of reasoning and demonstration, as is shown in the book on demonstration, it is reasonable that Socrates sought for reasoning and definition of the what it is. Since there is a reasoning without having a definition (see dialectical syllogisms), Aristotle claimed that dialectic at that time was not strong enough to infer, for instance, that pleasure is good without grasping the what it is and definition' (Alexander Aphrodisiensis, *In Aristotelis Metaphysica Commentaria* (Berlin, 1891), p. 718, ll. 4–11). Alexander thought that Socrates sought for a definition

Why was Socrates' dialectic 'not strong enough'? How did Aristotle strengthen it? The art of the dialogue, as Socrates understood it, aimed to acquire knowledge by reaching agreement with the interlocutor through examining his answer and seeking to formulate a definition. Once the latter was established, Socrates hoped to deduce further claims about the thing defined. This is why he said that without knowing what virtue is, one cannot examine whether virtue can be taught or not. In the same spirit he remarked that unless one knows what justice is, one cannot know whether the person who is just is happy or not (*Meno* 86d; *Resp.* 354c; cf. *Meno* 71b).

Aristotle, by contrast, developed a way of discussing opposed claims without asking, let alone answering, Socrates' 'What is F?' question (*chôris tou ti esti*). His basic approach is most clearly seen when he emphasizes that the dialectician should offer a contradictory pair of propositions to which one can reply 'Yes' or 'No' (158a14–17).[10] Consider, for example, his discussion of the proposition 'Knowledge of the opposites is the same.'

---

based on demonstration. What Aristotle criticizes, however, is the lack of power in Socrates' dialectic itself. It would be anachronistic for Alexander to contrast dialectic with a theory of demonstration which Socrates did not himself hold (987b1–22, 642a27–b4). Alexander Aphrodisiensis, ibid., p. 741. Cf. N. Gulley, *The Philosophy of Socrates* (London, 1968), p. 5.

[10] In *De Interpretatione*, Aristotle discusses the way in which the analysis of truth and falsity of an assertion is significant for dialectical practice. It is indispensable to formulate a question so as to be answered by either 'yes' or 'no'. Yes/no answers can be properly given to the contrary or contradictory pair of 'one affirmation' and 'one negation'. Aristotle says that 'To affirm or deny one thing of many, or many of one, is not one affirmation or negation, unless the many things together make up some one thing. I do not call them one if there exists one name but there is not some one thing they make up ... So if a dialectical question demands as answer either the statement proposed or one side of a contradiction (the statement in fact being a side of one contradiction), there could not be one answer in these cases. For the question itself would not be one question, even if true ... It is also clear that "What is a thing?" is not a dialectical question either; for the question must give one the choice of stating whichever side of the contradiction one wishes' (ch. 11, 20b14–27 with three gaps). Aristotle offers three classes of not formulating a contradictory pair of assertions. First, in the case of non-universal assertions made concerning universals in chapter 7, such as 'man is pale', both affirmation and negation could be true. Second, in chapter 8, a contradictory pair of assertions which were apparently simple, but in fact concealed two different claims such as 'cloak is pale', where the word 'cloak' applies to both man and horse, could furnish an affirmation and negation which are both false. A third class of exceptions is concerned with future singulars such as tomorrow's sea-battle in chapter 9.

The example of sea-battle which is a public event is chosen by Aristotle on purpose, because it is almost evident whether such an event takes place tomorrow or not. It is described as a kind of event 'for one to be more true (*mallon men alêthê*) than the other, yet not yet true or false (*ou mentoi êdê alêthê ê pseudê*)' (19a38). When he says 'more true', one part of contrary statements has higher possibility of truth. Thus he does not subscribe to the simple principle of bivalence but rather to a more fine-graded theory of potential degrees of truth value. Since a future singular assertion cannot constitute a contra-dictory pair, it is said that such assertion does not formulate the assertion of 'already true or false'. Commentators have missed seeing the context of the discussion of future singular event, that this is the third example to which the rule of contradictory pair of assertions cannot be applied.

Aristotle offers some *topoi* (points) in investigating whether the property at issue (being the same knowledge) belongs universally to knowledge of opposites (109b13–29). In this examination, one should not consider particular cases but ask rather whether in each species there is the same knowledge for each of the four kinds of 'opposites': (1) relative opposites (e.g. half and double), (2) contraries (e.g. just and unjust), (3) terms opposed as privation and possession (e.g. blindness and sight), and (4) contradictory terms (e.g. being and not-being). In a similar way, in the *topos* concerning contraries, he considers whether the contrary of the one follows from the contrary of the other (113b27–114a25). To establish and refute a view, we need to examine the relevant sequences of propositions about contraries 'by means of induction, so far as it may be useful' (113b29). This is a successor to the method Socrates employed when he set out contraries and investigated, for example, 'whether virtue is learnable or not' (as in the method of hypothesis in the *Meno*). Aristotle offered, in addition, points (*topoi*) by which to examine the opposites (e.g. 112a16–23, 147a29–148a9, 153a26–b24, 155b29–34). In this way, *topos* theory provides a method for examining opposite claims without directly engaging with the 'What is F?' question.

One of Aristotle's criticisms of Socrates is that he focused exclusively on ethical matters and neglected 'the world of nature as a whole' (987b2, cf. 642a27–31), so that the scope of his enquiry was limited. Definition was what Socrates sought in asking his famous 'What is F?' question. He aimed to find out what virtues such as piety and temperance are, thinking that knowing what a virtue is will be sufficient to make the enquirer virtuous. Aristotle, in developing his own account of knowledge based on the theory of demonstration (whose paradigm discipline is mathematics), thought it inappropriate to take ethical matters as the paradigm of knowledge.

Aristotle characterizes his own project at the end of the last book of the *Topics*, *The Sophistical Refutations*, and locates it in its proper historical context. He writes that, 'Our programme was to discover some faculty of syllogizing about any subject put before us from the most reputable premises that there are' (183a37f., cf. 100a29–b23). In this project, he nurtured 'the faculty' of 'being able to conduct an examination not only *dialectically* (*dialektikôs*) but also as a person who knows (*hôs eidôs*)' (183b2f.). Here he suggests that he established his results as 'a philosopher' (*tou sophou ergon*) who grasps wisdom and contrasts his approach with the art of sophist, 'the semblance of wisdom without the reality' (165a22f.). He characterizes the man who knows as one who is able 'to avoid falsities in the subjects he knows and to show up the man who makes them' (165a25–27). Aristotle places Socrates somewhere between the sophist and himself. 'For this reason, Socrates only questioned and never answered, because he confessed that he did not know. *But*, we have made clear, in the course of what precedes, the number with respect to which and the sources from which, this ['to defend a thesis' (183b5)] will be accomplished, and also from what sources we will find the way out from these issues' (183b6–12). In these remarks, Aristotle confirms that while he sees his own mission as a continuation of Socrates', he is confident that he has found a way to escape the difficulties which beset his predecessor. This is why he can contrast himself with Socrates as one who knows with one who did not (cf. *Top.* I.3).

Socrates' attempts to formulate definitions of what a thing is are, on occasion, favourably assessed as 'the first' (1078b19) sign of a project different from the physiologists' enquiry into elements: what a thing is made *of* (cf. 984a18f., 988b24ff., 993a11f.). In a similar passage, Aristotle says that the task of 'defining the what it was to be (*to ti ên einai*) in the sense of substance of the thing' was 'developed in the time of Socrates' (642a25, 28f.). Although Plato 'accepted' (987b4) the Socratic way of definition, his work is subject to the following comment: 'No one has articulated distinctly (*saphôs*) the what it was to be (*to ti ên einai*) in the sense of the substance of the thing. But those who believe in Forms mention it most' (988a34f.). This suggests that while, for Aristotle, there was a significant continuity in enquiry between himself, Socrates, and Plato, there were also areas in which, in his view, he had made important progress.

4 New Devices of Aristotelian Dialectic in the *Topics*

4.1 Proposition and Syllogism in Dialectic

Aristotle presents his own theory in the *Topics* as an attempt to build on the method of dialectic in the Academy. His accounts of the *topos* and of the dialectical syllogism are put forward to achieve this goal.

At the beginning of the *Topics* I.4 (see the quotations [A] and [B] below) Aristotle sets out an outline of his method, noting that 'The possession of a plan of enquiry will enable us more easily to argue about the subject proposed... The ability to puzzle on both sides of a subject will make us detect more easily the truth and error in any subject' (101a29–36 with a gap). In order for a questioner to facilitate agreement or disagreement, it is necessary to construct a theory which can be used in analysing and assessing arguments. Thus, it is important to confirm the number and characteristics of the bases from which arguments are composed. He sets these out in considering the dialectical syllogism. Aristotle writes as follows:

[A] First we must consider what the method consists of. If we could grasp how many and what kind of objects the arguments are directed to and of what bases they consist, and how we will find a way out (*euporêsomen*) of these issues, we should sufficiently attain the end which is set before us. Now the bases (*ek tinôn*) of arguments are equal in number and the same as, the things which syllogisms are about. For arguments are made from propositions, while the things about which syllogisms are concerned are problems. But every proposition and every problem makes known either a property (*idion*), a genus or an accident. (101b11–18)

This passage echoes the one just quoted in section 3 from the end of his book on dialectic (*Soph. El.* 183a37–b12). Constructing a *theory* of dialectic is a *sui generis* type of philosophical investigation. The frequent occurrences of the verb '*we* will find a way out (*euporêsomen*)' throughout this treatise show the situation in which Aristotle found himself (e.g. 101b13, 102a13, 104a2, 105a22, 108b14, 110b5, 111b33, 183b10). He was seeking to develop a new theory of dialectic to solve difficulties which had arisen in the Academy. The presence of the grammatical subject 'we' shows that he regards his as a joint venture he shared with the Academy. Nonetheless Aristotle makes his own individual contribution by creating a new set of terms which emerge from, but go beyond, the framework he had inherited. In this way his Academic colleagues could see him as continuing their own definitional practice while, at the same time, developing the basis for a new method to address their shared problems.

The bases of arguments are called 'propositions' and 'problems'. In the *Topics*, propositions and problems are to be understood in the context of dialectical practice examining a proposed problem by offering *pro* and *contra* syllogisms. 'The problems and propositions come about from these [pre-dicables]' (101b27f.). Aristotle suggests that all possible problems and prop-ositions arise from a limited set of components and that all arguments are based on this limited set. The classification of propositions and problems is made from the standpoint of formal (*logikos*) analysis. Since all propositions or problems are formed from one of these predicables, 'every proposition and every problem makes known either a property or genus or accident' (101b17f.). In Aristotelian dialectic, one cannot ask 'What is F?' directly. A dialectical problem must be set in a form to which it is possible to reply 'Yes' or 'No' (158a14–16). In a dialectical exchange, the person who examines a claim made by interlocutor must put a proposition in the form of a question: 'Is two-footed land animal the definition of man?' and 'Is animal the genus of man?' (101b32f.). The answerer is required to say just 'yes' or 'no'. Aristotle here mentions 'definition' (101b32) rather than 'defining-phrase', because an account to which true or false is ascribed is not a phrase but a proposition. The four predicables, to be considered in the next section, are basic ingredients of dialectical arguments of this type. A proposition must be composed of one of these four types of predicable. Similarly, a problem is made up of the same components. Problems should be put as follows: 'Is two-footed land animal the definition of man *or not?*' (101b32f.) because the dialectical syllogism is concerned with contradictory pairs of propositions. Arguments for both sides are to be presented for these contradictory conclusions which are expressed as one problem.

The theory of the dialectical syllogism is the engine of dialectical practice, underwritten by the results of theory as set out using *topoi*. 'Reputable opinion' (*endoxon*) is the opinion held 'by everyone or by the majority or by the wise' (100b21f.). If 'the wise people' give their opinion, it can be easily shared by ordinary people because of their authority (e.g. 104a11f., 33–37). Dialectical propositions must be endorsed by reputable opinion (cf. 104a3–11). Dialectical arguments begin with reputable opinion as a persuasive premise in a dialectical syllogism. Reputable opinion determines the limits of dialectic. For instance, if we were allowed to ignore the context of dialectical exchange (in which the examiner asks the premises in the interrogative form), we could put his examination of two contrary claims in two contrary syllogisms. 'Every pleasure is good' (cf. 119a39, 120a15) and 'Every pleasure is bad' by offering respectively *endoxic* premises: 'Anything which is pursued is good' and 'Anything which leads to excess is bad.' If these propositions are treated dialectically, by offering *pro* and *contra* arguments on the basis of reputable opinions, the practice will remain at the level of opinion.

4.2 Introduction of 'Essence' and 'Defining-Phrase'

Among Aristotle's methodological remarks in *Topics* I.5, we find perhaps the first use of the phrase 'the what it was to be' (*to ti ên einai*) and 'defining-phrase' (*horos*) in his extant writings. He continues his remarks quoted above as [A] as follows:

[B]   But every proposition and every problem makes known a property (*idion*), a genus or an accident. The differentia, since it is genus-like, should be classified together with the genus. But since of what is proper to anything, one sort of property signifies the what it was to be (*to ti ên einai*) and another sort does not, let us divide property into the two parts stated, and let us call (*kaleisthô*) the sort that signifies the what it was to be a defining-phrase (*to men to ti ên einai sêmainon horos*), while calling the remaining part a property (*idion*), in accordance with the common designation given to them. (101b17–23)

[A] and [B] form the context in which the phrases 'the what it was to be' (*to ti ên einai*) and 'defining-phrase' (*horos*) are first introduced. The imperative 'let it be called' (*kaleisthô*) (101b21) suggests that the term 'defining-phrase' (*horos*), as the name of the account signifying the what it was to be (*to ti ên einai*) is introduced or specified here for the first time.[11] However, no explicit explanation seems to be given for the latter phrase. Nonetheless, the terms 'property' and 'defining-phrase' offer a clue as to how it is to be understood. Since Aristotle had inherited terms such as 'property' and 'genus' from Plato and employed the term '*horos*' in a previous chapter (101a11), he did not think that his reader would be confused by the novelty of these expressions. The fact that he did not devise a new name for 'the remaining sort' of property suggests that while 'property' was already a familiar term, he was trying to create a more limited target for definitions, one whose characteristics would be accepted by his colleagues in the Academy.

Defining-phrase (*horos*) is to be understood in terms of the expression 'property', as it is said to be one sort of property. The common characteristic of 'property' shared by both 'defining-phrase' and 'the other property' is 'to

---

[11] In the context of Logic, Aristotle introduces another use of '*horos*' which is translated as 'term': 'I call a term that into which the proposition is resolved, i.e. both the predicate and that of which it is predicated, "is" or "is not" being added' (*An. Pr.* A.1, 24b16f.). Since an account which signifies the essence can be treated as a term, 'the term' is wider than 'the defining-phrase' in terms of its coverage (e.g. 91b2, 94a35). Cf. S. Peterson, '*Horos* (Limit) in Aristotle's *Nicomachean Ethics*', *Phronesis* 33.3 (1988).

be predicated convertibly'. Aristotle justifies his introduction of four predicables in I.8 by saying that 'it is necessary that anything which is predicated
about something must either be or not be predicated convertibly with its
subject' (103b7f.). This implies that 'defining-phrase' (*horos*) stands for
something, presumably a sub-sentential component, which is predicated
convertibly with its subject. We must keep in mind that this is the basic
characteristic of 'defining-phrase' (*horos*).

The term '*horos*' in ordinary Greek stands for the boundary of an area or a
landmark. This concrete meaning can be transformed to signify the line by
means of which one demarcates one thing from another. There is a common feature in these differing uses of the term: that of demarcating things or
marking their identity. In Plato's writings, the use of the term '*horos*'
meaning 'boundary' or 'line' is to be found in (e.g.) *Resp.* 551b; *Laws*
714c, 739d, 962d; *Polit.* 293e, 296e. We can see further examples of this
use in Aristotelian contexts similar to Plato's (e.g. *Pol.* 1280a7, 1271a35; *Nic.
Eth.* 1138b23).[12] In *Topics* I.2, Aristotle employs this term by itself and says
that 'the man with a fallacious proof infers neither on the basis of true and
primary premises nor of reputable opinions. For he does not fall inside the
boundary (*eis gar ton horon ouk empiptei*)' (101a9–11). The man who offers a
geometrical proof, whose 'manner seems to differ from' both a dialectical
syllogism and a demonstration, does not assume a premise from either of
them (a8f.). As a result, he does not fall into the same group as the
demonstrator and dialectician. Here, Aristotle has the ordinary meaning of
the word in mind. However, the demarcating role of a boundary can easily
be transferred in a philosophical context to the identifying role of a definition.

The word 'definition' (*horismos*) involves the idea of demarcation by
fixing the identity of a relevant thing. In the Academy, it is said that 'in
connection with definitions, we are greatly preoccupied with the issue of
whether things are the same or different' (102a7–9). Their attempt to
identify a thing is described as an answer to the 'What is F?' question.

---

[12] See E. Strycker's analysis of the word '*horos*' in Plato, 'Concepts-clés et terminologie dans les livre ii
à vii des *Topiques*', in *Aristotle, On Dialectic; The Topics*, ed. G. E. L. Owen (Oxford, 1968), p. 144.
Although it is true, as Strycker says, that 'Chez Platon, *horismos* fait entièrement défaut', we do find many
occurrences in its verbal form such as *horizesthai* in Plato (e.g. *Lach.* 194c8; *Gorg.* 453a7; *Resp.* 436b5,
474c).

This is confirmed by Aristotle's remark on the Academicians' common understanding of definition as what 'is *said* to be an account of the what a thing is' (*An. Post.* B.10, 93b29).

There is no doubt that the term '*horos*' in the present context has something to do with definition. It seems to be an abbreviation of the term '*horismos*'. Aristotle assigns a similar but different name '*horos*' to the account which signifies the what it was to be (*to ti ên einai*) itself captured by a new expression which is no doubt a variant of 'the what a thing is' (*to ti esti*). As an abbreviated word shows itself to be a part of an original word, we should understand *horos* as a sub-sentential component of definition (*horismos*). It is unfortunate that in English, 'boundary' and 'definition' do not have a similar lexical composition. It would have been helpful had there been a word in English like '*definion*' which stands to 'definition' as '*horos*' stands to '*horismos*'. '*Definion*' could have shown itself by its own lexical structure to be a partial component of a definition. When Aristotle gave a new name to this predicable, it is likely that he had this similarity in mind.

Both 'defining-phrase' (*horos*) and 'definition' (*horismos*) are said to be expressions ('*logoi*', cf. 101b38, 102a5), a term with a range of senses such as 'account', 'phrase', 'argument', 'speech', 'ratio', and 'understanding'. Given the problems that had arisen in the practice of definition in the Academy, the concept of definition (*horismos*) had to be refined. My suggestion is that Aristotle introduced the term 'defining-phrase' (*horos*) to do precisely this. Definition (*horismos*) was the expression given in answer to the 'What is F?' question in such affirmative formulae as 'Man is the two-footed animal' (101b30), stating what man is. On the other hand, 'defining-phrase' (*horos*) is the sub-sentential component whose role was to signify the what it was to be man: e.g. 'the two-footed animal'. If so, the expression (*logos*) when applied to a defining phrase (*horos*) must be understood in different terms from the ones appropriate for the whole definition (*horismos*). As a translation of expression (*logos*), I shall use 'account' to maintain the ambiguity between a whole sentence and its part (cf. *De Int.* ch. 4, 16b26–17a8).

Against this background, it seems appropriate to translate '*horos*' as 'defining-phrase'. This translation will be further supported by Aristotle's explanation of this term in I.5, which is considered in the next section.

Aristotle, by analysing the sub-sentential component of a definition, can offer points (*topoi*) to use in examining various attempts at definition. In his introduction of the four predicables, when contrasting his account with that used by the Academicians, he reminds his colleagues that 'It must not be unnoticed by *us* that all arguments about property, genus and accident are also appropriate in connection with definitions (*tous horismous*)' (102b27–29). Here, Academicians, again addressed by 'we', are told that what applies to the other three predicables also applies to definition. Aristotle claims that the other predicables offer some *topoi* useful for examining definitions, as each of them provides a necessary condition. 'Because, when we have proven that something fails to belong uniquely to the thing under the definition, . . . or that what is rendered as such in the definition is not the genus, or that things stated in the account do not belong, . . . then we shall have refuted the definition(*ton horismon*)' (102b29–33 with two gaps). We cannot achieve a successful definition if we negate the accident or fail to capture the genus or what uniquely belongs to the object in question. These mistakes all undermine a definer's attempt at definition. It is important to keep in mind that, as this passage shows, the term 'definition' contains an ambiguity between a definer's definitional practice, i.e. the act of defining, and its result, i.e. the definitional proposition that emerges (such as 'Man is the two footed animal').

Aristotle introduces his new terminology of 'the what it was to be' (*to ti ên einai*) and 'defining-phrase' (*horos*) to separate these from the other three predicables. In fact, 'genus' and 'property' are both called 'elements' (*stoicheia*) of the defining-phrase (120b11). The manner in which Aristotle introduces this phrase reveals that it is a part of 'property' and has the function of dividing the latter into two types. In this way, he can specify the role of the what it was to be (*to ti ên einai*) by offering various points (*topoi*) concerning these predicables, no matter what the precise meaning of the enigmatic phrase itself is.

5 The Theory of Four Predicables

5.1 *The Two Constituents of Defining-Phrase*

Aristotle proceeds to offer an explanation of 'what a defining-phrase is' (101b37) and of the other three terms in the set.

He notes the four ways in which predicate 'P' (either a name or a phrase) is predicated of subject 'F': the so-called 'predicables' (types of term).

The 'defining-phrase' is '(1) the account, on the one hand, which signifies the what it was to be (*to ti ên einai*); but (2) it is, on the other hand, given either by an account in place of a name or by an account in place of another account (*ê logos ant' onomatos ê logos anti logou*). For it is possible for some of the things which are signified by an account to be defined (*dynaton gar kai tôn hypo logou tina sêmainomenôn horisasthai*) (cf. *An. Post.* 82b36). But people who give only a name clearly do not give the definition of the thing in question, because every definition is an account of a certain kind (*logos tis*)' (101b38–102a5).

'Property' is 'what does not make known the what it was to be for some subject but belongs only to it and is predicated convertibly with it' (102a18).

'Genus', which includes differentia too (101b8), is 'what is predicated in the what a thing is of many things which are different in species' (102a31f.).

'Accident' is 'something which is none of these, not a defining-phrase, a property, or a genus, but yet belongs to the subject' (102b4f.) or 'what can possibly belong and not belong to one and the same thing, whatever it may be' (102b6f.).

In Aristotle's introduction of the four predicables, there is an asymmetry in expression. While defining-phrase is introduced with a semantic verb 'signify', the other predicables are presented as specifying certain kinds of entity in the world. This asymmetry arises because Aristotle coins the unaccustomed term 'defining-phrase' (*horos*) for the account which signifies the what it was to be. He can discuss the other cases without distinguishing between linguistic expressions and the corresponding entities in the world because these terms are already familiar in the Academy. Further, we can readily supply a corresponding linguistic expression in each case. For instance, 'property' or 'proper account' (140b10) signifies a property of the relevant thing in the world. On the other hand, 'defining-phrase' is introduced to specify *the account* which is supposed to signify the what it was to be. Since this predicable is new, it is important to note that this account has a referential role, signifying the corresponding entity. By contrast, the other three predicables have an already established referential usage in the practices of the Academy.

In his explanation of 'defining-phrase', the sentence, with its (1) on the one hand (*men*) and (2) on the other hand (*de*) structure, suggests that Aristotle is specifying two features of any account which is a 'defining-phrase'. While such an account is supposed to signify the what it was to be, it is also employed in the place of a name (or other name-like phrase). In other words, in order for a phrase to signify the what it was to be, it can be substituted for a name (or a name-like phrase). I shall call this 'the replacement condition'. The replacement of a name or a phrase by further phrase shows that they are strictly the same. Aristotle's argument for substitution between these expressions is, 'For it is possible for some of the things which are signified by an account [a phrase] to be defined (*dynaton tina horisasthai*).' The replacement is a necessary condition for a thing to be a definable. In the case of a fictitious entity such as Pegasus, the name 'Pegasus' can be substituted by the phrase 'half bird and half horse' but there can be no definition because there is no object to which the term refers. If a thing is to be definable, both the name and its replaced phrase must have the same signification and the what it was to be be referred to by these terms.

5.2 Signification and the Logical Form of 'Defining-Phrase'

In order to understand 'defining-phrase' in this introductory passage, we need to address two specific issues. The first concerns the role of signification, the second the relation between defining-phrase and definition.

Aristotle's introductory elucidation of defining-phrase can be understood in three ways: either (1a) a phrase 'P' conveys the sense of 'the what it was to be F', or (1b) 'P' refers to the what it was to be F in the world, or else (1ab) 'P' refers to the what it was to be F through the sense of 'F'. That is, the issue is whether the account (1a) is confined merely to the linguistic level or (1b) refers to a mode of being of a thing in the world or (1ab) refers to a mode of being of a thing in the world on the basis of the sense of the expression.

When Aristotle discusses a point (*topos*) about defining-phrases, he assumes that a name and an account are applied to a thing. He says that in order to reject a defining-phrase, one has to show 'that it is not true at all to apply the account to that to which the name is applied' (139a25f.). A defining-phrase is supposed to be an account of a thing in the world.

The semantic role of the word 'signify' can be clarified by examining a further remark in the *Topics*. While discussing some aspects of the term 'property', Aristotle explains the role of the signification of a name and an account. One must not employ a homonymous name or account due to their obscurity. He says that 'One must see whether any of the names given in the property is said in several senses, and whether the whole account signifies more than one thing. For if it does, the property will not have been correctly stated. For instance, since "to perceive" signifies more than one thing, namely, "to possess perception" and "to exercise perception", "to be by nature sentient" is not a property of animal' (129b30–35). It is evident from this passage, among others, that the initial role of the word 'signify' is to offer the meaning of the relevant word (cf. 139b19–31,162b36f.). In order to be taken as a property and thus a defining-phrase, a name or an account as a whole must have a single sense. It may also have a role of reference through the established meaning of the relevant word. That is, (1ab) a defining-phrase 'P' refers to the *what it was to be F* on the basis of the established sense of 'F'. Aristotle's theory of signification consists in the theory of meaning of the term whose role has both a sense and a reference in a favourable condition.

In sum: a linguistic expression, such as the name 'F', signifies F whose mode of being is the what it was to be F (in the world) on the basis of the established meaning of 'F' (if there is a thing F which satisfies certain conditions). By 'mode of being' I mean what is referred to by the phrase 'the what it was to be F': some way of being further specified in physical or metaphysical theory. But we should remember the task of the new method of dialectic is to offer a way of examining a proposition or problem without requiring that one knows the essence of the thing. It is enough for present purposes to confirm that if the expression is put forward as the defining-phrase, it must meet certain conditions. In this way we can argue about satisfactoriness of an account without already knowing what the essence in question is.

On this basis, we arrive at the following characterization of a defining phrase: (1ab') An account 'P' is called 'defining-phrase' of a thing F iff (i) 'P' signifies the what it was to be F & (ii) 'P' replaces the name 'F' (or a phrase 'the F') which signifies F & (iii) the what it was to be F is definable.

Aristotle introduces the word 'defining-phrase' and the phrase 'the what it was to be' as classificatory terms. When he speaks of them he is concerned with whether one '*says* the what it was to be' (*to ti ên einai*) or not so as to define it well with respect to the other predicables (e.g. 143a18, 146b32). In this context, the what it was to be (*to ti ên einai*) is not further explained and the term 'defining-phrase' is employed to indicate it (whatever it is). This is the initial baptism of the what it was to be.

But why didn't Aristotle explain what the what it was to be (*to ti ên einai*) more fully? One reason is that to enquire into 'what the what it was to be consists in and how it is by itself' (*Met.* Z.11, 1037a21, cf. 1025b28) is part of a metaphysical investigation of being, not required in constructing the theory of dialectic. If so, the role of 'the what it was to be' in the *Topics* is merely to differentiate it from the three other predicables. The phrase 'the what it was to be' functions simply as a sign to characterize and distinguish the defining-phrase. In fact, Aristotle discusses various points (*topoi*) about the defining-phrase by pointing to similarities with and dissimilarities from the other three predicables. But why did he need such a concept? The reason is, as I shall argue, that he wished to use it to pursue some aspects of Socratic enquiry without directly engaging with 'What is F?' question. If we keep in mind the Academic background, we will be better able to understand his enterprise.

5.3 The Replacement Condition of Defining-Phrase and its Relation with Definition

I shall now point to some characteristics of the term 'defining-phrase' and offer an interpretation of its relationship with 'definition'. The word 'given' in the sentence '(2) it is, on the other hand, given . . . by an account in place of a name' refers not to a whole definition which states what a thing is (such as 'Man is the two-footed animal') but rather indicates an account which occupies the place of a name.

Aristotle notes three types of sameness between a name and a phrase in I.7. He says that, 'The most strict and primary way of sameness is presented, when it is given either by a name or by a defining-phrase, as when "coat" is same as "cloak" or "two-footed land animal" as "man"' (103a26–28). In this case, a name can be replaced by its defining-phrase because both signify the same definable thing, that is, man. In the case of names such as 'coat' and 'cloak', what is signified is also strictly the same because their defining-phrases are the same (cf. 162b36f.). The substitution of defining-phrase for a name is justified if they signify strictly the same thing.

In the case of properties, it is possible that there are several necessary properties which belong to a relevant thing where each is predicated convertibly with the subject (103a29f.). Here, the replacement condition is not uniquely satisfied in this case, though the terms always signify the same thing (cf. 140a33–b2, section 8). In the case of accidents such as between 'Socrates' and 'the one sitting', the replacement condition is not strictly met either, even though both terms signify the same thing in some contexts (103a31).

Aristotle, in considering a point (*topos*) about 'whether one has defined and said *to ti ên einai* or not' (141a24f.), concludes from a formal (*logikos*) argument that there must be a single essence for the thing revealed in a single definition. He notes that 'there is a single being which is the very thing for each being (*hekastôi gar tôn ontôn hen esti to einai hoper estin*)' (141a35). If there were several definitions of the same thing, the object defined would be the same as the one represented in each of the definitions. Here I take 'the very thing for each of the beings' as identical with the what it was to be (*to ti ên einai*: 141a24).

The defining-phrase, because it captures this single essence of the object, can replace a name or name-like phrase (see examples of replacement, e.g. 110a4–6, 140b32–141a2, cf. *An. Pri.* A.39). Thus we can say that a defining-phrase is the sub-sentential component of a successful definition, which can replace the name for the thing signified. 'Defining-phrase' is a general name of an account which can replace a name and signify the what it was to be. This suggests that since 'defining-phrase' (*horos*) is the expression signifying a definable thing, it should be distinguished from definition (*horismos*), which consists in a defining-phrase predicated of the subject to be defined. Thus, I take 'defining-phrase' (*horos*) to be a proper component of a definition (*horismos*). For instance, if 'man' and 'two-footed land animal' signify the same definable object man, its successful definition composed of its defining-phrase will be that 'Man is the two-footed land animal'.

The expression 'defining-phrase' (*horos*) is employed to explain certain characteristics of definitions (*horismoi*). Consider the following passage: 'The examination from the point of view of greater degrees is of no use when a single definition (*horismos*) is compared with two things, or two definitions (*horismôn*) with one thing. For there cannot be one defining-phrase for two things or two defining-phrases (*horous*) of the same thing' (154a8–11). Here, Aristotle uses the term 'defining-phrase' to pick out certain aspects of definitional practice.

The defining-phrase also constitutes the goal of definitional practice. That is, the defining-phrase is introduced and described from the point of view of successful definitions. Aristotle, on occasion, suggests the possibility that a defining-phrase itself might be refuted, in the passage, 'It is obvious that a defining-phrase is the easiest of all [predicables] to refute but the most difficult to confirm' (155a27f., cf. 153a6–22). Here, it might look as if Aristotle is denying that 'defining-phrase' is always a success term. However, this sentence speaks of characteristics of defining-phrase as a point (topos) of contrast with the other three predicables. It is said to be the most difficult of all to affirm or construct, indicating the ideal nature of a predicable. In specific practices, this topos has the role of warning the people who try to define a thing. By 'defining-phrase', Aristotle sometimes refers to an account called 'the defining-phrase' ('what is purported to be the defining-phrase': ho lechtheis horos) (e.g. 139b36, 148a14, cf. 148a25). If so, the specific accounts mentioned do not have in fact to be defining-phrases. As 'something claimed to be a property' need not be a property, so something claimed to be a defining-phrase can also turn out not really to be one (132b32f.).

Aristotle, or so I have suggested, introduces his new theory of dialectic, with its own distinctive terminology, to overcome some difficulties which Academicians had faced in their enquiry into 'What is F?' Since he was constructing his account in this context, it is no wonder that he takes over the Academicians' term for definitions (or definitional practices) (horismos) as his own. Nonetheless, their practice needs to be grounded in his new theory of dialectic. By introducing 'defining-phrase', he has taken a step towards providing a better account of definitional practices.

My account differs from the standard view which fails to distinguish definition from defining-phrase. In his 'study of the defining-phrase', Aristotle states 'five' conditions which definitions 'must' (dei) satisfy (VI.1, 139a24–35). A definition must (1) be a universal and true predication of its definiendum; (2) put the definiendum in its proper genus and the differentiae, (3) be the proper account for its definiendum, (4) state the what it was to be (to ti ên einai) of the definiendum over and above the (1) (2) (3) conditions, and (5) define it well (kalôs). These remarks show that 'the defining-phrase' is to be understood in the context of the theory of the four predicables. As the term 'must', which appears three times (139a26, 28, 31) in this passage, reveals, definitions (or definitional practices), by contrast, can employ any of the four predicables and hence can fall short of issuing in a defining-phrase. Definitional practice in the Academy can issue in any of the possibilities just mentioned. This is why Aristotle needed to introduce and employ the term 'defining-phrase' (*horos*). There are about sixty occurrences of '*horos*' (defining-phrase) in the *Topics* altogether.[13] In these passages, there is a clear difference between the newly introduced word 'defining-phrase' and the traditional word 'definition'.

It is important to note that Aristotle leaves to other more accurate treatises the task of stating 'what a defining-phrase is'. He says that 'To say what a defining-phrase is (*ti estin horos*) and how it should be defined (*pôs horizesthai dei*) belongs to another more accurate enquiry' (153a11f.). The nature of a proper definition is the subject of further philosophical enquiry. In a treatise devoted to examining arguments, it is enough to note that, 'At present it concerns us only so far as is required for our present purpose' (153a12f.). By 'another more accurate enquiry', he seems to refer to the *Posterior Analytics* and the *Metaphysics*, where he develops the theory of definition on the basis of a theory of demonstration which aims to grasp the causal structure of the world.[14]

---

[13] Among about sixty occurrences of 'defining-phrase', we can divide its usages into roughly five groups. I shall offer text references of each of these groups, although some cases could be put into other group(s).

Aristotle employs '*horos*' in the following contexts:

(a) in discussing its function and ingredients (e.g. (1)01b22, 38, 02a26, 35a11, 40a27, 41b3, 53a12, 20, 21, 53a15, 16, 54a11);

(b) in enumerating it together with the other predicables (e.g. (1)01b25, 37, 03b5, 18);

(c) when its *topoi* are concerned with establishing and rejecting a proposed defining-phrase; (e.g. (1) 30a31, b14, 25, 31b37, 52b38, 53a2, 6, 8, b26, 26, 54a24, 35, 36, b1, 2, 55a3, 7, 10, 18);

(d) in relation to definitional practices as their guide (e.g. (1)39a24, 40a24, 41a34, 48a26, 32, b23, 49a29, 30 (I adopt the codex 'cu'), 54a11, 58a33);

(e) in giving examples (e.g. (1)18b21, 21a11, 39b25, 36, 40b2, 7, 29, 48a15, 20, 26, 49b26, 51b1, 58b16). The examples of defining-phrase are raised just for the sake of argument with respect to other predicables and discussing *topoi* on this predicable.

[14] I have argued elsewhere that Aristotle developed three types of defining-phrase in *Posterior Analytics* B.10 to establish a new theory of causal definition. Three defining-phrases connect the traditional method of definition in the Academy with his new scientific method of demonstration. Kei Chiba, 'Aristotle's Theory of Definition in *Posterior Analytics* B.10', *Journal of the Graduate School of Letters Hokkaido University* 3 (2008), pp. 1–17. See my web version http://eprints.lib.hokudai.ac.jp/dspace/handle/2115/32407.

Let me briefly confirm that the *Topics* type defining-phrase of signifying account can constitute an *Analytics* type definition of what a thing is. In B.10 Aristotle says in a parallel passage with *Topics* I.5, 101b38–2a5 that 'Since a definition is said to be an account of the what a thing is, it is obvious that the definition will be some account of what a name or else other name-like phrase signifies, for example, the what "the triangle" signifies is what triangle is, insofar as it is triangle' (93b29–32). The 'obviousness' of identifying 'some account of what a name signifies' with a definitional account comes from the formality of the four possible combinations between these two types of accounts. The four combinations are as

5.4 How are the Four Types of Predicables Chosen?

A feature shared by all predicables is that each has something to do with definition: 'all [predicables] are in a sense definitory (*horika*)' (102b34). I take it that since these all can be offered as definitions, Aristotle labels all predicables 'definitory (boundary marker)'. He introduces 'definitory (boundary marker)' in the context of offering and asking for a definition.

One may call 'definitory' such a remark as that 'the beautiful is the fitting', and likewise also the question, 'Are perception and knowledge the same or different?' For in connection with definitions, we are greatly preoccupied with the issue of whether things are the same or different. In a word, let it be called 'definitory' (boundary marker) everything that falls under the same method as the definitions. (102a5–10; see note 15)

Predicables, I take it, are chosen because they are in some way appropriate in the formulation of a definition (cf. 102b27–35). Anyone who claims that a predicable constitutes a definition of the relevant subject must claim that it is, in some way, the same as the object defined. In classifying the types of identity involving the predicables, the defining-phrase is to be preferred as it involves 'the most strict and primary way of the sameness' (103a25f.). 'Genus' proffers a loose identity with its species to the effect that for instance 'Man is animal' (cf. 102a35). 'Accident' also grasps a kind of identity 'as when the creature who is sitting, or who is musical, is called the same as Socrates' (103a30f.). At the end of his discussion of the four predicables in I.8, 'accident' is characterized as signifying anything which is not contained in definition of a subject but still belongs to it (103b16–19).

follows, where 'E' stands for the account of what a thing is and 'S' stands for the account of what a name signifies: (1) (E^+S^+), (2) (E^+S^-), (3) (E^-S^+), and (4) (E^-S^-). In B.7, 92b26–34, Aristotle discusses the possibility of (3) (E^-S^+) and explains its absurdity with three reasons. He says that 'Thus if the definer proves either what a thing is or what a name signifies, if there is certainly not a definition of the what a thing is, the definition must be an account signifying the same as a name. But this is absurd' (92b26–29). He raises a spurious alternative to choose between what a name signifies and what a thing is by separating the one from the other. In other words, he raises this on the assumption that the account of what a name signifies will never be taken as the account of what a thing is, although this assumption itself is not endorsed by anything. Given that a definer cannot deal with the what a thing is, a definer only proves what a name signifies. But this is absurd. See 92b29–34 for the three reasons of absurdity. Given the rejection of (3) (E^-S^+) in B.7 and the acceptance of (E^+) in his statement 'Since a definition is said to be an account of the what a thing is' in B.10, it becomes 'obvious' that among the accounts of what a name signifies, i.e. (1) (E^+S^+) and (3) (E^-S^+), 'some account' that is the account of (1) (E^+S^+) 'will be' a definition. A linguistic act of stating what a name 'triangle' signifies will be the account of what a triangle is, insofar as it signifies the triangle in the world.

An accident can be put forward as a candidate of definition because 'nothing prevents an accident from being a property at some specific time or in relation to something' (102b21f.). For instance, 'not retreating from the front in a battle' can be a property of courage in a certain context (*Laches* 190e, cf. 125b22, 151a2f.). Since there is a case in which courage can be identified as 'not retreating from the front in a battle', even an accident can be called 'definitory'. Nonetheless, immediately it becomes clear that the proposed definition is merely referring to an accident, it will be rejected. If one can show that the phrase 'not retreating from the front in a battle' can apply in other contexts to cowardice or recklessness, it is no more than an accident of courage. If the selection of predicables is understood in the context of a classification of possible definitions, we can see that Aristotle is attempting to refine the Socratic enquiry into *the what a thing is*. By separating various relevant predicables, he can avoid some of the confusions which trapped Socrates and his interlocutors.

Aristotle says, 'All the things we have enumerated would in a way be definitory (boundary marker). But we should not for this reason seek a single universal method for all cases' (102b33–36). His point is, once again, directed against the Socratic method of enquiry into definition. Aristotle continues, 'For it is not easy to find it and besides, if it were found, it would be thoroughly obscure and inconvenient for the study at hand' (102b36–38).[15] Instead, he offers exhaustive answers to that question corresponding to each division of predicables. Since the predicables are offered as exhaustive and mutually exclusive answers to the 'What is F?' question, we can

---

[15] R. Smith failed to notice the role of the 'definitory' in considering the predicables. He wrote that, 'The content [of I.6] is curious: first, Aristotle argues that we could really call all the "questions" definitory; next, he says that this is no reason for seeking a single procedure, citing the elusiveness and inconvenience it would have' (Smith, *Aristotle, Topics Books I and VIII*, p. 67). But there is nothing really 'curious' in this chapter. First, 'the problem' is called definitory because it concerns the classification of possible responses to 'What is F?' without directly asking the 'What is F?' question. Second, even if these accounts were all definitory, we should not seek a single universal method as in Socratic enquiry. It is Socrates' search for one universal method in finding definitions that is being criticized.

Since J. Brunschwig did not see the special significance of 'definitory' and failed to distinguish 'defining–phrase' from 'definition', he was forced to attribute his own misunderstanding to Aristotle when he claimed that there is a discrepancy in Aristotle's explanations of 'definitory' between I.5, 102a9f and I.6, 102b33–35. He says that 'les lignes [102b]33–35 contiennent une véritable erreur de la part d'Aristote ... Les considérations du chapitre 6 ne montrent nullement que les prédicables non-définitionnels soient justiciables de la même méthode que les définitions; elles montrent, ce qui est tout différent, que les définitions sont justiciables des mêmes méthods que les prédicables non-définitionnels.' J. Brunschwig, *Aristote Topiques I–IV* (Paris, 1967), p. lxxxi.

dispense with the simple Socratic 'What is F?' question and examine rather the forms of predication used in putting forward any proposition as definition.

My suggestion is that Aristotle developed his account of the predicables and of *topoi* more generally as part of his account of dialectic with the aim of analysing and refining Socratic enquiry into essence or definition. He offers a new terminology 'defining-phrase' (*horos*) and 'the what it was to be' (*to ti ên einai*) to capture what Socrates sought in his definition-directed enquiry, even though he lacked a proper method. Aristotle strengthens Socratic 'weak' dialectic by developing a theory of predicables and of points (*topoi*) to understand aspects of Socratic enquiry into definition 'without [directly asking] the "What is F?" [question]' (1078b26). These predicables are the exhaustive ingredients of any dialectical proposition put forward as possible answers to the Socratic 'What is F?' question, when considering 'how one ought to speak' by the method of formal argument (*logikôs*) about 'the what a thing is' (cf. 1030a27).

6 A Grammatical Analysis of 'the what it was to be' (*to ti ên einai*)

I shall now offer, against the background of Socratic enquiry, a grammatical analysis of the phrase 'the what it was to be' (*to ti ên einai*). In replying to the 'What is F?' (*ti esti;*) question, 'the what F is' (*to ti esti*) can provide a formal answer. In linguistic terms, 'the what F is' can be the response as any one of four predicables which is called 'definitory'. My suggestion is that the phrase 'the what it was to be' (*to ti ên einai*) is coined as a modified form of 'the what a thing is' (*to ti esti*) to refer to what it is to be the thing itself. When Socrates was given an answer involving one of three other predicables, he asked again for the thing itself using his 'What is F?' (*ti esti;*) question. I shall argue that the phrase 'the what it was to be' (*to ti ên einai*) is the one Aristotle used to capture the answer to Socrates' basic 'What is F?' question. It serves, *au fond*, as Aristotle's way of capturing the goal of Socrates' enquiry.

If my proposal is correct, we will have arrived at an account of this phrase on the basis of an understanding of the philosophical context in which it was introduced. In effect, Aristotle formulates the expression 'the what it was to be' (*to ti ên einai*) so that the interrogative sentence is prefixed by the article 'the' (*to*) to serve as a response to the Socratic question. If my proposal withstands criticism, it will not be the case, as M. Loux once suggested, that 'any account of the expression "what it was to be" (*to ti ên einai*) must remain conjectural' (see note 1).

Scholars have discussed the original form of the phrase ((1)) and the two 'be' verbs ((2) *einai* (3) *ên*). There is a debate, concerning (2), as to whether 'to be' (*einai*) is a 'predicate nominative' or an 'existential use'. The former is translated as 'to be F', the latter as 'for F to be'. The other issue which has been discussed, (3), is why the imperfect 'was' (*ên*) is employed.

First, I should like to clarify why and in what sense Aristotle used the infinitive phrase and the imperfect tense of the verb 'to be' ((2) (3)). I shall then seek to determine the original form (1) on the basis of my reading of (2) and (3).

There are many cases in which 'the what it was to be' (*to ti ên einai*) is complemented by a dative noun, such as for 'each thing' (*hekastôi*) or 'for the thing defined' (*horizomenôi*) (e.g. 139a33, 153a15, 1022a9, 1029b20, 1031b30, 1035b16) and sometimes by a genitive noun (e.g. 1032a2, b2). But it is not obvious whether the dative serves as the complement of (2) 'to be' (*einai*). Rather, the context suggests that the dative or genitive noun fixes the thing whose essence is at issue. Thus the translation should be 'the essence for F' or 'the essence of F'.

There is further evidence that (2) 'to be' (*einai*) should be complemented by a dative noun. There are cases in which the dative noun is put into the phrase like '*to ti ên ekeinôi einai*' (1031b7, 1030a2, 1029b27, 649b22), which should read, 'the what it was to be that thing' as a predicate nominative. There are two reasons for taking the phrase (2) 'to be' (*einai*) with the dative noun F as its complement as an example of the predicative use of 'to be' nominative.

First, Aristotle uses the dative noun with 'to be' (*einai*) and a definite article such as 'to be you' (*to soi einai*) (1029b14) interchangeably with 'the what it was to be' [the essence] (1029b18, 1041b6). Aristotle says that 'First let us say something about the essence by the way of formal argument (*logikôs*). The essence of each thing is what it is said to be in virtue of itself. For to be you is not to be musical' (1029b13–15). In many formal (*logikos*) expressions, the phrase signifies the essence, that is, the thing itself. When Aristotle says that 'For to be you (*to soi einai*) is not to be musical (*to mousikôi einai*)' above quoted, we should not understand this verb existentially. Nothing is gained by reading these two phrases 'for you to be' and 'for musical to be'. Simple or existential being is not at issue here. Rather we are concerned to discover whether to be you (which in fact belongs to the category of substance) and to be musical (which belongs to the one of quality) are identical.

Second, from the viewpoint of Socratic enquiry, the way to ask for the thing itself would be by the predicative use of 'to be' nominative. If, as sometimes has been suggested, Socrates did not always distinguish clearly between two questions: 'What does the word "F" signify?' and 'What is the thing F?' when using the 'What is F?' question, he may not have considered the existence or non-existence of the relevant thing.[16] For Aristotle, the first stage of enquiry is to know what the word signifies in order to reach to the grasp of essence through the grasp of its existence. Although Socrates only asked his 'What is F?' question in the area of ethics, his method of enquiry still offers a starting-point for the attempt to decipher the enigmatic phrase of 'the what it was to be' (*to ti ên einai*).

Although several interpretations of (3) the imperfect 'was' (*ên*) have been offered, I shall present an alternative on the basis of my previous discussion. While Socrates did not have anything apart from the expression 'What is F?', he did distinguish between questions which ask for examples and those which ask for the thing itself. When examples are given, Socrates is not satisfied and asks again, adding the particle 'then' (*pote*) as emphasis: 'What then is F?' Aristotle also uses 'then' (*pote*), when asking for the thing itself in the question 'What then is the thing said in itself?' (102b14). W. Goodwin comments on the imperfect 'was' (*ên*) which usually accompanies the particles 'then' (*pote* or *ara*) as follows: 'The imperfect "was" (*ên*) (generally with "*ara*") may express a *fact* which is just recognized as such by the speaker or writer, having previously been denied, overlooked, or not understood'.[17]

---

[16] D. Charles argues that Socrates did not distinguish accounts of what terms signify from accounts of the essences of the thing. D. Charles, 'Types of Definition in the *Meno*' in *Remembering Socrates*, ed. L. Judson and V. Karasmanis (Oxford, 2006), pp. 117ff.

[17] W. Goodwin, *Syntax of the Moods and Tenses of the Greek Verb* (London, 1929), p. 13. A typical example of dialectical imperfect is found in Aristophanes' *Birds* 279f.: 'Here is still another bird who is secured a crest. What kind of apparition is this? *Were* you then not the only hoopoe, but is he another hoopoe?' (*Ti to teras touti pot'estin; Ou su monos ar'êsth'epops, alla houtos heteros;*). We can find this type of imperfect in mathematical proofs reminding us of a fact which initially went unnoticed but was revealed in the process of proof (94a34). Similar usages of the imperfect are, e.g. 1051a23, 26, 92a16. When, in his

I shall call this use of imperfect the 'dialectical imperfect'. One example of this use in English is the following: 'what it was for the soul to be immortal has been, and still is the topic of discussion'. Goodwin's explanation can also be applied to the interrogative sentence. The role of 'then' (*ara*) in the interrogative form is sometimes said to express 'the anxiety of the question-er'.[18] When Socrates asks 'What is F?' and is not satisfied with the answer given, he asks again about F itself, which his interlocutor has overlooked or not understood. Given his dissatisfaction with the answer he has been given, his original intention in asking the 'What is F?' question is expressed by the imperfect 'was' (*ên*): that of asking for the thing itself again. So understood, this phrase is used to indicate the fact that Socrates, well aware that some-thing has been overlooked in the responses so far given, has throughout been searching for the thing itself. This is why the phrase is used in its modified form of 'the what it was to be' (*to ti ên einai*). If this is correct, there is no need to accept the metaphysical interpretations that have been offered which suggest that the imperfect 'puts an objective meaning', introduces 'timeless, separate forms', or expresses 'fundamental and eternal being' which precedes particular beings.[19]

If my interpretation of the two verbs 'to be' is correct, we may entertain a further conjecture about the original form (1). Ross took it that this phrase is a 'generalization' of an interrogative expression such as 'What was it to be blood for the blood itself?' (*ti ên autôi to haimati einai;*) (649b22). Arpe, Frede, and Patzig also suggest that the object F in the phrase 'the what it was to be' (*to ti ên einai*) originally appears twice with another dative with the definite article such as '[*to*] *ti ên tôi anthrôpôi anthrôpôi einai'.*[20] However, given our general approach, we should focus on the original form of the question posed in interrogative sentences such as 'What was it then for F itself to be F?' (*ti ara ên autôi to F einai;*). In this way, we can see the phrase as

commentary of *Topics* I.5 Alexander suggests that the imperfect tense is equivalent to the present tense 'is', it is not clear whether he has a dialectical imperfect in mind. He says that 'Now, "*ên*" is not used to express the time which has passed, but rather the "*esti*". This kind of use is customary. A man saying "*touto ên*" says the same as "*tout' esti*" and one can say "Who was knocking at the door?" instead of "Who is knocking at the door?"' Alexander Aphrodisiensis, *In Aristotelis Topicorum Libros Octo Commentaria*, ed. M. Wallies (Berlin, 1891), p. 42.

[18] Liddell & Scott, *Greek–English Lexicon* (Oxford, 1996), ad loc.

[19] Owens, *Doctrine of Being*, p. 183; C. Arpe, *Das ti en einai bei Aistoteles* (Hamburg, 1938), pp. 15, 18.

[20] D. Ross, *Aristotle's Metaphysics I* (Oxford, 1924), p. 127. Arpe, *Das ti en einai*, S. 18; Frede and Patzig, *Aristoteles Metaphysik Z Kommentar II*, S. 34, 'Was es für den Menschen heißt, ein Mensch zu sein'.

pointing to an appropriate response to the Socratic question about the thing itself.

We are now in a position better to understand the phrase 'the what it was to be' (*to ti ên einai*). The what it was to be (*to ti ên einai*) is the entity which Socrates was seeking for in asking the 'What is F?' question. Socrates was not satisfied with answers which used the other three predicables. A common feature of his enquiry is that when he initially asks his 'What is F?' question, he explains that he is not looking for an example of F but rather for what F itself is. The initial attempt to define the what it was to be (*to ti ên einai*) 'developed in the time of Socrates', consisted in investigating a number of questions of the form 'What is F?' (642a26–28). What was really sought in asking this question was in fact something which cannot be given by offering examples in the sense of accidents or 'elements [genus or differentia]' (cf. 120b12) but only by giving a defining-phrase. Socrates did not have any other way of asking for a definition than by raising the 'What is F?' (*ti esti;*) question. Aristotle coined the phrase 'the what it was to be' as part of his attempt to refine and build on Socratic dialectic by indicating the thing which Socrates was seeking in his enquiry.

It is important to note, in this context, that Aristotle urges his reader to consider a *topos* on 'what is defined' (*horizomenon*) whether 'the thing itself' or 'genus' (*auto ê kata to genos*) is mentioned in the definition (146a36–b12). Also in *Topics* V where various *topoi* concerning the property are enumerated, a defining-phrase is said to make clear 'the thing itself'. Aristotle says 'a thing itself reveals in every case to be itself, and that which reveals to be [itself] is not a property but a defining-phrase' (135a10–12). In this way, the defining-phrase in the *Topics* can be seen as what Socrates was seeking as an answer to his 'What is F?' question. The proper response to this question is a defining-phrase, which signifies the what it was to be (*to ti ên einai*).

7 Justification of Four Predicables and Ten Categories

7.1 Deduction of Four Predicables

In this section, I shall argue on the basis of an analysis of *Topics* I.8 and I.9 that Aristotle develops his new system of predications to resolve certain difficulties that arose for the Socratic enquiry into what a thing is. Aristotle argues in I.8 that all predications are composed of four types of predicables (103b2f.). In I.9, he introduces ten genera of predications in which these four types of predicables can be found. All possible predications are made up from these four types of mutually exclusive predicables. By dividing the Academy's traditional enquiry into what a thing is between ten categories of predications and entities, Aristotle refines the Socratic enquiry into what a thing is and attempts to overcome some of its shortcomings.

In I.8, Aristotle offers 'a warrant' (*pistis*) 'through induction' (103b3) and 'through deduction' (b7) that there are four and only four mutually exclusive predicables. Any proposition will contain one of the four predicables (exhaustive thesis (101b17f.)) and only one of them (exclusive thesis (101b23–25)) (cf. 101a18f., 101b38, 102a31f., 103b15f., 153a15–21). If this is correct, the theory based on the four predicables will provide the resources to examine all propositions, including those introduced in definitional practice.

Aristotle's inductive proof is that if anyone surveys propositions and problems one by one, they will find that each contains one of four predicables (103b3–6). His deductive proof is composed of three either–or questions whose range is successively narrowed. Aristotle deduces that there are four types of predicables on the basis of one general division: (A) 'every predicate of a subject must of necessity be either convertible with its subject or not' (103b7f.). I call this 'property condition', following the initial introduction of both 'defining-phrase' and 'property' (cf. 101b19). The property condition (A) prepares the way for further divisions. In the case of predicates which are convertible, the next criterion is (i) whether the term signifies the essence ('the what it was to be') or not. In the case of non-convertible predicates, the next criterion is (ii) whether it either is or is not one of the terms contained in the definition of the subject. Aristotle deduces the four predicables on this basis.

There is a common basis for the selection of criteria (i) and (ii). Aristotle has in his mind the following question: Is the predicate predicated of a subject in the what it is or not? (cf. 102a32, 153a18). I shall call this 'the what it is condition' (B). Through (A) the property condition, and (B) the what it is condition, we can confirm both the exhaustiveness and the exclusiveness of the four predicables: the defining-phrase (A^+B^+), the property (A^+B^-), the genus (A^-B^+), and the accident (A^-B^-).[21] In I.4–7 we saw that the introduction of four predicables is made on the basis of an analysis of possible answers to the Socratic 'What is F?' In I.8 Aristotle shows the centrality of the what it is condition in enumerating the four predicables. He attempts to prove that any way of saying what a thing is will employ one of the four predicables. On this basis he can go on in I.9 to establish a system of argument which can be applied to any subject-matter whatsoever.

7.2 Categories of Predications as a Frame of Dialectical Arguments

In I.9, Aristotle examines kinds of arguments by developing a theory of the categories of predications. The conclusion of the chapter says that, 'Therefore, these, then, and so many are the items which arguments concern and from which they are composed' (103b39f., cf. 105a20), where the items in question are types of predication which correspond to distinct types of entities. As 'being' and 'good' are classified in many ways in the *Metaphysics* and the *Nicomachean Ethics*, 'arguments', or rather their constituents, 'predications', will be classified in ten ways in this chapter. Aristotle distinguishes the genera of predications to which all four types of predicables belong by considering various ordinary interrogative forms with the aim of determining the kinds of dialectical argument.[22]

Aristotle begins the chapter as follows:

After these [discussions in I.8], the genera of the predications in the things which the four above-mentioned belong to (*en hois hyparchousin*) must be distinguished. These are ten in number, what a thing is, how much a thing is, how a thing is like, what relation, where, when, to-be-situated, to-have, to-do, to-be-affected. For the accident and the genus and the property and the definition (*horismos*) will always be (*estai*) in a single [predication] of these predications. For all propositions composed

---

[21] While Wagner and Rapp note this exclusive classification into four predicables, they do not consider the ground of the subdivision of (A) or explain why two further parallel questions (i), (ii) are raised. *Aristoteles Topik*, S. 276. Cf. A. Kitago, 'Predicables and Categories in Aristotle's *Topics* A.8–9', *TETSUGAKU, Annals of the Philosophical Society of Hokkaido University* 43 (2007), pp. 1–20.

[22] M. Frede, for instance, failed to see the connection between the predicables and the categories, when he says that, 'We are told in the first sentence of A.9 that having distinguished the predicables we next have to distinguish the categories. Obviously our understanding of what the categories are supposed to be would be greatly increased if we had a better understanding of why Aristotle thinks that we have to make this distinction, of how he thinks it is to be made. Unfortunately, Aristotle in the *Topics* does not enter into a discussion of either of these questions.' M. Frede, 'Categories in Aristotle', in *Essays in Ancient Philosophy* (Oxford, 1987), p. 47.

from these indicate either what a thing is or how a thing is like or how much a thing is or one of the genera of predications. (103b20–27)

I translate, following several other commentators, '*ta genê tôn katêgoriôn*' as 'the genera of the predications'.[23] There are four reasons for this. (1) The noun ('*hê katêgoria*') means predication or the act of predicating, as do its verbal forms such as '*katêgoreitai*' (107a3, 109b5, 141a4, 152a38, 178a5, 181b27).[24] (2) The fact that the first item on the list is not 'substance' but 'what a thing is' suggests that Aristotle is concerned to distinguish kinds of predications, which can be used to answer different types of question, rather than kinds of entity (166b10, 16). (3) The phrase 'the genera of predications' is used elsewhere to indicate that the genera in question are types of predication, made using a single word such as 'good' (107a3, a18, 152a38, 178a6; *An. Post.* 83b15). Here, the phrase is employed in the examination of a word's meaning at the linguistic level. Thus, Aristotle notes that while 'good' in the predication (proposition) 'the food is good' means 'productive of pleasure', in the predication 'the medicine is good' it means 'productive of health'. (4) Since English has the technical term 'category' to refer to genera or classes, we are naturally tempted to translate the literally corresponding Greek word '*hê katêgoria*' in this way. However, the Greek term is perfectly understandable without any such addition. Thus, Joachim translates it as 'predicating "being"' or 'predication of "being"' (*G. C.* 317b6).[25] If the context requires, Aristotle explicitly writes 'genus of being' (189a14, b24). Indeed, the Greek term '*ta genê*' rather than '*tôn katêgoriôn*' corresponds to the English term 'genus' or 'class' (cf. 165a38). Indeed, this is why in 103b20 Aristotle talks of the 'the genera of predications'.

Aristotle in I.9 addresses the question, 'In how many ways is *predication* said?' However, the expression 'the predication' (*hê katêgoria*) is act/result ambiguous: it can refer either to the act of predicating or to the result of that act, a proposition composed both of a subject and of a predicate. In this it

[23] Brunschwig, *Aristote Topiques I–IV*, ad loc., n. 2; Smith, *Aristotle, Topics Books I and VIII*, p. 74; L. A. Dorion, *Aristote: Les réfutations sophistiques* (Paris, 1995), p. 347.

[24] The term '*hê katêgoria*', which is found at least 11 times in the *Topics*, has received a number of interpretations, without a settled consensus emerging (103b20, b25, b27, b29, b39, 107a3, 109b5, 141a4, 152a38, 178a5, 181b27, cf. 107b18). The expression '*hê katêgoria*' has been taken to be the class or genus in the technical sense or to be the predication or sometimes the predicate. Cf. Frede, 'Categories in Aristotle'.

[25] H. H. Joachim, *Aristotle on Coming-To-Be and Passing-Away* (Oxford, 1922; Olms, 1970), p. 91.

resembles the term 'definition' which, as I have noted, can refer both to the act of defining and to the resulting definitional proposition (such as 'Man is a rational animal'). It is important to keep these two meanings in mind in what follows.

Aristotle, it appears, introduces his ten genera of predication which I call 'the categories of predications (CP)' on the basis of his examination of various ordinary interrogative forms. This is why he employs several interrogative expressions without changing their grammatical form or devising technical expressions to denote the categories (classes, genera, or kinds). Since, as Ackrill points out, 'The Greek [such as "*poion*", "*poson*"] is a word that serves both as an interrogative and as an indefinite adjective', we cannot determine to which grammatical form this expression belongs except by considering the context.[26] Since Aristotle is establishing a system for dialectic, these expressions have to be derived from a consideration of the questions raised. However, since the number of interrogative forms is limited, other types of predication which express the agent's or thing/event's state, possession, action, and how it is acted upon have to be introduced on the basis of an infinitive verb. These phrases are shorthand for 'How is F situated?', 'What does F have?', 'What does F do?', 'How is F affected?'

Aristotle seeks to justify his choice of ten genera of predication by offering an inductive argument, as is indicated by his employment of a singular future tense together with the adverb 'always' (103b23–25). He argues that one will always find one or other of the four predicables employed in one or other of these ten genera of predications and nowhere else. Since we are talking of predications, Aristotle employs the term 'definition' rather than 'defining-phrase' (b24). For the relevant predication is a whole proposition not one of its sub-sentential (or sub-propositional) components.

Aristotle next explains the connection between a predicable and a predication (proposition). He says, 'For all propositions made through these [four] indicate either what a thing is or how a thing is like or how much a thing is or some one of the other predications' (b25f.). If there are just four sub-sentential components (predicables) and all propositions (predications) made using these fall within one or other of the ten genera mentioned,

---

[26] J. Ackrill, *Aristotle's Categories and De Interpretatione* (Oxford, 1963), p. 76.

Aristotle will have shown the exhaustiveness of his list of categories. All propositions can be classified within one of these ten genera of predication.

Aristotle's choice of interrogatives is not arbitrary as they are distinguished in ordinary usage. The responses to these ten questions indicate 'what a thing is', 'how a thing is like', 'how much a thing is', and so on. In basing his account on these questions, Aristotle's approach is more systematic than Düring imagined when he wrote, 'Which forms of meaningful assertions can we make with respect to him (Koriskos)?'[27] For Aristotle can accommodate all propositions in one of the ten genera, depending on which question they answer. His list of interrogatives is confirmed, as we shall see in the next section, by the fact that the list of terms for entities introduced to answer these interrogatives (such as terms for substances, qualities, and times) is itself exclusive and exhaustive. He concludes that while there are only four sub-sentential components (predicables), there are ten genera of predications (propositions) which constitute all kinds of arguments.

7.3 Categories of Entities based on the Theory of Predications

Aristotle's next step is taken as follows:

It is clear from these discussions that the man signifying the what a thing is signifies (*ho to ti esti sêmainôn*) *sometimes* a substance, *sometimes* a quality [how a thing is like] and *sometimes* some of the other predications. For when a man is set before him and he says that what is set there is a man or an animal, he states what a thing is and signifies a substance; but when a white colour is set before him and he says that what is set there is white or is a colour, he states what a thing is and signifies a quality [how a thing is like]. Similarly, if a magnitude of a cubit is set before him and he says that what is set there is a magnitude of a cubit, then he states what a thing is and signifies a quantity [how much a thing is]. And likewise with the others. Because, as to *each* of such things, if either the very thing [*each*] is asserted of itself or if its genus is asserted of it, the predication indicates what a thing is, *but* when it [the *each*] is asserted of something else, the predication does not indicate what a thing is, but how much a thing is or how a thing is like or one of the other kinds of predications. (103b27–39)

Aristotle here proceeds to set out what and how many entities are signified by one engaged in stating what a thing is. He claims that the

[27] I. Düring, *Aristoteles Darstellung und Interpretation seines Denkens* (Heidelberg, 1966), S. 60.

man signifying, that is, indicating the what a thing is, signifies *sometimes* a substance, *sometimes* a quality [how a thing is like], and *sometimes* some of the other predications. Aristotle sets out his new list of categories which I call 'the categories of entities (CE)' as the conclusion of his previous discussion of the categories of predication (CP). In general terms, the new list of categories (CE) is his answer to the question 'In how many ways is the what a thing is said?' Further, in the present context, it is an answer to the question 'What are the entities about which the Socratic "What is F?" question can properly be raised?'

Given Aristotle's list of genera of predications, it is clear that some identifying terms will signify substances, others qualities, and so on. As it is indicated by 'sometimes', Aristotle inductively enumerates the ten genera of entities to which the what a thing is will be assigned depending on the category of predication involved. As a consequence, 'the what a thing is' can be said in many ways (cf. *Met.* Z.4, 1030a17).

Compare the case of 'change' which also can be said in many ways (cf. *Phys.* III.1). As there are four types of change according to the categories (substantial, qualitative, quantitative, and locomotive change), there will be ten types of identificatory predication (substantial, qualitative, identity, predication, and so on). In Aristotle's new system, each attempt to state what a thing is will employ one of his ten genera of entities: what a substance is will be stated using a substance term, what a quality is using a quality term, etc. The fact that the ten genera of predications (CP) are mutually exclusive and exhaustive is used in determining the number of entities over which the kinds of identity predications are distributed.

Since Aristotle wishes to classify (CE) all genera of entities on the basis of his framework of (CP) the categories of predications, he has to explain why the genera of entities (CE) correspond to the genera of predications (CP). In other words, he undertakes to specify more concretely the occasions of the correspondence between two kinds of categories which were previously left undetermined by the temporal indefinite adverbial 'sometimes'. To do this he first offers three examples and then explains it more generally based on his theory of predicables. First he identifies the entity signified by 'a man' as a substance (*hê ousia*), the entity signified by 'a colour' as a quality, and so on. When Koriskos is set before Callias and Callias states him to be 'a man' or 'an animal', he makes a predication in the first category (of predications) by saying what the thing (Koriskos) is. In this predication, the term 'man' or 'animal' signifies an entity (*hê ousia*) in the world: just what Koriskos is (103b22). However, the term 'man' has a dual function: it both says (S1) what Koriskos is (in the proposition 'Koriskos is a man') and refers (S2) to a corresponding entity in the world. The dual function is carried out by one single linguistic act of 'the man [Callias] signifying [(S2) in virtue of (S1)] the what a thing is' (103b27). It signifies (or indicates) that Koriskos is a man and signifies (or indicates) a substance, man, exemplified by Koriskos in the world.[28] Aristotle makes a similar point about a colour: when a white colour is set before Callias and he says that it is white or is a colour, he both states what a white is and the term he uses signifies a quality (an entity belonging to the ontological category of quality), i.e. how a thing is like. All definitional statements will have this dual function: they will both state (S1) what a thing is and refer (S2) to one of the types of entities (CE) Aristotle marks out.

On the basis of his theory of predicables, Aristotle explains more generally the reasons for the correspondence between (CP) and (CE). 'Each' (*hekaston*) term in these examples is part of a predication either (i) about itself or (ii) about something else.[29] This classification of predications is exhaustive, because while (i) the identity predication is constituted by a defining-phrase or a genus, (ii) the other predication is constituted by a property or an accident. If (i) 'the very thing' (*auto = hekaston*) is asserted of itself, or its genus is asserted of it (*hekaston*), the predication falls within the category of predication of what a thing is. There are ten different ways of stating what a thing is and to each of these will correspond a distinct type of entity (substance, quality, quantity, etc). By contrast, when (*hotan*) the term is asserted of (ii) another thing, the relevant predication does not indicate what the latter thing is but how it is like and so on.[30] For instance, when 'white' is predicated of 'bears', it indicates how

---

[28] Ackrill fails to understand the dual function, when he says that 'In this passage [102b29–35], where the question "what is it?" is thought of as addressed to items in any category, Aristotle can no longer use "what is it?" as a label for the first category but employs the noun for "substance".' Ackrill's claim is not true, because both categories (CP) and (CE) are at work in other places, as in *Metaphysics* Z.1 (1028a14, a36–b2). Ackrill, *Aristotle's Categories and De Interpretatione*, p. 80.

[29] Some commentators read 'each' in the sense of 'absolute adverbial phrase'. But Aristotle discusses each term as the component of two kinds of predications either as a subject or as a predicate. See M. Malink, 'Categories in *Topics* I.9', *Rhizai* 4.2 (2007), p. 278, n. 21.

[30] I disagree with Rijk, who takes the distinctions (i) and (ii) as the distinction concerning the two types of predications 'about concrete things'. Rijk says that 'The purport of this passage [103b29–39] is now understandable. To Aristotle's mind, each and every disputation is about concrete things... "Pale Socrates" is *either* addressed according to his very "this-ness" (*auto*), ... his individual being a man or an

bears are like. When either a property or an accident is predicated of another thing, the predication does not indicate what the thing is but rather signifies some other category of entity, corresponding to one of the other nine categories of predications, which it possesses.

Aristotle confirms that there is an asymmetry between substances and the other categories of entities. A substance term cannot be used in a predication of type (ii) since it cannot play the role of a predicate. If someone says that 'A snub-nose is animal', 'animal' cannot signify the what the snub-nose is nor how it is like nor any of the categories belonging to the snub-nose. Substance terms can only be used in predications of type (i) while other terms can be used in predications of both types (i) and (ii). Substances can never be predicated of other categories of entities, although other entities can be properly predicated of (i) themselves and (ii) substances.

By confirming this asymmetry, he specifies the occasions or situations characterized by 'sometimes' (103b28) when a man signifying what a thing is signifies the substance and when a man signifying what a thing is signifies the other kinds of entities. If a term can be used in both (i) and (ii), the term can be addressed by other proper interrogatives than the 'What is F?' question. In the cases of (i) and (ii), the relevant term cannot be a substance term. Substance terms are the only terms that can only be used in answering the 'What is F?' question, while all other terms can be used both in answering this question and in answering other questions as well. In this way, Aristotle establishes through the analysis of types of predications on a relevant term when a man signifying what a thing is signifies a substance.

On this basis Aristotle seeks to establish an important connection between the category of substance (CE) and the primary use of the 'what a thing is' type of predication (CP). Aristotle can claim that the category of substance (CE) corresponds to the category of what a thing is (CP). This is because substance terms are the only terms that can only be used in type (i) predication, while all other terms can be used in both type (i) and (ii) predications. Since the only role substance terms play is to specify what F is in answer to the

---

animal, *or* according to his being pale or being colored, which is something different from its proper being (*heteron*).' L. M. De Rijk, *Aristotle: Semantics and Ontology*, vol. 1. (Brill, 2002), p. 488. Given his aim in this chapter to determine the kinds of arguments, Aristotle is not merely concerned with the concrete things nor with their two modes of being. The distinction between being identical (*auto*) and being different (*heteron*) is based on his analysis of ten genera of predications about a term, i.e. 'each' (b36), which can be a universal term such as 'man' and 'white'.

'What is F?' question, they cannot be used to say what F is like or how big it is. By contrast, other types of term can be used both to say what something is (a quality etc.) and what something else is like and how big it is.

In fact, in *Metaphysics* Z.1, Aristotle carries out the *logikos* analysis of being and establishes the ontological primacy of substance and thus ontological asymmetry between the substance and the other entities. The Z.1 passage is a development of the relevant passage in *Topics* I.9, because the argument is offered by appealing to the dual function of stating what a thing is and the asymmetry of predications between the substance and other entities.

Aristotle says,

'Being' is said in many ways...Because, while it, on the one hand, signifies (S1) 'what a thing is' and (S2) some this (*tode ti*), on the other hand, (S1) 'how a thing is like' or 'how much a thing is' or 'each' of others predicated in this way. Since 'being' is said in these ways, it is evident that 'the what a thing is', by being the primary of these [expressions], is the one which signifies (S2) the substance. Because, when we say (S1) 'How is this (*tode*) like?', we say 'good' or 'bad', but not 'three cubits' or 'a man'. But when we say (S1) 'What is a thing?', we say not 'white' or 'hot' or 'three cubits', but 'a man' or 'a god'. (1028a10–18)

I shall here point out only two relevant claims with *Topics* I.9. First, some this (*tode ti*) which is signified by (S1) stating 'what a thing is' is (S2) the substance. When we reply to the question 'What is Callias?' by saying, 'He is (S1) a man', we simultaneously refer to (S2) some man (*tode ti*) instantiated by Callias. Aristotle claims the primacy of substance by pointing out that the identity predication primarily belongs to the substance. He says that 'the what a thing is', by being the primary of these [expressions] is the one which signifies (S2) the substance'. He limits the range of 'the what a thing is' which is supposed to be the general and abstract answer to the 'What is F?' question, by adding the subordinate clause 'which indeed signifies the substance'. By this modification, Aristotle limits the use of 'the what a thing is' only in the case of substance. Other entities can be predicated of 'this', insofar as the identity of substance is primarily fixed.

He explains the connection between the what a thing is and the substance by appealing to the distinction between the types of interrogatives and their corresponding terms. In this passage, Aristotle classifies the proper interrogatives to be addressed according to the genera of the corresponding terms of entities. We should not answer to the question of 'How is this like?'

by mentioning a substance term such as 'a man' or 'a god', but must answer by mentioning other kinds of terms such as 'white' or 'good'. Answering to the 'What is this?' question is primarily addressed to a substance. Among all kinds of entities, the primary being is the what a thing is which signifies the substance. Because unless the 'this' which is substance is fixed by an identity predication, any other entity such as a quality and a quantity cannot be predicated of the underlying 'this'.

In this way, in *Metaphysics* Z.1, Aristotle ontologically establishes the asymmetry of (i) the predication of what a thing is and (ii) the other types of predications. Also he establishes the correspondence between the categories of predications (CP), especially the what a thing is and the categories of entities (CE), especially the substance.

There are several advantages in considering what a thing is in terms of the system devised in *Topics* I.9 rather than in the simpler, undifferentiated, Socratic manner. In the *Meno*, Socrates asked what 'bee', 'virtue', 'colour', 'shape', 'tetragon' are without drawing any distinctions between the categories of entity involved (72a–82d). It appears as if Socrates thinks that he will find the same kind of answer to his 'What is F?' question, no matter which category of entity is involved. By contrast, within Aristotle's new framework, the enquirer will look for what a thing is in ways sensitive to the category of entity in which it falls. Second, Aristotle's distinction between the two functions of signification enables him to distinguish clearly between two types of account: one which connects (S1) two linguistic expressions, the other which connects (S2) a linguistic expression with an entity in the world. Once this distinction is drawn there can be no temptation to conflate accounts of what terms signify (which satisfy (S1)) with the things in the world which those terms signify (S2). Third, once we distinguish different types of predications, we will see that only some terms can be used to say what a thing is. Thus, for example, Laches' answer, 'not retreating from the front in a battle', to Socrates' question, 'What is courage?' indicates only an accident of courage. Laches addresses the question, 'How/What is courage like?' not, 'What is courage?' In this way, Aristotle can use his new system sharply to separate various features which are referred to in Socratic enquiry. In all these respects Aristotle can refine and clarify the Academicians' definitional practices on the basis of his own new theory of predication. If we are to engage properly in a dialectical debate, we should proceed in accordance with these distinctions.

8 Some Points concerning the Defining-Phrase and Definition

I shall finally consider some *topoi* (points) concerning defining-phrase and definition. First, 'finding differentiae' and 'examining likenesses' are 'the tools' which are useful in our search for the what a thing is (105a21–25). Since discovering *differentiae* requires us to grasp them and the relevant genus (107b39f.), 'the first thing to be laid down' in the definition must be the 'genus' (142b29, cf. 132a17–21). Enquiry into cases of likenesses proves useful for this purpose. Thus, calm at sea and windlessness in the air can both be regarded as cases of the genus of rest. When Aristotle says that 'those who deal in definitions (*hoi horizomenoi*) usually form them on this principle', he refers to the customary practice of definition in the Academy (108b28).

Once one has located the genus, the next thing to do is to find the differentiae. For instance, one has to consider ways in which justice differs from courage within the genus: virtue. The discovery of a relevant *differentia* is useful for the formation of syllogisms concerning 'sameness and difference' (108a38–b6). It is also useful for 'the recognition of what each thing is' (108a38–b1). As Aristotle remarks, 'we separated the proper account of the substance of each thing by means of the *differentiae* appropriate to it' (108b4–6). The theory of division rests on an enquiry into likenesses and into *differentiae*. It is the task of induction to use this practice to form definitions.

An important point (*topos*) concerns the question of whether a *differentia* is 'a *differentia* of genus' or 'a *differentia* proper to the subject' (143a29–b10). In the case of man, the *differentiae* (e.g. land-dweller, two-footed) signify the essence (*to ti ên einai*) more effectively than those (e.g. capable of grammar) which belong to a species (132a1–9). The former differentiates the genus animal, making it possible to articulate a relevant defining-phrase. Here, we see definition made on the basis of the theory of division: a 'habit' (108b6, b29) acquired in the Academy.

It is useful to consider a point (*topos*) by which Aristotle distinguishes a characteristic of the defining-phrase from that of a property: the method of addition and removal. He says, 'See if, though the additional matter is proper (*idion*) to the given subject, yet when it is taken away the rest of the account too is proper and makes clear the substance. Thus, in the account of man, the addition "capable of receiving knowledge" is superfluous; for take it away, and still the account is proper and makes clear the substance. Speaking generally, everything is superfluous if on its removal the remainder leaves the term being defined clear' (140a33–b2, cf. b7 ('defining-phrase')). That is, while there could be plural properties, there must be a single essence of the relevant object. A characteristic of 'the property' as 'convertibility' (102a18) merely means that if a property x exists, then it exists only in a specific subject y. That is, unless x exists in y, it does not exist. The convertibility consists in that y is the only thing to which x belongs and x is the thing which belongs only to y. On the other hand, a characteristic of essence consists in that if an essence z exists, then a thing y whose essence is z exists and vice versa: z exists if and only if y exists.

Let us also examine a point (topos) about defining a thing 'well or not' (kalôs ê ou kalôs). To do it well, one has to define it 'through terms that are prior and more intelligible' (141a29f.). At this point, Aristotle introduces two definitional conditions: priority and intelligibility or knowability simpliciter (141a33, 142a7f.). On their basis, we can see that it is not possible to have several different definitions of the same thing because there is only one essence which is prior to other properties. This is the ontological commitment implicit in the claim that 'for each entity there is a single essence' (141a35). The unity of the essence is required if the definition offered is to be 'well said'.

In the Topics these definitional conditions work within the traditional framework of division theory. The notion of intelligibility simpliciter is illustrated by three examples. The first, drawn from arithmetic, is that of the unit, which is prior to number in terms of intelligibility. The second, taken from geometry, is that of the point which is prior to the line in terms of intelligibility, as the line is prior to the plane and the plane is so to the cube. The third, an example drawn from linguistics, is of the letter which is prior to the syllable (141b6–8). Aristotle notes the priority relations between these items when he says that 'the unit is prior to and a principle of all numbers' (141b8) as the reason for priority in intelligibility in these cases. What is prior in terms of composition is prior in terms of intelligibility simpliciter (141b5f.).

Aristotle sees a parallelism with respect to the priority and the intelligibility of the account between the theory of demonstration and the theory of division. He says that 'We come to know things by taking not any random terms, but such as are prior and more intelligible, as is done in demonstrations. For so it is with all teaching and learning' (141a28–30). He claims here that the concept of the prior and more intelligible feature employed in definition by division is in harmony with the one established in demonstration. Indeed, since definition based on division does not involve any causal story about the relevant object, it seems to require addition from the theory of demonstration to establish the relevant priority among the elements of the definition.

In *Posterior Analytics* B.10, Aristotle developed a new theory of definition based on demonstration in an attempt to overcome deficiencies within the *Topics* division-based type of definition (*An. Post.* B.10; see my paper in note 14). Aristotle argues there that division-based types of definition can only succeed as definitions if they rest on demonstrations which establish both the existence of the relevant object and its causal ground. But he retains the idea that enquiries based on division and on demonstration generate the same knowledge. Thus, for example, the account of what thunder is might be given in terms of the genus 'noise' and the differentia 'fire being quenched in the clouds'. This differentia will reflect the causal ground captured in the demonstration: 'because fire is quenched in the clouds' (94a4f.). Aristotle claims, on the basis of this example, that 'the same account is said by another way, first as a continuous demonstration and second as a definition' (94a6f.). This type of definition is called 'a syllogism of the what it is, differing in arrangement from the demonstration' (94a12f, cf. 153a14f.).

In the *Topics*, these definitional conditions remain part of a *topos* (point). Depending on the situation in a dialogue, it is, 'as occasion requires' (142a13, a33), permissible to 'frame the account through terms that are intelligible to them' (141b18f.). For example, although a plane is prior to a solid *simpliciter* in terms of the order of intelligibility, it is possible to define 'a plane' as 'a limit of solid' (141b22). Aristotle next remarks that, 'One must, however, not fail to observe that those who define in this way cannot make known the essence of what they define, unless it so happens that the same thing is more intelligible both to us and also *simpliciter*' (141b23–25). This remark implies two things. First, while Aristotle, as a philosopher, is committed to the existence of a definitional order based on what is prior *simpliciter*, in constructing his theory of dialectic, he has to acknowledge that a dialectician can carry on an examination without relying on this ontological assumption. Second, 'what is intelligible to us' and 'what is intelligible *simpliciter*' can, on occasion, refer to the same thing. For persons whose thinking is 'more accurate' (*akribesterois*), something which is remote from the object of sense-perception is more intelligible (142a3, 141b10). This shows that it is possible for something which is more intelligible *simpliciter* to be more intelligible to us. But insofar as there is a single essence, the priority must be determined in terms of composition.

The *Topics* offers several *topoi* (points) concerning the way to establish and reject propositions within the framework defined by genus-species trees. In dialectical discipline, enquiry into the causal structure of a thing is inappropriate. It is not the task of induction, in moving from particular to universal, to elucidate the causal structure of a thing (156a4–6).

We can sum up the characteristics of the expression 'what it was to be' (*to ti ên einai*) in the *Topics* as follows. (1) It enables us, at the formal/general (*logikos*) level, to classify things and characterize what is grasped in successful definitions. (2) It picks out a single item for each thing F which is identical with F itself. (3) It picks out a mode of being which is referred to in the 'the defining-phrase'. (4) It may be defined by the theory of division through genus and differentiae. But (5) it, as well as the defining-phrase, should be studied by another enquiry more accurate than dialectic.

Aristotle, in his explicit characterizations of 'what it was to be' (*to ti ên einai*) in the *Topics*, has in mind, or so I have argued, the Socratic method of enquiry. Indeed, he introduces his concepts of essence and defining-phrase to set out what Socrates was seeking for in his dialectic. The theory of predicables is part of a theory constructed to refine and reform Socratic enquiry. This project sets the context for Aristotle's initial introduction of the phrases 'what it was to be' and 'defining-phrase'. Once we see these linguistic expressions in their proper historical context, we can understand why they were subsequently applied, in his metaphysical discussions, to entities such as forms.

9 Conclusion: A Prospect

One task of the *Topics* is to develop a theory of permissible enquiry into what something is. It achieves this goal by outlining a number of points (*topoi*), designed to facilitate the process of establishing and refuting propositions put forward in the practice of dialectic. *Topos* theory employs the theory of division taken from the Academy and operates in the logical space defined by genera and species grasped by induction. Induction, as I have noted, plays a limited role in elucidating the causal structure of things. Indeed, even if induction happens to grasp a cause which is prior to its effect in the order of being, it cannot grasp it *as* the cause, since that requires demonstration. For instance, suppose 'man' is properly defined by division as 'mortal, footed, two-footed, wingless animal' (92a1). Although division, based on induction, may hit on the cause in this case, it cannot determine which is causally prior: 'two-footed' or 'wingless'. In division-based 'defining-phrases', the question 'Why is it so?' can always be asked (91b39). Such definitions cannot explain the unity of the components of the *definiens*, even if all the relevant components are, in fact, present (cf. 92a29–34, 92b19–25).

In the *Posterior Analytics* the theory of demonstration outlines the explanatory conditions which establish what is prior, overcoming the limitations in the theory of division. We acquire knowledge by grasping the relevant causal structure. In this way, the *Topics* account of essence based on the theories of predicables and categories is supplemented using causal definition based on the theory of demonstration. My suggestion is that traditional division-based enquiry into the what a thing is, set out in the *Topics* on the basis of practice in the Academy, supplies the terminology later used to characterize causal definition in the *Posterior Analytics* and to formulate the proper goal for all definitions: to say what it was to be the thing in question (*to ti ên einai*). Aristotle carried this project further in the *Metaphysics* when he sought to answer the question 'What does the essence consist in?' (*Met.* E.1, 1025b29) within his hylomorphic theory in terms which invoke his theory of demonstration. At this point, form is identified with essence and further investigated (*Met.* Δ.2, 1013a27; Z.7, 1032b2–4; *Phys.* II.3, 194b27). However, the foundation for all his subsequent enquiry into essence was laid in the *Topics*.[31]

[31] Some parts of an earlier version of this paper were read in the 49th Japan Association of Classical Studies (May 1998, Osaka), at a seminar organized by Christopher Rapp (March 2005, Berlin), at two Oxford Workshops ('Essence and Substance: Historical Perspectives', June 2005, and 'Ancient and Modern Essentialism', June 2006), and at the conference 'Aristotle on Predication' at Rutgers University (October 2008) organized by Alan Code. I should like to thank many participants for their helpful comments, especially Tsutomu Okabe and Christopher Shields. I should also like to express my gratitude to David Charles, with whom I have discussed these topics for more than twenty years. This work is supported by International Collaborative Activities/Joint Project grants between the British Academy and the Japan Society for the Promotion of Science (D. Charles and K. Chiba, 'Essence and Explanation: Aristotle and Modern Scientific Essentialism', 2005–7).

Bibliography

J. Ackrill, *Aristotle's Categories and De Interpretatione* (Oxford, 1963).

Alexander Aphrodisiensis, *In Aristotelis Analyticorum Priorum Librum I Commentarium*, ed. M. Wallies (Berlin, 1883).

Alexander Aphrodisiensis, *In Aristotelis Metaphysica Commentaria*, ed. M. Hayduck (Berlin, 1891).

Alexander Aphrodisiensis, *In Aristotelis Topicorum Libros Octo Commentaria*, ed. M. Wallies (Berlin, 1891).

C. Arpe, *Das ti en einai bei Aistoteles* (Hamburg, 1938).

J. Barnes, review of *Aristotle, On Dialectic; The Topics*, ed. G. E. L. Owen, *Philosophical Review* 79.4 (1970), pp. 558–65.

J. Barnes, *Aristotle's Posterior Analytics* (Oxford, 1993).

E. Berti, 'Does Aristotle's Dialectic Develop?', in *Aristotle's Philosophical Development*, ed. W. Wians (Lanham, MD, 1996).

H. Bonitz, *Index Aristotelicus* (Berlin, 1870).

D. Bostock, *Aristotle Metaphysics Books Z and H* (Oxford, 1994).

J. Brunschwig, *Aristote Topiques I–IV* (Paris, 1967).

M. Burnyeat, *A Map of Metaphysics Zeta* (Pittsburgh, 2001).

D. Charles, *Aristotle on Meaning and Essence* (Oxford, 2000).

D. Charles, 'Types of Definition in the *Meno*', in *Remembering Socrates*, ed. L. Judson and V. Karasmanis (Oxford, 2006).

K. Chiba, *Aristotle on the Possibility of Metaphysics: Complementary Development between Dialectic and Natural Philosophy* (Keiso Shobo, 2002).

K. Chiba, 'Aristotle's Theory of Definition in *Posterior Analytics* B.10', *Journal of the Graduate School of Letters Hokkaido University* 3 (2008).

L. A. Dorion, *Aristote: Les réfutations sophistiques* (Paris, 1995).

I. Düring, *Aristoteles Darstellung und Interpretation seines Denkens* (Heidelberg, 1966).

J. D. G. Evans, *Aristotle's Concept of Dialectic* (Cambridge, 1977).

M. Frede, 'Categories in Aristotle', in *Essays in Ancient Philosophy* (Oxford, 1987).

M. Frede and G. Patzig, *Aristoteles Metaphysik Z Kommentar* (Munich, 1988).

W. Goodwin, *Syntax of the Moods and Tenses of the Greek Verb* (London, 1929).

N. Gulley, *The Philosophy of Socrates* (London, 1968).

P. M. Huby, 'The Date of Aristotle's *Topics* and its Treatment of the Theory of Ideas', *Classical Quarterly* 12 (1962).

T. H. Irwin, *Aristotle's First Principles* (Oxford, 1988).

H. H. Joachim, *Aristotle On Coming-To-Be and Passing-Away* (Oxford, 1922; Olms, 1970).

A. Kitago, 'Predicables and Categories in Aristotle's *Topics* A.8–9', *TETSUGAKU, Annals of the Philosophical Society of Hokkaido University* 43 (2007).

J. M. Le Blond, *Logique et Méthode chez Aristote* (Paris, 1939).

M. Loux, *Primary Ousia: An Essay on Aristotle's Metaphysics Z and H* (Ithaca, NY, 1991).

I. Ludlam, 'Defining Terms in Aristotle's *Topics*: *horos* or *hor◁ism▷os?*' *Mnemosyne* 53.3 (2000).

M. Malink, 'Categories in *Topics* I.9', *Rhizai* 4.2 (2007).

S. Mansion, 'La notion de matière en Métaphysique Z10 et 11', in *Étude Sur La Métaphysique D'Aristote* (Paris, 1979).

G. E. L. Owen, 'Tithenai ta phainomena', in *Logic, Science and Dialectic* (London, 1986).

J. Owens, *The Doctrine of Being in the Aristotelian Metaphysics* (Toronto, 1963).

S. Peterson, 'Horos (Limit) in Aristotle's *Nicomachean Ethics*', *Phronesis* 33.3 (1988).

I. Philoponus, *In Aristotelis Analytica Priora Commentaria*, ed. M. Wallies (Berlin, 1905).

I. Philoponus, *Commentaria in Aristotelem Graeca*, ed. M. Wallies (Berlin, 1909).

L. M. De Rijk, *Aristotle: Semantics and Ontology*, vol. 1 (Brill, 2002).

D. Ross, *Aristotle* (Oxford, 1923).

D. Ross, *Aristotle's Metaphysics I* (Oxford, 1924).

D. Ross, *Aristotle's Metaphysics II* (Oxford, 1924).

G. Ryle, *Plato's Progress* (Cambridge, 1966).

R. Smith, *Aristotle, Topics Books I and VIII* (Oxford, 1997).

R. Sorabji, *Necessity, Cause, and Blame: Perspectives on Aristotle's Theory* (London, 1980).

E. Strycker, 'Concepts-clés et terminologie dans les livre ii à vii des *Topiques*', in *Aristotle, On Dialectic; The Topics*, ed. G. E. L. Owen (Oxford, 1968).

T. Wagner and C. Rapp, *Aristoteles Topik* (Stuttgart, 2004).

M. Wedin, *Aristotle's Theory of Substance* (Oxford, 2000).

7

Nominal Definition in Aristotle

DEBORAH MODRAK

Aristotle discusses definition in many places; sometimes his interest seems to be in linguistic definitions, definitions of the terms of ordinary language, at other times, his focus is on technical definitions of one sort or another.[1] The diverse motivations that drive Aristotle's approach to definition in different contexts threaten the cogency of his thought on this topic. This problem has historical roots. Socrates and Plato had elevated definition to a central place in philosophy without achieving a clear consensus about the character of definition. Because Aristotle appeals to seemingly different notions of definition in different contexts, a careful reader is likely to be left baffled and wondering whether Aristotle has a theory of definition that encompasses all the cases of definition he discusses from nominal definitions to definitions expressing essences. Is there a single set of criteria that a good definition must meet? Is the sole difference between types of definition, according to him, the terms that are defined, as, for instance, a definition in biology might differ from a definition of an ordinary-language term solely in taking as a definiendum a term that, although used in common parlance, is useful to biologists? Or, are the criteria more stringent for a scientific definition? Does Aristotle ultimately decide in favor of a narrow, technical conception of definition that does not apply to many of the terms of ordinary language?

The origins of the core problem in Aristotle's account of definition can be found in his philosophical predecessors' treatment of definition. Socrates, Aristotle tells us, was the first philosopher to turn his attention to definition

---

[1] For the moment, the notions of linguistic and technical definition will be left somewhat open-ended. Roughly speaking, a linguistic definition is the definition that one might find in a dictionary; it is an expression of the linguistic knowledge required for the common usage of a natural-language term. A technical definition is a definition that is employed within a specific discipline, e.g. mathematics.

(987b1–3). The early Platonic dialogues present Socrates' quest for exception-less definitions of moral concepts. This practice assumes that terms naming virtues have objective meanings that can be found by examining our moral and linguistic intuitions. Moral knowledge consists in grasping the actual significance of the terms. Socrates' attempts to arrive at satisfactory definitions always end in *aporia*. In later dialogues, Plato pursues a different strategy for definition—the method of division. This method, too, starts from linguistic intuitions with the goal of arriving at an epistemically adequate definition that might differ markedly from the accepted linguistic definition. All three (Socrates, Plato, and Aristotle) recognize this possibility, at least implicitly. This is the crux of the tension between the nominal definitions capturing linguistic meaning and real definitions expressing actual natures.

In the *Posterior Analytics*, Aristotle lays out the conditions that a definition must meet in order to satisfy the requirements of a demonstrative science. These requirements are more stringent than those of ordinary language. They may also be more stringent than those appealed to by Aristotle in his scientific treatises.[2] Aristotle envisages definitions that capture the essences of the things defined. The criteria for these definitions are discussed in the *Metaphysics*. In both the *Posterior Analytics* and the *Metaphysics*, Aristotle mentions a type of definition that is merely terminological; it is merely an account of what the name signifies. He distinguishes this account from definition in the strict sense. He proceeds to discuss strict definition in earnest and largely ignores the broader notion of linguistic definition. Yet the broader notion would seem to be exactly what is needed for a general account of definition for a natural language. The broader notion specifies what the term signifies without placing any constraints on the object signified. The narrow notion also specifies what the term signifies but there are additional constraints. The sole requirement that Aristotle places on the relation between the definiendum and definiens in merely termino-logical definitions is synonymy. The account may be substituted for the name in a sentence without altering the meaning of the sentence. Synony-my is the principle upon which numerous dictionaries are constructed.

---

[2] It was once a commonplace that the requirements for demonstration in the *Posterior Analytics* were more stringent than those actually employed by Aristotle elsewhere but this commonplace has been challenged of late. For a helpful discussion of definition in Aristotle's biological treatises, see D. Balme, J. Lennox, R. Bolton, and A. Gotthelf in *Philosophical Issues in Aristotle's Biology*, edited by A. Gotthelf and J. Lennox, Cambridge, 1987.

Consider definitions of 'centaur', viz. 'horse with human body, arms and head, taking the place of its neck and head', and 'cat', viz. 'any member of genus Felis'.[3] To substitute the defining account of centaur for 'centaur' in a sentence would not change the meaning of the sentence nor its truth value. Synonymy does not guarantee that the definiens capture a real nature or that it even refer to any existent, however inadequately.[4] Thus, the conception of definition in the strict sense and the notion of linguistic definition seem to pull apart.

I Linguistic Definition in the *Posterior Analytics*

In *Posterior Analytics* II 7, Aristotle asks whether definitions are of the essence or only signify what the name means (92b26–28). It would be absurd, he suggests, to say that the account signifying the same as the name is a definition. Aristotle goes on to claim (a) that definitions in the latter sense would hold of non-substances and non-existents and (b) that they would be such that all expressions would have a definition, for instance the *Iliad*, and finally (c) that one cannot demonstrate that a name has a particular meaning (92b26–33). One might suppose, and Aristotle does, that a definition of essence would not be such that either (a) or (b) apply to it. Definitions of essence will turn out not to be demonstrable. More puzzling from the standpoint of natural language is Aristotle's apparent rejection of the nominal definition, namely, the formula signifying the same as the name.[5] A language with terms only for substances and simple concepts and with no way to speak about non-existents such as centaurs would be a truly impoverished language.[6] Aristotle seems to agree since only a few lines earlier he had distinguished between knowing what an expression or

---

[3] *The Concise Oxford Dictionary of Current English*, ed. H. W. and F. G. Fowler, fifth edition revised by E. McIntosh and G. Friedrichsen, Oxford, 1964.

[4] Meaning, for Aristotle, is closely tied to reference. Aristotle recognizes that an apparently significant term such as goat-stag that does not have a referent poses a problem for him. This case will be discussed below.

[5] In the discussion that follows I will use the traditional label, 'nominal definition', for the merely terminological definition that Aristotle mentions in the *Posterior Analytics* (92b5–8, b26–32, 93b29–31) and *Metaphysics* (1030a7–10, b7–10, 1045a12–14).

[6] There is a tension between Aristotle's characterization of nominal definition in a way that would seem to fit linguistic definitions of all sorts and his desire to have a notion of signification and definition that is specific to problematic cases of significant terms such as goat-stag or *Iliad*.

name signifies and knowing what the object named is (92b6–8). His example is goat-stag (*tragelaphos*), a mythical creature that was half goat and half stag. To know what something is, as distinguished from knowing how to use its name, is possible only when one knows that it exists.

The puzzle is not that Aristotle draws a distinction between what a name signifies and what the thing named is but rather why in II 7 he seems to restrict definition to the latter.[7] Part of the explanation may lie with Plato. In the *Sophist*, the Eleatic stranger twice makes a point of the difference between his and Theaetetus' having a name, 'sophist', in common and their grasping the thing itself or its *logos* (218c, 221b). Another part of the explanation may be that in the *Posterior Analytics* definition is discussed in connection with the theory of demonstration. Aristotle is not primarily concerned with definition in the context of natural language but rather with the requirements for definition in the context of a demonstrative science. Here definition must state what the thing is and not merely say what the name signifies. Even in this context, however, there would seem to be an earlier stage of enquiry where it would be important to express a concept in a preliminary way in order to discover whether the concept is instantiated.[8] Yet Aristotle seems to dismiss nominal definitions as absurd and thus presumably useless to the scientist (92b28). In order to resolve this problem, some commentators have argued that, strictly speaking, only an object that exists can have a nominal definition and others have argued that the nominal definition should be distinguished from a mere account of a name.[9] The disagreement arises because Aristotle's examples of accounts of a name suggest a minimalist conception of nominal definition; in this case, nominal definitions would be at best only one type of linguistic definition. The paradigm case of linguistic definition would, by contrast, seem to be an account of an ordinary-language term that had an existent as a referent and that got it roughly right about the characteristics of its referent. There is also considerable evidence for this conception of linguistic definition in Aristotle's writings.

---

[7] One solution to this puzzle is to argue as Charles does (2000, p. 69) that to take Aristotle to rule out nominal definitions on the basis of *Posterior Analytics* II 7 is to seriously misconstrue the aporetic structure of II 7.

[8] See the very helpful discussion of this topic in Charles (2000), pp. 40–55.

[9] Bolton (1976) takes the first position and DeMoss and Devereux (1988, pp. 133–54) the second.

Rather than addressing this tension immediately, let us use the traditional term, nominal definition, for the definition stating what the name signifies and let us consider the various cases that Aristotle includes under this notion. His examples are: (a) definitions of mythical creatures such as goat-stags (92b7–8), (b) an account that can be substituted for the name, for instance, the poem taken as the definition of its title in the case of the *Iliad* (92b32, 93b35–37; *Met.* 1030a7–10, b7–10, 1045a12–14), and (c) the linking by disjunction of expressions that collectively cover all the instances to which the term applies, for example, the different characteristics labeled *megalop-suchia* (pride) (97b15–26).[10] In the case of a disjunctive nominal definition, Aristotle recommends that we should look for a common characteristic. If a common characteristic cannot be found, then we should acknowledge that there are different types of the item in question. For instance, the effort to reduce the number of characteristics labeled *megalopsuchia* results in the recognition of two distinct forms or senses. While advocating precision with respect to cases where a word has several senses, Aristotle does allow for the use of the same term. The nominal definition of *megalopsuchia*, even after clarification, would be disjunctive.[11] Definitions of types (b) and (c) involve various ways (conjunction and disjunction) of producing a single account; these devices are contrasted by Aristotle to the inherent unity of a definition of essence. From the standpoint of Aristotle's philosophy of language, including all three cases as cases of nominal definition makes sense as many of the definitions of ordinary language exhibit the types of unity in question in (b) and (c). Since mythical figures and other non-existents are spoken about, including case (a) is also helpful because it allows a name of a fictional object or a name of a non-existent object that is believed to exist to have significance for speakers. Including all these cases of nominal definition as instances of linguistic definition makes sense, but Aristotle may fear that doing so would make non-standard cases of signifi-cation normative for linguistic definition.

---

[10] In *Posterior Analytics* II 7, Aristotle mentions both (a) and (b); (c) is discussed in II 13 in a context in which he is not distinguishing between nominal and strict definition; his treatment of (c) leaves little doubt, however, that it would fall under the former.

[11] The constraints he places on simple names in *De Int.* 2 would not rule out disjunctive definitions. Aristotle may, nonetheless, believe that in a truly well formed natural language one would not find different senses correlated with the same simple term.

Aristotle needs a type of definition that will cover cases where an existent is grasped but not adequately grasped. He gives a number of examples of such definitions in the *Posterior Analytics* (93a23–24): 'thunder is a noise in the clouds', 'an eclipse is a privation of light', 'man is a kind of animal', and 'the soul is a self-moving entity'. All of these definitions are, according to Aristotle, partially right and approximate the definition of essence. Although Aristotle does not explicitly identify these definitions as cases of nominal definition, they are offered in *Posterior Analytics* II 8 as part of the effort to clarify the puzzles raised in II 7 and so it seems reasonable to take them as examples of the constructive use of an account signified by a name in an investigation of the question of what the object is. Once the investigation is concluded, the investigator is often in a position to construct a syllogism that displays but does not prove the definition.

Therefore one type of definition is an indemonstrable account of the essence, another is a deduction of an essence, differing in aspect from demonstration; a third type is the conclusion of a demonstration of essence. (II 10, 94a11–14; cf. 75b30–32)

Aristotle illustrates the second type of definition using a syllogism, the conclusion of which is 'thunder is a noise in the clouds' (93b8–14). The form of what is initially grasped only as a nominal definition may turn out to be such that it can be the conclusion of a syllogism that displays its cause, namely, the extinction of fire, which is the middle term through which the conclusion is drawn.

In the discussion of the acquisition of universals in II 19 and *Metaphysics* I 1, Aristotle also seems to envisage an initial stage where an enquirer has some handle on the concept in question, i.e. she has some sort of definition at her disposal. At a later stage the cognitive grasp on the object is total, if all has gone well. This, too, would suggest a necessary role for linguistic definitions in enquiry. Like the partial definitions of *Posterior Analytics* II 8, this role provides further evidence that definitions for Aristotle fall along a continuum from minimalist nominal definitions of names of mythical creatures to strict definitions of essences of existents. Aristotle faces the challenge of accounting for the knowledge of indemonstrable principles in the final chapter of the *Posterior Analytics*. His answer is to sketch a cognitive process that issues in the grasp of basic universals. To have a basic concept of this sort is to have a fully adequate cognitive grasp of the object; it is ipso facto to grasp the definition of the essence of the object.[12] The second of the four descriptions of this process strongly suggests an initial grasp of the object that is typically not fully adequate.

Then out of perception memory, as we say, comes to be and out of memory occurring frequently with respect to the same thing experience comes to be. For memories that are many by number make up one experience. And out of experience or out of the universal resting as a whole in the soul, the one beside the many, which is one and the same in all of these, comes to be the first principle of art and science—of art, if it concerns coming to be, of knowledge if it concerns being. (100a3–9)

The picture is one where memory and experience stabilize and amplify an object as initially perceived. After many perceptions of the same kind of object, a rudimentary concept is formed when many memories cohere to form a single experience. Exactly how this works is clearer from a similar discussion in *Metaphysics* I. As Aristotle explains there, 'To have an opinion that when Callias was ill with this disease this helped him and similarly Socrates and many other individuals, is to have experience' (981a7–9). The opinion about Callias is a generalization based on a number of perceptions. It requires a grouping of a number of particulars, Socrates, Callias, and other ill individuals, together as sufferers of the same disease and as beneficiaries of the same treatment. In order to group the particulars, the person of experience has recognized similarities both in terms of illness and in terms of responsiveness to a particular medication. Many perceptions have coalesced to form one experiential judgement. This judgement, however, remains tied to the particulars that provide its warrant and it could in principle be reduced to a lengthy conjunction of the sort Aristotle uses.[13] The meaning of a general term grasped through experience would correspond to the extension of the term. The experiential judgement falls short of the grasp of causes that would warrant the unqualified judgement that this medication always benefits patients suffering from such and such illness. Although the cases are grouped together on the basis of similarities by experience, at the level of experience the person does not fully grasp the grounds for the

---

[12] See Modrak (1987), ch. 7 for a full defense of the interpretation of II 19 summarized here. For an alternative line of interpretation, see Charles (2000), pp. 149–53.

[13] For a different interpretation of the character of experience, see Butler (2003), 329–50, which argues that experiences are guess-beliefs about natures.

groupings. 'To recognize that this has helped such-and-such persons, marked off in one class, when they were ill with a particular disease, is to have art' (981a10–11). To grasp this notion is to comprehend the same phenomenon in a more adequate way than the person of experience does. Experience relies on overt similarities to group memories together and these might be misleading. The art of medicine specifies the grounds for the experiential judgement; these have to do with the causes of the disease and the relevance of body type (e.g. phlegmatic) to treatment protocols.

'Art arises when one universal opinion about a number of similar cases arises from many experiential notions' (981a5–7). In order to play this role, experience must get the particulars more or less right. The person of experience has a cognitive handle on the particulars but lacks the deeper understanding of them that comes of subsuming the particulars under the appropriate universal. Aristotle uses the same term, *hupolepsis*, to describe both what the person of experience has and what the knower has. The *hupolepseis* in question are different because their contents are different. In the former case, the content is provided by a series of particular observations; in the latter case, it is a fully articulated universal. As Aristotle remarks in *Posterior Analytics* II 13, 'for the doctor does not say what is healthy for some individual eye, but for every eye or by defining a specific kind of eye' (97b26–28). That there are two distinct yet similar *hupolêpseis* envisaged by Aristotle makes it clear that one is a partial grasp of the phenomenon and the other, a full grasp. The nominal definition and the real definition would seem to stand in the same relation to each other. The cognitive grasp that is constitutive of the art would be the apprehension of the definition of essence. The nominal definition is not mentioned as such in these passages, and thus the question becomes: is the experiential notion the counterpart of a nominal definition?

There are grounds for a positive response. Aristotle uses terms such as 'human' to illustrate the progression from perception to art and science. Presumably, what is at issue is the grasp of the concept corresponding to the term. This concept defines the term for the person in question. Grasping the concept might well involve several stages, an initial stage where the language-user grasps the concept implicit in her natural language and a later stage where as a trained biologist she grasps the essence of human. The definitions of the significant words of a natural language fit the description 'account of what a name signifies'. They would also be likenesses of objects in the world (16a3–8). The concepts of natural kinds that are required for a natural language are based on observations of particulars. They may, but they need not, capture the essence of the kind. Aristotle envisages an evolution of knowledge in *Metaphysics* I that begins with perceptions and over time develops into the understanding of essences and the most universal objects (981b13–26). On this picture, language users would begin with concepts that yield nominal definitions and in the favored cases (and perhaps many generations later) end with concepts that yield definitions of essence.

On balance, there is more evidence that Aristotle embraces a type of linguistic definition in addition to the definition of essence than evidence against it. Linguistic definitions have a genuine heuristic role in Aristotelian science. A definition specifying what something is that lacks the precision of a genuine definition of essence is a step towards the discovery of the essence. The only text in *Posterior Analytics* II that seems to deny that the account corresponding to a name is a definition occurs early in the discussion of definition (92b26–34). It is best construed as raising the question of what constraints the objects of definition of all sorts should meet. Need the objects of definition exist? Can any account, for instance a poem, count as a definition? Aristotle's ultimate answer to these questions is best considered in light of the discussion of definition in *Metaphysics* VII.

II Definition in *Metaphysics* VII

In *Metaphysics* VII, Aristotle discusses definition in the strict sense (*haplōs*) in chapters 4–6 and 10–12. Such definitions are used to differentiate between substance and non-substance, for only substances have essences and hence definitions strictly and primarily (1030a28–32).

Therefore there is an essence only of those things whose formula (*logos*) is a definition (*horismos*). And there is a definition not where a formula is identical in meaning to a word . . . but where there is a formula of something primary (*prōtou*); and primary things are those which do not imply the predication of one element of another. Therefore essence will not belong to anything that is not a species of a genus but to these alone for these are thought not to involve predication by participation or as an attribute or by accident. But of everything else also, if it has a name, there will be a formula (*logos*) that signifies something, namely that this attribute belongs to something, or instead of the simple formula there may be a more accurate account. However there will be neither a definition (*horismos*) nor an essence. (VII 4 1030a6–17)

These remarks, while occurring in a context where the topic is substance, have important implications for Aristotle's theory of definition. At first glance, the continuum between linguistic and scientific definition suggested by passages in the *Posterior Analytics* seems to have been replaced by a sharp dichotomy between nominal and real definition. A mark of substance is having an intrinsically unified definition. Aristotle sharply distinguishes definition in the ordinary sense, i.e. an expression that signifies the same thing as the word, from definition in the strict sense. A nominal definition has unity only in a weak sense. The source of its unity is conjunction interpreted as mere continuity. The conditions on strict definition are much more rigorous: the object defined must be simple and primary; the definition must possess unity in the strict sense; and the definition must express an essence. These conditions are not independent. It is precisely because the object of definition is simple and primary that it is an essence and its definition possesses inherent unity. The strict definition is said *kath' hauto* of its object. A definition meeting these conditions will also satisfy the requirements for being a premise of a demonstrative science as set out in the *Posterior Analytics*. Because its object is simple and primary, the definition is the expression of a concept of the sort envisaged in *Posterior Analytics* II 19. To grasp the concept of the object is to grasp the definition and hence to possess a starting-point for demonstration.

Despite these advantages, the definition of essence as characterized in VII 4 is too narrow a concept to apply to very many cases. Aristotle frets about whether items in the categories other than that of substance will have definitions (1030a17–32). He eliminates such useful terms as snub as candidates for definition. He sets aside linguistic definition as only an account (*logos*) of what a name signifies. This seems a high price to pay for the strict notion unless, despite initial appearances, Aristotle does have a broad notion of definition as well and a story to tell about the relation between the broad and narrow notions. He hints at a middle ground at 1030a14–16 when he mentions an account possessing a degree of accuracy but still falling short of being a definition. The first attempt at expanding the notion of the defin-able occurs at 1030b3–7 where Aristotle concedes that, even if, in one sense, only substances have definitions, in another sense, items in the other categories are definable. Having extended the notion of definition to non-substances, Aristotle goes on to suggest that in yet another sense composites, such as pale human, are definable (1030b12–13). The compound term 'pale human' had been arbitrarily labeled 'cloak' a few lines earlier in order to investigate the question whether every term has a definition (1029b27–8). This case appears to be the same as that of snub; here, too, is a single term that indicates a substrate, a human being, qualified by an attribute, paleness.[14]

Aristotle, however, raises a difficulty about extending the range of the definable to include composites. If definitions are allowed for cases that involve composition, then definitions will not be simple. In the definition of 'cloak', one thing is said of another (1030a3–7). Since the pale is not a *kath' hauto* predicate of human, this definition is not intrinsically unified. Some terms for composites, e.g. 'snub', are *kath' hauta* attributes of their substrates, however, and such terms cannot be defined without mention of their proper substrate, e.g. 'nose' in the case of snub (1030b16–22). This would seem to distinguish such *kath' hauta* predications from the way in which items in the non-substance categories are defined. But Aristotle extends this objection to 'pale' and other items in the non-substance categories by noting that even if they are not per se attributes of their particular substrates, they do have proper substrates, e.g. surface, which must be mentioned in their definition. In short, all such terms will violate the simplicity constraint on definition. This leads Aristotle to reaffirm the position that only substances are definable strictly speaking but in another sense items in the other categories will be definable (1031a7–14). They are definable because 'one' has as many senses as 'being' does (1031b10–12).

According to *Categories* 2, there are four types of existents. There are *onta* (things that are) that are neither present in nor said of anything else and hence are fully independent (viz. primary substances) and *onta* that are present in but not said of anything else (viz. primary attributes); these are the subjects of which other terms are predicated and to which they refer. Primary substance and primary attributes are individuals existing in the

---

[14] Later Aristotle notes a difference between these cases. Snubness is found only in noses; it is a proper attribute of noses, whereas paleness is found in many other types of substrata and is proper not to human beings but to surfaces (1030a16–22).

world as subjects or things present in subjects; secondary substances and secondary attributes are kinds and properties under which the primary substances and attributes fall. General terms name secondary substances and secondary attributes, and their definitions determine the reference class of objects to which the terms correctly apply. Predicates fall into ten basic types. These categories apply not only to beings but also to linguistic items. 'Of the things said without any combination, each signifies either a substance or a quantity or a quality or a relation or where or when or being in a position or having or acting or being acted upon' (*Cat.* 4 1b25–27). The very same list of categories—with one exception—is found in *Topics* I 9. On this list Aristotle substitutes 'what something is (*ti esti*)' for 'substance (*ousia*)'; clearly he takes the two descriptions to be synonymous. The ontology presupposed by linguistic signification coincides with the ontology of things. This would explain both why Aristotle allows items in non-substance categories to have definitions possessing unity and also why he rejects the possibility of defining wholes arrived at by conjunction. The picture is not quite this simple, however, as items in the non-substance categories are definable by addition (1031a2–5), and thus Aristotle must (at least tacitly) distinguish between different cases of definition by addition.

When Aristotle extends the notion of strict definition to simple items in the non-substance categories, he does not intend to extend it to composite items such as pale man nor to his favorite example of a nominal definition, viz. the poem signifying the same thing as its title.[15] It is not completely clear whether Aristotle is entitled to draw the distinction between a mere account signifying the same as a name and a proper definition where he draws it. Aristotle grants that definition of items in the non-substance categories is by addition (1031a2–5). Having implicitly distinguished between types of definition by addition, he fails to give an account of how to draw the line between legitimate cases of definition by addition and indefinable cases. Since the *Iliad* has a very weak form of unity due to conjunction, it does not put the same pressure on the distinction as do single terms that express composite notions, for instance, 'cloak' used arbitrarily for 'pale human'. If 'pale' cannot be defined without reference to surface, what makes the

---

[15] Aristotle initially entertains the suggestion that items such as 'pale human' are definable but in a different way than items in the non-substance categories (1030b12). However, the discussion of composite items in VII 5 reaffirms the unity constraint on definition.

account of 'cloak' more complex than that of 'pale'? Aristotle does not have a good answer to this question in VII 4. Happily, his discussion of the parts of definitions in chapter 10 provides one.[16]

Turning now to the account of what a name signifies, we might wonder to what extent unity and simplicity apply to such accounts. In *Metaphysics* VII, Aristotle uses these characteristics to restrict strict definition to substance. In *Posterior Analytics* II 10, Aristotle notes that an account may be one in two ways, either by conjunction or by making one thing clear of another thing non-accidentally (93b35–37). Linguistic definitions could easily meet the first condition since any defining account, however lengthy, can be unified by the use of conjunction. The second condition seems to be equivalent to Aristotle's restricting proper definitions to *kath' hauta* predicates. In this instance, neither the defining formula nor the object defined may contain extraneous elements. Aristotle's examples of definitions that violate this constraint are 'pale human' as the definition of 'pale' and 'pale' as the definition of 'pale human' (1029b29–1030a2). Thus construed, unity of the second type might be possessed by a linguistic definition of a natural-kind term, if the definiens expresses a conceptually simple concept. The *De Interpretatione*'s discussion of signification makes signification depend upon there being a single coherent (i.e. unified) concept corresponding to the term. According to the thumbnail sketch of meaning in *De Interpretatione* I, significant terms signify psychological states that are likenesses of things. Existents are either simple or complex; simple things fall under one or another of the categories. Thus, at the most fundamental level, the objects of natural language are the same as the objects of strict definition. Linguistic definitions of existents will differ, if at all, from strict definitions only in lacking precision. However, there are many items for which there are only linguistic definitions. These include terms that signify in a way according to Aristotle, such as terms for fictional entities (16a16–18), terms that do not have significance but play an important role in language, for instance, syntactic terms such as 'and', 'or', and 'not' (1456b37–1457a10), and compound terms that contain significant components. The question then becomes what constraints, if any, besides being a single concept apply to linguistic definition?

---

[16] See section III below.

The broad notion of linguistic definition admits definitions that contain added elements. Is this sufficient to make the poem a genuine linguistic definition of its title? Is connection by conjoining (*sundesmô*) the same as unity by addition (*ek prostheseôs*)?[17] The terminology is different but it is hard to know how to construe the latter in a way that excludes the former. In this effort, Aristotle might emphasize the (weak) intrinsic unity of the other cases where the elements of the definition are bound together by one element being a per se attribute of the other element. In the case of mere conjunction of the sort holding the lines of the *Iliad* together, there is no intrinsic conceptual unity involved, even if the poem has rhetorical unity. The poem is merely a continuous piece.[18] While it is true that the poem can be substituted for the title without affecting the truth value of a sentence containing the title, this, too, seems to have no bearing on the issue of unity. If this is his position, then Aristotle would be refusing to allow synonymy to be the sole criterion for evaluating the adequacy of a linguistic definition. On the other hand, the suggestion that the poem is held together by conjunction may be intended to provide some basis for allowing definitions of this sort.

The *De Interpretatione's* account of signification supports certain restrictions on definition.[19] These constraints, however, are looser than those imposed on strict definition elsewhere. Aristotle claims that some apparently meaningful expressions lack signification (and hence a proper linguistic definition) or have it only in a derivative sense.[20] These include terms such as 'not-man', which is said to signify something indefinite (16a29–31, b11–15, 19b9) and 'man-and-horse' which when taken as a whole signifies nothing (18a18–25). 'Goat-stag', by contrast, is significant in some sense (16a16–18). In the case of indefinite signification, there would seem to be no definition possible, or, possibly only a definition by disjunction. The concept of 'not-man' is indeterminate, because it does not delineate all the different things that are not human but marks them off in a derivative way

---

[17] The former is used at *Post. An.* 93b36 and 1030b9 in connection with the *Iliad*; the latter is used at 1029b30 in reference to accounts of composites such as pale human and at 1031a2–5 with reference to defining items belonging to the non-substance categories.

[18] In *Metaphysics* V 6, Aristotle mentions the continuous as one of the cases where things are one in their own nature (*kath' hauta*) (1015b34–1016a17). Thus construed, unity would hold of all linguistic definitions including the proposed definition of 'Iliad'.

[19] Definitions in the *De Interpretatione* are accounts of what terms signify.

[20] See Modrak (2001), ch. 1, section 2.

by marking off all the things that are human and distinguishing them from everything else. 'Not-man' does, however, possess a kind of unity, as it is a coherent notion. In the *De Interpretatione*, coherence is a necessary condition for signification, and the concept's being a likeness of a *pragma* is another. Aristotle believes 'not-man' meets the first but not the second of these conditions. 'Man-and-horse' either is not a single notion but two, i.e. 'man' and 'horse', or it is a single notion but one that has no signification. There is nothing in the world for the notion in question to be a likeness of nor can it be derived by conjunction, since the conjunction of actual likenesses would yield 'man' and 'horse'.

Why then would Aristotle say that 'goat-stag' and by implication 'centaur' are significant? These terms seem to be composite in just the same way as 'man-and-horse'. Aristotle's best answer would be to extend the notion of a *pragma* to include not only existents but also any term that has a clearly demarcated referent within a context of discourse.[21] There is a fictional context in which to find referents for 'goat-stag' and 'centaur'.[22] There is no independent context of discourse in which to locate the arbitrarily constructed 'man-and-horse', or the arbitrarily assigned 'cloak'.

Aristotle's account of real definition is clearly marked by Platonic language and concerns, and this background also influences the account of linguistic definition. The weak unity condition on linguistic definition makes considerable sense, if the ultimate goal of natural language is to carve reality up at its proper joints, as Plato supposes. 'Mustn't the name giver also know how to embody in sounds and syllables the name naturally suited to each thing?' (*Cratylus* 389d3–4).[23] For Aristotle, as well as for Plato, there is a fact of the matter about the structure of reality and hence a fact of the matter about whether our linguistic concepts correspond to actual classifications of beings. A necessary, although not sufficient, condition on

[21] *De Interpretatione* 17a37–b1 states that some *pragmata* are universal and others individual; Aristotle uses *anthropos*, a secondary substance, as an example. This suggests a willingness to extend the notion somewhat. But in this case the *pragma* is a secondary, simple existent and whether Aristotle would extend it still further is unclear.

[22] The question of the signification of 'goat-stag' and similar terms will be reconsidered in section III below.

[23] In the *Cratylus*, Plato makes the name the tool for carving reality up and treats the name as an encapsulation of the definition. Aristotle's account of the relation between name and associated definiens is different. The name is a conventional sign; there is no right or wrong name as such. However, he, too, takes the goal of language to be articulating real natures. These are specified in accounts or definitions.

such correspondence is that terms having unqualified signification pick out genuine objects. If the definition of a term satisfies the weak unity condition, the term will pick out a definite object. On the face of it, weak unity would not seem to be sufficient to guarantee existence; however, Aristotle may believe it does. His stock example of a fictional object, the goat-stag, has a compositional character and might be thought to fail even the weak unity constraint.

The Platonic theory of division provides a further motivation for the unity condition on linguistic definitions. Division is a method for defining a term by finding the broadest concept under which it falls, for instance, 'art' in the case of sophistry, and then determining all the conceptual links between the generic term and the kind in question on a tree structure where each lower concept is achieved by an exclusive division of the concept immediately preceding it on the tree.[24] Art is divided into acquisitive and productive arts and then the productive arts are divided into human and divine ones, etc. In the case of the final and definitive definition of sophistry in the *Sophist*, a series of divisions yields the definiens: 'the art of contradiction-making, descended from an insincere kind of conceited mimicry of the semblance-making breed, derived from image-making, distinguished as a portion, not divine but human, of productive <art>' (268cd). Even though he criticizes Plato for thinking that the method of division demonstrates the truth of the resulting definition, Aristotle admires the method for the conceptual clarity that it yields. Aristotle embraces definition by division as an analytic tool.

To establish a definition by division, one should aim for three things—grasping that which is predicated in what the thing is, ordering these as first or second, and establishing that these are all there are. (97a24–27)

A successful division maps the relations among the component concepts making up a definition. It links the genus to the species through a series of successive differentiations of the genus that define successively narrower sub-genera until the species is reached.

[24] Several later dialogues provide detailed illustrations of the method of division; see *Sophist* 221c–232a and 264e–268d; *Statesman* 258b–267c; and *Philebus* 16c–17a. Aristotle discussed this method at length in *Posterior Analytics* II 5, 13–14; *Metaphysics* VII 12; and *Parts of Animals* I 2–3.

The usefulness of the method of division depends upon the existence of properly formed linguistic concepts having a degree of internal coherence. Even a disjunctive definition of the sort mentioned in the *Posterior Analytics* could be illustrated on a tree that led from the genus under which the term falls to several, different definitions. This happens in the first series of definitions in the *Sophist* (221c–232a). When exploring the conceptual divisions between the generic term 'art' and the specific term 'sophistry', which falls under 'art', Socrates initially generates six different definitions. Plato takes this proliferation of definitions as evidence that none of the original definitions capture the core notion of sophistry. Aristotle would certainly agree in the case of real definition.

The discussion of *megalopsuchia* in *Posterior Analytics* II 13 seems designed to extend linguistic definition to the case where the same word has different, distinct and singly unified senses. Aristotle's willingness to allow the division of a linguistic concept to yield several, irreducibly different definitions, may also be a moral he drew from reflecting on the results of applying the Platonic method of division to ordinary-language concepts. Each of the first six definitions of 'sophist' does indeed seem to fit historical examples of people labeled sophists in ordinary contexts.[25] As a matter of linguistic practice, each definition states a sufficient condition for the application of 'sophist'. Just as in the case of the first six definitions of 'sophist', the division of *megalopsuchia* is motivated by considering the extension of the term as ordinarily used with the consequence that different conceptual cuts are made in order to cover different individuals (97b15–26). Socrates' *megalopsuchia* is found to be of a different sort than Alcibiades'. It is indifference to good and bad fortune whereas Alcibiades' is intolerance of insults. If a common feature cannot be found, the process of division will have established that the same term covers two types of character traits and thus clarified the (disjunctive) linguistic definition. Of the original six definitions by division in the *Sophist*, the first five are jointly coextensive with the final definition of sophist. The final definition differs from the earlier ones in stating a necessary and sufficient condition for application of the concept, according to Plato. It is a normative definition that excludes one of the original definitions based on linguistic practice. For Aristotle, definitions of

[25] For a defense of this reading of the *Sophist*, see Modrak (2001), pp. 85–95.

essence are also normative and might (but need not) lead to the reform of linguistic practice.

For Plato, the method of division provides the justification for the definition that results. The definition is true and expresses the essence of the concept defined. To achieve conceptual unity, Plato recommends dichotomous divisions of a single genus. Aristotle rejects division's claim to be a method for discovering truths. A division is not a demonstration, he says, because both the starting-point and decisions about cuts are governed by assumptions that are not discharged in the course of the division (91b18–27). In the *Posterior Analytics*, Aristotle recommends dividing the right differentia in the right order, e.g. animal, footed, two-footed (96b30–35, cf. 91b28–30). In the *Parts of Animals*, he emphasizes the importance of respecting natural groups when applying the method of division (642b9–20). Aristotle argues that dichotomous division does not always work for natural groups and that in some cases there will be more than one differentia to be divided (643b13–24). Aristotle seems to be recommending a strategy for division that would not proceed from the genus through the dichotomous division of one differentia to the species but rather the division of several differentiae to the final differentia in each column for the species in question.[26] The species would then be defined by all the final differentiae rather than being identified with a single final differentia. This may, in part, explain why Aristotle does not, at the end of the day, make the unity of a real definition solely dependent upon the application of the method of division.[27] Aristotle's goal is to reform the method of division rather than reject it. Division is a tool for uncovering and displaying conceptual unities that correspond to realities in the best case and to linguistic concepts in the second best case. The reformed use of division advocated by Aristotle provides a procedure for making linguistic definitions more precise and hence better approximations to strict definitions (definitions capturing real natures). Moreover, division would offer a way to clarify the nature of the unity possessed by a linguistic definition. In some instances, a series of divisions would ultimately reveal a single core concept; in others, it would not.

---

[26] Balme (1972) correctly argues that Aristotle's criticisms are aimed at a particular way of applying the method of division and are not intended as a blanket rejection of the method (pp. 101–19).

[27] See discussion of this point in section III below.

Definitions expressing essences possess unity in the strict sense. Nevertheless, unity also has a normative role to play in linguistic definition as is clear from Aristotle's discussion of the method of division. Finally, even a minimally adequate account of what a name signifies will have some sort of unity, however contrived.

III Relation between Linguistic and Real Definition

The prospects for linguistic definition and its relation to real definition are still open questions at the end of *Metaphysics* VII 6. In VII 10–12, Aristotle brings the distinction between form and matter to bear on the topic of definition. A consequence of hylomorphic analysis is that only forms (or essences) will be non-composites; particular substances and their species names will be composites of matter and form.

But 'human' and 'horse' and terms which are thus applied to individuals but universally, are not substance but a whole composed of this particular formula and this particular matter treated as universal; and regarding the individual, Socrates is already composed of ultimate matter and similarly in all other cases.[28] (*Met.* 1035b27–31; trans. follows Ross; cf. 1037a7)

The universal terms 'human' and 'horse' predicate both the substance (the form) and the material substrate of the concrete individual. These composites are distinct from the substance as form, which is predicated only of matter not individual substance (1049a34–36; cf. 1038b4–6). A species name such as 'human' or 'horse' refers to the species construed as a universal composite of form and matter. Are there, then, several definitions of 'human'—one of which applies to the species name, and another to the species essence? Is the former the same as the nominal definition; is the latter the same as a technical definition of the species? If the species name refers to the species studied by the scientist, then it would appear that the scientific definition of the species would fall short of possessing strict unity. Since the

---

[28] I have followed Ross's translation (1924) of the phrase (τὰ οὕτως ἐπί τῶν καθ᾽ ἔκαστα) as 'terms which are thus applied to individuals'. This wording better captures Aristotle's meaning than do other recent translations. Gill (1989, p. 122) translates this phrase 'the entities thus related to particulars'. See also Charles (1994, p. 78), and Irwin (1990, pp. 249 and 571 n. 5), which takes 1035b27–31 to be about Aristotle's universal forms.

linguistic definition of 'human' is also a definition of a generalized composite, the line between linguistic and technical definition would seem to blur. This would be problematic, because the technical definition, unlike the nominal one, embodies knowledge. Yet it appears unlikely that any definition, however rigorous, of a universalized composite could satisfy the unity condition for real definition.[29]

If, on the other hand, the biologist's technical definition of the species 'human' is a definition in the strict sense, a puzzle arises about the relationship between the definition of the species and the definition of the essence of a human being.[30] The definition of a natural kind shares many characteristics with the definition of essence. In both the *Posterior Analytics* and *Metaphysics*, Aristotle is willing to use his term for definition proper, *horismos*, for the definition of a natural kind. Science as distinguished from metaphysics requires definitions of this sort as premises. Like definitions of essence, these definitions specify essences. However, they do so by construing the essence as the essence of a certain kind of body (1035b14–18). The definition of 'soul' is an interesting case in point. In the *Metaphysics*, Aristotle takes 'soul' to be essence, i.e. to have the simplicity and unity required of the object of a strict definition of essence, and he contrasts 'soul' with 'human', a term for a natural kind. In the *De Anima*, Aristotle identifies the soul of an animal with the embodied essence of the biological kind and defines it in terms of its characteristic attributes (*De An.* 403b7–19; cf. 403a25). A definition of this sort articulates an essence but not without reference to bodily activities and functions. In contrast, the metaphysician frames definitions of essence without reference to body (403b15–16). Putting this notion of a metaphysical definition together with the use of 'soul' in the *Metaphysics*, we seem to be left with a distinction between strict definition and scientific definition.

The only apparent difference between a scientific definition of a natural kind and a definition of essence is that the former but not the latter makes some reference to matter.

---

[29] Cf. Gill (1989), pp. 120–44.

[30] One way to avoid this puzzle is to argue, as Frede does (1990, pp. 113–29), that Aristotle only admits natural science definitions in terms of form and matter in a qualified way and that as characterized in *Metaphysics* VII the definition of substance makes no reference to matter. The difficulty with this solution is that it would seem to undermine the epistemic warrant of definitions in natural science.

Since the soul of animals (for this is the substance of the ensouled creature) is the substance according to the formula and the form and the essence of such a body (at least if each is well defined, it will not be defined without its function, which does not belong without perception) so that the parts of this will be prior, either all or some to the composite animal. (1035b14–19)

Only substance construed abstractly as essence or form satisfies the strictest Aristotelian notion of unity. Precisely because its object is species form as realized in individuals, the definition of a natural kind has something important in common with linguistic definition. But as an object of knowledge, the definition of a natural kind has something equally important in common with the definition of essence as form. Aristotle is thus pressed on several fronts to bring together the disparate elements in his account of definition.

In order to fill out Aristotle's conception of definition and its implications for definition in natural science as well as for linguistic definition, we should revisit the strong unity requirement for definitions of essence. Were a definition completely simple conceptually, there would be no question about its unity. The problem is that such a definition would not do the work it needs to do. The real definition furnishes an analysis; it is an expression of the essence of the object. The dilemma Aristotle faces is the one raised towards the end of Plato's *Theaetetus*.

But in fact there is no formula (*logos*) in which any of the primary things can be expressed; it can only be named, for a name is all there is that belongs to it. But when we come to things composed of these elements, then, just as these things are complex, so the names are combined to make a formula, a formula being precisely a combination of names. (*Theaetetus* 202b1–5; trans. follows Cornford)

While a thinker may have an immediate cognitive hold on a simple entity, this cognition provides no analysis. It yields no definition. An account of any sort requires the combination of simples. Aristotle explores the relationship between the components of a definition and the definition as a unified whole.

Since a definition is a formula, and every formula has parts, and as the formula is to the thing (*pragma*), so is the part of the formula to the part of the thing, the question already arises whether the formula of the parts must be in the formula of the whole or not. (VII 10, 1034b20–23)

The upshot of this discussion is a picture on which certain parts are allowed in the definition of essence because they are parts of the formula (1035a4).

Thus the letters that make up a word are part of its formula, if the letters are abstractly conceived, but not if they are waxen or audible (1035a14–17). This constraint on the proper parts of a definition gives Aristotle a way to distinguish between the definition of an entity in a non-substance category and other items having composite definitions such as pale human. The parts of the definitions of such composites would not be proper parts of the formula of the thing. As parts of the account of the composite item labeled 'cloak', the terms 'pale' and 'human' bear no intrinsic relation to each other and have only a stipulated relation to 'cloak'.

Aristotle may also believe that an analogous account of proper parts should be applied in order to distinguish between properly formed linguistic definitions and other sorts of accounts corresponding to names; however, he does not address that topic here. Aristotle's recognition of the intrinsic compositionality of formulae enables him to admit a similar degree of complexity in the case of the analogous notion of form. This is an important step towards a solution, but Aristotle is not yet satisfied. He ends the discussion of definition in VII 11 on an aporetic note.

And in the case of definitions, how the elements in the formula are parts of the definition, and why the definition is one formula (for the thing is clearly one, but in virtue of what is it one thing, since it has parts?); this must be considered later. (1037a17–21)

Aristotle's reservations stem from his conception of strict definition. The elements of the formula are not merely terms but are also the things predicated by those terms, and thus a definiens consisting of several terms seems to presuppose distinct ontological elements. What is needed is an account of definition where the relation between part and whole is such that the parts of the definition are the analysans of the concept defined and yet they are not ontologically prior to the definition. Turning to the method of division in the effort to account for unity in VII 12, Aristotle grants that if the final differentia contains all the preceding differentiae and all are ordered properly, the method of division will display the unity of the definiens. Nevertheless, he remains skeptical about the implications of this for the unity problem.[31]

---

[31] The worry cited at 1038a33–34 is that unity should not depend on order. Elsewhere Aristotle argues that there are multiple differentiae and hence the goal of finding a final differentia that contains the others is wrongheaded in the case of complex biological species (*Parts of Animals* 643b9–26). See discussion in section II above.

The ontological and definitional aspects of the relation between parts and whole are discussed in VII 17. Aristotle argues that form and matter should not be seen as two components of one composite. The composite substance is one, because the form is realized in the matter not as another element or constituent (1041b25–32). The bricks are a wall, not because the form of the wall is another constituent of the wall, but because the bricks are structured in a particular way, i.e. collectively they have a particular form. In the first three chapters of VIII, Aristotle continues the discussion of substance as a composite of matter and form and does so in light of various kinds of definitions. 'Bricks and timbers in such and such a position' answers the question 'What is a threshold?' (1043a7–8). Aristotle notes that this answer is in terms of matter and position. This illustration and similar examples are used to extend a point made earlier about the nature of sensible substance to the definition of sensible substance. Sensible substances are composites of matter and form. A word such as 'house' is ambiguous in that its meaning may include material elements or may only indicate the form.

sometimes it is not clear whether a name signifies the composite substance, or the actuality or form, e.g., whether 'house' is a sign for the composite thing, 'a covering consisting of bricks and stones laid thus and thus', or for the actuality or form 'a covering' ... and whether an animal is 'a soul in a body' or 'a soul'; for soul is the substance or actuality of some body. (VIII 3 1043a29–36)

While it is possible to offer definitions in terms of matter only, which are, strictly speaking, definitions of the potential substance, or ones of the form or actuality alone (1043a14–19; *De An.* 403a25–b9), the most complete definition will mention both form and matter (*De An.* 403b7–9; *Phys.* 194b10–13, cf. 200b7–8).

Returning to the question of unity in VIII 6, Aristotle declares that what makes a definition one is that its object is one (1045a14; cf. 1037b25–27). He then argues that the way to explain the unity of natural substances, such as humans, is in terms of form and matter.

If one element <in the definition> is matter and another is form, as we say, and one is potentially and the other actually, the question <about unity> will no longer be thought a difficulty.[32] (1045a23–25)

---

[32] Even though Aristotle makes this remark in a context where he is, among other things, criticizing Platonic definitions, this is Aristotle's solution to the problem of unity that he faces.

The beauty of hylomorphic analysis, for Aristotle, is that it allows him to view natural substances as both analyzable into form and matter, soul and body in the case of living things, and as essential unities. Because the relationship between form and matter is one of actuality to potentiality, the composite of form and matter is one. Similarly, in the case of definition, what makes the definition unified is its having a structure that mirrors the relation between form and matter in the object. The 'material' component of the definition specifies a range of potentialities that are necessary for the realization of the formal component. The ability to hear, a psychic capacity, can only be realized in confined air (*De An.* 420a9–19). The definition of hearing specifies the range of material potentialities in which the capacity to hear may be realized. In *Metaphysics* VIII 6, Aristotle uses the definiens 'round bronze' to illustrate this point. As the matter in which round is realized in the bronze sphere, bronze is a material possessing the potentiality to constitute a sphere. This mode of analysis is also applicable, Aristotle notes, to abstract objects. His second example, viz. 'circle is a plane figure', is a partial definition that mentions intelligible matter (1045a34–36).[33] In a definition by specific differentia and genus, the genus is the matter. The feature a genus has in common with a specific material such as bronze is that both genera and matter, whether corporeal or intelligible, are conceptualized by Aristotle as specifications of ranges of potentialities. 'Animal' specifies the range of potentialities that may be realized as a four-footed or a two-footed or a footless living creature. The species form accounts for the actualization of a specific potentiality, e.g. the potential to be a two-footed animal.

This provides Aristotle with a strategy for a seamless transition from the definition of an infima species that meets the requirements of VII 4 to the natural science definition of the same concept. There is, for instance, a smooth transition from the metaphysical definition of the human soul to the definition of the human soul as species form of human beings. Aristotle allows the specification of the form in a definition of a natural kind to contain a reference to appropriate matter, which is construed as the material element of the definiens (*Phys.* 200b7–8). The transition between metaphysically correct definitions and scientifically correct ones is in fact so

---

[33] The conception of geometrical objects as shapes that bound extension may have been suggested to Aristotle by Socrates' defining figure in the *Meno* as the limit of a solid (76a).

seamless that Aristotle scarcely notices it, apart from admonishing the natural scientist to recognize the priority of form to matter (*Phys.* 194a16–18; *De An.* 403b7–15; *Part. An.* 640b4–641b11).

The strict definition of the species form of a natural kind is the core notion in the definition of a natural kind that also includes a generalized reference to the matter of the kind. The species form is such that it presupposes matter, but an account of it need not make reference to particular matter. The form of the word contains its constituent vowels and consonants but not particular audible or legible matter (1035a14–17; cf. 1034b26, 1041b11–16). The definitions of essence used by the natural scientist will meet the requirements of strict definition in the *Metaphysics*, not because they make no reference to parts or potential matter, but because they make no reference to particular matter. They are like words abstractly conceived as ordered arrangements of letters but not as made up of particular written or spoken syllables. This is how Aristotle proposes to close the gap that is opened in VII 4 between the definitions of substance that are used by the natural scientist and the description of strict definition. This, of course, still leaves the problem of the definitions of all the items in the non-substance categories. To explain in what way these items are definable, Aristotle could appeal to his account of the proper parts of a definition. He seems content, however, with his earlier response that in one sense such items do not have strict definitions and in another they do. Insofar as such entities are considered without matter, Aristotle takes them to be essential unities (1045a36–b1). That said, the paradigm instance of strict definition is the definition of a non-composite substance, an infima species. A weakened notion of definition will extend to the definition of genera, attributes, and relations.

The status of linguistic definition remains unclear. The name of a natural kind, horse, for instance, is used, as Aristotle notes, as a universal that contains a generalized reference to both the form and matter of individuals. When Aristotle takes the species name to signify particular form and particular matter as universal at 1035b27–31, his subject is linguistic definition. As the object of science, 'horse' is defined in terms of the species form; as the object of ordinary language, it may be defined in terms of the natural kind, construed as a type of concrete substance. A linguistic definition may coincide with the scientific definition but it need not. Indeed linguistic definitions seem to cover a range of cases. In some cases, ordinary language and science agree; in other cases, the linguistic definition and the scientific definition have the same object but the linguistic definition is less precise, because it includes accidental features due to the material constitution of individual instances of the kind; and in still other cases, the object of definition is such that there is no scientific definition, because its object is not simple and its definition involves conjunction or disjunction.

Aristotle cannot afford to ignore the challenge posed by linguistic defin-ition. When he tackles a topic for investigation, Aristotle typically treats the relevant linguistic definitions as legitimate starting-points. In practice he recognizes a continuum between the terms of natural language and the terms of natural science and their respective definitions. In *Physics* I 1, the undefined, universal term is associated with a whole, a kind of universal with fuzzy edges that is grasped through perception (184a23–26). Aristotle contrasts the name signifying a whole indeterminately with the definition of the term that demarcates its proper referents (184a26–b14). The definition specifies the proper conceptual parts of the whole and thus circumscribes the range of application of the term. Aristotle gives two examples. The first is 'circle' and its definition; the definition at issue is the geometer's.[34] The second is that of a child learning to use words correctly. The child at first applies 'father' to all adult males and 'mother' to all adult females but later discriminates among adults, using the terms appropriately. At this point the child tacitly possesses the linguistic definition.

The paradigmatic case of linguistic definition is a definition that expresses (at least partially) the nature of the existent signified by the word. A word has the meaning it has, because it is a mediated sign of the object it represents, as is clear from the description of signification in *De Interpreta-tione* 1–3.

Spoken words are the symbols of affections of the soul and written words are the symbols of spoken words. And just as written signs are not the same for all humans neither are spoken words. But what these primarily are signs of, the affections of the soul, are the same for all, as also are those things of which our affections are likenesses. (16a3–8)

---

[34] The definition of circle is implied but not stated at *Physics* 184b12–13. It is typical of Aristotle, however, to illustrate his notion of strict definition (*horismos*) by appealing to geometrical terms and definitions.

Signification by means of a natural language builds on a relation between the language-using creature and the objects in its environment. The relative stability of the objects fixes meanings and guarantees their stability. A natural-language term is a phonetic sign that is meaning-bearing. Since the referent of the term is the source of the concept that is associated with the phonetic sign, it is likely (or so Aristotle thinks) that the meaning of the term will correspond to (at least some of) the actual properties of the object. This places the linguistic definition on a continuum with the scientific definition. The more advanced the level of knowledge about the world is among the members of a particular linguistic community, the more closely the linguistic definitions of the community will track the world. If there is a perfect fit between the linguistic definition and the world, the distinction between linguistic and real definition will collapse. The linguistic definition in those instances will meet the criteria of strict definition (*horismos*).

However, linguistic definitions often express real characteristics of their objects but fail to state the essence fully or precisely. They may capture accidental rather than essential features of the object. In these cases, the natural-language term has a *logos* but not a *horismos* in the technical sense. A linguistic definition may also fail because its object lacks the simplicity and natural coherence of an object of scientific definition. This happens when the object is constructed out of other notions by conjunction or disjunction. There are also *logoi* that seem to be cases of strings of words that correspond to single terms that Aristotle takes to be examples of nominal definition by conjunction. The name of a poem does have the poem as its associated *logos* but this *logos* is a far cry from the simple expression of an essence in a scientific definition.

Sometimes a name signifies only an account and not an existent. Aristotle views this case as a defective instance of signification and one that is dependent upon the normative case.[35] 'Goat-stag' is significant for members of a particular linguistic community, because they share a common account

---

[35] Charles (2000) attributes a three-stage view to Aristotle where signification, existence, and essence are distinct. Although all three factors figure in Aristotle's thinking about definition, the picture for him (I believe) is one in which signification in the strict sense implies existence. However, Aristotle also recognizes that some account must be given of linguistically significant terms that seem to refer to non-existents or to other constructed items.

of what the word means.[36] 'Goat-stag' is significant within the context of a particular natural language.[37] The existence of the natural language will depend upon the satisfaction of the normative conditions on signification. A term referring to a fictional entity will fail to meet these conditions and will have signification only in a derivative way. To have an account of 'goat-stag' is to combine in thought two concepts derived from linguistic experience.[38] Both 'goat' (*tragos*, literally male goat) and 'stag' (*elaphos*) signify existing objects; by abstracting from these notions, a language user is able to form a minimal concept to correspond to the name 'goat-stag' (*tragelaphos*). A shared mythology allows the speakers of the natural language to fill out the minimal concept.

Sometimes a name signifies an account that is one merely by conjunction. Aristotle's favorite example of this type of *logos* is the poem that is called the *Iliad* (*Post. An.* 92b30–32; *Met.* 1030a7–10). Here Aristotle emphasizes the difference between a *logos* that signifies an object that is intrinsically unified and one that signifies an object that is one only by conjunction (*An.* 93b35–37; *Met.* 1030b6–12). Although he does not directly address this issue, he would seem to be committed to the view that no properly formed linguistic definition would be one in this very attenuated sense (*Met.* 1045a12–14). If this is right, then one might wonder why Aristotle uses the *Iliad* as an example of a nominal definition. He does so in contexts where his strategy is to push the notion of nominal definition as far as he can in order to discredit its claim to be strict definition. This need not commit him to the view that linguistic definition must be so loosely defined that any sort of *logos* counts as a definition.[39]

Without weakening the epistemic constraints on strict definition Aristotle is able to accommodate linguistic definitions. He does this by making signification dependent upon a general correspondence between linguistic concepts and extra-linguistic realities. Strict definition thus becomes the model for all definition. A real or strict definition meets the requirements of

[36] Aristotle uses 'goat-stag' as a stock example of a non-existent yet familiar object for which there is a natural-language term (*De Int.* 16a16–18; *Pr. Anal.* 49a24; *Post. Anal.* 92b5–8; *Phys.* 208a30).

[37] According to Liddell and Scott (*Greek–English Lexicon*), Κένταυρος was originally a term for a member of a tribe of fierce horsemen living in Thessaly; only later did it acquire a mythological significance. This evolution of the use of Κένταυρος fits Aristotle's picture of how signification works for mythological notions.

[38] Cf. Plato, *Rep.* 488a, 'just as painters paint goat-stags by combining the features of different things'.

[39] As noted above, Aristotle hints at this possibility at 1030a14–16 when he mentions an account that is more accurate than the account that merely indicates what a name signifies.

demonstrative science in the *Posterior Analytics*. Its objects satisfy the ontological requirements set out in the middle books of the *Metaphysics*. Linguistic definitions often fail on both counts. Nonetheless, if they are not vacuous, such definitions approximate real definitions. In several places, Aristotle reserves the use of *horismos* for definition in the strict sense (*Post. An.* 92b26–33; *Met.* 1030a6–12). He has a broader term for definition, *logos*, however, that is consistently used for 'definition' in linguistic contexts. In short, Aristotle's final position with respect to the status of linguistic definition is that the closer a linguistic definition approximates a strict scientific definition, the stronger its claim becomes to be a proper definition. Only the definition of essence is a definition in the strictest sense, but in another sense, the nominal definition also is a definition.

IV A Different Approach

Aristotle is drawn to a normative conception of definition that puts pressure on his minimal conception of nominal definition as merely terminological. The early Stoics are also pulled between the competing demands of ontology and language. A brief look at the way the theory of definition develops in Stoic hands provides an interesting contrast with Aristotle's attempt to balance a minimalist conception of definition with a metaphysical one. Initially the Stoics follow the Aristotelian/Platonic approach that takes its starting-point from Socrates' search for definition.[40] Socrates asks the *ti esti* question (What is <courage, justice, etc.>?) and then rejects any answer that fails to express necessary and sufficient conditions for the use of the term in question. He also seems to place further requirements on definition in certain contexts.[41] These include unity and capturing the essence construed as a cause or rational ground.

In a similar vein, the Stoics specify definitions for key ethical concepts.[42] Cicero speaks admiringly of Chrysippus' renderings of 'courage' as 'scientific

---

[40] The topic of definition was of considerable interest to other earlier philosophers as well. Plato mentions Prodicus in this regard (*Laches* 197d; *Cratylus* 384b) and Aristotle attributes an account of definition to Archytus of Tarentum (*Met.* 1043a21).

[41] In the *Euthyphro*, even though the definition of piety as that which is god-loved is coextensive with piety, it is rejected on the grounds that it fails to give the reason why (10d).

[42] The lists of titles attributed to Chrysippus provide evidence of a broad interest in definition in logical as well as ethical contexts (D.L. 7.189, 199–200).

knowledge of matters requiring persistence' and 'a tenor of the soul fear-lessly obedient to the supreme law in enduring and persisting' (*Tusc.* 4.53). As part of a critique of the dogmatists' approaches to the definition of ethical concepts, Sextus cites several definitions that he attributes to Stoic philoso-phers. 'Happiness is the equable flow of life' according to Zeno, Cleanthes, and Chrysippus (S.E., *M.* 11.30). 'Good is utility or not other than utility', as defined by the Stoics appealing to common notions (S.E., *M.* 11.22). Although the Stoics recognize that 'good' has different senses, they insist that these are closely related in that the first sense contains the second and so forth (S.E., *M.* 11.30). The attempt to unify their notion of good as evidence of the strong hold that the unity constraint on definition accepted by Socrates, Plato, and Aristotle continued to have.

Not content merely to frame definitions, the Stoics grounded this prac-tice in a theory of definition. Over time several different descriptions of definition (*horos*) were offered.

Chrysippus says that a definition is a representation of a peculiar characteristic, i.e. that which expresses the peculiar characteristic. Antipater the Stoic says: 'A defin-ition is a statement expressed with necessary force, i.e. with reciprocal force.' (*SVF* 2.226)

Galen adds to these: 'A definition is a statement of analysis matchingly expressed or a definition is a brief reminder that brings us to a conception of the things underlying the words' (*Def. Med.* 19.348.17–349.4; Long and Sedley trans.). These descriptions were in turn said to be equivalent (*SVF* 2.228).

A definition that had reciprocal force would be such that the definiens would provide both necessary and sufficient conditions for the use of the definiendum. In addition, the claim that the definition is a representation of a peculiar characteristic would meet the further Socratic requirement that the definition capture the unique, intrinsic character of the object in question. The peculiar characteristic of an existent is a feature of the world. The definition that expresses it is the Stoic analogue of an Aristo-telian definition of essence. That it is possible to grasp a definition that captures just what its object is is a constant feature of philosophical notions of definition from Socrates to Chrysippus.

Chrysippus' claim that the definition is a representation of the peculiar characteristic introduces an ontological element, because the peculiar characteristic of an existent is itself a reality; it is not simply a linguistic artifact.[43] This raises the question of how the mind bridges the gap between the peculiar characteristic of an existent and its expression in the definition. The Stoic doctrine, mentioned by Galen, that a definition is a reminder of a conception underlying our words may have been intended as an answer to this question. At birth the mind is blank; conceptions (*ennoiai*) are inscribed on it by the senses (SVF 2.83). Later through memory and experience, attention and instruction, further conceptions are inscribed. Conceptions arising without conscious shaping by us are called preconceptions (*prolêpseis*) and assigned a foundational role.[44] Through such conceptions, the mind grasps underlying realities. As a shorthand way of expressing a conception, the definition would prompt the thinker to recall the conception that was formed spontaneously on the basis of an encounter with the object in the world. The definition or, more precisely, the conception would be a representation of the peculiar character of the object. The artifice of the definition is offset by the naturalness of the conception. The definition when grasped in thought is a *lekton* but because, as a *lekton*, it would be dependent upon instruction and attention, the definition as such is not a foundational conception, although some of the preconceptions underlying meanings would be.[45]

Chrysippus' account of definition gives way to other formulations that are said to be equivalent to his but which, in fact, shift the account away from ontology to linguistic analysis. Antipater requires only that a definition have reciprocal or necessary force.[46] In any statement, it should be possible to substitute the definiens for the definiendum without changing the truth value of the sentence. The requirements for definition, thus formulated,

[43] Although the later Stoics tended to emphasize purely linguistic relations, I cannot agree with Hülser (1979) that the Stoics totally rejected the 'ontologisation of semantics' and made no attempt to justify language by appealing to the relation between terms and realities.

[44] Plutarch attributes *emphuton prolepseon* of good and evil to Chrysippus (*St. Rep.* 1041e). This need not be interpreted as Chrysippus' attributing innate *prolepseis* to minds. Its force might merely be to emphasize the naturalness of the ideas that accord with our natures. Cf. Sandbach (1971).

[45] Conception is the broader notion for the Stoics; preconceptions are a special category of conceptions that are more grounded in the nature of things and less an artifact of human thought processes than other conceptions (*SVF* 2.83; Cicero, *Acad.* 2.30–1).

[46] Long and Sedley (1987) interpret Antipater's formulation as adding the additional requirement that a definition be viewed as an identity statement (p. 194). However, since Antipater construes the notion of reciprocal force in terms of necessary force, it seems more likely that he is shifting the emphasis from capturing essences to necessary and sufficient conditions for the application of terms.

may hold for any term. A definition need only state necessary and sufficient conditions for the application of the term. Definitions need not carry existential commitments nor express real features of the world. This is a more modern picture of definition that marks an advance beyond the ontologically laden definitions of essence of earlier philosophers.[47]

More evidence of this shift toward an analytic approach to definition can be found in the Stoic employment of the method of division. Division is a method for displaying conceptual relations. It introduces analytic rigor in a context—that of framing definitions—where deductive inference is of limited usefulness. Aristotle recognized this feature of division and adopted it as a way to display relations among linguistic concepts. He nevertheless rejected it as a method of justification that could secure the epistemic warrant of definitions, thus arrived at. The Stoics even more strongly embrace the construal of the method of division as analysis shorn of ontological commitments. While accepting the traditional characterization of division as the dissection of a genus into proximate species, they defined other types of division, including contra-division, the dissection of a genus into a species and its opposite, in order to make division even more precise.[48] In their hands, the method of division becomes a very flexible device but the licensing of a variety of strategies diminishes the likelihood that a particular application of the method will provide independent justification of the sort that Plato envisaged.

As is clear, hopefully, from this all too brief sketch of their handling of definition, the Stoics move away from the earlier conception of real definition and embrace in its stead the modern, analytic conception of definition. A linguistic definition provides an analysis of the meaning of a term. By contrast, Aristotle, Plato, and Socrates, each in his own way, strive for linguistic definitions that at least approximate real definitions. Plato and Aristotle hope ultimately to eliminate nominal definitions of existents in

[47] Hülser (1979) argues that the Stoics were skeptical about the ontologization of semantics by earlier Greek philosophers. In the case of definition, however, this skepticism is expressed in later Stoic treatments of definition. Chrysippus seems to embrace the same ontological commitments as his predecessors.

[48] Division proper is the dissection of a genus into proximate species, e.g. 'animal' into 'rational' and 'non-rational'. Contra-division is a dissection of a genus into a species in relation to its opposite, e.g. 'existents' into 'good' and 'not good'. Subdivisions of both division and contra-division are also defined (D.L. 7.61–2).

favor of strict definitions of essence. This is not a hope shared by modern philosophers nor by the Stoics.

Bibliography

Balme, D., 1972, *Aristotle's* De Partibus Animalium I *and* De Generatione Animalium I, translation with notes, Oxford: Clarendon Press.

———1987, 'Aristotle's Use of Division and Differentiae', in *Philosophical Issues in Aristotle's Biology*, ed. A. Gotthelf and J. Lennox, 69–89.

Bolton, R., 1976, 'Essentialism and Semantic Theory in Aristotle's *Posterior Analytics* II. 7–10', *Philosophical Review* 85, 515–45.

———1987, 'Definition and Scientific Method in Aristotle's *Posterior Analytics* and the *Generation of Animals*', in *Philosophical Issues in Aristotle's Biology*, ed. A. Gotthelf and J. Lennox, 120–66.

Butler, T., 2003, 'Empeiria in Aristotle', *Southern Journal of Philosophy* 41, 329–50.

Charles, D., 1994, 'Aristotle on Names and Their Signification', in *Companion to Ancient Thought*, vol. 3: *Language*, Cambridge: Cambridge University Press.

———2000, *Aristotle on Meaning and Essence*, Oxford: Clarendon Press.

DeMoss D., and Devereux D., 1988, 'Essence, Existence and Nominal Definition in Aristotle's *Posterior Analytics* II 8–10', *Phronesis* 33, 133–54.

Frede, M., 1990, 'The Definition of Sensible Substances in *Met. Z*', in *Biologie, Logique et Metaphysique chez Aristote: Seminaire CNRS-N.S.F. 1987*, ed. D. Devereux and Pierre Pellegrin, Paris: Centre National de la Recherche Scientifique, 113–29.

Gill, M., 1989, *Aristotle on Substance: The Paradox of Unity*, Princeton: Princeton University Press.

Gotthelf, A., 1987, 'First Principles in Aristotle's *Parts of Animals*', in *Philosophical Issues in Aristotle's Biology*, ed. A. Gotthelf and J. Lennox, 167–98.

Gotthelf, A., and Lennox, J. (eds.), 1987, *Philosophical Issues in Aristotle's Biology*, Cambridge: Cambridge University Press.

Huffman, C., 2005, *Archytus of Tarentum: Pythagorean, Philosopher, and Mathematician King*, Cambridge: Cambridge University Press.

Hülser, K., 1979, 'Expression and Context in Stoic Linguistic Theory', in *Semantics from Different Points of View*, ed. R. Baüerle, U. Egli, and A. von Stechow, Berlin: Springer Verlag, 284–303.

Irwin, T. H., 1990, *Aristotle's First Principles*, Oxford: Oxford University Press (reprint, first published 1988).

Lennox, J., 1987, 'Divide and Explain: The *Posterior Analytics* in Practice', in *Philosophical Issues in Aristotle's Biology*, ed. A. Gotthelf and J. Lennox, 90–119.

Long, A. (ed.), 1971, *Problems in Stoicism*, London: Athlone Press.

Long, A., and Sedley, D. (eds.), 1987, *The Hellenistic Philosophers*, vols. 1 and 2, Cambridge: Cambridge University Press.

Modrak, D., 1987, *Aristotle: The Power of Perception*, Chicago: University of Chicago Press.

——2001, *Aristotle's Theory of Language and Meaning*, Cambridge: Cambridge University Press.

Ross, W. D., 1924, *Aristotle's Metaphysics*, 2 vols., Oxford: Oxford University Press.

Sandbach, F., 1971, '*Ennoia* and *Prolepsis*', in *Problems in Stoicism*, ed. A. Long, 22–37.

8

Definition and Explanation in the *Posterior Analytics* and *Metaphysics*

DAVID CHARLES

My aim in this paper is to outline (in sections 1 to 5) Aristotle's approach to definition and explanation in *Posterior Analytics* B and to consider (in sections 6–8) its more general philosophical significance. Aristotle's strategy has, I shall suggest, been misunderstood by friends and critics alike. Rightly interpreted, it constitutes a distinctive and challenging account of these issues.

1 Some Questions in the *Analytics*

Near the beginning of *Post. An.* B, Aristotle writes:

In all these cases, it is clear that what it is and why it is are the same. What is an eclipse? Privation of the light from the moon by the screening of the earth? Why is there an eclipse? Or why is the moon eclipsed? Because the light leaves it when the earth screens it. What is harmony? An arithmetical ratio of high and low. Why does the high harmonise with the low? Because there is an arithmetical ratio between them. (*Post. An.* B.2, 90a14ff.)

Later, in a key chapter on definition, he returns to this theme with another example:

'Why does it thunder?' Because the fire is extinguished in the clouds. But 'What is thunder?' Noise of fire being quenched in the clouds. Hence the same account is used in different ways: in one way as a continuous demonstration, in the other a definition. (*Post. An.* B.10, 94a4ff.)

In this passage, Aristotle considers two questions:

(1) What is thunder?, and
(2) Why does it thunder?

His answer to question (1) is:

noise [A] in the clouds [C] brought on by the fire being quenched [B].[1]

The complete specification of *definiens* and *definiendum* in (1) runs:

thunder is noise in the clouds brought on by the fire being extinguished,

which, properly expanded, is equivalent to the claim:

thunder is the type of noise in the clouds that is brought on by fire being quenched.[2]

Question (2) has to be further articulated to obtain the right *explananda*. Aristotle replaces 'thunder' with 'noise in the clouds' and then asks the question,

(2)★ Why does noise [A] occur in the clouds [C]?

to which the answer is:

because fire is quenched [B].

In this case, the complete specification of *explanandum* and *explanans* runs:

a certain type of noise in the clouds occurs because fire is quenched.

where 'a certain type of noise' refers to a determinate type of noise (yet to be fully specified).[3]

There are important points of similarity between the answers Aristotle offers to questions (1) and (2). Both involve

(a) a causal middle term [B] (e.g. fire being quenched), as Aristotle emphasizes in 90a24, and

---

[1] '[A]', '[B]', and '[C]' stand for terms used in the definition or demonstration.

[2] In this essay, I am concerned with kinds or with individuals qua members of those kinds. It is a further issue whether (i) individuals themselves are essentially members of these kinds and (ii) whether they are essentially the very particulars they are.

[3] Compare: sharks are a certain kind of fish. For further discussion of this issue, see 'The Paradox in the *Meno* and Aristotle's Attempts to Resolve it' (this volume, pp. 143–7).

(b) the same [A] and [C] terms. In (1), 'noise in the clouds' is used as part of the definition, in (2) as the *explanandum*.

From a demonstration which explains why noise of a certain type (viz. thunder) occurs,

[E.1]   Noise belongs to all fire-quenchings.
         Fire-quenching belongs to the clouds.
         _____

         Noise belongs to the clouds. (93b9–12)

one can read off the answer to question (1): thunder is the type of noise in the clouds that is caused by fire being quenched. On occasion, Aristotle explicitly identifies the cause (e.g. fire being quenched in the clouds), marked out by the middle term, with the essence (90a1, 90a15, 93b8). In this, he identifies the cause with what makes the phenomenon the one it is (its basic essence).[4]

While there are important differences between the answers to Questions (1) and (2), I shall focus on the first point of similarity already noted. Two questions immediately arise:

[Qu. 1]   Why does definition involve a grasp on the explanatory (or causal) middle term?
[Qu. 2]   Why does explanation begin with an element which is central to definition?

In answering these questions we will come to grasp Aristotle's account of the connections between the practices of definition and explanation (at least in the cases of the phenomena considered in the *Analytics*).

---

[4] Aristotle elsewhere uses the phrase 'what it is to be the thing' (*to ti ên einai*) to refer to the entity referred to as the basic cause by the middle term in the demonstrative syllogism: see, for example, *Metaphysics* Z.17, 1041a28–31. In *De Anima* 430b28, he notes that there is a way of talking about what a thing is (*ti estin*) which refers just to what it is to be the thing (*to ti ên einai*). This latter usage explains why sometimes in the *Analytics*, Aristotle identifies the cause with what a thing is (90a15: *to ti estin*), where the latter is to be identified with what it is to be the thing (see 93a18–20: *to ti ên einai*). This usage should be distinguished from another in which specifying what a thing is involves both the basic causal term and what is explained by it (see 94a5). In this essay, I shall use the phrase 'basic essence' to refer to the basic cause, marked out by the relevant middle term.

2 The Interdependence of Definition and Explanation (Demonstration) in the *Analytics*

The Order of Definitional Priority Rests on the Order of Causal Priority

Aristotle offers two syllogisms in *Post. An.* B.8 to illustrate the connection between the practice of definition and of demonstration. One, [E.1], has already been cited. The other runs as follows:

[E.2] Being eclipsed belongs to all being cases of being screened by the earth.
Being screened belongs to the moon (or to all moons of kind K).

Being eclipsed belongs to the moon (all moons of kind K).
(93a30–31)

While in both [E.1] and [E.2] an effect is demonstrated, the conclusions do not themselves contain definitions. Even when the term to be defined (e.g. 'eclipse') appears in the conclusion, the conclusion itself is not a definition of eclipse (or even of eclipse of the moon).

Why is this method a good one? We can begin to answer this question by comparing these demonstrations with the 'general deductions' (*logikoi syllogismoi*), which Aristotle had considered in *Post. An.* B.4 and B.6. In [E.1] and [E.2] the middle term (e.g. 'fire-quenching') specifies the efficient cause of

(1) an eclipse of the moon, and
(2) noise occurring in the clouds.

We can answer the 'Why?' question by giving the efficient cause of the phenomenon specified in the conclusion. In the case of thunder, the quenching of fire is causally more basic than the occurrence of noise in the clouds, because the former is the efficient cause of the latter.[5] This asymmetry is captured in [E.2], but not in a general deduction. For in the syllogism:

Noise in the clouds belongs to all fire quenchings.
Fire-quenching belongs to all thunder.

Noise in the clouds belongs to all thunder.

---

[5] In this essay, I use interchangeably as translations for '*aition*' cause, causal explanation, and explanation. The term refers to grounds as well as causes.

the middle term is not the cause of noise in the clouds belonging to thunder. Indeed, it is difficult to see what could possibly cause it to be the case that noise in the clouds belongs to thunder. Thunder, after all, just is a kind of noise in the clouds. Further, the general deduction gives us no ground for treating the second premise (or the terms in it) as prior to the conclusion (as Aristotle notes in B.6, 92a10ff.). By contrast, on the basis of [E.2], we can grasp which feature is definitionally prior: the one that is prior in the order of efficient causation. The quenching of fire is the start of a causal process which culminates in noise occurring in the clouds.

Why, for Aristotle, should our definitional practices depend on the causal explanations we uncover of the relevant phenomena? It is not merely that we *know* that certain features are definitionally prior because they are causally prior (B.8, 93a3–5). Rather, as he remarks in A.2, 71b31,

things are prior (i.e. by nature) since they are causes.

The order of definitional priority is metaphysically dependent on the order of causation. Fire being quenched is definitionally prior to noise in the clouds because it is causally prior. It is the efficient cause. *The what it is to be something* (as captured in the definition) and the basic relevant cause are one and the same (see B.2, 90a14–15 and note 4 above). The dependence of our practice of definition on that of explanation depends on the identity of basic essence and basic cause.[6]

Other features of Aristotle's approach reflect the same viewpoint. Consider his discussion of 'immediate propositions' (see B.8, 93a30–36). We reach, in giving explanations, an immediate proposition when there is no further cause which connects (e.g.)

(1) deprivation of light and the earth screening, or
(2) noise and fire being quenched.

If there were a further cause, our investigation would be incomplete until we discovered it (93b12–14). Immediate propositions are bedrock from a causal point of view. They describe direct, unmediated, causal connections.

---

[6] I use the terms 'practice of defining' and 'practice of explaining' to separate what we do in giving definitions or explanations from the subject-matter of such definitions and explanations: essences and *explananda/explanantia* (or causes/effects).

No further cause accounts for the connection they express.[7] In Aristotle's discussion of demonstration in B.8 two features are central:

(1) In discovering the answer to the 'Why?' question, we trace the pattern and order of efficient causation.

(2) In discovering the answer to the 'Why?' question, we find at the end of our enquiry an immediate proposition. At this point, there is no further causal relation to be discovered relevant to the effect in question.

By finding the basic efficient cause, we come to know the basic essence of the phenomenon in question. Here, as before, what is definitionally prior (viz. the basic essence) is metaphysically dependent on what is causally prior.

A similar approach, as already noted, is clear in Aristotle's identification of *the* essence with *the* cause in B.2 90a9–15. If one traces the relevant causal line back from the effect, one will find *one* feature (*the* cause) which explains why (in the case of thunder) noise occurs in the clouds. This feature will explain why thunder possesses its other necessary properties: why it is accompanied by lightning (for example), or why it is noisy. The presence of these latter properties is explained because the fire, when quenched, produces noise and flashes of light. There is *one* efficient cause which brings into existence the other necessary properties of thunder. This efficient cause would be discovered whichever of the relevant necessary properties had been the starting-point of enquiry. As the essence, it is the one common cause of all the kind's derived necessary properties. The presence of this prior feature underwrites the unity of the kind in question. In the case of thunder, it is one unified type of phenomenon because there is *one* common (efficient) cause which explains the presence of its necessary properties. (Had there been several unconnected causes of necessary distinct properties, thunder would not have been a unified kind. If there had been no essence to

---

[7] In these examples of immediate propositions, we find two distinct phenomena which are immediately related. The cause in these cases is other than the phenomenon caused (93b19, cf. 93a7), as *fire being extinguished* is other than *noise*. As such, immediate propositions of this type are different in kind from the cases discussed in B.9, where Aristotle is concerned (93b21–25) with primary objects which are identical with their causes or essences. It is crucial to separate immediate or primary *objects* (which are identical with their essences: 93b21–25) from immediate *propositions* which state unmediated (causal) connections between distinct phenomena. (There may be a class of immediate propositions which are concerned with the relation between primary objects and their essences. If so, they will be a sub-class of immediate propositions, whose other species will involve cases where the kinds or objects are distinct from their causes, but are non-mediately connected with them.)

hold together its necessary properties, it would have been an accidental unity.)

In his previous discussion Aristotle had asked: Why do all the following properties belong to man:

footed, two-footed animal (92a30)

and

featherless, footed, two-footed, mortal animal (92a1)?

He now has the resources to answer this question. All such properties belong to man because there is one common cause which explains man's possession of them: a cause which underwrites the unity of the kind. The relevant cause will, in this model, be captured by the middle term of a syllogism in which each proposition says one thing of one thing non-accidentally (93b36f.; cf. 72a9). By contrast, there is no one cause which explains why something is both musical and literate. The latter is an accidental unity since the feature which explains one property fails to explain the other. Although Aristotle introduces his account in discussing thunder and eclipse, the model he has described can (with the right type of casual material) extend to the case of substances.

Aristotle's account of scientific enquiry rests on a picture of reality. Enquiries are successful when there is one common cause prior in the way specified to the other features of the kind. In the cases of thunder and eclipse, the efficient cause is the definitionally prior feature. However, this account can, in principle, be extended to other causal modes. There the definitionally prior feature will be the basic common cause in whichever causal mode is appropriate for the kind in question (e.g. teleological or grounding: see *Post. An.* B.11, discussed below). The presence of this causally basic feature will ground the unity of the phenomenon in question.

In sum: in Aristotle's model, certain features are definitionally basic because they are causally prior, the common cause of all the other relevant features of the kind. The latter (or some of them) may be included in our definitions as the causal consequences (in the relevant causal mode) of this basic common cause.

Explanation and Definition: A More Complex Story

Is Aristotle's causal story independent of and prior to all definitional concerns? Are essences simply the starting-points of causal explanation? Can we come to know them just by tracing patterns of causal explanation (understood independently of all definitional concerns) back to their beginnings? There are reasons to doubt that this was Aristotle's considered view.

In B.11, Aristotle discusses cases in which there are several causal stories explaining the same phenomenon. He suggests, for example, that there could be both efficient and teleological explanations of the occurrence of thunder (94b31–34) as there are for a variety of other natural phenomena (94b35–37). However, only one of these causes is basic for the definition of the kind or feature in question, *the what it is to be the kind or feature itself.* What makes one (and only one) of them to be the right one for this definitional role? There has, it seems, to be some further factor at work (over and above simply being the starting-point of a causal explanation) which makes one (and only one) of these definitionally basic. What is the additional factor in Aristotle's account?

Definitions, if successful, give us knowledge of what the kind in question is (see B.3, 90b16; *Topics* Z.4, 141a27ff.). The feature marked out in a definition determines what the thing in question is.[8] It is the feature cited in answer to the 'What is F?' question which makes the kind the one it is. I shall describe the feature needed for this role (in the *Analytics*) as the one which fixes the identity of the kind.

In the case of thunder, the efficient and not the teleological cause plays this additional definitional role. Why is this? Aristotle remarks in *Metaphysics* Z.17 (1041a30ff.) that in the case of things that come to be, the efficient cause is the essence. Here, definitional concerns relating to the genus (or type) of phenomenon are at work marking out which cause is the relevant one. But why is the efficient, not the teleological, cause relevant for this type of phenomenon? Why is it the identity-fixer?

The efficient cause, fire's being quenched, has a distinctive explanatory role. It explains, as we have already noted, why thunder, the kind, has the other genuine features it has: being a noise, being accompanied by lightning, occurring under certain atmospheric conditions. There is a specific efficient causal explanation of why thunder has all these features, some of which have further consequences (e.g. frightening people). Contrast the possible teleological cause (to threaten those in Hades), which Aristotle

---

[8] Aristotle uses the phrase 'just what the thing is' (*hoper ti estin*) in describing the basic essence (*to ti ên einai*): see *Metaphysics* 1030a3. More fully, the basic essence is just the sort of thing the thing in question is. Indeed, it is what makes the particular in question a particular of the kind it is. (There are interesting issues at stake here which require further study.)

mentions (99b33–34). This does not by itself explain why thunder occurs in the clouds or in certain atmospheric conditions, even if it explained why thunder was noisy. It does not give a specific explanation of why thunder has all the genuine features it does. Indeed, those unfortunate enough to be in Hades might have been threatened by a different type of noise! Is the efficient cause's role as the one specific common cause sufficient to mark it out as the identity-fixer?

There are reasons to doubt that this proposal can accommodate all the cases Aristotle considers. In another of his examples, that of the house, there is an efficient cause (the art of house-building) and a teleological cause (safety for goods etc.), each of which appears specific enough to account for the relevant necessary features of a house. However, since (in Aristotle's view) only the teleological cause tells us 'what a house is', it cannot do so solely in virtue of its being the common cause of all the relevant features of the house.[9] For the efficient cause also plays that common causal role. The definitional, identity-fixing, role of a given feature cannot rest solely on its being a specific common cause of the kind's necessary features.

In Aristotle's account, if the efficient cause is the art of house-building, the builder's actions must be guided by an idea of what a house is for (the relevant teleological goal): providing security and protection for the occupier and his/her goods. The goal is definitionally prior both to the art of house-building and to the houses thus built. For the teleological goal makes the art of house-building the type of art it is.[10] There is, it seems, a definitional order in which the teleological cause is prior both to the art and to its product. But what general principles govern definitional order (in this case and others)?

One answer runs as follows: a causal starting-point will be definitionally prior (to other causal starting-points) if it meets the following conditions:

[I]   It is what it is independently of any other relevant causal feature (contrast the efficient cause in the case of the house).

---

[9] See, for example, *Metaphysics* H.2, 1043a15ff. Aristotle discusses the house in *Post. An.* B.10, 94b10f.

[10] If someone were to produce a building (e.g.) with the same structure as our houses and do so by the same techniques as we use in house-building, but without thinking it appropriate to use this building for human shelter, he would not have built a house. (Perhaps he regards it as too holy or too profane to be a dwelling place!) His product might have been a house-like structure (perhaps an art object), but would not have been a house. He would only have built a house if he saw his building as one to be used for some specific human purposes.

[II] The other elements in the causal story are defined in terms of it. What makes a collection of bricks a house and a given art the art of house-building is that both are directed (in different ways) towards the teleological goal.

In the definitional order:

(1) goal: securing the safety of oneself and one's belongings
(2) house
(3) the art of house-building

(1) is definitionally prior to (2) and (3) because what it is to be a house and what it is to be the art of house-building are both defined in terms of the teleological goal. The definitional order captures the order of metaphysical priority: the goal is what makes the house and the art the ones they are. It fixes their identity (as the object and craft they are).

Consider the attempt to reverse the definitional order and begin with the efficient cause. This could not be defined as the art of house-building as this is not (definitionally) independent of houses (and their goals). It would need to be defined in terms of (e.g.) certain movements of hands and implements while the resulting building would be defined (simply) as the product of these hand (and implement) movements. There would, it seems, be no definitional connection between the resulting building (so defined) and the goal of securing the safety of oneself or one's belongings. There are several inadequacies in this account. First, it does not adequately define what a house is, if this is something built for a certain purpose (such as safety). Second, in failing to capture the connection between houses and their goal, it loses one of the definitional connections visible if one begins with the teleological goal. Third, the bodily movements (as described above) do not adequately capture the skill of the house-builder. For what he was doing was attempting to build a house and this goal determined which movements he made on this occasion. Indeed, in other circumstances, he might have moved differently to achieve the same goal.

To generalize: what makes some feature the basic essence is that it is prior *both* in some causal order (whether efficient or teleological) *and* in the order of definition. While definitional priority requires the item in question to be prior in some causal order, being definitionally prior does not rest solely on causal priority. To be prior in definition the basic cause must meet conditions [I] and [II] above. When something meets these further conditions, it is the (basic) essence of the phenomenon in question: that which makes the thing the thing it is. In the case of thunder, the efficient cause is prior in definition to other possible causal starting-points. What makes the souls in Hades frightened in the way they are is thunder, a phenomenon whose identity has to be fixed on other causal grounds. Fear requires one to be frightened of something. In the present example, thunder is definitionally prior to its psychological effects in Hades, but definitionally dependent on its efficient cause. It is the latter which makes this type of noise (and the type of fear) the one it is.

3 Four Aspects of This Account

The (basic) essence, in Aristotle's account, simultaneously defines what it is to be house and explains why the house is as it is: why it possesses those properties it must have to be a house. The requirement that there is one feature which plays both these roles is of central importance for his account of definition and of explanation in the *Analytics*. While in the next section I shall give examples of the work it does there, in the present section I shall note some of its distinctive aspects.

Definition

If there is one feature that both fixes the identity of a kind and explains its necessary properties, grasping it will serve to make the structure of the kind thoroughly known to us (see B.3, 90b16; *Topics* Z.4, 141a27ff.). We can now understand why that kind could not lack its necessary properties. Their presence is causally explained (whether efficiently or teleologically) by the presence of a feature which fixes the identity of the kind: one which makes the kind the one it is.

In Aristotle's example of thunder, being noise in the clouds is a necessary property of thunder because it is an efficient causal consequence of fire being quenched (in the clouds), the cause which makes thunder the phenomenon it is. Further, its being caused in this way is what makes it the type of noise in the clouds it is. The cause simultaneously defines the phenomenon in question and explains why it possesses its distinctive necessary properties.[11]

Two conditions are central in Aristotle's account of definition:

(1) *Unity condition*: there has to be one feature (cited in the definition). If there are two unconnected features, there would need to be an explanation of why these two features necessarily go together. Without that, we would not have grasped what fixes the identity of the kind in question. The identity-fixer underwrites the unity of the kind. To play this role, the feature cited in the definition must itself be a genuine unity. Aristotle meets this condition by requiring that the feature in question be one cause (for example, in the case of thunder, one efficient cause.)

(2) *Priority condition*: the feature cited in the definition must be prior to the kind and its necessary properties. Aristotle meets this condition by requiring that the feature in question be prior in some causal order (such as efficient causation in the case of thunder).

These two conditions, Unity and Priority, show the extent to which Aristotle's account of definition in the *Analytics* B.8–10 rests upon a metaphysical basis. The (basic) essences required as objects of definition have to be causally prior unities if the resulting definitions are to be adequate.

Explanation

Aristotle's suggestion that there is one feature which fixes the identity of the kind and explains its necessary properties is central for his account of demonstration. Consider his claim that there cannot be demonstrative explanatory chains of infinite length (A.19, 82a8).[12] He argues for this as follows: if there were such chains, one could not arrive at knowledge of what the kinds are or of their definitions (A.22, 82b37–83a1). This argument, at first sight, appears weak. What prevents there being explanations of infinite length which do not begin with definitions? Why does definition play a central role in the practice of demonstration?

The argument of the previous section provides an answer. Demonstrations, as Aristotle conceives them, must begin with statements concerning

---

[11]   Or at least as many of these as are relevant to the definition. Other definitional constraints may be at work selecting some but only some necessary features as definitional. This issue is left open here.

[12]   I am indebted at this point to discussion with Henry Mendell.

the essences of the kinds in question. This is a constraint on what demonstrating is: to demonstrate is to give an argument which begins with a statement about a causally basic (non-demonstrable) feature which can be invoked to answer the 'What is F?' question. If demonstrations are to make the kind (or subject-matter) fully intelligible to us, they must begin with definitions which reveal the relevant essences.

Aristotle's strategy is not first to argue that every science must contain a set of basic (underivable) propositions and then to claim that these propositions must be definitions. That is, he does not impose non-definitional constraints on what is to count as the starting-point of a good explanation and then attempt to show that this role can only be played by definitions.[13] Rather, his basic claim is that demonstrations must begin with definitions: statements concerning essences. Demonstrations (in the basic case) are defined as essence-involving. The practice of demonstration is constrained (in his account) by considerations which flow from the practice of definition. Infinitely regressive (or circular) explanations are not demonstrations because they are not grounded in the essences of the kinds in question.

Definitional constraints, in this account, play a major role in Aristotle's account of demonstrative explanation. The starting-point in a demonstration is not merely the fundamental cause but also a feature which determines the identity of the phenomenon to be explained. On the basis of such demonstrations, the enquirer will fully understand the phenomenon in question. He (or she) grasps not only a feature which explains the presence of the necessary properties of (e.g.) thunder but also one which makes thunder the type of thing it is. Once he grasps this he can understand why (e.g.) thunder has to be a given way. Explanations of this type reveal in a

---

[13] For a contrasting view, see Robin Smith's paper 'Immediate Propositions and Aristotle's Proof Theory', *Ancient Philosophy* 6 (1986), pp. 47–55. Smith argues convincingly that Aristotle's arguments in *Post. An.* A.19–22 cannot depend on the claim that every regress of propositions must end in a basic set of premises which are self-evident or epistemically immediate. For Aristotle claims only that the starting-points are definitions which reveal essences, and makes no reference to the epistemic notion of self-evidence in this passage. However, Smith infers from this that the relevant starting-points must merely be ones not deducible from any other true proposition, and then notes that there is no obvious step from this claim to any which concern (non-demonstrative) knowledge of definitions. On my view, the starting-points are *non-demonstrable* because they are not the causal consequences of any further claim. Further, if they are to be *starting-points of demonstration*, they must (a) be non-demonstrable and (b) state the relevant basic essence. If the relevant essences are the objects of non-demonstrative knowledge (as emerges in *Post. An.* B.8–10), the starting-points of demonstration will themselves be capable of being known non-demonstratively.

perspicuous way the structure of thunder: why it must be the way it is if it is to be the thing it is. One might call this form of explanation 'structural causal explanation'. In it the efficient (or, in other cases, the final or grounding) cause is also the formal cause. Such explanations take as their starting-point basic essences which simultaneously fix the identity of a kind and explain its necessary properties. Such essences constitute the underlying nature of the kind.

Aristotelian enquirers, in seeking an explanation of this type, are governed by their search for essences. Thus, when they ask such questions as:

> Why do broad-leaved trees . . . not any object whatever but broad-leaved trees . . . behave in a given way? (98b36–38)

or

> What is it about *broad-leaved trees* which explains why they behave in this way . . . ?

or

> What is it in the nature of broad-leaved trees which explains why they react in this way in certain conditions?

they are looking for answers which point to distinctive features of broad-leaved trees, which they could not lack while being the kind they are, ones which constitute the essence (or nature) of such trees.[14] In a more specific case, grasp on the nature of the elm will enable them to understand why the kind could not lack certain features while remaining the kind it is. In grasping the essence of the elm, we come to understand why the elm could not lack its distinctive necessary features, while remaining the kind of tree it is. For the feature they grasp is (i) explanatorily basic and (ii) what

---

[14] Aristotle probably went further and took the nature of the elm to be what makes this object the one it is. At least, Aristotle seems committed to the idea that the object in question is essentially a 'this such', one which needs its suchness to be and to persist as the object it is. Its suchness is what makes the object in question the persisting unity it has to be to that very object. (This is not equivalent to the claim that its essence is what marks the object out as different from other objects.) Indeed, it is quite compatible with the account so far developed that there are quite different answers to the questions:

[1] 'What makes this the type of thing it is?'

[possible answer: its possession of a given type of nature] and

[2] 'What makes this the particular it is?'

[possible answers: its following the route it does/its having the matter it does/its having a particular Form/no answer (its particularity is not to be explained)].

fixes the identity of the kind. It simultaneously determines the filling of the two asterisked positions in the sentence:

'This is an instance of a tree of kind ★ which must act in way S★.'

In grasping which feature plays this role, Aristotelian enquirers gain a thoroughly perspicuous explanation of the kind and its distinctive activities (and features).

The Interconnection between Definition and Causal Explanation in Aristotle's Account

In the *Analytics*, two apparently distinct questions, 'What is G?' and 'Why is G as it is?', have the same answer: the basic essence (or underlying nature) of G. Why is this so?

Aristotle's emphasis on the interdependency of the practices of definition and of explanation is not to be expressed simply by the following (brute) bi-conditional:

E fixes the identity of kind G if and only if E explains in a given way why G is as it is.

For the connections between identity-fixing and explanatory roles are closer, resting (as we have seen) on two further claims:

[1]   To be an identity-fixer essentially involves being the starting-point in a given form of causal explanation. One cannot define what it is to be an identity-fixer independently of causal explanation precisely because part of what it is to be an identity-fixer is to be (in the way just explained) a cause of a given type (a causally prior unity).

[2]   To be a starting-point in the relevant form of (demonstrative) explanation essentially involves being an identity-fixer. One cannot specify what it is to be the starting-point in an appropriate demonstration independently of the relevant item's role as an identity-fixer. Part of what it is to be such a starting point is to be an identity-fixer.

In sum: when we seek, in Aristotle's account, to answer the 'What is G?' question we aim to find that which makes G what it is: G's basic essence. To be a basic essence (or underlying nature) is to be the one feature which *both* fixes the identity of thunder *and* explains thunder's necessary properties.

Aristotle's account of explanation and definition are both governed by the search for essences of this type. In his account, our practices of definition and of causal explanation are the right ones only because they aim at capturing rich essences of this type. It is not that such essences are required to meet conditions on good definition or good explanation arrived at on independent grounds. Rather, his ideas of good definition and good explanation themselves rest on the explanatorily rich and more basic idea of essence just outlined. He is, in effect, offering an essence-first account of both definition and the relevant type of explanation.

The significance of Aristotle's approach will be apparent if one compares it with the alternatives Plato considers in the *Phaedo*. Socrates, in turning away from the search for material (or material/efficient) and teleological causation (which had preoccupied him as a young man), connects the objects of definition (the forms) with a type of causation distinct from material, efficient, or teleological causation. In the *Phaedo*, the explanatory role of formal causes does not depend on their being material, efficient, or teleological causes. What makes something a formal cause is not its playing any causal role of the latter type.[15] The only alternatives Plato offers are (1) a 'scientific' account in terms of material or teleological causation unconstrained by definitional considerations and (2) a definitional account based on resources independent of material, efficient, and teleological causation. While Aristotle criticizes the latter approach in his discussion of the 'general deduction' (*logikos syllogismos*) in *Post. An.* B.4–6 (discussed above), he does not opt for the purely 'scientific' alternative (suggested by (1)). Rather, he develops an explanatory account dependent (in the ways we have examined) on definitional considerations and (*pari passu*) a definitional account dependent (as we have seen) on concerns drawn from the theory of teleological, material, or efficient explanation. It is just such a position, with its scientifically rich basic essences, that was passed over (apparently unseen) by Socrates when he moved immediately from a purely 'scientific' account (unconstrained by definitional concerns) to his own preferred 'second journey' grounded in forms and definitions alone.[16]

---

[15] Even if formal causes, in the *Phaedo*, are efficient causes, they are not formal causes in virtue of being efficient causes. (My remarks on the *Phaedo* are merely a 'thumbnail' sketch of complicated issues. For further details, see the essay by Vasilis Politis in this volume.)

[16] In the *Euthyphro*, Socrates assumes that there is just one relevant type of explanation at work connecting the pious and what is god-loved. He does not consider the possibility, so vivid to Aristotle,

Epistemological Issues

In the case of kinds we can (if all goes well) come to know that E is the relevant (basic) essence by seeing it as the starting-point in the distinctive type of causal explanation we have discussed above. We have initial grounds for taking E as the basic essence when we come to know that it is the starting-point in a causal explanation (e.g. an efficient explanation) of the kind's properties. These grounds will be confirmed when we come to see that this explanation is a demonstration, one whose starting-point fixes the identity of the kind in question. While essences are prior in nature, they are not prior in our order of discovery. We come to see that something is an essence on the basis of our understanding of the role it plays in causal demonstration. Aristotle spells this out clearly in *De Anima* A.1, 402b23ff. when he notes that 'when we are able to give an account of all, or at any rate most of the attributes, we shall be in a position best to define the substance in question. For the starting-point of each demonstration is what a thing is.'

This style of account can be generalized to other Aristotelian starting-points: we can come to see that, for example, the point or the monad are starting-points in a science if they simultaneously demarcate the subject-matter of that science and can be invoked to explain why the other elements in that domain have the necessary features they do. (It is because the point is thus and so that the line is thus and so.) These simples simultaneously fix the identity of their relevant domains (the ones whose starting-points they are) and explain why other elements in that domain have the necessary features they do.[17]

It is important, at this point, to guard against a common misunderstanding of Aristotle's account. Some have thought that if basic essences provide the starting-point for demonstrative explanations, the latter must have as their conclusions ones whose truth is entailed *a priori* by the definitions of the kind in question.[18] So understood, Aristotle's explanations are (as a consequence) restricted to deriving 'analytical truths': ones that follow *a priori* from the defining features of the kind. Indeed some have thought that,

---

that there might be several types of causal story (e.g. teleological or efficient) relevant to this case. It may be that here, as in the *Phaedo*, he thought that only a distinctive type of 'formal' explanation was relevant to his concerns.

[17] I discuss this issue in more detail in *Aristotle on Meaning and Essence*, Oxford, 2000, p. 307.

[18] Michael Ferejohn, *The Origins of Aristotelian Science*, Yale, 1991, pp. 177ff.

if the first principles are to play this role, they must contain within themselves all the material that can be derived from them.[19] Still others have thought that because of these difficulties Aristotle's model can only work for a limited set of cases and is inapplicable to the central case of substances.[20]

This pattern of (mis)understanding rests on the assumption that the relation between statements describing essences (cited in a definition) and the relevant conclusions in an Aristotelian explanation is that of *a priori* (or logical) entailment. However, if the interpretation presented above is correct, the relevant connections will be those of (e.g.) efficient causal explanation, tracing causal necessitation in reality. There is no reason to believe that these must be grasped *a priori* or that the premises must 'contain' all the information that is derived in the conclusion. If one sees demonstrations as involving causal explanation of this type, they will not be confined to deriving analytical consequences from their premises.

4 Examples of This Model at Work in the *Analytics*

Aristotle focuses on the connections between definition and demonstration in the chapters that follow *Post. An.* B.8–10. I shall consider three cases, drawn from his discussion of grounding, teleological, and efficient causation, which further illustrate his view. In these cases, the formal cause is identified with the grounding, teleological, and efficient cause respectively. In considering these examples, we can see the ambitions and difficulties in Aristotle's account.

Post. An. *B.11, 94a25ff.: The Grounding Cause and Definition*

Aristotle begins B.11 by discussing a geometrical example.

Why is the angle in the semicircle a right angle? What is the ground for its being a right angle? Let us attach the letter A to a right angle, B to half of two right angles, and Γ to an angle in a semicircle. The cause of Γ's (the angle in the semicircle) being A (a right angle) is B. For B is A and Γ is B because B is

[19] Richard McKirahan, *Principles and Proofs: Aristotle's Demonstrative Theory*, Princeton, 1992, pp. 111, 169.
[20] Owen Goldin, *Explaining an Eclipse*, Michigan, 1996, pp. 10–13.

half two right angles. The fact that B is half two right angles is the ground for
Γ''s being A, i.e. the angle in the semicircle being a right angle. B is the same
as the essence since it is what is signified in the account (proof). Indeed, the
essence has been shown to be a cause as it plays the role of the middle term.[21]

Why is the angle in a semicircle a right angle? According to Euclid III.20,
'In a circle the angle at the centre is double the angle at the circumference
when the angles have the same segment of the circumference as base.' Since
in the case at issue the angle in the centre of a circle is two right angles, the
angle at the circumference must be one right angle. The relevant proof
would run as follows:

(1)   The angle at the centre is double the angle at the circumference
      (Euclid III.20).
(2)   The angles at the centre (when combined) are (in the case described)
      two right angles.
So: The angle at the circumference is half of two right angles.
So: The angle at the circumference is one right angle.

In this proof, the fact that the angle at the centre is two right angles is the
specific ground (given Euclid's claim in III.20) for the angle at the circumference being one right angle.[22] But why should the former fact's figuring in
this proof make it an essential feature of this angle? For Aristotle, this proof
invokes the grounding cause. He claims that it is because the angles at the
centre add up to two right angles that the angle at the circumference is one
right angle. In this he assumes that there is a relevant asymmetry: the size of
the angle at the circumference is determined by the sum of the angles at the
centre (as the former is half of the latter). Given this pattern of grounding
causation, the starting-point of the demonstration is taken to be the essence
of the angle at the circumference: that feature which determines its size.
Demonstrations, as we have already noted, begin with essences. What
makes this feature (being half the sum of the angles at the centre) the

---

[21] So understood, this passage refers back to *Post. An.* B.10, 94a1–6 where the (basic) essence has been
shown to be the relevant causal middle term.

[22] An alternative proof is sketched in an interpolation to Euclid I.32. Since similar issues will arise
about it, I shall consider only the simpler proof set out in the main text. For discussion of Aristotle's use of
this example elsewhere, see H. Mendell 'Two Geometrical Examples from Aristotle's Metaphysics',
Classical Quarterly 34 (1984), pp. 359–72 and S. Makin, *Aristotle, Metaphysics Theta*, Oxford, 2006,
pp. 234–7.

relevant essence is that it is the basic grounding cause which determines the size of the angle.[23] Aristotle concludes:

> The essence has been established as a cause as it plays the role of the middle term (sc. in the relevant proof).

The order of the proof, in Aristotle's view, establishes the essence as the cause because it tracks the direction of grounding causation back to the determining cause. Indeed, the proof in question rests on the direction of grounding causation, whose starting-point is the basic essence of the phenomenon to be explained. In this example, the essence is identified with the starting-point in a demonstration of the type relevant for mathematics.

While Aristotle is attempting to extend the account he has worked out in B.8–10 to mathematical cases, his approach is not without difficulty. First, as already noted, there is an alternative proof that the angle at the circumference is half two right angles which proceeds from features distinctive of isosceles triangles. However, Aristotle does not suggest how to determine which proof tracks the grounding cause in cases where several proofs are available. Second, one could envisage a geometer proving, using Euclid III.20, that the angle in the centre is two right angles on the basis that (i) it is double the angle at the circumference and (ii) the angle at the circumference is one right angle. It would be a major task to show why one proof reveals the essence while the others do not. Aristotle does not himself attempt to do this, even though he is clearly attracted to the view that there is a natural order in geometry (*Physics* B.9, 200a17ff.). Perhaps he was mistaken on this point. However, if he was, this does not undermine his essentialist claims in other areas. Since he reserved his major efforts for the cases of processes and substances, it is in these areas that his version of essentialism should be assessed.

Post. An. B.11, 94b8ff.: The Teleological Cause and Definition

Aristotle's discussion in this passage is complex and baffling.[24] He writes:

---

[23] I take the grounding cause (in this case) as a determining sufficient condition and not (merely) as a necessary condition. In the *Analytics*, Aristotle appears to allow grounding causes to be sufficient conditions (see *Post. An.* 94b28–29). For a similar discussion of material causes, see also *Part. Anim.* 640a10ff., 642a14ff. Since in the *Analytics*, Aristotle does not invoke matter, it seems mistaken to understand the present discussion in terms of intelligible matter.

[24] Barnes, for example, describes the section on final explanation as 'miserably obscure' and one of its suggestions as 'Delphic' in *Aristotle, Posterior Analytics*, 2nd edn., Oxford, 1993, p. 228.

Suppose that making the foodstuffs not remain on the surface at the mouth of the stomach [B] holds of walking after dinner [C] and that this is healthy [A]. What is the cause of A, the goal or outcome, holding of C? It is B, the food's not remaining on the surface. And this is, as it were, an account of the latter [A]; for A will be elucidated in this way. (94b16–20)

The argument runs as follows: why is after-dinner walking [C] healthy [A]? The answer is: because walking [C] results in foodstuff not remaining on the surface at the mouth of the stomach [B]. Indeed, one can give 'a type of account' of being healthy in terms of foodstuff not remaining there. However, although this causal story invokes a middle term [B] which explains the healthiness of after-dinner walking, it appears to be an efficient (not a teleological) cause. Indeed, Aristotle says that the efficient cause can be used to give an account (of some type) of the kind of health resulting from such walks: the type brought about foodstuff being digested in this way. But why does he describe this as 'as it were' an account? And why does he invoke efficient and not teleological causation at this point?

Aristotle continues as follows in 94b20–22, using the same terms as before:

For what purpose does [B] belong to [C]? [What is the beneficial result of [B]'s attending [C]?] Because being in this state [B] is what being healthy is. (You should take the definitions instead and everything will be clearer.)

At this point, it appears, he has switched to taking the teleological cause [A]: health, as the middle term. This is the good to be achieved by food being digested [B] when one walks after dinner [C]. Aristotle further notes that if you look at the definitions, you will see that good health requires food not to remain at the mouth of the stomach and walking after supper. His idea is, I suggest, this: food not remaining at the mouth of the stomach is required for health and is defined as part of healthy digestion.[25] If so, the middle term ('health') picks out the basic teleological cause of the food's not staying at

[25] I take the phrase 'being in such a state is what being healthy is' (94b21) to define what the relevant state is. For a contrasting view, see Robert Bolton's 'The Material Cause: Matter and Explanation in Aristotle's Natural Science', in *Aristotelische Biologie*, ed. W. Kullmann and S. Follinger, Stuttgart, 1997, pp. 114–16. Bolton takes this phrase to define health in terms of its material (or efficient) cause and concludes that (for Aristotle) 'the occurrence of the final cause is scientifically and deductively explained by the material cause'. However, his conclusion appears to invert the priority normally given by Aristotle to teleological over material/efficient causation.

the mouth of the stomach, the cause which fixes the identity of what is going on: good digestion (the condition of the stomach when it digests well). Further, what is distinctive of walks after supper is that they are aimed at healthy digestion. Indeed, being so aimed is what makes them the type of walk they are. If so, there is definitional order [health: good digestion: post-prandial walking] which reflects the order of teleological causation.

Aristotle comments on his change of perspective:

Here the events occur in the opposite order from that required in explanations in terms of processes. (94b23ff.)

In teleological explanation health (the middle just mentioned) comes first (as the starting-point of the explanation) while in the efficient causal story (previously mentioned) it is mentioned last.[26] In the teleological case, health plays a basic role in the relevant type of explanation. At the first step it is what makes foodstuff's not remaining at the mouth of the stomach the phenomenon it is: a case of good (or healthy) digestion. At the second stage, the goal of health (or healthy digestion) explains why one walks after supper and makes such walks the ones they are. In both, the final cause plays a central role in the form of explanation on which the definitions of good digestion and post-prandial walking depend.

While, in this case, there are two types of causal order (efficient and teleological causation), Aristotle can take the teleological cause (health) definitionally as the (basic) essence because (i) it is what makes the state (the foodstuff not remaining at the mouth of the stomach) be the one it is: a state of good digestion and (ii) explains why that state is present (for the sake of health). By contrast, the efficient causal story gives only 'a type of account' of health: it may explain what produces health but does not tell us what health is. In this example, as in that of the house, the teleological cause is central for definitions because it fixes the identity of the other phenomena mentioned: foodstuff being absorbed into the stomach (part of the process of healthy digestion), walking after dinner (a goal-directed

---

[26] For a similar pattern of thought, see, for example, *Physics* 200a34ff. The contrast which Aristotle explicitly draws between different directions of causation suggests that he was aware that his first example (94b15–19) was not one of teleological causation. Indeed, it may have been introduced precisely to bring out the distinctive way in which teleological causation functions. The contrast, thus drawn, between these two modes of causation generates the issue on which Aristotle focuses in 94b27ff. Here, in outline, I follow the line of interpretation introduced by Pacius, *In Aristotelis Organon Commentarius Analyticus*, Frankfurt, 1597.

process). Aristotle, as elsewhere, introduces a definitional order to determine which of the two causal stories considered begins with the basic essence.[27]

Post. An. B.16, 98b19–21: The Efficient Cause and Definition

While in *Post. An.* B.11, Aristotle's example of efficient causation does not involve definition (94a36–b8), in *Post. An.* B.16, 98b19–21 he contrasts the syllogism which demonstrates the cause with one which merely demonstrates the fact. One example of the former is (A.13, 78a37f.):

> Things that are near do not twinkle.
> *The planets are near.*
> _____
> The planets do not twinkle.

By contrast, a syllogism which demonstrates the fact would be:

> Things that do not twinkle are near.
> *The planets do not twinkle.*
> _____
> The planets are near.

Planets fail to twinkle (according to Aristotle) because they are near. They are not near because they fail to twinkle. The causal order is fixed in the world.[28] In B.16, Aristotle makes a further remark about a similar case:

> It is clear that being screened by the earth (B) is the cause of the eclipse (A) and not vice versa: for B is specified in the account/ definition of A, so that it is obvious that the latter is known via the former and not vice versa. (98b21–24)

Here, the causal order seems clear because B (being screened by the earth) is specified in the account of A (eclipse). But isn't this to get things the wrong way round? Isn't B in the account of A because it is A's cause? Is Aristotle, contrary to my central hypothesis, now taking the order of definition to be independent of (and prior to) the order of causation.

It is important to note, at the outset, that Aristotle says (in this passage) only that the causal order is *clear* from the relevant definitions. He does not

---

[27] I have gained considerably in my understanding of this passage from the excellent discussion by Mariska Leunissen, *Explanation and Teleology in Aristotle's Philosophy of Nature*, Leiden, 2007, pp. 370–4. We differ in that Leunissen holds that, for Aristotle, ends cannot serve as middle terms in the relevant demonstrations but must always be part of the conclusion demonstrated.

[28] For further discussion of this case, see B. Brody 'Towards an Aristotelian Theory of Scientific Explanation', *Philosophy of Science* 39 (1972), pp. 20–31.

claim that the order of definition itself is independent of the order of causation. Indeed, given what he has said elsewhere, B (the screening) will appear in the definitional account of A (the eclipse) precisely because it is the relevant cause of A (the one which makes A the thing it is. But why is the causal order clear from the definition? One answer runs as follows: if we know the definitional account of an eclipse, we will grasp that screening (B) is the relevant cause because the latter fixes the identity of the type of light failure involved. Indeed, if an eclipse is defined as the distinctive type of failure of light that is caused by screening (B), we can read off the cause of the light failure from the definition. In such cases, where the efficient cause fixes the identity of the type of phenomenon that occurs, we will in grasping the latter's definition grasp its efficient cause. (By contrast, since the identity of the type of screening is not determined by the presence of the eclipse, its definition will not refer to the eclipse. Indeed, if we grasp its definition we will see that it is not caused by the eclipse but by something else.)

5 Definition in the *Metaphysics*

In the *Analytics*, Aristotle develops his interconnected account of definition and explanation by considering examples of natural processes such as eclipse and thunder. He does not attempt to show (in any detail) how his account applies to substances or to goal-directed processes. While he refers to substances (in B.9 and 13), he does not explicitly apply his basic account, as devised in B.8–10, to them. Nor does he introduce the notions of matter and form required for this project. However, in important chapters of the *Metaphysics*, he attempts to extend his *Analytics* explanation-involving account of definition to the case of substances, building on his *Analytics* style discussion of thunder and eclipse.[29] I shall consider a few examples of his approach.

---

[29] For discussion of his attempt to apply this strategy to goal-directed processes, see my 'Teleological Causation in the *Physics*', in *Aristotle's Physics: A Collection of Essays*, ed. Lindsay Judson, Oxford, 1991, pp. 117ff. Such processes are defined in terms of a goal which will be achieved if nothing intervenes. Typically, they are composed of stages which are also for the sake of the goal. (Compare the earlier discussion of walking after supper: these are made the type of walk they are by their teleological cause.)

Metaphysics *Z.17 and H.1–4: The First Move*

In *Metaphysics* Z.17 Aristotle makes the following suggestion:

consider the question 'Why does thunder occur?' [This is best put as] 'Why does noise occur in the clouds?' In this way the object of enquiry is why something belongs to something else. And, similarly, 'Why are these things, bricks and stones, a house?' It is clear that what is being sought is the cause. This is the essence to speak in general terms. In some cases it is the final cause, as probably in the case of the house or the bed, in others the efficient cause. For this is also the relevant cause (in some cases). (1041a24–30)

In this passage, he explicitly identifies the (basic) essence with the efficient cause in some cases, the final cause in others. In the case of thunder, discussed in the *Analytics*, the basic essence is the efficient cause (fire being quenched). Aristotle is attempting to extend this account from cases (such as thunder) of coming to be (1041a31–33) to those involving final causes, beginning with artefacts (such as the house) and ending with substances (such as man: 1041b7ff.: see 1041a20ff.). His goal, it seems, is to define substance within the general framework developed in his discussion of non-substances in the *Analytics*, employing his key physical notions of final causation, matter and form to do so.

In the *Analytics*, as we have seen, Aristotle uses the following demonstration to capture the basic essence of thunder:

[E.1]   Noise belongs to all fire-quenchings.
   Fire-quenching belongs to the clouds (all clouds of kind K).

   ———————————————————————————————

   Noise belongs to the clouds (all clouds of kind K). (93b9–12)

If he is to develop a comparable approach in the case of substances, he has to clarify (i) what needs to be explained and (ii) what is to play the role of the essential and explanatory middle term. As he himself comments, unless we set out (or 'articulate') the question in an appropriate way, we will not be able to find the basic essence (1141a33–b4).

Let us follow his discussion of the house. Aristotle formulates what needs to be explained as follows:

'Why are these things, bricks and stones, a house?' (1041a26–27: see 1041b5–6)

Since the bricks and stones are described as the matter, his question can be raised in the following form:

'Why is this matter a house?'

or, more generally still,

'Why is this matter some determinate thing?'[30]

employing his favoured notion of matter as one of the *explananda* (1041b7–8).
His answer is formulated in terms of 'what it is to be a house' (1041b6), which
he identifies with 'the form' (1041b8) which earlier he has identified (in this
case) with the final cause (1041a29). At this point, he has basis for a demonstration which parallels the one he gave for thunder:

[E.3]   House belongs to what it is to be a house.
        What it is to be a house belongs to matter of this type.
        ―――――――――――――――――――――――――――――――――――――――
        House belongs to matter of this type.

He is, it appears, looking for connections between explanation and definition paralleling those set out in the case of thunder, with teleological causes
replacing efficient ones. Does he carry this project through?

[E.3] is not his finished product. Aristotle needs to specify in more detail
(i) what it is to be a house (what will replace the middle term) and (ii) what
'house' signifies in the first premise and conclusion. Although he has said
that the answer to (i) is to be identified with the final cause, more has to be
done to spell this out. Similarly, while some demonstrations in the *Analytics*
speak of thunder in the conclusion (see 93b9), Aristotle preferred to speak of
noise at this point (93b11f., 94a5ff.). If he wishes to follow a similar model in
the present case, he must replace 'house' in the conclusion with an alternative expression. Both question and answer need to be articulated further.
Z.17 is not the end of the story.

Aristotle takes his project further in *Metaphysics* H.2, when he notes
that matter can be distinguished in terms such as 'being arranged thus'
(1042b19–20) in the case of thresholds and lintels and applies this suggestion
to the case of houses (1043a7f.). As thunder is noise in the clouds, so thresholds (and houses) are stones arranged in a given way. In the former case, the
(efficient) cause accounts for noise being in the clouds, in the latter the (final)

―――

[30] In 1041b5 some take the question to be 'Why is the matter as it is?' However, by 1041b8 it has been
rephrased as 'Why is the matter some definite thing?' I prefer to understand the question in 1041b4–5 as
'Why does this matter belong (*huparchein*) (sc. to a house)?' and that in 1041b6 as 'Why are these things
(bricks and stones) a house?'

cause accounts for stones being arranged in a given way (1043a8–9). The latter is the cause sought in Z.17 to explain why bricks and stones are a house. In H.2 Aristotle further articulates his Z.17 question by introducing various *differentiae* of matter and asking for an explanation of why specific matter (such as bricks and stones) is differentiated in the way it is. Further, in the case of the house, he points towards the type of teleological explanation (providing protection) required. The relevant type of basic essence is the form, the final cause of the matter being arranged in a given way. The example of the house, so understood, parallels that of thunder. As the latter is noise in the clouds caused by fire being quenched, a house will be bricks and stones (matter) arranged in a given way for the sake of protection (1043a9: for mention of the goal 1043a16f.). Although replacing efficient with teleological causation, Aristotle is keeping as close as possible to his *Analytics* model.

Although Aristotle does not consider the case of man in similar detail beyond Z.17, he does suggest that body will take the place of bricks and stones (1043a32–35), building on his earlier remark that the body is the relevant matter (1041b7). The nearest he comes to describing the relevant arrangement of the body is when the relevant animal is said to be 'two-footed' (1043b10–11), a phrase which may fill out what is intended by the elliptical 'with this feature' in 1041b7. He does, however, identify the soul as what it is to be a man (1043b3–4) and (it seems) takes this to be the cause of the animal in question being two-footed (1043b13f.). If one follows these suggestions, one arrives at the following syllogism, which parallels the one he developed for thunder:

[E.4]   Being two-footed belongs to what it is to be a man.
        What it is to be a man belongs to a body of this type.
        _____
        Being two-footed belongs to a body of this type.[31]

---

[31]   In this demonstration, the premises contain the following connections:

  (i) being two-footed belongs to what it is to be a man: the relevant teleological cause requires two-footedness;

  (ii) what it is to be a man belongs to a body of this type: the relevant teleological cause requires a body of this type.

In (i) being two-footed (in the relevant way) is defined in terms of what it is to be a man. (This is the type of two-footedness involved). In (ii) what it is to be a man defines the type of body involved. In the conclusion, two-footedness belongs to the body involved because they share a common (defining) cause. There are per se connections at each stage in this demonstration. For an alternative view of the relevant demonstrations, see Michael Wedin's *Aristotle's Theory of Substance*, Oxford, 2000, pp. 423.

In a more articulated version of [E.4] 'soul of a given type' replaces 'what it is to be a man' as the proper description of the final cause. In this account, it will be because of the requirements of a given type of soul (one which needs to walk etc.) that the body in question is two-footed. However, Aristotle is not concerned with the details of this case, perhaps confident that he has done enough with his other examples to indicate how they will go.[32]

In sum: in Z.17 and the early chapters of H Aristotle is, it seems, seeking to use matter, form, and final causation to extend the model of causal definition originally devised in the *Analytics* to the case of substance. This model, if successfully applied to the case of substances, enables him to address a number of epistemological and metaphysical issues. In the *Analytics*, it provides, *inter alia*, a way to account for our coming to know the essences of phenomena when we realized that they are the fundamental causes of their other features. In the *Metaphysics*, it allows us to come to know specific essences which are (i) unique to the kind in question and (ii) not made up of universals or other substances. They are knowable, even though unique to the kind, because they are the final cause (*arche*) of the substance's possession of its other properties.

Aristotle introduces material drawn from the *Analytics* material to escape from the *aporia* reached at the end of Z.16. The latter takes the form of a dilemma: either the essence is unique to the kind in question or it is composed out of universals (which apply more generally) or other substances (as succinctly stated in Z.13, 1039a14–19). Aristotle develops a battery of metaphysical arguments against the latter alternative in Z.13–16, suggesting (*inter alia*) that it is inconsistent with the unity of the kind (1039a15ff.).[33] However, as he notes, if one is forced back on to the first horn and has to accept that the essence is unique to the kind and not made

---

[32] He sometimes also considers 'animal' (presumably of this type) taking the place of 'body' (of this type) in the specification of the matter (1043b11) although he does not endorse this suggestion.

[33] The complex arguments of Z.15 invoke ideas of unity and priority. Thus, Aristotle objects to the idea of defining man as combination of universals which jointly mark out man (in part) because all the elements mentioned in the definition will be prior to man (1040a20–22). If so, the elements will continue to exist even if man ceases to exist. But, since, in Aristotle's account, the essence of man would cease to exist if there were no men, it cannot be identical with these elements. This proposal, like a similar one discussed in *Post. An.* B.13, fails to capture the required priority relations between the elements mentioned in the definition. (For further discussion of this point, see my *Aristotle on Meaning and Essence,*

up from universals, one is left with something which is indefinable, not describable in language (1040a10ff.), and unknowable (1040a25). All one can do is point at it. One will not know what it is.

Aristotle's basic dilemma in Z.13–16 can be presented as follows: either essences are composite or they are simple. If they are composite, they cannot underwrite the unity of the kind (in the way essences are required to do) as they will consist in a number of independent ingredients, themselves in need of unification. However, if they are simple, they will be unknowable.[34] Z.17 addresses this dilemma: the (basic) essence, even if unique to the kind, will be knowable in virtue of its being the specific final cause of the kind's possession of its other properties. As in *Analytics* B.8–10, one can grasp something as a basic essence in virtue of seeing it as the fundamental cause. Thus, for example, one can come to know the basic essence of thunder even if this is a unique kind of phenomenon (a certain kind of fire-quenching found nowhere else) when one sees it as the cause of noise in the clouds. Similarly, one can come to know the unique basic essence of a man (or a house) when one sees the human soul as the cause of the relevant matter's being organized in a given way. Basic essences, so understood, will be unities if they are single unified teleological causes. They are, like fire-quenching, a single unified cause even if they are not metaphysical simples (which cannot be described in general terms). The resulting full definition of man (two-footed body with soul of a given type) will be properly unified, held together by one causally basic feature (or *arche*) such as soul of a given type. Further, as in the *Analytics* model, the type of two-footed body in question (referred to in the definition) will be made the one it is by the presence of this type of soul (as the type of noise in the case of thunder is made the one it is by its being caused in a given way). In this way, the three features referred to in the definition of man (two-footed, body, soul of a given type), so far from being a set of independent components, will form

Oxford, 2000, pp. 225ff.) Further, this proposal, in which all the elements are actually present, cannot (in Aristotle's view) capture the appropriate specific unity of the kind (see 1039a15ff.).

[34] Stephen Menn discusses the second horn of this dilemma in his '*Metaphysics* Z10–16 and the Argument-Structure of *Metaphysics* Z', *Oxford Studies in Ancient Philosophy* 21 (2001) and correctly notes its connections with issues raised in the *Theaetetus*. Our interpretations differ only in that (i) I emphasize its first horn (with its epistemological aspect) and (ii) see its resolution as depending on the role of (e.g.) what it is to be a man as simultaneously the relevant teleological cause and the definitionally basic essence. (ii) is, in my view, crucial for Aristotle's discussion in Z.17 (and beyond).

an integrated unity in which the identity of the first two aspects is (partially) determined by the third, their relevant explanatorily basic starting-point.

Aristotle, it seems, motivates his introduction of the explanatory approach to definition in Z.17 by presenting it as the way to escape from the *aporia* reached at the end of Z.16. Without it, he does not have the resources to resolve (i) his epistemological problem ['How can one come to know an essence which is unique to a kind in question and capable of underwriting the unity of the kind?] or (ii) his metaphysical question ['How can one account for the distinctive unity of complex substances?']. If this is his strategy, he needs next to show that his approach applies to substances in a way consistent with the metaphysically based Unity and Priority Conditions (described in Section 3 above). I shall argue that this is what he seeks to do in some central sections of *Metaphysics* H and Θ.

Unity and Priority: Metaphysics *H.6 and Beyond*

In the *Analytics*, demonstrations reveal as the basic essence one feature, prior to those mentioned in the conclusion, capable of securing the unity of the phenomenon in question. Does what it is to be a man (being a soul of a given type) play this role? Is it immediately causally connected with the matter (body of this type)? Is it prior in the relevant ways? There are grounds for taking Aristotle as offering an affirmative answer to these questions in Z.17 and subsequent sections of H and Θ. Z.17 requires supplementation: while Aristotle is concerned in that chapter with the question of the unity of the kind (1041b11ff.) and suggests that seeing the form as the (final) cause of the body (or flesh) being a given way marks an important step towards resolving this issue (1041b25ff.), he does not spell out why this is so. Similarly, while he sees the relevant essence as the first (and so the prior) cause of the substance being as it is (1041b28), he does not set out his grounds. In these respects Z.17 is incomplete.

Aristotle returns to the question of unity in H.6 (1045a7–9) after his discussion of matter and its *differentiae* and of types of causation in H.2–5, and offers a solution, which requires (once again) the correct formulation of the relevant (definitional) question. He writes,

if, as we put it, there is on the one hand matter and on the other form, the one potentially the other actually, what is sought [viz: the cause of the unity of the kind] is no longer something insuperably problematic (an *aporia*). It would be like asking what is the cause of the bronze and roundness being one (in the case of the rounded bronze). This is no longer an insuperable problem because one is matter, the other the shape. What is the cause of what is potentially [a bronze sphere] being actually [a sphere] over and above the efficient cause in the case of things that come to be? There was no other [cause] other than the essence of each of them. (1045a25–33)[35]

Consider, first, the example of the house, using ideas drawn from the earlier chapters of H. The actuality (as we were told in 1043a8ff.) is [the matter's] being arranged in a given way: as a covering protecting property and bodies (1043a16–17). As Aristotle notes, one may include in this description reference to the final cause (1043a9), which we were previously told is the basic essence in this case (1041a29f.). Against this background, he suggests the problem of unity is no longer insuperable. The final cause makes the actuality the one it is by determining the specific arrangement in question: it makes it be a covering designed to protect one's belongings. It also determines which matter is present: the matter required to achieve this goal. What it is to be a house (the final cause) requires the presence of matter of this type (as the relevant potentiality). Indeed, when the house exists this potentiality is exercised. In this way, the final cause makes the shape (being arranged thus) and the matter (the one suitable to be arranged thus for this goal) be the ones they are.[36] It is the basic essence of both. No further cause is required to account for their unity. The essence (understood as the relevant final cause: see 1043a15, 1044b1) does this by itself. It simultaneously makes the building into a house and grounds the unity of its matter and form.[37] The basic essence, as in the *Analytics* model, accounts for the presence of the unified phenomenon in question with its necessary properties and makes it the thing it is. While in the *Analytics*, the basic essence was the efficient cause, here it is the final cause. Further, it is the final cause of the matter having a given arrangement (or shape).

Consider, next, the case of man. In [E.4] the basic premise is

What it is to be a man belongs to a body of this type.

---

[35] For further discussion of this passage, see Charles, *Aristotle on Meaning and Essence*, pp. 294–6.

[36] Aristotle may use shape and roundness in this context (1045a28–29) to focus on the spatial arrangement in question. (Compare his use of the phrase 'arranged thus' in 1043a8–9.)

[37] I defend this reading of this passage in *Aristotle on Meaning and Essence*, pp. 297ff.

If this is correct, there will be an immediate teleological connection: the type of soul which a man has requires a body of this type: one capable of locomotion, perception, etc. Man's distinctive goals determine both what it is to be a man and the type of body a man requires. There will be, as in the case of the house, one unified teleological cause which accounts for the arrangement of the body (e.g. being two-footed) and requires the matter (body) in question to be present. The basic essence, understood as the teleological cause, will ground the unity of the kind and explain why it has the features it does.

Caution is required. In H.6 Aristotle does not explicitly deploy the final cause nor spell out how talk of matter and form (or potentiality and actuality) interacts with his earlier emphasis on the importance of teleological causation (in, for example, Z.17 and H.2). Nor does he show how the priority condition can be satisfied when one introduces talk of potentiality and actuality. The latter problem is pressing since if actualities are taken as the realizations of potentialities, the latter seem to be prior. While H.6 may make progress with the Unity Condition, it cannot be the end of the story. Aristotle still has to spell out his use of final causation and secure the priority of the essence (conceived as actuality) over matter (conceived as potentiality). He still needs to show how his Priority Condition is satisfied in the case of substances.

Aristotle addresses these questions in his discussion of potentiality and actuality in Θ.7–8. I shall focus on just some of the issues raised by these chapters, aiming merely to indicate how they are intended to supplement the explanation-based definitional project begun in Z.17.[38] In Θ.8, Aristotle commits himself to the following claims:

[A] The goal for matter is to be enformed.
[B] To be enformed is an actuality (*energeia*) (1050a15–16).

From [A] and [B] he can infer:

[C] The goal for matter is an actuality (being enformed).

Aristotle reifies talk of form and actuality and permits himself to draw the further conclusion that

---

[38] For a fuller discussion of *Metaphysics* Θ.7–8, see my 'Some Questions Concerning Potentiality and Actuality', in *Essays in Honour of Allan Gotthelf*, ed. R. Bolton and J. G. Lennox, Cambridge, 2010.

[D] The form is an actuality (1050b2–3).

and finally

[E] The actuality is prior in being to the potentiality (1050b3–4).

In this discussion, final causation has two roles:

(1) Actuality is taken as prior to potentiality because the presence and nature of the latter is teleologically explained by the former, the goal in question (1050a9–19). Introducing talk of teleology gives Aristotle a reason for taking actualities as prior in being (and not merely in account) to potentialities. In this way, teleology provides him with the resources to meet the Priority Condition, which, as we have seen in the *Analytics*, is essential to his project.

(2) In Θ.8, teleological concerns underwrite Aristotle's comparison between matter and form and the capacity for change and change itself. In both, (i) the end-product (or result) is a goal, and (ii) since the end-product is an actuality, the resulting actuality is a goal. Their goal-like status allows Aristotle to present both types of result as actualities, even though they differ ontologically: in one case the goal is an activity (e.g. displaying knowledge: 1050a18), in the other a state (e.g. being a house or a statue). Against this background, he notes:

The result (in the case of action) is a goal, the actuality (*energeia*) is a result, and this is why the term '*energeia*' is predicated on the basis of what is the result [in the case of action: the activity] and extends to the perfected state (*entelecheia*).[39] (1050a21–23)

The goal-like status enjoyed both by activities (the result in the case of actions) and by perfected states entitles us to refer to both as 'actualities'

---

[39] For a similar line of thought, see Θ.3, 1047a30 where Aristotle notes that the name '*energeia*' is extended from a primary application to processes to refer (derivatively) to *entelecheiai* (that which has the goal in it: the perfected state). In 1050a21–23, he refines his earlier thought, noting that the term '*energeia*' is predicated of what is done in the case of action (either the action or the result of action) and together with this refers also to the perfected state. (In this translation, '*teinei eis*' can indicate 'refer to' (*Cratylos* 439b10–c1) when words 'stretch to' objects. The prefix '*sun-*' in '*sunteinei*' suggests (as in 1047a30) 'together with its basic reference'. The '*pros*' in '*pros ten enteleicheian*' may indicate that the direction in which the term '*energeia*' is stretched when it refers to the perfected state. '*Teinei pros ti*', however, can mean 'come near to' or 'be like' (*Theaetetus* 169b; *Rep.* 584d). While I have followed Ross in using the first translation of '*sunteinei*', an alternative would be to understand 1050a22–23 as follows: 'the term "*energeia*" comes to be like the term "*he entelecheia*".' Since the difference in sense between these two (acceptable) translations is not germane to my purposes, I shall not seek to adjudicate between them.)

('*energeiai*').[40] In the case of substance, the goal (final cause) determines both the nature of the perfected state (*entelecheia*) and its relevant potentiality (its matter). Indeed, both actuality and potentiality are defined (directly or indirectly) in terms of the relevant goal. The form (actuality) is the perfected state of the organism (its goal) and the matter (potentiality) is that which achieves that goal (if all goes well).

In this passage (and others) Aristotle seeks to secure the claim, basic to his definitional project, that the essence is prior to matter, by employing talk of final cause, potentiality, and actuality.[41] Indeed, these latter terms are well chosen to emphasize the role of teleological causation because both are defined (at least in part) in terms of their relevant goals. In this respect, the terminology of actuality/potentiality is superior to that of matter/form if (as appears to be the case) the latter terms are not tied directly to teleological concerns. (Form is, after all, often connected with geometrical notions such as shape; matter was introduced by pre-Aristotelian thinkers with no interest in teleology). The conception of essences as actualities is preferable because (so understood) they (i) are teleologically prior to potentialities, (ii) share a common goal with potentialities which grounds the unity of the kind, and (iii) are knowable as the specific final cause of the distinctive features of the kind in question. Aristotle (I conjecture) used talk of actuality and potentiality to carry through his explanation-involving definitional project, introduced in *Metaphysics* Z.17, in the case of substances. This terminology gave him the resources to satisfy (in a perspicuous and compelling way) his *Analytics*-based conditions of Unity and Priority in this metaphysically basic case. In central chapters of *Metaphysics* H and Θ Aristotle is engaged in showing how this is to be done.

6 Definition and Division

My discussion has focused on explanation-based definition in the *Analytics* and the extension of this account to definition in terms of matter and form

---

[40] The translation of '*energeia*' remains controversial. While I have used the term 'actuality' simply as a stand-in for '*energeia*' in this essay, it seems important to capture the idea of something's being '*en . . . ergoi*' (literally 'being in or at work'). If so, the basic sense should (perhaps) be tied to activity, but the term can extend to the product (work as in artwork).

[41] Michail Peramatzis discusses these issues further in his 'Aristotle's Notion of Priority in Nature and Substance', *Oxford Studies in Ancient Philosophy*, 35 (2008), pp. 187–247.

(or potentiality and actuality) in parts of the *Metaphysics*. A further issue concerns its connection with division-based definitions, which Aristotle considers in the *Analytics*, *Metaphysics*, and his biological works. While I shall make a few comments on this question as it arises in the *Metaphysics*, many important questions are left unaddressed.

Aristotle considers definition by genus and *differentia* in *Metaphysics* Z.12 and returns to this topic in *Metaphysics* H.2 and 6. His remarks are fragmentary, probably because he lays more weight on the explanatory type of definition we have so far considered.

Z.12 raises a question about definition by division also raised in *Post. An.* B.6:

'Why is two-footed animal a unity?' (1037b13–15, see *Post. An.* 92a29–30)

In Z.12 Aristotle's answer is to suggest that the final *differentiae* (here, being two-footed) gives the form and essence of the kind and entails other *differentiae* (such as being footed). He ends up by indicating definitions of the form: two-footed animal. However, he seems to treat his remarks as preliminary, concluding the chapter by remarking:

Concerning definitions obtained by divisions, then let this be said as a first shot as to what they are. (1038a34)

His caution is not difficult to understand. It is not clear how the method he outlines in Z.12 can apply to cases where there is a more complex set of *differentiae* such as

wingless, two-footed animal (1037b33),

since being wingless does not entail being two-footed (consider dogs) nor does being two-footed entail being wingless (consider birds). Nor has he said anything about how the final *differentia* is to be selected if it is to be the form and the essence (1038a26). Does Aristotle make progress with these pressing issues after Z.12?

In H.2, Aristotle comments that in the case of the house, the final cause will be found among the *differentiae* (1043a9), such as being arranged thus for the sake of safety (1043a15ff.), predicated of bricks and stones. As we have already seen, in this case the basic essence is the final cause and this requires (i) a certain arrangement of bricks and stones and (ii) the presence of bricks and stones (as the matter). If so, we can see how it will (teleologically) necessitate the presence of the other *differentiae* (being arranged thus) and the matter (which in H.2 plays the role of the genus). Aristotle, using the resources introduced in his preferred definitions in terms of matter and form, can, in this case, meet the requirements mentioned in Z.12. The final *differentia* (the form), conceived as the final cause, requires the presence of the other *differentiae*, even if the latter are complex. In this example, the final cause (safety) explains both why bricks and stones are arranged in a given way and why (e.g.) houses are situated in given positions etc.

In H.6 Aristotle returns to consider the case of man, asking (once more), 'Why is two-footed animal a unity?' (see 1045a15ff.). He now notes that this problem will only be soluble if it is set up in terms of matter and form (or potentiality and actuality: 1045a23f.). At this point he appears to consider formulations (like those in Z.17, 1041b7) involving specific bodies and fails to show how these will help with the issue of the unity of two-footed and animal. For, the genus animal cannot be identified with matter conceived of as body with a given shape. Since Aristotle does not develop his line of thought in any detail, we are left to speculate. There are, at least, three possible suggestions.

A conservative proposal, using the ideas canvassed in Z.12 and H.2, would run as follows. When we add the form of man (e.g. being rational in a given way) and treat this as the final *differentia*, it will require the presence of the other *differentiae* (being two-footed, wingless, capable of perceiving and moving, etc.). Further, a form of this type may require that the creature in question is an animal. In this way, the final *differentia* (the form) will require the presence of both the genus (animal) and the other *differentiae* mentioned in the definition (if there are any). Perhaps, in Aristotle's view, we would not have latched on to this way of thinking unless we had reconceptualized the problem in terms of matter and form; for we grasp the idea of form (and so of essence) by thinking of it as the feature which explains why the matter is arranged as it is. However, once this move has been made, we can fill the gaps left in the *Metaphysics* Z.12 account of definition.

There are more radical proposals. It may be that in H.6, once Aristotle has introduced his favoured talk of matter and form (potentiality and actuality), he finally dispenses altogether with genus/*differentiae* definitions of man. Or perhaps he now regards matter (and not animal) as the relevant genus, carrying further a project introduced in H.2.[42] Or perhaps he sees genus/ *differentiae* claims such as man is a biped animal as, at best, epistemically useful, preliminary non-definitional accounts, steps towards his preferred causal definitions in terms of matter and form.

These differing proposals suggest two different strategies: *either* Aristotle is concerned in *Metaphysics* H.6 to use matter–form style definitions as a new basis for definitions by division *or* the latter are discarded once the former have been introduced. However, whichever strategy is adopted, there is no inconsistency between division-based accounts of definition and Aristotle's preferred, explanatory, model. In one of the two ways just suggested, the explanatory model is the more basic. It may be that, once this basic point was established, Aristotle did not feel the need to adjudicate between these strategies.[43]

7 Some Misunderstandings of Aristotle's Essentialism

Aristotle, in identifying the answers to the 'What is F?' and 'Why is F as it is?' questions, rejects two important claims:

(1) that definitional questions can be satisfactorily answered without drawing on resources taken from scientific explanation, and

(2) that explanatory questions can be satisfactorily resolved without drawing on resources taken from our definitional practices.

---

[42] Richard Rorty pursued this suggestion in his 'Genus as Matter: A Reading of *Metaphysics* Z–H', in *Exegesis and Argument*, Phronesis Supplement 1, ed. E. N. Lee, A. P. D. Mourelatos, and R. M. Rorty, Assen, 1973, pp. 393–420.

[43] Similar questions can be raised about Aristotle's discussion of division-based definitions in *Post. An.* B.13. Some have taken these as preliminary accounts which may be useful en route to uncovering causally based definitions (of the type discussed in B.8–10). Others have suggested that his choice of *differentiae* (and genus) is determined by the causation-involving style of definition developed in *Post. An.* B.8–10. In one version of the latter view, the definition of thunder as noise in the clouds caused by fire being quenched could be caste in genus/*differentia* form (in H.2 style) with noise as the genus and in the clouds and caused in a given way as the *differentiae* (with the latter as the final *differentia*). For an example of the first approach, see Robert Bolton's 'Division, définition et essence dans la science aristotelicienne', *Revue Philosophique* 2 (1993), pp. 197–222. For an example of the second, see my *Aristotle on Meaning and Essence*, pp. 221–44.

It is a major paradox that Aristotelian essentialism has often been characterized, by friends and foes alike, precisely as the acceptance of one or other of these rejected claims. Here are three examples.

(1) Popper once suggested that the 'aim of all inquiry (for Aristotle) is the compilation of an encyclopaedia containing intuitive definitions of all essences'.[44] So understood, Aristotle's definitional concerns stand in the way of scientific progress. In a similar vein, Quine once spoke of 'the metaphysical jungles of Aristotelian essentialism' as a landscape cut off from, indeed standing in the way of, science.[45] Popper is the more explicit: he suggested that 'Aristotle held that...we possess a faculty, intellectual intuition, by which we can visualise essences and find out which definition is the correct one...' For these writers, definitional questions are (for Aristotle) to be resolved in ways independent of our scientific explanatory practices. Popper and Quine (and many others) find this unacceptable, taking scientific explanation as the proper route to knowledge (in the relevant areas).

(2) Nor is the latter view confined to Aristotle's critics. Kit Fine has recently defended a form of essentialism in which the role of the essence is to fix the identity of a kind (or object).[46] He sets out his account with a series of telling examples, noting (for example) that while it is necessary that Socrates belongs to the singleton Socrates, it is not essential to Socrates that he does so. His being a member of this set is not what fixes his identity. Throughout Fine addresses the definitional 'What is F?' question and not the explanatory question: 'Why is F as it is?'

Essences should be prior, in Fine's account, to other features of the object whose essence they are. But what makes something prior? Here there is, as Fine himself notes, a difficulty: is, for example, the human person prior to the human body and the human mind? Or is the human body prior to the others? Or the human mind? As Fine comments, 'philosophers can agree on modal facts and disagree on these questions...of the source of the necessity'. While fully aware of this difficulty, Fine does not suggest how it can be solved. Aristotle, I have suggested, thought that it could only be

[44] *The Open Society and its Enemies*, 2nd edn., London, 1952, vol. 2, p. 12.
[45] *Ways of Paradox*, New York, 1966, p. 174.
[46] 'Essence and Modality' in *Philosophical Perspectives*, vol. 8: *Logic and Language*, ed. J. Tomberlin, Atascadero, CA, 1994; 'The Logic of Essence', *Journal of Philosophical Logic* 24.3 (1995); 'Semantics for the Logic of Essence', *Journal of Philosophical Logic* 29.3 (2000).

resolved if one invokes causal (or explanatory) priority in material, teleological, or efficient modes. From his perspective, Fine's proposal (without
further addition) resembles that suggested by advocates of the general
deduction (discussed in *Post. An.* B.4–6) and appears to be subject to similar
criticism: one could take any of the features Fine mentions (human person,
human mind, human body) as prior and proceed to derive the others (if one
assumes that the human mind, body, and person always coexist). In Aristotle's own view, once we leave aside issues of teleological explanation,
nothing makes the relevant priority claims true.

Many have despaired of Aristotelian essentialism because, having sought
(like proponents of the method of 'general deduction') to elucidate definitions without relying on causal explanation, they have found no metaphysical
grounds for the distinction between necessary and essential features. As a
consequence, some have thought that, if we are to know which features are
definitionally basic, we will need to devise a route to knowledge of essences
which is not (*au fond*) dependent on our practices of explanation. While some
(optimists) invoke metaphysical intuition, claiming that we can simply see
which features are essential, many reject this account as mysterious, concluding that we lack the epistemic resources needed to know which features are
essential and which are necessary. Indeed, for these reasons, Aristotelian
essentialism has been widely regarded as a failure.

Aristotle, however, would (if I am correct) reject all versions of essentialism which rest on the assumption that it is possible to determine what is
essential independently of our practices of explanation. For such an approach rests on an idea of the nature (or essence) of a kind which is
independent of its role in explaining why the kind has certain features.
Further, it presupposes that our definitional practices are complete without
materials drawn from our understanding of the world's causal order. But
Aristotle, I have argued, explicitly challenges these assumptions. In the
Analytics, his fundamental idea of a good definition is that of an account
which captures the nature (or essence) of the phenomenon to be defined,
the feature which causes it to have certain derived necessary features. From
his viewpoint, in giving up this idea, we lose much of our ordinary
understanding of definition. Without it, we cannot (as he suggests in
considering the 'general deduction') simply appeal to definitional ideas
such as unity and priority, as these (in his view) need to be spelled out

(and grounded) using causal terms. In these respects, Aristotle's explanation-based account of definition (as developed in the *Analytics*) points to a form of essentialism different from the one which Quine (and many others) rejected and Fine has attempted to revive.

(3) Other recent essentialists have taken essences simply as scientifically basic features, the starting-points of scientific explanation. In their view, we can take as fundamental what counts as an adequate explanation (without resting on the idea of nature or essence as what fixes the identity of the kind) and then label the starting-points of such explanations as 'essences'. In effect, they take explanatory issues to be satisfactorily resolved without dependence on definitional practices or concerns. Indeed, some, like Brian Ellis in his monograph *Scientific Essentialism*,[47] take this project to be a form of Aristotelian essentialism.

From Aristotle's viewpoint, however, while one may able to account in the way just proposed for (e.g.) thunder's possession of certain properties (in this and close possible worlds), one will not be able to show why thunder *must* have such properties if it is to exist at all. Why is it part of the nature (or essence) of thunder to have such properties? It might, after all, only be a necessary feature of thunder in worlds like ours, consistent with its being different elsewhere. Without a satisfactory answer to this challenge, one will not be able, by focusing on essence-free explanation alone, to generate (distinctively Aristotelian) essentialist claims about thunder.[48] Aristotle, by contrast, proceeded from a different starting-point, taking as basic an essence-involving form of explanation. In his view, questions such as

'Why is it that *elms* shed their leaves?'

or

'Why does *salt* dissolve in water?'

---

[47] *Scientific Essentialism*, Cambridge, 2001.

[48] For an attempt to address this problem, see Alexander Bird's 'Necessarily, Salt Dissolves in Water', *Analysis* 61.4 (2001), pp. 267–74. Bird suggests that salt necessarily dissolves in water because of the existence of a specific higher-order law (Coulomb's Law) whose obtaining is (i) necessary for the existence of salt and (ii) sufficient to account for its dissolving in water. But how does one establish (i)? That is, why is Coulomb's Law necessary for the existence of salt in all possible worlds where it exists, not just in close possible ones? Couldn't the structure of salt be preserved in a world governed by a law in some ways different from Coulomb's? In such a world salt, it seems, would exist and dissolve because of its distinctive nature (even though the higher-order laws differed).

require answers which begin with the essence of elms or salt. Only in this way will one have explained why elms (not any old tree but *elms*) or salt (that very substance) behave in this way. One needs answers which appeal to the natures of elms or salt to answer these questions. Since some parts of our practices of explanation are essence-invoking, our idea of what is explanatorily basic (in these cases) rests on the thought that (e.g.) elms or salt have distinctive natures (or essences). If one refuses to engage in essence-invoking explanation, one is (from Aristotle's point of view) giving up a basic feature of our ordinary form of explanation.

For the contemporary 'scientific essentialist', once explanation has been separated from definition, it is we who choose to regard explanatorily basic features as constituting the essence of the kind. This choice reflects our preferences as definers, not any further metaphysical truth. Our choice, of course, is not an arbitrary one, since we may reasonably wish to have definitions which refer to explanatorily basic features. But, nonetheless, it is we who convert explanatorily basic features into essential ones. Talk of essences reflects our choices or conventions, not how the world is. For Aristotle, by contrast, essences are required as part of the causal order of the world, needed to ground satisfactory explanations of why (e.g.) elms (that very type of tree) behave as they do.

8 Aristotle's Essentialism: Some Remaining Queries

In the cases of the phenomena studied in the *Analytics*, two apparently distinct questions, 'What is F?' and 'Why is F as it is?' have the same answer: the nature of F, which can be picked out by two routes. The correct approach to explanation and to definition should be governed by the search for natures of this type. Aristotle's project, armed with this account, was to examine how far this model of definition extends and what happens when it fails to apply.[49]

The significance of Aristotle's approach should be clear. As we have seen, if one assumes that a full and determinate account of definition and of explanation can be given without dependence on each other, one is swiftly

---

[49] Consider the following problematic cases: (a) natural substances, (b) biological kinds, (c) artefacts, (d) collections of particulars such as bunches, heaps, and teams. Aristotle devoted considerable time to each of these types of case: they require further study.

led (if one wishes to maintain talk of essences) to an unpalatable choice between intuitionism and conventionalism. However, once this assumption is made explicit and challenged (in the way Aristotle did in the *Analytics*), one can resist the temptation to think that these are the only alternatives. Aristotle's positive account, understood on the basis for the systematic interconnections between the practices of explanation and definition noted in the *Analytics*, is a different, more interesting and perhaps more defensible form of essentialism than has so far been realized.[50]

Bibliography

J. Barnes, *Aristotle, Posterior Analytics*, 2nd edn. Oxford, 1993.

A. Bird, 'Necessarily, Salt Dissolves in Water', *Analysis* 61.4 (2001), pp. 267–74.

R. Bolton, 'Division, définition et essence dans la science aristotelicienne', *Revue Philosophique* 2 (1993), pp. 197–222.

R. Bolton, 'The Material Cause: Matter and Explanation in Aristotle's Natural Science', in *Aristotelische Biologie*, ed. W. Kullmann and S. Follinger, Stuttgart, 1997.

B. Brody, 'Towards an Aristotelian Theory of Scientific Explanation', *Philosophy of Science* 39 (1972), pp. 20–31.

D. Charles, 'Teleological Causation in the *Physics*', in *Aristotle's Physics: A Collection of Essays*, ed. Lindsay Judson, Oxford, 1991, pp. 101–28.

D. Charles, *Aristotle on Meaning and Essence*, Oxford, 2000.

D. Charles, 'Some Questions Concerning Potentiality and Actuality', in *Essays in Honour of Allan Gotthelf*, ed. R. Bolton and J. G. Lennox, Cambridge, 2010.

B. Ellis, *Scientific Essentialism*, Cambridge, 2001.

M. Ferejohn, *The Origins of Aristotelian Science*, Yale, 1991.

K. Fine, 'Essence and Modality', in *Philosophical Perspectives*, vol. 8: *Logic and Language*, ed. J. Tomberlin, Atascadero, CA, 1994, pp. 1–15.

K. Fine, 'The Logic of Essence', *Journal of Philosophical Logic* 24.3 (1995), pp. 241–73.

K. Fine, 'Semantics for the Logic of Essence', *Journal of Philosophical Logic* 29.3 (2000), pp. 543–84.

---

[50] I am indebted to discussions with Lucas Angioni, David Bronstein, Laura Castelli, Kei Chiba, Scott O'Connor, Hiro Ogino, Vassilis Karasmanis, Atsushi Kawatani, Michail Peramatzis, Nathaniel Stein, and Charlotte Witt on these and related topics. I should also like to thank the Oxford University Press anonymous commentator for his helpful comments on an earlier draft of this essay. Work on this essay was supported by a grant from the British Academy and the Japanese Society for the Promotion of Science.

O. Goldin, *Explaining an Eclipse*, Michigan, 1996.

M. Leunissen, *Explanation and Teleology in Aristotle's Philosophy of Nature*, Leiden, 2007.

R. D. McKirahan, *Principles and Proofs: Aristotle's Theory of Demonstrative Science*, Princeton, 1992.

S. Makin, *Aristotle, Metaphysics Theta*, Oxford, 2006.

H. Mendell, 'Two Geometrical Examples from Aristotle's *Metaphysics*', *Classical Quarterly* 34 (1984), pp. 359–72.

S. Menn, '*Metaphysics* Z10–16 and the Argument-Structure of *Metaphysics* Z', *Oxford Studies in Ancient Philosophy* 21 (2001), pp. 83–134.

Pacius, *In Aristotelis Organon Commentarius Analyticus*, Frankfurt, 1597.

M. Peramatzis, 'Aristotle's Notion of Priority in Nature and Substance', *Oxford Studies in Ancient Philosophy* 35 (2008), pp. 187–247.

K. Popper, *The Open Society and its Enemies*, 2nd edn., London, 1952.

W. V. O. Quine, *Ways of Paradox*, New York, 1966.

R. Rorty, 'Genus as Matter: A Reading of *Metaphysics* Z–H', in *Exegesis and Argument*, Phronesis Supplement 1, ed. E. N. Lee, A. Mourelatos, and R. Rorty, Assen, 1973, pp. 393–420.

R. Smith, 'Immediate Propositions and Aristotle's Proof Theory', *Ancient Philosophy* 6 (1986), pp. 47–55.

M. Wedin, *Aristotle's Theory of Substance*, Oxford, 2000.

9

Bios and Explanatory Unity in Aristotle's Biology

JAMES G. LENNOX

I Introduction

Aristotle articulates a form of essentialism in the *Posterior Analytics* (*APo.*) that is at once sophisticated and unlike what contemporary philosophers refer to as 'Aristotelian essentialism' (cf. Charles 2000, ch. 1). According to *APo.* II, the goal of scientific enquiry is knowledge of certain features of the objects of enquiry, both as features that make those objects what they are *and* as features that are causally responsible for most or all the other non-accidental features of those objects. That is, to know the essence of some-thing is not merely to know the defining features of that thing—one must know that those features causally necessitate that thing's other non-acciden-tal features. Precisely because of this dual role played by these features, Aristotle's summary statement of his position in *APo.* II.10 refers to a privileged kind of *definition* that is a rearrangement of the terms of a parallel *demonstration*. For example, in a scientific demonstration of why a certain noise (thunder) occurs in certain clouds, the middle term identifies the cause of the noise (extinction of fire). This demonstration provides the materials for a definition of thunder as a noise that occurs in certain clouds due to the extinction of fire (*APo.* II.10 93b38–94a9).

During the last three decades a great deal of work has been done to narrow the distance between the understanding of Aristotle's essentialism derived from the *Analytics* and the explanatory and definitional practices of the biological works (cf. Bolton 1987; Charles 2000; Detel 1997; Gotthelf

1985b; 1987; Kullmann 1974; Lennox 1987, 1990).[1] A major problem standing in the way of integrating theory and practice in the biological case arises from the absence, in the *Analytics* discussion of scientific definition and demonstration, of any reference to form or to the distinction between form and matter, concepts that are at the heart of biological definition and explanation. Moreover, while *APo.* relies heavily on examples from the science of nature—thunder, eclipses, leaf-shedding—there are few hints as to how that theory would apply to complexly integrated natural *substances*. On the face of it this is surprising, since Aristotle's most sustained scientific investigation of nature, his multifaceted investigations of animals, is focused on what is surely his paradigm case of the natural unity of matter and form. In the domain of living things form refers to the soul (ψυχή), the integrated set of an animal's living capacities, carried out by a complicated network of parts functioning as a coordinated whole. One would expect definitions of animals to differentially identify those capacities for life which explain why each kind of organism has the distinctive physical structure it has; moreover, one would expect those defining features to play a central role in accounting for the amazingly complex and organized process of *development*.[2]

In *Aristotle on Meaning and Essence*, David Charles makes a significant advance in envisioning how the *Analytics* program can apply to such a domain. He argues that the 'fresh start' to the question of primary substance initiated in *Metaphysics* Z.17 and reaching some sort of at least an interim conclusion in H.6 is designed to extend the *Analytics* model of essence and causal explanation (i.e. of definition and demonstration) to natural complexes of matter and form.

I have sketched an account in which explanation is central to Aristotle's strategy for defining unified composite substances. If this sketch is correct, he is attempting to

---

[1]   The goal of eventually finding explanations of attributes at the level of commensurate universality is central to the methodology of the *Historia Animalium* as well, as a great deal of detailed research has made clear (Balme 1987b; Gotthelf 1988; Lennox 1987, 1991). But the way in which this goal is pursued has serious implications for the kind of essentialism that can be reasonably defended on the basis of Aristotle's biological works.

[2]   As he tells us in two central texts, development is part of the process by which biological forms, souls, are endlessly replicated. It permits a living thing to 'participate in the eternal and divine'. It is the 'most natural' of an organism's formal capacities. Cf. *De an.* II.4 415a26–b7; *GA* II.1 731b18–732a1. In light of this most natural capacity, *Metaph.* Z.8 1033b26–1034a8 argues that there is no need to postulate Platonic forms as causes of natural substances.

apply to this case the style of definition developed for *eclipse* and *thunder* in the *Analytics*. If so, his answer to the 'What is F?' question will be given by invoking the basic feature in a teleological explanation of why the other genuine features of F are as they are. . . . Thus Aristotle will introduce form and matter (and later actuality and potentiality) in the *Metaphysics* as the conceptual resources needed to provide the metaphysical basis for his *Analytics* style of explanation involving definition. (Charles 2000, 304)

In the next chapter of his book, however, Charles raises serious questions about whether, in the face of the staggering complexity of the living world, this extension of the *Analytics* model to the domain of natural substance can work.

In support of the possibility of such an extension, notice the clear echoes of the *Analytics* program in the following summation of Aristotle's account of the heart:

Regarding the heart, then, *what sort of thing it is, what it is for the sake of*, and *the cause* owing to which it is present in those animals that have it, let so much be said. (*PA* III.4 667b13–14; emphasis added)

A scientific definition of the heart will identify, in fundamental terms, what the heart is *and* the cause on account of which animals with hearts have them. Indeed in this chapter, Aristotle's general account of the heart concludes (i) that the heart is present for the sake of originating blood and (ii) that it is thus the primary organ of the perceptive capacity of soul, the capacity essential to being an animal (*PA* III.4 666a34–36).[3] The definition of a heart is, as Charles's account would lead us to expect, based on a teleological explanation of why animals with hearts have hearts: definition and explanation are intertwined in precisely the way the *Posterior Analytics*, on Charles's account, would lead us to expect.[4]

That example also exemplifies one more complication in applying the *Analytics* model to the biological domain stressed by Charles: the tight connection between demonstration and definition defended in the *Analytics*

---

[3] It needs to be noted that it is part of Aristotle's explicit theory that many animals that perceive lack hearts. *PA* III.4, however, is part of the discussion of the internal organic parts of blooded animals. Aristotle turns to the bloodless animals in book IV, and when he does so he notes that they must have an analogue of the heart and blood (cf. *PA* IV.5 678b1–7).

[4] This claim of affinity between the *APo.* model and Aristotle's biological project has its critics of course. The most sustained and knowledgeable critic is Sir Geoffrey Lloyd; see for example Lloyd 1990 and Lloyd 1996, chs. 1–7.

must be integrated with Aristotle's insistence on the priority of 'the cause for
the sake of which' over motive causes and the priority of living form over
living matter defended in the first chapter of *On the Parts of Animals*. But can
this integration possibly work at the level of an account of the organism as a
whole? Aristotle appears to claim that it can in a passage in *PA* 1.5, where he
extends the explanatory priority of functional activity from organs to whole
organism:

Since every instrument is for the sake of something, and each of the parts of the
body is for the sake of a certain action, it is apparent that the entire body too has
been constituted for the sake of a certain complete action.[5] For sawing is not for the
sake of the saw, but the saw for the sake of sawing; for sawing is a certain use. So
the body too is in a way for the sake of the soul, and the parts are for the sake of the
functions in relation to which each of them has naturally developed. (645b15–20)

The connection between essence and explanation here is as intimate as it
was in the *Posterior Analytics*. The unity of matter and form in animals is to be
understood as the unity of an instrumental structure and its functional
capacity. The various features of a part are to be explained by reference to
the function or action for the sake of which that part came to be and exists;
the physical features of the animal as a whole are to be understood by
reference to some sort of 'complete' activity. The definition of a part that
corresponds to such an explanation will necessarily make reference to the
part's structure, but only in so far as that structure exists for the sake of
performing its function or functions (645a33–36). To be the heart of a
certain kind of animal is to be an instrument structured (and located)
appropriately for the nutritive and perceptive functions of that (kind of)
animal.

Yet, while *PA* II–IV provides extensive examples of both uniform and
non-uniform parts being provided with *Analytics* style, essence-based explanations, by that work's very nature as an explanation of *parts*, it might
well be doubted whether it will help at all in understanding the explanatory
relationship between the 'complete activity' of an animal of a certain kind

---

[5] The majority of the manuscripts and Michael of Ephesus read πλήρους (full, complete, whole)
πράξεως, though Peck (1945, 102) and Düring (1943, 122–3) both follow ms. **P**, which reads πολυμεροῦς.
I see no reason to follow **P**, given the substitution at b18 of 'soul' for the disputed phrase. Nevertheless,
since Aristotle will occasionally speak of 'parts' of the soul when referring to its integrated functional
capacities, either reading could yield a picture of the body as a whole organized for a unified soul.

and the instrumental body of that animal. The burden of the remainder of this paper will be to argue that it is by introducing an explanatory role for βίος that Aristotle evidences a concern to identify a single essential feature of organisms—their way of life—that accounts for the *integration* of the many physical and functional differences that make different kinds of animals what they are.

II *Βίος* and Unity

To this point I have provided ample evidence that the epistemological concerns of the *Posterior Analytics* remain central to Aristotle in his biological practice. It should not be surprising, then, if, in his extensive and systematic development of a science of animals, one of his primary concerns is to determine the source of *unity* for living things. The obvious candidate, of course, is soul, which Aristotle consistently portrays as the form of a living thing. Yet, while soul is an excellent candidate for the cause of unity of a living *body*, the soul itself is typically portrayed as a hierarchically organized complex of capacities, capacities which underlie an even more complex network of activities or functions (πράξεις or ἔργα), performed by a complex system of organic parts. Will there be any explanation for why a particular kind of animal has just the set of functions it has, or why we should think of that set as unified in the appropriate ways? Or will distinctive accounts of the parts by reference to their particular functions be explanatory bedrock for Aristotle? Here I will present evidence that an animal's many parts and corresponding activities are provided with a unified explanation by identifying their contributions to the one βίος, or 'way of life', of that animal.

As noted briefly in the previous section, the need for an account of biological unity is highlighted in chapter 12 of David Charles's *Aristotle on Meaning and Essence*. On his reading of the *Posterior Analytics* II, the goal of scientific enquiry is to find a single fundamental feature that will account for all of the other necessary features of a kind.[6] Using Aristotle's discussions of

---

[6] 'Thus he [Aristotle] insists that demonstrations must begin with one common cause and not a conjunction or disjunction of separate causes. These claims are natural if what is sought is the essence of the kind, a single cause which can provide the basis for the "What is F?" question' (Charles 2000, 217). In

fish as a test for whether the explanatory program of Aristotle's biology implements the theory of explanation outlined in the *Posterior Analytics*, Charles draws attention to how often references to the way of life of a fish account for its various features, and concludes:

The distinctive parts of fish should be just the ones required for its distinctive manner of life[7] and movement as a swimmer in water. (Charles 2000, 331)

And after quoting the crucial line from the passage in *PA* I.5 which we discussed near the end of section I, a passage, recall, which asserts that the body of an animal as a whole exists for the sake of one complete action, Charles resumes:

If the relevant action is swimming in water, this should explain, as in the passages cited, why the external and internal parts are as they are. (331)

There is a subtle difference between Charles's two formulations of this issue: in the first he conjoins 'distinctive manner of life' and 'movement as a swimmer in water'. But after discussing the reference to a single complex action of the body as a whole in *PA* 1.5, the βίος of fish, their way of life, is quickly reduced to the activity of swimming. In the end, Charles concludes that Aristotle failed to find that single unitary feature for each kind that could account for all their other distinctive features. This leads him to speculate on whether we are witnesses to 'the collapse of a brilliant research programme' (336). He concludes his discussion by suggesting a way in which Aristotle might rescue his biological project from collapse, a *via media* between the strict *Analytics* model of essence and explanation and its total abandonment. This middle way would be accomplished 'by taking the teleological factors as basic and relaxing the relevant unity condition' (343).

Independent of questions that might be raised about Charles's characterization of the *Analytics* model of unity, there are questions that need to be addressed about his picture of the unity that Aristotle is striving for in biology. Can an animal's 'way of life' be identified with a single, basic activity? As we will soon see, the evidence of the text tells strongly against

response to questions about why such a strong notion of unity is needed, Charles insists that without it you would lack an explanation for 'why all [a kind's] features are *interconnected* in the way they are' (emphasis added). I agree with Charles that Aristotle will not rest content without an explanation of that kind.

[7] I suppose that by 'manner of life' here Charles has in mind Aristotle's concept of βίος.

such a reduction. I therefore explore another option: that an organism's *βίος*, its way of life, explains the remarkable *integration* (or, to use Charles's term, 'interconnectedness') of its parts and activities. An organism's way of life appears to be the key to this interconnectedness. It is able to meet *Analytics* constraints on the unity of essence-based explanation *without* reducing an animal's way of life to a single basic activity.

III Two Roles for *Βίος*

The concept of *βίος* identifies one of the four overarching differentiae around which the *Historia animalium* (*HA*) is organized.[8] Immediately after its opening theoretical discussion of the ways in which things can be alike and different, a discussion which uses uniform and non-uniform parts as illustrations, he tells us:

The differences among animals are in accordance with their ways of life (κατὰ τε τοὺς βίους), their activities (τὰς πράξεις), their traits of character (τὰ ἤθη) and their parts. (*HA* I.1 487a11–12)

During these introductory chapters Aristotle provides illustrations of the use of division within each of these categories of difference; and then we have most of four books devoted to differences among parts, followed by five books devoted to activities (especially those related to generation), ways of life, and traits of character.[9] In *HA*, then, *βίος* is a fundamental tool for the comparative organization of information about animals at the most abstract level.

In *De partibus animalium* (*PA*) and *De generatione animalium* (*GA*), on the other hand, the concept is used for a very different purpose, as an explanatory concept. Identifying an animal's *βίος* helps us to understand why a general part or function is differentiated in one way rather than in another. In the next section of this paper, in fact, we will look at the way in which the external parts of different kinds of birds are accounted for in *PA* IV.12 by

---

[8] I will translate *βίος* with the English expression 'way of life'. I am putting aside one important use of the concept, typically in the genitive with διά, in which it refers to an organism's characteristic *period* of life, which is the sense embedded in terms such as μακροβίος.

[9] The word *βίος* appears explicitly 34 times in *HA*, and it is distributed just as these introductory comments would lead one to expect: there are 8 in book I, while the remainder are in V–VIII.

identifying the ways of life of those birds. The key to understanding that discussion is to notice that a bird's βίος is appealed to in order to account for coordination among its parts.

In both its data organization role and its explanatory role, a key question for this investigation is how an animal's βίος is related to its πράξεις. I will briefly discuss βίος in *HA* in this paper, but will focus attention here primarily on its explanatory role, since it is in that role that it provides a possible solution to the unity 'crisis' posed by Charles.[10]

IV *Βίος* as a Tool for Data Organization

According to *HA* I, one of the ways in which animals are differentiated from each other is by their ways of life. *Βίος*, *πρᾶξις*, and *ἦθος* are, however, complexly interwoven concepts.[11] In the introductory discussion in *HA* I Aristotle makes little effort to signal when he is discussing differences in way of life, activity, or character, likely because differentiating ways of life typically involves asking questions about an animal's habits and activities. This suggests a very complex relationship between an animal's way of life and its many activities.[12]

This complexity is reflected exactly in Books VII–VIII, with VII discussing βίος and πρᾶξις together and VIII discussing ἦθος (though often with reference to the animal's βίος). Aristotle apparently had greater difficulty in discussing activity and way of life separately.

In order to have a concrete idea of what differences are under consideration in these books, a list of some of the more important differences Aristotle has in mind is useful. The category of βίος includes such differences as: social/solitary, land-dweller/water-dweller/flyer, carnivorous/

---

[10] I spend more time on the former role in 'Bios, Praxis and the Unity of Life' in S. Föllinger, ed., *What is 'Life'? Aristotle on 'Life' and its Functions*, Philosophie der Antike (W. Kullmann, series editor), Stuttgart (2010).

[11] Interestingly, πρᾶξις is used in both a descriptive and an explanatory way as well. As a theoretical statement of its explanatory role we need look no farther than *PA* I.5: 'whenever there are actions that are for the sake of other actions, the things whose actions they are differ in the same way as their actions do. Similarly if some actions are in fact prior to, and the end of, others, it will be the same way with each of the parts whose actions are of this sort' (645b28–31). More on this later.

[12] At 487b32 we find a list of differences restricted to ways of life and activities, followed, at 488b12, by a list that is focused on differences in character.

frugivorous/omnivorous, hunting/gathering, storing, housebuilders/non-housebuilders, subterranean/terrestrial, nocturnal/diurnal. Notice that each one of these ways of life will be correlated with an indeterminate number of activities performed by many parts; and those activities will be performed in different ways depending on the animal's character, for example, whether it is spirited or sluggish, timid or aggressive, and so on. The complexity in Aristotle's characterization of the relationships among these differences reflects the complexity in animals' lives.

Differences in ways of life are in part differences in where, how, and when animals perform certain *activities*, especially those related to feeding and reproducing: fish swim (activity) either in schools or alone (way of life); birds feed (activity) either on flesh, seeds, or both (way of life). At least part of the information integrated by the concept of 'way of life' is that about *where, how, and when* an animal performs the various activities related to feeding and reproducing.

If that is right, then specific ways of life are *inherently relational*, tying many different modes of activity to an animal's overall way of interacting with its environment. To refer to an animal as aquatic or migratory relates a large number of distinct activities to a unified way of interacting with the animal's environment. And like all of Aristotle's universal differences, ways of life may be subdivided along a variety of axes, subdivisions made by reference to differences in an animal's activities and characters. At this point, however, the following caution needs to be flagged: the fact that a way of life is divisible along a variety of axes that make reference to activities does not entail either that it is *reducible* to those activities or that it is *non-unitary*. In fact the unity of the activities derives from the way they contribute to a way of life. Not surprisingly, given Aristotle's metaphysical commitments, it is the way of life of the whole animal that has conceptual priority. This viewpoint is present only by implication in *HA*, since it is a work that is pre-explanatory by design (see *HA* I.6 491a7–14). As we will see in the next section, it is explicit in the *De partibus animalium*.

Having said that, it is surely in part this complicated interdependency between activities and way of life that makes a Charles-style reduction tempting. Given the intimate connection between activity and way of life, why can we not get along perfectly well simply by listing the *activities* at the most general level and subdividing them? And in that case, when we turn to explanation, why not search for one of those activities as the

explanatorily fundamental core of an animal's way of life? After a brief look
at the way in which Aristotle structures his discussion of πρᾶξις and βίος in
HA VII–VIII, we will turn to the explanatory practices of *PA* II–IV to
answer that question.

The first point that I want to stress about these books is that a single βίος
appears to be correlated with a considerable number of activities related to
nutrition, reproduction, perception, and locomotion. Consistent with the
overall aims of *HA*, Aristotle doesn't directly discuss the causal/explanatory
relationships among these differentiae; nevertheless he will, by way of the
choice of prepositions he uses, make a certain relationship between way of
life and activities clear. The way of life of the animal appears to take
precedence over its particular activities, character traits, and parts.

An animal's way of life is identified in part by reference to its environ-
mental context—its *niche*, as we might say. As flyers, for example, all
birds share a number of physical and behavioral characteristics, and these
are differentiated *in a coordinated fashion* depending on the differentiation of
their βίος. The eyes, beaks, necks, wings, and legs of a carnivorous raptor—
and their activities associated with perceiving, eating, and locomotion—will
be *systematically* different from those of a shore bird. By stressing interrelations among these three categories of difference, *HA* V–VIII provide a basis
for the explanatory work of *PA* and *GA*.[13]

HA VII opens by remarking that 'the activities (αἱ πράξεις) and the ways
of life (οἱ βίοι) [of animals] differ in accordance with character traits (τὰ ἤθη)
and feeding' (588a17–19).[14] The evidence from the rest of the book indicates

[13] Throughout the next few pages I will be assuming the results of recent scholarship on the aims and
methods of the *Historia animalium*. Briefly, the conclusions of that scholarship are: [i] that *HA* is a crucial
part of Aristotle's systematic scientific study of animals; [ii] in terms of the views of the *Posterior Analytics*
about scientific investigation, it represents a primarily pre-causal, data organization part of that larger
enterprise—it seeks τὸ ὅτι rather than τὸ διότι; [iii] its form of organization is nevertheless dictated in
large part by Aristotle's aim of a demonstrative science of animals; [iv] the data are thus organized most
broadly in terms of general differentiae, and division is used systematically in order to find universal
correlations, including coextensive correlations, among more specific differentiae; [v] in so far as animal
kinds play a role in the discussion, they are loci for these related sets of differentiae; and finally, and
perhaps most controversially, [vi] it appears as if the *HA* took something like its current form after the
research for the *De partibus animalium* was completed, and may have been continuously added to
throughout Aristotle's second period in Athens. For some key contributions to this scholarship see
Balme 1987a, 1987b, 2002; Gotthelf 1988; Kullmann 1974; Lennox 1987, 1990, 1991, 1996.

[14] *Τροφή* in the context of discussing activities and ways of life appears to have the nuance of 'mode of
feeding' rather than 'nutrients' or 'nourishment'. That is, often, in phrases such as διὰ τὴν τροφήν
(589b17, b19, b22), the word appears to be a substitution for phrases such as τὸ τὴν τροφὴν ποιεῖσθαι
(589a17, a19) or λαμβάνειν τροφήν (589b26). The emphasis, that is, is more on the environment in which

that the plurals here range over all the animals—they should not be taken as a suggestion that the same animal has both many ways of life and many activities. In discussing animals with very simple lives, for example, Aristotle refers to 'the activities of their way of life' (κατὰ τὰς τοῦ βίου πραξεῖs) noting that their activities are all related to nutrition and generation, as if they were living the life of a plant (*HA* VII.1 588b23–28).[15] He goes on to say that in more complex organisms, however, *a single way of life will consist of many different activities related to feeding and procreating*, and differences related to feeding are correlated with differences in the natural material constitutions of the animals. Foods that accord more with their natures are more pleasant to animals, and that is what they by nature pursue (see 589a1–9, 590a11).

In both of these passages there is a pointed stress on the singularity of an animal's way of life, and the multiplicity of activities constituting it. These many activities will, in turn, differ with respect to character traits because character traits simply *are* dispositions to perform activities in certain ways, timidly, ferociously, cunningly, gregariously, etc. Thus the same activity will have a different 'valence' depending on the character of the animal performing it. We will see shortly that the characteristic way that an animal performs its activities is regularly related to the animal's overall way of life as well. But the introduction of *HA* VII also indicated that feeding behavior was of central importance in distinguishing one way of life from another. This suggestion is soon reinforced:

There are water animals of a different sort [than fish], *on account of the blend of their body and their way of life*, namely those that, though they receive air, live in water, as well as those that, though receiving water and having gills, progress to a dry environment and eat there. Up till now only one such has been observed, the one called 'cordylos'; for though it has not a lung but gills, yet it is four-legged as if in fact it had developed naturally to walk. (589b22–28)

Determining whether an animal is a 'water-dweller' or a 'land-dweller' is, as it turns out, no simple matter; it follows from (ἀκολουθεῖν) *three* other

the feeding takes place and the way it takes place rather than on the food itself. It turns out, however, that Aristotle sees a very tight connection between the material constitution of the food source and the environment in which an animal lives, which may explain the ease with which he makes this sort of substitution. More on this shortly.

[15] Cf. Aristotle often will characterize very simple animals, or an animal embryo during development, as 'living the way of life (βίος) of a plant'. Cf. *GA* II.3 736b13; III.2 753b28; V.1 779a2.

divisions: [1] whether it take in air or water, [2] the characteristic blend of its body, and [3] where it feeds.[16] That is, if it breathes air, *in that respect* it is a land-dweller; if it has dry, 'earthen' flesh, *in that respect* it is a land-dweller; if it feeds in the water, *in that respect* it is a water-dweller.[17]

While no kind falls on both sides of a particular division, it is entirely possible for an animal to be a water-dweller with respect to one division and a land-dweller with respect to another. Moreover, since there are two different respects in which animals that pass their time in water 'take in and expel water or air', things are more complicated still. Cetaceans breathe air; they only take in water through their mouths incidental to feeding in water; others take in water by means of gills as an *alternative* to breathing air, so that a differentiation of 'taking in water' is required (cf. 589a33–b7).

These passages do put pressure on the idea that the way of life of an animal kind is a *single* feature around which its activities are coordinated. Certain kinds of animals, as Aristotle would put it, 'tend toward both [ways of life]' (i.e. τὰ ἐπαμφοτερίζοντα). With respect to some of their activities and physical characteristics, they live one sort of way of life; with respect to others, they live another. These are, however, a special class of animals. It would be a mistake to try to determine his general notion of 'way of life' by focusing on this category.

In general, Aristotle's understanding seems to be that in determining the way of life for a kind of animal, one needs to investigate the kind of food it eats, where it feeds, where and by means of what does it cool itself, where and how it generates and cares for its young, in what medium it spends its time, and so on. That there is likely some priority given to the kind of food the animal needs in identifying and differentiating ways of life is strongly suggested by an important passage in the *Politics*.

But furthermore, there are many forms (εἴδη) of nutrition, for which reason there are also many ways of life (βίοι) both among animals and among human beings; for

---

[16] The last sentence of this passage states: 'For some follow in accordance with blend, nourishment and the taking in of either water or air, while others follow in virtue of blend and by ways of life (τοῖς βίοις) alone' (590a16–18). One might suppose the same subject with ἀκολουθεῖν as in the first sentence, οἱ βίοι. David Balme (in Balme 1991, 81) correctly takes it that τὰ μὲν . . . τὰ δὲ should be understood as 'Some animals . . . while other animals . . .'. There is a significant difference in the texts of two families of manuscripts compared to the third. I suspect the reading of the γ family reflects an editor's early conjecture that was intended to allow the subject to be 'way of life' throughout.

[17] Determination of whether an animal is a land or water dweller can be further complicated by considering where an animal generates (cf. *HA* I.1 487a14–23; VII.1 588b23–28, 589a1–9).

it is not possible to live without nutrition, so that differences in nutrition have made the ways of life of animals different. For among the wild animals some are nomadic and some are solitary, whichever is best suited to their nutrition, on account of some of them being carnivorous, some frugivorous and some omnivorous. So nature distinguishes their ways of life in relation to their preferences and inclination. But since what is by nature flavorful is not the same for each animal but different for different animals, even among those that are carnivorous or frugivorous ways of life are divided relative to one another. (*Pol.* I. 3 1256a20–29)

There is an implicit division within the category of 'way of life' here. Suppose an animal is a land-dweller. Land-dwellers may be either social or solitary, nomadic or stationary; which they are will depend on such things as whether they are flesh-eaters, fruit-eaters, or omnivores, for animals have a natural preference for different kinds of food. In virtue of being a living thing it requires nutrients and it must reproduce (it is worth remembering that *De anima* II.4 argues that the capacity for nutrition and generation are one and the same). The above passage from the *Politics* strongly suggests that any creature is a water-dweller because the foods that are naturally suited to its nutritional needs are found in water—and for that reason the many activities related to perception, locomotion, and reproduction must also be adapted to living in water, whatever kind of animal it is. There is a clear priority of way of life relative to their parts and activities, even before we consider how to explain these features; and it looks like nutritional preferences are critical in distinguishing one animal's way of life from another. That is the first important asymmetry between an animal's way of life and its activities.

The second asymmetry has to do with the way in which a way of life requires *coordination* among activities. As one looks at the long list of more-and-less differentiations of activities and parts that serve to differentiate one fish from another or one bird from another, one sees a coordination among these differentiae that has to do with ensuring they work together, a coordination regularly accounted for by identifying the kind's way of life. High-flying carnivores (raptors) have a special kind of vision, mode of flight, way of capturing prey, way of eating, way of perching, and so on. From the standpoint of the *Historia animalium* one simply notes that a single way of life is coordinated with a number of such differentiated features, variably repeated in every animal with that way of life, every hawk and eagle, let us say. It is only in the *De partibus animalium* that one begins to see that at any level of specificity it is the animal's way of life that *explains* that pervasive coordination, why the same pattern is repeated as you go from one raptor to the next, or from one shore bird to the next.[18]

In *HA* VIII Aristotle turns to discussing differences in respect of character (τὰ ἤθη). The term βίος is used in that discussion at least ten times in the sense we are interested in,[19] and in every case the message is the same: animals can perform activities related to feeding, mating, or care of offspring with greater or lesser intelligence, skill, resourcefulness, courage, gentleness, and so on, given their particular way of life. Thus variations in the nest-building of birds, in the web-construction of spiders, in the complexity of work relations in bees, are related to differences in way of life. One judges the (say) resourcefulness of a behavior relative to the animal's βίος.

The dwelling-places of the wild birds are devised relative to both their ways of life and the safety of their offspring. Some are good parents and care for the young, some are the opposite; some are resourceful in relation to their way of life while others are not. (614b32–34)

What distinction is Aristotle pointing to here? Well, nests are generally constructed to protect the eggs and the chicks. But how a bird goes about doing this is radically dependent on its way of life. The kinds of materials available, where the nest is located, what sorts of predators it needs to protect the clutch from, all these and more are dependent on the particular bird's way of life. This introduction to his discussion of differences in character is then followed by an account of the different environments that different kinds of birds nest in and character differences in their feeding, nest-building, and parenting, i.e. of how well or poorly these activities are carried out, given where and how the bird lives.

In short, we see the same sorts of asymmetry between βίος and ἤθος that we saw in the case of πρᾶξις—the character traits of animals are differentiated and coordinated in a complex fashion by reference to their ways of life.

---

[18] Though I hasten to add that since it is the *parts* of animals that are there being explained, one needs to recall that for Aristotle most variations in a part are for the sake of some variation in function or activity.

[19] Excluding one use where it simply means 'duration of life', they are: 610a34, 612b18, 614b32–34, 615a21, 616b21, 617a8, 619b22, 620b11, 622b24, 623b26, 629b4.

V *Βίος* as an Explanatory Concept

I turn now to the role of *βίος* as an explanatory concept in the *De partibus animalium*.[20] Since *βίος* refers to a category of differentia, there are many instances in *PA* II–IV of differences within that category (water-dweller, land-dweller) playing an explanatory role without the term itself being used. However, in *PA* IV.12 Aristotle seems to be self-consciously highlighting the way in which an animal's way of life accounts for its other differences, and for that reason he repeatedly refers to the category itself.

The last four chapters of *PA* return to the external parts of blooded animals, a topic from which Aristotle departed in *PA* III.2.[21] He turns to the remaining external parts of birds in chapter 12, and begins by noting the observable similarities and differences of their parts and correlations among them, treating these correlations as sufficient grounds for the groupings he mentions.

Among birds, differentiation of one from another is *by means of excess and deficiency of their parts, i.e. according to the more and less.* That is, some of them are long-legged, some short-legged, some have a broad tongue, others a narrow one, and likewise too with the other parts. (*PA* IV.12 692b3–6; emphasis added)

All birds have feathers and beaks, and these parts differ *by more and less*, while there are *analogous* parts in other animals—scales rather than feathers in fish, trunks rather than beaks in elephants (692b15–18). As he begins to discuss the neck, he notes correlations between its measurable variations and

---

[20] Allan Gotthelf notes (Gotthelf 1987, 192–3 and note 61) that *βίοι* are among the explanatory 'givens' that he is concerned to highlight as among the first principles of *PA* in that paper. Likewise *βίοι* are among the unexplained principles used to account for the trunk of the elephant discussed in Gotthelf 1997a; see e.g. p. 87.

[21] The organization is complex. After a lengthy introduction, Aristotle begins his discussion of animal parts with the uniform parts of blooded animals (roughly, our 'tissues'); at II.10 he turns to the non-uniform parts, arguing for a top-down strategy, as determined by human anatomy. When he gets to the neck, however (at the beginning of III.3), after announcing that its purpose is the protection of the windpipe and esophagus, he moves to a study of the internal parts, the viscera, and thus the *external* parts below the neck remain to be considered. When he has completed that discussion of the viscera at IV.4, instead of returning to the external parts of blooded animals, he discusses the bloodless animals. Only once that task is completed, at the beginning of IV.10, does he return to the remaining external parts of the blooded animals, which he discusses roughly in the order live-bearing land-dwellers, egg-laying land-dwellers, birds, fish, and some that don't fit neatly into these categories. (For further discussion of this structure see Gotthelf 1987, 172–8; Lennox 2001a, 220, 292, 314–15.

those of other parts, and begins offering explanations for these correlations. For example,

those that are long-legged have a long neck, while those that are short-legged have a short one ... for if the neck were short in those with long legs, the neck would not be of service to them for eating food off the ground; nor if it were long in those with short legs. *Again for those that eat flesh a long neck would be contrary to their way of life* (βίος) ... (692b19–693a6; emphasis added)

Eating flesh is an aspect of the way of life of the group of birds Aristotle elsewhere refers to as 'the crook-taloned [birds]' (τὰ γαμψώνυχα). This group of birds also has a type of *beak* that is correlated with talons, and this is because of their predatory way of life (693a10–13). By contrast, 'all birds whose way of life (βίος) is swamp-dwelling and plant-eating have a flat beak; for such a beak is useful both for digging up and cropping off their nourishment' (693a14–17). Again a single way of life is characterized in relation to a characteristic dwelling-place *and* a mode of nutrition typical of that environment.[22] The teleological/functional explanation for the flat beak is its usefulness for acquiring the kind of food these birds eat.[23] Reference to their specific way of life provides a more fundamental form of understanding: it explains why that is the kind of food these birds *must* be adapted to eating, and thus why they must have this specific sort of beak. Not all birds have *flat* beaks; not even all swamp-dwelling birds do, since for those who eat frogs and small fish a flat beak would not be useful. A full understanding of such a beak requires us to focus on the relationship between where these birds pass their time and what resources are available in that environment for nutrition.[24]

Among the features shared by all birds that are differentiated along more-and-less axes, Aristotle identifies a number as ἴδια of birds (feathers

---

[22] I'm using the word 'environment' here in the ecologist's sense, rather than the questionably 'absolutist' sense it has taken on in the popular literature. For a clear discussion see Andrewartha and Birch 1984, 3–18.

[23] To avoid making the point repeatedly: this passage appears in a treatise devoted to the explanation of animal parts, and thus it is parts, rather than activities, that are repeatedly related to ways of life in *PA*. But for Aristotle, terms for parts refer to *functional* parts, so I will assume throughout that explaining why a bird has a particular kind of beak implicitly explains the way the beak functions as well. For example, when referring to a flat beak, or bill, one is referring to a beak that does the sorts of things that bills do, not merely to a structure. That does not mean you have a full-blown teleological explanation of the part.

[24] This connection to nutrition, and the differences specified by terms that pick out a way of eating by reference to the source of nutrition (carnivorous, herbivorous) is highly reminiscent of the discussion of ways of life in *Politics* I.3 discussed on pp. 340–1, above.

(692b10), beaks (b15–16), and feathered wings (693a26)), and others as aspects of the being (οὐσία) of birds (being *blooded*, yet *winged* (693b5–7) and *able to fly* (693b12–13)). This conjunction of features identified as aspects of a bird's being further necessitates their peculiar form of bipedalism (693b5–14). For our purposes we will focus on what it is that is explained when Aristotle says that something is 'on account of an animal's way of life'. I shall argue that it is the *coordination* in an organism's functional anatomy, the fundamental fact that all the parts are structured so as to ensure that they perform as an integrated unity.[25]

It is here that *difference* in βίος becomes a central explanatory concept. Each form of bird has *each* of the kind's essential and distinctive parts differentiated for its own way of life, or βίος. This requires the biologist to take a certain perspective on the animal's functional activities. Each function must be viewed within the wider context of the animal's overall way of life. A hawk is essentially a carnivore that hunts by soaring at great heights; this means it must fly (i.e. its wings must function) in a way that fits the way of life of a bird that captures and kills prey of a certain kind; but doing that requires eyes that see very clearly at a great distance, a digestive system suited to raw flesh, hooked talons so that it can pick up the prey that it dives to capture, and so on. All of these parts and their activities will differ in degree (and *only* in degree) from those of other birds, and these differences in such a bird's activities and parts must be integrated into a single, functional unit. The structure of *each* part will be explained teleologically, as present for the sake of its particular function; but all of these 'structure/function complexes' must work together in a coordinated fashion if such a bird is to survive and flourish. The eyes, talons, hooked beak, strong, short neck, thick, streamlined wings, short tail feathers, and so on, must be organized in an *integrated* manner, since they typically work together in fulfilling the animal's needs. An example of this coordinating function of βίος can be seen in the following passage:

The beak differs according to the use to which it is put and the protection required. For all birds called crook-taloned have their beak hooked because they are carnivores and eat no seeds; such a beak is by nature useful for mastering prey and is

---

[25] Though due to space limitations the subject must be set aside, this leads to an intimate connection between division and explanation in Aristotle's biology (cf. *PA* I.5 645b1–3; Gotthelf 1987, 215–30 and 1997b, 215–29; Lennox 2001a, 175 and 2001b, 7–38).

more powerful. *But their strength lies both in this part and in their talons, which is why they also have their talons more curved. And in each of the other birds the beak is useful for its way of life* (βίος); for example, for the woodpeckers, crows and crow-like birds the beak is strong and hard, while for the small birds it is hollow for collecting seeds and grasping mites. (*PA* III.1 662a34–b9; emphasis added)

There is an equally important and quite distinct explanatory role for βίος. Take the explanation of the elephant's trunk, for example, an explanation mined for a related purpose by Allan Gotthelf.[26] The explanation for this most peculiar of all noses begins as follows:

This animal is by nature *at once a swamp-dweller and a land-dweller.* So, since on occasion it gets its nourishment from the water and, being a blooded land-dweller, must breathe, and on account of its size, is unable to make the transition from the moist to the dry environment as quickly as some of the live-bearing, blooded animals do, necessarily it uses the water as it does the land. (*PA* II.16 659a3–6; emphasis added)

The primary reason for the elephant having this strange nose is so that it can breathe air even when it is submerged in water; but why does it need to be able to do that? Because elephants are at once land-dwellers and swamp-dwellers: they pass their time in two different environments, a crucial fact about their βίος and one which plays a fundamental role in this explanation. Similarly, as David Charles notes in the discussion I referred to earlier, though the *term* βίος is not used in the chapter on the external parts of fish, we are told that 'it is on account of being swimmers that [fish] have fins and on account of not being land-dwellers that they do not have feet; for the addition of feet is useful in relation to movement on land' (695b20–22). Initially it is puzzling that Aristotle appeals to the fact that fish are swimmers to explain the presence of fins, but then switches to the negative fact that they are *not* land-dwellers to explain the absence of feet—but given his wide-ranging knowledge of the ways of life of animals it makes perfect sense. There are animals that swim quite well by means of legs, and these have no fins. Fish, however, do not have legs, because they are not land-dwellers; thus it is essential to fish (though not to all swimmers) that they have fins for swimming, since other options for swimming (legs with webbed feet, for example) are not available to them. Swimming is accom-

---

[26] Gotthelf 1997a.

plished by means of fins because fish are in essence water-dwellers rather than land-dwellers. It is the way of life that is fundamental to this explanation and accounts for the way they swim.

Aristotle insists that explanations by reference to way of life should also be forthcoming for internal parts, though in practice there are relatively few in *De partibus*:

Moreover, just as the use of the external parts is not the same for all animals, but has been provided in a particular way to each of them in relationship to their ways of life and movements, in the same way too the internal parts are by nature different in different animals. (*PA* III.4 665b1–5)

In fact not long after this passage, just such an explanation is used to account for differences in the organs for cooling in the blooded animals, the gills and the lungs. Gills and lungs serve the same function, cooling the region around the heart. They share, then, the same teleological explanation. Why, then, is cooling sometimes performed by lungs and sometimes by gills? Animals have a lung on account of being land-dwellers (διὰ τὸ πέζον εἶναι), that is, on account of their way of life. The cooling function must be performed in a way that fits with other aspects of an animal's life. And the connection made in *HA* VII, between an animal's way of life and its 'bodily blend', is here invoked to account for the surprising fact that some water-dwellers have lungs and breathe—they pass most of their time in water *on account of* the blend of their body (διὰ τὴν τοῦ σώματος κρᾶσιν), and are thus among those animals that tend toward being both a land-dweller and a water-dweller. Similarly, the *differences* among lungs are in part explained by reference to a combination of their material make-up and their way of life (669a24–b8). This discussion closes by suggesting that perhaps animals with lungs should be a γένος, a kind, for possession of a lung is in the substantial being of these animals (669b8–13).[27]

As Allan Gotthelf indicated many years ago in 'The Elephant's Nose', when one attempts to spell out a complete explanation for a part and its differentiations, one sees how remarkably complex and rich the explanations actually are. The way of life common to a kind allows one to see unity in this complexity, the principle around which all of the differences in the various organs designed for different contributions to different soul func-

---

[27] ... ἐν τῇ οὐσίᾳ ὑπάρχει τὸ πλεύμονα ἔχειν. (669b13)

tions are organized. Differences in the perceptual modalities, locomotive organs, digestive organs, modes of generating and raising young are integrated around the animal's way of life.

PA III.4 665b1–5, quoted above, indicates that Aristotle has a strong commitment to the idea that both the external and internal parts of animals 'have been provided in a particular way to each of them in relationship to their ways of life and movements'. An animal's βίος is occasionally identified as a fundamental feature of its *being*; and particular *divisions* of ways of life as general differentiae are likewise aspects of the essences of *forms* of those kinds.

From this brief look at the explanatory deployment of βίος in *PA* it seems clear why Aristotle concentrates on the differentiae water-dweller and land-dweller at the beginning of *HA* VII. These differences identify organisms by reference to the feature of the environment that most significantly impacts their other differences. This, in turn, allows us to account for some of the defining differences *between* kinds. Thus the specific *differentiations* of these general differences are not only crucial to understanding the differentiation of forms within kinds; ways of life are fundamental in differentiating the great kinds *from each other*. Some of the most puzzling combinations of differentiae found in animals, moreover, result from the fact that certain animals, such as dolphins, whales, and seals, are caught between different ways of life, often because of their nutritional needs. It is perhaps indicative of the place of βίος in *De partibus animalium* that this work concludes with a discussion of the many features of 'the dolphins, whales and all such cetacea' that differ from the fish. 'They are', Aristotle concludes, 'in one way land-dwellers and in another way water-dwellers; for they take in air as do land-dwellers but they are footless and seize their nourishment from a moist environment just as water-dwellers do' (697a28–30). This leads him to comment on other animals that partake of more than one way of life— seals, bats, and the Libyan ostrich (697b1–27).

VI *Βίος*, Explanation, and Unity

It is now time to return to the discussion of the *unity* of definition and explanation with the results of our exploration of βίος in hand (cf. pp. 330–5,

above). Given the importance of the concept of βίος in both the organization of biological information in *HA* and its explanation in *PA*, one would
expect that, in his philosophical introduction to the study of animals, *De
partibus animalium* I, a significant amount of time would be spent discussing
this concept and arguing for its centrality in a scientific study of animals.
Such expectations are not fulfilled. Recall the passage near the end of *PA* I
that David Charles rightly recognized as indicating Aristotle's concern about
explanatory unity in biology.

Since every instrument is for the sake of something, and each of the parts of the
body is for the sake of a certain activity, it is apparent that *the entire body too has been
constituted for the sake of a certain complete activity.* For sawing is not for the sake of the
saw, but the saw for the sake of sawing; for sawing is a certain use. So *the body too is
in a way for the sake of the soul*, and the parts are for the sake of the functions in
relation to which each of them has naturally developed. (645b15–20; emphasis
added)

By comparing the two italicized phrases above, the reader would appear
licensed in the substitution of 'soul' for 'certain complete activity', each as
that which the animal's body is for. Moreover, the resulting teleological
unity of matter and form can be understood at any level of generality, a
point stressed when, just prior to this passage, Aristotle extends the
account of levels of likeness, developed in chapter 4 for parts, to activities.
It is worth stressing, however, Aristotle's tentative mode of expression in
this passage. The body is for the sake of 'a certain (τινός) complete
activity' and 'in a way (πῶς) for the sake of soul'. He does not elaborate
at all on this point, and his tentativeness suggests that he is not here
prepared to do so.

   If one is tempted to substitute βίος for 'a certain complete activity' here,
then, one should resist that temptation. The aforementioned substitution of
'soul' for 'complete activity' in this passage and the fact that the explanatory
pattern adumbrated is teleological speak strongly against it. In virtually all
passages in which an animal's way of life plays an explanatory role, it is
explanation of the type said to be best at 640a33–34: 'since this is what it is to
be X, on account of (διὰ) this it has these things'. The way of life of the
'crook-taloned birds' demands an integrated set of features functioning in an
integrated way: if a hawk had all its other features, but lacked the crook

talons to grasp its prey, it would not be able to live the life of a hawk. That is what it is to be a hawk.[28]

Aristotle closes the first book of *De partibus animalium*, his philosophical introduction to the study of animals, with a brief sketch of how teleological explanations are to be prioritized:

So it is clear, then, that whenever there are activities that are for the sake of other activities, the things whose activities they are differ in the same way that their activities do. Similarly, if some activities are in fact prior to, and the end of, others, it will be the same way with each of the parts whose activities are of this sort. And thirdly, there are things that are necessarily present because others are. (645b28–33)

Here we are provided with a picture of a complex web of explanatory priorities among an animal's parts and activities, following the earlier and tentative expression of the idea of a similar explanatory relationship between the whole body and the soul.

What explanatory role does βίος play in Aristotle's biology that is not captured in this discussion? I have argued that it accounts for the unity that *integrates* the many parts of an animal's body and the many different activities those parts perform. That understanding comes from the recognition that an animal's functional parts *must* make *coordinated* contributions to a single way of life.

The teleological relationship between body and soul abstractly sketched in the second half of *PA* I.5 is *not* the integration accomplished by means of the concept of βίος.[29] The way of life of an animal demands a coordination

---

[28] This is, then, an appeal to the essence of being a form of crook-taloned bird. I resist referring to this as a 'formal cause explanation' because of Aristotle's insistence that the form of a living thing is its soul. While there is a complex and interesting connection between an animal's way of life and its soul-capacities, they are not to be identified.

[29] In *PA* IV.12 there are two passages that might be thought to suggest that way of life explains teleologically, as a goal, but neither of them is definitive. The first asserts of the wings of flesh-eating birds that 'it is a necessity for them to be able to fly [well] on account of their way of life, so for the sake of (ἕνεκα) this they have both many feathers and large wings' (694a1–3). But here I take it that it is *for the sake of flying well* that they have many feathers and large wings, while it is on account of their βίος that they must fly well. Here then, the only teleological explanation runs from flying well to feathers and large wings, while their way of life necessitates their flying well. The second asserts, of webbing in the feet of water fowl, that it happens both on account of various material necessities and 'it is *on account of* the better (διὰ τὸ βέλτιον) that waterfowl have such feet, *for the sake of* (χάριν) their way of life—*in order that* (ἵνα) since they live in water where wings are useless, they will have feet that are useful for swimming' (694b6–9). This is a vexed passage in many respects, raising questions about explanations that appeal jointly to the necessary and the better *and* about explanations that are 'layered' in the way that this one is: 'G has p *on account of* the better, *for the sake of* X, *in order that* Z.' I stress the need for caution here. Aristotle tends to

of the many 'structure/function complexes' that make up the animal. Without that coordination, as Georges Cuvier and Richard Owen so well understood, you do not have an organism, i.e. a living unity. There is a good reason why both of them had boundless admiration for Aristotle.[30]

It is an outstanding puzzle why, given its importance at both the level of data organization and the level of explanation, Aristotle does not discuss the concept of βίος in PA I. Its absence may provide support for David Balme's thought that the HA that has come down to us looks toward a more complex explanatory biology than we see in our PA.[31] For this passage certainly calls out for the invocation of βίος as the explanatory ground for the coordinated unity of structure and function that is so characteristic of Aristotle's study of animals.

VII Conclusion

In this essay I have argued that the concept of βίος plays two fundamental roles in Aristotle's biology. The first role is that of a fundamental category of differentia, one of four around which the entire *Historia animalium* is organized. The discussion of differences in ways of life in HA I, VII–VIII, and of their relationship to differences in activities (πράξεις) and traits of character (ἤθη) provided evidence of the way in which an animal's way of life demands a coordination of its many activities and the parts that perform them. Ways of life are typically identified by terms that relate the animal's life to its environment: water-dweller, flesh-eater, nomadic (i.e. one that

use χάριν in a much more flexible manner than he does ἕνεκα, often when he wishes to avoid the implication of a causal relationship; moreover, it is reasonable to take this passage to be saying that since the way of life of waterfowl is aquatic, it is better that they have feet that are useful for swimming. That is, the actual teleological explanation, spelled out in the ἵνα clause and against the background of the fact that waterfowl are water-dwellers as well as flyers, is from swimming to webbed feet. I thank Devin Henry and David Charles for pressing me for further discussion of these passages.

[30] Richard Owen, in his Hunterian Lectures on Comparative Anatomy, for example, wrote: 'Zoological Science sprang from his [Aristotle's] labours, we may almost say, like Minerva from the Head of Jove, in a state of noble and splendid maturity' (Sloan 1992, 91). On the same page Owen quotes some typical praise for Aristotle from Cuvier.

[31] Compare his discussion of the project sketched in PA I.5 and its relationship to the analysis of differentiae in HA on the final page of 'The Place of Biology in Aristotle's Philosophy' (Balme 1987a, 20), with the discussion of the same relationship in 'Aristotle's Use of Division and Differentiae' (Balme 1987b, 80) both in Gotthelf and Lennox 1987.

regularly changes dwelling-place). Consistently, kinds of animals are said to have one way of life around which their activities related to nutrition and reproduction are organized. The 'dualizers', those unusual creatures that are caught between two ways of life, are the exceptions that prove the rule.

The second fundamental role played by βίος is explanatory. An animal's way of life accounts for the sort of unity of its parts and activities that David Charles, in *Aristotle on Meaning and Essence*, feared might be absent in the realm of animals and threaten the applicability of the *Analytics* model of essence-based explanation to biology. Ways of life do not provide a *teleological* account of that unity, however. *PA* I.5 spells out a complex web of teleological relationships that may be found among parts and their activities, examples of which populate the remainder of that work. But the way in which the parts function in a coordinated manner is consistently said to be due to (or on account of, διά) an animal's way of life. The unexplained explainers in this case are not basic ends, but the way of life around which any organic system of functional parts and goal-directed activities is organized and to which they are tuned.

That Aristotle does not believe that ways of life are reducible to a collection of activities is clear. I hope I have also made clear *why* he does not: the way of life of an animal demands that there be coordination among its parts and activities. It is that coordination around the animal's way of life that accounts for such things as the convertible relationship between crooked talons and hooked beaks, fins and gills, long necks and long legs. It is by grasping an animal's way of life that we grasp the underlying unity in organic complexity.

Consider a concept that is in many ways analogous, the concept of a career. A social scientist with reductionist tendencies may be inclined to say a career is exhaustively characterized by a complete list of the activities in which it consists. An Aristotelian social scientist will disagree. A career in, say, finance or film, requires that many, many goal-directed activities be carried on in an integrated and coordinated manner over the full length of a person's working life. One will fail to grasp the unity in all those activities until you first understand the nature of the career—the concept of 'career' has both conceptual and explanatory priority over the activities that constitute it. So it is with a way of life.

I shall end with two puzzles. To the first I have already alluded, the complete lack of any discussion of 'way of life' in the philosophical preamble to Aristotle's animal studies, *PA* I. It is especially surprising that its last chapter, which presents a stirring integration of his previous discussions of explanation and division, is silent on the concept. Without much conviction, I noted that if indeed David Balme is correct that the *HA* is actually composed late in Aristotle's life, and looks forward to a significant revision of his explanatory enterprise, the concept of βίος might have played as central a role in that revision as it does in the organization of *HA*.

The second puzzle is of a very different nature. I noted passages from the *Historian animalium*, *De partibus animalium*, and *Politics*, all pointing to a dependence of an animal's way of life on the sort of food it is by nature suited to eat. This dependence points to something that may in the end stand to an animal's way of life as I am claiming an animal's way of life stands to its many activities, namely the relationship between its 'bodily blend' and the kind of food it is inclined to eat. These connections are rarely mentioned and never explored in detail in the texts we have, though Aristotle makes occasional references to a work περὶ τροφῆς where they may have been.[32] Whatever connection Aristotle might have seen between differences in diet and ways of life, it would not, as far as I can see, affect the relationship between way of life and activities that I've been discussing here.

Bibliography

Andrewartha, H. G., and Birch, L. C. 1984. *The Ecological Web*, Chicago.

Balme, D. M. 1987a. 'The Place of Biology in Aristotle's Philosophy', in Gotthelf and Lennox (eds.), 9–20.

——1987b. 'Aristotle's Use of Division and Differentiae', in Gotthelf and Lennox (eds.), 69–89.

——1991. *Aristotle: History of Animals: Books VII–X* (text and translation, prepared for publication by Allan Gotthelf), Cambridge, MA.

——2002. *Aristotle: Historia Animalium*, vol. 1: *Books I–X: Text* (prepared for publication by Allan Gotthelf), Cambridge.

Bolton, R. 1987. 'Definition and Scientific Method in Aristotle's *Posterior Analytics* and *Generation of Animals*', in Gotthelf and Lennox (eds.), 120–66.

Charles, D. 2000. *Aristotle on Meaning and Essence*, Oxford.

---

[32] e.g. *De an.* II.4 416b31; *PA* II.3 650b10; *GA* V.4 784b2; *De som.* 3 456b5.

Detel, W. 1997. 'Why All Animals Have a Stomach. Demonstration and Axiomat-
ization in Aristotle's Parts of Animals', in Kullman and Föllinger (eds.), 63–84.

Devereux, D., and Pellegrin, P. (eds.) 1990. *Biologie, Logique et Métaphysique chez
Aristote*, Paris.

Düring, I. 1943. *Aristotle's De Partibus Animalium: Critical and Literary Commentaries*,
Göteborg.

Föllinger, S. (ed.) forthcoming. *What is 'Life'? Aristotle on 'Life' and its Functions*,
Philosophie der Antike (W. Kullmann, series editor).

Fortenbaugh, W. W., and Sharples, R. W. (eds.) 1988. *Theophrastean Studies*, vol. 3,
New Brunswick, NJ.

Gotthelf, A. (ed.) 1985a. *Aristotle on Nature and Living Things: Philosophical and
Historical Studies*, Pittsburgh and Bristol.

—— 1985b. 'Notes towards a Study of Substance and Essence in Aristotle's *Parts of
Animals* ii–iv', in Gotthelf (ed.), 27–54.

—— 1987. 'First Principles in Aristotle's *Parts of Animals*', in Gotthelf and Lennox
(eds.), 167–98.

—— 1988. 'Historiae I: Plantarum et Animalium', in Fortenbaugh and Sharples
(eds.), 100–35.

—— 1997a. 'The Elephant's Nose', in Kullmann and Föllinger (eds.), 85–96.

—— 1997b. 'Division and Explanation in Aristotle's Parts of Animals', in Günther
and Rengakos (eds.), 215–30.

Gotthelf, A., and Lennox, J. G. (eds.) 1987. *Philosophical Issues in Aristotle's Biology*,
Cambridge.

Günther, H.-C., and Rengakos, A. (eds.) 1997. *Beiträge zur antiken Philosophie.
Festschrift für Wolfgang Kullmann*, Stuttgart.

Kullmann, W. 1974. *Wissenschaft und Methode: Interpretationen zur aristotelischen
Theorie der Naturwissenschaft*, Berlin.

Kullmann, W., and Föllinger, S. (eds.) 1997. *Aristotelische Biologie: Intentionen,
Methoden, Ergebnisse*, Stuttgart.

Lennox, J. G. 1987. 'Divide and Explain: The *Posterior Analytics* in Practice', in
Gotthelf and Lennox, 90–119 (reprinted in Lennox 2001b, 7–38).

——1990. 'Notes on David Charles on *HA*', in Devereux and Pellegrin (eds.),
169–84.

——1991. 'Between Data and Demonstration: The *Analytics* and the *Historia
Animalium*', in *Science and Philosophy in Classical Greece*, ed. Alan Bowen,
New York, 261–94 (reprinted in Lennox 2001b, 39–71).

——1996. 'Aristotle's Biological Development: The Balme Hypothesis', in Wians
(ed.), 229–48.

—— 2001a. *Aristotle: On the Parts of Animals* (translation with commentary), Oxford.

—— 2001b. *Aristotle's Philosophy of Biology: Essays on the Origins of Life Science*, Cambridge.

Lloyd, G. E. R. 1990. 'Aristotle's Zoology and his Metaphysics. The Status Questionis. A Critical Review of some Recent Theories', in Devereux and Pellegrin (eds.), 7–36.

—— 1996. *Aristotelian Explorations*, Cambridge.

Peck, A. L. 1945. *Aristotle: Parts of Animals* (text and translation), Cambridge, MA.

Pellegrin, P. P. 1986. *Aristotle's Classification of Animals*, Berkeley.

—— 1987. 'Logical Difference and Biological Difference: The Unity of Aristotle's Thought', in Gotthelf and Lennox (eds.), 313–38.

Sloan, P. 1992. *Richard Owen: The Hunterian Lectures in Comparative Anatomy*, Chicago.

Wians, W. (ed.) 1996. *Aristotle's Philosophical Development: Problems and Prospects*, Lanham, MD.

PART III
Post-Aristotelian Writers on Definition

10

The Stoics on Definitions

PAOLO CRIVELLI

The present study is a reconstruction of the Stoic theory of definition. The topic is vast and the sources are scarce. My focus is on the epistemological and semantic aspects of the Stoic theory of definition.

The study's first section explains how important definitions were for the Stoics. The second section expounds the different locations of the study of definitions within the Stoic system of philosophical disciplines. The third section discusses the epistemological side of the theory of definitions on which one of these locations relies. In particular, it addresses two roles played by definitions: sharpening our conceptions in such a way that they are more successfully applied to or withheld from entities, and endowing our conceptions with a systematic structure that makes them suitable for instruction. The fourth section discusses the link between definition and essence: it argues that the Stoics do not think that definitions reveal the essence of what is defined. The fifth section discusses the position of definitions within Stoic philosophy of language: definitions are not linguistic expressions, but sayables of a special kind (distinct from statables).*

* Many friends and colleagues helped me to shape my views on many of the issues addressed by this study, and alerted me to points where improvement was needed. Early drafts of parts of the study were presented in Oxford and Pisa: I am grateful to the audiences for their insightful criticisms. I owe a special debt of gratitude to David Charles, who offered extensive written comments on the penultimate version. The responsibility for the remaining shortcomings is of course only mine.

I The Importance of the Study of Definitions for the Stoics

Definitions in the Stoics' Philosophical Practice   In antiquity the Stoics were famous for their use of definitions.[1] Within the Stoa, the ability at framing definitions was considered a mark of distinction: Cicero reports that the Stoics regarded Sphaerus as 'extremely good at framing definitions' (*Tusc.* 4.24,53), and Diogenes Laertius (7.32) records that Zeno's earliest philosophical exploit on his arrival in Athens as a young man was to define the end. The discovery of definitions was a school-enterprise in which different individuals made contributions.[2]

That the Stoics attributed importance to definitions is clear by their philosophical practice. For instance, the account of Stoic ethics in Stobaeus, after an introductory classification (whereby beings are divided into those which are good, bad, and indifferent, good beings are divided into those which are virtues and those which are not, and bad beings are divided into those which are vices and those which are not),[3] shoots a salvo of ten definitions of the four primary virtues and the four primary vices (one primary virtue and one primary vice are defined twice) followed by a definition of virtue in general.[4] Immediately afterwards, the distinction is drawn between primary and subordinate virtues, whereupon nineteen definitions of the subordinate virtues are offered.[5] This sums up to thirty definitions within a portion of text that could be printed on two pages of an ordinary modern book.

Collections of Definitions   The titles of lost works of Stoic philosophers provide a further indication of the importance attributed by the Stoics to definitions.

Many Stoic treatises were about definitions. Some were collections of definitions. Some such collections were about logic: Chrysippus is said to have written one work of *Dialectical Definitions* (to Metrodorus, in six

---

[1] D.L. 8.48; Cic. *Tusc.* 4.5, 11; Hippol. *Haer.* 1.21,1; Front. *ad Ant.* 146 Naber (cf. Ph. *Aet. Mund.* 52).

[2] S.E. *M.* 7.227–41; Stob. *Ed.* 2.7, 6ᵃ (2. 75, 11–76, 15 W.); Olymp. *in Gorg.* 12.1; Simp. *in Cat.* 350, 15–16.

[3] Stob. *Ed.* 2.7, 5ᵇ (2. 58, 5–59, 3 W.).

[4] Stob. *Ed.* 2.7, 5ᵇ ¹ (2. 59, 4–60, 5 W.).

[5] Stob. *Ed.* 2.7, 5ᵇ ² (2. 60, 9–62, 6 W.).

books).[6] Others focused on ethics: Chrysippus reportedly authored three works of *Definitions of the Good*, *Definitions of the Bad*, and *Definitions of the Intermediate* (each dedicated to Metrodorus and in two books) (the definitions of virtues and vices mentioned in the preceding subsection might stem from the first two of these works).[7] Were the catalogue of Chrysippus' works not mutilated, we would probably have titles of collections of definitions concerning physics.

Contributions to the Theory of Definition   Other Stoic treatises concerning definitions appear to have been contributions to the theory of definition. Sphaerus is reported to have written one work *On Definitions*.[8] Chrysippus is credited with one work *On Definitions* (to Metrodorus, in seven books),[9] one *On Incorrect Objections to Definitions* (to Laodamas, in seven books),[10] and one of *Plausible Views for Definitions* (to Gorgippides, in two books—the position of this treatise within the catalogue of Chrysippus' works suggests that it was a contribution to the theory of definition: either an examination of plausible views about definitions, or a study of how plausible views can contribute to framing definitions).[11] Antipater seems to have authored one work *On Definitions* (in more than one book).[12]

Other Stoic treatises concerned issues closely connected with the theory of definition. Cleanthes is said to have authored a work *On Peculiarities*.[13] Sphaerus reportedly wrote one work *On Similarities*.[14] Chrysippus is credited with one work *On Similarities* (to Aristocles, in three books), one *On Species and Genera* (to Gorgippides, in two books), one *On Divisions* (in one book), one *On Contraries* (to Dionysius, in two books), and one on *Plausible Views relating to Divisions and Genera and Species and what concerns Contraries* (in one book).[15]

---

[6] D.L. 7.65; 71 (where, following Gigante (1982), 269 and 536, I read '*ἐν τοῖς Διαλεκτικοῖς* <*ὅροις*>'); 189. Gal. *Diff. Puls.* 8.578, 18–579, 3 K. probably refers to Chrysippus' *Dialectical Definitions*.

[7] D.L. 7.199.

[8] D.L. 7.178.

[9] D.L. 7.60; 199; [Plu.] *Plac.* 885B (323ᵃ11 Diels); Stob. *Ecl.* 1.5,15 (1. 79, 3 W.) (*v.l.*).

[10] D.L. 7.199.

[11] D.L. 7.200.

[12] D.L. 7.60.

[13] D.L. 7.175.

[14] D.L. 7.178.

[15] D.L. 7.199–200.

Diogenes Laertius registers two further titles of works by Chrysippus which must have been concerned with definitions: *Definitions of Things Determined according to the Genus* (to Metrodorus, in seven books)[16] and *Definitions of Things corresponding to Other Arts* (to Metrodorus, in two books).[17] It remains unclear what these works were about—even the translation of their titles is dubious. In particular, one cannot tell whether they were collections of ethical definitions (as their position within the catalogue suggests) or contributions to the theory of definition.

II Definitions within the Stoic System of Philosophical Disciplines

The Tripartition of Philosophical Disciplines   The Stoics hesitate about the location of the study of definitions within their system of philosophical disciplines. Let me first say something about this system. Diogenes Laertius reports:

T 1   They [sc. the Stoics] say that philosophical discourse is tripartite [τριμερῆ εἶναι τὸν κατὰ φιλοσοφίαν λόγον]: some of it is physical, some ethical, and some logical. (7. 39)[18]

Diogenes Laertius reports the Stoic view by using the sentence 'Philosophical discourse is tripartite', which may be found also in other sources.[19] For the Stoics this sentence was not a mere stylistic variant of 'Philosophy is

---

[16] D.L. 7. 199. The text of this title is dubious: two of the main MSS (B and P, followed by H.S. Long) have 'ὅρων τῶν πρὸς Μητρόδωρον κατὰ γένος'; the third main MS (F) skips to a title further down the list ('περὶ τῶν ὅρων πρὸς Μητρόδωρον'); von Arnim emends to 'ὅρων τῶν πρὸς Μητρόδωρον <τῶν> κατὰ γένος'; Hicks and Marcovich (whom I have followed in my translation above) have 'ὅρων τῶν κατὰ γένος πρὸς Μητρόδωρον'. One passage (Stob. *Ecl.* 2.7, 9 (2. 86, 19–87, 2 W.)) makes it plausible to suggest that 'definitions according to the genus' are definitions 'from the top down' that specify a genus by means of a differentia, and are contrasted with 'definitions according to the species', which are 'from the bottom up' and amount to disjunctions of the species of what is defined.

[17] D.L. 7. 199. This title is omitted by F.

[18] Diogenes Laertius goes on to say that 'Zeno of Citium was the first to divide in this way' (7. 39). He probably means that Zeno was *the first Stoic* to divide in this way: for Zeno's teacher Xenocrates (cf. below. n.89) is reported to have divided philosophy into physics, ethics, and logic (see S.E. *M.* 7.16 and Cic. *Ac.* 1.5,19 with Hadot (1979), 206). Recall that Aristotle in the *Topics* (1.14, 105ᵇ19–21) distinguishes three kinds of propositions and problems: ethical, physical, and logical. Some late sources (Atticus *apud* Eus. *PE* 11.1, 1; 11.2, 1; August. *C.D.* 8.4) credit Plato himself with a tripartition of this sort, but they are probably influenced by Stoicism (cf. Hadot (1979), 211–12).

[19] Ph. *Agr.* 14; Stob. *Ecl.* 2.7,2 (2. 42, 7–13 W.).

tripartite': for Diogenes Laertius reports that some Stoics, among them Zeno of Tarsus (Chrysippus' successor at the lead of the school), dissented from the mainstream position by saying that 'these [*sc.* the parts under discussion] are not parts of discourse, but of philosophy itself' (7.41). What did most Stoics mean when they used the sentence 'Philosophical discourse is tripartite'?

One answer[20] to this question relies on the assumption that the Stoics used 'philosophical discourse' to refer to the presentation of philosophical matters in teaching. The Stoic position would then have been that while no statable pertaining to philosophy could be assigned to a single part of the discipline, because it belongs to other parts as well, the teaching of the discipline must follow a certain tripartite order.

A different answer[21] relies on the assumption that the Stoics used the expression 'philosophy' in a way different from ours. A clue for reconstructing the Stoic use comes from a startling testimony by Sextus Empiricus:

T2 The true is said to differ from truth [διαφέρειν τῆς ἀληθείας τὸ ἀληθές] [. . .] in substance because the true is incorporeal (for it is a statable and a sayable)[22] while truth is a body (for it is knowledge assertive of all that is true, and knowledge is the dominating part of the soul in a certain condition, just as a fist is the hand in a certain condition, and the dominating part of the soul is a body, for according to them it is breath). (*P.* 2.81)[23]

The Stoics therefore hold that truth is knowledge, which is the dominating part of the soul in a certain condition. In PHerc 1020 (an early Stoic text often attributed to Chrysippus)[24] we encounter three characterizations of philosophy:

---

[20] Cf. Hadot (1979), 215.

[21] Cf. Ierodiakonou (1993), 58–61.

[22] 'Sayable' and 'statable' translate, respectively, 'λεκτόν' and 'ἀξίωμα'.

[23] Cf. *M.* 7.38–45; [Gal.] *Hist. Philos.* 13 (606, 12–17 Diels); Stob. *Ed.* 1.5,15 (1. 79, 5–12 W.). Truth (ἀλήθεια) is not the quality responsible for something's being true (ἀληθὲς εἶναι): in that case it ought to be a quality of a statable (because it is statables that are true), and therefore could not be a body. Rather, truth (ἀλήθεια) is the quality responsible for someone's being truthful (ἀληθεύειν): since only the wise are truthful (S.E. *M.* 7.432), being truthful does not coincide with saying something true (also fools sometimes say something true, S.E. *M.* 7.42), but is a much more robust and rare condition. Note however that the Stoics occasionally use 'ἀληθεύειν' to mean 'to say something true' (S.E. *M.* 8.73). Recall that according to Stoic orthodoxy qualities are breath and the dominating part of the soul is also breath, so that for a Stoic it is perfectly reasonable to say that the quality truth is the dominating part of the soul in a certain condition.

[24] Cf. Baldassarri (1984–7), II 42.

T 3 Philosophy is either care for the correctness of discourse,[25] or knowledge [sc. of the correctness of discourse], or study mainly of discourse [ἔστιν ἡ φιλοσοφία, εἴτ᾽ ἐπιτήδευσις λόγου ὀρθότητος εἴτ᾽ ἐπιστήμη ἢ μάλιστα περὶ λόγον πραγματεία]. (PHerc 1020 col. In [=OxMa] 12–17)[26]

The second of T 3's characterizations of philosophy describes it as know-ledge of a certain sort. Given their view that knowledge is the dominating part of the soul in a certain condition, the Stoics are probably committed to the claim that philosophy, at least according to one acceptable conception of it, is the dominating part of the soul in a certain condition. Perhaps, as they applied 'truth' and 'true' (respectively) to the dominating part of the soul in a certain condition and certain statables, so they applied 'philosophy' and 'philosophical discourse' (respectively) to the dominating part of the soul in a certain condition and a certain system of statables. Given such a usage, the claim which we would make with the words 'Philosophy is tripartite' would have been made by a Stoic with the words 'Philosophical discourse is tripartite'. Some of our sources report the Stoic position by using a sentence like 'Philosophy is tripartite':[27] they are probably using 'philosophy' not in the Stoic sense, but in their own.

The Location of the Study of Definitions In the seventh book of his *Lives and Opinions of Eminent Philosophers* Diogenes Laertius offers two accounts of Stoic logic: in the first (7.41–8) he expounds Stoic logic 'summarily [κεφαλαιωδῶς]' (7.48), in the second (7.49–83) he does this 'in detail [κατὰ μέρος]' (7.48). The passage that constitutes the beginning of Diogenes Laertius' first account of Stoic logic shows that the Stoics hesitated about the location of the study of definitions within their system of philosophical disciplines:

T 4 And some say that the logical part [sc. of philosophical discourse] divides into two sciences, into rhetoric and dialectic [τὸ δὲ λογικὸν μέρος φασὶν ἔνιοι εἰς δύο διαιρεῖσθαι ἐπιστήμας, εἰς ῥητορικὴν καὶ εἰς διαλεκτικήν]. But some say it divides also into the definitional species, that concerning yardsticks and criteria [τινὲς δὲ καὶ εἰς τὸ ὁρικὸν εἶδος, τὸ περὶ κανόνων καὶ κριτηρίων]. Some however eliminate the definitional part [ἔνιοι δὲ τὸ ὁρικὸν περιαιροῦσιν].

---

[25] Cf. Isidor. Pelus. *Epist.* v 558 (PG 78 col. 1637); Clem. Al. *Paed.* 1.13, 101,2.
[26] I am following the text in *FDS* I 88.
[27] S.E. *P.* 2.13; *M.* 7.16; D.L. 7.84.

They adopt the part concerning yardsticks and criteria for the sake of discovering truth: for here they adjust the differences between presentations [τὸ περὶ κανόνων καὶ κριτηρίων παραλαμβάνουσι πρὸς τὸ τὴν ἀλήθειαν εὑρεῖν· ἐν αὐτῷ γὰρ τὰς τῶν φαντασιῶν διαφορὰς ἀπευθύνουσι]. Similarly, they adopt also the definitional part for the sake of the discernment of truth: for things are grasped through conceptions [καὶ τὸ ὁρικὸν δὲ ὁμοίως πρὸς ἐπίγνωσιν τῆς ἀληθείας·[28] διὰ γὰρ τῶν ἐννοιῶν τὰ πράγματα λαμβάνεται].[29] (7.41–2)

T 4 poses a philological problem. In its second sentence the reading 'τὸ περὶ κανόνων', handed down by the MSS, presupposes that the definitional species should encompass or coincide with the study of yardsticks and criteria. This is problematic for two reasons. Firstly, T 4's second half seems to discuss the definitional part and that concerning yardsticks and criteria as if they were distinct. Secondly, T 4's third sentence goes on to say that some Stoics 'eliminate the definitional part'. Wouldn't these Stoics then be upholding the same position as those mentioned in the first sentence? In view of these problems, some commentators suspect a lacuna;[30] others instead adopt an emendation, either Usener's 'τό <τε> περὶ κανόνων' or Apelt's '<καὶ> τὸ περὶ κανόνων'.[31]

However, the text of the MSS (preserved by Hicks, H.S.Long, and Hülser) can be defended. The first difficulty can be solved by assuming that T 4's second half explains why the study of yardsticks and criteria is a subsection of a section of the logical part that is called 'definitional'. It is because the study of yardsticks and criteria is grouped together with that of definitions (a grouping justified by the fact that yardsticks and criteria as well as definitions contribute to the discovery of truth), and the whole section encompassing these two disciplines as subsections derives its name 'definitional' from the second. This solution presupposes that the Stoics used 'definitional' both for the study of definitions and for the discipline that encompasses both the study of yardsticks and criteria and that of definitions. Such a double use of a single expression within the same division has parallels within Stoic philosophy.[32]

---

[28] For the phrase 'ἐπίγνωσις τῆς ἀληθείας' cf. Epict. Diss. 2.20,21; S.E. M. 7.259.

[29] I translate 'ἔννοια' by 'conception' in order to preserve the contrast with 'ἐννόημα' ('concept').

[30] Rieth (1933), 40.

[31] Usener's emendation is adopted by Baldassarri (1984–7), III 16; Long and Sedley (1987), II 186; and Marcovich (1999–2002).

[32] Cf. below, n.69 and text thereto.

As for the second difficulty, T4 could be reporting the historical development of the Stoic views about the division of the logical part of philosophical discourse. I shall now attempt to reconstruct this development.

Originally the logical part was divided into two sciences, namely dialectic and rhetoric. Zeno himself favoured this division.[33]

With regard to Cleanthes we have two apparently conflicting reports. On the one hand, he is said to have divided the philosophical disciplines into six parts: the dialectical, the rhetorical, the ethical, the political, the physical, and the theological.[34] According to this report, Cleanthes' position was different from that of Zeno: Cleanthes did not recognize a single logical part, whereas Zeno did.[35] On the other hand, we are told that Zeno and Cleanthes 'divided both the logical and the physical part' (D.L. 7.84). This report suggests that Cleanthes shared Zeno's view that there is a single logical part that comprises dialectic and rhetoric. The most plausible solution to this conflict consists in abandoning its second horn. In other words, we may assume that although both Zeno and Cleanthes 'divided both the logical and the physical part' (D.L. 7.84), they did this in different ways: Zeno carried out his division in such a way as to leave single overarching parts comprehensive of their subdivisions (i.e. a single logical part covering dialectic and rhetoric, and a single physical part comprehending physics in a narrow sense and theology), whereas Cleanthes carried out his divisions in such a way as to eliminate single overarching parts comprehensive of the subdivisions. Despite the elimination of a single overarching logical part, Cleanthes' position was close to that of his teacher: for the subdivisions which Cleanthes introduced while eliminating the single overarching logical part were the same as those introduced by Zeno while retaining the single overarching logical part.[36]

After Zeno and Cleanthes, someone proposed a tripartition of the logical part into dialectic, rhetoric, and the study of definitions. The author of this innovation called these three subdivisions 'species'. According to Diogenes Laertius (7.39), Chrysippus and Eudromus used 'species' for the three main

[33] Cic. *Fin.* 2.6, 17 (cf. D.L. 7.84). Zeno is reported to have contrasted rhetoric with dialectic by comparing them, respectively, with an open hand and a fist (see Cic. *Orat.* 32, 113; *Fin.* 2.6, 17; S.E. *M.* 2.7; Quint. *Inst.* 2.20, 7). Zeno was perhaps following the lead of his teacher Xenocrates (see S.E. *M.* 2. 6–7).

[34] D.L. 7.41.

[35] Cf. above, n. 18 and text thereto.

[36] Cf. Pearson (1891), 236; *SVF* I 108; Hülser (1979), 285.

parts of philosophical discourse. Therefore the Stoic who proposed the tripartition of the logical part into dialectic, rhetoric, and the study of definitions was probably either Chrysippus or Eudromus. We know very little about Eudromus: Diogenes Laertius reports that he authored a text of *Elements of Ethics* where he endorsed the traditional division of philosophical discourse into three main parts (7.39), that he called these three main parts 'species' (7.39), and that he recommended that they should be taught in the succession logic–physics–ethics (7.40). It is unlikely that such a minor author focusing on ethics introduced an important novelty in the division of the logical part. We may therefore plausibly identify Chrysippus with the Stoic who proposed the tripartition of the logical part into dialectic, rhetoric, and a definitional part.[37]

Finally, after Chrysippus, some Stoics 'eliminate the definitional part'. This can mean either that they gave up completely the study of definitions, or that they abolished the study of definitions as one of the main parts of logic. In view of the importance attributed by the Stoics to definitions,[38] the first alternative is unlikely. Given that the Stoics in question abolished the study of definitions as one of the main parts of logic, what did they do with it? Did they subsume it under one or more other parts of logic, or did they transfer it to some discipline other than logic?

The Study of Definitions as Ancillary to Ethics The mutilated catalogue of Chrysippus' works handed down by Diogenes Laertius (7.189–202) is clearly structured. Each main section divides into several large 'areas' ('τόποι'), to which titles are attached. Each 'area' divides into numbered but untitled 'collections' ('συντάξεις'). Each 'collection' lists a small number of works (at most 13).

The works concerning definitions are listed not in the logical but in the ethical section. Specifically, they are listed in the second and the third 'collection' of the 'area' entitled 'Ethical area[39] dealing with the articulation of ethical conceptions' (7.199–200). So, according to the catalogue of Chrysippus' works, the study of definitions not only does not constitute one of the

---

[37] Cf. Gourinat (2000), 56.
[38] Cf. section 1.
[39] Reading 'ἠθικοῦ τόπου' ('ethical area') instead of the 'ἠθικοῦ λόγου' ('ethical discourse') (7.199) handed down by the main MSS and printed by some editors.

main divisions of the logical part, but does not even fall within the logical part: it belongs to ethics because it contributes to articulate ethical conceptions.

There are reasons for thinking that Chrysippus is not the author of the catalogue of his own writings. To be sure, some ancient authors (Galen, for example) did compile catalogues of their own works. However, in the catalogue of Chrysippus' writings three works are described as spurious (7.195–6), one as apparently such (7.195). One can just swallow the hypothesis that Chrysippus included in the catalogue of his own writings works which he regarded as spurious and described as such, but it is incredible that he would have described one work as 'appearing to be spurious'. The author of the catalogue has been tentatively identified with either Apollodorus of Seleucia (second century BC, a pupil of Antipater) or Apollonius of Tyre (second and first century BC).[40] If either of these identifications is correct, the catalogue was compiled at least four or five decades after Chrysippus' death. Hence the catalogue cannot be confidently taken to reflect Chrysippus' own arrangement of his works, and provides no grounds for crediting Chrysippus with the view that the study of definitions does not fall within the logical part.[41] All we can say is that the author of the catalogue of Chrysippus' works held that the study of definitions falls under ethics.

The Study of Definitions as Part of the Study of Vocal Sound   A different location of the study of definitions is recorded by Diogenes Laertius in a passage shortly after T 4, still within the first of Diogenes Laertius' two accounts of Stoic logic:

T 5   A specific area of dialectic is also the one, previously mentioned, about vocal sound itself [αὐτῆς τῆς φωνῆς], which expounds articulate vocal sound [ἐγγράμματος φωνή] and what the parts of speech are, and is about solecism, barbarism, poems, and ambiguities, and about euphonic vocal sound, about music, and about definitions, according to some, divisions, and utterances [καὶ περὶ ὅρων κατά τινας καὶ διαιρέσεων καὶ λέξεων]. (7.44)

Thus, according to T 5, some Stoics regarded the study of definitions as belonging to the part of dialectic concerning vocal sound (the Stoics divided

[40] Cf. Barnes (1996), 170–2 and Gourinat (2000), 97–103, who analyze the evidence and discuss earlier views about the catalogue's authorship.

[41] Brunschwig (1991), 81 more optimistically thinks that the catalogue of Chrysippus' works is fundamentally faithful to Chrysippus.

dialectic into two parts, one of the them dealing with vocal sound, the other with what is signified by vocal sounds).[42] In fact, in Diogenes Laertius' second, more extensive and detailed account of Stoic logic, the discussion of definitions is a part of that of vocal sound (the discussion of vocal sound extends over 7.55–62, and definitions are discussed in 7.60). Note that in Diogenes Laertius' second, more extensive and detailed account of Stoic logic, definition and division are treated between poems (7.60) and ambiguity (7.62). Thus, Diogenes Laertius' two accounts of Stoic logic are inconsistent with regard to the position of the study of definitions within the part of dialectic which deals with vocal sound. This inconsistency could be due simply to carelessness on Diogenes Laertius' or his sources' part; but it could also reflect a disagreement between Stoics.[43]

Definitions which Map Ambiguities   One reason why some Stoics placed the study of definitions within that of vocal sound could be that in their view definitions are about linguistic expressions because they contribute to distinguish the significations of words. For example, part of the Stoic position perhaps was that what gets defined is the word 'dog' (rather than the species dog or some other item which is not a linguistic expression) because definitions of the word 'dog' contribute to distinguish its various significations.

We have some conjectural evidence for attributing such a view to some Stoics. [a] In Diogenes Laertius' detailed account of Stoic logic, the discussions of definition and division (7.60–2) immediately precede that of ambiguity (7.62).[44] [b] Some documents describe the Stoics as using definitions to distinguish the significations of a word.[45] If the Stoics' logical theory reflected their logical practice, it would recognize the distinction of significations of words as one of the tasks of definitions.

Stipulative Definitions   Another reason why some Stoics placed the study of definitions within that of vocal sound could be that in their view a definition serves the purpose of establishing that a certain linguistic expression is going to be used in a certain (possibly technical) sense, and is therefore concerned with that linguistic expression. An inspection of the extant

---

[42] D.L. 7.43; 62; S.E. *P.* 2.214; Sen. *Ep.* 89,17.
[43] Cf. Atherton (1993), 132.
[44] Cf. Rieth (1933), 37; Gourinat (2000), 51–2.
[45] Stob. *Ecl.* 1.19,3 (1. 165, 21–3 W.).

fragments of Stoic philosophy shows that it is rich in new technical terminology: consider, for instance, their use of 'συμπεπλεγμένον' as a noun for
conjunctive statables—but examples could be multiplied. Since new technical terminology can be established only by using stipulative definitions,
the Stoics must have made abundant use of stipulative definitions. This is
confirmed by Galen:

> T6   [Archigenes did not write] a book about his own language [βιβλίον περὶ τῆς
> ἰδίας διαλέκτου], as Chrysippus did with regard to the names he assigned in
> dialectic [ὑπὲρ ὧν ἔθετο κατὰ τὴν διαλεκτικὴν ὀνομάτων]: only in this way
> could we understand him. (*Diff. Puls.* 8.579, 1–3 K.)

If T6 is alluding to Chrysippus' *Dialectical Definitions*,[46] it tells us that this
collection of definitions was about names whose usage would otherwise
have been obscure, namely technical terms. In fact, Galen scorned the Stoics
for their legislating about linguistic usage:

> T7   While he [*sc.* Chrysippus] legislates on names [νομοθετεῖ ... ὀνόματα] more
> than Solon fixes for the Athenians customs by means of the law-tables, he
> himself is the first to confuse them. (*Diff. Puls.* 8.631, 3–5 K.)[47]

Thus, if the Stoics' logical theory reflected their logical practice, it would
acknowledge the existence of stipulative definitions concerning linguistic
expressions. A stipulative definition normally either associates a sound
which is not yet an expression of the language with a certain signification,
or assigns a new signification to a sound which already is an expression of the
language, or selects one of the significations of a sound which already is an
expression of the language to the exclusion of others. Stipulative definitions of
this last sort accomplish a sort of disambiguation: they tell us in which of the
received senses a received expression will be used. In this respect, the Stoic
use of stipulative definitions could also have been connected with ambiguity:
not with describing ambiguities, but with eliminating them.

The Stoics' Hesitation   We have found three Stoic views about the position
of the study of definitions within philosophy: firstly, the view, probably
going back to Chrysippus, that the study of definitions is one of the main

---

[46]   Cf. above, n.6.
[47]   Cf. Gal. *Inst. Log.* 4,6 (11, 5–14 Kalbfleisch); Alex. Aphr. *in Top.* 181, 2–6; 301, 22–3; *Fat.* 173, 20–1;
174, 1–3.

sections of the logical part and contributes to the discovery of truth; secondly, the view, endorsed by the author of the catalogue of Chrysippus' works, that the study of definitions falls under ethics; thirdly, the view that the study of definitions falls under the section of dialectic that deals with vocal sound. The rest of this study will concentrate on some epistemological and semantic issues raised by the first view.

III Definitions and Conceptions

Definitions, Conceptions, and the Discernment of Truth   T4 reports that the Stoics pursue the study of definitions 'for the sake of the discernment of truth: for it is through conceptions that things are grasped'. The view thus attributed to the Stoics presupposes, firstly, that definitions are intimately connected with conceptions, and, secondly, that in virtue of this connection the study of definitions will help one to discern what is true. How are definitions and conceptions connected? How can this connection bring it about that the study of definitions will help one to discern what is true?

I begin by discussing the Stoic view about conceptions. This is most easily achieved by means of the following diagram, which shall be discussed in the following subsections:

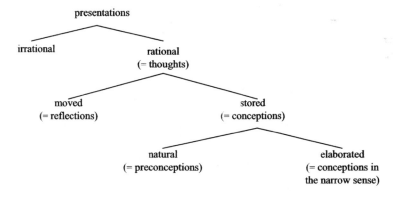

Rational vs. *Irrational Presentations*   The Stoics take conceptions to be presentations of a special sort. Within the Stoic school there was some debate as to the nature of presentations:

T 8   A presentation [φαντασία] is an imprint within the soul [τύπωσις ἐν ψυχῇ], that
       is an alteration [ἀλλοίωσις], as Chrysippus lays down in the second book of his
       work *On the Soul* (for one should not regard the imprint as the engraving of a
       ring, because it is inadmissible that many engravings should come to be in the
       same thing at the same time). (D.L. 7.50)

The Stoics offer several classifications of presentations. The one that is
relevant for our purposes divides presentations into two subordinate kinds:
rational and irrational presentations. Here are the most important witnesses:

T 9   Among presentations, some are rational [λογικαί], others irrational [ἄλογοι]:
       rational are those of rational animals, irrational those of irrational animals.
       Rational presentations are thoughts [νοήσεις],[48] whilst irrational presentations
       have no name. (D.L. 7.51)
T 10 The Stoics [...] say [...] that rational is a presentation in accordance with
       which what is presented can be put forward in discourse [λογικὴν εἶναι
       φαντασίαν καθ᾽ ἣν τὸ φαντασθὲν ἔστι λόγῳ παραστῆσαι]. (S.E. *M.* 8.70)

T 9 is often interpreted as recording the Stoic definition of rational and
irrational presentations. According to this interpretation, the Stoics would
be committed to two claims: that rational are all and only those presentations that occur in rational animals (namely adult humans and gods), and
that irrational are all and only those presentations that occur in irrational
animals.[49] Since, as we shall later see, the Stoics hold that each rational
presentation has exactly one sayable as its content, they would be committed to the claim that each presentation which occurs in a rational animal
has exactly one sayable as its content. This claim is however wildly implausible: it seems not to be the case that each presentation which occurs in a
rational animal has exactly one sayable as its content. Consider the perception I am having in this very moment: it is a presentation that occurs in a
rational animal, but it seems not to be the case that it has exactly one sayable
as its content. For what would this sayable be? Would it be the sayable
which can be signified by an utterance of 'This is white'? That which can be
signified by an utterance of 'This is a sheet of paper'? Or would it be some
other sayable? It therefore seems safe to reject the interpretation of T 9
according to which it is recording the Stoic definition of rational and

---

[48] Cf. [Gal.] *Def. Med.* 19.381,13 K.
[49] Cf. M. Frede (1983), 153–4; Annas (1992), 75; M. Frede (1994), 112.

irrational presentations. It is more plausible to assume that T9 is offering a Stoic exemplification of rational and irrational presentations: T9 is explaining what a rational presentation is by pointing out that many or most or the most typical of the presentations which in fact occur in rational animals are rational presentations, and it is explaining what an irrational presentation is by pointing out that most or even all of the presentations which in fact occur in irrational animals are irrational presentations.

It is T10 that contains the Stoic definition of a rational presentation: rational is a presentation where 'what is presented can be put forward in discourse'. It is when 'what is presented', namely the presentation's content, can be expressed in discourse that the presentation itself, and the animal which has it, is called 'rational' ('λογικός', the Greek expression of which 'rational' is my English rendering, is connected with 'λόγος', one of whose meanings is 'saying'). In the case of a rational presentation 'what is presented', namely the presentation's content, is a sayable, in particular, either a complete sayable (for example, a statable) or an incomplete sayable (for example, a predicate—it remains unclear whether all incomplete sayables are predicates). For example, in this moment I am having a rational presentation about this pen which has as its content a complete sayable which is a statable. This statable can be said by uttering the sentence 'This is a pen'. Moreover, this rational presentation contains or involves another rational presentation which has as its content a predicate. This predicate can be said by uttering the words '. . . is a pen'.

As we learn from T9, rational presentations coincide with thoughts.

Conceptions vs. *Reflections*   The Stoics divide thoughts, or rational presentations, into two subordinate kinds: conceptions, which they characterize as 'stored' thoughts, and reflections, which they characterize as 'moved' thoughts. Here are the most important witnesses:

T11   All of these [*sc.* logical abilities] belong to all animals, as doubtless does what concerns thoughts [νοήσεις], which if stored they call 'conceptions', whilst if moved they call 'reflections' [ἃς ἐναποκειμένας μὲν 'ἐννοίας' καλοῦσι κινουμένας δὲ 'διανοήσεις']. (Plu. *Soll. Anim.* 3, 961C–961D)[50]

---

[50] Cf. *Comm. Not.* 47, 1085A–1085B; [Gal.] *Def. Med.* 19.381,12 K.; Porph. *Abst.* 3.22, 17–18.

T 12 The creator of all things, who possesses and always uses conception and reflection [ἔννοιαν καὶ διανόησιν], the most stable powers [βεβαιοτάτας δυνάμεις], the first being stored thought, the second transition of thought [τὴν μὲν ἐναποκειμένην οὖσαν νόησιν, τὴν δὲ νοήσεως διέξοδον], observes from above his own works. (Ph. Deus Immut. 34)

Thus, conceptions are stored thoughts, namely stored rational presentations. The contrast between conceptions as 'stored' thoughts and reflections as 'moved' thoughts is puzzling: I forgo interpreting it now but I shall return to it later. Note that conceptions are presentations of a special sort.[51]

Conceptions as Registrations on the Dominating Part of the Soul Further traits of the Stoic theory of conceptions are reported by ps.-Plutarch:

T 13 The Stoics say: When human beings are born, the dominating part of their soul is like a small papyrus which is apt for registrations [ὥσπερ χαρτίον εὐεργὸν εἰς ἀπογραφήν]. On this they register for themselves each of the conceptions [εἰς τοῦτο μίαν ἑκάστην τῶν ἐννοιῶν ἐναπογράφεται]. The first type of record is that through perceptions [πρῶτος ... τῆς ἀναγραφῆς τρόπος ὁ διὰ τῶν αἰσθήσεων]. For when they perceive something, for example something white, they have a memory [μνήμην] of it when it has gone away. And when many memories of the same kind have come to be, then we say they have experience [ἐμπειρίαν]: for experience is a plurality of presentations of the same kind.★★★[52] Among conceptions, some come to be naturally [φυσικῶς γίνονται] in the aforesaid ways [κατὰ τοὺς εἰρημένους τρόπους], that is in a non-technical way [ἀνεπιτεχνήτως], others instead come to be through our instruction and diligence [δι' ἡμετέρας διδασκαλίας καὶ ἐπιμελείας]: these are called only 'conceptions', the former are also called 'preconceptions' [αὗται μὲν οὖν 'ἔννοιαι' καλοῦνται μόνον, ἐκεῖναι δὲ καὶ 'προλήψεις']. (Plac. 900B–C (400ᵃ4–22 Diels))[53]

T 13 concerns events within the dominating part of the human soul which are somehow analogous to events of registration on a papyrus.[54] Moreover, it describes conceptions as outcomes of something like events of making a

---

[51] Cf. Plu. Comm. Not. 47, 1084F.

[52] For this lacuna see below, n.61 and text thereto.

[53] Cf. [Gal.] Hist. Philos. 92 (635, 19–636, 1 Diels).

[54] The comparison of the dominating part of the soul with a papyrus recalls Plato's description of mental events in the *Philebus* (38E–39A), where he says that memories matching perceptions and 'other affections concerning these [. . .] write discourses in our souls'.

registration.[55] T13's description of conceptions as outcomes of something like an operation of making a registration on a papyrus fits well with the Stoic view that conceptions are presentations (cf. the last subsection): for all presentations are imprints (cf. T8), and the operation of making a registration on a papyrus recalls that of producing an imprint on a wax-tablet.

Immediately after saying that human beings 'register for themselves each of the conceptions' on the dominating part of their soul, T13 mentions 'the first type of record'. Since the expression 'the first type of record' occurs so close to the expression 'register for themselves each of the conceptions', it is natural to assume that 'the first type of record' is here elliptical for 'the first type of record of conceptions'. If this is correct, T13 commits the Stoics to the view that there are more ways than one in which human beings can register for themselves conceptions on the dominating part of their soul.

Conceptions Based on Perceptions   According to T13, the first type of record of conceptions is based on perceptions of individual items. Some perceptions of individual items give rise to memories of those items, and some of these memories go to constitute an experience, which consists of many memories of the same kind, i.e. many memories of previously perceived individual items which resemble one another. This description of experience is followed by the reappearance of conceptions, of which it is said that they 'come to be naturally in the aforesaid ways'. One wonders what the relation between experiences and conceptions is. Is a conception identical with the corresponding experience? Or is it the corresponding experience insofar as it has given rise to a certain disposition? Or is it distinct both from the corresponding experience and from each of the memories that constitute it? Different commentators opt for different solutions,[56] and the evidence does not enable one to reach any sure result. But one hint gives the edge to the third solution. For every conception is a presentation (cf. the penultimate subsection): on the basis of the plausible (albeit not unassailable) assumption that no collection of memories is itself a presentation, one may infer that a conception is distinct both from the corresponding experience and from each of the memories that constitute it. This, in turn, suggests that

---

[55] Cf. Cic. *Ac.* 1.11,42; 2.7, 21–2; Plu. *Comm. Not.* 47, 1084F.

[56] The first solution is favoured by Gould (1970), 60; the second is presented (albeit not endorsed) by Brittain (2005), 170; Sandbach (1930/71), 25 and Brittain (2005), 170–1 support the third.

at least some conceptions are formed by some sort of induction or abstraction based on memories of previously perceived individual items.[57] Neither T 13 nor any other document reports the Stoic view as to how this induction or abstraction works.

Conceptions Not Based on Perceptions   Do the Stoics maintain that every conception is formed by an induction or abstraction based on a collection of memories of previously perceived individual items? The answer is probably negative. For there is evidence for crediting the Stoics with the following two claims: firstly, that human beings have a preconception of the good;[58] secondly, that human beings reach for the first time a conception of the good by an analogical inference.[59] Since, as T 13 informs us, every preconception is a conception (because preconceptions are those conceptions which are formed in a natural way), the evidence just mentioned strongly suggests that according to the Stoics human beings form the preconception of the good by an analogical inference.

In order to understand what the Stoics have in mind when they talk of an analogical inference, we must consider the following report of the Stoic classification of what is thought of:

T 14   Of items thought of, some are thought of by confrontation, others by similarity, others by analogy, others by transposition, others by combination, others by opposition [τῶν νοουμένων τὰ μὲν κατὰ περίπτωσιν ἐνοήθη, τὰ δὲ καθ᾿ ὁμοιότητα, τὰ δὲ κατ᾿ ἀναλογίαν, <τὰ δὲ κατὰ μετάθεσιν,> τὰ δὲ κατὰ σύνθεσιν, τὰ δὲ κατ᾿ ἐναντίωσιν]. Things perceived are thought of by confrontation. By similarity are thought of those that are thought of by moving away from something present, like Socrates on the basis of a picture. Things thought of by analogy are thought of sometimes by magnification, as in the case of Tityos and Cyclops, sometimes by diminution, as in the case of the Pigmy. The centre of the earth is also thought of by analogy on the basis of smaller spheres. Things thought of by transposition are like the eyes on the chest. A horse-centaur is thought of by combination; death by opposition. Some things also are thought of by transition, like sayables and place [νοεῖται δὲ καὶ κατὰ μετάβασίν τινα, ὡς τὰ λεκτὰ καὶ ὁ τόπος]. Moreover, something

---

[57]   Cf. Gourinat (1996), 53.

[58]   Epict. *Diss.* 1.22,1; 2.17,12 (cf. D.L. 7.53; Plu. *Stoic. Rep.* 17, 1041E; Simp. *in Cat.* 213, 11–14; *in Epict.* 68, 19–22).

[59]   Cic. *Fin.* 3.10, 33; Sen. *Ep.* 120, 3–4.

just and good is thought of in a natural way. And some things are thought of by privation, for example, what lacks hands. Such are the things they decree with regard to presentations, perceptions, and thoughts [περὶ φαντασίας καὶ αἰσθήσεως καὶ νοήσεως]. (D.L. 7.52–3)

The very last remark of T14 makes it clear that the points made in what precedes concern the objects about which rational animals have thoughts (summaries of the Stoic views on presentations and perceptions were offered in the passages from Diogenes Laertius' report that come before T14: presentations in sections 50–1, perceptions in section 52). T14 reports a list of ways in which a rational animal can make epistemic contact with objects it is thinking about: in some cases the rational animal is directly confronted with these objects, i.e. perceives them; in other cases it makes contact with them by inferences based on similarity, analogy, transposition, combination, or opposition. Perceptions and inferences based on similarity, analogy, transposition, combination, or opposition seem to be on a par: they enable a human being to think of items of various sorts. Since some conceptions are formed by some types of induction or abstraction based on collections of memories of previously perceived individual items, the Stoics perhaps think that if some conceptions are formed by means of analogical inferences, these analogical inferences play a role analogous to that of perceptions for conceptions of other types: they provide the starting-points from which memories are formed on which some sort of induction or abstraction is performed. As we have seen, the Stoics probably think that human beings form the preconception of the good by analogical inference. Since, as T13 informs us, every preconception is a conception, we can plausibly conclude that according to the Stoics not all conceptions are formed by inductions or abstractions based on collections of memories of previously perceived individual items: some are formed by some sort of induction or abstraction based on collections of memories of items which were grasped by analogical inference.[60]

This conclusion has two welcome consequences. Firstly, it provides independent confirmation of a lacuna in T13 which had been suspected by F.H. Sandbach on the basis of the observation that the plural 'in the aforesaid ways' at the beginning of T13's second half seems to presuppose

---

[60] Cf. Sandbach (1930/71), 27–9; Todd (1973), 51–3; Gourinat (1996), 59–60.

that experience is only one of several ways in which conceptions can be formed in a natural way.[61] Secondly, it provides us with an explanation of T 13's expression 'the first type of record': for, as I argued earlier, this expression seems to commit the Stoics to the view that there are more ways than one in which a man can register for himself conceptions on the dominating part of his soul, and now we are in a position to expound what some of these ways are.

Conceptions and Universals   T 13's progression from perceptions to memories and from similar memories to experience reminds one of Aristotelian views in this area. Here is one of Aristotle's passages which most closely resemble the Stoic position:

T 15   Memory [μνήμη] comes to be from perception [ἐκ αἰσθήσεως], as we say, and experience [ἐμπειρία] from a frequent memory of the same thing: for memories that are numerically many are one experience. And from experience, or from the whole universal that has made a stand in the soul [ἐκ ἐμπειρίας ἢ ἐκ παντὸς ἠρεμήσαντος τοῦ καθόλου ἐν τῇ ψυχῇ], the one over the many, whatever, one and the same, is present in all of them, comes to be a principle of art and knowledge. (Arist. *APo.* 2. 19, 100ᵃ3–8)[62]

According to T 15, it is at the stage of experience that universals are grasped.[63] Although the Stoics probably rejected some of Aristotle's views on universals, it cannot be excluded that they preserved others, and in particular that they retained the association of experience with mental states whereby one grasps universals. Since T 13 attributes to the Stoics the view that some preconceptions are records which are formed on the basis of experiences, the Stoics perhaps held that some preconceptions are mental states by virtue of which one grasps universals. If this is correct then, for example, the Stoics would grant that every adult human being has an experience-based preconception whereby he grasps the universal whiteness, and an experience-based preconception whereby he grasps the universal man.[64]

---

[61] Cf. Sandbach (1930/71), 25–6.

[62] Cf. *Metaph.* A 1, 980ᵃ27–981ᵃ7; Sandbach (1985), 51–2.

[63] I take the 'or' ('ἤ', 100ᵃ6) linking the clauses 'from experience' and 'from the whole universal that has made a stand in the soul' as epexegetic (cf. Barnes (1994), 264).

[64] Cf. Gourinat (1996), 53–4.

The suggestion that according to the Stoics some preconceptions are mental states whereby one grasps universals is confirmed by Chrysippus' authority:

T 16   In the first book of *On Reason* Chrysippus says that criteria are perception and preconception (and a preconception is a natural conception of universals [ἔστι δ' ἡ πρόληψις ἔννοια φυσικὴ τῶν καθόλου]). (D.L. 7.54)[65]

In fact, T 16 makes it plausible to credit the Stoics with a stronger claim: that all preconceptions are mental states whereby one grasps universals. Given that, as we shall soon see, for the Stoics those conceptions which are not preconceptions are obtained by refining and sharpening conceptions, we may perhaps allow ourselves to attribute to the Stoics an even stronger view: that all conceptions are mental states whereby one grasps universals.

Conceptions and the Capacity to Predicate   As we shall soon see, the Stoics appear to hold that conceptions can be applied to or withheld from entities which are being perceived or otherwise thought of. Thus, the Stoics seem to associate conceptions with a rational animal's capacity to make affirmative and negative predications. So they probably think that by having a conception one has a capacity to form thoughts whereby one describes things as being, or not being, in a certain way. For example, by having a conception of whiteness one has a capacity to form thoughts whereby one describes things as being, or not being, white (thoughts which could be expressed by uttering sentences like 'This is white' or 'This is not white'); by having a conception of man one has a capacity to form thoughts whereby one describes a thing as being, or not being, a man (thoughts which could be expressed by uttering sentences like 'This is a man' or 'This is not a man').

Let us now consider the following three claims, claims which we may plausibly attribute to the Stoics: firstly, conceptions are associated with the capacity to make predications; secondly, conceptions are thoughts of a particular kind; thirdly, thoughts by their very nature have a content which is a sayable. Since predicates are one of the main kinds of sayables,

---

[65] Von Arnim excludes the final gloss 'ἔστι ... καθόλου' from fragment *SVF* II 105, which breaks off immediately before it. Such an exclusion seems unjustified (cf. Brittain (2005), 169). Different possible translations of the phrase 'ἔννοια φυσικὴ τῶν καθόλου' are mentioned and dismissed by Sandbach (1930/71), 35.

we can plausibly credit the Stoics with the view that conceptions are precisely those thoughts which have predicates as their contents.[66]

Conceptions vs. *Reflections (again)*   I can now return to a problem I had set to one side for later discussion: the interpretation of the Stoic distinction between reflections as 'moved' thoughts and conceptions as 'stored' thoughts. One might be inclined to interpret this distinction as one between thoughts which are events of thinking that occur over a relatively short period of time, on the one hand, and thoughts which are memories which can be actualized over and over again and remain for a relatively long period of time, on the other hand.[67] However, this at first attractive interpretation faces a difficulty. For suppose this interpretation is correct: the distinction between reflections and conceptions is that between thoughts which are events of thinking that occur over a relatively short time and thoughts which are memories which can be actualized over and over again and remain for a relatively long time. Suppose, secondly, that conceptions are precisely those thoughts which have predicates as their contents (as I suggested in the last paragraph). Suppose, thirdly, that the division of thoughts into reflections and conceptions is exhaustive (a likely assumption). It then follows that those thoughts which have (not predicates, but) complete sayables as their contents remain homeless. On these grounds I reject the suggested interpretation of the Stoic distinction between reflections and conceptions.

As an alternative, I tentatively suggest that what the Stoics have in mind when they distinguish between conceptions as 'stored' thoughts and reflections as 'moved' thoughts is that a thought is a conception just if it has exactly one predicate as its contents whereas a thought is a reflection just if it has exactly one complete sayable as its contents. As for the description of conceptions as 'stored' and of reflections as 'moved', it could be the case that reflections are regarded as 'moved' because they involve predication, which is the application of something to something (all complete sayables can be plausibly taken to involve some predication), whereas conceptions are regarded as 'stored' because they lack the movement of predication. The terminology adopted by the Stoics does endow this suggestion with some

---

[66] Cf. M. Frede (1983), 156. Brittain (2005), 173–4 argues that the contents of conceptions are not predicates, but statables. However, as he himself readily admits, the arguments for this conclusion are not compelling.

[67] This is more or less the interpretation which seems to be favoured by Gourinat (1996), 51.

plausibility: for '$\delta\iota\alpha\nu\acute{o}\eta\sigma\iota\varsigma$', the Stoic technical term I translated with 're-flection', recalls '$\delta\iota\acute{a}\nu o\iota\alpha$', which is used by Aristotle in speaking of thoughts involving predication.[68]

Note however that an alternative strategy might be reasonably adopted: one might retain the interpretation of the Stoic distinction between reflections and conceptions suggested in the penultimate paragraph, according to which the distinction between reflections and conceptions is that between thoughts which are events of thinking that occur over a relatively short time and thoughts which are memories which can be actualized over and over again and remain for a relatively long time, and give up the view that for the Stoics conceptions are precisely those thoughts which have predicates as their contents. Were one to adopt this alternative strategy, one would perhaps take the Stoic position to be that conceptions comprise both thoughts which have predicates as their contents and thoughts which have complete sayables as their contents. My preference for the solution adopted in the last paragraph is due to the fact that the link between conceptions and predicates seems very tight.

Preconceptions vs. *Conceptions in the Narrow Sense*   In the last part of T 13 the Stoics are portrayed as distinguishing two senses of 'conception': alongside the wide sense, which is prominent in the first part of the passage and covers both conceptions which arise in a natural way and conceptions which 'come to be through our instruction and diligence', there is a narrow sense, which covers only conceptions which 'come to be through our instruction and diligence'. Conceptions in the narrow sense are therefore opposed to those which arise in a natural way, for which the Stoics reserve the term 'preconception'.[69]

---

[68] *Metaph.* Γ7, 1012^{a}2–5; *EN* 6.2, 1139^{a}21. Aristotle does use '$\delta\iota\alpha\nu\acute{o}\eta\sigma\iota\varsigma$' (*Pol.* 7.3, 1325^{b}20).

[69] The Stoics often use the same expression in a wide and in a narrow sense within the same theoretical context. Other examples are the Stoic distinctions of wide and narrow senses of 'conclusive' ('$\pi\epsilon\rho\alpha\nu\tau\iota\kappa\acute{o}\varsigma$': see D.L. 7.78), 'impulse' ('$\acute{o}\rho\mu\acute{\eta}$': see Stob. *Ed.* 2.7,9 (2. 86, 19–87, 2 W.); Orig. *inMat.* 10. 4), 'predicate' ('$\kappa\alpha\tau\eta\gamma\acute{o}\rho\eta\mu\alpha$': see D.L. 7.64 with Brunschwig (1986–94), 66, Schubert (1994), 67, and Gaskin (1997), 92–3), 'good' ('$\dot{\alpha}\gamma\alpha\theta\acute{o}\nu$': see S.E. *M.* 11.25–7, 30), 'prudence' ('$\phi\rho\acute{o}\nu\eta\sigma\iota\varsigma$': see Plu. *Stoic. Rep.* 7, 1034C), 'soul' ('$\psi\upsilon\chi\acute{\eta}$': see S.E. *M.* 7.234), and 'qualified item' ('$\pi o\iota\acute{o}\nu$': see Simp. *in Cat.* 212, 12–213, 1). Note that whereas the Stoics take 'predicate', 'good', 'soul', and 'qualified item' to apply in their narrow senses to the *most important* members of the extensions of these expressions in their wide senses, they adopt the opposite stance in the case of 'conclusive': they take 'conclusive' to apply in its narrow sense to the *least important* members of the extension of 'conclusive' in its wide sense. Cf. Aristotle's distinction of a wide and a narrow sense of 'peculiarity' ('$\acute{\iota}\delta\iota o\nu$') at *Top.* 1.4, 101^{b}17–25 (cf. below, n.131 and text thereto).

A passage from Galen gives us plausible grounds for believing that the distinction between preconceptions and conceptions in the narrow sense goes back at least to Chrysippus:

T 17 [In your *Therapy of Passions*, Chrysippus, you say that] 'there are parts of the soul of which reason, which is in it, is constituted', reminding us perhaps of the things written in the books *On Reason*, things you recounted in detail. that 'it is a collection of certain conceptions and preconceptions [ἔστιν ἐννοιῶν τέ τινων καὶ προλήψεων ἄθροισμα]'. (*Plac. Hippocr. Pl.* 5.3,1 (304, 33–5 DeLacy))[70]

Galen's report is confirmed by Plutarch:

T 18 By coming between them [*sc.* Arcesilaus and Carneades], Chrysippus with his rejoinders to Arcesilaus stopped in its tracks also Carneades' cleverness, on the one hand by leaving to perception many succours, as it were, against siege [πολλὰ μὲν τῇ αἰσθήσει καταλιπὼν ὥσπερ εἰς πολιορκίαν βοηθήματα], on the other hand by eliminating entirely the confusion that surrounds preconceptions and conceptions, by articulating each of them and assigning it to its proper place [τὸν δὲ περὶ τὰς προλήψεις καὶ τὰς ἐννοίας τάραχον ἀφελὼν παντάπασι διαρθρώσας ἑκάστην[71] καὶ θέμενος εἰς τὸ οἰκεῖον]. (*Comm. Not.* 1, 1059B–1059C)

In T 18 Plutarch credits Chrysippus with two important contributions to the defence of the Stoic position against the attacks of Academic philosophers: the first contribution consists in 'leaving to perception many succours, as it were, against siege', the second in 'eliminating entirely the confusion that surrounds preconceptions and conceptions, by articulating each of them and assigning it to its proper place'. Chrysippus' first contribution is relatively easy to understand: it is a defence of the reliability of perception against Academic attacks. Chrysippus' second contribution is hard to understand. Surely it has to do with preconceptions and conceptions. Moreover, as we shall see,[72] the verb 'to articulate' ('διαρθρόω'), used by Plutarch in his

---

[70] Cf. Brittain (2005), 169.

[71] Note that 'ἕκαστος' can be used with regard to two items (see Smyth (1920), 96). Also note that whenever two or more groups of items have been mentioned, 'ἕκαστος' in the singular can be used to refer not only to each single item in the union of the groups, but also to each of the groups themselves (see Gal. *Sympt. Diff.* 7. 55,12–16 K.). Hence the occurrence of 'ἑκάστην' at the end of T 18 may be taken to refer either to each single preconception and conception, or to each of those two groups which are the group of preconceptions and that of conceptions.

[72] Cf. below, nn.90–3 and text thereto.

description of Chrysippus' second contribution, is probably a technical term of Stoic logic and is connected with the processes of definition and division. We may therefore safely infer that Chrysippus' second contribution has to do with defining and dividing. What remains unclear with regard to Chrysippus' second contribution is what it is about. Does Chrysippus' second contribution consist in having produced a definition and a division of each single preconception and conception involved in the debate with the Academics?[73] Or does it consist in having produced a definition of what a preconception is, a definition of what a conception is, and a division whereby preconception and conception are assigned to their proper places within a classification of epistemological concepts?[74] Since Chrysippus' first contribution seems to be of an epistemological nature and to concern perception in general (rather than single perceptions), it is likely that Chrysippus' second contribution should also be of an epistemological nature and should concern preconception and conception in general (rather than single preconceptions and conceptions). This gives the edge to the second solution. T18 therefore makes it plausible to assume that part of what Chrysippus did was to draw the distinctions which in the last part of T13 are attributed to unnamed Stoics.

The Stoics seem to think that certain conceptions, and in particular certain preconceptions, are shared by all human beings. Such universally shared conceptions and preconceptions, which they call 'common conceptions' ('κοιναὶ ἔννοιαι') and 'common preconceptions' ('κοιναὶ προλήψεις'),[75] play important roles in their theory of knowledge.

Definitions as Links between Preconceptions and Conceptions in the Narrow Sense The distinction between preconceptions and conceptions in the narrow sense is particularly important for the Stoic theory of definition: for definitions seem to be associated with the transformation of preconceptions into conceptions in the narrow sense. Here are some pieces of evidence:

---

[73] For this solution see Long and Sedley (1987), II247.
[74] For this solution see Sandbach (1930/71), 22, 31; Brittain (2005), 169.
[75] Plu. *Stoic. Rep.* 17, 1041F; *Comm. Not.* 3, 1060A; 4, 1060C; 8, 1062A; 29, 1073D; 31, 1074F; 46, 1084D; S.E. *M.* 9.124; Epict. *Diss.* 4.1,42; Alex. Aphr. *Mixt.* 227,11 (cf. Sandbach (1930/71), 23–5; Brittain (2005), 175–9).

T 19   [...] of these things [...] there is a certain pattern marked and impressed by
the intellect [*quaedam conformatio insignita et impressa intellegentia*], which I call
'conception' ['*notionem' voco*]. Often in the course of argumentation it must be
explained by means of a definition [*definitione explicanda est*]. (Cic. *Top.* 5, 27) I
call 'conception' ['*notionem' appello*] what the Greeks sometimes call '*ἔννοιαν*',
sometimes '*πρόληψιν*'. Whatever it is of, it is a notion that is stored and was
previously obtained by the soul but needs elucidation [*ea est insita et animo
praecepta cuiusque cognitio enodationis indigens*]. (7, 31)

T 20   Study the definitions of courage and you will understand that it does not
require ill-temper. Courage is 'a state of the soul obedient to the supreme
law in matters requiring endurance'. Or 'the preservation of stable judgement in undergoing and warding off things that seem fearsome'. Or 'scientific knowledge of things fearsome, contrary to fearsome, or to be
completely ignored, preserving stable judgement of those things'. Or, in
Chrysippus' briefer formulation (for the preceding definitions were by
Sphaerus, a man—the Stoics think—extremely good at framing definitions:
for they are all pretty much similar, but some more successful than others at
explaining our common conceptions [*declarant communes notiones alia magis
alia*])—how, then, does Chrysippus define it? 'Courage', he says, 'is knowledge of matters requiring persistence, or a state of the soul fearlessly
obedient to the supreme law in enduring and persisting'. However we
may attack these men, as Carneades used to, I am afraid they may be the
only real philosophers. For which of those definitions fails to disclose the
hidden and tangled conception of courage we all have [*quae istarum defin-
itionum non aperit notionem nostram, quam habemus omnes de fortitudine tectam
atque involutam*]? (Cic. *Tusc.* 4.24, 53)[76]

T 21   [Theopompus] censures Plato for wishing to define everything [*ἔκαστα
ὁρίζεσθαι*]. For what does he say? 'Did none of us before you ever say
"good" or "just"? Or, without attending what each of these is, we uttered
the sounds without meaning and emptily?' Who tells you, Theopompus, that
we do not have natural conceptions [*ἐννοίας φυσικὰς*], namely preconceptions [*προλήψεις*], of each of these things? But it is not possible to apply the
preconceptions to the corresponding entities without having articulated
them and without having examined precisely which entity should be subsumed under each of them [*οὐχ οἷόν τ' ἐφαρμόζειν τὰς προλήψεις ταῖς*

---

[76] Cf. Cic. *Off.* 3.19,76; 20,81; *Orat.* 33, 116; *Top.* 22,83; Mart. Cap. 4.349.

καταλλήλοις οὐσίαις μὴ διαρθρώσαντα αὐτὰς καὶ αὐτὸ τοῦτο σκεψάμενον, ποίαν τινὰ ἑκάστῃ αὐτῶν οὐσίαν ὑποτακτέον].[77] For go and say something of this sort to doctors: 'Who of us did not say "healthy" and "diseased" before Hippocrates was born? Or were we uttering these sounds emptily?' For we have some preconception also of the healthy, but we are unable to apply it [ἔχομεν γάρ τινα καὶ ὑγιεινοῦ πρόληψιν, ἀλλ᾽ ἐφαρμόσαι οὐ δυνάμεθα]. For this reason one says 'Abstain from food', another 'Give nourishment'; again, one says 'Cut a vein', another 'Use the cupping-glass'. What is the cause? Is it anything but that one is unable to apply finely the preconception of the healthy to particulars [τὴν τοῦ ὑγιεινοῦ πρόληψιν καλῶς ἐφαρμόσαι τοῖς ἐπὶ μέρους]? (Epict. Diss. 2.17, 5–9)

T 22 [When people see craftsmen acting not in accordance with their arts, they conclude that they are poor craftsmen. By contrast, when they see a man acting not in accordance with his philosophical principles, they do not conclude that he is a poor philosopher, but that being a philosopher is pointless.] What, then, is the reason for this? It is because we cultivate the preconception [τὴν πρόληψιν πρεσβεύομεν] of the carpenter and that of the musician, and so also of all other craftsmen, but not that of the philosopher, but, since it is confused and unarticulated [συγκεχυμένην καὶ ἀδιάρθρωτον], we judge only from externals. (Epict. Diss. 4.8, 10)

T 23 ... when the articulation has already occurred [γενομένης τῆς διαρθρώσεως], the presentation [φαντασία] becomes clear [τρανής] and brought to exactness [διηκριβωμένη] ... (Hierocl. El. Mor., PBerol inv. 9780v col. VII 53) ... confused [συγκεχυμένος] and making use of a rough imprint [ὁλοσχερεῖ τῇ τυπώσει χρώμενος] ... (col. VII 60)

T 24 The Stoics, although intensely keen on the ability to discuss, which they call 'dialectic', thought that it should be drawn from bodily perceptions, claiming that it is from these that the soul forms its conceptions, which they call 'ἔννοιας', namely of those things which they explain in definitions [earum rerum quas definiendo explicant]; from here the whole system of learning and teaching is derived and organized [hinc propagari atque conecti totam discendi docendique rationem]. (August. C.D. 8, 7)

---

[77] The verb 'to subsume' ('ὑποτάττειν') is probably a technical term of Stoic logic (cf. Crivelli (1994a), 193–4): Stoic logicians seem to use it to describe the placing either of a species under its genus (see D.L. 7.92) or of a definite statable under a corresponding indefinite one (see S.E. M. 8.297; 11.11; Epict. Diss. 4.1,61; Alex. Aphr. in APr. 348, 5).

In T 21 Epictetus defends Plato's interest in definitions against Theopompus.[78] This defence presupposes that when we have definitions we are able to articulate our preconceptions in such a way that they become more likely to be successfully applied or withheld. This fits with the thesis advanced in T 19: preconceptions are in need of elucidation, and this is achieved by means of definitions (T 19 does not attribute this thesis to the Stoics, but its terminology is Stoic).[79] T 24 provides one last important bit of information: the explication which definitions provide of those conceptions which are derived from the senses, namely of preconceptions, makes those conceptions suitable for the construction of the system of teaching and learning. If we recall that, according to T 13, conceptions in the narrow sense are distinguished from preconceptions in that they are associated with instruction, it becomes likely to assume that the explication of preconceptions by means of definitions transforms those preconceptions into conceptions in the narrow sense.[80]

One might want to attribute to the Stoics a different account of the relationship between preconceptions and conceptions in the narrow sense. According to this alternative account, preconceptions would be conceptions formed merely on the basis of experiences whereas conceptions in the narrow sense would be conceptions formed by inferential processes (which turn on similarity, analogy, transposition, combination, or opposition).[81] This alternative account differs from the one I attributed to the Stoics in the last paragraph in that it recognizes no role for definitions in the development of conceptions in the narrow sense. However, this alternative account cannot be plausibly attributed to the Stoics: as I argued earlier,[82] the Stoics probably maintain that preconceptions are formed not only on the basis of experiences, but also by inferential processes.[83]

The evidence reviewed so far enables us to credit the Stoics with the following views: there are two stages in the formation of conceptions; the first stage leads to the formation of preconceptions, which constitute

---

[78] The Theopompus in question was an orator active in the second half of the fourth century BC. He wrote an *Attack on Plato's Way of Life*.

[79] Cf. Pauli (1986), 235–6; Gourinat (2000), 47–8.

[80] Cf. Gourinat (2000), 47–8; Brittain (2005), 179–81.

[81] Cf. Togni (2006), 79.

[82] See above, subsection to n. 58.

[83] I find no evidence supporting the interpretation of Watson (1966), 24–8, according to whom preconceptions are natural capacities to organize the data of perception.

the first subordinate kind of conceptions; the second stage transforms pre-conceptions into conceptions in the narrow sense, which constitute the second subordinate kind of conceptions; definitions play a role in the second stage.

Two Purposes of Definitions   According to Sextus Empiricus, the 'dogmatists' think that definitions serve two purposes:

T 25   Now while the dogmatists think that definitions serve many purposes, you will perhaps find that two are the highest heads which they say embrace all their necessity: for in all cases they represent definitions as necessary either for comprehension or for instruction [ἢ γὰρ ὡς πρὸς κατάληψιν ἢ ὡς πρὸς διδασκαλίαν]. (*P.* 2.205–6)

Although Sextus does not identify the 'dogmatists' he mentions in T 25 as Stoics, his claim that 'the dogmatists [. . .] represent definitions as necessary either for comprehension or for instruction' chimes with what the documents reviewed so far tell us with regard to the Stoics. For our documents enable us to single out two purposes which, according to the Stoics, definitions are supposed to serve: firstly, to improve one's ability to apply or withhold conceptions; secondly, to endow one's conceptions with a systematic structure suitable for instruction. In what follows I shall discuss at some length these two purposes.

The First Purpose of Definitions: Improving One's Ability to Apply or Withhold Conceptions   T 21 clearly displays one of the purposes which the Stoics take definitions to serve: to improve a person's mental state in such a way that the conceptions stored in that person's soul will be more likely to be successfully applied (affirmed) or withheld (denied). More precisely, the Stoics seem to think that a definition can contribute to induce a change in a person's mental state: it can contribute to bring a person to pass from a mental state where there are certain preconceptions, which the person is relatively likely to apply unsuccessfully to or withhold unsuccessfully from entities, to a mental state where some of those preconceptions have evolved into conceptions in the narrow sense, which the person is less likely to apply unsuccessfully to or withhold unsuccessfully from entities. This evolution of preconceptions into conceptions in the narrow sense could perhaps be understood in analogy with the improvement of a tool which enables it to perform its function more effectively: just as a rudimentary knife of stone can be sharpened and otherwise modified so as to perform its function (cutting) more successfully, and the transformation could be described as an evolution of a 'pre-knife' into a 'knife in the narrow sense', so also a rudimentary conception can be so modified as to perform its function (being applied to or withheld from entities) more successfully.

One might wonder what the success in applying or withholding a conception consists in. This problem becomes clear when one realizes that one might claim that conceptions cannot be applied unsuccessfully: given that a conception is a private mental state, specifically, a thought stored in the dominating part of one's soul, what could the unsuccess of its being applied to or withheld from entities amount to? Could one not claim that a conception is successfully applied to whatever entity one in fact applies it to, and is successfully withheld from whatever entity one in fact withholds it from?

The sources do not indicate that the Stoics were aware of this problem, nor do they therefore report a Stoic answer to it. The sources however do provide some indication of what moves the Stoics would probably have made in answering this problem, had they addressed it. In fact one can detect two kinds of strategies which the Stoics would have been likely to adopt.

The first Stoic answer to the problem of what the success in applying or withholding a conception could consist in transpires at the end of T21. Here the Stoics insist that a result of the transformation of one's preconceptions into conceptions in the narrow sense is the harmonization of the conceptions of different members of a community: for Epictetus suggests that different people who have not articulated their preconceptions of health by means of a definition will easily disagree on the cure they will recommend for someone who is unwell.[84] T4 confirms this. For, in T4, Diogenes Laertius reports, first, that the Stoics develop the study 'concerning yardsticks and criteria for the sake of discovering truth' because 'here they adjust the differences between presentations', and, then, that they believe something analogous with regard to definitions. Thus, the

---

[84] The idea of definitions effecting a harmonization of a disagreement in the application of preconceptions returns in Epictetus: see *Diss.* 2.17, 10–22.

harmonization of the conceptions of different members of a community is one of the purposes of definitions.

The important idea here is that the reason why conceptions are not successfully applied to or withheld from whatever entity they are in fact applied to or withheld from is that they are associated with linguistic expressions. If Dio applies to a particular whale the conception, stored in the dominant part of his soul, which he associates with the word 'fish', but Theo withholds from that whale the conception, stored in the dominant part of his soul, which he associates with the word 'fish', and if this disagreement remains after Dio and Theo have carefully examined the particular whale in question, the conclusion which one can reasonably draw is that something is wrong in the conceptions recorded in the dominant parts of the souls of Dio and Theo. In general, if the stored conception which one man associates with a certain word is (not only numerically, but also) qualitatively different from the stored conception which another man associates with that same word, the possibility is open that the first man could apply the conception he associates with the word to an entity from which the second man will withhold the conception he associates with the word. What such a situation calls for is some sorting-out of the conceptions, so that this disagreement about what they get applied to and withheld from is eliminated. Such harmonization is achieved by means of definitions.

Plato in the *Sophist* seems to attribute to definitions a role comparable to the one I have just outlined:

T 26 I think you need to begin with me the investigation from the sophist—by searching for him and clarifying what he is by means of an account. Now in this case you and I only have the name in common, and perhaps we have each applied it to a different thing. In every case, though, we always need to be in agreement about the thing itself by means of accounts, rather than doing without any account and merely agreeing about the name. (*Sph.* 218B7–218C5)

Here definitions are supposed to bring about an agreement in the use of expressions (in particular of the noun 'sophist') by different speakers. Note that Plato's views on definition probably influenced Stoicism.[85]

---

[85] Cf. below, n. 89 and text thereto.

The second Stoic answer to the problem of what the success in applying or withholding a conception could consist in may be inferred from T 20, T 22, and T 23. In T 20 Cicero seems to hint that for the Stoics one of the roles of definitions is to 'disclose' or 'explain' conceptions which would otherwise remain 'hidden and tangled'. In T 22 Epictetus describes a certain preconception as 'confused and unarticulated'. The fragment of Hierocles' *Elements of Ethics* reported as T 23 suggests that articulation, which in other Stoic fragments is associated with definition, transforms a confused presentation into a clear one.[86] I suspect that what the Stoics have in mind when they speak of presentations and conceptions being confused is that some of our conceptions have fuzzy borders: they leave their owner undecided as to whether they should be applied to or withheld from certain entities. It may well be the case that a certain amount of fuzziness is unavoidable, but some of our conceptions may quite obviously need some sharpening because they leave us undecided about too many and important cases. One of the purposes of definitions will then be to sharpen the borders of a person's conceptions in such a way that the number of entities is increased which the conception can be applied to or withheld from. In sharpening the borders of a conception, one will probably have to take into account how the linguistic community uses the linguistic expression with which one associates the conception in question: one cannot sharpen borders in any arbitrary way. The definition will therefore have to reflect how the linguistic community uses the associated linguistic expression.

One can now see why (as we learn from T 4) the Stoics 'adopt the definitional species for the sake of the recognition of truth': definitions enable us to articulate our conceptions in such a way that we are more likely to apply and withhold them successfully, and thereby assent to presentations which are true. By the same token, one can see why (as we learn from T 25) one of the purposes which the 'dogmatists' attribute to definitions is to contribute to comprehension, which, according to the Stoics, is assent given to a comprehensive presentation, namely a presentation which (among other things) is true.[87]

---

[86] Galen occasionally associates 'confusion' with 'lack of articulation': see *de Diff. Febr.* 7. 365; *de Dign. Puls.* 8.836 K.

[87] S.E. *M.* 7.151–5; 8.397; 11.182; *P.* 3.242; Alex. Aphr. *de An.* 71, 10–12 (cf. Cic. *Ac.* 2.47,145; Chrysipp. PHerc 1020 col. ın (=OxMa) 7–10; Gal. *An. Pecc. Dign.* 5.60, 4–5 K.; Clem. Al. *Strom.* 8.5,16, 2; Sedley (2002), 151–2).

The Second Purpose of Definitions: To Organize One's Conceptions in a System Suitable for Instruction   As I said, the evidence reviewed so far enables one to single out two purposes which the Stoics take definitions to serve. The first of these purposes was discussed in the last subsection: to improve a person's mental state in such a way that the conceptions stored in the soul will be more likely to be successfully applied or withheld. The second purpose is to organize a person's conceptions in a system suitable for instruction. This is particularly clear in T24's claim that 'it is hence [*sc.* from conceptions explicated by means of definitions] that the whole system of learning and teaching is derived and organized'. How can definitions, as conceived by the Stoics, serve this purpose?

One plausible answer appeals to the tight link which the Stoics believe to obtain between definition and division. This link is variously attested: in Diogenes Laertius' report of Stoic logic, definition and division are treated in immediate succession (7.60–2);[88] in the catalogue of Chrysippus' works handed down by Diogenes Laertius, the titles concerning definition immediately precede those concerning species, genera, and division (7.199–200); Sextus Empiricus (*M.* 11.8–14) reports some views of Stoic logicians inspired by Chrysippus which presuppose a close association between definitions and divisions. Since Zeno probably attended the lectures of the Academics Xenocrates and Polemon,[89] there is some likelihood to the suggestion that the link between definition and division was bequeathed by the Academy to the founder of Stoicism and was never dissolved by his followers.

The link between definition and division is confirmed by T21's terminology. For T21 uses the verb '*διαρθροῦν*' ('to articulate') to describe the process whereby definitions transform our preconceptions. The verb '*διαρθροῦν*' and other expressions etymologically connected with it are often used to formulate this idea. [a] Epictetus himself in other passages uses '*διαρθροῦν*', '*διάρθρωσις*', and '*διαρθρωτικός*' to describe the transformation of preconceptions by means of definitions,[90] and in T22 he employs

---

[88] Cf. 7.44.

[89] On Zeno as a student of Xenocrates see D.L. 7.2; Eus. *PE* 14.5, 11. On Zeno as a student of Polemon see D.L. 7.2; 25; *Suda s.v.* '*Ζήνων ὁ Μνασέου*'; Cic. *Ac.* 1.9,35; *Fin.* 4.2, 3; Eus. *PE* 14.5, 11; 14.6, 7. For a discussion of the plausibility of the information that Zeno attended the lectures of Xenocrates and Polemon see Alesse (2000), 87–104.

[90] *Diss.* 2.11,18; 12,9; 17,11; 17,13; *Ench.* 52,1.

'ἀδιάρθρωτος' ('non-articulated') alongside 'συγκεχυμένος' ('confused') to describe certain preconceptions. [b] In the catalogue of Chrysippus' works handed down by Diogenes Laertius, one of the 'areas' within the ethical section bears the title 'Ethical area[91] dealing with the articulation [διάρθρωσις] of ethical conceptions' (7.199). Chrysippus' works concerning definitions are listed in the second and the third 'collection' of this 'area'. [c] The fragment of Hierocles' *Elements of Ethics* reported as T 23 again uses 'διάρθρωσις' alongside 'συγκεχυμένος'.[92] Now, the verb 'διαρθροῦν' brings to one's mind Plato's use of the noun 'ἄρθρον' ('joint') in a famous passage from the *Phaedrus* where he claims that in dividing a genus one should 'be able to cut according to species along the joints [κατ' ἄρθρα], where it is natural' (265E1–2).[93]

Given that for the Stoics definition is tightly linked to division, one can see on what grounds the Stoics held that definitions serve the purpose of organizing a person's conceptions in a system suitable for instruction and science: for division yields a systematic organization of a person's conceptions, and a systematic organization of this sort will help instruction and science.

Meno's Paradox   Hellenistic and late-ancient philosophers appealed to preconceptions in order to answer Meno's paradox. Here is the main evidence:

T 27   According to the sage Epicurus it is not possible either to search or to doubt without a preconception [οὔτε ζητεῖν ἔστιν οὔτε ἀπορεῖν ἄνευ προλήψεως]. (S.E. *M.* 11.21)[94]

T 28   That there is a real problem as to whether it is possible to search for something and find it, as the *Meno*'s challenge goes: for neither do we search for and find things which we know (for it would be pointless), nor things which we do not know (for even if we encounter them, we shall be unaware of it, as with chance things). The Peripatetics contrived the potential intellect. [. . .] The Stoics postulate natural conceptions [οἱ δὲ ἀπὸ τῆς Στοᾶς τὰς φυσικὰς ἐννοίας αἰτιῶνται]. [. . .] The Epicureans instead postulate preconceptions [οἱ δὲ

---

[91]   Cf. above, n. 39 and text thereto.
[92]   Cf. Gal. *Differ. Febr.* 7.365,6 K.; *Diff. Puls.* 8.647, 7–8 K.; *Dignosc. Puls.* 8.836,2–3 K.; Stob. *Ecl.* 2.7, 6ᵃ (2. 76, 1 W.).
[93]   Cf. *Plt.* 287C3; Gourinat (2000), 48–9.
[94]   Cf. 1.57; 8.337–331a; D.L. 10.33; Cic. *N.D.* 1.16,43; Clem. Al. *Strom.* 2.4,16,3.

Ἐπικούρειοι τὰς προλήψεις]. (Plu. fr. 215 *apud* Olymp. *in Phd.* 156, 1–11 Norvin)

T 27 and T 28 testify that Epicurus appealed to preconceptions in order to solve Meno's paradox.[95] Cicero (*N.D.* 1.17,44) reports that Epicurus was the first philosopher to use 'preconception' as a technical term, and there is no reason to doubt this witness. The Stoics, and in particular Chrysippus, probably took 'preconception' over from the Epicureans (there is no indication that Zeno used 'preconception').[96] As we know (cf. T 13), for the Stoics natural conceptions are preconceptions. So, when T 28 tells us that the Stoics 'postulate natural conceptions' to solve Meno's paradox, the solution attributed to them is probably either close or identical to Epicurus'. The Stoic solution for Meno's paradox is probably roughly along the following lines: a preconception of an object enables one to set up a search for that object and to recognize that object in case one encounters it; once one has encountered that object and recognized it, one can make further enquiries about it and thereby achieve a conception in the narrow sense of it.[97]

There is evidence that at some point the Stoic distinction between preconceptions and conceptions in the narrow sense was transformed in such a way as to fit in the mould of the Platonic doctrine of recollection: preconceptions, being conceptions formed in a natural way, were identified with the buried inborn memories which in the present life a soul has of what it contemplated in its disembodied prenatal existence; conceptions in the narrow sense were identified with the result of the exhumation of these buried memories.[98] In the *Meno* Plato introduced the theory of recollection to back a solution to Meno's paradox.[99] There is some likelihood in assuming that after the early Stoics employed the distinction between preconceptions and conceptions in the narrow sense to solve Meno's paradox, some later thinkers (middle-Platonists and, perhaps, Stoics from the Imperial period) found it natural to interpret Plato's theory of recollec-

[95] Cf. Long and Sedley (1987), 189–90; Barnes and Schenkeveld (1999), 196.
[96] Cf. Pearson (1891), 72; Sandbach (1930/71), 30–2; Long and Sedley (1987), 188–9.
[97] Cf. Gourinat (2000), 53–4; Brittain (2005), 179–80.
[98] Cic. *Tusc.* 1.24,57; *N.D.* 2.4, 12; Epict. *Diss.* 2.11,1–3; 6; Plu. *Plat. Quaest.* 1, 1000D–1000E; Anon. *in Tht.* col. 47,37–48,7; Albin. *Intr.* 6, 150, 21–3 H.; Alcin. *Intr.* 4, 155, 17–29 H.; 25, 178, 7–10 H.; Porph. *Marc.* 10.
[99] *Men.* 80E1–81E2.

tion in terms of the distinction between preconceptions and conceptions in the narrow sense. The identification of preconceptions with inborn memories of what was contemplated in a disembodied prenatal existence was favoured by the circumstance that the adjective 'ἔμφυτος', which the early Stoics occasionally used to describe the natural formation of preconceptions,[100] could be taken to mean 'inborn'.[101]

Sketches The Stoics connect definitions with sketches (ὑπογραφαί).[102] The main witness on the Stoic views about sketches is again Diogenes Laertius:

T 29   A sketch [ὑπογραφή] is an account which introduces one to things in outline [λόγος τυπωδῶς εἰσάγων εἰς τὰ πράγματα],[103] or an account that takes on the capacity of a definition in a simplified manner [λόγος ἁπλούστερον[104] τὴν τοῦ ὅρου δύναμιν προσενηνεγμένος]. (7.60)

According to the Stoics no sketch is a definition.[105] We have an example of a sketch and a definition of the same item: a sketch of a statable was probably something like, 'A statable is what is either true or false,'[106] whilst a definition of statable was probably something like, 'A statable is a complete thing capable of being asserted in so far as it itself is concerned.'[107]

---

[100] Epict. *Diss.* 2.11,3; Plu. *Stoic. Rep.* 17, 1041E; 1042A.

[101] Cf. the use of 'ἔμφυτος' at Plu. *Plat. Quaest.* 1, 1000E and Porph. *Marc.* 10.

[102] Different technical expressions are attested as alternatives to 'ὑπογραφή': 'λόγος ὑπογραφικός', 'ὅρος ὑπογραφικός', and 'ὑποτύπωσις' (see *Schol. in Dionys. Thr.* 114, 14–15; Gal. *Diff. Puls.* 8. 708, 16–709, 5 K.; Simp. *in Cat.* 22, 16; 29, 21–2; 34, 4). Also cf. below, n. 111 and text thereto.

[103] Cf. *Suda s.v.* 'ὅρος'; [Gal.] *Def. Med.* 19. 349, 18–350, 1 K. (where, following the suggestion made by von Arnim *apud SVF* II 227, I read 'τὴν τοῦ δηλουμένου πράγματος' instead of Kühn's 'τὴν δηλουμένην τοῦ πράγματος'); 350, 1–2 K.; S.E. *P.* 2.212. Brittain (2005), 188 suggests that the first of the two accounts of sketches reported in T 29 is describing not sketchy accounts, but introductory textbooks (which are sometimes referred to as 'sketches', cf. D.L. 7.199), and that T 29 is therefore getting out of the way an ambiguity in 'sketch'.

[104] The MSS and most editors read 'ὅρος ἁπλούστερον'. Since the sources report that sketches are not definitions (cf. below, n. 105 and text thereto), emendation seems to be called for: von Arnim (*apud SVF* III Antipater 24) proposes 'λόγος ἁπλούστερον', Sedley (*apud* Long and Sedley (1987), II 191–2) suggests instead 'ὅρου ἁπλούστερον'. I adopted von Arnim's emendation because it yields smoother syntax.

[105] *Schol. in Dionys. Thr.* 115, 29–31; 116, 1–2; Gal. *Diff. Puls.* 8. 709, 3–5; 720, 5–7 K.; Porph. *in Cat.* 64, 15–16.

[106] S.E. *M.* 8.12. Cicero (*Ac.* 2.30,95) is probably inaccurate when he describes 'A statable is what is either true or false' as a definition.

[107] D.L. 7.65; S.E. *P.* 2.104; Gel. 16.8,4. The Stoic account of emotion (πάθος) is described as a definition by one document (Gal. *Plac. Hippocr. Pl.* 4.2,8 (240, 11–13 DeLacy)) and as a sketch by others (Stob. *Ecl.* 2.7, 10^a (2. 89, 14–16 W.); Gal. *Plac. Hippocr. Pl.* 4.5,14 (262, 10–12 DeLacy)): this is probably due to our sources' carelessness (cf. above, n. 106). Other Stoic examples of sketches have been preserved: S.E. *M.* 8.245; 314; 454; 11.25; Stob. *Ecl.* 2.7, 5^b 13 (2. 68, 22–3 W.); 2.7, 5^d (2. 70, 3–5 W.); Ph. *Leg. All.* 1. 63.

As we have seen, definitions serve to improve a person's mental state in such a way that some preconceptions stored in that person's soul are transformed into conceptions in the narrow sense. This seems to require that definitions should be something more than accounts describing or reporting the contents of preconceptions. Some documents suggest that according to the Stoics an account describing or reporting the contents of a preconception is (not a definition, but) a sketch.[108] To be sure, T 29 does not connect sketches to preconceptions. Such a link may however be plausibly established on the basis of further evidence. Firstly, some sources report that sketches express what is common to all human beings.[109] This fits well with their being accounts expounding preconceptions, some of which were regarded by the Stoics as being shared by all human beings.[110] Secondly, Ammonius (in Porph. 55, 2–7) describes sketches as revealing their objects in a non-articulate manner (οὐ διηρθρωμένως), and contrasts them with definitions which instead present their objects clearly (σαφῶς). This again fits well with sketches being closely associated with preconceptions, which, as we have seen, are often contrasted with conceptions in the narrow sense in that they lack articulation (διάρθρωσις). Thirdly, some ancient sources record 'ὅρος ἐννοημματικός' as an alternative technical expression (not necessarily adopted by the Stoics) for 'ὑπογραφή'.[111] Once again, this fits well with sketches being closely associated with preconceptions.

The sources provide no indication as to what role the Stoics attributed to sketches. One guess is that a sketch was regarded as the starting-point of a research leading to the discovery of a definition, which was obtained by elaborating and expanding on the sketch. A hint that this guess could be on the right track is Stobaeus' report (Ecl. 2.7,6ᵃ (76, 1–2 W.)) that after Zeno defined the end as living consistently, his successors, 'by way of articulating further' ('προσδιαρθροῦντες'), defined it as 'living consistently with nature': this presupposes that for the Stoics the process of articulation could lead from one definition to a further definition, more accurate or otherwise superior (of course, if Zeno's original account was a definition, it could not be a sketch: the important point of Stobaeus' report is that the Stoics

---

[108] Cf. Gourinat (1996), 61; (2000), 53.
[109] Gal. Diff. Puls. 8. 708, 16–709, 1 K.
[110] See above, n.75 and text thereto.
[111] Schol. in Dionys. Thr. 114, 14–15; Gal. Diff. Puls. 8. 708, 16–709, 5K.

recognized the possibility of improving an account by transforming it into another account).[112]

IV Definition and Essence

Antipater and Chrysippus in a Passage by Alexander   The most important document concerning the Stoic views on definition and essence is a passage from Alexander of Aphrodisias' *Commentary on Aristotle's Topics*. Let me introduce the passage in question by summarizing its immediate context. The passage is part of Alexander's discussion (*in Top.* 41, 20–43, 8) of Aristotle's claim that 'a definition is an account that signifies the what it was to be' ('ἔστι [...] ὅρος [...] λόγος ὁ τὸ τί ἦν εἶναι σημαίνων', *Top.* 1.5, 101[b]39). Alexander begins (41, 21–8) with some general remarks about definitions: he asserts that the definition is more perfect than the other predicables, and he offers an etymology of 'definition'. He then (41, 29–42, 12) turns to Aristotle's characterization of a definition as 'an account that signifies the what it was to be'. He explains that the formula 'what it was to be' refers to what being amounts to for the item which is being defined, and he claims that the imperfect tense 'was' as used in this formula is equivalent to the present 'is'. He then (42, 12–43, 8) argues that the 'to be' portion of the formula 'what it was to be' is not superfluous. Had it been superfluous, 'what it was to be' would have been equivalent to 'what it was', which would in turn have been equivalent to 'what it is' (because, as Alexander has just said, 'was' as used in the formula is equivalent to 'is'). But, had this been correct, any formula attributing one of the 'predicates in the what it is' would have been a definition. For example, someone who had placed a species within its genus would thereby have defined the species. Alexander regards the obvious falsity of this consequence as a proof that the 'to be' portion of the formula 'what it was to be' is not superfluous. At this point comes the passage reporting Stoic views:

T 30   Therefore 'was' was not enough, as some believe (Antisthenes seems to have been the first of these, then came some Stoics), but it is reasonable that 'to be' should be added [οὐκ ἄρα αὔταρκες τὸ ἦν, ὥς τινες ἡγοῦνται, ὧν δοκεῖ

---

[112] Cf. above, n. 2 and text thereto.

πρῶτος μὲν Ἀντισθένης εἶναι, εἶτα δὲ καὶ τῶν ἀπὸ τῆς Στοᾶς τινες, ἀλλὰ εὐλόγως τὸ εἶναι πρόσκειται]. For the account that reveals what to be is for it [ὁ τί ἐστι τὸ εἶναι αὐτῷ δηλῶν λόγος] is not the one that predicates of it the genus or something else from its 'what it is': for to be for the species is not this, for its genus to be predicated of it, because the species is not identical to its genus. And what is said is equivalent to 'account revealing the substance of the thing, namely that by virtue of which it has being'. But those who say that a definition is an account formulated analytically and fittingly [οἱ δὲ λέγοντες ὅρον εἶναι λόγον κατὰ ἀνάλυσιν ἀπαρτιζόντως ἐκφερόμενον], calling 'analysis' the unfolding of what is defined, namely of the heading, 'fittingly' the lack of excess and defect ['ἀνάλυσιν' μὲν λέγοντες τὴν ἐξάπλωσιν τοῦ ὁριστοῦ καὶ κεφαλαιώδους,[113] 'ἀπαρτιζόντως' δὲ τὸ μήτε ὑπερβάλλειν μήτε ἐνδεῖν],[114] would say that a definition does not differ in any way at all from the rendering of a peculiarity [οὐδὲν ἂν λέγοιεν τὸν ὅρον διαφέρειν τῆς τοῦ ἰδίου ἀποδόσεως]. For even 'animal capable of laughter' is an account, and it explains man without excess or defect [ἀπερίττως τε καὶ ἀνελλιπῶς σημαίνει[115] τὸν ἄνθρωπον]: for it is neither larger nor smaller than man. But an account rendered by means of a peculiarity differs to the greatest extent from a definition because it does not indicate what to be for a man consists in [μὴ σημαίνει ἐν τίνι ἐστὶ τὸ εἶναι τῷ ἀνθρώπῳ]. For that being for a man does not consist in being capable of laughter is clear from the fact that the activities by virtue of which each one is bring it to perfection: but laughing is not a perfection for man. (in Top. 42, 20–43, 8)

In the first part of T 30 Alexander contrasts a position which he attributes to Antisthenes[116] and some Stoics, according to which a definition is an account that signifies the what it was, with Aristotle's position, according to which a definition is an account that signifies the what it was to be. The

---

[113] Here (43,1) the reading handed down by most MSS is 'καὶ κεφαλαιωδῶς' (B omits 'καί'). The words 'καὶ κεφαλαιωδῶς' appear also in the parallel Suda s.v. 'ἀνάλυσις'. This reading makes no sense. Three emendations have been suggested: Diels (followed by von Arnim apud SVF III Antipater 24) proposes '[καὶ] κεφαλαιώδη'; Rieth (1933), 42, 43–5 suggests 'καὶ κεφαλαιωδῶς <δηλουμένου>'; Pauli (1986), 233 favours 'καὶ κεφαλαιώδους' (with epexegetic 'καί'). This third emendation is more plausible than the others: several sources attest that the Stoics used 'κεφαλαιῶδες' as a technical term (see Epict. Diss. 2.12, 9–10; Simp. in Cat. 52,32–3; 66,6–10; 181, 33–4; Procl. in Ti. 1. 240,28–241,3; Schol. in Dionys. Thr. 107,30–108, 3).

[114] The noun 'ἐξάπλωσις' ('unfolding') occurs both in Galen (Art. Med. 1.305 K., where it is connected with the theory of definition and with 'ἀνάλυσις') and in Sextus Empiricus (M. 7.51, where it means 'paraphrase').

[115] For 'σημαίνειν' meaning 'to explain' see LSJ s.v. 'σημαίνω' III2.

[116] Cf. D.L. 6.3.

wording of T 30 suggests that Antisthenes and some Stoics advanced the thesis that a definition is an account that signifies the what it was as a criticism of Aristotle's characterization of a definition as an account that signifies the what it was to be. This however is extremely unlikely because Antisthenes seems to have lived between 445 and 365 BC,[117] and it is not plausible that before 365 BC he could have criticized Aristotle for his characterization of a definition. Three solutions are possible. The first is to assume that the characterization of a definition as an account that signifies the what it was to be was around in the Academy before Aristotle's time, early enough for Antisthenes to criticize it (Antisthenes could have criticized what we now call 'the Aristotelian position' without criticizing Aristotle himself). The second solution is to assume that T 30 is sloppily formulated: the truth of the matter is that Antisthenes first characterized a definition as an account that signifies the what it was without having in mind the Aristotelian position, and some Stoics later picked up Antisthenes' characterization and used it as a criticism of the Aristotelian position, but Alexander in his account mixed matters up by describing Antisthenes as a critic of the Aristotelian position. The third solution is to interpret T 30 as saying merely that Antisthenes and some Stoics characterized a definition as an account that signifies the what it was, without the further twist of this being a criticism of Aristotle. The first solution should be discarded because it lacks independent evidence: there is no trace of a pre-Aristotelian use of the formula 'the what it was to be'. The third solution should be preferred to the second on the grounds of charity towards Alexander.

T 30 also mentions a view about definition which it attributes to unnamed thinkers: that 'a definition is an account formulated analytically and fittingly'. It then goes on to claim that whoever holds such a view about definition is committed to granting that 'a definition does not differ in any way at all from the rendering of a peculiarity'. We are fortunate enough to be in a position to attribute to Antipater the view that 'a definition is an account formulated analytically and fittingly'. Moreover, there are documents which attribute to Chrysippus the claim that a definition is 'the rendering of a peculiarity'. Thus, T 30 is implicitly referring to Stoic views about definition.

---

[117] For the dates of Antisthenes' birth and death see Decleva Caizzi (1966), 118; Giannantoni (1990), IV 199–201.

Chrysippus' Characterization of Definitions   The following passage from Diogenes Laertius is the most important witness on Chrysippus' and Antipater's views on definitions:

T 31   And a definition, as Antipater says in the first book of *On Definitions*, is an account formulated analytically and fittingly [ὅρος δέ ἐστιν, ὥς φησιν Ἀντίπατρος ἐν τῷ πρώτῳ Περὶ ὅρων, λόγος κατ' ἀνάλυσιν ἀπαρτιζόντως ἐκφερόμενος],[118] or, as Chrysippus says in *On Definitions*, the rendering of a peculiarity [ἤ, ὡς Χρύσιππος ἐν τῷ Περὶ ὅρων, ἰδίου ἀπόδοσις].[119] (7.60)

For chronological reasons I discuss first Chrysippus' characterization of a definition as a 'rendering of a peculiarity'. At least two interpretations are possible: the *pneumatic* interpretation, according to which the 'rendering of a peculiarity' mentioned by Chrysippus is the description of a quality, which is a portion of breath,[120] and the *dialectical* interpretation, according to which the 'rendering of a peculiarity' mentioned by Chrysippus is the indication of an attribute to which 'peculiarity' can be applied in one of the senses in which this expression is used by Aristotle in dialectical contexts (especially in the *Topics*).[121]

Support for the pneumatic interpretation is provided by the fact that the Stoics apply the adjective 'peculiar' ('ἴδιος') to certain qualities which they thereby contrast with others to which they apply 'common' ('κοινός').[122]

---

[118] Cf. [Gal.] *Def. Med.* 19.349,1–2 K.; *Suda s.v.* 'ὅρος'; *s.v.* 'ἀπαρτιᾶν'; *s.v.* 'ἀνάλυσις'; Alex. Aphr. *in Top.* 42, 27–43, 1 (where Antipater is not mentioned). In the scholia to Dionysius Thrax we read: 'ὁ δὲ Ἀντίπατρος ὁ Στωϊκὸς λέγει· "ὅρος ἐστὶ λόγος κατ' ἀνάγκην ἐκφερόμενος", τουτέστι κατ' ἀντιστροφήν· καὶ γὰρ ὁ ὅρος ἀντιστρέφειν θέλει' (107, 6–8). As von Arnim already realized (see the note to *SVF* II 226), 'κατ' ἀνάγκην' is probably corrupt. However, his suggested emendation 'κατ' ἀνάλυσιν' is unsatisfactory: 'ἀνάλυσις' has nothing to do with convertibility (cf. Rieth (1933), 42). It is better to correct 'κατ' ἀνάγκην' into 'κατ' ἀπαρτισμόν', an expression which seems to have been used in the sense of 'precisely' and 'fittingly' by Chrysippus and Posidonius (see Stob. *Ecl.* 1.8,42 (1. 106, 1 and 1. 106, 17 W.)).

[119] The words 'ἤ, ὡς ... ἀπόδοσις' are entirely omitted by F, one of the three main MSS whereby Diogenes Laertius has been handed down to us; of the other two main MSS, B reads 'ἤ, ὡς ὁ Χρύσιππος ἐν τῷ Περὶ ὅρων, ἡ ἀπόδοσις' (cf. *Suda s.v.* 'ὅρος'), whilst P has 'ἤ, ὡς Χρύσιππος ἐν τῷ Περὶ ὅρων, ἡ ἀπόδοσις'. The reading adopted in the main text above is the result of von Arnim's emendation (based on *Schol. in Dionys. Thr.* 107, 5–6, the only other document that attributes to Chrysippus a characterization of definitions), and has been endorsed by all later eds. (Hicks, H.S. Long, Baldassarri, Hülser, and Marcovich). Chrysippus' characterization of definitions is repeated (with no mention of Chrysippus) by Alex. Aphr. *in Top.* 42, 27–43, 1, and is echoed by Clem. Al. *Strom.* 8.6,21,3. For Chrysippus' work *On Definitions* see above, n.9 and text thereto.

[120] Cf. Goldschmidt (1953), 164; Reesor (1972), 284; Brittain (2005), 187, 189, 191.

[121] Cf. Bréhier (1908), 30.

[122] D.L. 7.58; A.D. *Pron.* 105, 18–19; Plu. *Virt. Mor.* 2, 441B.

A peculiar quality[123] is a portion of breath which by imbuing a lump of matter gives rise to a peculiarly qualified item. A peculiarly qualified item remains the same for so long as its peculiar quality continues to exist and remains unchanged, and its peculiar quality is distinct from that of every other peculiarly qualified item. Thus, the peculiar quality of a peculiarly qualified item is tied both to its identity and to its distinctness. This has to do with our ability to recognize peculiarly qualified items. When we meet a peculiarly qualified item we can form a memory of it which is based on its peculiar quality. If we encounter that peculiarly qualified item again, we can recognize it because its peculiar quality is still there unchanged for us to spot, and whenever we spot that peculiar quality we may infer that the peculiarly qualified item is the same.[124] A common quality is probably a portion of breath different parts of which imbue different lumps of matter so as to give rise to commonly qualified items of the same sort. The fact that according to the Stoics at least some qualities can be described by using the adjective 'peculiar' speaks in support of the pneumatic interpretation of Chrysippus' characterization of a definition as 'the rendering of a peculiarity', according to which what Chrysippus means is that a definition is a description of a quality. Given that the peculiar quality of a peculiarly qualified item is tied both to its identity and to its distinctness, one can see that the pneumatic interpretation of Chrysippus' characterization of definitions credits Chrysippus with something like the view that a definition is an account of a thing's essence.

Three considerations speak in favour of the dialectical interpretation of Chrysippus' characterization of definitions. [a] In the *Topics* Aristotle employs the phrase 'to render a peculiarity' ('ἴδιον ἀποδοῦναι'),[125] and he uses the noun 'rendering' ('ἀπόδοσις') to describe what is going on when one offers a definition.[126] Such a usage recalls Chrysippus' characterization of a definition as 'the rendering of a peculiarity' ('ἰδίου ἀπόδοσις'). [b] When Alexander in T 30 introduces the characterization of definitions which other

[123] My reconstruction of the Stoic views on the first and the second category is close to David Sedley's: see Sedley (1982), 255–67, 271–4; Long and Sedley (1987), 1172–3; Sedley (1999), 402–4 (cf. Lewis (1995), 90–7).

[124] Cf. Schubert (1994), 219; Lewis (1995), 91–3.

[125] *Top.* 5.1, 128ᵇ22; 128ᵇ34–5; 129ᵃ6; 2, 129ᵇ6; 130ᵃ16; etc.

[126] *Top.* 1.5, 102ᵃ3; 18, 108ᵇ9; 108ᵇ20; 4.6, 128ᵃ24; 6.8, 147ᵃ5; 12, 149ᵇ13–14. The phrase 'rendering of a peculiarity' never occurs in Aristotle, but it is relatively common in Alexander's *Commentary on Aristotle's Topics* (see 376, 34; 380, 12; 382, 3; 12; 25; 383, 1; 21; 401, 2; 514, 5; 14).

sources attribute to Chrysippus, he treats it as if 'peculiarity' were used in one of the senses we encounter in Aristotle's *Topics*. In fact, Alexander does not even suggest that the characterization of a definition as 'the rendering of a peculiarity' had been offered by some thinker: it is we who on the basis of independent evidence identify this characterization of definitions with Chrysippus'. Alexander merely says that those who hold that 'a definition is an account formulated analytically and fittingly' are committed to the claim that a definition is 'the rendering of a peculiarity', and in saying this he is using 'peculiarity' in an Aristotelian sense. Note that the dialectical interpretation does not require that Chrysippus should have read Aristotle's *Topics* (the evidence does not enable us to establish whether Chrysippus read any of the treatises within the *Organon*).[127] The *Topics* are probably the codification of dialectical practices which were common in the Academy: Chrysippus could have encountered some of the views codified in the *Topics* not by reading the work but by being acquainted with an Academic tradition. [c] The Stoic use of the adjective 'peculiar' in connection with qualities is attested only with regard to peculiar qualities.[128] Thus, if what Chrysippus means when he characterizes a definition as 'the rendering of a peculiarity' were that a definition is a description of a quality, he would be expressing himself in a way which suggests that a definition is a description of a peculiar quality. Such a suggestion would be infelicitous: if definitions are descriptions of qualities, it is surely not the case that they are descriptions only of peculiar qualities and not also of common qualities.

The considerations supporting the dialectical interpretation are more convincing than those supporting the pneumatic interpretation. The dialectical interpretation should therefore be preferred, according to which when he characterizes a definition as 'the rendering of a peculiarity', Chrysippus is using 'peculiarity' in one of the senses in which it is used by Aristotle in the *Topics*.

Three facts are worth noting about Aristotle's use of 'peculiarity' and his conception of peculiarities in the *Topics*:

---

[127] Cf. Barnes (1999).

[128] To be sure, Simplicius (*in Cat.* 222, 32) credits the Stoics with the use of the noun 'peculiarness' ('ἰδιότης') in connection with common qualities. But the passage within which this ascription occurs (*in Cat.* 222, 30–3) is so obscure that not much can be made of it.

[a] Every peculiarity has a necessary link to what it is a peculiarity of. More specifically: not only is it the case that y is a peculiarity of x only if y holds of all and only the individuals of which x holds; it is also the case that y is a peculiarity of x only if it is necessary that y should hold of all and only the individuals of which x holds.[129]

[b] In order for a peculiarity to be rendered finely, the peculiarity rendered must be more familiar than what it is a peculiarity of. This is because the purpose of rendering a peculiarity of an item is to make that item more familiar, namely to enable someone to come to know that item better.[130]

[c] There are two senses of 'peculiarity': a strong and a weak sense. In its strong sense, 'peculiarity' applies to y with respect to x just if it is necessary that y should hold of all and only the individuals of which x holds but y does not reveal the essence of x. In its weak sense, 'peculiarity' applies to y with respect to x just if it is necessary that y should hold of all and only the individuals of which x holds (it is not ruled out that y could reveal the essence of x).[131]

Aristotle's commitment to [a] makes it plausible to understand Chrysippus as postulating that a necessary link should obtain between the attribute corresponding to the *definiendum*-expression and the one corresponding to the *definiens*-expression. In other words, Chrysippus is probably committed to the view that it is always necessary that for every individual v, the attribute corresponding to the *definiendum*-expression holds of v just if the attribute corresponding to the *definiens*-expression holds of v.

Aristotle's commitment to [b] makes it plausible to credit Chrysippus with the view that the attribute corresponding to the *definiens*-expression should be better known than the one corresponding to the *definiendum*-expression and should help one to come to know the attribute

---

[129] *Top.* 1.5, 102^{a}22–30; 5.1, 129^{a}3–5; 3, 131^{a}27–131^{b}4; 4, 133^{a}12–23 (cf. Pflug (1908), 7–8; Verbeke (1968), 264–5; Barnes (1970), 137–9).

[130] *Top.* 5.2, 129^{b}2–29; 130^{a}4–5; 3, 130^{b}38–131^{a}26 (cf. Verbeke (1968), 262–70).

[131] *Top.* 1.4, 101^{b}17–25 (cf. 5, 102^{a}18–19; 8, 103^{b}2–19; 4.1, 120^{b}12–13; 5.3, 131^{b}37–132^{a}9; 4, 132^{b}35–133^{a}11; 133^{a}18–23; 5, 135^{a}11–12; 6.1, 139^{a}31–2; 139^{b}3–5; 3, 140^{a}33–140^{b}26; 7.5, 154^{a}37–154^{b}2; 155^{a}7–10; 155^{a}17–22; *APr.* 1.27, 43^{b}6–8; *APo.* 1.4, 91^{a}15; 2.4, 91^{a}14–18; Barnes (1970), 140–2; Brunschwig (1986), 146–7; 153–5). Brittain (2005), 187 seems to suggest that on one of the two senses of 'peculiarity' distinguished by Aristotle, 'peculiarity' applies to y with respect to x just if it is necessary that y should hold of all and only the individuals of which x holds and y reveals the essence of x. No such sense of 'peculiarity' appears to be operating in the *Topics*.

corresponding to the *definiendum*-expression. Note that such a view about definitions is very reasonable, and fits well within the Socratic and Platonic tradition: it is at least part of what lies behind the well-known requirements that definitions should not be circular and should help one to come to know what something is (knowing something is often equated with knowing what it is).

As for [c], no confident answer can be reached for the question in which of Aristotle's two senses Chrysippus is using 'peculiarity'. On the one hand, one might argue that if Chrysippus acknowledges that some things have essences, it would be strange for him to use 'peculiarity' in Aristotle's strong sense, whereby it applies to y in its relation to x just if it is necessary that y should hold of all and only the individuals of which x holds but y does not reveal the essence of x: why should all definitions avoid revealing the essence? If instead Chrysippus holds that no things have essences, it would be awkward for him to use 'peculiarity' in Aristotle's strong sense (just as a scientist who believes that there are no goblins would avoid using a word in a sense whose elucidation would involve the phrase '... and not a goblin'). On the assumption that Chrysippus has a position with regard to essences, i.e. holds either that some things have essences or that no things have essences, it may be plausibly inferred that he does not use 'peculiarity' in Aristotle's strong sense. On the other hand, one might argue that Chrysippus is using 'peculiarity' in Aristotle's strong sense precisely to make (obliquely) the point that no things have essences.

One final ambiguity in Chrysippus' characterization of a definition should be noticed. According to a first interpretation, Chrysippus maintains that the attribute corresponding to the whole *definiens*-expression is a peculiarity. For example, if one defines man by using the *definiens*-expression 'rational mortal animal', one's definition counts as 'the rendering of a peculiarity' because the attribute rational-mortal-animal, signified by the whole *definiens*-expression 'rational mortal animal', is itself a peculiarity of man. According to a second interpretation, Chrysippus maintains that a peculiarity is an attribute corresponding (not to the whole *definiens*-expression, but) to a constituent of it: according to this second interpretation, by saying that a definition is 'the rendering of a peculiarity' Chrysippus means that a definition is completed or accomplished only when a peculiarity is rendered, namely when an attribute is mentioned which is a peculiarity of the item which is being defined. For example, if one defines man by using the *definiens*-expression 'animal capable of laughter', one's definition counts as 'the rendering of a peculiarity' because after mentioning the genus man one has completed or accomplished the definition by mentioning that peculiarity of man which is the attribute capable-of-laughter. The two interpretations of Chrysippus' characterization of a definition as 'the rendering of a peculiarity' correspond to two different conceptions of definitions which were both rather widespread in antiquity. On the one hand, Cicero seems to echo the idea that the attribute corresponding to the whole *definiens*-expression is a peculiarity;[132] on the other hand, Quintilianus and Marius Victorinus favour the view that a peculiarity is an attribute corresponding to a constituent of the *definiens*-expression.[133]

T 30 seems to opt for the second interpretation of Chrysippus' characterization of a definition, according to which a peculiarity is an attribute corresponding to a constituent of the *definiens*-expression. For it considers 'animal capable of laughter' as a possible *definiens*-expression for man. Alexander normally mentions capable-of-laughter, not animal-capable-of-laughter, as an example of a peculiarity.[134] Hence in T 30 the peculiarity is probably the attribute capable-of-laughter, which is signified by a constituent of the *definiens*-expression 'animal capable of laughter'. Despite this, I have a slight preference for the first interpretation of Chrysippus' characterization of a definition: for the second interpretation requires a rather strained and unnatural reading of the sentence 'A definition is the rendering of a peculiarity' (it must mean something like 'A definition is accomplished when a peculiarity is mentioned').

Antipater's Characterization of Definitions Antipater's characterization of a definition as a 'λόγος κατ' ἀνάλυσιν ἀπαρτιζόντως ἐκφερόμενος' presents us with a difficulty of literal interpretation: how should 'κατ' ἀνάλυσιν' and 'ἀπαρτιζόντως' be construed with respect to one another? On one interpretation, adopted by some scholars, 'κατ' ἀνάλυσιν' and 'ἀπαρτιζόντως' are coordinate adverbial modifications of 'ἐκφερόμενος'. Accordingly, Antipater's view would be that a definition is 'an account formulated analytically

---

[132] Cic. *Top.* 6, 29; *Part.* 12, 41.

[133] Quint. *Inst.* 7.3, 3; Mar. Vict. *Def.* 8, 6–27 Stangl. On the two ways of conceiving the relationship between definitions and peculiarities in antiquity see Pauli (1986), 229–33.

[134] *In Top.* 40, 4–7; 43, 23–8; 45, 19–24; 45, 27–8; 60, 15–17; 132, 11–12; 133, 5–8; 137, 15–16; 192, 4–7; 322, 19–22; 373, 7–9; 375, 24–6; 387, 22–4; 416, 21–3; 516, 3–5; 517, 3–11.

and fittingly'.[135] On a second interpretation, which seems to be favoured by Mariano Baldassarri, '*κατ' ἀνάλυσιν*' modifies '*ἀπαρτιζόντως*'. Accordingly, Antipater's view would be that a definition is 'an account formulated fittingly with respect to the analysis', that is an account whose analysis (the phrase supposed to do the explicating or clarifying) neither omits any necessary characteristic nor includes any superfluous one.[136] On a third interpretation, which, as far as I can see, has not been offered by anyone, '*κατ' ἀνάλυσιν*' modifies '*ἀπαρτιζόντως*' in a way different from the one suggested by the second interpretation. A fragment of Stoic ontology preserved in Simplicius' *Commentary on Aristotle's Categories* uses expressions connected with the adverb '*ἀπαρτιζόντως*' to express the idea of something fitting something,[137] and there the expressions in question are construed with '*κατά*' followed by a noun phrase in the accusative in such a way that the '*κατά*'-phrase introduces the item with respect to which the fit is supposed to obtain.[138] If we import this construal back into the interpretation of Antipater's characterization of definitions, the result is that according to Antipater a definition is 'an account formulated fittingly with respect to the analysis': an account whose 'analysis' (the phrase supposed to do the explicating or clarifying) fits, that is neither exceeds nor falls short of, the item for which the explication or clarification is being offered.

The parallel with the fragment of Stoic ontology preserved in Simplicius' *Commentary on Aristotle's Categories* might be thought to give the edge to the third interpretation. However, the resulting characterization of definitions is uneven: why should only one of the items be mentioned between which the fit is supposed to obtain? From a purely linguistic point of view, the first interpretation seems more plausible: thus, in accordance with the first interpretation, I shall assume that according to Antipater a definition is 'an account formulated analytically and fittingly'. This makes it all the more important to clarify the meaning of the phrase '*κατ' ἀνάλυσιν*', which I rendered simply by 'analytically'. If in this matter we may trust Alexander of Aphrodisias' witness, those who endorsed Antipater's characterization of definitions called '"*ἀνάλυσις*" the *ἐξάπλωσις* of what is defined' (*in Top.* 42,

---

[135] Long and Sedley (1987), I 190–1; Hülser *apud FDS* II 715.

[136] Baldassarri (1984–7), I 101.

[137] Cf. '*συναπαρτίζω*' (Simp. *in Cat.* 212, 14; 212, 34; 213, 6; 215, 1; 226, 23—cf. 184, 21–2); '*ἀπαρτίζω*' (Simp. *in Cat.* 212, 24; 212, 25; 212, 34); '*ἀπηρτισμένως*' (Simp. *in Cat.* 212, 22–3; 212, 24).

[138] *in Cat.* 212, 22–4; 212, 25–6.

28). The noun '$\dot{\epsilon}\xi\dot{\alpha}\pi\lambda\omega\sigma\iota\varsigma$' ('unfolding') was perhaps used already by Zeno within the phrase '$\dot{\epsilon}\xi\dot{\alpha}\pi\lambda\omega\sigma\iota\varsigma$ $\tau\hat{\omega}\nu$ $\delta\alpha\kappa\tau\dot{\upsilon}\lambda\omega\nu$' ('unfolding of fingers') in order to explain the difference between dialectic and rhetoric: Sextus Empiricus (*M.* 2.7) reports that Zeno used the clenching of his fist to indicate the compact and concise character of dialectic, the unfolding of his fingers to allude to the breadth of rhetoric. If we follow the lead of Zeno's use of '$\dot{\epsilon}\xi\dot{\alpha}\pi\lambda\omega\sigma\iota\varsigma$', the result is that according to Antipater a definition is an account formulated by way of expansion and fittingly. This interpretation of the phrase '$\kappa\alpha\tau'$ $\dot{\alpha}\nu\dot{\alpha}\lambda\upsilon\sigma\iota\nu$' is rather plausible also on historical grounds: it turns out that by using this phrase Antipater wanted to point out that a definition must provide an expansion of what is defined, and this requirement can be regarded as corresponding, at least in part, to Aristotle's postulate that the *definiens*-expression should always be a phrase (never a single word).[139]

The Relationship between Chrysippus' and Antipater's Characterizations of Definitions   In T 30 Alexander treats the characterization of definitions which we have reason to attribute to Antipater as equivalent to that which we have reason to attribute to Chrysippus. However, since Antipater lived about 80 years after Chrysippus, and since Antipater's characterization of definitions sounds quite different from Chrysippus', one is inclined to think that Antipater was taking himself to be improving on Chrysippus' characterization. It is not clear what the improvement was supposed to consist in. One possibility is that by requiring that the item that does the defining should simply fit, namely neither exceed nor fall short of, the item defined, Antipater was dispensing with the modal component of Chrysippus' characterization which was implicit in his borrowing Aristotle's conception of a peculiarity: Chrysippus was committed to the view that for every individual it is always *necessary* that the item that does the defining should hold of it just if the item defined holds of it; on Antipater's characterization, all that is required is that the item that does the defining should hold of all and only the individuals of which the item defined holds.[140]

---

[139] *Top.* 1.5, 102^{a}2–5; 6.11, 149^{a}1–2; *Metaph.* Z 10, 1034^{b}20; H 3, 1043^{b}25–6; 6, 1045^{a}12–14.

[140] Brittain (2005), 187 interprets Antipater's characterization of definitions in such a way that it requires that a definition specify a necessary attribute which is unique to the thing defined. As far as I can tell, the evidence does not warrant the modal component of this interpretation.

Definitions Do Not Disclose Essences In whichever of Aristotle's two senses Chrysippus is using 'peculiarity', he is not committed to the claim that a definition reveals the essence of the thing defined.[141] We have also seen that Antipater's characterization of definitions is surely not stronger than Chrysippus': if anything, it is weaker because it gives up the modal component of Chrysippus' characterization. Thus, we can safely assume that in his characterization of definitions Antipater is also not committed to the claim that a definition reveals the essence of the thing defined. We can therefore plausibly conclude that the Stoics do not require definitions to disclose essences. This position chimes with what we have seen so far of the Stoic view on definitions: if the role of definitions is to sharpen our conceptions, namely the rational presentations whereby we grasp universals, there is no reason why definitions should disclose essences.

It is worth recalling that according to Aristotle certain definitions reveal what something is by explaining what certain linguistic expressions (usually nouns or noun-phrases) signify.[142] Since for Aristotle a definition which is merely an account of what a certain linguistic expression signifies need not disclose an essence, Aristotle would probably have accepted that certain definitions reveal what something is without disclosing the essences of the items defined.

One might still doubt that the Stoics can coherently detach definitions from essences. One reason for having doubts of this sort could be based on the fact that the Stoics attribute an important role to definitions in teaching and learning (cf. T24). But—one might argue—teaching and learning are intimately connected with proofs, which surely must use essences in their providing explanations of facts. However, on reflection, the Stoic position is consistent. For, according to one Stoic characterization, a proof is a conclusive argument where the premises are apprehended while the conclusion used not to be apprehended but has become apprehended,[143] and arguments

[141] Long and Sedley (1987), I 194 claim that 'there seems no doubt' that in Chrysippus' characterization of a definition the expression 'peculiarity' is 'intended [...] to apply only to features which are not just unique but also essential'. But the evidence mentioned by Long and Sedley to buttress their claim (Alex. Aphr. *in Top.* 1,8–14; D.L. 7.103; Sen. *Ep.* 76,9–10; Cic. *Tusc.* 5.28, 81–2) is far from conclusive.
[142] *APo.* 2.10, 93^{b}29–32 (cf. 7, 92^{b}26–8).
[143] Cic. *Ac.* 2.8,26 (cf. D.L. 7.45).

of this sort need not provide explanations of the statables asserted as their conclusions.[144]

Another reason for doubting that the Stoics can coherently detach definition from essence has to do with the roles they attribute to qualities. As I pointed out earlier,[145] qualities are tied to an entity's identity over time and to its distinctness from other entities. So, qualities play a role rather similar to that which other philosophical systems ascribe to essences. Given that qualities enable us to recognize the entities which have them, would it not be reasonable to require that definitions somehow capture or describe the qualities (or essences) of what is being defined? I think that this consideration does carry some weight. Nevertheless I resist crediting the Stoics with the view that definitions reveal the qualities (or the essences) of the things they are defining. For our documents present absolutely no explicit indication that they took such a line, and there is a small bit of further independent evidence suggesting that they kept clear from it. For one striking feature of the Stoics' practice is that they often offer several different definitions of the same thing:[146] this would be strange if definitions were to reveal the essences of the things defined.

V Definitions, Sayables, and Statables

What Is a Definition?   Are definitions linguistic expressions or sayables? If they are sayables, are they statables or sayables of a different sort (on a par with questions, commands, etc.)?

Let me begin by addressing the question whether for the Stoics definitions are linguistic expressions or sayables. Four documents are relevant to it.

---

[144] Sextus Empiricus (*P.* 2.135–43, *M.* 8.300–14) reports different characterizations of proof which probably go back to the Stoics. I cannot pursue here these alternative characterizations, but I think it could be shown that they also do not require that a proof provide an explanation of the statable asserted as its conclusion.

[145] Cf. above, paragraph to n. 122.

[146] D.L. 7.42 (dialectic); 7.58 (verb); 7.64 (predicate); 7.94 (the good); 7.135 (surface and line); Sen. *Ep.* 89,5 (wisdom); Cic. *Tusc.* 4.24,53 (courage); etc. It cannot be ruled out that sometimes our sources misdescribe as a definition what the Stoics would regard as a sketch (cf. above, n. 106 for an example). But it would be quite extraordinary if all the alleged cases of multiple definitions of a single item were due to a misdescription of our sources.

[i] Definitions and Indefinite Conditionals in Chrysippean Dialectic The first relevant document is the following passage from Sextus Empiricus:

T 32 All philosophers who seem appropriately to expound the elements [of the ethical part of philosophy], and most notably of all those of the Old Academy and the Peripatetics, and the Stoics too, are accustomed to make a division by saying that of beings some are good, others bad, others between these (these last they also call 'indifferent') [εἰώθασι διαιρούμενοι λέγειν τῶν ὄντων τὰ μὲν εἶναι ἀγαθά, τὰ δὲ κακά, τὰ δὲ μεταξὺ τούτων, ἅπερ καὶ ἀδιάφορα λέγουσιν]. Xenocrates, however, in a way rather peculiar with respect to the others, and employing singular cases, said: 'Every being either is good or is bad or neither is good nor is bad' [ἰδιαίτερον δὲ παρὰ τοὺς ἄλλους ὁ Ξενοκράτης καὶ ταῖς ἑνικαῖς πτώσεσι χρώμενος ἔφασκε· 'πᾶν τὸ ὂν ἢ ἀγαθόν ἐστιν ἢ κακόν ἐστιν ἢ οὔτε ἀγαθόν ἐστιν οὔτε κακόν ἐστιν']. [. . .]

Although the fact that the distinction of beings is threefold seems to be agreed in all quarters, some people invent specious arguments by granting, on the one hand, that the distinction of beings is more or less of this sort, and yet, on the other hand, attacking in a sophistical fashion the division set forth. And we will be clear about this if we take it up from a little further back.

The technical writers [τεχνογράφοι] say that a definition differs from a universal claim[147] merely in composition, but is the same as far as force is concerned [τὸν ὅρον ψιλῇ τῇ συντάξει διαφέρειν τοῦ καθολικοῦ, δυνάμει τὸν αὐτὸν ὄντα].[148] And reasonably: for he who says 'Man is a rational mortal animal' and he who says 'If something is a man, it is a rational mortal animal' say the same as far as force is concerned, but something different as far as sound is concerned [ὁ εἰπὼν 'ἄνθρωπός

---

[147] I adopt 'universal claim' as a translation of the noun 'καθολικόν'. I reserve 'universal' for 'καθόλου'. One of the reasons for the choice of 'universal claim' as a translation is to avoid prejudging the question whether the items denoted by 'καθολικόν' are linguistic expressions or sayables.

[148] Most translators render the occurrences of 'δύναμις' in T 32 by 'meaning' (see Bury (1933–49), III 389; Long and Sedley (1987), 1180–1; Bett (1997), 4). However, as far as I can see, in no other fragment of Stoic logic is 'δύναμις' used in the sense of 'meaning'. By contrast, several fragments display occurrences of 'δύναμις' within contexts that recall those of T 32, occurrences that require the translation 'force'. For example, we find 'δύναμις τῶν λημμάτων' meaning 'strength of the premises' (see S.E. P. 2. 143; M. 8.310, cf. M. 8.308), and 'δύναμις λόγου' meaning 'strength of reason' (see Plu. Stoic. Rep. 10, 1037B; Aud. Poët. 11, 31E).

ἐστι ζῷον λογικὸν θνητόν’ τῷ εἰπόντι ‘εἴ τί ἐστιν ἄνθρωπος, ἐκεῖνο
ζῷόν ἐστι λογικὸν θνητόν’ τῇ μὲν δυνάμει τὸ αὐτὸ λέγει, τῇ δὲ φωνῇ
διάφορον].¹⁴⁹ And that this is so is plain from the fact that not only is
the universal claim inclusive of the particulars, but the definition also
extends over all the species of the thing rendered, that of man, for
example, over all specific men, and that of horse over all horses.¹⁵⁰ And
if one falsehood is subsumed under either of the two (the universal
claim or the definition), it becomes faulty [ἑνὸς ὑποταχθέντος ψεύδους
ἑκάτερον γίνεται μοχθηρόν, τό τε καθολικὸν καὶ ὁ ὅρος].

Well then, just as these, although they differ as far as sounds are
concerned, are the same as far as force is concerned [ταῦτα φωναῖς
ἐξηλλαγμένα κατὰ δύναμίν ἐστι τὰ αὐτά], so also, they say, a complete
division, which has a universal force, differs from the universal claim in
composition [ἡ τέλειος διαίρεσις, δύναμιν ἔχουσα καθολικήν, συντάξει
τοῦ καθολικοῦ διενήνοχεν]. For he who divides in this way, ‘Of men
some are Greeks, others barbarians’ [‘τῶν ἀνθρώπων οἱ μέν εἰσιν
Ἕλληνες, οἱ δὲ βάρβαροι’], says something equivalent [ἴσον τι λέγει]
to ‘If some are men, they are either Greeks or barbarians’ [‘εἴ τινές
εἰσιν ἄνθρωποι, ἐκεῖνοι ἢ Ἕλληνές εἰσιν ἢ βάρβαροι’]. For if some man
is found who is neither Greek nor barbarian, it is necessary both that
the division should be faulty and that the universal claim should
become false [ἀνάγκη μοχθηρὰν μὲν εἶναι τὴν διαίρεσιν, ψεῦδος δὲ
γίνεσθαι τὸ καθολικόν].

Hence, too, what is said in this way, ‘Of beings some are good,
others bad, others between these’, is, according to Chrysippus, as far as
force is concerned, a universal claim like ‘If some things are beings,
they either are good or are bad or indifferent’ [καὶ τὸ οὕτω λεγόμενον
‘τῶν ὄντων τὰ μέν ἐστιν ἀγαθά, τὰ δὲ κακά, τὰ δὲ τούτων μεταξύ’
δυνάμει κατὰ τὸν Χρύσιππον τοιοῦτόν ἐστι καθολικόν· ‘εἴ τινά ἐστιν
ὄντα, ἐκεῖνα ἤτοι ἀγαθά ἐστιν ἢ κακά ἐστιν ἢ ἀδιάφορα’]. But such a
universal claim is false if something false is subsumed under it [τὸ

¹⁴⁹ For the Stoic classification that lies behind the definition ‘Man is a rational mortal animal’ see Ph.
Agr. 139. A Latin version of ‘If something is a man, it is a rational mortal animal’ appears in Cic. Ac. 2.7,
21.
¹⁵⁰ According to the Stoics ‘a most specific [sc. species] is what, being a species, does not have a species
[εἰδικώτατόν ἐστιν ὃ εἶδος ὂν εἶδος οὐκ ἔχει], like Socrates’ (D.L. 7.61). Thus for the Stoics individuals
also are species.

τοιοῦτον καθολικὸν ψεῦδός ἐστιν ὑποτασσομένου τινὸς αὐτῷ ψεύδους].
For, they say, if two things are given, one of them good and the other
one bad (or one good and the other indifferent, or one bad and the
other indifferent), 'This, among beings, is good' is true, but 'These are
good' is false: for it is not the case that they are good, but one is good
and the other one bad. And, again, 'These are bad' is false: for it is not
the case that they are bad, but one of them is. Similarly with indiffer-
ents: for 'These are indifferent' is false, as 'These are good or bad' is. So
this is, more or less, the objection, but it appears not to affect Xenocrates because he did not employ plural cases, which would have
resulted in the division being falsified by the indication of items of
different kinds. (*M.* 11.3–14)

T 32 brings on the stage several characters that remain unidentified: in its
second paragraph it mentions certain people who invented 'specious arguments'; at the beginning of its third paragraph it mentions certain technical
writers; near the beginning of its fourth paragraph it vaguely refers to certain
people by means of the sentence 'they say'. The people vaguely referred to
near the beginning of the fourth paragraph must be the same as the technical
writers mentioned at the beginning of the third paragraph: for the technical
writers are introduced by means of the sentence 'φασὶν οἱ τεχνογράφοι', the
people vaguely referred to near the beginning of the fourth paragraph are
introduced by means of a simple 'φασί', and it is natural to supply the subject
for the 'φασί' from the preceding 'φασὶν οἱ τεχνογράφοι'.[151] At the beginning of T 32's fifth paragraph Chrysippus is mentioned in a way that
presupposes his being committed to the views attributed to the people
mentioned near the beginning of the fourth paragraph, who, as we have
just seen, can be plausibly identified with the technical writers. This makes it
likely to assume that these technical writers were Stoic authors of introduc-
tions to dialectic[152] who were expounding Chrysippean theories.[153] T 32
discusses at some length an objection to the division 'Of beings some are

---

[151] According to Bett (1997), 55–7, the people mentioned near the beginning of the fourth paragraph
are not the third paragraph's technical writers, but the unidentified authors of specious arguments
mentioned in the second paragraph. This interpretation seems to me implausible for the linguistic
reasons mentioned in the main text above.
[152] Cf. S.E. *M.* 8.428.
[153] Cf. Long and Sedley (1987), II 185; Crivelli (1994b), 497–8; Spinelli (1995), 158; Bett (1997), 54–6.

good, others bad, others between these', a division that employs plural cases, and it claims that the objection does not apply to Xenocrates' division 'Every being either is good or is bad or neither is good nor is bad', a division that employs singular cases. The ultimate source of T 32's discussion could be Chrysippus' work *On Incorrect Objections to Definitions* (in seven books):[154] definitions and divisions, although distinct, are so intimately linked that an incorrect objection to a division could well be discussed in a work dedicated to incorrect objections to definitions (note that T 32 itself introduces definitions in its discussion of objections to divisions). Who are then the authors of specious arguments mentioned in T 32's second paragraph? They could be people who actually produced specious objections to Xenocrates' division and were criticized by the technical writers who were followers of Chrysippus; however, if the specious objections to Xenocrates' division were invented by Chrysippus in his critical exposition of incorrect objections to divisions and definitions, the authors of specious arguments could well coincide with Chrysippus and the technical writers who were following him (it is they who made up the objections and then criticized them).

What kind of item is the definition discussed in T 32's third paragraph? Is it the linguistic expression 'Man is a rational mortal animal'? Or is it the sayable signified by this linguistic expression, namely the sayable **«man is-a-rational-mortal-animal»**?[155]

Two remarks made in T 32's third paragraph could induce one to think that the definition under discussion is a linguistic expression: firstly, the

---

[154] D.L. 7.199.

[155] In my presentation of sayables, I rely on a primitive and unexplained distinction between simple and complex linguistic expressions (note that certain phrases, like 'is running' and 'it is', are to count as simple linguistic expressions). I take any utterance of any simple linguistic expression to signify an item which I denote by a name written in boldface (and, if appropriate, hyphens): for instance, an utterance of 'runs' signifies the predicate **runs**, and an utterance of 'is walking' signifies the predicate **is-walking**. I take any utterance of any complex linguistic expression to signify the concatenation (with association on the right) of the items signified by the utterances of simple linguistic expressions that are its components: for instance, an utterance of 'Dio is walking' signifies **Dio + is-walking** (namely the concatenation of **Dio** with **is-walking**), and an utterance of 'Not Dio is walking' signifies **not + (Dio + is-walking)** (namely the concatenation of **not** with the concatenation of **Dio** with **is-walking**). No item signified by any utterance of any simple linguistic expression is the concatenation of anything with anything. (For a presentation of the theory of concatenation see Tarski (1933), 173–4, for its development see Corcoran et al. (1974), 625–8, 635–6.) I use a sequence of occurrences of names enclosed in chevron quotes ('«' and '»') as an abbreviation of the expression obtained by inserting occurrences of the concatenation symbol between those occurrences of names (with parentheses added to express association on the right): for instance, '**«not Dio is-walking»**' is an abbreviation of '**not + (Dio + is-walking)**'.

remark that 'a definition differs from a universal claim merely in composition' (the expression translated by 'composition', 'σύνταξις', could also be rendered by 'syntax'); secondly, the remark that a definition and a universal claim 'say the same as far as force is concerned, but something different as far as sound is concerned'. However, a bit of reflection shows that these two remarks provide no compelling evidence in favour of the interpretation they are supposed to support. Firstly, the remark that 'a definition differs from a universal claim merely in composition' is neither here nor there because 'composition' could refer to the way sayables are constructed from more elementary components—such a usage of 'composition' is attested in fragments of Stoic logic.[156] The remark in question could therefore amount to the observation that a definition and the corresponding universal claim are distinct sayables differently assembled from the same components. Secondly, the remark that a definition and a universal claim 'say the same as far as force is concerned, but something different as far as sound is concerned' could be a somewhat clumsy formulation of the view that a definition and a universal claim, which are distinct sayables, have the same force (whatever this may amount to: see below) despite the fact that the difference of their linguistic formulations might induce one to think otherwise.

In fact, I am inclined to believe that the definition discussed in T32's third paragraph is a complete sayable (an incorporeal item signified by an utterance of a complete sentence). For, according to the Stoics, it is only statables that, properly speaking, are true or false.[157] Now, in T32's fourth paragraph we are told that 'if some man is found who is neither Greek nor barbarian, it is necessary both that the division should be faulty and that the universal claim [sc. either an utterance of the linguistic expression "If some are men, they are either Greeks or barbarians" or the statable signified by this utterance] should become false'. Moreover, in T32's fifth paragraph

---

[156] Plutarch (Col. 22, 1119F) mentions the 'composition of sayables' ('λεκτῶν σύνταξις'). Dionysius of Halicarnassus (Comp. 4,22 U.–R.) reports that two works of Chrysippus, both entitled On the Composition of the Parts of Discourse, were about dialectic and concerned, among other things, the 'composition of statables' ('ἀξιωμάτων σύνταξις'). Chrysippus wrote works On the Composition of Things Said and On the Composition and the Elements of Things Said (D.L. 7.192–3): since 'things said' probably are sayables, these works were probably concerned with how sayables are built from more elementary components. Fragments of Stoic logic speak of 'composing' ('συντάσσειν') a predicate with a case or a name (see D.L. 7.58; 64; Ammon. in Int. 44,29; 45,4), a statable from other statables by means of connectives (see D.L. 7.72), and an argument from statables (see D.L. 7.80; 81).

[157] S.E. M. 8.12; 74; 207; D.L. 7.65; 66; 68; Cic. Ac. 2.30,95.

we are also told that 'such a universal claim [*sc.* either an utterance of the linguistic expression "If some things are beings, they either are good or are bad or indifferent" or the statable signified by this utterance] is false if something false is subsumed under it'. Thus, T 32's fourth and fifth paragraphs are giving conditions under which the universal claims referred to are false. Hence these universal claims are probably statables (and therefore sayables). This makes it plausible to assume that the universal claim mentioned in T 32's third paragraph also is a statable: the statable «**if something is-a-man it is-a-rational-mortal-animal**». Such a result agrees with evidence coming from other sources: some documents suggest that the Stoics used the term 'universal claim' to describe statables «**if something π it ρ**» (where π and ρ are predicates);[158] and some remarks by Cicero[159] seem to presuppose that Chrysippus used the phrase 'indefinite conditional' to describe statables «**if something π it ρ**».

So, the universal claim mentioned in T 32's third paragraph is probably a statable. Since this universal claim and the definition corresponding to it are described as being 'the same as far as force is concerned' and as differing merely 'in composition', we have reason to believe that the definition corresponding to the universal claim is a sayable: it would be awkward if such a close affinity were affirmed of items as different as a linguistic expression (which, according to the Stoics, is a body) and a statable (which is a sayable, and therefore an incorporeal item).[160] In other words, the definition corresponding to the statable «**if something is-a-man it is-a-rational-mortal-animal**» is probably the sayable «**man is-a-rational-mortal-animal**», signified by an utterance of the complete sentence 'Man is a rational mortal animal.' Since it is probably a sayable signified by an utterance of a complete sentence, «**man is-a-rational-mortal-animal**» is probably a complete sayable.

---

[158] Epict. *Diss.* 2.20, 2–3 (where universal claims «**if something π it ρ**» are described as true or false): S.E. *M.* 1.86; Gal. *Inst. Log.* 18, 6–8 (46, 21–47, 17 Kalbfleisch).

[159] *Fat.* 8, 15 (where, following Szymański (1985), I read: '... *neque eos usuros esse con<exis sed con>inctionibus, ut <non> ita sua percepta pronuntient* ...'), cf. 6, 12. In *de Simplicium Medicamentorum Temperamentis ac Facultatibus* (11.498, 14–501, 9 K.) Galen seems to attribute to 'those around Chrysippus' the use of the expression 'conditional statable' ('ἀξίωμα συνημμένον') to denote statables like «**if something is-pungent this is-rough**».

[160] S.E. *M.* 8.12.

Given that the definition discussed in T 32's third paragraph is a complete sayable, we have some reason to believe that according to the Stoics all definitions are complete sayables.

[ii] Antipater's Characterization of Definitions The result suggested by T 32, that according to the Stoics definitions are complete sayables, is in agreement with what we can infer from Antipater's characterization of definitions, which is the second document that is relevant to the question whether for the Stoics definitions are linguistic expressions or sayables. Antipater characterizes a definition as 'an account [λόγος] formulated [ἐκφερόμενος] analytically and fittingly'.¹⁶¹ Now, the Stoics regularly use the verb 'to formulate' ('ἐκφέρειν') in such a way that its object, or the subject of its passive form, is a designation of a sayable.¹⁶² Thus, the occurrence of 'formulated' ('ἐκφερόμενος') in Antipater's characterization of definitions suggests that according to the Stoics definitions are sayables.¹⁶³

[iii] Genera, Species, and Sayables The third document that is relevant to the question whether for the Stoics definitions are linguistic expressions or sayables is a passage in Diogenes Laertius:

T 33 They [sc. the Stoics] say that dialectic divides into the area concerning what is signified and that concerning vocal sound; and that the area of what is signified divides into those of presentations and of sayables that subsist depending on these: statables, complete sayables, predicates and similar active and passive items, genera and species, and similarly arguments, modes, syllogisms, and sophisms that depend on vocal sound or on things. (7.43)

T 33 attributes to the Stoics the view that the study of sayables includes that of genera and species. This is a rather surprising view because for the Stoics

¹⁶¹ See above, T 31 with n.118. Also cf. S.E. *M.* 7.232 ('ἐξενεχθέντα ὅρον').

¹⁶² S.E. *M.* 8.96; 97; 102; 110; 297; D.L. 7.49; Chrysipp. *Quaest. Log.*, PHerc 307 col. v15–16; 19 (cf. the use of 'ἐκφορά' at D.L. 7.63; 67). The Stoic use of 'ἐκφέρειν' ('to formulate') must not be confused with that of 'προφέρειν' or 'προφέρεσθαι' ('to utter'), which requires that the objects of the verbs, or the subjects of their passive forms, should denote utterances (see S.E. *M.* 8.80; 275; D.L. 7.57; Ammon. *in Int.* 43, 11–12; Gal. *Plac. Hippocr. Pl.* 2.2, 11 (106, 2 De Lacy)). Schenkeveld (1990), 94–5 is wrong when he claims that the occurrence of 'ἐκφερόμενος' in Antipater's characterization of definitions 'hampers the treatment of ὅρος under the *topos* of σημαινόμενα'.

¹⁶³ Note that the Stoics do use 'λόγος' (which, in the present context, I translate by 'account') to denote sayables: for they apply 'λόγος' to arguments (see D.L. 7.76), which in their view are sayables (see S.E. *P.* 3.52; D.L 7.63).

universals, which comprise genera and species, are not sayables (according to the Stoics universals are non-somethings, whilst sayables are some-things).[164] So, on what grounds can the Stoics claim that the study of sayables includes that of genera and species? Since for the Stoics genera and species are closely connected to division, and therefore to definition,[165] the Stoics' reason for claiming that the study of sayables includes that of genera and species could be that for the Stoics definitions are complete sayables. It must however be admitted that one could offer interpretations of T33 which do not bring definitions in: the Stoics' reason for claiming that the study of sayables includes that of genera and species could be that a predicate is what most closely corresponds to a universal within a sayable; alternatively, the reason could be that among incomplete sayables there are cases signified by utterances of nominal expressions, which bear to one another relations of subordination which warrant the application to them of the expressions 'genus' and 'species'.

[iv] Chrysippus on Contraries   The fourth document that is relevant to the question whether for the Stoics definitions are linguistic expressions or sayables is in Simplicius:

T34   Since the same thing can be said both by an incomposite vocal sound ('wisdom' and 'stupidity', for example) and by a definition ('knowledge of things which are good, bad, and neither' and 'ignorance of these', for example) [ὄντος δὲ δυνατοῦ τὸ αὐτὸ καὶ κατὰ ἀσύνθετον φωνὴν εἰπεῖν, οἷον φρόνησιν ἀφροσύνην, καὶ δι᾿ ὅρου, οἷον ἐπιστήμην ἀγαθῶν καὶ κακῶν καὶ οὐδετέρων καὶ ἄγνοιαν[166] τῶν αὐτῶν], they inquire whether contraries are only the items corresponding to what is simple or also those corresponding to definitions [ζητοῦσιν πότερον <ἐναντία> ἐστὶν τὰ κατὰ τὰ ἁπλᾶ μόνον ἢ <καὶ τὰ> κατὰ τοὺς ὅρους]. And Chrysippus establishes that perhaps appel-latives and simple items only are contraries, whilst the others [*sc.* definitions and non-simple items corresponding to them] are not: for in these we include many items together with articles, connectives, and other interpret-ative particles, each of which one would be hard put to bring under the

---

[164] For the Stoics' view that universals are non-somethings see Simp. *in Cat.* 105, 9–11. For their view that sayables are somethings see S.E. *M.* 10.218; Plu. *Col.* 15, 1116B.

[165] On the connection between definition and division see above, text to n.89.

[166] The MSS and eds. have 'καὶ τὴν ἀφροσύνην ἄγνοιαν'. I excise 'τὴν ἀφροσύνην' (389,20).

definition of contraries.[167] For this reason he says that while wisdom is contrary to stupidity, the definition of the one is no longer contrary in the same way to the definition of the other, but, by referring them to those, they oppose definitions too, by association. (*in Cat.* 389, 18–28)

T 34 is a difficult passage. Fortunately, I do not need to reconstruct the view concerning contraries it attributes to Chrysippus. I can restrict myself to noting that according to one *prima facie* plausible interpretation of it, T 34 presupposes that according to the Stoics a definition is a linguistic expression (because it suggests that according to the Stoics 'the same thing can be said both by an incomposite vocal sound [. . .] and by a definition'). This would go against the position which in the preceding subsections I tentatively attributed to the Stoics.

However, on reflection, one realizes that T 34 does not upset the picture outlined so far. For in T 34 the expression 'definition' ('ὅρος') is used in a sense which is quite different from the one in which it was used in the preceding subsections: in T 34 'definition' means something like '*definiens*-expression', and therefore denotes subsentential expressions, whilst in the preceding subsections 'definition' was used in a sense according to which it denotes either complete sentences or complete sayables signified by utterances of complete sentences. This circumstance suffices to doubt T 34's relevance to the issue addressed in the preceding subsections.

Are Definitions Statables or Complete Sayables of Some Other Sort? The arguments of the preceding subsections show that the documents make it plausible to credit the Stoics with the view that definitions are complete sayables. The next question is whether according to the Stoics definitions are statables or complete sayables of some other sort. The only document that is relevant to this question is T 32, which, regrettably, is ambivalent.

---

[167] My usage of 'name' and 'appellative' conforms to Chrysippus'. Zeno distinguished four parts of speech: his first part of speech comprises proper names, common nouns, and adjectives, his remaining three parts of speech are verbs, connectives, and articles. Zeno's term for the first of his four parts of speech was 'ὄνομα' ('name') (see D.H. *Dem.* 48, 232–233 U.-R.; *Comp.* 2,7 U.-R.). Chrysippus modified Zeno's classification by distinguishing five parts of speech: Chrysippus' first part of speech comprises only proper names, his second part of speech comprises common nouns and adjectives, and his remaining three parts of speech are verbs, connectives, and articles. Chrysippus reserved 'ὄνομα' ('name') for the first of his five parts of speech, that is for proper names, and he chose 'προσηγορία' ('appellative') for the second, that is for common nouns and adjectives (see D.L. 7.57). On the development of the Stoic classification of parts of speech cf. Pinborg (1975), 99–100; Brunschwig (1984–94), 40.

On the one hand, in support of the line that definitions are statables, one could emphasize that the definition «**man is-a-rational-mortal-animal**» and the statable «**if something is-a-man it is-a-rational-mortal-animal**» are described as being 'the same as far as force is concerned' and as differing merely 'in composition'. One could regard this as an indication that the definition also is a statable. If this were correct, what the Stoic logicians have in mind when they say that the definition and the universal claim are 'the same as far as force is concerned' would probably be that the definition and the universal claim are logically equivalent statables, namely statables that are reciprocal consequences of one another; and what they have in mind when they say that the definition and the universal claim differ merely 'in composition' would probably be that they are distinct statables constructed from the same components arranged differently.

On the other hand, other considerations support the line that definitions are sayables of a different kind from statables. One can first of all dispute the argument in favour of the first interpretation. For the presence of the phrase 'the same as far as force is concerned' does not guarantee that definitions should be statables. It could be the case that what the Stoic logicians want to say by using such a phrase is merely that whatever job one wants a definition (which is a sayable but not a statable) to perform within an argument can be equivalently performed by the corresponding universal claim (which is a statable). Just consider what one finds in many modern textbooks of mathematics: definitions are introduced with some sort of special status which seems to distinguish them from proper assertions which play an analogous role of unproved starting-point for proofs (namely axioms), but when definitions are used in the course of proofs they are treated as universally quantified biconditional assertions. It would not be out of place to describe such a practice by saying that a definition is 'the same as far as force is concerned' as a universally quantified biconditional assertion. Analogously, it could be the case that what the Stoic logicians want to convey when they say that the definition differs from the universal claim merely 'in composition' is that the definition and the universal claim are distinct sayables constructed from the same components arranged differently.

Apart from this destructive argument, there is also a positive consideration in support of the interpretation that definitions are sayables of a different kind from statables. No fragment of Stoic logic describes definitions as 'true' or 'false': at most definitions are called 'faulty'.[168] Now, 'valid' ('ὑγιής') and 'faulty' ('μοχθηρός') are used in Stoic logic as generic expressions of praise and blame. Sometimes 'valid' or 'faulty' is applied to items which could well be described as 'true' ('ἀληθής') or 'false' ('ψεῦδος').[169] On other occasions, however, 'valid' or 'faulty' is applied to items for which 'true' and 'false' would be inappropriate: to arguments,[170] argument-forms,[171] and divisions.[172] These facts about linguistic usage in Stoic logic do suggest that for the Stoics definitions are not statables.

If definitions are complete sayables but not statables, what kind of sayables are they? Although our sources never use an expression like 'definitional sayable', some documents acknowledge explanatory (διασαφητικά) sayables alongside statables, questions, commands, etc.[173] Since the Stoics probably thought that an explanatory sayable is something that can be said in providing an explanation or a clarification, and since one of the functions attributed by the Stoics to definitions is to explain and clarify our preconceptions, there is some plausibility in assuming that the Stoics regarded definitions as explanatory sayables.

Bibliography

AA. VV. 1986, *Energeia: Études aristotéliciennes offertes à Mgr Antonio Jannone*, Paris.
Abrusci, V. M., Casari, E., and Mugnai, M. (eds.) 1983, *Atti del Convegno Internazionale di Storia della Logica (San Gimignano, 4–8 dicembre 1982)*, Bologna.
Alesse, F. 2000, *La Stoa e la tradizione socratica*, Naples.

---

[168] S.E. *P.* 2.209; *M.* 7.237; 11.9; 37.

[169] S.E. *P.* 2.43; 105; 111; *M.* 8.248; 10.94; 11.9.

[170] S.E. *P.* 1.116; 2.150; 153; 154; 156; 175; *M.* 8.121; 292; 294; 433; 452; 10.110. The Stoics allow themselves to apply 'true' and 'false' also to arguments (see D.L. 7.79), but the senses of 'true' and 'false' involved in such applications are secondary and derivative with respect to their basic senses, according to which they apply only to statables (cf. above, n.157).

[171] S.E. *P.* 2.146; 147; *M.* 8.429; 432; 444; 445.

[172] S.E. *M.* 11.10; 15. Of course, 'valid' and 'faulty' are also applied outside logic (in medicine, for example, and in ethics).

[173] Anon. *Proleg. Hermog. Stat.* 187, 10–11 Rabe; *Schol. in Aphton.* 662, 13–14 Waltz. I follow Nuchelmans (1973), 63–4 in assuming that explanatory sayables are not statables (Schenkeveld (1984), 305 instead takes them to be a special kind of statables).

420 PAOLO CRIVELLI

Algra, K. A., Barnes, J., Mansfeld, J., and Schofield, M. (eds.) 1999, *The Cambridge History of Hellenistic Philosophy*, Cambridge.

Algra, K. A., van der Horst, P. W., and Runia, D. T. (eds.) 1996, *Polyhistor: Studies in the History and Historiography of Ancient Philosophy Presented to Jaap Mansfeld on His Sixtieth Birthday*, Leiden, New York, and Cologne.

Annas, J. 1992, *Hellenistic Philosophy of Mind*, Berkeley, Los Angeles, and London.

Atherton, C. 1993, *The Stoics on Ambiguity*, Cambridge.

Baldassarri, M. 1984–7, *La logica stoica: testimonianze e frammenti*, 8 vols., Como.

Barnes, J. 1970, 'Property in Aristotle's Topics', *Archiv für Geschichte der Philosophie* 52: 136–55.

—— (trans. and comm.) 1994, Aristotle, *Posterior Analytics*, 2nd edn., Oxford.

—— 1996, 'The Catalogue of Chrysippus' Logical Works' = Algra, van der Horst, and Runia (1996), 169–84.

—— 1999, 'Aristotle and Stoic Logic' = Ierodiakonou (1999), 23–53.

Barnes, J., and Schenkeveld, D. M. 1999, 'Language' = Algra et al. (1999), 177–225.

Bäuerle, R., Egli, U., and von Stechow, A. (eds.) 1979, *Semantics from Different Points of View*, Berlin, Heidelberg, and New York.

Bett, R. (trans. and comm.) 1997, Sextus Empiricus, *Against the Ethicists*, Oxford.

Bréhier, E. 1908, *La théorie des incorporels dans l'ancien Stoïcisme*, 3rd edn., Paris 1997.

Brittain, C. 2005, 'Common Sense: Concepts, Definition and Meaning in and out of the Stoa' = Frede and Inwood (2005), 164–209.

Brunschwig, J. 1984–94, 'Remarks on the Stoic Theory of the Proper Noun' = Brunschwig (1994), 39–56.

—— 1986, 'Sur le système des "prédicables" dans les *Topiques* d'Aristote' = AA. VV. (1986), 145–57.

—— 1986–94, 'Remarks on the Classification of Simple Propositions in Hellenistic Logics' = Brunschwig (1994), 57–71.

—— 1991, 'On a Book-Title by Chrysippus: "On the Fact that the Ancients Admitted Dialectic along with Demonstrations"', *Oxford Studies in Ancient Philosophy*, Supplementary Volume: 81–95.

—— 1994, *Papers in Hellenistic Philosophy*, trans. J. Lloyd, Cambridge.

Bury, R.G. (ed. and trans.) 1933–49, *Sextus Empiricus in Four Volumes*, 4 vols., Cambridge, MA and London.

Corcoran, J., Frank, W., and Maloney, M. 1974, 'String Theory', *Journal of Symbolic Logic* 39: 625–37.

Crivelli, P. 1994a, 'Indefinite Propositions and Anaphora in Stoic Logic', *Phronesis* 39: 187–206.

—— 1994b, 'The Stoic Analysis of Tense and of Plural Propositions in Sextus Empiricus, *Adversus Mathematicos* x 99', *Classical Quarterly* n.s. 44: 490–9.

Decleva Caizzi, F. (ed. and comm.) 1966, *Antisthenis fragmenta*, Milan and Varese.

Epp, R. H. (ed.) 1985, *Spindel Conference 1984: Recovering the Stoics, Southern Journal of Philosophy* 23, Supplement.

Everson, S. (ed.) 1994, *Language*, Cambridge.

FDS = Hülser, K. (ed.), *Die Fragmente zur Dialektik der Stoiker*, 4 vols., Stuttgart and Bad Cannstatt 1987–8.

Frede, D. and Inwood, B. (eds.) 2005, *Language and Learning: Philosophy of Language in the Hellenistic Age. Proceedings of the Ninth Symposium Hellenisticum*, Cambridge.

Frede, M. 1983, 'Stoics and Skeptics on Clear and Distinct Impressions' = Frede (1987), 151–76.

—— 1987, *Essays in Ancient Philosophy*, Oxford.

—— 1994, 'The Stoic Notion of a *Lekton*' = Everson (1994), 109–28.

Gaskin, R. 1997, 'The Stoics on Cases, Predicates and the Unity of the Proposition' = Sorabji (1997), 91–108.

Giannantoni, G. (ed. and comm.) 1990, *Socratis et Socraticorum reliquiae*, 4 vols., Naples.

Gigante, M. (trans. and comm.) 1982, Diogene Laerzio, *Vite dei filosofi*, repr., Milan 1993.

Goldschmidt, V. 1953, *Le système stoïcien et l'idée de temps*, 4th edn., Paris 1989.

Gould, J. B. 1970, *The Philosophy of Chrysippus*, Leiden.

Gourinat, J.-B. 1996, *Les stoïciens et l'âme*, Paris.

—— 2000, *La dialectique des stoïciens*, Paris.

Hadot, P. 1979, 'Les divisions des parties de la philosophie dans l'Antiquité', *Museum Helveticum* 36: 202–23.

Hicks, R. D. (ed. and trans.) 1929, Diogenes Laertius, *Lives of Eminent Philosophers*, 2 vols., Cambridge, MA and London.

Hülser, K. 1979, 'Expression and Content in Stoic Linguistic Theory' = Bäuerle, Egli, and Schenkeveld (1979), 284–303.

Ierodiakonou, K. 1993, 'The Stoic Division of Philosophy', *Phronesis* 38: 57–74.

—— (ed.) 1999, *Topics in Stoic Philosophy*, Oxford.

Lewis, E. 1995, 'The Stoics on Identity and Individuation', *Phronesis* 40: 89–108.

Long, A. A. (ed.) 1971, *Problems in Stoicism*, London and Atlantic Highlands, NJ.

Long, A. A., and Sedley, D. N. 1987, *The Hellenistic Philosophers*, 2 vols., Cambridge.

Long, H. S. (ed.) 1964, Diogenis Laertii, *Vitae Philosophorum*, 2 vols., Oxford.

LSJ = Liddell, H. G., Scott, R., and Jones, H. S., *A Greek–English Lexicon*, 9th edn., with a Revised Supplement, Oxford 1996.

Marcovich, M. (ed.) 1999–2002, Diogenis Laertii, *Vitae Philosophorum*, 3 vols., Stuttgart and Leipzig.

Nuchelmans, G. 1973, *Theories of the Proposition: Ancient and Medieval Conceptions of the Bearers of Truth and Falsity*, Amsterdam and London.

Owen, G. E. L. (ed.) 1968, *Aristotle on Dialectic: The* Topics. *Proceedings of the Third Symposium Aristotelicum*, Oxford.

Pauli, H. 1986, 'Ἀπόδοσις τοῦ ἰδίου: Zur Geschichte eines Mißverständnisses', *Rheinisches Museum für Philologie* 129: 227–47.

Pearson, A. C. 1891, *The Fragments of Zeno and Cleanthes*, Cambridge.

Pflug, I. 1908, 'De Aristotelis Topicorum Libro Quinto', diss., Leipzig.

Pinborg, J. 1975, 'Classical Antiquity: Greece' = Sebeok (1975), 69–126.

Reesor, M. E. 1972, 'Poion and Poiotes in Stoic Philosophy', *Phronesis* 17: 279–85.

Rieth, O. 1933, *Grundbegriffe der stoischen Ethik: Eine traditionsgeschichtliche Untersuchung*, Berlin.

Sandbach, F. H. 1930/71, 'Ennoia and Prolēpsis in the Stoic Theory of Knowledge' = A. A. Long (1971), 22–37.

—— 1985, *Aristotle and the Stoics*, Cambridge.

Scaltsas, T. and Mason, A. (eds.) 2002, *Zeno of Citium and His Legacy: The Philosophy of Zeno*, Larnaka.

Schenkeveld, D. M. 1984, 'Studies in the History of Ancient Linguistics, II: Stoic and Peripatetic Kinds of Speech Act and the Distinction of Grammatical Moods', *Mnemosyne* 37: 291–353.

—— 1990, 'Studies in the History of Ancient Linguistics, III: The Stoic *TEXNH ΠΕΡΙ ΦΩΝΗΣ*', *Mnemosyne* 43: 86–108.

Schubert, A. 1994, *Untersuchungen zur stoischen Bedeutungslehre*, Göttingen.

Sebeok, T. A. (ed.) 1975, *Current Trends in Linguistics*, XIII.I, The Hague and Paris.

Sedley, D. 1982, 'The Stoic Criterion of Identity', *Phronesis* 27: 255–75.

—— 1999, 'Hellenistic Physics and Metaphysics' = Algra et al. (1999), 355–411.

—— 2002, 'Zeno's Definition of *Phantasia Kataleptike*' = Scaltsas and Mason (2002), 135–54.

Smyth, H. W. 1920, *Greek Grammar*, 2nd edn., Cambridge, MA 1956.

Sorabji, R. (ed.) 1997, *Aristotle and After*, London.

Spinelli, E. (ed., trans., and comm.) 1995, Sesto Empirico, *Contro gli etici*, Naples.

SVF = von Arnim, J. and Adler, M. (eds.), *Stoicorum Veterum Fragmenta*, 4 vols., repr., Stuttgart 1978–9.

Szymański, M. 1985, 'De fato 8,15: Can *Coniunctio* Mean Implication?', *Hermes* 113: 383–4.

Tarski, A. 1933, 'The Concept of Truth in Formalized Languages' = Tarski (1956), 152–278.

—— 1956, *Logic, Semantics, Metamathematics: Papers from 1923 to 1938*, trans. J. H. Woodger, 2nd edn., ed. J. Corcoran, Indianapolis, IN 1983.

Todd, R. B. 1973, 'The Stoic Common Notions: A Re-Examination and Reinterpretation', *Symbolae Osloenses* 48: 47–75.

Togni, P. 2006, 'Rappresentazione e oggetto nella gnoseologia stoica', *Dianoia* 11: 41–83.

Verbeke, G. 1968, 'La notion de propriété dans les *Topiques*' = Owen (1968), 257–76.

Watson, G. 1966, *The Stoic Theory of Knowledge*, Belfast.

11

The Ancient Commentators on Concept Formation

RICHARD SORABJI

Aristotle's account of scientific method in his *Posterior Analytics* sees it as starting from definitions of the things studied by science (e.g. points, lines, thunder, lunar eclipse), and then deducing, with the help of those definitions, explanations of the further, non-definitional, properties of the things. But how do we discover the definitions? The subject is postponed to the very last chapter of the work, 2.19, where Aristotle explains how we acquire universal concepts, both everyday concepts and—his eventual interest— the expert concepts which the scientist expresses in scientific definitions. The ancient commentators on Aristotle were equally interested in scientific and non-scientific concept formation. My account will have three parts.

I Aristotle, *Posterior Analytics* 2.19

I shall start by saying how I have taken Aristotle's account of concept formation in *Posterior Analytics* 2.19, in order to contrast the ancient commentators, who take it quite differently. Aristotle is providing an alternative to Plato by showing how concepts can be formed on the basis of sense perception. There is in that case no need, he thinks, for Plato's alternative, argued in *Phaedo* 72E–77A, of concepts stored in the mind from the soul's existence before birth. In 100a3–8, Aristotle says that many memories of the same type of perceived thing, let us say of oxen, constitute experience (*empeiria*) of oxen. And then, on my interpretation, he uses the word 'or' (*ē*), to equate experience, or many memories, with a rudimentary universal concept of oxen. At any rate, he speaks of experience, or (*e*) the whole universal (*katholou*) in the soul. Admittedly, the word 'or' can mean 'or rather'. But if he were here talking of experience *or rather* the whole universal, he would have left unexplained the very thing he is trying to explain, how, contrary to Plato's view, remembered sense perceptions are enough to give us at least a rudimentary universal concept. The explanation is that to have a rudimentary universal concept of oxen *just is* to have enough memories of oxen to react with experience to them. It is not a further step beyond many memories.

However, a rudimentary universal concept falls short of the concepts required by an expert or by a scientist. An example that Aristotle has given in *Posterior Analytics* 2.8 is that the rudimentary concept of lunar eclipse is that it is *some sort of* familiar loss of light by the moon. It is only the scientist who knows that it is a lunar loss of light due to the earth's shadow. And special ability is needed to recognize this, as he explains in 100b5–12. He here talks of intellectual *spotting*—I believe this is sometimes the force of his talk of *nous*—and rightly says that *spotting* may be what has to happen if we are to grasp the universal defining feature of a natural kind, *An. Post.* 2.19, 100b12; 15. He also speaks of being good at spotting, *ankhinoia*, *An. Post.* 1.34. Reasonably again, he says, *An. Post.* 1.31, that we might spot (*noēsai*) how the burning glass works in all cases, just from seeing light passing through pores in the glass.

Reasoning, *logismos*, *logos*, is mentioned at 100b7 and 10 and reasoning is standardly treated by Aristotle as different from spotting, because it is a process of working something out step-by-step. One kind of reasoning is induction (*epagōgē*), that is, generalizing from one or more instances, and this turns out to play a role in concept formation at 100b3, since it is by induction that one passes from individual oxen to the concept of ox (such species are 'primary' and 'without parts'), and thence to the concept of animal in general.

The intervening discussion in 100a14–b5 is part of a restatement that Aristotle offers, on the ground that his initial description of how we form rudimentary concepts was not clear enough. In the restatement, important new ideas are introduced about the contribution of sense perception. It turns out that although one perceives a particular, sense perception is nonetheless, in some sense, perception of a universal. This is true even of a single act of perception without the mediation of many memories. It is not of Callias, the man, but of man. The ancient commentators offer quite plausible accounts of what Aristotle means. But they regard it as his only statement in this chapter of how sense perception contributes to concept formation. They do not regard the appeal to many memories of perceived oxen as having provided an earlier explanation, now to be superseded.

It is sometimes asked whether, when Aristotle talks of universals (*katholou*), here, he is talking of universal propositions or universal concepts. The answer is both. For to have the concept of lunar eclipse is to know a certain proposition, that lunar eclipse is so-and-so. This is not to say that Aristotle is talking of propositions quite generally. I do not agree with Themistius that he is even talking of all scientific generalizations, *in An. Post.* 63,15. He is talking about the first premises of the sciences which supply the definitions of the key concepts.

Let me turn to what the commentators say, after first quoting the passage in Aristotle.[1]

(1) Aristotle, *An. Post.* 99b35–100b12
Animals are born with (*sumphutos*) a capacity (*dunamis*) for discrimination (*kritikê*), which is called perception (*aisthêsis*). Granted that they possess this faculty, in some of them the sense image (*aisthêma*) lasts, while in others it does not. Apart from perceiving, those in which it does not last have no knowledge (*gnôsis*) at all, or no knowledge of the things whose perceptions do not last. On the other hand, some animals are able to keep [the image] in their soul after they perceive something. When many occurrences of this sort take place, there is a further distinction (*diaphora*): from the lasting of this kind of things there results in some animals a rational account (*logos*), while in others there does not. Now memory (*mnêmê*) results from perception (*aisthêsis*), as we say, and experience (*empeiria*) [results] from many memories of the same thing, since memories that are many in number constitute a single experience. From experience, or (*ê*) from the whole universal (*katholou*) when it has become stable in the soul—the one beside the many, whatever is one identical thing in them all—[results] a principle (*arkhê*) of art

   [1] This chapter is reprinted, with changes, from Frans de Haas, Mariska Leunissen, and Marije Martijn, eds., *Ancient Interpretations of Aristotle's Posterior Analytics*, forthcoming. Translations are based on those by the following translators, whose names are indicated in the text by initials as follows: Richard McKirahan (RMcK), R. W. Sharples (RWS), Robert Todd (RBT), William Charlton (WC), John Dudley and Koenraad Verrycken (JDud, KV), Jan Opsomer (JO), John Dillon (JD), David Sedley (DNS), Gerard Bechtle (GBe), Frans de Haas (FDH), Glenn Morrow (GM), Charles Hagen (CH), L. G. Westerink (LGW), Richard Sorabji (RRKS). I have also benefited in one of my own translations from that of Harold Tarrant.

(*tekhnê*) and scientific understanding (*epistêmê*): of art if [the subject in question] is in the realm of coming to be, and of scientific understanding if it is in the realm of what is. So the states are not [innate] in (*enuparkhein*) [animals] in a determinate form nor do they come from higher cognitive states (*gnôstikôteros*), but from perception, as happens when a rout has occurred in a battle, and when one man has stopped, another stops and then another, until it reaches the original position (*arkhê*). The soul is the kind of thing that can undergo this.

[100a14] But let us say again what was just said, but not said clearly. When one of the indiscriminables (*adiaphoros*) has stood still, the first universal is in the soul. (For to be sure one perceives the particular, but the perception is of the universal, for instance of man and not of Callias the man.) Again, a stand is made in these until the things that are without parts (*ameres*) and universal stand still: for example, first such and such an animal, and then animal, and also similarly here. So it is clear that we must come to know (*gnôrizein*) the primary things by induction (*epagôgê*); for that is how perception plants the universal in us too. Since some of the cognitive states (*hai peri tên dianoian hexeis*) with which we apprehend the truth are always true while others, like opinion (*doxa*) and calculation (*logismos*), admit falsity—while scientific understanding (*epistêmê*) and intellect (*nous*) are always true; and since no other kind is truer than scientific understanding except for intellect; and since first principles have higher cognitive status (*gnôrimôteros*) than demonstrations; and since all scientific understanding depends on a rational account (*logos*)—there cannot be scientific understanding of first principles. And since nothing except intellect can be truer than scientific understanding, it follows that the state that knows first principles is intellect. (RMcK)

II The Ancient Commentators and the Roles Ascribed to Perception, Reason, Intellect, and Imagination

Aristotle died in 322 BC. The commentators I shall refer to include Alexander, head of the Aristotelian school in Athens at the end of the second century AD. The others are all Platonists, starting with the Middle Platonist Alcinous in the mid-second century AD, and continuing in sequence with Porphyry in the late third century, his probable pupil, Iamblichus, around 300 AD, Themistius in the late fourth century, in the fifth century the Athenians Plutarch of Athens, Syrianus and Proclus and Syrianus' pupil in Alexandria, Hermeias, then in the sixth century Philoponus (I shall write

'Philoponus?' when the text may or may not be by him), Simplicius and Olympiodorus and finally around 1100, Eustratius.[2]

Role of Perception

Only some of these wrote commentaries directly on Aristotle's *Posterior Analytics*, but these ones discount Aristotle's talk of memories being experience and of experience *or* the universal in the soul. 'Philoponus?', *in An Post.* 2, 436,2–12,[3] substitutes talk of 'experience and the whole sense image (*aisthêma*)', as if memories did not yet give us a universal concept, but only an image. Eustratius, *in An. Post.* 264,10–13, takes 'or' in the sense of 'or rather', as if memories and experience were different from the universal concept. They think the role of perception in concept formation is not explained until we come to the restatement, according to which perception is perception of the universal.

(2) Ps.-Philoponus, *in An. Post.* 2 436,2–12

'Or [100a6]' should be understood as standing for 'and'. It goes like this: 'from experience and from the whole sense image (*aisthêma* [but Aristotle says 'from the whole universal']) when it has become stable in the soul' and settled there, comes knowledge (*gnôsis*) of 'the universal (*katholou*), the one beside the many', which is something different besides the particulars (*merika*), and 'is one' universal 'in them', i.e. one and the same thing becomes manifest in all those particulars. Such a universal, which is on the one hand something different besides the particulars and on the other hand is observed in them, comes to be 'a principle (*arkhê*) of art (*tekhnê*) and scientific understanding (*epistêmê*).' If this universal is gathered together (*episunagein*) from things 'in the realm of generation (*genesis*),' i.e. things that are subject to generation and perishing, it is a 'first principle' of art, but if it is 'in the realm of what is,' i.e. if it is gathered together from things that are always in the same way, i.e. eternal, it is a first principle 'of scientific understanding'. (RMcK)

---

[2] I am glad to have the opportunity of going beyond what I wrote in *The Philosophy of the Commentators 200–600 AD*, London, 2004, because that was scattered between vol. 2 (ch. 3, sec. (g), texts 4–13, and ch. 5) and vol. 3 (ch. 5, sec. (c) and ch. 12 secs (a) and (b)), and it also used only part of the Porphyry passage. Universals, in addition to universal concepts, are discussed in my 'Universals Transformed: The First Thousand Years after Plato', in *Universals, Concepts and Qualities*, ed. Peter Strawson and Arindam Chakrabarti, Aldershot, 2006.

[3] I have argued that this text just might be by Philoponus in my preface to Owen Goldin's translation, *Philoponus(?): On Aristotle Posterior Analytics 2*, London, 2009.

(3) Eustratius, *in An. Post.* 264,10–13
He meant that 'from experience' (*empeiria*) [results] 'a first principle' (*arkhê*) 'of art (*tekhnê*) and scientific understanding (*epistêmê*)'. But since experience is something less complete and insufficient to serve as a first principle of art and science, he added 'or from the whole universal when it has become stable,' i.e. when it has come to a stand and is fixed and made firm in the soul. (RMcK)

When 'Philoponus?' comes to Aristotle's restatement at 100a14–b5, which, like other commentators he considers the real starting-point, he reintroduces his sense image (*aisthêma*) into the discussion and explains quite plausibly (*in An. Post.* 2, 437,15–438,2) that it bears not only the marks of the particular qualities of the person seen, of their being long-haired and pale, but also the marks of the shared characteristics, such as being a rational animal. And all this information is sent along in the first instance to the imagination.

The universal that perception apprehends, according to Themistius, *in An. Post.* 64,2–9 and Eustratius, *in An. Post.* 266,14–29, is a universal not properly separated out from the characteristics of particular instances. Eustratius cites Aristotle's idea from *Physics* 1.1, 184b3–5, that a little child at first calls all men 'Daddy', before it separates out the distinctive characteristics of its father.

(4) Ps.-Philoponus, *in An. Post.* 2, 437,15–438,2
Perception acts upon certain particulars, which are undifferentiated in species, and then once and for all implants and imprints this sense image (*aisthêma*) in the imagination which not only bears the marks of certain distinctive (*idiotêtes*) and incidental features, of which the particulars consist (*sunistasthai*) and by which they are recognized, but also takes some mark from the universal. The universal is the common nature which all the particulars have in common. Sense perception sees Socrates and Alcibiades, and takes an impression not only of the particular distinctive qualities (*merika idiômata*) in them (the particular distinctive qualities are one man's being long-haired and pale, the other not), but also of one of the shared characteristics that it finds in them, that is, their being animals, or rational, or something of that sort. It then sends this along in the first instance to the imagination. When the first sense image is imprinted in the soul, it also creates in the soul a dim knowledge of the universal. Similarly the second sense image and the third and the fourth, being alike, and possessing along with the distinctive (*idiômata*) and incidental qualities in the particulars something of the common features in them, get imprinted in the imagination too and also create in the soul knowledge of the universal. For sense perception grasps not only particulars (*merika*), that is, the

accidental (*sumbebêkota*) and distinctive qualities (*idiotês*) of which the particulars consist (*ex hôn sunestêkasin*), but also the universal man, that is, some of the things of which the universal man consists (*sunistasthai*). (RRKS)

(5) Themistius, *in An. Post.* 64,2–9
For when sense perception perceives Socrates, it simultaneously apprehends human, and when [it perceives] this particular white it simultaneously perceives white. For it does not perceive Callias and man together as entirely the same thing; [if it did,] it would not have called anything but Callias a man. But when it sees Socrates it also sees in him something that is similar and common to other people. And so perception is of the universal too in a way, but not in such a way as to separate (*khôrizein*) it and abstract (*aphairein*) it and know (*gnônai*) it in its own right, but as confused (*sunkekhumenos*) with the particular and rather turned towards it. (RMcK)

(6) Eustratius, *in An. Post.* 266,14–29
When Socrates is known perceptually, our perception simultaneously apprehends human, though it does not abstract (*aphairein*) human from the particular but confusedly (*sunkekhumenôs*) recognizes (*gnôrizousa*) human too in the particular. And it is clear that it transmits this to the reason (*logos*) in the soul. (RMcK). For if perception did not recognize human at all, the soul would not be able to move through its own recognition to the apprehension and recognition of human and to assemble (*athroizein*) the universal in itself. But this is what happens to it, so it perceives [human].

[266,20] And perception is in a way of what is common, even if not as common, but as particular. Or one might say that it is of the particular more as something common than as something particular. For if perception by itself were able to discriminate particulars from each other, it would have been thought to be of them as particulars. But as it is, it encounters them indiscriminately and recognizes them confusedly. (RRKS)

[266,15] An indication (*sêmeion*) is that children call all men father and all women mother, since they operate (*energein*) only on the level of perception and do not yet possess a disposition that can distinguish (*diakritikê hexis*) the distinctive features (*idiômata*) of each one. And so the perception that perceives Callias does not in virtue of its own capacity (*dunamis*) recognize (*gnôrizein*) him as Callias, but only as a human. (RMcK)

Role of Reason

Reason (*logos*) plays a role as well as perception. According to Eustratius, *in An. Post.* 266,14–29, just quoted, when perception confusedly recognizes the universal 'human' in the particular, it sends the information along to reason, whereas pseudo-Philoponus had only told us that in the first instance the information was sent to the imagination. Reason or thought (*dianoia*) is also used, according to Hermeias, *Commentary on Plato's Phaedrus* 171,8–25, for the process of assembling (*sunathroizein*) what is common to Socrates and Plato into a universal concept that is then stored in reason. The commentators on Aristotle use a number of words for describing how these rudimentary universal concepts of Aristotle are empirically assembled— *sunageirein, sunagein, episunagein, athroizein, sunathroizein, sullegein, kephalaiousthai*[4] from the perception of a number of particulars.

(7) Hermeias, *in Phaedr.* 171,8–25 (Couvreur)

'For the human being must be capable of' (249b6–7) assembling (*sunathroizein*) by means of thought (*dianoia*) the later-generated (*husterogenē*) universal (*katholou*) from the common traits distributed in individuals (*apo tôn en tois kathekasta katatetagmenôn koinotêtôn*), i.e. from what is common in Socrates and Plato and the like—for this is what 'to understand' (249b7) means. From these [the human being must] project (*proballein*) the universals (*katholou*) that are present in the soul in virtue of its essence, through which as images he will recollect the Forms in the intelligible realm. The animal soul cannot do this, for it is not capable, upon seeing this, that and yet another horse, of assembling in reason the later-generated universal 'horse'. (FDH)

[16] This is so because [the animal soul] does not even possess in virtue of its essence and as innate the concepts (*logoi*) and the substantial universals (*katholou*) of these things. Consequently only the human and the humans' rational soul can do this, viz. assemble from this and that equal thing which are not precisely equal (for what enmattered thing is precise?) the later-generated universal and precise concept of equal. From these it provides to hand (*prokheirizesthai*) and projects (*proballein*) the universal concepts in virtue of its essence.

Then [the human's rational soul] from these images (*eikones* [the later-generated universals]) is reminded (*anamimnêskesthai*) of all the forms (*eidê*) in the Demiurge's Intellect. For neither the soul itself nor things here in the world of coming to be would possess the forms, if the Demiurge's Intellect had not had them long before, always fixed the same way and having real being. (RRKS)

---

[4] Themistius, *in An. Post.* 64,24–65,2; Hermeias, *in Phaedr.* 171,8–25, Couvreur; Philoponus, *in Phys.* 12,24–8; 'Philoponus', *in An. Post.* 436,2–12; Simplicius, *in Phys.* 1075,4–20; Eustratius, *in An. Post.* 266, 14–19. I owe to Christoph Helmig the reference to *kephalaiousthai*, which is in Themistius, *in An. Post.* 64,16 and to *kephalaiôma*, which is later in Proclus, *in Parm.* *Athroismos* is also in Sextus, *adv. Math.* 7.224.

Roles of Different Intellects

In some contexts, I took it above, reason (*logos*) differs from *nous* as step-by-step reasoning differs from intellectual spotting. But the commentators do not take *nous* to refer to spotting in Aristotle's *Posterior Analytics* 2.19. They take it to refer to the three or more intellects, which, starting with Alexander, they attribute to Aristotle, on the basis of Aristotle's brief chapter *On the Soul* 3.5. Alexander distinguishes the three intellects, for example, at *DA* 88, 23–4, and, if this part of the *Mantissa* is by him, at *Mantissa* 107, 21–34 and III, 29–32. We have a material intellect (*alias* potential or passive intellect), which gets its proper disposition (*hexis*) from the active intellect (*alias* productive intellect) in us and so becomes the dispositional intellect. The dispositional intellect, according to Alexander, *DA* 85,20–86,6, is where we store (*apokeisthai*) our concepts.

But whereas Alexander says in his *On the Soul* (*de Anima*, or *DA* for short), 85,20–86,6; 87,19–21, that the material intellect can already separate out concepts from matter, in the *Mantissa* he, or the author of that part, says that only the active or productive intellect enables the material intellect to perform that separation, *Mantissa* 108,19–24. It does so by constituting an example of a matterless form for reference (*anaphora*). The idea mentioned here of 'intellect from outside' is taken from the discussion in Aristotle, *On the Generation of Animals* 736b28 of the baby's intellect's not arising solely from changes in the womb.

The role given to *nous* here is one that Aristotle does not even mention in *Posterior Analytics* 2.19: the separation of form from matter. That idea is itself ambiguous. According to Aristotle, in thinking of geometrical figures one thinks of the form (shape) without even *thinking of* the matter in which it is found. But in thinking of objects in nature like a stone, one has to *think of* their matter; it is merely that what one *receives* into one's mind is only the form of a stone, not its matter (*On the Soul* 3.8, 431b29–432a1). This is in the first place a theory about what happens when one thinks, and is not expressed by Aristotle as primarily a point about concept formation. But if Alexander sees it in the latter way, he will have made the separation of form from matter a central part of concept formation. Certainly Porphyry treats the separation of form from matter as occurring somewhere in the process of concept formation in the passage to be quoted below.[5] The initial concept has to be turned into a universal in order that the form may be deposited immaterially in the soul, and this work is assigned to imagination. Themistius and Eustratius in passages cited below[6] think that separation of the universal from the particular is what is required for concept formation, because although perception apprehends the universal human, it apprehends it muddled up with the particular characteristics of, e.g. Socrates. The role given to *nous* by Themistius, however, is not this separation, but completing the inductive process by recognizing that all the cases belong together, first giving the same name to simple things, then combining them into complexes and finally defining them (64,18–21; 25–6; 65,15–66,3).

(8) Alexander(?), *Mantissa* 107,21–34
Another [type of intellect] is that which is already intelligising and possesses the disposition of intelligising, and is able to grasp the forms of intelligible things by its own power, being analogous to those among craftsmen who possess the disposition [for their craft] and can perform the actions of the craft by themselves. The first [type of intellect] was not like these, but more like those who are able to take up the craft and *become* craftsmen. And this [second type of intellect] is the material intellect when it has already acquired the disposition and actual intellection. This sort of intellect is in those who are already more perfect and are intelligising. So this is the second [type of] intellect.

[107.29] The third [type of] intellect besides the two already mentioned is the productive (*poiêtikos*), on account of which the material [intellect] comes to have the disposition, this productive [intellect] being analogous, as Aristotle says, to light. For as light is the cause for colours that are potentially visible of their becoming actually visible, so this third [type of] intellect makes the potential and material intellect [become] intellect in actuality, by creating in it the disposition of intellection. (RWS)

(9) Alexander, *DA* 85,20–86,6
The disposition (*hexis*) of this sort is produced in the intellect initially by a transition from the continuous activity (*energeia*) over sense objects, with the intellect taking from the sense objects a sort of theoretical vision, as it were, of the universal. At first, the universal is called a thought (*noêma*) or concept (*ennoia*), but once it has grown and become complex and versatile, so that it can do this even without a leg-up from perception, it is by that time intellect. For when through continuous activity it has

---

[5] Porphyry, *Commentary on Ptolemy's Harmonics* 14,10–11.
[6] Themistius, *in An. Post.* 64,2–9; Eustratius, *in An. Post.* 266,14–29.

acquired such a disposition as to be able thereafter to act through itself, then the intellect spoken of as a disposition comes into being. It is analogous to the knower who is between the so-called potential knower and the one who is active (*energein*) as regards knowledge, and who overtakes the potential knower as much as he is thought to fall short of the one who is active as regards knowledge. But when this disposition is active, it becomes the intellect in actuality (*kat' energeian*). For the dispositional intellect is in a way the thoughts (*noêmata*) that are stored (*apokeimena*), assembled and at rest. (RRKS)

(10)   Alexander, *DA* 87,19–21
Intellect makes the essence and the forms of composites intelligible to itself by separating them from what accompanies their being. (RRKS)

(11)   Alexander(?), *Mantissa* 108,19–24
This thing that is both intelligible in its own nature and intellect in actuality (*kat' energeian*) is the cause of the material intellect's, by reference (*anaphora*) to such a form, separating and imitating and intelligising each of the enmattered forms as well, and making it intelligible. It is the intellect said to be 'from outside', the active intellect, not being a part or power of our soul, but coming to be in us from outside, whenever we think it. (RWS)

There are alternatives to Alexander's view of the role of intellect. Themistius, *in DA* 98,35–99,10, thinks that the productive intellect turns into universal concepts the imprints which are received from perception and imagination and which are stored in the potential intellect.[7] Pseudo-Philoponus draws not on Aristotle's chapter on intellect, but on Plato's *Philebus* 39B, when he says that active intellect inscribes the imprints of all things in the potential intellect like a painter. But in Plato, it was perception and memory that made the inscriptions, and the painter came along afterwards and painted pictures of what had been inscribed.

(12)   Themistius, *in DA* 98,35–99,10
As light when supervening on potential sight and potential colours produces both actual sight and actual colours, so too this actual (*energeiai*) intellect advances the potential intellect, and not only makes it an actual intellect, but also constitutes its potential objects of thought as actual objects. These are the enmattered forms and universal concepts (*noêmata*) assembled from particular objects of perception. Up to this point the potential intellect cannot distinguish between them, or make transitions from one to the other, or combine and divide them. Instead like a storehouse

---

[7]   His further account of the role of *nous* at *in An. Post.* 65,15–21 is less informative.

(*thesauros*) of concepts, or rather as their matter, it stores the imprints (*tupous*) from perception and imagination through the agency of memory. But when the productive (*poiêtikos*) intellect comes upon it and takes hold of this matter of thoughts, the potential intellect becomes one with it, and becomes able to make transitions [from one concept to another], and to combine and divide concepts, and to examine some on the basis of others. (RBT)

(13) Pseudo-Philoponus, *in DA* 538,4–10
It should be known, then, that actual intellect is said to make all things because it inscribes the imprints of all things in potential intellect. That is why Plato too likens it to a painter [*Philebus* 39B] and Aristotle straight off proposes that it is a painter [an interpretation of *DA* 3.4, 430a1; 3.5, 430a15–17]. For if potential intellect becomes all things, actual intellect makes all things. So this can belong to the human intellect. For it is not Intellect from outside that inscribes all things in potential intellect, but actual intellect in us. (WC)

Role of Imagination

So much for perception, reason, and intellect. But a role in concept formation was also given to imagination. We have already seen Themistius saying that the potential intellect receives imprints from perception and imagination. And we have seen 'Philoponus?' *in DA* likening actual intellect to Plato's painter in the soul. A role in concept formation had already been given by Aristotle's own school to imagination and artistry in the soul, according to Sextus, *Against the Mathematicians* 7.221–2. But 'Philoponus?' quoted above from *in An. Post.* 2, 437,15–438,2 goes into much more detail about the imagination, which he mentions three times in lines 17, 26, and 30. It is in the imagination that perception imprints an image both of the individuating features of what is perceived (someone's being long-haired and pale) and of the universal features (being a rational, mortal animal).

Porphyry goes further still and makes the imagination not just a passive recipient of imprints, but an active ability to add precision to the data of sense. This is in a passage which Harold Tarrant has translated and discussed and considers to be partly drawn by Porphyry from the much earlier Middle Platonist, Thrasyllus.[8] In his *Commentary on Ptolemy's Harmonics*, Porphyry's account starts off at 13,21–14,14, echoing Aristotelian ideas to a considerable extent, just as he does also at *in Cat.* 91,2–5. But he finishes up with Platonist

---

[8] Harold Tarrant, *Thrasyllan Platonism*, Ithaca, NY, 1993, ch. 5.

ones. First, using sense perception, the soul tears forms in an Aristotelian way off external matter and draws them into itself. Second, a faculty connected with opinion gives a name to the sensory datum and inscribes it in words on the writing tablet of the soul, in the manner of Plato's *Philebus*. Third comes imagination (*phantasia*), which performs a new role of correcting the input, working out an accurate version and storing it in the soul. This is already a concept (*ennoia*). But the universality of the concept is due to the form received being stored in a non-material way. And it seems that imagination performs this function too, of separating the form from matter. When that has been done, one has scientific knowledge (*epistêmê*), but not yet *nous*. *Nous* arises like a light kindled by leaping fire and the scientific knowledge is made firm by *epibolê*, which might be a kind of mental concentration, although Tarrant takes it to be a kind of accumulation.[9] Neither the spark nor the mental concentration is further explained, any more than Aristotle explains his intellectual spotting, which is also *nous*, and which indeed cannot be further explained. Tarrant conjectures that the confirmation is produced by the assembly of many similar inputs, but one might expect that to have happened, if at all, before the stage of scientific knowledge.

Then after a digression, Porphyry reverts at 15,1–5, to a much more Platonist account of how the reason (*logos*) within us has a pre-conception of the form received from matter, and uses its previously possessed conception to supplement and correct the received form. This appears to be a second corrective process quite distinct from that carried out by imagination, and based on the prior possession by reason of concepts in a Platonic manner possibly through recollection. The apparently inconsistent appeal to imagination may be due to borrowings from Thrasyllus, while the appeal to recollected concepts may represent Porphyry's more orthodox view. I have based the following translation on Tarrant's with my own variations.

(14) Porphyry, *Commentary on Ptolemy's Harmonics* 13,21–14,14 and 15,1–5
When matter has been given form by the aforementioned rational principle (*logos*), it happens that the soul attends to the entities and as it were tears the forms (*eidê*) again off the matter and receives them into itself and in some way restores them, so that discrimination (*krisis*) can become immaterial. For at first (1) grasping is done

⁹ Tarrant, *Thrasyllan Platonism*, pp. 128–30.

by sense perception, which as it were touches the entity and tries to recover the forms and as it were announce them and introduce them into the soul, like a guide, or usher. After that, (2) supposition (*hupolēpsis*, defined by Aristotle, *On the Soul* 3.3, 427b25 as including opinion) of the opiniative sort (*doxastikē*) receives what has been brought in, names it and inscribes it through words (*logos*) in the soul as if upon a writing tablet present in it. The third after this (3) is a faculty that copies the distinctive qualities (*idiōmata*) and is genuinely pictorial or plastic, namely, imagination (*phantasia*) which is not satisfied with the form produced by naming and inscribing, but is like those who descry people coming to shore, or who scrutinize matching identity tokens, and work out the exact details of the likeness. In this way imagination also works out (*eklogizesthai*) the entire structure (*morphē*) of the thing and when in this way it makes it exact, then it deposits the form in the soul. And this is the concept (*ennoia*).

[14,3] When the concept has been installed and firmed up, the disposition of scientific knowledge (*epistēmē*) is installed. From this, like light kindled from a leaping fire, *nous* appears like exact vision for assailing true reality.

[14,6] The soul began (1) through the grasping and learnt the form embedded in matter, then (2) accepted through supposition that this, the revealed, is the same as what revealed it, and then (3) through imagination worked out by making a copy that the external thing was like the copy. And it (4) passed through the concept to the universal for the immaterial depositing of the form.

[14,11] After the depositing, scientific knowledge has acquired a firming up through concentration *epibolē* and receives *nous* which concentrates in a pure and then universal state. And that is why there comes to be *nous* of that of which there is also scientific knowledge and a concept, [that is,] of the form which supplies all the structure to matter. . . .

[15,1–5] But reason (*logos*) by acting in a formal way without matter, finds all that is being discriminated, and as having the form exactly in itself, contemplates [the form of] what is being investigated in a more exact state than it has in perceptible objects. Thence reason also adds what is missing from the form and straightens what is crooked. It could not do that without possessing the form first. (RRKS)

Passive Intellect = Imagination

The role of imagination here might seem to be in competition with the enormous role given by other commentators to Intellect (*nous*). But in fact, some commentators from Proclus onwards allow a very un-Aristotelian overlap between *nous* and imagination, since they identify passive intellect with imagination. Proclus' reference to someone having called imagination passive intellect is probably not to an earlier commentator, but to Aristotle himself, as Proclus interprets him. The equation between imagination and passive intellect is thereafter found in Proclus' pupil Ammonius and in Ammonius' pupils, Philoponus and Asclepius, as well as in pseudo-Philoponus and pseudo-Simplicius.[10] The equation cuts across Aristotle's classifications, because in *On the Soul* 3.3, Aristotle classifies imagination as a function of perception, not of intellect. It means that to give a role in concept formation to passive intellect is to give a role to images derived from sense perception.

(15)   Proclus, *in Eucl. 1*, 51,20–52,20

Imagination (*phantasia*), by virtue of its formative movement and by having its existence along with and in the body, produces impressions that are always particularized and divided and possess shape, and everything it cognizes has this kind of existence. That is why someone has not shrunk from calling it passive intellect. Yet if it is intellect, how could it be other than impassive and immaterial? But if its activity is accompanied by being affected (*pathos*), how could it be rightly called intellect any longer? Indeed, impassivity is the hallmark of intellect and the intellective nature, whereas the possibility of being affected is far removed from a being like that. But in my view he wanted to emphasize its intermediate position between the highest and the lowest types of knowledge, and therefore he called it both 'intellect', because of its resemblance with the highest, and 'passive' because of its kinship with the lowest. For, on the one hand, cognitions that are without any shape or form contain the objects of intellection within themselves and their activity is self-directed [i.e. directed towards themselves]. They are one with the objects of their cognition and free of any impression or affect (*pathos*) reaching them from the outside. The lowest types of cognition, on the other hand, work through the sense organs, and they are more like affects (*pathēmata*), receiving their information [i.e. knowledge and opinions] from the outside and moving passively along with their objects. Such are sense perceptions, which 'arise out of violent affects (*pathēmata*)', as Plato says [*Tim.* 42A]. (JO)

[10] Besides Proclus, Ammonius, *in Int.* 6,4–14; 26,1–2; Philoponus, *in de Intellectu* p. 13 Verbeke (Corpus Latinum Commentariorum in Aristotelem Graecorum), ms. lines 00–6; Philoponus, *in DA* 5,38–6,4; 11,7–11; Asclepius, *in Metaph.* 280,14–17; pseudo-Philoponus, *in DA 3*, 523,29–31; pseudo-Simplicius, *in DA* 248,6–10. Most are translated in Richard Sorabji, *The Philosophy of the Commentators 200–600 AD*, London, 2004, vol. 1, 3j.

III Did Aristotle Agree with the Platonic Truth Espoused by Platonist Commentators, or Was He by their Criteria just Wrong?

I have now reviewed the roles in concept formation assigned by the ancient commentators to perception, reason, intellect, and imagination. What remains is to consider how they handled the disagreement between Plato and Aristotle. For some Platonist commentators wanted to present Plato and Aristotle as in harmony. But Syrianus and Proclus were ready to condemn Aristotle, and the condemnation left traces in later commentators too.

Recollected Concepts Ascribed to Aristotle

Some commentators go much further in assimilating Aristotle to Plato, and really remove the centre-point of his opposition to Plato's account of concept-possession, by making him accept Plato's idea of concepts recollected from the soul's life before birth. This is true of the Neoplatonists Iamblichus, Plutarch of Athens (not the author of *Lives* and *Moralia*), and Philoponus. Thus Plutarch is criticized by pseudo-Philoponus for thinking that Aristotle agrees with Plato that the intellect of children already has concepts (*logoi*) of things. According to Philoponus, Aristotle's comparison of the potential intellect with a blank writing tablet (*On the Soul* 3.4, 430a1–2) is not a denial that it already contains within the thinkable forms—it does, but it needs them brought to light because of the unconsciousness caused by incarnation. Iamblichus is most explicit of all. Aristotle's comparison of the child's potential intellect with a writing tablet on which nothing is written must be taken to mean only that the writing is faint. Thus Aristotle comes out agreeing with Plato that concepts are within us waiting to be recollected.

(16) 'Philoponus', *in DA* 3, 520,1–12

Plato is the person who thinks that the intellect of children is dispositional and has concepts (*logoi*) of things, not Aristotle. But Plutarch thinks that Aristotle too says this. How can he not be speaking falsely when Aristotle refutes him? He [Aristotle] says that the intellect of children is like a writing tablet on which nothing is written, because it is suitable (*epitêdeios*) for receiving the rational accounts of things but has not already actually received them. Alexander and Plutarch, then, err both severally and together. So now let us say what is true. It should be known that we are of the opinion that intellect is always form. For the intellect of children is form, potentially receptive of forms, and insofar as it is form it is not potential, as Alexander thinks, but insofar as it is potentially receptive of forms it does not have the rational accounts of things, as Plutarch thinks. (WC)

(17)   Philoponus, *in de Intellectu* pp. 38–40 Verbeke (Corpus Latinum Commentariorum in Aristotelem Graecorum), ms. lines 99–43

[38,99]   But to this it may be replied that we ought to interpret what Aristotle says here carefully and thoughtfully with regard to his whole thought and to what he says everywhere about the intellect. If we have shown a thousand times over, quoting Aristotelian texts, that he wants the rational soul to be separate and immortal, it is plain that even if he here likens it to an uninscribed thing we write on, he does not mean that it has forms in potentiality in the first sense (the sense in which semen is a man in potentiality). But a certain latitude (*latitudo*) must be recognized in both meanings of 'potentiality'. For we say that prime matter is in potentiality a man, and also the elements and semen and all the things which are in potentiality in the first sense, that is, by virtue of suitability; but they are not in potentiality in the same way but some are closer to the thing and some more remote. A similar latitude, then, must be recognized in connection with potentiality in the second sense, i.e. by way of disposition. Both the sleeping geometer and the one who is awake are said to be [one who knows] in potentiality, but the waking geometer is closer to the actuality; and the geometer who is asleep or drunk because he is held down by sleep or intoxication, resembles the man who does not have the disposition at all. So in the same way even if he says the soul resembles an uninscribed thing you write on, he calls it this because of the holding down of cognition by the passions which makes it seem as if it did not have forms at all. And when it has already become a knower he still calls it 'in potentiality'. For he says: 'When it becomes particular things as one who knows in actuality is said to [even then it is in potentiality in a way]' [Aristotle *DA* 3.4, 429b5–7].

[39,21]   That he means it to be everlasting and immortal he has said plainly before more than once, and he now pronounces it to be separate from all matter. And a little later he again plainly says it is immortal. But these earlier words are sufficient: 'Concerning the intellect and the contemplative capacity the position is not yet clear; but this seems to be a different sort of soul, and it falls to this alone to be separated as that which is everlasting from that which is destructible [*DA* 2.2, 413b24]'. And later he says that just as the sun makes colours which are in potentiality, i.e. colours at night, to be colours in actuality [*DA* 3.5, 430a15–17], so intellect which is in actuality, i.e. the teacher's intellect and the Divine Intellect, makes intellect in potentiality intellect in actuality.

[40,30]   The Philosopher's meaning is plain from the model itself. Just as the rising sun does not provide existence for the colours, but makes manifest colours which

exist there but are not evident, and does not make them to be colours (for they were just as much colours during the night), but makes them visible, so intellect which is in actuality perfects intellect which is in potentiality and brings it to actuality not by putting into it forms which are not there, but by bringing to light forms which are non-evident and hidden because of the state of swoon which is the effect of birth. And it is this that he calls 'potentiality' in the first sense. For there is a difference between the geometer who is in a cataleptic swoon though he still possesses [knowledge] dispositionally, or who is asleep, and one who is in none of these conditions but is not exercising the disposition; the one has both the disposition and the actuality hidden and is not capable of functioning; the other functions when he wants without being impeded by anything. The intellect which enters the world of becoming is like a person asleep or delirious. (WC)

(18) Iamblichus ap. 'Philoponum', *in DA 3*, 533,25–35
Iamblichus says: 'And see that he says "writing tablet [Aristotle *DA* 3.4, 430a1]" and not "sheet of papyrus". For it is not called a "writing tablet" if it does not have written letters on it. He says this meaning that the souls of children, which are potential intellect, have the accounts of things. So if he likens it to a writing tablet, clearly it has accounts of things, just as the writing tablet has written letters. If he calls it "on which nothing is written", it stands for "ill written" because it has faint, non-evident written letters, as also we say of a tragic actor with a bad voice "He has no voice". So Aristotle too (says he), like Plato, is of the opinion that objects of intellect are in the soul and accounts of all things, and that there is recollection, not learning.' He says this to show that Aristotle too is of the same opinion as he. (WC)

Recollected Concepts Alongside Aristotle's

Another less startling view is that Aristotle's empirically gained concepts can be accepted alongside the concepts that Plato postulated as being recollected from the soul's existence before birth. This view is already found in the mid-second century in Alcinous' handbook of Platonism, the *Didaskalikos*. Alcinous, like the Stoics, thinks of reason (*logos*) as a collection of concepts (*logoi*). But the concepts gained empirically in Aristotle's manner through sense perception constitute opiniative reason (*doxastikos logos*), whereas the concepts recollected from before birth in Plato's manner constitute scientific reason (*epistêmonikos logos*).[11]

---

[11] Charles Brittain has compared other Middle Platonist texts for acceptance of both types of concept, the *Anonymous Commentary on Plato's Theaetetus*, cols. 23 and 46–8 and Plutarch, *Platonic Questions* 1.4, 1000D–E, and for opiniative reason Plutarch, *On the Generation of the Soul in the Timaeus* 1024 ('"Middle"

I have pointed out above that Porphyry also combines an Aristotelian account of concepts being acquired from external matter initially through perception with a Platonic account of reason providing a correction through concepts which it possesses in advance. The acceptance of both kinds of concept is found also in a passage translated above from the *Commentary on Plato's Phaedrus*, 171,8–25. Of Hermeias, who was professor in Alexandria. In general, the Alexandrian school stuck closer to Porphyry in philosophy of language, I believe, than did the Athenians.

(19) Alcinous, *Didaskalikos* ch. 4, 154,25–29
This latter [reason (*logos*)], too, has two aspects: one concerned with the objects of intellection, the other with the objects of perception. Of these, the former, that concerning the objects of intellection, is science (*epistêmê*) and scientific reason (*epistêmonikos logos*), while that concerning sense-objects is opinion (*doxa*), and opiniative reason (*doxastikos logos*). (JD)

(20) Alcinous, *Didaskalikos* 154,40–155,5
Opinion is the combination of memory and perception. For when we first encounter some perceptible, and from it we get a perception, and from that a memory, and later we encounter the same perceptible again, we connect the pre-existing memory with the subsequent perception and say within ourselves 'Socrates!', 'Horse!', 'Fire!', etc. And this is called opinion (*doxa*)—our connecting (*suntithenai*) the pre-existing perception with the newly produced perception. (DNS)

Aristotle's Concepts Rejected or Downgraded

A commoner view among the Platonists was that Aristotle's idea of empirically gained concepts is to be rejected. The fact they are standardly cited in lists of types of *logos*, common feature, or universal, does not mean that they are endorsed. The attack is already launched by Proclus' teacher, Syrianus, *in Metaph.* 12,28–13,3; 95,13–17; 95,29–38, and continued in Proclus' *Commentary on Euclid Book 1*, 12,9–13,27, and his *Commentary on Plato's Parmenides*, and thereafter in Simplicius, *in Phys.* 1075, 4–20 and Olympiodorus *Commentary on Plato's Phaedo*, lecture 12.1, lines 9–25, Westerink.

Platonists on Academic Scepticism', in *Greek and Roman Philosophy 100 BC to 200 AD*, ed. Richard Sorabji and R. W. Sharples, Bulletin of the Institute of Classical Studies Supplement 94, 2 vols., London, 2006). For opiniative reason, A. A. Long has cited Ptolemy, *On the Criterion* 18,12–19,6; 21,8–10; Sextus Math. 7.111.

The objections to Aristotle's idea that we gain concepts from what we perceive are numerous and some of them are good. Syrianus complains that we do not see every shape, and that the shapes we do see are not precise. If it be replied that they could be made precise, he has a very good answer: how would we know what changes to make except through our possessing precise concepts recollected in Plato's way from before birth? Porphyry had already addressed this problem to some extent in the passage quoted above, but in a way that fluctuates perhaps because of borrowings from Thrasyllus.[12] First he speaks as if imagination could make forms more precise, which simply raises Syrianus' problem how it knows how to do so. But later (15,1-5), he gives an answer somewhat like Syrianus', that it is reason that adds precision and that it can only do so by first having an exact form within itself. Objections to Aristotle are repeated by all but Ammonius, who has left no writing on the subject, in a chain of teachers and pupils stretching from Syrianus, through his pupil Proclus, to his pupil Ammonius and his two pupils Simplicius and Olympiodorus, and the present objection recurs in Proclus and Olympiodorus. An answer could presumably be supplied by Aristotle's active intellect which, like Plotinus' undescended intellect, resides within us continuously thinking the intelligibles. Had Aristotle wished, he could have made the active intellect the source of precision. But then he would have conceded to the Platonists their main point: the need for concepts beyond those gained empirically.

Proclus is drawing on his teacher, Syrianus, when he raises his objections to Aristotle. He complains in his commentary on Euclid that the geometrical figures we peceive are neither precise nor certain. Precision and certainty have to be added by the soul. Further, there is nothing in the perceptible world which, like geometrical entities, lacks parts, breadth, and depth. We do not find there equal radii, fixed ratios of sides, or right angles. (The *Parmenides* commentary adds, Helmig points out, that we do not see precise triangles.) Proclus' *Parmenides* commentary argues that there is a gap when we generalize by induction from what is true of one or more perceived instances to what is necessarily true of all. How can we know of the necessity, unless we have concepts recollected in Plato's manner from before birth, *in Parm.* 981,5-9?

[12] Porphyry, *Commentary on Ptolemy's Harmonics* 13,21-14,14; 15,1-5.

Simplicius makes the related complaint that there is an infinity of particulars so that universals could not be assembled from them, and Helmig reports this objection from Proclus' *Parmenides* commentary as well.[13] Olympiodorus, *Commentary on Plato's Phaedo*, lecture 12.1, lines 9–25, Westerink, objects that adding a grain of sand makes no difference to the equality of merely perceptible objects. In comparing degrees of beauty, we must be appealing to some internal concept as a standard. Without internal forms, we could not mentally supply the deficiencies in what we see, nor pass in thought from one thing to another. Finally, the cause of our longing to know precise forms that we do not perceive must be the fact that they are lurking within us. The attacks on Aristotle's account of concept formation are extensive and I shall finish by quoting a good selection.

(21) Syrianus, *in Metaph.* 12,28–13,3 (Kroll)
Therefore, by saying that there are many ways in which these things [numbers, lines, figures, points] *are*, we bring to light both their being and their substantiality. For even in the sensible works of nature one could see figure, number, physical surface and its limits; in addition, these things are established also in our imagination and opinion, either being grasped by means of abstraction from the sensibles, as he [Aristotle] prefers, or in our judgement being perfected by the substantial forms of the soul. Thus these things in imagination and opinion (*phantasta, doxasta*) participate in being, but are not substances; that is why they might also fall under quantity rather than quality or any other category; but the substantial concepts (*ousiôdeis logoi*) of soul which contain these things are already substances. But if someone might also see their models in intellect and in the intelligibles, one could view number, figures, and magnitude itself as counted amongst the very first substances. (GBe)

(22) Syrianus, *in Metaph.* 95,13–17 (Kroll)
But one might wonder at Aristotle who even in these cases of succession puts the universals on the same level as the mathematicals; for as the universals are, so the mathematicals are, too. In reality both are in the substantial formal principles (*logoi* [concepts]) of the soul but according to him they are in the sensibles and in the concepts (*epinoiai*) which abstract the common natures (*koinotêtes*) from the sensibles. (RRKS)

---

[13] Christoph Helmig, 'Proclus' Criticism of Aristotle's Theory of Abstraction and Concept Formation in *Analytica Posteriora II.* 19', in *Interpreting Aristotle's* Posterior Analytics *in Late Antiquity and Beyond*, ed. F. de Haas, M. Leunissen, and M. Martijn, Leiden, 2010.

(23) Syrianus, *in Metaph.* 95,29–38

Generally one should bring against his [Aristotle's] whole theory, both (1) that we have not seen among the sensibles every geometrical shape or every number that the mathematical sciences deal with, and (2) that it is impossible to employ such precision (*akribeia*) on what is grasped from sensibles. If it is claimed that we supplement what is lacking in them and make them more precise and consider them in that condition, it is necessary to state first where the capability to perfect them comes from. We cannot find another more truthful explanation than the one stated by the ancients, viz. that in virtue of its essence the soul has preconceived (*prolambanein*) the concepts (*logoi*) of everything.

Moreover, if we add something to abstractions from sensibles, we shall end up making them not more precise and truthful but rather more fictitious. (FDH)

(24) Proclus, *in Eucl.* 1 12,9–13,27

In the first place, if we say that mathematical forms (*eidē*) are derived from sense objects—that the soul, from seeing material circles and triangles, shapes in herself the later-generated (*husterogenòs*) form of circle and the form of triangle—whence come the precision (*akribeia*) and certainty that belong to our concepts (*logoi*)? Necessarily either from sense objects or from the soul. But they cannot come from sense objects, for then there would be far more precision in sense objects than there is. They come therefore from the soul, which adds perfection to the imperfect sensibles and precision to their impreciseness. For where among sensible things do we find anything that is without parts, or without breadth, or without depth? Where do we see the equality of the lines from centre to circumference? Where the fixed ratios (*logoi*) of the sides? Where the rightness of angles? Do we not see that all sensible things are confused with one another and that no quality in them is pure and free of its opposite, but that all are divisible and extended and changing? How, then, shall we get the stable substance which unchangeable principles have, if they are derived from things that are ever changing from one state to another? For it is admitted that anything which results from changing beings receives from them a changeable character. And how can we get the precision of precise and irrefutable forms (*eidē*) from things that are not precise? For whatever yields knowledge that is steadfast has that quality itself in greater degree.

[13,7] We must therefore posit the soul as the generatrix of mathematical forms (*eidē*) and concepts (*logoi*). And if we say that the soul produces them by having their patterns (*paradeigmata*) in her own essence and that these offspring are the projections (*probolai*) of forms previously existing in her, we shall be in agreement with Plato and shall have found the truth with regard to mathematical being. If, on the other hand, she weaves this enormous immaterial fabric and gives birth to such an imposing science without knowing or having preconceived (*proeilēphuia*) these

concepts (*logoi*), how can she judge whether the offspring she bears are fertile or wind eggs [Plato *Theaetetus* 151E; 157D], whether they are not phantoms instead of truth? What canons could she use for measuring the truth in them? And how could she even produce such a varied mass of concepts without having their essence (*ousia*) in herself? For thus we should be making their being (*hupostasis*) come about by chance, without reference to any standard. If, therefore, mathematical forms (*eidē*) are products of the soul and the concepts of the things that the soul produces are not derived from sense objects, mathematicals are their projections (*probal-lesthai*), and the soul's travail and her offspring are manifestations of eternal forms (*eidē*) abiding in her. (GM)

(25) Proclus, *in Parm.* 981,5–9; 24–41
In demonstrations and definitions the particular must be entirely subordinate to the universal and the definition. Definitions of common features in particulars do not comprehend the particulars as a whole. (. . .)

If we are, then, to discover the definition which will serve as the principle of a demonstration, the definition must be of an entity of such a sort as to comprehend everything more particular than itself. Such things are the forms (*eidē*) in us, and not those inherent in particulars. Therefore, if these are abolished, definition will no longer be possible. So the science of definition will disappear, along with that of demonstration, departing from the range of human thought. Furthermore, follow-ing on these, the science of division will become a mere name; for divisions do nothing other than distinguish the many from the one, and separate off those things preexisting in a unified manner in the whole into their proper differentiae, not adding the differentiae from without, but viewing them as being within, in the genera themselves, dividing off the species from one another. Where, then, would be the task of this science, if really-existent forms were not present in us? (FDH)

(26) Simplicius, *in Phys.* 1075,4–20
This, then, is the way Alexander explained [it], wishing the universal and the cognition of the universal to be assembled (*sunagesthai*) from the particulars, and he said that it was stated that 'it somehow knows the particulars through the universal [knowledge]' as a sign that the cognition of the universal is assembled (*athroizesthai*) by means of the particulars, since the universal knowledge is of each of the things [falling] under the universal (and it has been assembled from these), for the particulars are comprehended in the knowledge of the universal, on the grounds that that [knowledge] comes to be from them and in dependence on them.

[1075,10] On the other hand, if it is not possible for universals to be assembled (*sunagesthai*) from particulars, since those are infinite, nor for the cognition in the sensory and imaginative [parts] to be capable of bringing scientific understanding

into existence in the intellect, [this cognition] being much inferior to [scientific understanding, which is] superior, one must rather, I think, explain in a simpler and truer way what has been stated by Aristotle. The intellect always has knowledge of the universals in actuality (whether ready to hand (*prokheiron*) or not), but of the particulars [only] potentially. Whenever perception strikes the particular, at that time, then, the intellect actually knows (*ginôskei*) the particulars through the universal. 'For an individual human being is a human being too', as [Aristotle] himself stated elsewhere. [Cf. *An. Post.* 2.19, 100a16–b1] For this reason too he added the 'somehow' (*pôs* [247b6. It is not clear whether Simplicius here read Aristotle as saying 'particulars are somehow known by the universal' or 'the universal . . . somehow . . . by particulars']), because the cognition of the universal is not on the same level as that of the particular; rather, the particular is known (*ginôsketai*) 'through the universal [knowledge]' because the particular is encompassed by the universal. (CH)

(27) Olympiodorus, *on Phaedo*, lecture 12.1, lines 9–25, Westerink
The second argument is that the approximate must be preceded by the precise (*akribes*), and the vague rough and ready (*amudrês, holoskherês*) by the well-defined, and the forms (*eidê*) in this world are not exact (precise: *akribês*): two magnitudes that are equal will remain so when a quantity the size of a grain of sand is added or removed [74b7–c6]. Since, however, these arguments prove the existence of Ideas (*ideai*) no less than that of concepts (*logoi*) in the soul, let us give some additional proof of the existence of such concepts in the soul. If the human soul distinguishes between forms (*eidê*) in this world and calls the one more beautiful, the other less so, it evidently pronounces these judgements by referring to a certain standard and a certain form; it could not distinguish between things of which it does not have the concepts within itself. We should not believe the Peripatos [Ar., *An. Post.* II 19, 99b35] when it declares that we discern these things by means of something called the capacity of judgement (*kritikê*): the human soul does not act by mere natural instinct (*phusikôs*), as a spider makes its web. Besides, if it makes additions and passes from one thing to another, it must evidently have certain forms within itself, otherwise there would be no question of passing on to other things, or of supplying deficiencies, without such forms; a man who sees Socrates' portrait without having seen Socrates before cannot go beyond the portrait. Lastly, if the soul aspires to the knowledge of exact (precise: *akribês*) forms and its aspiration is not in vain, the cause of this longing can only be the presence in it of forms, which it tries to learn. (LGW)

Overview

To look back in overview, it has become clear that the ancient commenta-tors force us to look much more closely at Aristotle's text than we would otherwise do, whether or not we believe their interpretations. They are surely right that very important new information is added by Aristotle when he offers to state his point more clearly. They grapple, as not all modern scholars have, with Aristotle's unprecedented statement that even a single act of perception is of the universal, and they make some plausible sense of it. They add in their own conviction that Aristotle's talk of *nous* must refer to the three kinds of intellect that Alexander read into Aristotle's *De anima* 3.5. They do not accept my suggestion (but neither so far do contempor-aries) that Aristotle is only thinking of intellectual 'spotting'. In surprising combination with this stress on the three kinds of intellect, some of them gave a large role to imagination, which Aristotle refers to at best obliquely in his earlier reference to many memories. For him imagination belonged on the other side of a divide from intellect. As the great biological taxonomist, he saw imagination as belonging to the perceptual faculties, intellect to the rational. The Platonism of most commentators (Alexander was an Aristotel-ian) was not like that. It saw the rationality of humans as permeating their other psychological capacities. Some Platonists, we saw, even identified imagination, in a way that would make Aristotle scream, with the lowest kind of intellect. Our probable disagreement does not prevent us from learning far more from these interpretations than we could if left to our own devices.

Bibliography

P. Adamson, 'Posterior Analytics II.19: a Dialogue with Plato?', in *Aristotle and the Stoics Reading Plato*, ed. V. Harte, M. M. McCabe, R. W. Sharples, and A. Sheppard, Institute of Classical Studies, forthcoming.

V. Caston, 'Something and Nothing: The Stoics on Concepts and Universals', *Oxford Studies in Ancient Philosophy* 17 (1999), pp. 145–213.

O. Goldin, trans., *Philoponus(?): On Aristotle Posterior Analytics 2*, London, 2009.

F. de Haas, 'Recollection and Potentiality in Philoponus', in *The Winged Chariot*, ed. M. Kardaun and J. Spruijt, Leiden, 2000, pp. 165–84.

C. Helmig, 'Proclus' Criticism of Aristotle's Theory of Abstraction and Concept Formation in *Analytica Posteriora II.* 19', in *Interpreting Aristotle's* Posterior Analytics *in Late Antiquity and Beyond*, ed. F. de Haas, M. Leunissen, and M. Martijn, Leiden, 2010.

I. Mueller, 'Aristotle's Doctrine of Abstraction in the Commentators', in *Aristotle Transformed*, ed. R. Sorabji, London, 1990, pp. 463–79.

F. H. Sandbach, '*Ennoia* and *prolēpsis* in the Stoic Theory of Knowledge', *Classical Quarterly* 24 (1930), pp. 44–51.

D. Sedley, 'Faculties of Judgement in the Didaskalikos', *Mnemosyne* 44 (1991), pp. 347–63.

D. Sedley, 'Alcinous' Epistemology', in *Polyhistor, Studies in the History and Historiography of Ancient Philosophy Presented to Jaap Mansfeld on His Sixtieth Birthday*, ed. K. Algra, P. van der Horst, and D. Runia, Leiden, 1996, pp. 300–12.

R. Sorabji, *The Philosophy of the Commentators 200–600AD*, 3 vols., London, 2004.

R. Sorabji, 'Universals Transformed: The First Thousand Years after Plato', in *Universals, Concepts and Qualities*, ed. Peter Strawson and Arindam Chakrabarti, Aldershot, 2006, pp. 105–23.

H. Tarrant, *Thrasyllan Platonism*, Ithaca, 1993.

12

Galen's Aristotelian Definitions

JANE HOOD

This paper will argue that Galen takes a sophisticated and broadly Aristotelian stance on definition. There is, however, a significant divergence in his account from Aristotle's at the level of the first stages in definition-, or concept-, formation. In order to examine this I shall concentrate in particular on sections of Galen's text *De Pulsuum Differentiis* IV (Kühn VIII). In this book he gathers together his more theoretical views on definition, with some practical points thrown in for good measure on the way.

Galen's stance on definition initially seems particularly difficult to pin down. It is closely connected with his views on first principles and axioms and also with his acknowledgement that experiential knowledge, which is crucial for the doctor, is of a different type from knowledge of logic. It is also tied to his Platonism and adoption of Platonic theories of essence and division (as discussed by Barnes 1971, 51 n. 7),[1] and yet also to his general underlying acceptance of Aristotelian taxonomy and that the doctor must have experience as well as theory in order to heal his patients. I clearly cannot even begin to address all these interrelated complexities here. However, it does seem that Galen's theory of definition can give us a first indication of how to emerge from the epistemological maze he has created.

Jonathan Barnes (1991, 73) discusses Galen's loathing for definitions as most employ them. Galen complains that doctors seem themselves to have caught a disease: 'definitionitis' (*philoristia*, *Diff. Puls.* VIII 698). They seem unable to begin to do their work without playing with definitions and words in a way completely unrelated to the business of healing. As Galen puts it, some of them couldn't even buy a cabbage without defining it first

---

[1] See, for instance, Galen, *Against Lycus* 3.7 (*SVF* 2.230).

(*Diff. Puls.* VIII 698). Barnes points out that Galen, when in this mood, looks on the business of forming definitions as merely a dialectical exercise for logicians or rhetoricians. Whether names are used correctly or incorrectly is irrelevant for the survival of the patient. Indeed, he uses the opportunity of this discussion to attack his old enemies the Methodists in, for instance, *Meth. Med.* X 30, on the grounds that they are arguing about words whilst their patients suffer, rather then getting down to the business of healing them and advancing their medical knowledge.

It is important to note that Galen is not arguing that all definitions are pointless but rather that it is just that doctors should concentrate their efforts on producing definitions that actually advance scientific knowledge which will aid them in healing the individual patients who come to them. They should not waste their time on the obvious. This is one of his complaints at the start of *Diff. Puls.* IV (VIII 696–7): there is no need to define 'pulse' since it is not a nonsense word that needs a definition to be understood. Writers on medicine should stop making fools of themselves by concentrating on such things. Just in case we had not got this point, he then goes through the faulty definitions of 'pulse' by various schools and individuals, including some of the medical hall of fame such as Herophilus, Erasistratus, and Praxagoras (702–3).

Galen's aim is not just rhetorical. He is telling us something important about definition. At the scientific level we are interested in, definition is not merely about the signification of terms, as practised by those suffering from definitionitis. We are not interested in the interrelation of words: what we are interested in, as medical practitioners, is what we can learn about the human body and how it reacts within itself and with the external world so that we can diagnose and, if at all possible, heal. Definitions, therefore, are concerned with the nature of the substance(s) we are dealing with. When different essential definitions are proposed, the mistake will be a theoretically driven one.

τὸν ὁρισμὸν οὖν εἴπερ ὅλην τὴν οὐσίαν ἀκριβῶς τοῦ πράγματος μέλλει δηλώσειν, οὐδὲν αὐτῆς τῶν κυριωτάτων παραλείπειν προσήκει· τῆς δ' οὐσίας ἀμφισβητουμένης, ἀναγκαῖον ἔσται καθ' ἑκάστην αἵρεσιν ἴδιον ὁρισμὸν γίνεσθαι·

If the definition is intended to make clear accurately the entire essence, it must not leave out any aspect of its principles; but when there is a debate about the essence, it will be the case that a particular definition arises philosophical school by school. (*Diff. Puls.* K. VIII 703, 16–704, 1)

Of course, the same empirical evidence has always (more or less) been available to everyone, and so differences (and hence mistakes) arise from the assumptions made by medical theorists. Galen wants to make a deeper point: the different schools also have different notions of what is required for a scientific definition.

Galen first gives us a two-fold notion of definition:

καὶ τούτου γ᾽ ἔτι μᾶλλον ἀναγκαῖον ἐγνῶσθαι δύο γένη τὰ πρῶτα τῶν ὁρισμῶν εἶναι, τὸ μὲν ἕτερον ἐξηγούμενον σαφῶς τὴν τοῦ πράγματος ἔννοιαν, ἣν ἔχουσιν οἱ ὀνομάζοντες αὐτό, τὸ δ᾽ ἕτερον, ὡς εἴρηται, τὸ τὴν οὐσίαν διδάσκον. ἀρετὴ δ᾽ ἑκατέρου τῶν ὅρων ἰδία τοῦ μὲν τὴν ἔννοιαν ἑρμηνεύοντος ὁμολογεῖσθαί τε πᾶσι τοῖς ὁμοφώνοις καὶ μὴ προσάπτεσθαι τῆς οὐσίας τοῦ πράγματος, τοῦ δὲ τὴν οὐσίαν διδάσκοντος ὁμολογεῖν μὲν τῷ κατὰ τὴν ἔννοιαν, ἕτερον δὲ ὑπάρχειν αὐτῷ.

And it is still more necessary than this (i.e. realizing that there are different definitions for different schools) to grasp that there are two primary types of definition, one of which clearly sets out the general notion of the matter, which those who name it hold, and the other, as it is said, teaches us what the essence is. Each of the definitions has its own virtue: that which expresses the general notion is accepted by all who speak the same language, but it does not grasp hold of the essence of the matter; but that which is explanatory of the essence is accepted in as much as it is in accordance with the general notion, but the essential definition is not of the same type as it (i.e. the *ennoia*). (*Diff. Puls.* K. VIII 704, 6–15)

Galen's two-fold distinction of types of definition is not in the same vein as the distinction he made between those with definitionitis and those who give essential definitions: both of these types of definition have an excellence or virtue. The virtue of one is that of setting out the *ennoia*, the virtue of the other is that it gives us the essence.

The *ennoia*-type of definition is clearly tied to language use and is accepted by ordinary language users. An example of such a definition may be, in fact, the kind of definition Galen himself gives us of 'pulse' at *Diff. Puls.* VIII 706, where he captures the general notion used by the general body of language users who would employ this term on the basis of what can be clearly observed. What such an *ennoia*-type definition amounts to will become clearer as Galen's account unfolds. Although not a full scientific, essential, definition, the *ennoia*-type of definition is not a mere waste of time if it enables us to move to the second type of definition: that is, from a definition reliant simply on our grasp of language to one which tells us the essence of the kind in question. As Galen makes clear, there is a connection between the *ennoia*-type definition and the essential definition, although they are of a different type. We have already seen why: Galen has made it clear that it is only the essential definition which does not 'leave out any aspect of the relevant principles', i.e. it sets out the necessary and sufficient conditions for that substance being the substance it is and acting as it does.

Galen does not make clear here how these two 'primary' types of definition are interrelated. The Aristotelian picture would be that, in successful cases of pinpointing a natural kind (such as picking out and naming the kind 'water' as opposed to mistakenly naming the non-existent kind of 'goat-stags'), enquiry into the nature of the kind picked out by the name leads to discovery of the underlying essence.[2] This might involve many refinements on the way as we find out that the essence is more complicated (and so we need to exclude some of what was previously taken to be 'water' from our definition of 'water') or more simple (and so our definition becomes more inclusive) than at first was thought. Such a picture would explain how the two types of definition are related, representing, as they do, stages in the acquisition of knowledge of the essential from the starting-point of the *ennoia*. This would tally with his statement at *Meth. Med.* X 39, that in each enquiry one should replace a name with a definition, when understood as a scientific, essential one.

However, before we are carried away with a possible unifying explanation linking these two types, it is necessary to heed Galen's warning about our understanding of definitions:

πρῶτον οὖν τοῦτό σοι γιγνέσθω γνώρισμα τῶν εἰκῆ φλυαρούντων, ὅταν ἕνα τοῦ προκειμένου πράγματος ἀκούσῃς αὐτῶν λεγόντων ὅρον.

This, therefore, will be the first signal to you of those who are foolish and vain, when you hear them speaking of a single definition for the matter under consideration. (*Diff. Puls.* K. VIII 704, 16–18)

However much we may see them as linked, that they are different *types* of definition is made especially clear. This is because the *ennoia*-type and essential definitions have fundamentally different functions, as he sets out. The *ennoia*-type is concerned with our initial naming and then

---

[2] On the difficulties in interpreting Aristotle's position on the definition of non-existent kinds, see Charles 2000, 28–33. Galen makes it clear that definitions must latch onto necessary features of the kind, not the accidentals he takes Aristotle to argue as sufficient for a nominal definition (*Diff. Puls.* K. VIII 705, 7–706, 3: see below).

how we employ those names in our language, whereas the essential definition works in the domain of science.

At this point, however, Galen is not satisfied that he has captured
everything that is required by means of his two-fold distinction and so
introduces a four-fold set of distinctions (I have numbered them below):

ἐπὶ τινῶν μὲν γὰρ οὐ δύο μόνον, ἀλλὰ καὶ τρεῖς καὶ τέτταρας ἄμεινόν ἐστι ποιεῖσθαι·
[1] πρῶτον μὲν τὸ ὁμολογούμενον ἅπασι τοῖς ὁμοφώνοις, ὅστις οὐδὲν ἀποφαίνεται
περὶ τῆς τοῦ πράγματος οὐσίας, ἐπὶ ψιλῆς καταμένων τῆς ἐννοίας· [2] ἕτερον δ᾽ ἐπ᾽
αὐτῷ, βραχὺ μέν τι τῆς ἐννοίας ἀποχωροῦντα, βραχὺ δέ τι καὶ τῆς οὐσίας
ἐφαπτόμενον· [3] καὶ τρίτον ἐπὶ τῷδε, πλέον μὲν ἤδη τῆς ἐννοίας, πλέον δὲ καὶ
τῆς οὐσίας ἑρμηνεύοντα· [4] καὶ τέταρτον ἐπ᾽ αὐτοῖς τὸν τὴν οὐσίαν ὅλην
διδάσκοντα.

For there are not only two types of definition, but it is better to have three and even
four. [1] First of all there is the definition which is accepted by all who speak the
same language, but which reveals nothing of the essence of the matter, but nakedly
sets out the general notion. [2] The second moves away from this general notion a
little, and grasps to some small degree something of the essence. [3] And the third
moves on from this, moving further from the general notion, and further sets out
the essence. [4] And, after this, the fourth sets out the essence in its entirety. (*Diff.
Puls.* K. VIII 704, 18–705, 7)

The progression between the types of definition, and their interconnection,
is explicit. The first type of definition here seems to correspond to the
ennoia-type definition of Galen's two-fold distinction. It is accepted by all
who speak the same language, as was the *ennoia*-type. Indeed, it is said to set
out the *ennoia*.[3] In this four-fold distinction, this type of definition is said to
set out the *ennoia* nakedly, revealing nothing of the essence at all. It seems
that Galen is again referring to our ability as language users to employ terms
in our language even if we do not understand anything of the nature of the
underlying kind.

It is distinction [4] above which seems most closely to correspond with
the essence-type of definition in Galen's two-fold distinction, as in both
cases he is speaking of the essence for scientific purposes. In his two-fold
distinction, he is keen, however, to point out that the essential definition
is not contrary to the *ennoia*-type. This connection seems to explain
his employment of a four-fold distinction whose aim is to set out how

---

[3] Note the Stoic phrase of the ʾkoinai ennoiaiʾ (*SVF* 2.154.29; 3.5.41): see Schofield 1980, 294.

the *ennoia* and essential definitions are connected. The four-fold distinction does not render redundant or mistaken Galen's earlier two-fold distinction, it rather sets out in more detail how the *ennoia*-type and essential definitions (the 'primary' definitions) are connected. The passage which follows in Galen's text makes the nature of the connection clear, and he explicitly claims this as a broadly Aristotelian account:

τοῦτον μὲν οὖν δείκνυσθαι δεῖ τὴν ἀναφορὰν ἐπὶ τὸν τρίτον ἔχοντα, τοῦτον δ' αὖ πάλιν ἐπὶ τὸν δεύτερον, κἀκεῖνον αὖθις ἐπὶ τὸν πρῶτον, αὐτὸν δὲ τὸν πρῶτον ἐξ αὐτοῦ πιστεύεσθαι, φαινομένων ἐναργῶς πραγμάτων ἑρμηνείαν ἔχοντα. διὸ καὶ λόγον αὐτὸν ὀνοματώδη κέκληκεν ὁ Ἀριστοτέλης, ὡς εἰ καὶ λόγον ὀνόματος ἑρμηνευτικὸν εἰρήκει. τὸν δ' ἕτερον ὅρον, οὐσιώδη τινὲς ἐκάλεσαν, λόγον εἶναί φησιν τὸν τί εἶναι δηλοῦντα. τί μὲν γάρ ἐστιν ἑκάστῳ τῶν ὁριζομένων τὸ εἶναι τοῦτον ἑρμηνεύειν φησὶ, τὰ συμβεβηκότα δὲ ἰδίως αὐτῷ συνδιέρχεσθαι τὸν ἐννοηματικόν. ὑπολαμβάνει δὲ καὶ ἄλλον ὁρισμὸν εἶναι τὸν καὶ τὴν οὐσίαν τοῦ πράγματος διδάσκοντα. καὶ τί με δεῖ λέγειν μακρότερον ἔτι περὶ τηλικούτων πραγμάτων, ἃ δυοῖν ἐδεήθη βιβλίων, τοῦ τρίτου καὶ τετάρτου τῶν ὑπομνημάτων ὧν ἐποιησάμην εἰς τὸ δεύτερον Ἀριστοτέλους τῶν δευτέρων ἀναλυτικῶν.

It is necessary, therefore, that this fourth definition makes clear the connection it has to the third, and this third again its connection to the second, and the second again its connection to the first, but the first definition gains its acceptability from itself, with its discovery coming clearly from the appearance of things. And so Aristotle called it a *nominal* definition,[4] as if even the definition of the name set out something interpretative. But the other [type of] definition, some called it *essential*, he says is a definition making clear *the what-it-is*. For he says that this definition explains that which is essential to each definition, but the nominal definition in itself specifically goes together through the accidentals. It is thought that it is a different definition that also teaches the essence of the matter. And yet what I should say is still rather brief concerning these issues, which needed two books, the third and fourth books of commentary which I wrote on the second book of Aristotle's Posterior Analytics. (*Diff. Puls.* K. VIII 705, 7–706, 3)

Several important points can be gained from this passage:

Firstly, the different types of definition are explicitly seen as interconnected, and they are interconnected in the process of learning or discovering the underlying essence, beginning with our grasp of the name. This seems to be

---

[4] Ar., *An. Post.* 93b29–32: ὁρισμὸς δ' ἐπειδὴ λέγεται εἶναι λόγος τοῦ τί ἐστι, φανερὸν ὅτι ὁ μέν τις ἔσται λόγος τοῦ τί σημαίνει τὸ ὄνομα ἢ λόγος ἕτερος ὀνοματώδης, οἷον τί σημαίνει [τί ἐστι] τρίγωνον.

what should be understood by a connection being made from one type of a definition to the previous one, as we move towards the essential.

Secondly, the essential definition is the point from which Galen sets out this interconnectedness, perhaps as that is the end-point in investigation, but it must be tied to the first, *ennoia*-type definition.

Thirdly, the starting-point for the first type of definition is the *phainomena*, the appearances, clearly, *enargôs*. This seems to relate back to the *ennoia* capturing in language what would be accepted by all language users, but we learn that what is captured in language is that which is apparently clear through perception.

Fourthly, at this point, Galen separates what he has to say about definition from Aristotle. Where he has an *ennoia*-type first type of definition, Aristotle is credited with nominal definition. The nominal is somehow meant to be interpretative,[5] as opposed to the *ennoia*-type. It seems that Galen understands Aristotle's nominal definition to be one which lists the accidents of the subject, rather than being a definition which gains acceptability through language use. This seems to be a mistake in Aristotelian interpretation on Galen's part of *An. Post.* 93b30–33, and one which separates him from the Aristotelian position of definition, especially through Aristotle's commencement of definition through the pre-conceptual mapping of similarities over individuals, as originating in perception. For it may be the case that Aristotle does accept that accidents form a part of definitions such as that of 'goat-stag', as it is only the accidents of goats and stags which can be enumerated in Aristotle's first-stage definitions, but they are accidents belonging to no essence, giving the signification of the name only. These accident-listing definitions may only truly list accidents when what Galen

---

[5] It seems that Galen uses 'interpretive' as 'explanatory': Galen, *Inst. Log.* Kalbfleisch 17, 9, 3: ἐν γὰρ τούτῳ τῷ λόγῳ τὸ μὲν ἐκ τῆς <ἀλήθεια> φωνῆς σημαίνεσθαι λόγον ἑρμηνευτικὸν τῶν ὄντων ἐξήγησίς ἐστι τοῦ σημαινομένου πρὸς τῆς ἀλήθεια φωνῆς, τὸ δὲ πάντη ἀληθεύειν Δίωνα ἐν χώρᾳ τοῦ καθόλου ἀξιώματος εἴληπται, τὸ δὲ <συμπέρασμα τόδε> εἰ πάντα ἀληθεύει Δίων, ἔν δέ τι <ὧν φησι> καὶ τοῦτ' ἔστι τὸ μαντικὴν εἶναι, ἀλη(θές) ἐστι καὶ τοῦτο. In *Hippocratis Aphorismos Comentarii VII*, XVIIIa, 187,5: ἀλλ' ὅτι τῶν ἐπὶ μέρους τινὸς ὁ λόγος οὗτος ἑρμηνευτής ἐστιν, εἴρηται δ' ὡς ἐκ καθόλου, διὰ τοῦτο τὴν ἀπορίαν παρέσχεν. Galen appears to be distancing his opinion from his understanding of Aristotelian 'nominal' definitions as in themselves able to to provide a link to the understanding of the essence, once those 'nominal' definitions have passed the experiential test of picking out existent kinds, as opposed to the non-existent 'goat-stags'. The reason that Galen's first-level definitions can be linked to the second level, and so on, is that they gain validity from the reception of concepts at the moment of perception by means of *phantasia*. Galen understands Aristotle's 'nominal' definitions to indentify mere accidents, and so provides no reliable or explanatory connection to the more sophisticated levels of definition to which science aims to progress.

perhaps understands by 'interpretation' takes place, and the signification of the name is linked to our further understanding of the underlying essence.

It is important at this point to understand the status accorded to perception and *phantasia* in definition-formation by Galen and Aristotle.

Aristotle indicates that the content of the images of the faculty of *phantasia* are distinguishable from the content of our rationally assessable human judgements. Like the Müller-Lyer illusion, things can appear to us one way whilst we believe that they are of a quite different nature. The sun, for instance, can look a foot across to us, and at the same time as it looks that way to us, we can believe that it is an entirely different size:

φαίνεται δὲ καὶ ψευδῆ, περὶ ὧν ἅμα ὑπόληψιν ἀληθῆ ἔχει, οἷον φαίνεται μὲν ὁ ἥλιοφς ποδιαῖος, πεπίστευται δ' εἶναι μείζων τῆς οἰκουμένης

And also there are false appearances about which there is at the same time a true supposition, such as the sun appears a foot across, but it is believed to be larger than the inhabited world. (*De Anima* Γ.3, 428b2–4)

This should not lead us to think, however, that *phantasia* and the suppositions (*hypolepseis*) are entirely independent of one another. The faculty of *phantasia* is in fact claimed to be a prerequisite for the ability to make suppositions,[6] as the content of *phantasia*, the *phantasma*, is a necessary condition for *hypolepsis*, the *phantasma* being the image which enables us to make judgements:

εἰ δή ἐστιν ἡ φαντασία καθ' ἣν λέγομεν φάντασμά τι ἡμῖν γίγνεσθαι καὶ μὴ εἴ τι κατὰ μεταφορὰν λέγομεν, μία τίς ἐστι τούτων δύναμις ἢ ἕξις, καθ' ἣν κρίνομεν καὶ ἀληθεύμεν ἢ ψευδόμεθα

If indeed imagination is that in virtue of which we say that an image is present to us, and if we are not speaking metaphorically in any way, it is one of those things, a faculty or a disposition, in virtue of which we make judgements, and assess truth and falsity.[7] (*De Anima* Γ.3, 428a1–4)

It seems that *phantasia* is acting as an informational system, which is providing data from perception. The *phantasma* it provides can then be assented to as representing the truth or rejected as representing what is false on the basis of further considerations (such as the belief that the sun is not a

---

[6] φαντασία γὰρ ἕτερον καὶ αἰσθήσεως καὶ διανοίας· αὐτή τε οὐ γίγνεται ἄνευ αἰσθήσεως, καὶ ἄνευ ταύτης οὐκ ἔστιν ὑπόληψις. De Anima Γ.3, 427b14–16.

[7] Cf. *De Anima* Γ.3, 428a12–15.

foot across, even though it might look that way). Such a judgement concerning a *phantasma* does not change its content, however: the *phantasma* of the sun still represents the sun as being a foot across, even when we do not believe the sun to be so. *Phantasia* is nevertheless open to being truth-assessed by humans with the ability to form *hypolepseis*. This distinction is due to the fact that *hypolepsis* is part of the intellectual faculty, whereas *phantasia* is part of the perceptual faculty, and of the intellectual only incidentally.[8] For *hypolepsis* is concerned with true/false judgements which must therefore be capable of being set out in propositional form and assessed inferentially, as are the propositions of belief.[9]

καὶ διὰ τὸ ἐμμένειν καὶ ὁμοίας εἶναι ταῖς αἰσθήσεσι, πολλὰ κατ' αὐτὰς πράττει τὰ ζῷα, τὰ μὲν διὰ τὸ μὴ ἔχειν νοῦν, οἷον τὰ θηρία, τὰ δὲ διὰ τὸ ἐπικαλύπτεσθαι τὸν νοῦν ἐνίοτε πάθει ἢ νόσιος ἢ ὕπνῳ, οἷον οἱ ἄνθρωποι.

And because images remain in us and are similar to their perceptions, animals carry out many actions under their influence, some because they do not have intellect, such as wild animals, others because sometimes intellect is obscured by a condition either in illness or in sleep, as in the case of humans. (*De Anima* Γ.3, 429a4–8)

In this passage, animals and humans seem to be able to respond in action on the basis of things looking a particular way, a form of discrimination

---

[8] *Mem.* 450a12–14: ἡ δὲ μνήμη καὶ ἡ τῶν νοητῶν οὐκ ἄνευ φαντάσματός ἐστιν. ὥστε τοῦ διανοουμένου κατὰ συμβεβηκὸς ἂν εἴη, καθ' αὑτὸ δὲ τοῦ πρώτου αἰσθητικοῦ. But memory, also of the objects of thought, is not without imagery. The result seems to be that it belongs incidentally to the intellectual faculty, but in itself to the primary sense-faculty.

Cf. *De Anima* Γ.8, 432a12–18, where the *noemata* of thought are said to be distinct from the images of *phantasia*, but *phantasmata* are a necessary condition for *noemata*.

[9] *De Anima* Γ.3, 427b16–21: ὅτι δ' οὐκ ἔστιν ἡ αὐτὴ [νόησις] καὶ ὑπόληψις, φανερόν. τοῦτο μὲν γὰρ τὸ πάθος ἐφ' ἡμῖν ἐστιν, ὅταν βουλώμεθα (πρὸ ὀμμάτων γὰρ ἔστι τι ποιήσασθαι, ὥσπερ οἱ ἐν τοῖς μνημονικοῖς τιθέμενοι καὶ εἰδωλοποιοῦντες), δοξάζειν δ' οὐκ ἐφ' ἡμῖν· ἀνάγκη γὰρ ἢ ψεύδεσθαι ἢ ἀληθεύειν. It is clear that this [i.e. imagination; not reading νόησις] is not the same thing as supposition. For imagination is an affection that is in our power whenever we want (for it is possible to produce something before the eyes, just like those who set things down in mnemonic systems and form mental pictures), but believing is not up to us; for that must be either true or false.

As Ross states ad loc., the unnamed subject of the sentence quoted above is φαντασία. νόησις was bracketed by Madvig as the comparison is between φαντασία and ὑπόληψις. As Hicks points out, confusion about the exact interpretation of νόησις goes back a long way, as Themistius substitutes φαντασία for νόησις in his paraphrase, and the second hands of MSS. C and U, as well as Simplicius' lemma have ἡ αὐτὴ φαντασία. The sentence, as Ross points out, reads better without either νόησις or φαντασία, with φαντασία as the subject continued from the sentence before, and the subject of the following sentence.

Cf. *De Anima* Γ.3, 428a–b: the truth-assessibility of φαντασία is not of the same rigour as that open to thought, which is concerned with the truth functions of syllogistic reasoning (*De Anima* Γ.8, 432a12–18); it seems that although *phantasiai* can be true/false, they do not have to be accepted by the subject as true.

which does not involve the use of propositions. Nor is the ability to form rationally assessable propositions something that Aristotle believes we have throughout our lives:

διὸ οὔτε ἐν τοῖς ἄλλοις ζῴοις ἐστὶν ἡ προαίρεσις οὔτε ἐν πάσῃ ἡλικίᾳ οὔτε πάντως ἔχοντος ἀνθρώπου· οὐδὲ γὰρ τὸ βουλεύσασθαι, οὐδ᾽ ὑπόληψις τοῦ διὰ τί, ἀλλὰ δοξάσαι μὲν εἰ ποιητέον ἢ μὴ ποιητέον οὐθὲν κωλύει πολλοῖς ὑπάρχειν τὸ δὲ διὰ λογισμοῦ οὐκέτι.

So the capacity of deliberate choice is not present in the other animals, nor in humans at every stage or condition in life; for no more is the capacity of deliberation, nor supposition of the cause, but nothing prevents there being for many the capacity of forming beliefs as to whether to do or not do something without the capacity to form such a judgement through reasoning. (EE B.10, 1226b21–5)

Humans at certain stages of life, we learn, like animals, do not have the capacity of deliberate choice, any more than they can employ reasoning (logismos) or hypolepseis. The same can be said for εἰδότι at NE Γ.1, 1111a22, where children and animals are said to *know* particulars, and as a result voluntary action can be attributed to them.[10] Animal and child voluntary action need commit Aristotle to no more than behaviourally guided action for which one is nevertheless held responsible (as the voluntary is concerned with the assignment of praise and blame, for instance at NE Γ.1, 1110b1). The images of *phantasia* are the material from which humans come to make epistemic claims (*hypolepsis*). The material of *phantasia*, the images with their origin in perception, can also provide the starting-point for subsequent epistemic claims in our immediate contact with the world. *Phantasiai* are clearly, therefore, the material out of which propositions can be formed, but humans and animals can act voluntarily without the faculty of rational thought. Thus, the content of perception is not itself propositional or automatically governed by rational assessment.

Galen, however, seems to take a different, Stoic view on the content of perception as is indicated by the fact that the first stage in definition is that of the *ennoia*-type. Plutarch informs us that *ennoiai* are a type of *phantasia*.[11]

---

[10] NE Γ.1, 1111a22–4: τὸ ἑκούσιον δόξειεν ἂν εἶναι οὗ ἡ ἀρχὴ ἐν αὐτῷ εἰδότι τὰ καθ᾽ ἕκαστα ἐν οἷς ἡ πρᾶξις.

[11] Plutarch, *Comm. Not.* ch. 47, 1084F (SVF 2.847): φαντασία γάρ τις ἡ ἔννοιά ἐστι, φαντασία δὲ τύπωσις ἐν ψυχῇ. Cf. 1085A; Cf. Cicero, *De Fin.* III 21 on moral development and learning, and the grasp of *ennoiai*. See Schofield 1980, 291–308 on the nature of preconceptions.

A passage from Aëtius is useful in understanding how these *ennoiai/phantasiai* relate to conceptualizations and definition-formation:

οἱ Στωικοί φασιν· ὅταν γεννηθῇ ὁ ἄνθρωπος, ἔχει τὸ ἡγεμονικὸν μέρος τῆς ψυχῆς ὥσπερ χάρτην εὔεργον εἰς ἀπογραφήν· εἰς τοῦτο μίαν ἑκάστην τῶν ἐννοιῶν ἐναπογράφεται. πρῶτος δὲ ὁ τῆς ἀναπογραφῆς τρόπος ὁ διὰ τῶν αἰσθήσεων. αἰσθόμενοι γάρ τινος οἷον λευκοῦ ἀπελθόντος αὐτοῦ μνήμην ἔχουσιν· ὅταν δὲ ὁμοειδεῖς πολλαὶ μνῆμαι γένωνται, τότε φαμὲν ἔχειν ἐμπειρίαν· ἐμπειρία γάρ ἐστι τὸ τῶν ὁμοειδῶν φαντασιῶν πλῆθος. τῶν δὲ ἐννοιῶν αἱ μὲν φυσικῶς γίνονται κατὰ τοὺς εἰρημένους τρόπους καὶ ἀνεπιτεχνήτως, αἱ δὲ ἤδη δι᾽ ἡμετέρας διδασκαλίας καὶ ἐπιμελείας· αὗται μὲν οὖν ἔννοιαι καλοῦνται μόνον, ἐκεῖναι δὲ καὶ προλήψεις. ὁ δὲ λόγος, κατ᾽ ὃν προσαγορευόμεθα λογικοὶ ἐκ τῶν προλήψεων συμπληροῦσθαι λέγεται κατὰ τὴν πρώτην ἑβδομάδα.

The Stoics say [this]: when a person is born, he has the commanding part of the soul like a sheet of paper well-disposed for writing on: onto this he writes each one of his conceptions [*ennoiai*]. And the first manner of inscription is the one by means of the senses. For by perceiving something, for example white, when it [i.e. the thing perceived] has gone away they have a memory of it: and when many memories of a similar kind have come about, then we say we have experience. And some conceptions [*ennoiai*] come about naturally in the ways stated and without the use of skill [*techne*], but others come about through our instruction and concern: so these latter are called only conceptions [*ennoiai*], but those former are also called preconceptions. And reason [*logos*] according to which we are called rational is said to be completed from our preconceptions by the age of seven. (Aëtius 4.11 (*SVF* 2.83))

This passage concerns itself with our ability to learn in a way highly reminiscent of Ar., *Met.* A.1. It has, however, the Stoic distinction of separating preconceptions from conceptions. It seems as though the umbrella term '*ennoiai*' is used for preconceptions and conceptions, but conceptions, *ennoiai* strictly speaking, are the established notions given to us through teaching and instruction. As Schofield points out when discussing this Aëtius passage (1980, 293–4), 'preconception is a notion or concept; not any concept, but a general concept (DL VII 54); not any general concept, but a particularly basic sort of general concept'. As he also points out, preconceptions are linked to language by means of the reference to reason in Aëtius. Further, Galen quotes Chrysippus as stating that reason is a collection of certain conceptions/notions (*ennoiai*) and preconceptions (*prolepseis*), *SVF* 2.228.31–2. When reason can operate on these conceptions/

preconceptions, they are the sort of thought which can be expressed in propositional form. Such conceptual thought which can be set out in propositional form can be employed in a full range of inferences. Such propositional thought and inference is, of course, also able to be universally communicated and is clearly independent of the perspective of any individual who has that thought. Both *ennoiai* and *prolepseis* are thus such as to satisfy Gareth Evans's generality constraint for concept-formation (1982, 104), such that 'if a subject can be credited with the thought that *a* is *F*, then he must have the conceptual resources for entertaining the thought that *a* is *G*, for every property of *G* of which he has a conception'.[12]

Stoic *ennoiai* arise from clear *phainomena*, from our perceptions.[13] Galen's understanding of our first definitional concepts is therefore of concepts possessed at the point when we gain perceptual *phantasiai*. These concepts are such that they conform to the generality constraint and so we gain full, if primitive, concepts at the point of these perceptual *phantasiai*. A possible justification for conceptualization at this point is that conceptual contents are required to stand in inferential relations.[14] In order to fulfil this function, the contents of experience must be conceptual. Perceptual illusions of whatever sort, and so the possibility of error in perception, are the difficulties for a conceptualist account of this type. It also perhaps leaves us with little to be gained by the other stages of Galen's definitions: if we do have a primitive concept given to us at the point of perception, what is it that is actually achieved by the subsequent levels? It seems as though we are in the

[12] Evans 1982, esp. 100–12. Under the Generality Constraint, conceptual thought ascribes predications to an object in a way that rests on the commitment that to be able to understand the proposition that *a* is *F* is part of a *structured ability* to understand also that *a* is *G*. There is also the commitment that there is a *common explanation*, which rests on conceptual structure, for the ability to understand not only that *a* is *F* and that *a* is *G*, but also that *a* is *F* and that *b* is *F*, even though the thought that *a* is *G* or that *b* is *F* may not be explicitly entertained, as long as that non-entertainment is not due to any conceptual error. The ability to structure our thoughts in such a way as to be able to relate an individual to a general property is what Evans sees as the ability that will account for the fact that someone can understand all these different propositions involving different tokens being ascribed to a type.

[13] Augustine, *City of God* 8.7 (*SVF* 2.106): Stoici, qui cum vehementer amaverint sollertim disputandi, quam dialecticam nominant, a corporis sensibus eam ducendam putarunt, hinc asseverantes animum concipere notiones, quas appellant ἐννοίας, earum rerum scilicet quas definiendo explicant; hinc propagari atque conecti totam discendi docendique rationem.

[14] Cf. McDowell 1994, 7: 'We can not really understand the relations in virtue of which a judgement is warranted except as relations within the space of concepts: relations such as implication or probabilification which hold between potential exercises of conceptual capacities. The attempt to extend the scope of justificatory relations outside the conceptual sphere cannot do what it is supposed to do.'

position of Sosa's 'Lucky Strikes', someone who is struck by lightning and, at the moment that the lightning strike, receives his full conceptual apparatus *de novo* (Sosa and Bonjour 2003, 115). Sosa even allows that this unfortunate need not receive all of his concepts in one flash, but could gain them over a series of such incidents. Sosa claims that the 'knowledge' of Lucky Strikes does not 'qualify as the sort of knowledge to which humans can aspire, as reflective beings or even as animals' precisely because it is divorced from the means and processes by which we can claim to be epistemically justified: 'knowledge is not just hitting the mark [of truth] but hitting the mark somehow through means proper and skilful enough' (2003, 105). It is *justification* which comes about via the route of appropriate human learning which ties our explanatory account to our interaction with the world. Perhaps Galen took it that science needs us to make explicit the necessary and sufficient conditions which set out the essence of the kind, but if the grasp of the *ennoia* allows us to heal, what more could the doctor actually need to know? Perhaps, further, Galen seeks an encyclopaedically complete *logos* in order for us to be able to make fully justified epistemic claims.[15] Such a *logos* would be communicable in a way that no longer relied on the *phantasiai* of the individual, even though those *ennoiai* were themselves able to be communicated in propositional form.

A related question concerns the distinction between Galen's *ennoia*-type definitions and Aristotle's *nominal* definitions. It is not clear why Galen does not discuss *ennoia*-type definitions attached to names which lack a referent (as in the case of 'goat-stags', unicorns, etc.). Of course we can give verbal definitions of terms such as 'unicorn', for instance, 'a horse with the horn of a rhino and the wings of a bird'. Grasp of these terms does not have epistemological significance, as Aristotle discusses at *An. Post.* 93b30–2. Indeed, those who think they do are perhaps to be included amongst

---

[15] Plato's *logoi* cut nature at the joints (*Phaedrus* 265e1: τὸ πάλιν κατ᾽ εἴδη δύνασθαι διατέμνειν κατ᾽ ἄρθρα ᾗ πέφυκεν). At *Gorgias* 464e2–465a6, the *logos* of a craft is required to be in terms of the *cause* (ἡ αἰτία), as also at *Gorgias* 501a2, a6. The account given should also be set out with complete technical accuracy, but what those accurate terms are, are subject to change. In the *Republic* (522c5–8) enumerable accuracy is the *telos* of a *techne*; in the *Phaedrus* (270b–d), the elemental accuracy is that of the combination of the powers of action and passion; in *Philebus* (27e5–9) there is the accuracy of the correct point on the otherwise sliding scale of pleasure and pain, since comparative pleasure and pain form a continuum that admits of 'the more and the less'. Further, in the *Theaetetus*, the philosopher studies astronomy and practises geometry, seeking the precise nature of every thing as a whole, never being concerned with the particular (*Theaetetus* 173e6–174a2: κατὰ Πίνδαρον 'τᾶς τε γᾶς ὑπένερθε' καὶ τὰ ἐπίπεδα γεωμετροῦσα, 'οὐρανοῦ θ᾽ ὕπερ' ἀστρονομοῦσα, καὶ πᾶσαν πάντῃ φύσιν ἐρευνωμένη τῶν ὄντων ἑκάστου ὅλου, εἰς τῶν ἐγγὺς οὐδὲν αὐτὴν συγκαθιεῖσα).

those suffering from Galen's definitionitis. Galen talks of his two-volume commentary on the *An. Post.*, so he clearly knew about this point. The answer seems to lie in his conceptualist point that we gain concepts that fulfil the conditions of the generality constraint at the point of perceptual *phantasiai*. If, in fact, we gain such concepts, however primitive, at the level of *ennoiai*, then the supposed definitions such as those attributed to the term 'goat-stag' are not to be classed as definitions at all; all one can have is an account of what the terms signify.[16] These would never be *ennoiai*, as *ennoiai* pick out underlying kinds in order to both fulfil Evans's generality constraint and also be such as can progress stage-by-stage into a full account of the essence. Even though the *ennoiai*-type of definition is said to reveal nothing of the essence, it is connected in our definitional progression to the second, which does grasp the essence, if only to a partial degree. This also explains his divergence from Aristotle over the nominal essence. According to Galen, a name is not interpretative in the Aristotelian view unless it does grasp the kind, in the sense that it does grasp an underlying kind, and from that point scientific discovery can proceed. That, of course, is not clear in Aristotle's terms, as verbal, nominal, definitions can be given of those terms ('goat-stag') which are not linked to underlying kinds at all.

Perhaps, further, Galen in his conceptualist vein is someone who demands that the way we perceive things is restricted by the conceptual resources we have, and so is relying on an argument such that we would not be able to perceive, or remember, something *as* being the case, unless there were a conceptual scheme to give the subject a way of appreciating the world.[17] This, however, seems to be, as Martin points out (1992, 756), an entirely arbitrary restriction on how we perceive the world. Just because we can only formulate certain propositions about the world as perceived or remembered dependent on the sophistication of our conceptual repertoire, does not mean that that limited propositionally reportable set is all that we do perceive/remember of the world.[18]

---

[16] This position I am attributing to Galen is the basic position taken on Aristotle's definitions of terms such as 'goat-stag' by Robert Bolton (1976 and 1991) and Richard Sorabji (1980, 196).

[17] This argument for the conceptually-driven restriction on how we appreciate the world is attributed to the conceptualists for instance by Peacocke 1983, 7; cf. Martin 1992, 756.

[18] This is especially so in the appreciation, as compared with the reporting, of a complexity of shades of a colour. It is not because one cannot be bothered to classify the different colours that this is difficult, it is rather that one does not have concepts which are sufficiently fine-grained to do so. This is not to deny that one can gain a basic indexical concept by pointing to 'that shade'; this is, however, a different point

Further, at *Diff. Puls.* K. VIII 574, Galen makes it plain that he takes it that definitions are of things not of words.[19] This would also account for there being accounts of what terms such as 'goat-stag' signify, in Galen's definitional theory, although there could be no definition of such terms. Perhaps his conceptualism is also driven by the *things* that the doctor perceives, the individuals, their symptoms, the drugs they are given. If so, then the merely verbal nonsense spoken about goat-stags is not only (in its medical equivalent) misleading medically, but also further fuels definitionitis, this time about that which will only distract further from the business of healing and scientific enquiry.

It seems, therefore, that Galen is trying to take a stance which respects the chief philosophical views on the subject available to him, as usual. Here, he adopts a broad Aristotelian position on definition in medical science, but he also accepts the Stoic idea that our *phantasiai* are fully conceptual, so he seeks a complete set of necessary and sufficient conditions. In this way, Galen hopes to gives us a progression in learning in science, where we move from a naive grasp of the concept to a fully scientific, essential one. This is opposed to Aristotle's move from experiential grasp of common characteristics across individuals of a kind (of the 'this is like that' variety, *Met.* A.1, 981a7–9)[20] that are pre-conceptual to the grasp of the essential definition of the kind at the fully scientific level. Aristotle's scientific learning begins at the pre-conceptual level of experience, although he does seem to allow for definitions of non-existent kinds (*An. Post.* 93b30–2 'goat-stags': where a (clearly conceptual) definition is given of a concept, it is just the case that that concept has no referent). Galen takes it, in the Stoic tradition, that scientific learning can only commence when it can fit into a nexus of interrelated concepts, the reliability of those concepts arising with the *phantasiai* of perception, thus guaranteeing that there are no definitions of notions with no referent. The Aristotelian position instead seems to allow

to conceptual structure limiting one's ability to appreciate the world in any way at all, as on the conceptualist claim it is conceptual structure which delimits the ability to appreciate the world; cf. Martin 1992, 757 n. 14, and 759. If one needs a conceptual structure in order to appreciate an aspect of the world, however, it is unclear how one can learn such concepts in the first place.

[19] Cf. Galen gives us the Stoic definition of 'definition' as 'that which, by a brief reminder brings to us a conception of the things underlying words'. Galen, *Def. Med.* 19.348, 1–349, 4: ὅρος ἐστὶ διὰ βραχείας ὑπομνέσεως εἰς ἔννοιαν ἡμᾶς τῶν ὑποτεταγμένων ταῖς φωναῖς πραγμάτων.

[20] *Met.* A.1, 981a7–9: τὸ μὲν γὰρ ἔχειν ὑπόληψιν ὅτι Καλλίᾳ κάμνοντι τηνδὶ τὴν νόσον τοδὶ συνήνεγκε καὶ Σωκράτει καὶ καθ' ἕκαστον οὕτω πολλοῖς, ἐμπειρίας ἐστίν.

for mistakes at the conceptual level,[21] but experiential interaction with the kind, or acknowledgement that there is no such kind, will iron out those conceptual faults. Galen ultimately rests his theory of definition on the Stoic notion that perception automatically provides us with infallible, if basic, concepts, whereas Aristotle rests his view of scientific discovery on the work we do with the materials available to us, and success with those material kinds will enable us to refine our definitions and so heal still more successfully.

It thus seems to be the case that Galen and Aristotle are in agreement about what an essential definition is and how the grasp of that definition is central to scientific understanding and progress. They clearly have opposed views of how the definitional progression to the essential definition commences and what its origin is based on. As a result, their notions of what is demanded from a nominal definition are different.

Bibliography

Barnes, J. (1971) 'Aristotle's Concept of Mind', *Proceedings of the Aristotelian Society* 72, 101–14.

Barnes, J. (1982) 'Medicine, Experience and Logic', in Barnes, J., Brunschwig, J., Burnyeat, M. and Schofield, M. (eds.), *Science and Speculation: Studies in Hellenistic Theory and Practice*, Cambridge: Cambridge University Press, 24–68.

Barnes, J. (1991) 'Galen on Logic and Therapy', in Kudlein, F. and Durling, R. J. (eds.), *Galen's Method of Healing*, Leiden: Brill.

Bolton, R. (1976) 'Essentialism and Semantic Theory in Aristotle: Posterior Analytics II, 7–10', *Philosophical Review* 85, 514–44.

Bolton, R. (1991) 'Aristotle's Method in Natural Science', in L. Judson (ed.), *Aristotle's Physics*, Oxford: Oxford University Press, 1–29.

Bywater, L. (ed.) (1894) *Aristotelis Ethica Nicomachea*, Oxford Classical Texts, Oxford: Clarendon Press.

Charles, D. (2000) *Aristotle on Meaning and Essence*, Oxford: Oxford University Press.

Evans, G. (1982) [McDowell, J. (ed.)] *The Varieties of Reference*, Oxford: Oxford University Press.

---

[21] See *Phys.* A.1, 184b12–14: καὶ τὰ παιδία τὸ μὲν πρῶτον προσαγορεύει πάντας τοὺς ἄνδρας πατέρας καὶ μητέρας τὰς γυναῖκας, ὕστερον δὲ διορίζει τούτων ἑκάτερον.

Hankinson, R. J. (1991a) 'Galen on the Foundations of Science', in López-Férez, J. A. (ed.), *Galeno: Obra, Pensamiento e Influencia*, Madrid: UNED.

Hankinson, R. J. (1991b) 'Galen's Anatomy of the Soul', *Phronesis* 36, 197–233.

Hankinson, R. J. (1998) *Galen on Antecedent Causes*, Cambridge: Cambridge University Press.

Helmreich, G. (ed.) (1893) *Clandii Galeni Pergameni Scripta Minora*, vol. 3, Leipzig: Teubner.

Hicks, R. D. (1965) *Aristotle: De Anima*, Amsterdam: Adolf M. Hackkert.

Kühn, C. G. (1821–33) *Galeni Opera Omnia*, 20 vols., Leipzig: Cnobloch.

Kühn, D. C. G. (1828) *Medicorum Graecorum Opera Quae Exstant*, Leipzig: Cnobloch.

Kühn, J.-H. and Fleisher, U. (1989) *Index Hippocraticus*, Göttingen: Vandenhoeck & Ruprecht.

Lloyd, G. E. R. (1996) 'Theories and Practices of Demonstration in Galen', in Frede, M. and Striker, G. (eds.) (1996) *Rationality in Greek Thought*, Oxford: Oxford University Press.

McDowell, J. (1994) *Mind and World*, Cambridge, MA: Harvard University Press.

Martin, M. G. F. (1992) 'Perception, Concepts and Memory', *Philosophical Review* 101, 745–63.

Peacocke, C. A. B. (1983) *Sense and Content*, Oxford: Clarendon Press.

Ross, W. D. (ed.) (1961) *Aristotle: de Anima*, Oxford: Clarendon Press.

Ross, W. D. and Minio-Paluello, L. (eds.) (1964) *Aristotelis Analytica Priora et Posteriora*, Oxford Classical Texts, Oxford: Clarendon Press.

Schofield, M. (1980) 'Preconception, Argument and God', in Schofield, Burnyeat, and Barnes, *Doubt and Dogmatism*.

Schofield, M., Burnyeat, M., and Barnes, J. (eds.) (1980) *Doubt and Dogmatism: Studies in Hellenistic Epistemology*, Oxford: Oxford University Press.

Sorabji, R. (1980) *Necessity, Cause and Blame*, London: Duckworth.

Sosa, E. and Bonjour, L. (2003) *Epistemic Justification: Internalism vs. Externalism, Foundations vs. Virtues*, London: Blackwell.

13

Essence and Cause in Plotinus' *Ennead* VI.7 [38] 2: An Outline of Some Problems

ANNAMARIA SCHIAPARELLI

Introduction

The concepts of essence and cause are widely discussed in philosophy: they are central themes of philosophical speculation in Antiquity as well as nowadays. In Antiquity, the concept of definition was closely connected to that of essence: at least from Aristotle onwards, it was generally assumed that the definition indicates or expresses the essence. However, these concepts are highly problematic: although many attempts have been made, it is still difficult to capture and understand them fully. Furthermore, when one tries to analyse the relation between essence and cause, the task becomes even more challenging.

Given the complexity of these philosophical problems, in this paper I shall focus on some aspects of the concepts of essence and cause as they are presented in Plotinus' *Ennead* VI.7 [38] 2. In some passages of this treatise, Plotinus' philosophical speculation has two aspects: as one would normally expect, there is an important Platonic background, but Plotinus also makes use of some Aristotelian theses about knowledge of the essence and knowledge of the cause. Since scholars have already explored the significance of the Platonic background,[1] I shall consider the influence of Aristotle's viewpoint on Plotinus' discussion. For this reason, some Aristotelian texts will also be

[1] e.g. Hadot [1988], D'Ancona Costa [1992].

presented. My aim is to bring evidence in support of the view that Plotinus is interested in applying part of the Aristotelian conceptual apparatus in his analysis on the causality of Forms.

1   The Platonic Background: The Causal Structure of Sensible Phenomena

Since, as I have said, the Platonic background of Plotinus' views on causation has been widely explored, I shall restrict myself here to a brief outline of that background.

Some of the main themes of Plotinus' discussion in VI.7 [38] 2 are introduced in the first chapter of the treatise, where Plotinus engages himself in certain exegetical problems arising from Plato's *Timaeus*. In VI.7 [38] 1, the starting-point of Plotinus' philosophical speculation is Plato's description of the activity of the craftsman and the other gods when the world's body, i.e. the sensible universe, was formed.[2] Plotinus is also concerned with the formation of the human body and its sense organs. However, he does not seem to be interested in the details of how this formation came about; for example, he is not interested in how the gods assembled head and limbs. Rather, he addresses the question of whether the fact that a human body has sense organs depends on some forethought present in the gods' minds.[3] The answer is clear and straightforward: Plato's suggestion that there is some planning in the gods' minds should not be taken literally. For, according to Plotinus, there is forethought in the case of neither living things nor the universe (VI.7 [38] 1.30).

The question of what causes the sensible universe to have a certain structure is left open: if Plotinus dismisses the idea of there being any forethought in the case of the intelligible world, he needs to provide us with an alternative suggestion. If this is the case, then one of Plotinus' tasks is to search for an account of how in the sensible world there are certain

---

[2] A detailed reconstruction of the significance and the role of the *demiurgos* in the neo-Platonic tradition can be found in O'Meara [1975].

[3] The *Timaeus* passage that Plotinus seems to have in mind is the following: 'Our present subject must be treated in more details and its preliminaries, concerning the generation of bodies, part by part, and concerning soul, and the reason and the forethought of gods producing them—of all this we must go on to tell on the principle of holding fast to the most likely account' (*Ti.* 44c4–d1, Cornford translation).

characteristics; he needs to provide an account of the causal structure of sensible phenomena. His view can be only partially summarized here: his interesting proposal is that the natural phenomena's causal structure will provide us with a certain image of the intelligible world. This image will not be complete for two reasons: the first is that, due to the nature of our soul, we could never reach a complete grasp of the intelligible world; the second is that the sensible world contains a number of contingencies that are foreign to the intelligible world.

The issues that arise from Plotinus' exegetical task in VI.7 [38] 1 and 2 are intertwined with a philosophical reflection on the concept of causality. Since it remains unclear from the outset what type of causality Plotinus has in mind, I shall need to mention some more Platonic background. In particular some passages in the *Phaedo* will be briefly examined. I shall focus only on the issues that are related to our discussion.

In a well known section of this dialogue, Plato says that Socrates was looking for the causes of sensible things and natural phenomena. However, he was not looking for their material or mechanical causes. As a result of his investigations, Plato offers two accounts of the concept of *aitia*. Both accounts are said to present a safe (ἀσφαλῆ) *aitia*. However, the first is a safe but trivial (ἀμαθῆ) *aitia*, whereas the second is a safe and cleverer (κομψοτέρα) *aitia*. In his description of the safe but trivial *aitia*, Plato claims 'the one thing that makes the other things beautiful is the presence of or the association (. . .) with absolute beauty'. That is to say, it is only by referring to the Form and to the relation between the Form and a particular that we can understand better what causes the particular to have a certain characteristic (*Phaedo* 100c6–7, 101c4–5).[4]

The case of the safe and cleverer *aitia* is different. For example, if one were to ask by virtue of what a body becomes hot, the answer would no longer be that it becomes hot by virtue of its association with heat. This answer would be true but trivial. The appropriate answer is that a body becomes warm in virtue of a certain relation with the fire (*Phaedo* 105b8–c1). It is clear that the difference between the two accounts of *aitia* can be expressed along the following lines: the account of the safe but trivial *aitia* mentions the relation between a particular and the Form directly

---

[4] The role of the Forms in Plato's *Phaedo* has been the subject of much discussion: see (e.g.) Vlastos [1968], Bostock [1986], Fine [1987], Matthews/Blackson [1989], Irwin [1995].

responsible for a certain characteristic that the particular possesses. The account of the safe and cleverer *aitia* presents a more complex picture, which introduces a third factor alongside the particular with its characteristic and the Form; however, it remains unclear whether the third factor is a further Form.

In both accounts, the concept of *aitia* is not fully characterized, and there are at least two problems. The first is that it is difficult to find a suitable translation: the English word *cause* is perhaps the closest. However, the concept of causality that is here involved suggests something more than a form of rational explanation. This brings us to the second problem. One is led to wonder in what sense, for Plato, Forms are *aitiai* of the characteristics that particulars possess by participating in them. Several answers are possible, and it is hard to choose between them. Still, the following can be argued with some plausibility. The Forms play the metaphysical role of providing the 'ontological ground' of particulars, that is to say, particulars depend on the Forms for their being and for being what they are; it is in this sense that Forms can be called causes of particulars.[5] Furthermore, these metaphysical entities have an epistemological function: as we read in *Republic* V, Forms are the objects of knowledge, and it is by virtue of their epistemological function that they do the explanatory work.

In Plotinus' discussion we find a trace of these problems. In the context of VI.7 [38] 1 and 2, the concept of *aitia* is not fully characterized, and one wonders what concept Plotinus has in mind when he speaks of *aitia*. Plotinus does not seem to distinguish between different senses of this term, and this strikes us as perplexing because there is evidence that Plotinus is acquainted with the Aristotelian discussion about the different ways in which something can be the cause of something else.

Plotinus' outlook on the causal structure of the sensible world can be summarized by saying that sensible items and natural phenomena are ontologically dependent on the intelligible world. Therefore, it is at the intelligible world that we should look if we want to find the causes of sensible phenomena, in the Platonic sense of 'ontological ground'. Plotinus presents some details of how this has to be understood in a difficult discussion in VI.7 [38] 2.

---

[5]   This interpretation is based on Vlastos's detailed reconstruction of the central section of the *Phaedo* in his [1968] influential paper 'Reason and Causes in the *Phaedo*'.

2 Essences and Causes in *Ennead* VI.7 [38] 2: The Identity between Something and its Cause

At the beginning of VI.7 [38] 2 Plotinus holds that in the intelligible world there is no distinction between Forms and their causes: he expresses this point by saying that in the intelligible world the 'that' (ὅτι) coincides with the 'why' (διότι).[6]

However, for us in the sensible world it is not possible to grasp the structure of reality in the way in which it is present in the intelligible world. For, we have a different mode of thinking. In general, it is a characteristic of our mode of thinking that we do not gain knowledge by immediate apprehension. Our mode of thinking involves a transition from one thought to another. In virtue of this characteristic, we do not grasp something and its cause together. That is to say, paraphrasing Plotinus, we need to distinguish, at least conceptually, between the 'that' (ὅτι) and the 'why' (διότι).

In VI.7 [38] 2, Plotinus seems to introduce a parallel between the intelligible world and our sensible world. He says:

Text (1)   VI.7 [38] 2

> Ἐκεῖ δ᾽ ἐν ἑνὶ πάντα, ὥστε ταὐτὸν το πρᾶγμα καὶ τὸ "διά   10
> τί" τοῦ πράγματος. Πολλαχοῦ δε καὶ ἐνταῦθα τὸ πρᾶγμα
> καὶ τὸ "διὰ τί" ταὐτόν, οἷον τί ἐστιν ἔκλειψις.

But there all are in one, so that the object and the reason why of the object are the same. But in many cases here too the object and the reason why are the same, as for example what an eclipse is.

Let us begin the analysis of these lines with some philological and terminological observations. No variant readings are printed in the editions of Henry and Schwyzer. In this chapter, Plotinus seems to use interchangeably διὰ τί, διὰ τοῦτο, and αἴτιον, the last of which I translate with 'cause' whilst reserving 'the reason why' for the other two; in my discussion,

---

[6] When Plotinus draws the distinction between the 'that' and the 'why', he uses Aristotelian terminology: the distinction between διότι and ὅτι was introduced in *APo.* 78ᵃ22. From line 9 to the end of the chapter, Plotinus uses διὰ τί in place of διότι. Grammatically, διότι is equivalent to διὰ τοῦτο, ὅτι ('on account of this, that . . .'). They both refer to the same philosophical concept, i.e. the concept of cause. In this context διότι and διὰ τί seem to be merely stylistic variants.

however, I shall follow Plotinus' lead and use 'cause' and 'reason why' interchangeably. I have rendered πρᾶγμα with 'object': in a daringly loose paraphrase, one could render τὸ πρᾶγμα καὶ τὸ "διὰ τί" τοῦ πράγματος as 'x and the cause of x'.

One reading of the passage suggests the following interpretation. In the first sentence of our text, Plotinus states that in the intelligible world (ἐκεῖ) there is identity between something and its cause. This is a consequence of the fact that in the intelligible world there is the unity of all things, and this unity is one of the basic tenets in the Plotinian metaphysics. It seems plausible to suggest that when he talks about identity between something and its cause in the intelligible world, Plotinus means that x and the cause of x are identical; since in the intelligible world there is no distinction between something and its essence, then Plotinus' claim seems to be that, in the intelligible world, essence and cause are identical. In the second sentence, Plotinus turns his attention to the sensible world (ἐνταῦθα). In particular, he is concerned with one aspect of the sensible world. He seems to be interested in the cases in which there is identity between something and its cause (τὸ πρᾶγμα καὶ τὸ "διὰ τί" ταὐτόν). This identity would be a feature that the sensible world shares with the intelligible world. Furthermore, Plotinus' words suggest that the example of the eclipse should constitute a paradigmatic case that will show how it is possible to speak about identity between something and its cause in the sensible world.

It is very likely that when Plotinus refers to the case of the eclipse, he has in mind a piece of Aristotelian doctrine. Let me briefly recall this piece of doctrine. It is well known that the case of the eclipse is one of Aristotle's favourite examples in his discussion of the practices of definition and demonstration in the *Posterior Analytics*.[7] In *APo.* 90ᵃ14–16, Aristotle writes: 'For in all these cases it is clear that what it is and why it is are the same. What is an eclipse? Privation of light from the moon by the screening of the earth. Why is there an eclipse? Or why is the moon eclipsed? Because the light fails it when the earth screens it.' Furthermore, Aristotle uses the example of the eclipse in the *Metaphysics* when he examines the general structure of an explanation. In *Metaph. H* 4, 1044ᵇ10, he writes: 'The formal

---

[7] Aristotle talks about the eclipse in two different contexts. In one case, he investigates the eclipse as an astronomical event. In the other, he defines the eclipse as deprivation of light, and he uses this example in his discussion of the relationship between cause and essence. We are interested in the latter.

principle is the account, but it is obscure if it does not include the cause. For example, What is an eclipse? Deprivation of light. But if we add "by interposition of the earth", this is the account which includes the cause.' The Aristotelian doctrine, which Plotinus refers to, has been interpreted in many different ways.[8] On the interpretation of it adopted here, Aristotle claims that the 'what it is' of the eclipse is the privation of light from the moon because of the screening of the earth. Then, the cause of the eclipse is the screening of the earth.

Let us go back to our text (1), and let us see whether it is possible to say something more about the claim that 'in many cases here too the object and the reason why are the same, as for example what an eclipse is'. It is important to note that, at the beginning of line 11, it is clearly stated that in the sensible world the identity between something and its cause holds *in many cases* (πολλαχοῦ). One then wonders in what other cases, in the sensible world, this identity holds. A highly attractive possibility is that Plotinus refers at least to the other cases mentioned by Aristotle. Thus, if this is correct we have a collection of things in the sensible world for which the identity with their causes hold. At this point, one would be tempted to enquire even more into the nature of this collection of things. However, this would not be a fruitful route to take: for, as we shall see shortly, Plotinus is ready to make this collection even wider.

Let me consider again this interpretation of our text (1). This reading suggests that Plotinus introduces the parallel between intelligible and sensible world to make an ontological distinction. If this is the case, then Plotinus is distinguishing between intelligible realities and items in the sensible world. He is saying that the intelligible realities are one and the same with their causes (lines 10–11). He then adds that in many cases items in the sensible world also are one and the same with their causes (lines 11–12).

However, as it stands, the claim that items in the sensible world are one and the same with their causes can raise a difficulty. For, in a Plotinian perspective, the cause, i.e. the ontological ground, of a sensible item cannot itself be a sensible item. A sensible item has its cause, i.e. its ontological ground, in the intelligible world. It is not possible that the sensible item is one and the same with its cause in the same sense in which a Form is one and the same with its cause. Hence, the claim that there is identity between

---

[8] A detailed reconstruction of this Aristotelian doctrine is to be found in Charles [2000].

items in the sensible world and their causes needs to be properly qualified. In order to get a better understanding of Plotinus' claim, it is helpful to have a closer look at this concise and difficult passage.

It is possible that Plotinus is here saying something along the following lines. In the intelligible world, everything is in unity, thus, in particular, the object and its cause, i.e. its ontological ground, are in unity. In the sensible world also there is unity between an object and its cause: just consider the eclipse, where the cause, i.e. the screening of the earth, is in the essence, i.e. the privation of light from the moon because of the screening of the earth. However, there are some important differences between the object–cause unity as it presents itself in the intelligible world and the object–cause unity as it presents itself in the sensible world. For, on the one hand, in the intelligible world the object–cause unity is the unity of the object with its ontological ground. On the other hand, in the sensible world (since the ontological ground of an object in the sensible world is a Form, and therefore is on a different level from it) the object–cause unity is *not* the unity of the object with its ontological ground, rather it is a unity with a cause which is not an ontological ground. In this sense, the cause of an object in the sensible world is itself sensible.

It is important to note that when Plotinus states that in the intelligible world there is identity between an object and its cause, he emphasizes the fact that in the intelligible world everything is in unity (ἐν ἑνὶ πάντα). This claim plays an important role, for it indicates a crucial feature that characterizes the intelligible world. As we shall see below, this claim suggests something along the following lines: in the intelligible world everything is something like a constituent part of a unified whole, and each 'part' is interconnected with the whole. One should note that it is not possible to talk about complete and absolute unity because in Plotinus' system complete or absolute unity belongs only to the One that is at the level above the Intellect: in the Intellect we find a reflection of the unity that is proper to the One. It is then possible to suggest that, according to Plotinus, in the sensible world some form of unity, namely a form of unity that is similar to that of the intelligible world, is preserved. However, given the ontological difference between the intelligible and the sensible world, there will be a difference in the unity of something with its cause. A possible suggestion is that in the sensible world, there is a weaker form of unity because it is based on containment, in the sense that you find the διὰ τί in the τί ἐστιν: in the sensible world the τί ἐστιν contains features that are not present in the intelligible world. By contrast, the unity of an object with its cause in the intelligible world is strict identity. It is very likely that the unity of an object with its cause in the sensible world is a reflection of the unity between a Form and its cause in the intelligible world. Furthermore, the difference between the kind of unity that is present in the intelligible world and the unity of the sensible world can also be explained by referring to the process of 'derivation' from the One, which is the principle of unity: the intelligible world is closer to the One than the sensible world, i.e. it is a higher level of beings and thus it possesses a kind of unity that is stronger than what we find in the sensible world. In any case, for our present discussion the following should be noticed: it remains that an important difference between the intelligible and the sensible world is that in the intelligible world everything is in unity, whereas in the sensible world the unity seems to obtain only between an object and its cause.

There is another possible interpretation of text (1). For, if Plotinus introduces the parallel between intelligible and sensible world to draw some sort of epistemological distinction, then another interpretation opens up. The idea is that Plotinus is talking about an object, which comes to be apprehended in two different ways. When an object is known in the Intellect (ἐκεῖ), there is identity between it and its cause. Strictly speaking, at the level of the Intellect there is no distinction not only between an object and its cause, but also between knowing and being: for something to be known is the same as for it to be. The distinction between knowing and being, as it applies to the Intellect, is drawn by our discursive thought. When an object is apprehended in the sphere of our discursive thought (ἐνταῦθα), a separation between the concept of cause and that of essence is introduced. However, this second reading faces some difficulties. For example, one would be committed to the view that in the Intellect we find something like the eclipse. And, to say the least, this is controversial. Moreover, given that here (ἐνταῦθα) too there is identity between an object and its cause, one wonders what the difference between here (ἐνταῦθα) and there (ἐκεῖ) is. Given these difficulties, we can conclude that this interpretation is more problematic and should not be endorsed.

Let us consider again Plotinus' claim that here, i.e. in the sensible world, there is some form of identity between an object and its cause. This claim is far from being intuitive and it has to be argued for. Plotinus finds support for his claim in a piece of Aristotelian doctrine. One wonders why Plotinus finds the Aristotelian example attractive. For Plotinus is certainly interested in the epistemological implication of the Aristotelian doctrine, the claim that at least in some cases to know the essence is to know the cause. However, Plotinus cannot introduce an essence of the Aristotelian kind: he cannot accept some of the fundamental tenets of Aristotelian essentialism. On the contrary, it is well known how Plotinus strongly criticizes some of the basic aspects of the Aristotelian concept of essence.[9] Hence, one wonders what it is that Plotinus appeals to in order to explain the relation between something and its cause. I am not sure I can provide a satisfactory answer to all these difficult problems, but I shall try to see what suggestions can be offered by our text.

It seems to me that Plotinus' idea will become clear later in the continuation of our passage, especially at lines 12–19. Nevertheless, it is important to mention and briefly characterize this idea in advance. At line 18, Plotinus refers explicitly to the Forms that are playing an important role in the argument as well as in the entire treatise. When Plotinus is talking about Forms and their causes in the intelligible world, he has in mind something like Platonic Forms. Let me try to clarify this point. Platonic Forms are revisited as thoughts in the Divine Mind. They are ontologically similar to Platonic Forms, for they are self-sufficient; they also are, in a certain way, cause of being for the sensible things. But there is something more: Plotinus' Forms bear a certain relation with each other, with the primary *genera*, and with the totality of the intelligible world. That is to say, Plotinus' Forms are interconnected in the order that is present in the intelligible world. For this reason, the whole of the intelligible world is perfect and complete (VI.7 [38] 3, 21).

It is also true to say that Plotinus' Forms share a feature with the Aristotelian natural kinds: at a discursive level, Plotinus' Forms are known in a way that is similar to the one whereby Aristotelian natural kinds are known, i.e. in a way that shows the identity between essence and cause.

Thus, Plotinus is interested in Aristotle's essentialism and, in particular, in the example of the eclipse because they constitute a useful device to

---

[9] This point is discussed in (e.g.) Chiaradonna [1999], 36. Chiaradonna says that Plotinus criticized in particular the fact that Aristotle identified the essence with certain predicates of the sensible, i.e. corporeal, being.

illustrate his important and difficult view that in the sensible world there is a certain kind of unity between object and cause. Given that this unity is a reflection of the unity between a Form and its cause, they also illustrate how Forms in the intelligible world depend on the primary *genera* and are reciprocally connected.

3 Three Further Claims

It is useful to read and analyse the sequel of our text (*1*) to see more precisely what kind of move Plotinus is prepared to do.

Text (2)   VI.7 [38] 2

> Τί οὖν κω-
> λύει καὶ ἕκαστον διὰ τί εἶναι καὶ ἐπὶ τῶν ἄλλων, καὶ τοῦτο
> εἶναι τὴν οὐσίαν ἑκάστου; μᾶλλον δὲ ἀνάγκη· καὶ πειρω-
> μένοις οὕτως τὸ τί ἦν εἶναι λαμβάνειν ὀρθῶς συμβαίνει. Ὃ   15
> γάρ ἐστιν ἕκαστον, διὰ τοῦτό ἐστι. Λέγω δὲ οὐχ ὅτι τὸ εἶ-
> δος ἑκάστῳ αἴτιον τοῦ εἶναι —τοῦτο μὲν γὰρ ἀληθές— ἀλλ'
> ὅτι, εἰ καὶ αὐτὸ τὸ εἶδος ἕκαστον πρὸς αὐτο ἀναπτύττοις,
> εὑρήσεις ἐν αὐτῷ τὸ "διὰ τί".

(i) Then, what prevents also that each thing be the reason why in the others too, and this be the essence of each thing? Rather it is necessary: (ii) and for those who try to grasp the essence in this way things work out correctly. For what a thing is, (sc. this) is the reason why. But I do not mean that the Form is the cause of being for each thing—this is of course true—but (iii) that if you also unfold each Form back upon itself, you will find the reason why in it.[10]

Let us begin the analysis of this text with some philological and terminological observations. At line 15, Plotinus uses the Aristotelian technical expression τὸ τί ἦν εἶναι that indicates the essence. At line 18, the text presents a minor textual variant in that the family of codices x omits εἰ. If we accept the reading in x, the clause would sound grammatically harsh. None of the scholars I have consulted adopts this reading.

---

[10] The division of the text is mine. At line 17, I read αἴτιον not as an adjective meaning 'responsible', but as a substantive meaning 'cause'. An analysis of the origin and the usage of αἴτιον (and διὰ τί) can be found in Frede [1987].

In our text (2), Plotinus puts forward several philosophical suggestions. Let us focus on the points that are relevant to our discussion, namely (i) the (revisited) identity between an object and its cause, (ii) the thesis whereby certain attempts to grasp the essence provide the correct result, and (iii) the claim that in the analysis of each individual Form, it is possible to find its cause. Let us now analyse each of the three claims in turn.

4 The Identity between Objects and their Causes Revisited

Let us begin our analysis with (i) the (revisited) identity between an object and its cause. So far Plotinus claimed that in many cases it has been recognized that in the sensible world there is identity between an object and its cause; he referred to the eclipse as an example of these cases. In what follows Plotinus restates this identity and widens his claim: the identity between an object and its cause holds also in the other cases.

Lines 12–14 are cryptic. Although the syntax is not convoluted, the style is extremely concise and the meaning is difficult to disclose. The sentence has an interrogative form. However, when one reads it carefully in its context, one realizes that it is not a genuinely open question and a negative answer is expected.

In lines 12–14 there are two main problems. The first concerns the expression ἐπὶ τῶν ἄλλων (line 13). The second problem concerns the meaning of the two clauses ἕκαστον διὰ τί εἶναι and καὶ τοῦτο εἶναι τὴν οὐσίαν ἑκάστου. Let us begin with the expression ἐπὶ τῶν ἄλλων that I have rendered as 'in the others' in order to maintain the ambiguity of the Greek text. It is not clear what τῶν ἄλλων refers to. There are several candidates. First, as some scholars suggested (e.g. Henry and Schwyzer *in apparatu*, Harder, and Hadot), τῶν ἄλλων can indicate all the sensible things other than the eclipse, which was already considered. This is the most natural reading of the Greek. However, this does not provide a sufficient understanding: for the set of all the things other than the eclipse is very large and crowded. Moreover, it does not consider the fact that, at line 11 in text (1), Plotinus has already mentioned many cases such as the eclipse for which the identity holds.

It is a second possibility that τῶν ἄλλων refers to the examples mentioned at the beginning of the chapter (at lines 6–8), where one reads: 'but there (ἐκεῖ) there is man and the reason why it is man (. . .) and eye and the reason why it is eye'. If this is correct, then one needs to understand what the examples of man and eye would add to the argument. They are clearly arbitrary examples of intelligible things that are present in the Intellect together with their causes.[11] Although this option has the advantage that it restricts the set of 'the other things' (τῶν ἄλλων) to intelligible beings, it is not a straightforward reading of the Greek; for the referent of τῶν ἄλλων is far away in the text. Another objection comes from the fact that Plotinus has already said that, in the case of the intelligible realities, the identity holds.

A third possibility is that Plotinus has in mind the other cases, apart from the eclipse, mentioned by Aristotle, e.g. the example of thunder. This third option seems less likely: it sounds highly conjectural and the evidence is extremely scanty. Moreover, as I argued above, it is likely that Plotinus referred to the Aristotelian list above, i.e. at line 11 in our text (1), when he mentions that the identity between a thing and its cause holds in many cases (πολλαχοῦ).

Let me then suggest that τῶν ἄλλων refers to items in the sensible world, but τῶν ἄλλων refers to all the cases other than those of the Aristotelian list because they were already considered. I shall try to explain better this point: the idea is that there is a collection of things for which the thesis of the identity between essence and cause holds. This collection contains items from the Aristotelian list together with other items in the sensible world. Still, at this stage, it remains difficult to give a full-fledged description of this collection.

Let us now focus on the clauses ἕκαστον διὰ τί εἶναι and καὶ τοῦτο εἶναι τὴν οὐσίαν ἑκάστου. Suppose that Plotinus is talking about sensible items, as suggested above. Then he is saying that each sensible item is its cause, and this, i.e. its cause, is its essence.

It seems that here Plotinus is making two identity statements. He is saying that a sensible item is one and the same with its cause. He then adds that the cause is one and the same with its essence. This portion of the text suggests at least two interpretations.

---

[11] The reading that the expression τῶν ἄλλων refers to intelligible beings has been accepted by Schwyzer and Cilento. Bréhier, MacKenna, and Armstrong leave the ambiguity that is present in the Greek. In his Latin translation, Ficino leaves out the expression ἐπὶ τῶν ἄλλων.

First, Plotinus is talking about cause in the sense of ontological ground. If this is the case, then Plotinus is saying that a sensible item is one and the same with its ontological ground. However, as I have already said, the claim that there is strict identity between a sensible item and its cause, in the sense of ontological ground, is extremely problematic. For this reason, this interpretation is very difficult to accept.

There is a second and more likely interpretation. Plotinus is talking about cause not in the sense of ontological ground, but in the sense of 'sensible cause'. If this is the case, we need to understand what he means when he says that each sensible item is one and the same with its cause. As we noted above, the object–cause unity in the sensible world is different from the object–cause unity in the intelligible world. For, in the sensible world, the unity of an object with its cause is based on containment and not on strict identity as in the intelligible world. Hence, a sensible item is one and the same with its cause only in a certain qualified way. That is to say, the cause of a sensible object is *in* the object. Accordingly, the cause is the essence of the object in the sense that the cause is *in* the essence of the object.

It is possible to offer a concluding suggestion for the interpretation of the expression καὶ τοῦτο εἶναι τὴν οὐσίαν ἑκάστου. It seems to me that the passage will be clearer if we understand the καὶ not as 'and', i.e. as a conjunction, but as 'or rather', i.e. with an epexegetic value. Then, the whole sentence would be constructed as follows: what prevents each thing being its cause, or rather this, i.e. cause, being the essence of each thing? In other words, the claim that each sensible thing contains, in some way or other, its cause is more precisely formulated in the claim that the cause is in the essence of each thing.[12]

5 Grasping Essence and Cause: An Aristotelian Attempt?

Let us move to (ii), namely to the thesis that certain attempts to grasp the essence provide the correct result. It is easy to see that lines 14–15 can be

---

[12] Here Plotinus seems to suggest that there is a certain kind of identity between an item and its essence. This position is reminiscent of another Aristotelian thesis, namely the claim that we find in *Metaphysics Z* 6, according to which there is identity between something and its essence.

understood in more than one way. The expression πειρώμενοι λαμβάνειν occurs elsewhere in the *Enneads*: it occurs at VI.2 [43] 1, 5 where it refers to Plotinus and his pupils. It occurs also at V.8 [31] 9, 12 and at VI.4 [22] 16, 6 where it refers to others than Plotinus and his pupils. The expression πειρώμενοι λαμβάνειν is used in a generic way and very little can be known about its referent. I shall put forward two alternative suggestions.

A first option is the following. One could choose to render the clause πειρωμένοις οὕτως τὸ τί ἦν εἶναι λαμβάνειν as 'when we try to grasp the essence in this way'.[13] In this case, the participle πειρωμένοις refers to Plotinus and, possibly, to his pupils. Then, the next clause, i.e. ὀρθῶς συμβαίνει, says that things work out correctly.

Unfortunately, this reading faces a difficulty that arises from a terminological consideration: one wonders why Plotinus is adopting the technical Aristotelian expression τὸ τί ἦν εἶναι. If he were simply explaining his own doctrine, he could have kept the term οὐσία that occurs on the previous line.[14] One is advised to see whether a preferable interpretation can be found.

A second option is the following. One could choose to translate the clause καὶ πειρωμένοις οὕτως τὸ τί ἦν εἶναι λαμβάνειν as 'and when they try to grasp the essence in this way'. In this case, the participle πειρωμένοις refers to others than Plotinus and his pupils. We know that it is standard Aristotelian doctrine to say that when one knows the essence, one knows also the cause (*APo.* 90ᵃ31–4, 93ᵃ4–5). Thus, it is likely that πειρωμένοις refers to Aristotle and, more in general, to the Peripatetics holding this view.[15] If this is the case, the usage of the Aristotelian jargon τὸ τί ἦν εἶναι is most appropriate: it explains why Plotinus shifts from οὐσία (line 14) to τὸ τί ἦν εἶναι (line 15). Moreover, this reading would fit very well with our previous passage (text *1*) as it continues the reference to the Aristotelian

---

[13] This interpretation seems to be implied in Armstrong's and Cilento's translation. In Sleeman/Pollet [1980], p. 590, ll. 11–12, the meaning of λαμβάνειν is 'apprehend'. At line 15 I read οὕτως following H-S¹.

[14] Plotinus uses τὸ τί ἦν εἶναι only four times and mainly when he is referring to a piece of Aristotelian doctrine. This expression occurs at II.1 [40] 6, 29, where Plotinus discusses and rejects the Aristotelian 'fifth element', and at VI.7 [38] 4, 18, and 26, where Plotinus is addressing some problems on the relation between essence and definition in Aristotle's *Metaph.* Z 4–5. It occurs also at VI.7 [38] 3, 21, where the text reads as follows: καὶ ἡ οὐσία καὶ τὸ τί ἦν εἶναι καὶ τὸ διότι ἕν. It is highly plausible that the second καί has an epexegetical value; hence, the sentence is rendered as 'and the essence, i.e. the form (τὸ τί ἦν εἶναι) and the cause are one'.

[15] The same suggestion is present in Hadot [1988], 89 and 201. Hadot (having the broader task of translating and commenting the entire treatise) does not discuss alternative interpretations on this point.

position. In other words, when Plotinus says καὶ πειρωμένοις οὕτως τὸ τί ἦν εἶναι λαμβάνειν, he means 'and when the Peripatetics try to grasp the essence in this way . . .' The expression 'in this way' renders the adverb οὕτως, and it is important to clarify what it means in this context. The adverb οὕτως refers to what precedes: it refers to the thesis whereby there is identity between cause and essence of a thing (τοῦτο [sc. διὰ τί] εἶναι τὴν οὐσίαν ἑκάστου). The entire clause can be spelled out as follows: when the Peripatetics try to grasp the essence in this way, i.e. in a way that also captures the cause, things work out correctly, i.e. they grasp it correctly.

For a moment, let me pause and expand on the proposal that the participle πειρωμένοις refers to Aristotle and, more generally, to the Peripatetics. This proposal contains some elements that are helpful for our discussion now and at a later stage of the paper.

It is important that we briefly focus on Aristotle's view about the relation between essence and cause and that we recall some of his conceptual machinery. Both in the *Metaphysics* and in the *Posterior Analytics*, Aristotle tells us how it is possible to find the cause: there are two alternatives. On the one hand, it is possible to establish the cause through the search for definitions: in this case, the cause will be included in the definitory account of the essence. For Aristotle says that x's essence is one of the causes of x (*APo.* 94^{a}35–36), and that the definition indicates the essence (*APo.* 91^{a}1). On the other hand, it is possible to find the cause through the practice of demonstrations: in this second case, the cause will be expressed in the middle term of the syllogism. The concept of cause is further analysed as follows: Aristotle says that 'we understand something when we know its cause, and *there are four sorts of cause* (. . .), all of them are proved through the middle term' (*APo.* 94^{a}20–23; the italics is mine). In both cases, i.e. in definitions and demonstrations, the crucial role is played by the middle term: for it is in the middle term that we find the *four sorts of cause*.[16]

This brief digression contains two main points of interest. The first is that Aristotle theorized two methods by which it is possible to grasp the cause. Since for Aristotle the definition that mentions the cause is nothing but a

---

[16] The formal, final, and efficient causes are undoubtedly present here. There has been disagreement among scholars as to whether the material cause has to be included in the group. I follow Barnes's interpretation, according to which the fourth type of cause introduced here by Aristotle is the material one. Barnes [1993] *contra* Ross [1949].

rearrangement of the demonstration (*APo.* 94ᵃ6–8), we can safely assume that the distinction of the four types of causes can be imported in Aristotle's conception of essence. The second point concerns the concept of cause: Aristotle tells us how the concept of cause, expressed by the middle term, has to be intended: he refers to his own, and most famous, conception of the causes as he develops it in *Phys.* B3, *Metaph.* A3 and *Δ* 2.

We know that Plotinus is interested in the Aristotelian thesis of the interdependence between knowledge of the essence and knowledge of the cause. One wonders to what extent the Aristotelian conception of cause can be maintained by Plotinus. Unfortunately, our text does not offer enough evidence for a complete answer to this question. Nevertheless, the following can be argued with some plausibility: Plotinus is interested in preserving the epistemological thesis of the interdependence between knowledge of the essence and knowledge of the cause, and he seems to feed in a modified conception of cause.

It is clear that the second reading of claim (ii), whereby the participle πειρωμένοις refers to Aristotle and, more generally, to the Peripatetics, has two advantages: it avoids the difficulties of the first reading and it presents an interesting insight into the Aristotelian tradition. This insight leads to some questions concerning the role of the Peripatetic tradition in Plotinus' philosophy.

Let us analyse now lines 15–16, where the text reads: Ὃ γάρ ἐστιν ἕκαστον, διὰ τοῦτό ἐστι. Here the γάρ refers to the previous sentence and it has an explicatory role. There is more than one way to read this extremely dense portion of the text. I shall present three alternative readings. A first possibility is as follows: the expression ὃ ἐστιν ἕκαστον has a strong sense, it means 'what each thing is', and it indicates the essence of that thing. Then, the next clause, i.e. διὰ τοῦτό ἐστι, means 'this (i.e. what each thing is, namely the essence) is the reason why'. In this case, the entire sentence expresses the Aristotelian thesis of the identity between essence and cause.

There is a second possibility. The expression ὃ ἐστιν ἕκαστον has a weaker meaning: the ἐστιν expresses not the relationship between a thing and its essence, but the relation of a thing to its essential predicates, e.g. Socrates and man. The τοῦτο in διὰ τοῦτό ἐστι picks up the relative clause ὃ ἐστιν ἕκαστον, and it means 'whatever each thing essentially is, it is because of this that it is', e.g. 'Socrates is a man, and man is the cause of Socrates'. In this case, lines 15–16 are a concise summary of Plotinus' position.[17]

It seems to me that there is a third possibility if one gives to the ἐστιν in ὃ ἐστιν ἕκαστον an even weaker meaning. That is to say, the ἐστιν in ὃ ἐστιν ἕκαστον is a generic expression of predication and it covers both essential and accidental predication. The referent of τοῦτο in διὰ τοῦτό ἐστι is τὸ τί ἦν εἶναι that occurs in the previous line. According to this reading Plotinus is saying that 'whatever each thing is, it is because of *this* (i.e. the essence: τὸ τί ἦν εἶναι) that it is so'. There is further evidence in support of this reading. For at VI.5 [23] 2.24–26, Plotinus says: 'Since in all cases the starting-point is the what it is, and in the case of those who have defined well it is said that they know most of the accidental properties.'[18] It is extremely likely that here Plotinus is referring to the thesis that Aristotle offers in (e.g.) *De An.* 402[b]17–18: 'to know the essence is helpful in the search of the causes of the substances' accidental properties' (τὸ τί ἐστι γνῶναι χρήσιμον εἶναι πρὸς τὸ θεωρῆσαι τὰς αἰτίας τῶν συμβεβηκότων ταῖς οὐσίαις).

To sum up briefly, so far I have offered three readings of lines 15–16. One reading, i.e. the second, represents a concise summary of Plotinus' position, whilst the other two, i.e. the first and the third, refer to the Aristotelian view.

It is hard to choose between these three readings, as each of them is grammatically justified and philosophically appealing. Still, I am more inclined to endorse the third reading for the following reasons: first, as I have shown above, there is textual evidence for claiming that Plotinus was interested in this piece of Aristotelian doctrine. Second, the third reading explains better the reason why Plotinus introduced the case of the eclipse and made use of a certain Aristotelian conceptual apparatus.

In order to complete our understanding of the passage, let us now move to lines 16–19: 'But I do not mean that the form is the cause of existence for each thing—this is of course true—but that, if you also open each individual form itself back upon itself, you will find the reason why in it' (Armstrong's translation). The Greek text is the following: Λέγω δὲ οὐχ ὅτι τὸ εἶδος

---

[17]   This reading was suggested to me by Michael Frede in a conversation, while I was discussing with him an earlier version of this paper in spring 2006.

[18]   The Greek text is: ἐπειδὴ πανταχοῦ τὸ τί ἐστιν ἀρχή, καὶ τοῖς καλῶς ὁρισαμένοις λέγεται καὶ τῶν συμβεβηκότων τα πολλά γινώσκεσθαι.

ἑκάστῳ αἴτιον τοῦ εἶναι —τοῦτο μὲν γὰρ ἀληθές— ἀλλ᾽ ὅτι, εἰ καὶ αὐτὸ τὸ εἶδος ἕκαστον πρὸς αὐτὸ ἀναπτύττοις, εὑρήσεις ἐν αὐτῷ τὸ "διὰ τί".

The expression λέγω δέ suggests that Plotinus is about to offer an explanation of his position. This expression introduced two clauses, namely τὸ εἶδος ἑκάστῳ αἴτιον τοῦ εἶναι, and εἰ καὶ αὐτο τὸ εἶδος ἕκαστον πρὸς αὐτὸ ἀναπτύττοις, εὑρήσεις ἐν αὐτῷ τὸ "διὰ τί". Let us consider the first clause. These lines have been interpreted in the following way: the occurrence of τὸ εἶδος at line 16 means 'intelligible Form'. Accordingly, in this clause Plotinus says that the Form is the cause of being for each sensible item that partakes of it.[19] Then, he qualifies this claim as true.

I would like to suggest an alternative, and perhaps more daring, reading: the occurrence of τὸ εἶδος at line 16 is used not to mean 'intelligible Form', but as the equivalent of τὸ τί ἦν εἶναι, i.e. sensible or immanent form. In this case, the entire clause can be paraphrased as 'x's form is the cause of x being (say) F'. Then, at line 17, Plotinus says that this is true.

However, according to Plotinus, this is not the complete account of his doctrine. Hence he adds the second clause: in order to provide a fuller presentation of his position, he suggests that we turn to αὐτὸ τὸ εἶδος ἕκαστον, i.e. to each intelligible Form by itself. It is important to note the presence of αὐτὸ that marks the contrast between the occurrence of τὸ εἶδος at line 16, which in my suggestion is used to mean the immanent form, and the occurrence of τὸ εἶδος at line 18, which is used to mean 'intelligible Form'. In this last portion of the text, Plotinus focuses on the concept of intelligible Form, and he makes two related points. The former concerns the possibility of unfolding a Form (αὐτὸ τὸ εἶδος ἕκαστον πρὸς αὐτὸ ἀναπτύττοις); the latter turns to the concept of cause (ἐν αὐτῷ τὸ "διὰ τί"). According to this suggestion, Plotinus has something like the following in mind: consider the Form. If you analyse the Form in a way that you fully understand it, then you will find the reason why in it. That is to say, you will find in it the reason why of the particular (in a certain way, i.e. by participation or because the immanent form of a sensible object is a certain reflection of the intelligible Form). But, more importantly, in the intelligible Form you will find *its* reason why. More precisely, when one unfolds a Form, one shows what a Form is. The idea is that a Form is what it is because it is constituted in a certain way and because it is in some relation

---

[19] See Hadot [1988], 89, and Adamson [2002], 134.

with other Forms and, in particular, with the primary *genera*. In this way, a Form is connected with the whole intelligible world.

These two related points are clearly stated a few lines below in this chapter, where Plotinus draws some of his argument's conclusions. For, at lines 37–38 we read: 'so much more *there* (ἐκεῖ) must all things—each of them—be in relation to the whole and each in relation to itself' (Armstrong's translation slightly modified).

6. Definition and *Logos* as 'Formative Principle'

We saw that Plotinus' reference to the case of the eclipse enabled him to make use of a certain Aristotelian conceptual apparatus. We know that when Aristotle discussed the case of the eclipse, he was interested in the search for definitions. It is then useful to spend some words on what Plotinus has to say about Aristotelian definitions. A full treatment of this issue would require an extensive study on its own. Still, for the sake of the present discussion, it will suffice to note that while in some cases Plotinus seems to accept a requirement that holds for a certain type of Aristotelian definition, i.e. that a definition has to indicate the essence of the thing defined,[20] in others he expresses unhappiness with this type of definition.

Plotinus' suggestion that in some cases a definition that indicates the essence is not sufficient may give rise to perplexity. For when we speak of definitions we usually distinguish between conceptual definitions, namely conceptual analyses of the things to be defined, and real definitions, namely propositions that give the essences of the things to be defined. It is well known that both Plato and Aristotle seemed to prefer real definitions. Their approach appears to presuppose that real definitions are the 'strongest' ones available. The initial perplexity can be (at least partly) eased if we consider that Plotinus' conception of definitions differs from his predecessors': it depends on his multi-level ontology and his own understanding of the concept of *logos*.

Some of Plotinus' remarks on Aristotelian definitions are expressed in a couple of passages that it is helpful to read. The first is in *Ennead* VI.7 [38] 4

---

[20] See e.g. *Top.* V.130^{b}26, *APo.* 73^{a}38, *Metaph.* 1003^{b}24.

(that is to say, two chapters below the texts analysed in sections 2–5): the details of Plotinus' overall argument are too complex to be discussed here, and I shall focus on some points of interest for our present discussion.[21] Plotinus is trying to answer the question 'who this man here below is'; he says that he is looking for the logos of man. Several possibilities are considered. In particular, he tells us that the composite of soul and body cannot be the logos of man. At 16–18, we read: 'For, this logos will be indicative (δηλωτικός) of what is going to be, not the sort we say man-in-itself is, but more like a definition (ὅρῳ), and the kind of definition which does not indicate the essence. For it is not even a definition of the form in matter, but indicates the composite which already exists' (Armstrong's translation revised).[22] The expression 'definition that indicates the essence' is strongly reminiscent of the way in which Aristotle characterizes a definition. For example, in Top. I.101ᵇ37–8 Aristotle says that a definition is an account that indicates the essence (ἔστι δ' ὅρος μὲν λόγος ὁ τὸ τί ἦν εἶναι σημαίνων). In ancient Greek the verb δηλοῦν can have the same meaning as σημαίνειν, namely 'to indicate' or 'to·signify'. Thus, in the present passage, it would initially seem that Plotinus accepts a strong type of account, i.e. an account that indicates the essence. However, he later adds that, at least in some cases, e.g. in the case of 'the man here below', accounts that indicate the essence will not be adequate: for, in these accounts there is no grasp of 'the formative principle itself which has made (τὸν λόγον αὐτὸν τὸν πεποιηκότα) for instance man' (line 25). The concept of logos as formative principle will be illustrated shortly.

The second passage is Ennead II.7 [37] 3, 7–10, and it belongs to the treatise that chronologically precedes Ennead VI.7. Here Plotinus distinguishes between logos as a definition that indicates the essence of the thing (ὁρισμὸς δηλωτικὸς τοῦ τί ἐστι τὸ πρᾶγμα) and a logos that produces the thing (λόγος ποιῶν πρᾶγμα). It is easy to see that, as in the text quoted above, the expression 'definition that indicates the essence of the thing' is reminiscent of the Aristotelian discussion of a certain type of definition (in the Aristotelian corpus, ὁρισμός can be used interchangeably with ὅρος).[23] For present purposes, it will be enough to say that in this text Plotinus is arguing against the

---

[21] A more extensive discussion of this passage and its context can be found in Hadot [1988], 207–23.

[22] The Greek text is as follows: Ἔσται γὰρ ὁ λόγος οὗτος δηλωτικὸς τοῦ ἐσομένου, οὐχ οἷος ὅν φαμεν αὐτοάνθρωπος, ἀλλὰ μᾶλλον ἐοικὼς ὅρῳ, καὶ τοιούτῳ οἵῳ μηδὲ δηλωτικῷ τοῦ τί ἦν εἶναι. Οὐδὲ γὰρ εἴδους ἐστὶ τοῦ ἐνύλου, ἀλλὰ τὸ συναμφότερον δηλῶν, ὅ ἐστιν ἤδη.

[23] Smith [1997], 58.

(seemingly) Peripatetic view that corporeity is *simply* a universal contained in the definition that indicates the essence of bodies. Rather, it is a *logos* in the sense of a formative principle that produces bodies.[24]

To attain a better understanding of Plotinus' view, we need to consider that for him it would be difficult to hold that something in the perceptible world is what it is because it is a crude reflection of the content of the intelligible world. That is to say, it would be difficult, if not absurd, to hold that 'a man here below' is bestowed with sense perception because in the intelligible world there is the Form of Humanity that has sense perception. It is partly to face this difficulty that Plotinus introduces his peculiar concept of *logos*. In the passages quoted above, when he speaks of '*logos* that produces the thing', he is referring to the role of the so-called 'formative principle'. Although the details of how this works are complex, the general idea is that the Intellect gives the *logoi* to the Soul, and the Soul interprets what there is in the intelligible world: the Soul, in a process involving several stages, uses the *logoi* to bring order and determination in the sensible world.[25] The concept of *logoi* as formative principles has certain similarities with the Stoic concept of *logoi spermatikoi*. But whereas there are strong suggestions that Stoic *logoi* are corporeal, Plotinus' formative principles are not so.[26]

We could say that according to Plotinus, the Aristotelian doctrine about real definitions is not wrong, but it is incomplete. It is likely that Plotinus wants to add that in some cases, namely when we want to explain how things are at the level of the sensible world, we cannot simply refer to something like definitions that indicate the essence. Plotinus thinks that something else must be added, namely formative principles that organize different qualities into an ordered perceptible world.

Concluding Remarks on Division and Cause

Let me conclude the analysis of Plotinus' text, which was presented in sections 2–5 above, with some remarks. It seems to me that the concept

---

[24] Bréhier's introduction to *Ennead* II.7 contains a brief but informative note on this chapter with references to Peripatetic texts.

[25] A discussion of the role of *logoi* in the sensible world can be found in Kalligas [1997].

[26] Witt [1931], 106.

of 'unfolding' plays an important role in Plotinus' discussion. However, if one were to provide a full account of the concept of 'unfolding', one would easily go far beyond the limits of the present paper. It will suffice to hint at some suggestions. At this stage of our analysis, one easily wonders what the method could be by virtue of which it is possible to 'unfold' what has been grasped. Since our text (2) does not provide an answer, let me make a tentative suggestion. In I.3 [20], Plotinus illustrates the method of dialectic that consists in the Platonic method of division (τῇ διαιρέσει τῇ Πλάτωνος). This method was presented as the means by which it is possible 'to distinguish the Forms, to determine the essence of each thing, and to find the primary kinds'. In other words, dialectic through the method of division reveals what the Forms are, i.e. it reveals their definition. The method of division is therefore a suitable candidate for the activity of unfolding the Forms, for it can reveal the way in which each Form is related to the others, and hence to the whole of the intelligible world.

Let us now focus our attention on the concept of cause. For, it would be natural to ask what kind of causal role is to be ascribed to the Forms. Given the complexity of this problem, it is only possible to draw a map of the suggestions presented in some of the texts analysed in this paper.[27] In particular, according to our text (2), it is possible to find the following characterization of the Forms' causality. The general idea is that there are at least two ways in which one can say that Forms are causes. The first is that Forms are causes for sensible items. It is a possibility that Plotinus is here referring to something like the Platonic view that sensible items partake of Forms: Forms provide the ontological grounds of particulars that partake of them. But it is more plausible to suspect that Plotinus could offer his personal elaboration about the relationship between Forms and sensible items: the essence of a sensible object could be determined by reflection of an intelligible Form.[28] If this is correct, then it is in this latter sense that, according to Plotinus, Forms are the ontological grounds of the particulars. However, given that it is not Plotinus' primary concern to go into the details of the relationship between Forms and sensible items in the last lines of our text (2), we can turn to the second way in which Forms are causes.

---

[27] The topic of the Forms' causality is discussed (among others) in Wagner [1985] and in D'Ancona Costa [1992].

[28] This point is discussed in Kalligas [1997], 399–400.

This second way in which Forms are causes is still difficult to define. We are dealing with a different kind of causality, as sensible items are not involved: this is the kind of causality that one finds when one unfolds a Form.

When we focus on this second way in which Forms are causes, a complex picture presents itself. For our present purposes, it suffices to delineate only some of its traits. A characteristic feature of Plotinus' Forms is that they do not depend on other things that are not intelligible beings. Still, at the same time, Forms should not be taken in isolation: they are to be taken in their mutual relations, in particular in their relations with the primary *genera*, and hence in their interconnection with the whole of the intelligible world. Hence, there is a certain kind of dependence of the Forms on the intelligible world. Accordingly, when one comes to grasp the essence and the cause in the unfolding of the Form, one understands what the Form is by grasping how it is related to (and dependent on) other Forms, and, in particular, to the primary *genera*. One thereby grasps the connections and the interrelations between different elements of the intelligible world. If one were to push this view even further, one would be tempted to see in Plotinus a holistic view of universals.[29] However, this thesis needs to be more extensively argued for, and it constitutes an interesting and fruitful starting-point for new research.[30]

Bibliography

P. Adamson, 2002, *The Arabic Plotinus*, Duckworth.

J. P. Anton, 1992–3, 'Plotinus and the Neoplatonic Conception of Dialectic', *Journal of Neoplatonic Studies* 1, 3–30.

A. H. Armstrong, 1966–88, intro. and trans., *Plotinus*, 7 vols., Harvard University Press.

---

[29] Plotinus' holism has recently been discussed in Emilsson [2007], 199–207.

[30] I would like to thank the many colleagues and friends who read previous drafts of this paper and made extremely helpful suggestions. I am particularly grateful to David Charles, Paolo Crivelli, Pavlos Kalligas, and the anonymous referee. I gratefully acknowledge the time that Michael Frede spent discussing the content of this paper in spring 2006.

M. Atkinson, 1983, *Ennead V.1: On the Three Principal Hypostases*, Oxford University Press.

J. Barnes, 1993, trans. and comm., *Aristotle: Posterior Analytics*, Clarendon Press.

H. J. Blumenthal, 1971, *Plotinus' Psychology: His theory of Embodied Soul*, Martinus Nijhoff.

E. Bréhier, 1924–38, intro., ed., trans., and notes, *Plotin: Ennéades*, 7 vols., Les Belles Lettres.

R. Bolton, 1993, 'Division, definition et essence dans la science aristotelicienne', *Revue philosophique de la France et de l'Etranger* 183, 197–222.

D. Bostock, 1986, *Plato's* Phaedo, Clarendon Press.

R. Chiaradonna, 1999, '*ΟΥΣΙΑ ΕΞ ΟΥΚ ΟΥΣΙΩΝ*. Forma e sostanza sensibile in Plotino (*Enn.* VI 3, 4–8)', *Documenti e studi sulla tradizione filosofica medievale* 10, 25–57.

—— 2002, *Sostanza, Movimento, Analogia: Plotino critico di Aristotele*, Bibliopolis.

D. Charles, 2000, *Aristotle on Meaning and Essence*, Oxford University Press.

C. D'Ancona Costa, 1992, '*ΑΜΟΡΦΟΝ ΚΑΙ ΑΝΕΙΔΟΝ*. Causalité des formes et causalité de l'Un chez Plotin', *Revue de Philosophie Ancienne* 10, 69–113.

E. K. Emilsson, 1988, *Plotinus on Sense Perception*, Cambridge University Press.

—— 1991, 'Plotinus and Soul–Body Dualism', in *Companions to Ancient Thought*, 2: *Psychology*, ed. S. Everson, Cambridge University Press, 148–65.

—— 1995, 'Plotinus on the Objects of Thought', *Archiv für Geschichte der Philosophie* 77, 21–41.

—— 2007, *Plotinus on Intellect*, Oxford University Press.

G. Fine, 1987, 'Forms as Causes: Plato and Aristotle', in *Mathematics and Metaphysics in Aristotle*, ed. A. Graeser = *Mathematik und Metaphysik bei Aristoteles*, Haupt, 69–111.

M. Frede, 1987, 'The Original Notion of Cause', in *Essays in Ancient Philosophy*, Clarendon Press, 125–50.

P. Hadot, 1988, intro., comm., and notes, *Plotin: Traité 38. VI,7*, Cerf.

R. Harder, 1956–71, intro., ed., and trans., *Plotinus Schriften*, continued by R. Beutler and W. Teiler, Felix Meiner.

P. Henry and H.-R. Schwytzer, 1951, 1959, 1973, intro. and ed., *Plotini Opera*, 3 vols. (vol. 1, Edition Universelle, *Enneads I–III*; vol. 2, Edition Universelle and Desclée de Brouwer, *Enneads IV–V*; vol. 3, Desclée de Brouwer and Brill, *Ennead VI*) = H-S¹ *editio maior*.

P. Henry and H.-R. Schwyzer, 1964, 1976, 1982, intro. and ed., *Plotini Opera*, 3 vols., Clarendon Press (vol. 1, *Enneads I–III*; vol. 2, *Enneads IV–V*; vol. 3, *Ennead VI*) = H.-S.² *editio minor*.

M. Hocutt, 1974, 'Aristotle's Four Becauses', *Philosophy* 49, 385–99.

T. Irwin, 1995, *Plato's Ethics*, Oxford University Press.

R. W. Jordan, 1983, *Plato's Arguments for Forms*, Cambridge Philological Society.

P. Kalligas, 1997, 'Logos and the Sensible Object in Plotinus', *Ancient Philosophy* 17, 397–410.

A. C. Lloyd, 1955, 'Neoplatonic Logic and Aristotelian Logic I', *Phronesis* 1, 58–79.

—— 1956, 'Neoplatonic Logic and Aristotelian Logic II', *Phronesis* 2, 146–60.

—— 1986, 'Non-Propositional Thought in Plotinus', *Phronesis* 31, 258–65.

—— 1990, *The Anatomy of Neoplatonism*, Clarendon Press.

S. MacKenna, 1962, trans., *Plotinus: The Ennead*, Faber.

G. B. Matthews and T. A. Blackson, 1989, 'Causes in the *Phaedo*', *Synthese* 79, 581–91.

D. O'Meara, 1975, *Structure hiérarchiques dans la penseé de Plotin*, Brill.

R. Radice and G. Reale, 2003, *Plotino: Enneadi*, trans. R. Radice, intro. and comm. G. Reale, Arnoldo Mondadori Editore (1st edn. 2002).

W. D. Ross, 1949, trans. and comm., *Aristotle's Prior and Posterior Analytics*, Oxford University Press.

L. P. Schrenk, 1993, 'The Middle Platonic Reception of Aristotelian Science', *Rheinisches Museum für Philologie*, n.s. 136, 343–59.

—— 1994a, ed., *Aristotle in Late Antiquity*, Catholic University of America Press.

—— 1994b, 'Proof and Discovery in Aristotle and the Later Greek Tradition: A Prolegomenon to a Study of Analysis and Synthesis', in Schrenk [1994a], 92–108.

F. M. Schroeder, 1992, *Form and Transformation: A Study in the Philosophy of Plotinus*, McGill-Queen's University Press.

J. H. Sleeman and G. Pollet, 1980, *Lexicon Plotinianum*, Brill.

R. Smith, 1997, trans. and comm., *Aristotle: Topics Books I and VIII*, Clarendon Press.

G. Vlastos, 1968, 'Reason and Causes in the *Phaedo*', *Philosophical Review* 78, 291–325.

M. F. Wagner, 1982, 'Vertical Causation in Plotinus', in *The Structure of Being: A Neoplatonic Approach*, ed. R. B. Harris, International Society for Neoplatonic Studies, 51–165.

—— 1985, 'Realism and the Sensible World', *Ancient Philosophy* 5(2), 269–92.

—— 1996, 'Plotinus on the Nature of the Physical Reality', in *The Cambridge Companion to Plotinus*, ed. L. P. Gerson, Cambridge University Press 130–70.

R. E. Witt, 1931, 'The Plotinian *Logos* and its Stoic Basis', *Classical Quaterly* 25, 103–11.

N. P. White, 1992, 'Plato's Metaphysical Epistemology', in *The Cambridge Companion to Plato*, ed. R. Kraut, Cambridge University Press, 277–310.

14

Sceptical Enquiry

GAIL FINE

1 In *Outlines of Pyrrhonism* (*PH*) I 7, Sextus says that 'the sceptic (*skeptikê*) way, then, is also called "enquiring" (*zêtêtikê*), from its activity of enquiring and investigating (*skeptesthai*)'.[1] And he begins *PH* II by saying: 'Since we have reached our enquiry about (*pros*) the dogmatists, let us inspect, concisely and in outline, each of the parts of what they call philosophy, having first answered those who always allege that sceptics can neither enquire into nor, more generally, think about (*noein*) the things about which they [i.e. dogmatists] hold opinions (*dogmatizomenôn*).' Sceptics may be *called* 'enquirers' and 'investigators', but the dogmatists challenge the appropriateness of these labels. They argue that sceptics can't enquire into or investigate the things the dogmatists discuss; indeed, they can't even think about them. If so, the enquiry Sextus has just said he'll undertake can't get off the ground. Hence, before embarking on it, he attempts to rebut the dogmatic challenge to his ability to do so.

The dogmatists' challenge to the possibility of sceptical enquiry recalls a famous passage in the *Meno*, in which Meno challenges Socrates' ability to enquire. Socrates claims not to know what virtue is; as a result, he says,

---

[1] Here and elsewhere in citing the *Outlines of Pyrrhonism*, I generally use the translation by J. Annas and J. Barnes, *Sextus Empiricus: Outlines of Scepticism* (Cambridge: Cambridge University Press, 1994), though I have occasionally altered it, sometimes without comment. The verb I translate 'investigate' is *skeptesthai*, which is cognate with *skeptikos*, sceptical. In Sextus' day, it meant 'investigate', 'enquire', or 'consider', rather than 'sceptic' in our sense, of one who suspends judgement as to whether, or who denies that, knowledge or justified belief, either as such or in some area, is possible. So when Sextus says the Pyrrhonists are the only genuine *skeptikoi*, he means they are the only genuine enquirers. Hence the claim that sceptics cannot enquire challenges the appropriateness of one of the most fundamental descriptions of Pyrrhonism.

neither does he know whether virtue is teachable or, indeed, anything at all about virtue (71ab). For, in his view, one can't know anything at all about F (including what things are F) unless one knows what F is. Nonetheless, he claims he is willing, indeed eager, to enquire into what virtue is (80d1–4). Meno asks Socrates how he can do so if, as he says, he doesn't at all know what virtue is (80d5–8). Socrates adds that there also seems to be a problem about the possibility of enquiry if one does know (80e1–5). Let us call this the *paradox of enquiry*. I have discussed Plato's presentation of, and reply to. the paradox of enquiry elsewhere.[2] Here I focus on Sextus' formulation and reply in *Outlines of Pyrrhonism (PH)* II 1–11. At various stages, I compare Sextus' and Plato's accounts. As we shall see, Sextus associates the version of the paradox of enquiry that he considers here with the Stoics; hence we shall also need to consider some of their views.

2 Here, to begin with, is the relevant passage from PH II:[3]

[2] They say that sceptics either do, or do not, apprehend (*katalambanei*) what the dogmatists talk about (*legomena*). If they apprehend it, how can they be puzzled (*aporoiê*) about what they say they apprehend? If they do not apprehend it, they do not even know how to talk about (*oide legein*) what they have not apprehended. [3] For just as someone who does not know (*eidôs*) what, for example, the removal <argument> or the theorem in two complexes is cannot even say anything about them, so someone who does not recognize (*gignôskôn*) any of the things the dogmatists talk about cannot enquire in opposition to them about things which he does not know (*oiden*). In neither case, therefore, can sceptics enquire into what the dogmatists talk about. [4] Now those who put this argument forward must tell us how they are here using the word 'apprehend'. Does it mean simply 'to think', without any further affirmation of the reality (*huparxeôs*) of the things about which we are making our statements? Or does it also include a positing of the reality of the things we are discussing? If they say that 'apprehend' in their argument means 'assent to an apprehensive appearance' (an apprehensive appearance comes from something real, is imprinted and stamped in accordance with the real thing itself, and is such as would not come from anything unreal), then they themselves will perhaps be unwilling to allow that they cannot enquire into things which they have

---

[2] In 'Inquiry in the *Meno*', in R. Kraut (ed.), *Cambridge Companion to Plato* (Cambridge: Cambridge University Press, 1992), 200–26; reprinted, with minor revisions, in my *Plato on Knowledge and Forms: Selected Essays* (Oxford: Clarendon Press, 2003), ch. 2.

[3] I omit the end of section [6], as well as sections [7]–[9].

not apprehended in this way. [5] For example, when a Stoic enquires in opposition to an Epicurean who says that substance is divided or that god does not show providence for things in the universe or that pleasure is good, has he apprehended these things or has he not apprehended them? If he has apprehended them, then in saying that they are real he utterly rejects the Stoa; and if he has not apprehended them, then he cannot say anything against them. [6] And similar things are to be said against those who come from the other schools, when they want to enquire into the beliefs of those who hold different beliefs (*heterodoxai*) from themselves. Thus they cannot enquire into anything in opposition to one another. Or rather, to avoid talking nonsense, practically the whole of dogmatism will be confounded and the sceptical philosophy will be firmly established, if it is granted that it is impossible to enquire into what has not been apprehended in this way.... [10] If they say they mean that it is not apprehension of this sort, but rather mere thinking which ought to precede enquiry, then it is not impossible for those who suspend judgement about the reality of what is unclear to enquire.[4] For a sceptic is not, I think, barred from having thoughts, if they arise from things which give him a passive impression (*hupopiptontôn*) and appear clearly to him[5] and do not at all imply the reality of what is being thought of. For we can think, as they say, not only of real things (*huparchonta*) but also of unreal things.[6] Hence someone who suspends judgement maintains his sceptical condition while enquiring and thinking. For it has been made clear that he assents to any impression given by way of a passive appearance, insofar as it appears to him. [11] And consider whether in actual fact the dogmatists are not barred from enquiry. For those who agree (*homologousi*) that they do not know (*agnoein*) how objects are in their nature (*pros tên phusin*) may continue without inconsistency to enquire into them, whereas those who think they know (*gignôskein*) them accurately (*ep'akribes*) may not. For the latter, the enquiry is already at its end, as they suppose, whereas for the former, the reason why any enquiry is undertaken—that is, the idea (*to nomizein*) that they have not found the answer—is fully present.

---

[4] Alt.: 'it is not impossible for those who suspend judgement to enquire into the reality of what is unclear'.

[5] I follow Annas and Barnes in omitting *logô(i)/logôn*. The main MSS have *logôn*, which is used in the Teubner (= vol. 1 of *Sextus Empirici Opera*, 2nd edn., ed. H. Mutschmann, rev. J. Mau, Leipzig, 1958). There is also some manuscript warrant for *logô(i)*, which is used in the Loeb (ed. R. Bury, *Sextus Empiricus: Outlines of Pyrrhonism* [Cambridge, MA: Harvard University Press, 1933; repr. 1990 = Loeb Classical Library, vol. 1 of Sextus]), and assumed by many translators. In favor of Annas and Barnes's omission is the fact that the end of section [10] plainly recalls this remark, but it doesn't contain either *logôn* or *logô(i)*.

[6] Cf. *M* VIII 334a–336a; *M* IX 49.

Sextus presents the paradox of enquiry[7] in sections [2] and [3]; subsequent sections contain his reflections on it. Let's look first at his account of the paradox. It may be formulated as follows:[8]

1. For any x enquired into by a dogmatist, the sceptic either does, or does not, apprehend (*katalambanei*) x.
2. If the sceptic apprehends x, he isn't puzzled about x.
[3. If the sceptic isn't puzzled about x, he can't enquire into x.]
4. Therefore if the sceptic apprehends x, he can't enquire into x.
5. If the sceptic doesn't apprehend x, he doesn't know how to talk about x.
6. If the sceptic doesn't know how to talk about x, he can't enquire into x.
7. Therefore if the sceptic doesn't apprehend x, he can't enquire into x.
8. Therefore, whether the sceptic does, or does not, apprehend x, he can't enquire into x.

Before evaluating the argument, it will be helpful to make a few preliminary points about the nature of enquiry, as it is conceived of here. Firstly, in *PH* II 11, Sextus says that one enquires only when one has the idea (*nomizein*) that one hasn't found the answer. Similarly, in *M* VII 393 he says that 'if everything were evident, there would be no enquiry or being puzzled; for one enquires into and puzzles over (*aporei*) what is unclear (*adêlon*) to one, but not about what is apparent'.[9] To be puzzled about something—that is, to be in a state of *aporia* about it—involves suspending judgement either way. As Sextus says, the sceptical persuasion was called aporetic 'either (as some say) from the fact that it puzzles over (*aporein*) and enquires into everything, or (*êtoi*) from its being at a loss (*amêchanein*) whether to assert or deny' (*PH* I 7).[10]

---

[7] Or perhaps we should call it the paradox of *sceptical* enquiry. For the dogmatists don't mean to challenge either the possibility of enquiry as such or their own ability to enquire, but just the sceptics' ability to enquire. (Whether they succeed in challenging just the sceptics' ability to enquire is, of course, another question, and one Sextus considers in due course.) By contrast, Socrates, in his rephrasing of what Meno says, considers a challenge to the possibility of enquiry as such.

[8] Premises enclosed in square brackets are tacit.

[9] Here it's worth asking: What if one thinks one doesn't know the answer, but does in fact know it (assuming that's possible, an issue about which there is controversy)? Is enquiry then possible? Similar questions arise at various stages, but I shall generally bypass them here.

[10] I assume that the second clause is meant to elucidate the first; if so, then, if one is in a state of *aporia* with respect to something, one suspends judgement about it. Even if the second clause gives a different explanation from the first, both aim to explain why sceptics are called aporetics, and so one explanation of the label is that sceptics suspend judgement either way. As such, to be in a state of *aporia* with respect to p is not to doubt whether p is true, if (as is sometimes thought) doubting whether p is true involves an

Secondly, enquiry involves directed, systematic search. Happening upon what one was looking for isn't enquiry; nor is apprehending something directly or immediately.[11]

Thirdly, for Plato, at any rate, the goal of enquiry is to acquire knowledge one lacks.[12] That is also how the Stoics conceive the goal of enquiry. In the *Academica*, for example, Cicero says that, according to them, 'enquiry (*quaestio* = *zêtêsis*) is the impulse (*adpetitio*) for knowledge (*cognitio*), and the aim (*finis*) of enquiry is discovery (*inventio*) . . . Discovery is the opening up of things previously hidden' (II 26 = *SVF* 2.103). Clement explains the Stoic view of enquiry along similar lines: 'enquiry is an impulse towards *katalêpsis*, an impulse that discovers the subject through some signs. Discovery is a limit and cessation when enquiry has arrived at *katalêpsis*' (*Strom.* VI 14 p. 801 Pott = *SVF* 2.102). The opening lines of *PH* suggest that sceptics also enquire in order to discover the truth: 'When people are enquiring into any subject, the likely result is either a discovery, or a denial of discovery and a confession of inapprehensibility, or else a continuation of the investigation. This, no doubt, is why in the case of philosophical enquiries, too, some have said that they have discovered the truth, some have asserted that it cannot be apprehended, and others are still investigating' (*PH* I 1–2). Sextus goes on to say that dogmatists think they have discovered the truth; Academics claim it cannot be apprehended; and sceptics are still enquiring—sc. (or so it seems) in an effort to discover the truth.[13] Diogenes Laertius, at any rate, explicitly says that sceptics were called enquirers (*zêtêtikoi*)

---

inclination to believe that p is false. Cf. B. Mates, *The Skeptic Way* (New York: Oxford University Press, 1996), 5, 30–2.

[11] Of course, one might stumble across what one was looking for in the course of an enquiry; but doing so isn't itself a proper part of enquiry. As Plutarch says, 'one can't enquire into something if one has no conception of it, nor could one discover it—at least, not through enquiry. For we do say that someone who happens upon something also discovers it' (Fr. 215 (e) in vol. 15 of the Loeb Classical Library's edition of Plutarch's *Moralia* [Cambridge, MA: Harvard University Press, 1969], ed. and trans. F. Sandbach = sect. 279 in L. G. Westerink (ed.), *The Greek Commentaries on Plato's Phaedo* [Amsterdam: North Holland, 1977], vol. 2). The latter part of this fragment makes the point that there are ways of discovering something other than through enquiry.

[12] See, e.g. *Ch.* 165b–c. Cf. Aristotle, *EN* 1142b: 'we do not enquire about what we already know (*ou gar zêtousi peri hôn isasin*)', sc. but do enquire so as to acquire knowledge we don't have.

[13] To say that sceptics are searching in order to discover the truth should not be taken to imply that they are committed to thinking that any dogmatic claims are true. Rather, they enquire in order to discover which *if any* dogmatic claims are true. By contrast, Plato and the Stoics believe there are truths in what Sextus characterizes as the dogmatic realm.

because they were always enquiring for the truth (*zêtein tên alêtheian*) (DL 9.70).[14]

Fourthly, we should ask what one can enquire into: that is, about possible substituends for 'x'. Sextus initially gives two examples: the removal argument and the theorem in two complexes. Unfortunately, it's not clear what the removal argument is.[15] But presumably enquiring into an argument involves asking whether it is valid or invalid, sound or unsound.[16] The theorem in two complexes is the argument or inference schema 'If p then q; if p, then not q; therefore not p'.[17] Sextus goes on to give further examples of possible objects of enquiry: he asks whether Stoics can enquire into such Epicurean claims as that being is divided, or that god doesn't have foreknowledge, or that pleasure is good (II 5). These are all single propositions. Enquiring into an individual proposition presumably involves asking whether it is meaningful and, if it is, whether it is true or false. One can also enquire into its grounds: the reasons why, for example, the Epicureans believe that pleasure is good. One can also enquire into what something is. In *M* VII 426, for example, Sextus says that sceptics enquire into what apprehensive appearances are.[18] Enquiring into what something is involves attempting to articulate a satisfactory concept or definition of it. Accordingly, Sextus spends a great deal of time investigating various dogmatic concepts and definitions: for example, of proof (II 134–92), man (II 22–34), and time (III 136–50). One can also enquire about things or states of affairs. For example, one can enquire about Socrates' whereabouts, or whether that is Socrates over there in the distance.[19] Possible substituends for 'x' are

[14] For a challenge to the view that discovering the truth, or acquiring knowledge, is the goal of sceptical enquiry, see J. Palmer, 'Sceptical Investigation', *Ancient Philosophy* 20 (2000), 351–75. For a reply to Palmer, see C. Perin, 'Pyrrhonian Scepticism and the Search for Truth', *Oxford Studies in Ancient Philosophy* 30 (2006), 383–401.
[15] See Annas and Barnes, note ad loc.; Mates, *The Skeptic Way*, 265. According to Mates, MS T says that the removal argument is 'omnis triangulus habet tres angulos equales duobus rectis', which is half of theorem 32 in Book I of Euclid's *Elements*. Bury, note ad loc., speculates that the removal argument is some form of the Sorites.
[16] If the removal argument is a theorem rather than an argument (see last note), then Sextus doesn't here give an example of enquiring into an argument. Nonetheless, arguments are possible objects of enquiry, and enquiring into them involves asking about validity and soundness.
[17] So Annas and Barnes, note ad loc.; Mates, *The Skeptic Way*, 265. Mates also suggests that perhaps it is rather 'the metatheoretic assertion that all instances of the schema are sound'. An account of this theorem is given in Origen, *Contra Celsum* VII 15.
[18] I discuss apprehensive appearances briefly below.
[19] See *PH* III 173–4; DL 10.33 (on Epicurus).

therefore quite broad; and different questions arise, depending on what sort of thing one is enquiring into. Be that as it may, Sextus for the most part focuses on propositions, and I shall follow suit. However, at some stages it will be useful to consider other substituends for 'x'.

3   These preliminaries out of the way, let's now ask how good the argument is.   In this section, I provide my own assessment, by looking at the argument in the abstract, as it were. In subsequent sections, I return more directly to Sextus.

If 'apprehend' is used univocally, the argument is valid.[20] For it is then essentially a constructive dilemma:

1'.   p or not-p.
4'.   p implies q.
7'.   Not-p implies q.
8'.   Therefore q.

That is, for any x enquired into by a dogmatist, the sceptic either does, or does not, apprehend x. Whichever of these two exclusive and exhaustive options obtains, the sceptic can't enquire into x. Therefore, sceptics can't enquire into any x enquired into by a dogmatist.

Let's assume for now that the argument is of this form. Not only is it then valid, but (1) is also then non-problematically true: the sceptic either does, or does not, apprehend x; *tertium non datur.* To know whether the argument is sound, we therefore need to look at (4) and (7). Since (4) is supported by (2) and (3), and since (7) is supported by (5) and (6), we also need to look at them. Let's look first at (2)–(4):

2.   If the sceptic apprehends x, he isn't puzzled about x.
3.   If the sceptic isn't puzzled about x, he can't enquire into x.
4.   Therefore if the sceptic apprehends x, he can't enquire into x.

This argument is clearly valid.[21] But is it sound? I shall assume that (3) is true. For we said that one enquires only into what is unclear to one, and so only into something one is in some sense puzzled about. And that seems to be all (3) means.

---

[20] More accurately, (1), (4), (7), and (8) then constitute a valid argument. However, since (4) and (7) are supported by sub-arguments, the argument as a whole (1–8) might not be valid.

[21] Again assuming that the key terms are used univocally.

What, however, about (2)? Let's assume first that to apprehend something is to have some knowledge about it, and that an individual proposition p is being enquired into. There are then readings of (2) on which it is true, and readings of it on which it is false. (2) is true if it means that if the sceptic knows that p is true, she can't be puzzled about whether it is true.[22] (2) is also true if it says that if the sceptic understands what p means, she can't be puzzled about what it means.[23] However, (2) is false if it says that if the sceptic understands what p means, she can't be puzzled about whether it's true.[24] (2) also seems false if it means that if the sceptic knows that p is true, she can't be puzzled about why it's true.[25] In Aristotle's terms, even if one knows the *that*, one can be puzzled about, and search for, the *why*. Indeed, Aristotle thinks that one must know (or believe) that something is so in order to enquire why it is so.[26]

What if to apprehend something is to have some knowledge about it, where an object is being enquired into? In this case, (2) seems false: one might know some things about Socrates (such as who he is, where he is, that he was an associate of Plato's), but seek to know more about him (for example, whether he was truly virtuous, or had or took himself to have any knowledge).

Let's now suppose that apprehending something is knowing not just something, but everything there is to know, about it. In this case (2) seems true no matter what the sceptic purports to enquire into: a single proposition, an argument, an object, or something else again. If the sceptic

---

[22] Suppose the sceptic in fact knows that p is true, but doesn't believe she knows it but, on the contrary, thinks she doesn't know it. Couldn't she in that case be puzzled as to whether p is true and enquire whether it is? Cf. n. 9. It's worth noting that the Stoics might think this is the sceptics' position. At least, the Stoics think that everyone has some knowledge, whether or not they take themselves to do so.

[23] However, one might argue that one could have a partial understanding of what p means, and seek a deeper understanding.

[24] It's sometimes thought that there are some propositions such that, if one understands what they mean, one thereby knows that they are true. But even if some propositions are like this, not all are.

[25] Plato would jib here. For he thinks that one can't know anything about F, including what things are F, unless one knows what F is (*Meno* 71b). One can't know, for example, whether Euthyphro's action of prosecuting his father is pious unless one knows what piety is. If one knows what piety is, one will be able to explain why Euthyphro's action is (or is not) pious. Hence, one can know that it is (or is not) pious only if one knows why it is (or is not) pious.

[26] See esp. *APo.* II 1–2, 8–10. For an illuminating discussion of Aristotle on this issue, see J. L. Ackrill, 'Aristotle's Theory of Definition', in E. Berti (ed.), *Aristotle on Science: The Posterior Analytics* (Padua: Editrice Antenore, 1981), 359–84. My phrasing in the text slides over an important distinction: it's one thing to say that one needs to *know* that something is so in order to enquire why it is so, and quite another to say that one must *believe* that something is so in order to enquire why it is so.

knows everything there is to know about Socrates or virtue or the removal argument, there is nothing left for her to be puzzled about.

What if apprehending something is just having some idea or other about it? In this case, (2) seems false. The sceptic might, for example, have the idea that water is a liquid, but wonder exactly what sort of liquid it is, or what its chemical constitution is. She might have the idea that Goldbach's conjecture is a mathematical conjecture, but be puzzled about whether it is true.[27]

There is, then, no simple answer to the question whether (2) is true. It depends partly on what apprehension amounts to here: is it partial or complete knowledge, or something else again? It also depends partly on what the cognitive attitude is directed towards: an object or a proposition and, if the latter, whether one is attempting to enquire into its meaning, its truth value, or its explanation.

Despite these complexities, we've seen that (2) is true if it means that if the sceptic knows that p is true, she is not puzzled about whether it is true; and, on this reading, (2)–(4) is a sound sub-argument (given that (3) is true).[28] If we so read (2)–(4), and if (1) is of the form 'p or not p', then, in order for the entire argument (i.e. (1–8)) to be valid, 'not apprehending', in (5)–(8), must mean 'not having any knowledge'. Suppose we assume that is what it means. We then preserve validity. Moreover, (6) seems true, if it means that, if one can't engage in systematic discussion about something, one can't enquire into it.[29] However, (5) is then false. For contrary to (5), one doesn't need to apprehend (i.e. *know*) anything about x in order to

---

[27] One might argue that, to think about x at all (and so to have an idea about it), one must have available a uniquely referring description. On this view, if all one can say about Goldbach's conjecture is that it is a mathematical conjecture, one can't, properly speaking, think about, or have an idea about, *it*. Although this is an objection to the example, it doesn't affect the basic point. All I need for it is that one can have an idea about something without having complete knowledge of it, without knowing everything there is to know about it; and that seems reasonable, even if, to have an idea about something, one must be able to identify it uniquely.

[28] As we've seen, there are also other readings of (2) on which it is arguably true. But I believe the basic moral would be the same in any case.

[29] This assumes that 'know how to talk about x' just means 'being able to talk about x', where genuine knowledge is not at issue (but just, say, an ability that doesn't involve genuine knowledge). If, however, genuine knowledge is at issue, then, if knowing how to talk about x involves having some knowledge about x, (5) would be true. For it would then say that if one doesn't apprehend something—that is, if one doesn't have any knowledge about it—one doesn't know how to talk about it. And, of course, if one knows nothing at all about x, one doesn't know how to talk about x, if doing so involves knowing something about x. Though (5) so read is true, (6) would then be false. For (as I shall argue) one doesn't need knowledge for enquiry. It doesn't matter for my purposes whether we take (5) to be true and (6) to be false, or whether we take (5) to be false and (6) to be true.

engage in systematic discussion about it. More generally, one doesn't need to *know* anything at all about virtue or Goldbach's conjecture in order to be able to discuss them intelligibly. As Plato argues in the *Meno*, someone who doesn't know the way to Larissa can still get there if she has, and relies on, relevant true beliefs (97ab).[30]

Suppose, however, that 'not apprehending' means: not having a clue, being in a complete blank. One doesn't merely lack knowledge about the matter to hand. One also lacks any beliefs about it; one doesn't even understand what the terms involved mean. On this reading, (5) and (6) are true. For in order to be able to enquire into something, one must have some sort of grasp of it, some clue about what one is enquiring into. If one has no idea at all about x, not even a rudimentary concept, no initial beliefs or hypotheses, no understanding, even, of what 'x' means, then it's difficult to see how one can enquire into it. If, however, that is how we understand 'not apprehending', then, for the overall argument to be valid, 'apprehension', in (2)–(4), would have to mean 'having an idea about, not drawing a complete blank'. As we've seen, however, if that is how we understand 'apprehension', (2) is false: having an idea about x doesn't mean one isn't puzzled about it. For, again, one might have the idea that Goldbach's conjecture is a mathematical conjecture, but be puzzled about whether it is true. Hence on this reading, (2)–(4) (and so (1)–(8)) is unsound.

We can, then, read (5)–(7) so that it is a sound sub-argument. We can also read (2)–(4) so that it is a sound sub-argument. But if we so read both (2)–(4) and (5)–(7), the argument as a whole is invalid. For it is then of the following form: p or not p (= (1)); r implies q (= (2)–(4)); s implies q ((5)–(7)); so q ((8)).[31] We can restore validity by retaining the readings of (2)–(4) and of (5)–(7) on which they are sound, and revising (1) to say: 'For any x, the sceptic either knows x, or draws a complete blank with respect to it.' But then the argument is unsound. For if (1) is so read, it is false: knowing something, and drawing a complete blank with respect to it, are not

[30] See Fine, 'Inquiry in the *Meno*'; cf. Introduction to *Plato on Knowledge and Forms*, 1–5. Plato focuses on arguing that having and relying on true beliefs is sufficient for enabling one to enquire; but he seems to think that having and relying on relevant true beliefs is also necessary for enquiry. Although he thinks that one can enquire if and only if one has and relies on relevant true beliefs, he doesn't think one must be aware of which of one's beliefs are true, which false. Beliefs don't come ready-labelled 'true' or 'false'. Nor, in requiring true belief for enquiry, does Plato mean that one must have the true belief that p is true in order to enquire whether p is true; he means only that one must have some relevant true beliefs.

[31] I assume that p, q, r, and s are all different, non-equivalent propositions.

exhaustive options. For example, there are also (true) beliefs. We can avoid this difficulty by again making (1) an instance of the law of the excluded middle, and reading 'apprehension' univocally. The argument is then again valid. But, in this case, either (2)–(4) or (5)–(7) is unsound. I conclude that the argument is either valid but unsound, or else has all true premises but is invalid.[32]

4   If the argument is so bad, one might be tempted to conclude that the dogmatists' challenge to the possibility of sceptical enquiry is easily disarmed. However, this conclusion would be premature. For even if the argument as a whole can't be read so as to be sound, we've seen that it contains two sub-arguments, each of which can be read so as to be sound. We should therefore ask whether sceptics are vulnerable to either of these sub-arguments when they are so read. In order to decide about this, we need to know what the sceptic's cognitive condition is: or, more precisely, what he takes it to be. For my concern here is not whether sceptics can in fact enquire, but how they reply to the paradox of enquiry. For that, the, or a, relevant issue is what they take their cognitive condition to be, not what it actually is.[33]

There is, however, to say the least, considerable dispute about what cognitive condition sceptics take themselves to be in. Here we may contrast the *No Belief View* with the *Some Belief View*.[34] According to the No Belief View, sceptics take themselves to lack all beliefs.[35] According to the Some Belief View, sceptics take themselves to have beliefs. Among those who favor the No Belief View, there is dispute about what nondoxastic cognitive condition sceptics take themselves to be in.[36] Among those who favor the Some Belief View, there is dispute about what beliefs sceptics take

---

[32] In 'Inquiry in the *Meno*', I reach the same verdict about the *Meno*'s paradox of enquiry. There are further options beyond those I consider in the text. But I think the same moral still applies.

[33] There are other important relevant issues as well; but I shall largely focus on cognitive condition.

[34] I introduced these labels in 'Scepticism, Existence, and Belief', *Oxford Studies in Ancient Philosophy* 14 (1996), 273–90, at 284ff. Others sometimes use other labels, for these or related positions.

[35] One might well ask what it would be to take oneself to lack all beliefs, but I shall not pursue that matter here.

[36] By a nondoxastic cognitive condition, I mean one that falls short of belief (*doxa*). For example, it might appear to me that the oar is bent in water, without my believing that it is bent in water; it might appear to me that an argument is sound, without my believing that it is. As the second example is meant to show, nondoxastic appearances are not restricted to perceptual appearances. Nor need the content of a nondoxastic appearance be nonconceptual. It can appear to me that the oar is bent in water only if I have a concept of oar; it can appear to me that an argument is sound only if I have a concept of soundness.

themselves to have. Among defenders of both views, there is dispute about the operative sense of 'belief'.

If the No Belief View is correct, Plato's reply to the paradox—that one can enquire even if one lacks knowledge, so long as one has and relies on relevant true beliefs—is not available to the sceptics. Indeed, one might think that, if the No Belief View is correct, sceptics are vulnerable to the second sub-argument, (5)–(7), when it is read so as to be sound. As we've seen, on this reading it says that if one's mind is a complete blank with respect to something, if one doesn't have a clue about it, one can't enquire into it. And it might seem that, if sceptics disavow all beliefs, and correctly describe their situation, then their minds are complete blanks. In that case, they would instantiate the antecedent of (5), and so be vulnerable to (5)–(7).

It might seem, by contrast, that if the Some Belief View is correct, Sextus could reply to the paradox as Plato does. However, to know whether the Some Belief View (if it is correct) allows an escape route from the paradox, we need to know more than that sceptics take themselves to have some beliefs. We also need to know what they claim to have beliefs about, and in what sense of 'belief' they claim to have beliefs. For example, if their beliefs are minimal enough, it's not clear they can enquire. Animals and infants are sometimes said to have beliefs. But it's not clear that having the sorts of beliefs they have is sufficient for being able to enquire whether god exists, or whether there are atoms.[37] Even if the sceptics' beliefs are not as low-level as those of animals or infants, it might matter what their beliefs are about. Perhaps their beliefs are irrelevant to particular enquiries they claim to undertake. For example, it's not clear that having sophisticated theological beliefs enables one to enquire into the basis of physics.[38]

Not only, then, is the paradox of enquiry challenging in its own right. But looking at Sextus' reply may also help us decide between the No Belief

---

[37] It's worth mentioning that in *PH* I 62–78, Sextus argues that dogs (which, according to Sextus, were thought by some to be the lowest animals of all: 63) are much more cognitively sophisticated than was sometimes supposed. For example, contrary to what was sometimes supposed, dogs do not lack reason; they can even engage in dialectic (69)—and so, presumably, they can enquire. The point, here, is not that dogs can engage in dialectic in some reduced sense, but that they can do so even as the Stoics conceive of dialectic. But it's not clear how seriously Sextus intends his arguments here. He says he is offering them in addition to other, more substantial, arguments, because 'we do not rule out a little ridicule of the deluded and self-satisfied dogmatists' (62).

[38] Which is not to say that sceptics take themselves to have sophisticated theological beliefs. I ask later what if any beliefs they accord themselves. The point for now is just that having some beliefs or other doesn't guarantee that one can enquire in a given domain.

View and the Some Belief View. Hence it promises to shed light on one of the most vexed issues about Pyrrhonism.

With these issues in mind, let's now look at Sextus' reply to the paradox.

5 Sextus begins in just the right way, by asking, in section [4], what apprehension is. He initially mentions two possibilities:

(a) to apprehend is simply to think, without affirming the reality (*huparxis*) of what one is thinking about; or

(b) to apprehend is to think, and to posit the reality of what one is thinking about.

He then abruptly mentions a third possibility:[39]

(c) to apprehend is to assent to an apprehensive appearance (*phantasia kataléptikê*), that is, to an appearance that 'comes from something real, is imprinted and stamped in accordance with the real thing itself, and is such as could not come from anything unreal'.[40]

I consider (a) in the next section; here I focus on (b) and (c). (b) construes apprehension as belief, in the sense of taking something to be true.[41] As such, it captures, or comes close to capturing, the Stoic notion, not of

---

[39] J. Brunschwig, 'Sextus Empiricus on the *kritérion*: The Sceptic as Conceptual Legatee', in J. M. Dillon and A. A. Long (eds.), *Questions of Eclecticism* (Berkeley: University of California Press, 1988), 145–75, reprinted in his *Papers in Hellenistic Philosophy* (Cambridge: Cambridge University Press, 1994), ch. 11 (latter pagination), 228, thinks Sextus distinguishes just two senses of 'apprehend', or two kinds of apprehension ((a) and (c)). Cf. Mates, *The Skeptic Way*, 264, 47. Thanks to Roald Nashi for suggesting to me that Sextus distinguishes three sorts of apprehension. Perhaps, however, (c) is an instance of (b). If this is so, there is a sense in which Sextus mentions just two possibilities ((a) and (b)), and a sense in which he mentions three ((a), (b), and (c)), though at places he focuses on (a) and (c).

[40] For the view that apprehension is assent to an apprehensive appearance, see also *M* VII 151–2; *M* VIII 397; *M* XI 182; *PH* III 241. *M* VII 154, by contrast, says that apprehension is assent to an *axíoma*. For the definition of apprehensive appearances, see *M* VII 248, 402, 426; DL 7.46; Cicero, *Acad.* II 77–8. In the passage cited in the text, Sextus uses a three-clause definition; there is also an earlier two-clause definition. There's dispute about whether the addition of the third clause signifies a change in Stoic epistemology, or just spells out more clearly what they intended all along; this issue doesn't matter for our purposes here.

[41] Cf. *PH* I 14. I discuss this familiar account of belief in 'Sceptical *Dogmata*: *PH* I 13', *Methexis* 13 (2001), 81–105. In saying that belief involves taking a proposition to be true, I don't intend anything fancy by 'proposition', but just believing that something or other is so. Perhaps one should say that belief is taking a proposition to be true *with the aim of its being true*: see D. Velleman, *The Possibility of Practical Reason* (Oxford: Clarendon Press, 2000), ch. 11. He argues that imagining something, for example, also involves taking something to be true, though not with the aim of getting its truth-value right. Nonetheless, for convenience I shall generally speak just of taking p to be true, where that is meant to capture belief in particular. It may be relevant to note that Sextus speaks of positing and affirming that

apprehension (*katalêpsis*), but of assent (*sunkatathesis*).[42] In their view, to assent to p is to take p to be true. They recognize two species of assent: *doxa* (which for them is *mere* belief, not belief as such), and *katalêpsis*, which they understand, not in way (a) or (b), but in way (c). In their view, one has *katalêpsis* that p when one assents to an apprehensive appearance that p. Not only does one then believe p (in the sense of taking it to be true), but p is also true and indeed is 'such as could not come from anything unreal'; that is, it is guaranteed to be true. *Katalêpsis* so construed goes beyond mere true belief; it is, at the minimum, reliably true belief, or true belief that is caused in the right way. Though not everyone thinks that having such beliefs is sufficient for knowledge, I think the Stoics do so.[43] Whether or not they in fact do so, that is how Sextus seems to understand them here. For in II 3 he uses *katalêpsis* (in sense (c)) and its cognates interchangeably with *eidenai* and *gignôskein* and their cognates.[44] Hence, when I have *katalêpsis* in sense (c) in mind, I'll sometimes just speak of 'knowledge'.

The Stoic account of *katalêpsis* (i.e. of knowledge) as assent to an apprehensive appearance is controversial; Philo of Larissa, for example, does not seem to accept it.[45] The fact that Sextus explains *katalêpsis* in distinctively Stoic terms suggests he is considering a Stoic version of the paradox of

something is true: perhaps, even if taking something to be true isn't distinctive of belief, positing and affirming that something is true is.

[42] For some relevant passages on Stoic epistemology, see A. A. Long and D. N. Sedley, *The Hellenistic Philosophers* (Cambridge: Cambridge University Press, 1987), sections 39–42. For general discussion, see J. Annas, 'Stoic Epistemology', in S. Everson (ed.), *Companions to Ancient Thought*, 1: *Epistemology* (Cambridge: Cambridge University Press, 1990), 184–203; Long and Sedley, *Hellenistic Philosophers*, vol. 1, pp. 256–9; M. Frede, 'Stoics and Skeptics on Clear and Distinct Impressions', in his *Essays in Ancient Philosophy* (Minneapolis: University of Minnesota Press, 1987), 151–76, at 169–70; and his 'Stoic Epistemology', in K. Algra et al. (eds.), *The Cambridge History of Hellenistic Philosophy* (Cambridge: Cambridge University Press, 1999), ch. 9.

[43] To be sure, as they conceive of *katalêpsis*, it is not as such the highest form of knowledge, for which *epistêmê* is reserved. But they seem to take *katalêpsis* to be knowledge, insofar as it is truth entailing but goes beyond mere true belief (for example, accidentally true belief doesn't count as *katalêpsis*). Whether Plato would agree that bare *katalêpsis* counts as knowledge, or whether he has more demanding criteria for knowledge, is another matter.

[44] *Gignôskein* can be used for mere recognition in a sense that falls short of knowledge (when knowledge is taken to be a truth-entailing cognitive condition that goes beyond mere true belief); but *eidenai* is generally used for knowledge. Since Sextus uses the words interchangeably here, both seem to indicate knowledge.

[45] See e.g. *PH* I 235; Cicero, *Acad.* II 18. For discussion, see G. Striker, 'Academics Fighting Academics', in B. Inwood and J. Mansfeld (eds.), *Assent and Argument* (Leiden: Brill, 1997), 257–76; and C. Brittain, *Philo of Larissa: The Last of the Academic Sceptics* (Oxford: Clarendon Press, 2001). Nor is the specifically Stoic notion involved when the Cyrenaics claim (or are alleged to have claimed) that only *pathê* are *katalêpta* (see e.g. *PH* I 215).

enquiry. Moreover, Sextus immediately goes on to give the example of a Stoic enquiring into an Epicurean claim; and then, in [6], he says that a similar argument can be used against other sects. That too suggests that he's discussing a specifically Stoic challenge to sceptical enquiry.[46]

Sextus proceeds to focus on apprehension in senses (b) and (c). He asks, that is, whether, when the Stoics say that sceptics don't apprehend, and so can't enquire into, their opponents' claims, they mean that one must know or believe that p is true, in order to enquire whether it is true.[47] If that's what the Stoics mean, and if one must in fact know or believe that p is true in order to enquire whether it is, then the sceptics may be in trouble. For they suspend judgement about the truth of their opponents' claims; hence they don't take themselves to know or believe them. Suppose they don't know or believe them. In that case, they instantiate the antecedent of (5), and so fall prey to (5)–(7).

Sextus' first reply is *ad hominem*: he argues that the Stoics shouldn't advance this argument, for it has repercussions they wouldn't welcome. For suppose that in order for a Stoic to enquire whether (as the Epicureans believe) pleasure is good, he must know or believe that it is. If he knows that pleasure is good, then pleasure *is* good, since knowledge (assent to an apprehensive appearance) is truth-entailing. Even if he merely believes that it is, still, he takes it to be true that it is. Hence, if one can enquire whether p is true only if one already knows or believes that it is, a Stoic could enquire into the truth of Epicurean claims only if those claims were true or, at least, only if he believed they were. Of course, no Stoic would want to accept this; nor, *mutatis mutandis*, would any dogmatist want to do so. For were they to do so, they would need to either embrace contradictory claims (their own, as well as those of their opponents), or abandon their

---

[46] Cf. G. Striker, '*Kritêrion tês alêthês*', *Nachrichten der Akademie der Wissenschaften zu Göttingen* I. Phil.-hist. Klasse 2 (1974), 48–110), reprinted as ch. 2 in her *Essays on Hellenistic Epistemology and Ethics* (Cambridge: Cambridge University Press, 1996) (latter pagination), 65. (However, F. Grgic, 'Sextus Empiricus on the Possibility of Inquiry', *Pacific Philosophical Quarterly* 89 (2008), 436–9, thinks we should suspend judgement about whether the argument is Stoic (439). I regret that Grgic's paper appeared too late for me to be able to take it into account.) Interestingly enough, in *M* VIII 337–336a Sextus considers a version of the paradox of enquiry that he says is due especially (*malista*) to the Epicureans. I discuss it in 'Concepts and Inquiry: Sextus and the Epicureans', in B. Morison and K. Ierodiakonou (eds.) (Oxford: Clarendon Press, forthcoming).

[47] Hence although, as we've seen, substituends for 'x' in the paradox of enquiry can be quite broad—that is, although one can enquire into many sorts of things—Sextus is now focusing on propositions.

own claims.[48] Obviously neither option is attractive. Hence, the dogmatists shouldn't say that one can enquire whether a given claim is true only if one already knows or believes that it is. The dogmatists wanted to argue that it's just sceptics who can't enquire. Sextus argues that if their argument succeeds, it shows that neither can the dogmatists enquire—at least, not into their opponents' claims.

Sextus allows that the Stoics might well agree: 'they themselves will perhaps be unwilling to allow that they cannot enquire into things which they have not apprehended in this way' (II 4). But it's not clear whether Sextus is suggesting that they antecedently require knowing, or believing, that p is true for enquiring whether it is, but will willingly abandon that view in the face of Sextus' argument; or whether he admits that they never intended that view in the first place. It is, in any case, worth asking, if only briefly, whether the Stoics require one to know or believe that p is true, in order to enquire whether it is. I shall focus initially on asking whether they require knowledge for enquiry and, if so, exactly how they do so.

According to Plutarch 'The Stoics make natural concepts (phusikai ennoiai) responsible <for our ability to enquire>'.[49] Cicero also suggests that the Stoics think that:[50]

from this class [i.e. mental perceptions in general] concepts (notitiae) of things are imprinted on us, without which there can be no understanding (intellegi) or inquiry (quaeri) or discussion (disputari) of anything. (Acad. 2.21 = Long and Sedley (LS) 39C)

---

[48] Thanks to Roald Nashi for this way of putting the point.

[49] SVF 2.104 = Fragment 215(f) in vol. 15 of the Loeb Classical Library's edition of Plutarch's Moralia, ed. Sandbach = Fr. 280 in Westerink; see n. 11. The fragment continues: 'If these are potential, we shall say the same things <against the Stoics as against the Peripatetics>. But if they are actual, why do we enquire into what we know? And if we start from them <, to inquire> into other things we don't know, how do we <inquire into> what we don't know?' Plutarch seems to level a dilemma against the Stoics: natural concepts are either potential or actual. If they are potential, the Stoics have to explain how we can enquire if we don't know. If they are actual, the Stoics have to explain how we can enquire if we do know. He suggests one possibility: we use what we know, to enquire into what we don't know. But he suggests that collapses into the first horn. He doesn't say how the Stoics would reply to his dilemma.

Plutarch doesn't suggest that the Stoics think either that one needs a natural concept of x in order to enquire into x, or that one needs to know that p is true in order to enquire whether it is. For all he says here, the Stoics might think we have a small set of natural concepts, which enables us to inquire into a variety of things. Epictetus, Diss. 2.11 and 17, suggests one way in which this could work: we could apply natural concepts to particular cases. Armed with a general account of what justice is (a natural concept of justice), we can enquire whether this or that person is just. Alternatively, one could articulate or fill in a natural notion; I consider an example of this from Antipater below.

[50] I take it that notitiae are natural concepts, not any old concept.

On this view, we need natural concepts in order to enquire. And, according to the Stoics, everyone rational—that is, everyone (normal) who has reached the age of reason[51]—has a set of these natural concepts; indeed, having reason, or being rational, consists in having such concepts. According to Michael Frede, the Stoics also think that 'if we have a natural notion of human beings, we know that if something is a human being, it is mortal'. He goes on to say that '[p]art of the motivation for such a conception of reason [as consisting in the having of natural notions which, in turn, involves having knowledge] clearly is the conviction that we can only come to know something if, in some sense, we already know what we are coming to know'.[52] Thus, according to Frede, the Stoics reply to the Meno's paradox of enquiry by saying that we need antecedent knowledge of what we're enquiring into.[53] One might infer that the Stoics believe that one can enquire whether p is true only if one already knows that p is true.

However, this inference should be resisted.[54] In the first book of On the Gods, for example, Antipater says (Plutarch, St. Rep. 1051F; SVF 3.A.33):[55]

Prior to our whole discourse (logos), we can briefly call to mind the clear evidence (enargeian) (von Arnim: ennoian, concept) that we have about god. Well, we conceive (nooumen) of god as a blessed imperishable animal that is beneficent to men.

---

[51] Which is either 7 (Aetius 4.11.1–4 = SVF 2.83 = LS 39E) or 14 (DL 7.55 = LS 33H).

[52] Both quotations are from his 'The Stoic Conception of Reason', in K. J. Boudouris (ed.), Hellenistic Philosophy (Athens: IAGP, 1994), 50–63, at 54.

[53] Frede thinks that Plato and Aristotle also favor this solution: 'The Stoic Conception of Reason', 54.

[54] Nor does Frede clearly make the inference. For one thing, he says that the Stoics think one can come to know something only if one already knows it 'in some sense'. Unfortunately, he doesn't say what the relevant sense is. But perhaps the sense he has in mind doesn't commit the Stoics to the view that, to come to know that p, one already needs to know that p is true.

C. Brittain argues that the Stoics think 'there is a sense in which the inquirer already knows the conclusion: as Plutarch suggested, it is potentially there in the inquirer's set of preconceptions' ('Common Sense: Concepts, Definitions and Meaning in and out of the Stoa', in D. Frede (ed.), Language and Learning (Cambridge: Cambridge University Press, 2005), 164–209, at 183). Plutarch doesn't seem to me to say exactly this: see n. 49 above. Nor am I sure what it means to say that the conclusion is potentially there in one's preconceptions (i.e. in one's natural concepts). If it means that one can come to know the conclusion, that falls short of already actually knowing it. If, however, it means that one has tacit or latent knowledge of it, that might be a way of already actually knowing the conclusion: though whether it is would depend on precisely how one spells out the notion of tacit or latent knowledge. Be that as it may, when Sextus considers the view that one can enquire whether p is true only if one has katalêpsis that p is true, he seems to have in mind conscious, explicit katalêpsis that p is true. Brittain rightly doesn't attribute that view to the Stoics.

[55] My account of Antipater follows Brittain, 'Common Sense', 180ff. ennoian is a conjecture of Wyttenbach's, adopted by Pohlenz and von Arnim. However, the MSS have enargeian, which Cherniss favors in his Loeb edition. Even if we read enargeian rather than ennoian, some sort of concept is at issue.

We then use this concept in order to help us arrive at the final definition of god, which alone captures its (whole) real essence—perhaps:[56]

God is an immortal rational animal, perfect or noetic in happiness, un-receptive of any evil, and providential of both the cosmos and the things in it. (DL 7.147; *SVF* 2.1021)

The concept we begin with is an outline account of what god is; enquiry involves trying to articulate it more fully, so as to discover god's full real essence.[57]

If this interpretation is right, Antipater, at any rate, doesn't think one needs to know (or, for that matter, even believe) that p is true in order to enquire whether it is. For the proposition one grasps at the beginning of the enquiry differs from the proposition one knows (or believes) at the end of it (if all goes well). They are about the same thing, god; but they say different, if overlapping things, about god.

Sextus would be right to say that the Stoics think that enquiry requires us to have some knowledge. For they think it requires us to have natural concepts, and they seem to think that having them confers knowledge. However, even if they think we can enquire whether god is perfect or noetic in happiness only if we have a natural concept of god, they don't think we need to know that god is perfect or noetic in happiness, in order to enquire whether he is.

Of course, even if they don't think one needs to know that p is true, in order to enquire whether it is, they might think one needs to believe that p is true, in order to enquire whether it is. But I see little reason to ascribe this view to them either. In the example from Antipater, for example, the enquirer doesn't antecedently believe that the proposition she discovers is true; she comes to believe it in the course of her enquiry.[58]

---

[56] As Brittain explains ('Common Sense', 180–1 and n. 64), it's not clear that Antipater takes this to be the final definition. But that shouldn't obscure the crucial point, which is just that the proposition one has at the beginning of an enquiry is not identical to the one one grasps at the end of a successful enquiry.

[57] Not all enquiries aim to discover essence. I focus on just one case that does, to support my general claim that the Stoics aren't committed to the view that one needs to know that p is true, to enquire whether it is.

[58] One might argue that one can enquire whether p is true, only if one knows or believes it in the sense of understanding what it means. But that's not what Sextus has in mind here. I discuss what's involved in understanding what a proposition means below.

Returning now to Sextus: he makes a good philosophical point, for, as I shall argue more fully below, one doesn't need to know or believe that a given proposition is true in order to enquire whether it is. But he would be wrong to say that the Stoics are committed to the offending view. However, as we've seen, it's not clear he says this.

So far, Sextus has not argued either that any premise of the paradox is false or that any inference it contains is invalid. He has argued only that the dogmatists should not use (5)–(7) against the sceptics if, by 'apprehend', they mean 'know' or 'believe'. For in that case, they themselves face unwelcome consequences. Sextus is right about the consequences of his *ad hominem* argument. But since his opponents don't hold the view he attributes to them, they need not worry.

6   In [10] Sextus turns to (a), on which to apprehend is simply to think (*to noein haplôs*). He says that sceptics apprehend dogmatic claims in this way, and that is sufficient for enquiring into them.

Sextus is making two related points. Firstly, he is now disarming (2)–(4): there is a sense in which sceptics apprehend dogmatic claims; and so there is a sense in which they satisfy the antecedent of (2). But the way in which they do so does not preclude them from enquiring; on the contrary, it enables them to do so. Secondly, he is challenging the truth of (7), if 'apprehension', in it, is knowledge or belief: contrary to (7), one doesn't need to apprehend (know or believe) that p is true, in order to enquire into it. For sceptics don't (claim to) know or believe that dogmatic claims are true; yet they can enquire into them. If (7) is false, then, to avoid commitment to it, one must reject at least one of (5) and (6) (given that the argument is valid). I assume Sextus is targeting (5), either in his own right in some sense or in an *ad hominem* way. At least, we've seen that (5) is in fact false, if it says that one needs to *know* something in order to engage in systematic discussion about it. For knowledge isn't needed for systematic discussion or enquiry: (true) belief will do.

Looking at the paradox as a whole ((1)–(8)), we can now say that Sextus allows[59] that it is valid, if to apprehend a proposition is simply to think about

---

[59] In speaking of what Sextus allows—or argues or claims—I don't mean to imply that he is committed to what he says, in the sense of taking it to be true. In some cases, his arguments are *ad hominem*. In other cases, he might be propounding arguments to set in opposition to those of the dogmatists, so as to achieve equipollence on the issue of whether sceptics can enquire: the dogmatists

it. He then says that sceptics apprehend dogmatic claims in this way, and so satisfy the antecedent of (2). But (2) so read is false; and so, despite the truth of (3), we need not infer (4). He also allows that the paradox is valid if apprehension is knowledge or belief; in this case, however, (7) and, presumably, (5) are false. Either way, the paradox is unsound.

How should we characterize the way in which sceptics think about dogmatic claims, if they neither know nor believe them? Sextus says they think about them without taking them to be true.[60] That this is what he means seems clear from II 4 and II 10. As we've seen, II 4 distinguishes three accounts of apprehension. We've looked at two of them, knowledge and belief. The third is 'simply "to think"', without any further affirmation of the reality (huparxeôs) of the things about which we are making our statements'. Throughout, Sextus has been focusing on propositions; and for a proposition to have huparxis is for it to be true (see e.g. M VIII 10). If sceptics think about dogmatic claims without affirming their reality, they think about them without affirming that they are true. Similarly, in II 10 Sextus says that 'a sceptic is not, I think, barred from having thoughts if they arise from things which give him a passive impression and appear clearly to him and do not at all imply the reality of what is being thought of. For we can think, as they say, not only of real things but also of unreal things.' Once again, given Sextus' focus on propositions, he seems to be saying that sceptics think about dogmatic claims without taking them to be true. There are a variety of ways in which one can do so: one can entertain a proposition, or wonder whether it is true, or consider it, and so on. We do this all the time. I read a philosophy article and wonder whether its main claims are true; scientists test new hypotheses; and so on. Moreover, having such an 'acceptance attitude' to a proposition is sufficient for enquiring into it; one doesn't need to know or believe that it is true.[61]

---

argue that sceptics can't enquire; here's an argument that says they can enquire. Conflicting appearances are equipollent; the result is suspension of judgement. In some cases, he might be saying how things nondoxastically seem to him to be. Be that as it may, my main concern is to ask how good a case can be made for the claim that sceptics can enquire, if they are in the cognitive condition that defines scepticism. I leave largely to one side Sextus' own attitude to the defense he suggests.

[60] At least, they don't take them to be true with the aim of their being true: see n. 41. Cf. G. Striker, 'Review of H. Tarrant, *Scepticism or Platonism?*', in *Ancient Philosophy* 11 (1991), 202–6. I thank Striker for calling my attention to this review, which I saw only after completing the main argument of this paper.

[61] On acceptance attitudes, see e.g. R. Stalnaker, *Inquiry* (Cambridge, MA: MIT Press, 1979). Entertaining a proposition and so on are perhaps best called *mere* acceptance attitudes, to distinguish them from belief, which in addition involves taking a proposition to be true (with the aim of its being true).

Insofar as Sextus replies to the paradox by saying that one can think about, and enquire into, a claim without knowing or believing that it is true, he is absolutely right. Moreover, Plato is often taken to say that one can enquire into a proposition only if one already knows that it is true. And it's arguable that Sextus and others interpret the Stoics this way.[62] If that interpretation of Plato and the Stoics were correct, then, on this point, Sextus would have the edge. As indicated above, however, my own view is that neither Plato nor the Stoics think that enquiry requires one to know, or even believe, that the very proposition whose truth one is enquiring into is true. They agree with Sextus that one can enquire whether p is true even if one doesn't already know or believe that it is true.

However, as we've seen, the Stoics seem to think that one needs some knowledge or other (*katalêpsis* in sense (c) above) to enquire; and Plato thinks one needs some true beliefs.[63] We haven't yet asked what Sextus says about this. Nor, more generally, have we asked whether the passage sheds any light on the debate between the Some Belief View and the No Belief View. To say, as Sextus does, that sceptics think about and enquire into claims they neither know nor believe to be true is to say that they disclaim *some* beliefs. But it isn't to say that they disclaim *all* beliefs. Nor is it to say that they take themselves to have any beliefs.

Whatever Sextus says on the matter, one might think that one can in fact enquire only if one has some knowledge or beliefs. In particular, one might argue that one can enquire whether a given proposition is true only if one understands what it means. And, on one familiar view, to understand what a proposition means is to know what it means, where this involves knowing what its constituent concepts mean. On this view, understanding a proposition requires what we may call *conceptual knowledge*. If Sextus accepts this view, he is committed to the Some Belief View.[64]

---

[62] But as we saw above, Sextus may admit that this isn't really the Stoic view. As we also saw above, Frede and Brittain may interpret the Stoics this way; but it's not clear whether they do so. Aristotle and the Epicureans are, I think, sometimes taken to believe this—or, at least, to believe that one can enquire only if one has some knowledge—but they fall outside the scope of the present paper. I discuss Aristotle on this issue in 'Aristotle's Reply to the *Aporêma* in the *Meno*', in V. Harte and M. M. McCabe (eds.), *Aristotle and the Stoics Reading Plato* (BICS, forthcoming). I discuss Epicurus on this issue in 'Concepts and Inquiry'.

[63] I briefly discussed the Stoics on this above. On Plato, see n. 30.

[64] He would be committed to the view that sceptics have not only belief but also knowledge. For the view that sceptics have, and take themselves to have, not only belief but also knowledge, see Frede, 'The

And he is sometimes thought to accept it. R. J. Hankinson, for example, in commenting on II 10, says: 'Sceptics, then, are allowed conceptual knowledge . . . [T]he Sceptic has no qualms about allowing himself to understand, for instance, the content of the Stoic concept of cataleptic impression—all he doubts is whether such a concept is instantiated.'[65]

However, I don't think II 10 accords sceptics anything that Sextus, at any rate, wants to call conceptual *knowledge*. He does say that sceptics think (*noein*); and thinking involves having concepts.[66] But Sextus doesn't seem to mean that thinking, or having concepts, is a kind of *knowledge*.[67]

It is true that '*noein*' can be used for knowledge. In the *Republic*, for example, Plato uses *noêsis* for the highest level of cognition in the Divided Line (511d; contrast 533e); and at the end of *Posterior Analytics* II 19, Aristotle (in my view) uses *nous* for a cognitive condition that is at least as cognitively strong as one is in when one has *epistêmê* (100b8ff.). But *noein* certainly need not be so used and often isn't. Nor do I think Sextus means to suggest that sceptics think in a high-level sense. For one thing, he suspends judgement as to whether there is any *katalêpsis* in the Stoic sense. Hence he is unlikely to mean that sceptics are in an even higher-level cognitive condition, whether

Sceptic's Beliefs', in *Essays in Ancient Philosophy*, ch. 10, at 179–80 (though his reasons are not those just mentioned).

[65] *The Sceptics* (London: Routledge, 1995), 281. I discuss Hankinson more fully in 'Scepticism, Existence, and Belief'. Cf. H. Maconi, who says that Sextus 'did not cut himself off from conceptual knowledge: his *epochê* was compatible with the possession and use of concepts' ('Nova Non Philosophandi Philosophia', *Oxford Studies in Ancient Philosophy* 6 (1988), 231–45, at 244). The claim that follows the colon doesn't obviously imply the claim that precedes it: perhaps one can have and use concepts without having anything properly called *knowledge*.

[66] See, for example, *M* VIII 337, where Sextus either equates thinking (*noêsis*) with having concepts (*ennoia*, *epinoia*, and *prolêpsis* are all used) or at least takes the former to imply the latter.

[67] If Sextus did accord sceptics conceptual knowledge, his position would be interestingly similar to Descartes'. In the Sixth Set of Objections, it is argued that 'from the fact that we are thinking it does not seem to be entirely certain that we exist. For in order to be certain that you are thinking you must know what thought or thinking is, and what existence is; but since you do not yet know what these things are, how can you know that you are thinking or that you exist?' (Adam and Tannery (AT) VII 413/ Cottingham, Stoothoff, and Murdoch (CSM) II 278). Descartes replies that '[i]t is true that no one can be certain that he is thinking or that he exists unless he knows what thought is and what existence is' (AT VII 422/CSM II 285). But, he goes on to say, '[t]his internal awareness of one's thought and existence is so innate in all men that, although we may pretend that we do not have it if we are overwhelmed by preconceived opinions and pay more attention to words than to their meanings, we cannot in fact fail to have it'. The knowledge at issue here is what Descartes calls 'internal awareness' as opposed to 'reflective knowledge'. Cf. the Appendix to the Fifth Objections and Replies, at AT IXA 206; and, for different but interestingly related points, AT VIII A 37–8/CSM I 220f. and AT V 152/CSM III 337. If Descartes but not Sextus exempts the meanings of terms from the scope of his scepticism, there is a way in which his scepticism is less extensive than Sextus'.

about the meanings of dogmatic claims or about anything else. Further, he uses *noein* here as an alternative to *katalêpsis* in senses (b) and (c): that is, as an alternative to belief and to knowledge (where the former involves taking a proposition to be true, and the latter is understood in the distinctively Stoic sense of *katalêpsis*, as assent to an apprehensive appearance). Sextus is suggesting, that is, that sceptics think in a way that doesn't involve knowledge or belief.

It's also worth noting that, contrary to Hankinson, Sextus' scepticism extends beyond doubting—or, perhaps more accurately, suspending judgement as to whether[68]—various dogmatic concepts are instantiated. In II 22–8, for example, he argues that (so far as what the dogmatists say goes) man is not only inapprehensible but also inconceivable (22: *anepinoêtos*); indeed, 'what they say is actually unintelligible' (22: *asuneta*). This seems to question whether dogmatic concepts are ultimately coherent. This too might suggest that Sextus doesn't take sceptical thoughts about dogmatic claims to consist in any sort of knowledge: perhaps he thinks that to do so would misleadingly imply commitment as to the adequacy, or at least the coherence, of the concepts involved. To be sure, perhaps one can know (where knowledge goes beyond true belief) what a concept means, without being committed to the concept's being fully satisfactory or adequate, and even if the concept is not in fact fully satisfactory or adequate. It's less clear whether one can know what an unintelligible concept means. For if it is unintelligible, it has no meaning.[69]

Even if sceptics don't claim to *know* what dogmatic claims and concepts mean, might they claim to have *beliefs* about what they mean? II 10 does imply that sceptics have *some* beliefs. For the end of this passage says that 'it has been made clear that he [the sceptic] assents to any impression given by way of a passive appearance, insofar as it appears to him'. This refers back to I 13, the only passage in which Sextus explains the sense in which sceptics have, and lack, *dogmata*. The interpretation of this passage is much disputed.

---

[68] See n. 10.

[69] However, perhaps in saying that man, for example, is *anepinoêtos* (so far as dogmatic attempts to say what man is goes) and that what the dogmatists say is *asuneta*, Sextus means to say not that what the dogmatists say is literally unintelligible, but just that it is unsatisfactory in some weaker way. Certainly, despite saying that man, for example, is *anepinoêtos*, Sextus discusses various *epinoiai* of man. However, perhaps this is just an example of his concessive strategy: strictly speaking, man is *anepinoêtos*. But if you aren't persuaded by that, consider various purported concepts of man; various difficulties still result. Alternatively, perhaps there can in some sense be an *epinoia* of x even if x is *anepinoêton*.

I argue elsewhere that it says that sceptics have beliefs about how they are appeared to, though not about anything unclear.[70] So, for example, if it appears to a sceptic that the sky is blue, she believes that it appears to her that the sky is blue; but she suspends judgement as to whether the sky is blue. This is a version of the Some Belief View, one I take Sextus to be adverting to here.

However, though Sextus implies in II 10 that sceptics have beliefs about how they are appeared to, I don't think he does so in order to suggest that sceptics also have beliefs about what dogmatic claims or concepts mean. For one thing, he doesn't seem to mention sceptical beliefs about how one is appeared to as a direct explanation of how sceptics can enquire; he seems to mention them only in order to defuse the objection that sceptics don't rely on their nondoxastic appearances. The reply is that so far from rejecting their appearances, they believe they have them.[71] But it seems to be the mere having of, and reliance on, the appearances, rather than the fact that sceptics believe they have them, that, so to speak, does the work of the reply. Further, again, Sextus is aiming to articulate a notion of thinking that differs not only from knowledge (*katalêpsis* in sense (c)) but also from belief (*katalêpsis* in sense (b)).

But how can sceptics think about dogmatic claims and concepts if they don't know or even have beliefs about what they mean? Sextus seems to say that sceptics can do so in the sense that they have nondoxastic appearances about them, where this seems to mean not just that they don't affirm their truth or meaningfulness, but also that it merely nondoxastically seems to them that they have a given meaning. The sceptical thoughts at issue here, that is, are nondoxastic appearances. Sextus' point is that having nondoxastic

---

[70] See Fine, 'Sceptical *Dogmata*'.

[71] Cf. *PH* I 19, where the context is the *apraxia* argument. The charge is that since sceptics reject their appearances, they can't act. The reply includes the claim that so far from rejecting their appearances, sceptics rely on them. The similarity between the present passage and I 19 is hardly surprising. For the paradox of enquiry is an *apraxia* argument: it alleges that there is something sceptics cannot do, viz. enquire. In this connection, it's interesting to note that Margaret Wilson has argued that having beliefs about how one is appeared to is sufficient for action, and so for dissolving the *apraxia* argument. See her *Descartes* (London: Routledge, 1978), 48. (She is discussing Descartes, not Sextus; but I argue in 'Descartes and Ancient Skepticism: Reheated Cabbage?', *Philosophical Review* 109 (2000), 195–234, that similar issues confront them both, and that their replies are more similar than they are sometimes taken to be.) Of course, even if having beliefs about how one is appeared to is sufficient for some actions, it doesn't follow that it is sufficient for enquiry into dogmatic claims in particular.

appearances is a kind of thinking; since sceptics have nondoxastic appearances about dogmatic claims and concepts, they think about them.

Whatever we might think of this point ourselves, the Stoics should concede it. For they think that all the appearances of those who have reached the age of reason are thoughts.[72] Hence, if sceptics have nondoxastic appearances, they think—contrary to what the dogmatists allege in II 1.[73]

Even if one concedes that having a nondoxastic appearance about what a proposition means is a kind of thinking, one might argue that it doesn't involve understanding what that proposition means. One might then argue that enquiry requires one to understand what the propositions one relies on mean; and one might then infer that the sorts of thoughts Sextus accords sceptics aren't sufficient for enquiry.

The first step of this argument—that having a nondoxastic appearance about what a proposition means is not sufficient for understanding it—will appeal to anyone who thinks that to understand what a proposition means, one must know or have true beliefs about what it means. And that is certainly a familiar view about what is involved in understanding a proposition. However, Dean Pettit has recently argued that 'to understand a bit of language with a certain meaning it is sufficient that it *seem* to the speaker to have that meaning, even if the speaker does not believe (tacitly or otherwise) that it does'.[74]

However, it's not clear that Sextus can use Pettit's argument. Firstly, Pettit appeals to nondoxastic appearances only in a very local and limited way. He focuses on understanding a word in a foreign language, and on cases in which a person has relevant associated true beliefs, though not about what the word at issue means. In a variant on one of his examples, someone knows (and so has a true belief about) what 'water' means, but doesn't know (or have a true belief about) what 'l'eau' means, though she has a normal repertoire of true beliefs about what water (the stuff) is, and though she has a

<hr/>

[72] See, for example, DL 7.49–51 (= LS 39A). For some discussion, see Frede, 'The Stoic Conception of Reason'.

[73] The Stoics also think that everyone who has reached the age of reason has *katalêpsis*, and so some thoughts that are guaranteed to be true. So the Stoics will have to allow that, whatever the sceptics may say about their own cognitive condition, they in fact have some *katalêpsis*.

[74] 'Why Knowledge is Unnecessary for Understanding Language', *Mind* 111 (2002), 519–50, at 543. See the reply by S. Gross, 'Linguistic Understanding and Belief', *Mind* 114 (2005), 61–6, and Pettit's reply to Gross, 'Belief and Understanding: A Rejoinder to Gross', *Mind* 114 (2005), 67–74.

correct nondoxastic appearance about what 'l'eau' means. Perhaps, for example, it nondoxastically appears to her that 'l'eau' means water, but she doesn't believe that it does, because she believes she is being manipulated by a neurologist in such a way that she systematically associates the wrong meanings with various words. Pettit argues that she nonetheless understands what 'l'eau' means; her correct nondoxastic appearance is sufficient, in the circumstances, to confer linguistic understanding. Pyrrhonists, however, don't claim to know or have beliefs either about what '*hudôr*' (or 'water' or 'l'eau') means or about what water is. Their disclaimer of belief is far wider than that considered in Pettit's examples. Sextus could use something like Pettit's argument only if he were willing to extend it far more widely than Pettit himself does.

Secondly, it's crucial to Pettit's account that, though the speaker doesn't believe that p means what it in fact means, his nondoxastic appearance is (as it happens, and unbeknownst to the speaker) accurate. Sextus, however, can't claim that sceptical nondoxastic appearances about meaning are correct. It's one thing for a third party to say that someone else's nondoxastic appearances are correct; it's another thing for one to say this about one's own nondoxastic appearances. If one says this about one's own appearances, they are beliefs, not nondoxastic appearances. Perhaps sceptics in fact understand what dogmatic claims mean, precisely because their nondoxastic appearances are correct. And saying this would have some *ad hominem* force, if the Stoics believe that sceptical nondoxastic appearances are by and large accurate. But the sceptics can't say this from the inside, as it were, using only their own resources.

But does Sextus claim that sceptics not only think about but also understand dogmatic claims? According to Benson Mates, he doesn't do so.[75] But in saying this, Mates seems to have in mind a rather robust notion of understanding. For though he says that sceptics don't understand dogmatic claims, he also says that they "catch on", to some extent, to what the dogmatists are talking about'.[76] Perhaps this amounts to some sort of understanding.

There are, at any rate, different levels or degrees of understanding. Even if sceptics don't claim to understand dogmatic claims about, say, proof in the

---

[75] *The Skeptic Way*, 30–2. Despite saying this, he translates *noeite*, in a parallel argument in *M* VIII 337aff., as 'understand' (*The Skeptic Way*, 25).

[76] *The Skeptic Way*, 25.

way in which a nonsceptical expert logician might claim to do so, perhaps they understand them in a weaker sense. Tyler Burge, for example, distinguishes minimal from greatest competence, where the former 'consists in conformity to the practice of others'.[77] Sceptics say they conform to the practices of others; they follow *bios*, ordinary life. So, for example, at *PH* I 21–4, Sextus describes the sceptical four-fold way of life, which includes following ordinary customs and laws. Perhaps this enables them to understand dogmatic claims.

But just as there is a difficulty in Sextus' using something like Pettit's argument in order to defend the claim that sceptics understand, so there is a difficulty in his appealing to Burge's argument for that purpose. For I've argued elsewhere that Sextus is an External World Sceptic, in the sense that he suspends judgement as to whether anything exists other than his states of being appeared to.[78] If so, he's not in a position to claim that sceptics conform to the practices of others. Perhaps sceptics do understand dogmatic claims, if they in fact conform to the practices of others; but this isn't something sceptics can say from the inside. Moreover, just as Pettit requires the nondoxastic appearances that confer understanding to be correct, so Burge assumes that the practices of others are coherent, and involve correct normative practice; they by and large correctly distinguish how things are from how they merely seem to be.[79] In both cases, externalism, coupled with certain assumptions about correctness, are needed in order explain how sceptics can understand.

Sextus can, however, turn to the offensive. He can say that if dogmatic practice is incoherent, then neither sceptics nor dogmatists can understand or, therefore, enquire. If, however, as the Stoics believe, we all have knowledge that allows us to enquire, and if, as the Stoics also think, there is an external world and everyone by and large stands in the right causal connections to things, then sceptics can enquire just as well as dogmatists can. That's not to say that sceptics can enquire. It's to say only that if dogmatists can enquire, so too can sceptics. Further, the argument achieves this result only by saying that

---

[77] 'Intellectual Norms and the Foundations of Mind', *Journal of Philosophy* 83 (1986), 697–720, at 702.

[78] 'Sextus and External World Scepticism', *Oxford Studies in Ancient Philosophy* 24 (2003), 341–85.

[79] As Pettit acknowledges, he is indebted to Burge's arguments. Thanks to David Charles for emphasizing to me the importance of the point that relying on the practices of others won't help sceptics understand dogmatic claims unless those practices are coherent, and unless they involve drawing a roughly accurate distinction between how things seem and how they are.

sceptics could enquire if they were in the cognitive condition the Stoics take them to be in. It falls short of saying that sceptics could enquire if they lack knowledge and beliefs as widely as they say they do.

Further problems might arise about the possibility of sceptical enquiry, if sceptics suspend judgement as to whether dogmatic claims and concepts are even meaningful. Here, however, one might note that although Berkeley, for example, argues that materialism is incoherent or meaningless, he nonetheless manages to talk about it and to argue against it. As Jonathan Bennett says: 'In declaring materialism to be incoherent or meaningless ... Berkeley does not treat it as mere gabble. He rightly concedes that it has enough structure for us to be able to operate with it in a fashion, and to pretend that it is consistent in order to criticize it in other ways.'[80] However, it's not clear that Sextus can say this. Berkeley might be happy to say that materialism is not 'mere gabble'; nor does he disclaim belief to the extent that sceptics do. The beliefs he has might allow him to talk about materialism even if there's a sense in which he takes the position to be ultimately incoherent. It's less clear whether sceptics can consistently allow that dogmatic claims are not mere gabble. And if they are mere gabble—which the sceptics allow is possible—it's not clear that one could use them as the basis for an enquiry.

One might then argue, as Mates does, that even if sceptics don't understand dogmatic claims, they can enquire into them—but only because sceptical enquiry 'turns out to be, in most cases, nothing more than the raising of questions about the meaning and seeming implications of Dogmatic assertions purporting to be true'.[81]

---

[80] *Learning from Six Philosophers* (Oxford: Clarendon Press, 2001), vol. 1, p. 135; cf. 142–5. Thanks to Nick Sturgeon for suggesting both the parallel and the reference.

[81] *The Skeptic Way*, 32. Mates doesn't describe the nature of the few cases of sceptical enquiry that aren't like this, nor does he say whether sceptics can consistently claim to enquire in these further cases. Nor is it clear why Mates thinks one can enquire into the meaning and implications of claims one doesn't understand, or why, if one can do so, one can't also engage in further enquiries.

Others have also argued that sceptical enquiry is limited. M. F. Burnyeat, for example, says that sceptics don't have 'an active programme of research' ('Can the Sceptic Live his Scepticism?', in M. Burnyeat and M. Frede (eds.), *The Original Sceptics* [Indianapolis: Hackett, 1997], 56). Cf. Hankinson, *The Sceptics*: 'The Sceptic's continuing investigation will not amount to a research program—rather it will be a gentle sort of pottering about comparing and contrasting things' (299). I'm not sure why they think sceptics can't have (active) research programs. (Burnyeat uses 'active', Hankinson doesn't.) At least, Sextus says that sceptics can teach kinds of expertise (*PH* I 24). Perhaps Burnyeat and Hankinson mean that sceptics don't engage in research in the sense that they aren't committed to the truth of the claims they teach. It's not clear, though, whether that's necessary for engaging in research.

But perhaps we can allow that even if sceptics don't understand dogmatic claims, or do so only in the thin sense just described, they can nonetheless enquire in a more robust sense than Mates allows. Here again we might appeal to Burge, who argues that conforming to the practices of others is 'sufficient for responsible ratiocination'[82]—and perhaps that, in turn, is sufficient for enquiring more deeply, or broadly, than Mates thinks sceptics are able to do. We can also once again say that, whether or not Sextus can offer this argument in his own right in some sense, it has *ad hominem* force, insofar as the Stoics have to concede that sceptics conform to the practices of others, and so should concede that they can enquire. But this is to some extent unsatisfying, since Sextus seems to have the more ambitious aim of explaining, from within sceptical resources, how sceptics can enquire even if they don't know, or have beliefs about, the truth or meaning of dogmatic claims, and even if those claims are in fact meaningless.

7 Having argued that sceptics can enquire, Sextus next (in section [11]) turns to the offensive and argues that it's the dogmatists who can't enquire.[83] It's not inconsistent for those who agree that they do not know how objects are in their nature to enquire. But dogmatists think they know such things accurately; and that is inconsistent with enquiry. For, as Sextus says, one enquires only when one has the idea (*nomizein*) that one hasn't found the answer.

Sextus' argument is open to criticism. Of course, if to have accurate knowledge of how something is in its nature is to have complete knowledge of it, one can't enquire into it.[84] But dogmatists don't typically think everyone has complete knowledge; the Stoics, for example, don't think there are any wise men.[85] If, however, knowing how things are in their nature is weaker than complete knowledge, there is room for inquiry. To be sure, if one thinks one accurately knows that pleasure is good, one won't

---

[82] 'Intellectual Norms', 713.

[83] Earlier Sextus argued that, if the dogmatists insist that one must know or believe that p, in order to enquire whether p is true, they couldn't enquire whether their opponents' claims are true. He is now suggesting a different argument for the claim that dogmatists can't enquire, at least in a certain range of cases. I again leave to one side Sextus' attitude to the cogency of his argument.

[84] At least, this is so if enquiry is aimed at acquiring knowledge one lacks. See section 2.

[85] So at least Sextus says: *M* IX 133–4 (= LS 54D2). Not that it's clear that a wise man, were one to exist, would have complete, as opposed to very synoptic, knowledge. But if not even the wise man's knowledge would be complete, then, *a fortiori*, such knowledge as others possess isn't complete.

inquire whether it is. But one could inquire about the implications of the claim. Moreover, we've seen that, though the Stoics require some knowledge for inquiry, they don't claim to know the truth-values of all the propositions they inquire into. Part of Sextus' criticism seems to rest on this inaccurate understanding of the Stoics.[86]

A more important issue for our purposes is what Sextus means in saying that sceptics have the idea (*nomizein*) that they have not found the answer. Elsewhere, Sextus seems to use *nomizein* for belief.[87] If that's how he's using it here, then he's claiming that sceptics believe they have not found the answers. I've suggested that sceptics claim to have beliefs about how they are appeared to. But the belief that one hasn't found the answer doesn't seem to fall under this rubric. If it doesn't, then Sextus is now ascribing a further kind of belief to the sceptics. This might seem to be a very modest increase in the sceptics' repertoire of beliefs. But it might be the thin end of the wedge. Perhaps once we see what is really involved in enquiry, we will see that it requires more beliefs than is at first apparent, perhaps more beliefs than sceptics are willing to admit they have. On the other hand, if *nomizein* just indicates a further non-doxastic appearance, we can ask whether, if it merely nondoxastically seems to the sceptic that he doesn't know the answer, he can enquire, or whether enquiry requires him to believe that he doesn't know the answer.[88] We can also ask whether, if it merely seems to him that he doesn't know the answer, it likewise only seems to him that he enquires.

8   Whatever the exegetical value of Sextus' arguments against the Stoics, he at any rate makes some good philosophical points. In particular, he's right to say that one can enquire whether p is true without knowing, or even believing, that it is true; one can enquire whether p is true by, for example, entertaining p. Although this is a good point in itself, it isn't enough, by itself, to vindicate the possibility of sceptical enquiry. To be sure, if we

---

[86] If some other dogmatists hold the offending view, Sextus would have a good criticism of them. However, I've suggested that at least Plato doesn't hold this view. Nor do I think that Aristotle or the Epicureans do so, though I again leave them to one side here.

[87] Sextus doesn't use *nomizein* very often. But at *PH* III 218 (cf. 219) he uses it of those who believe in the traditional gods. In *M* XI 147, it also seems to indicate belief: cf. *kata doxan*.

[88] Similarly, in the last section we asked whether enquiry requires more beliefs than sceptics accord themselves, in particular, beliefs (or knowledge) about what dogmatic claims mean.

appeal to the Stoic view that we all have a stock of natural concepts which confers some sort of knowledge, then perhaps sceptics can enquire—so long as having this knowledge, as opposed to thinking one has it, will do. And this gives Sextus a good *ad hominem* argument against the Stoics: the Stoics can't say that they can enquire but that sceptics can't do so. However, the sceptics can't affirm the Stoic position in their own right. Yet it's less clear whether Sextus can defend the possibility of sceptical enquiry from the inside: on the assumption, that is, that sceptics in fact lack all the beliefs they disclaim. But perhaps Sextus doesn't mean to do so. After all, in *PH* I 4 he says that the rest of *PH* just records how things seem to him to be. So, as good sceptics, we should continue the enquiry into the possibility of sceptical enquiry further.[89]

Bibliography

J. L. Ackrill, 'Aristotle's Theory of Definition', in E. Berti (ed.), *Aristotle on Science: The Posterior Analytics* (Padua: Editrice Antenore, 1981), 359–84.

C. Adam and P. Tannery (eds.), *Oeuvres de Descartes*, rev. edn. (Paris: Vrin/CNRS, 1964–76).

J. Annas, 'Stoic Epistemology', in S. Everson (ed.), *Companions to Ancient Thought*, 1: *Epistemology* (Cambridge: Cambridge University Press, 1990), 184–203.

J. Annas and J. Barnes (trans.), *Sextus Empiricus: Outlines of Scepticism* (Cambridge: Cambridge University Press, 1994).

J. Bennett, *Learning from Six Philosophers*, vol. 1 (Oxford: Clarendon Press, 2001).

C. Brittain, *Philo of Larissa: The Last of the Academic Sceptics* (Oxford: Clarendon Press, 2001).

C. Brittain, 'Common Sense: Concepts, Definitions and Meaning in and out of the Stoa', in D. Frede (ed.), *Language and Learning* (Cambridge: Cambridge University Press, 2005), 164–209.

[89] An earlier version of this paper was read at the B-Club in Cambridge University, in May 1998. I thank the audience on that occasion for helpful discussion. Thanks too to Charles Brittain, David Charles, and Terry Irwin for helpful and detailed written comments as well as for discussion; and to Susanne Bobzien, Lesley Brown, Al-Quassim Cassam, David Sedley, Dominic Scott, Gisela Striker, Kate Woolfit, and the students in my seminar on ancient scepticism held at Cornell in the spring of 2004, for helpful discussion. I have also greatly benefited from work by, and discussion with, Roald Nashi. The present version of this paper dates primarily from 2004. I've added references to a few articles that appeared later; but I haven't been able to take them all into account.

J. Brunschwig, 'Sextus Empiricus on the *kritêrion*: The Sceptic as Conceptual Legatee', in J. M. Dillon and A. A. Long (eds.), *Questions of Eclecticism* (Berkeley: University of California Press, 1988), 145–75. Reprinted in his *Papers in Hellenistic Philosophy* (Cambridge: Cambridge University Press, 1994), ch. 11.

T. Burge, 'Intellectual Norms and the Foundations of Mind', *Journal of Philosophy* 83 (1986), 697–720.

M. F. Burnyeat, 'Can the Sceptic Live his Scepticism?', in M. Schofield, M. Burnyeat, and J. Barnes (eds.), *Doubt and Dogmatism* (Oxford: Clarendon Press, 1980), ch. 2. Reprinted in M. Burnyeat and M. Frede (eds.), *The Original Sceptics* (Indianapolis: Hackett, 1997), ch. 2.

J. Cottingham, R. Stoothoff, and D. Murdoch (trans.), *The Philosophical Writings of Descartes*, 2 vols. (Cambridge: Cambridge University Press, 1985).

G. Fine, 'Scepticism, Existence, and Belief', *Oxford Studies in Ancient Philosophy* 14 (1996), 273–90.

G. Fine, 'Descartes and Ancient Skepticism: Reheated Cabbage?', *Philosophical Review* 109 (2000), 195–234.

G. Fine, 'Sceptical Dogmata', *Methexis* 13 (2000), 81–105.

G. Fine, 'Inquiry in the *Meno*', in R. Kraut (ed.), *Cambridge Companion to Plato* (Cambridge: Cambridge University Press, 1992), 200–26. Reprinted, with minor revisions, in G. Fine, *Plato on Knowledge and Forms: Selected Essays* (Oxford: Clarendon Press, 2003), ch. 2.

G. Fine, 'Sextus and External World Scepticism', *Oxford Studies in Ancient Philosophy* 24 (2003), 341–85.

G. Fine, 'Aristotle's Reply to the *Aporêma* in the *Meno*', in V. Harte and M. M. McCabe (eds.), *Aristotle and the Stoics Reading Plato* (BICS, forthcoming)..

G. Fine, 'Concepts and Inquiry: Sextus and the Epicureans' (in preparation)..

M. Frede, 'The Sceptic's Beliefs', in *Essays in Ancient Philosophy* (Minneapolis: University of Minnesota Press, 1987), ch. 10.

M. Frede, 'Stoics and Skeptics on Clear and Distinct Impressions', in *Essays in Ancient Philosophy* (Minneapolis: University of Minnesota Press, 1987), 151–76.

M. Frede, 'The Stoic Conception of Reason', in K. J. Boudouris (ed.), *Hellenistic Philosophy* (Athens: IAGP, 1994), 50–63.

M. Frede, 'Stoic Epistemology', in K. Algra; J. Barnes, J. Mansfeld, and M. Schofield (eds.), *The Cambridge History of Hellenistic Philosophy* (Cambridge: Cambridge University Press, 1999), ch. 9.

F. Grgic, 'Sextus Empiricus on the Possibility of Inquiry', *Pacific Philosophical Quarterly* 89 (2008), 436–9.

S. Gross, 'Linguistic Understanding and Belief', *Mind* 114 (2005), 61–6.

R. J. Hankinson, *The Sceptics* (London: Routledge, 1995).

A. A. Long and D. N. Sedley, *The Hellenistic Philosophers*, 2 vols. (Cambridge: Cambridge University Press, 1987).

H. Maconi, 'Nova Non Philosophandi Philosophia', *Oxford Studies in Ancient Philosophy* 6 (1988), 231–45.

B. Mates, *The Skeptic Way* (New York: Oxford University Press, 1996).

J. Palmer, 'Sceptical Investigation', *Ancient Philosophy* 20 (2000), 351–75.

C. Perin, 'Pyrrhonian Scepticism and the Search for Truth', *Oxford Studies in Ancient Philosophy* 30 (2006), 383–401.

D. Pettit, 'Why Knowledge is Unnecessary for Understanding Language', *Mind* 111 (2002), 519–50.

D. Pettit, 'Belief and Understanding: A Rejoinder to Gross', *Mind* 114 (2005), 67–74.

Plutarch, *Moralia*, ed. and trans. F. Sandbach, vol. 15 (Cambridge, MA: Harvard University Press, 1969).

Sextus Empiricus, *Sextus Empirici: Opera*, ed. H. Mutschmann and J. Mau, rev. J. Mau, 2nd edn. (Leipzig: Teubner, 1958).

Sextus Empiricus, *Outlines of Pyrrhonism*, vol. 1, trans. R. Bury (Cambridge, MA: Harvard University Press, 1933; reprinted 1990).

Sextus Empiricus, *Outlines of Pyrrhonism*, trans. J. Annas and J. Barnes as *Sextus Empiricus: Outlines of Scepticism* (Cambridge: Cambridge University Press, 1994).

R. Stalnaker, *Inquiry* (Cambridge, MA: MIT Press, 1979).

G. Striker, 'Review of H. Tarrant, Scepticism or Platonism?', *Ancient Philosophy* 11 (1991), 202–6.

G. Striker, 'Kritérion tés aléthés', *Nachricthen der Akademie der Wissenschaften zu Göttingen* I. Phil.-hist. Klasse 2 (1974), 48–110, reprinted in her *Essays on Hellenistic Epistemology and Ethics* (Cambridge: Cambridge University Press, 1996), ch. 2.

G. Striker, 'Academics Fighting Academics', in B. Inwood and J. Mansfeld (eds.), *Assent and Argument* (Leiden: Brill, 1997), 257–76.

D. Velleman, *The Possibility of Practical Reason* (Oxford: Clarendon Press, 2000), ch. 11.

L. G. Westerink (ed. and trans.), *The Greek Commentaries on Plato's Phaedo* (Amsterdam: North Holland, 1977), vol. 2.

M. Wilson, *Descartes* (London: Routledge, 1978).

Index Locorum*

Plato

Apology
 23a 163

Charmides
 165b–c 497

Cratylus
 384b 280
 385b2 120
 389d3–4 266
 439b10–c1 318

Euthyphro
 4b4–e2 31, 46
 5d8–e2 44, 186
 6a7–d4 31
 6d9–e6 32
 7b7–c9 180
 9a1–d5 44
 9e1–3 31
 10a1–5b 31, 36, 38, 46, 49, 50,
    58, 60, 61
 10a5–c12 34–5, 36, 37,
    42, 43
 10d1–8 34, 41, 46, 49, 280
 10d9–10 37
 10e2–5 48, 51
 10e6–8 48, 50, 51
 10e10–11a3 33, 48, 51–3
 11a3–5 53
 11a6–b1 32
 13c6–d3 45
 15a5–6 45
 16d2ff 33

Gorgias
 453a7 218
 454c6ff 120
 463a1–c5 154
 464e2–465a6 165, 462
 501a1–6 165, 462

Hippias Major
 294b1f 8

Laches
 125b22 229
 152a2f 229
 190d7 120
 190e 229
 194c8 218
 197d 280

Laws
 714c 218
 739d 218
 962d 218

Meno
 71a2–b6 6, 13, 115, 124, 127, 212,
    494, 500
 71d5 120
 71e1–72a5 186
 72b3–8 4, 123
 74b9–11 123
 72c5–7 127
 72c7–d1 3, 5, 6, 13, 119
 74e11f 121, 122, 124, 125
 75a3–5 121, 122, 123, 124, 126
 75b7–c1 122, 123, 124, 125, 126
 75d2–7 5, 9, 13, 126

---

* I would like to thank Kei Chiba and Keisuke Furudate for their invaluable help in preparing the indices.

Index Nominum

General Index